Intelligence Collection

Intelligence Collection

Robert M. Clark

SAGE | CQPRESS

Los Angeles | London | New Delhi
Singapore | Washington DC

Los Angeles | London | New Delhi
Singapore | Washington DC

FOR INFORMATION:

CQ Press
An Imprint of SAGE Publications, Inc.
2455 Teller Road
Thousand Oaks, California 91320
E-mail: order@sagepub.com

SAGE Publications Ltd.
1 Oliver's Yard
55 City Road
London EC1Y 1SP
United Kingdom

SAGE Publications India Pvt. Ltd.
B 1/I 1 Mohan Cooperative Industrial Area
Mathura Road, New Delhi 110 044
India

SAGE Publications Asia-Pacific Pte. Ltd.
3 Church Street
#10-04 Samsung Hub
Singapore 049483

Publisher: Charisse Kiino
Editorial Assistant: Lauren Johnson
Associate Editor: Nancy Loh
Production Editor: Olivia Weber-Stenis
Copy Editor: Michelle Ponce
Typesetter: C&M Digitals Ltd.
Proofreader: Scott Oney
Indexer: Sheila Bodell
Cover Designer: Michael Dubowe
Marketing Manager: Erica DeLuca
Permissions Editor: Jennifer Barron
Illustrator: ronwilsonillustration.com

Library of Congress Cataloging-in-Publication Data

Clark, Robert M.

Intelligence collection / Robert M. Clark, University of Maryland

pages cm
Includes bibliographical references and index.

ISBN 978-1-4522-7185-9 (alk. paper).

Intelligence service—Methodology. I. Title.

JF1525.I6.C57 2014
327.12—dc23   2013006588

13 14 15 16 17 10 9 8 7 6 5 4 3 2 1

Contents

Part III. Collection Management and Strategy

Figures and Tables

Preface

This book addresses the complete spectrum of intelligence collection. My previous book, *The Technical Collection of Intelligence,* as the title suggests, is aimed at individuals who need a better understanding of various technical collection disciplines. *Intelligence Collection* encompasses information from the former but places equal emphasis on nontechnical collection. The text is written at a level that should be understandable and make sense to practitioners in both areas.

Why treat seemingly disparate fields in one text? Because solutions to the most critical intelligence problems today demand that collectors across the board have a basic understanding of each other's disciplines. It would be a mistake for readers to imagine that only Part I or only Part II applies to their particular work situation. Collectors need to know how other collectors function in order to help them and be helped in turn. Analysts, as well, have to understand the potential and limitations of collection assets in order to intelligently use them and use the results in solving analytical problems.

The purpose of this book is to

- explain specific collection systems, including the potential and limitations of each,

- help collectors and analysts to function across organizational boundaries, and
- highlight the value of sharing approaches between collection disciplines.

Intelligence Collection discusses how collectors in all disciplines garner the raw intelligence that is used by all-source analysts in finished intelligence production. It will be of value to

- *professors* who teach undergraduate- and graduate-level collegiate courses in intelligence or political science;
- *collection practitioners and managers* who must work cooperatively across collection *stovepipes*—a term widely used in the United States to refer to the specialization and compartmentation practices of collection organizations;
- *all-source analysts* who need to better understand how to task and collaborate with their collection partners and be able to evaluate collection and participate actively in it;
- *customers* of intelligence who need to understand the capabilities and limitations of collection when the results are cited to support intelligence conclusions; and
- *recruiters* for the intelligence community who bring in the talented people who develop collection systems and engage in collection activity.

This book is intended to serve these readers as a reference, or for university students, a textbook on intelligence collection. It covers terminology and important issues in collection performance and its utility for intelligence. It focuses especially on the function and process, to include single-source analysis of collected material. It does not go into the **all-source analysis** of such information. That subject is covered in a companion book, *Intelligence Analysis: A Target-Centric Approach.*

A Few Basic Definitions

All intelligence collection disciplines have their specialized jargon, or shorthand for communicating concepts. Some of these terms are explained in the appropriate chapters of this book, and many additional terms are included in the Glossary. A few terms are common to almost all collection, and their definitions are given below.

Raw versus finished intelligence: The end product of intelligence collection is referred to as raw intelligence. Finished intelligence is the term customarily applied to the product of all-source analysis (described below).

Collection: This term has two meanings in practice, and both meanings are used in this book. It can mean the entire process, from the planning stage to the dissemination of raw intelligence—which is the meaning that is applied in this book's title. Or it can mean one step in the process where information or something else of intelligence value is physically acquired. The context usually signals which meaning is relevant.

INTs: Collection disciplines are often called "INTs" as shorthand, because they have a common suffix, for example, COMINT, ELINT, and HUMINT. This practice has led to many terms, some half-serious, for specialized collection and analysis techniques; so terms such as TrashINT appear in this book.

Collateral: This term has a very specific meaning in all collection organizations. It refers to material or information that is extrinsic to the organization, usually reporting or intelligence that is produced by another INT. A **communications intelligence (COMINT)** organization that used imagery to supplement a COMINT report would refer to the imagery as collateral. Conversely, an **imagery intelligence (IMINT)** organization would refer to any COMINT used in its reporting as collateral.

Clandestine versus covert: These two terms are often confused by the layman. An operation is *clandestine* if the opponent or **target** is not supposed to know that it happened at all. Traditional espionage, for example, is intended to be clandestine. An operation is termed *covert* if the opponent or target is aware that it happened but cannot identify the source of the operation (or the source has plausible deniability). A coup attempt, for example, is obvious to many people, but the identity of a foreign intelligence service supporting the coup attempt should not be apparent.

Legacy systems: Over time, collection programs develop established means of collecting intelligence and a set of customers for the product. The term *legacy system* is used to describe such an ongoing collection effort, usually where customer demand makes it difficult to terminate the effort. The term is often used in a pejorative sense, because legacy systems can consume a collection organization's entire budget and leave no room for new initiatives.

Single-source versus all-source analysis: All-source analysts, as the name implies, make use of all relevant sources of intelligence in producing what is described as *finished intelligence.* Their function is detailed in *Intelligence Analysis: A Target-Centric Approach* (4th ed., CQ Press, 2012). But collection organizations also have analysts who specialize in exploiting, analyzing, and reporting the collection product, for example, COMINT analysts, open source analysts, and imagery analysts (today often called **geospatial intelligence [GEOINT]** analysts). The functions performed by these single-source analysts are described in this book.

Multi-INT versus all-source analysis: The difference between these two terms is a controversial issue. Some authors argue that there is no difference. Others distinguish multi-INT analysis (often called multi-INT fusion) as being the merging, or fusion, of raw intelligence from different collection sources, usually to support combat operations.

Competitive intelligence: This is conducted by businesses to assess the strengths and weaknesses of current and potential competitors. This is not the same as *business intelligence* or *market intelligence*. The terms are often confused. Business intelligence has an inward focus. Market intelligence is concerned with customers and the market for products. Neither makes use of collection methods that are generally associated with intelligence.

Acknowledgments and Disclaimer

Many people in the U.S. intelligence communities and academia have provided wisdom that I have incorporated; I cannot name them all, but I appreciate their help. A large part of Chapter 3 (HUMINT) was originally drafted by my colleague at the University of Maryland University College, Professor Peter Oleson. Peter also provided extensive input to Chapter 18 (Managing Intelligence Collection). I am grateful to him for allowing me to use his material.

I am especially grateful to reviewers within and outside the U.S. intelligence community who have contributed their time to improving the text. I especially want to thank Charisse Kiino at CQ Press for her unstinting support and the staff at Sage/CQ Press for shaping the finished product. And most special thanks to my wife and partner Abigail, who edited this text and revised it extensively to make it better reading for you.

All statements of fact, opinion, or analysis expressed are those of the author and do not reflect the official positions or view of the Central Intelligence Agency (CIA) or any other U.S. government agency. Nothing in the contents should be construed as asserting or implying U.S. government authentication of information or Agency endorsement of the author's views. This material has been reviewed by the CIA to prevent the disclosure of classified information.

Robert M. Clark
Wilmington, North Carolina

Acronyms

Acronym	Description
ACINT	intelligence collected from underwater sound
ACOUSTINT	intelligence collected from sound in air
AEOS	Advanced Electro-Optical System
AESA	active electronically scanned array
AFMIC	Armed Forces Medical Intelligence Center (now the National Center for Military Intelligence)
AGI	advanced geospatial intelligence
ALCOR	ARPA Lincoln C-band Observable Radar
ALTAIR	ARPA Long-range Tracking and Identification Radar
AMAN	Military Intelligence Directorate (Israel)
BBC	British Broadcasting Company

BE	Basic encyclopedia or bombing encyclopedia
BIMA	Biometrics Identity Management Agency
BMD	ballistic missile defense
BW	biological warfare
C&C	Command and control
CB	Citizen's band (radio)
CBW	chemical and biological warfare
CCD	charge-coupled device or coherent change detection
CCS	collaborative collection strategies
CDAA	circularly disposed antenna array
CIA	Central Intelligence Agency
CNA	computer network attack
CNE	computer network exploitation
COBRA	Collection by Remote Assets
COMINT	communications intelligence
CW	chemical warfare or continuous wave
D&D	denial and deception
dB	decibels
dBW	decibels above or below one watt
DF	direction finding
DCI	Director of Central Intelligence
DCID	Director of Central Intelligence Directive
DEA	Drug Enforcement Agency
DHS	Department of Homeland Security or Defense HUMINT Service
DIA	Defense Intelligence Agency
DNA	deoxyribonucleic acid
DNI	Director of National Intelligence
DoD	Department of Defense

DSP	defense support program
ECM	electronics countermeasures
ELINT	electronic intelligence
EM	electromagnetic
EMP	electromagnetic pulse
EMR	electromagnetic radiation
EO	electro-optical
EPL	ELINT parameters list
ERS-1	European remote sensing satellite
ESA	European Space Agency
FBI	Federal Bureau of Investigation
FDOA	frequency difference of arrival
FIRCAP	Foreign Intelligence Requirements, Categories, and Priorities
FISINT	foreign instrumentation systems intelligence
FLIR	forward-looking infrared
FM	frequency modulation
FOV	field of view
FSB	Federal'naya Sluzhba Bezopasnosti (Federal Security Service) (Russia)
GAO	Government Accountability Office
GCHQ	General Communications Headquarters (UK)
GDIP	General Defense Intelligence Program
GEO	geostationary orbit
GEODSS	ground-based electro-optical deep space surveillance system
GEOINT	geospatial intelligence
GMTI	ground moving target indicator
GPS	global positioning system
GRU	Glavnoye Razvedyvatel'noye Upravleniye (Main Intelligence Directorate) (Russia)
GSD	ground sample distance

GSM	global system for mobile communications
HEO	highly elliptical orbit
HF	high frequency
HIIDE	handheld interagency identity detection equipment
HPM	high power microwave
HSI	hyperspectral imaging
HUMINT	human intelligence
I&W	indications and warning
IC	intelligence community
IC-MAP	Intelligence Community Multi-intelligence Acquisition Program
ICARS	Intelligence Community Analysis and Requirements System
ICBM	intercontinental ballistic missile
ICM	Integrated Collection Management
IED	improvised explosive device
IEEE	Institute of Electrical and Electronics Engineers
IFOV	instantaneous field of view
IIR	intermediate infrared or intelligence information report
IMINT	imagery intelligence
IMS	International Monitoring System
IR	infrared
ISAR	inverse synthetic aperture radar
ISR	intelligence, surveillance, and reconnaissance
ITU	International Telecommunications Union
IUSS	integrated undersea surveillance system
JCMEC	Joint Captured Materiel Exploitation Center
JCMT	joint collection management tools
JSTARS	Joint Surveillance and Target Attack Radar System
JWICS	Joint Worldwide Intelligence Communication System

KGB	Komityet Gosudarstvennoy Bezopasnosti (Committee for State Security) (Russia)
KIQ	key intelligence question
LEO	low earth orbit
LFM	linear frequency modulation
LITINT	literature intelligence
LPI	low probability of intercept
LWIR	long wavelength infrared
MAD	magnetic anomaly detector
MANPADS	man-portable air defense system
MASINT	measurements and signatures intelligence
MATTS	Marine Asset Tag Tracking System
MEMS	micro electro-mechanical systems
MEO	medium earth orbit
MHz	megahertz
MICE	money, ideology, compromise (or coercion), ego
MRS	MASINT Requirements System
MSI	multispectral imaging
MTI	moving target indicator
Mv	visual magnitude
MWIR	mid-wavelength infrared
NASA	National Aeronautics and Space Administration
NCMI	National Center for Medical Intelligence
NCS	National Clandestine Service
NGA	National Geospatial-Intelligence Agency
NGIC	National Ground Intelligence Center
NGO	nongovernmental organization
NIC-C	National Intelligence Coordination Center
NIE	national intelligence estimate

NIH	not invented here
NIIRS	National Imagery Interpretability Rating Scale
NIPF	National Intelligence Priorities Framework
NIR	near infrared
NITC	National Intelligence Tasking Center
NOAA	National Oceanic and Atmospheric Administration
NORAD	North American Aerospace Defense Command
NPIC	National Photographic Interpretation Center
NRO	National Reconnaissance Office
NSA	National Security Agency
NSC	National Security Council
NSRP	National SIGINT Requirements Process
NTM	national technical means
NUCINT	collection of nuclear debris and radiation
ONIR	overhead nonimaging infrared
OPIR	overhead persistent infrared
OPTINT	collection of nonimaging optical intelligence
OSC	Open Source Center
OSINT	open source intelligence
OSRMS	Open Source Requirements Management System
OTH	over-the-horizon
PDA	personal digital assistant
PDD-35	Presidential Decision Directive 35
PED	processing, exploitation, and dissemination
PHD	phase history data
PLA	People's Liberation Army (China)
PRF	pulse repetition frequency
PRI	pulse repetition interval

QRC	quick reaction capability
R/V or RV	reentry vehicle
RADINT	radar intelligence
RCS	radar cross-section
RDT&E	research, development, test, and evaluation
RF	radio frequency
RFI	radio frequency interference
RFID	radio frequency identification
RMS	Requirements Management System
S&T	scientific and technical
SAM	surface-to-air missile
SAP	Special Access Program
SAR	synthetic aperture radar
SARS	severe acute respiratory syndrome
SBIRS	Space-Based Infrared System
SECAR	Surface-wave Extended Coastal Area Radar
SIGINT	signals intelligence
SIPRNet	Secret Internet Protocol Router Network
SIR-C	a SAR carried on the space shuttle
SIS	Secret Intelligence Service (also known as MI-6) (UK)
SLBM	submarine launched ballistic missile
SNR	signal-to-noise ratio
SOI	space object identification
SOSUS	sound surveillance system
SPOT	Satellite Pour l'Observation de la Terre (French imagery satellite)
STRATCOM	U.S. Strategic Command
SVR	Sluzhba Vneshney Razvedki (Foreign Intelligence Service) (Russia)
SWIR	short wavelength infrared

TDOA	time difference of arrival
TEL	transporter-erector-launcher
TEMPEST	name given to a process for shielding electronics equipment to suppress emissions
TIRA	tracking and imaging radar
TPED	tasking, processing, exploitation, and dissemination
TRADEX	Target Resolution and Discrimination Experiment radar
TT&C	telemetry, tracking, and commanding
UAV	unmanned aeronautical vehicle
UHF	ultra high frequency
USI	ultraspectral imaging
UV	ultraviolet
VHF	very high frequency
VLWIR	very long wavelength infrared
WAN	wide area network
WHO	World Health Organization
WMD	weapons of mass destruction

1. Introduction

This book is organized into three parts, as shown in Figure 1.1: Parts I and II address literal intelligence and nonliteral intelligence. Part III concerns managing intelligence collection.

The logic of the literal/nonliteral intelligence division has been recognized by other writers about intelligence. British author Michael Herman, as quoted in Figure 1.1, has written that there are two basic types of collection: One produces access to human thought processes (literal). One produces evidence in the form of observations and measurements of things (nonliteral).[1]

In other words, one type of collection produces **literal information** in the form that humans use for communication. Analysts and customers generally understand how we collect and use literal information. It requires no special exploitation after the processing step (translation) to be understood. It literally speaks for itself.

Nonliteral information, in contrast, usually requires technical expertise applied in processing and exploitation in order for analysts to make use of it. Many customers don't understand it.

Functionally, intelligence collection produces either literal or nonliteral intelligence. Each is treated quite differently by analysts, customers, and collectors. It's worth taking a moment to discuss the distinctions they tend to make.

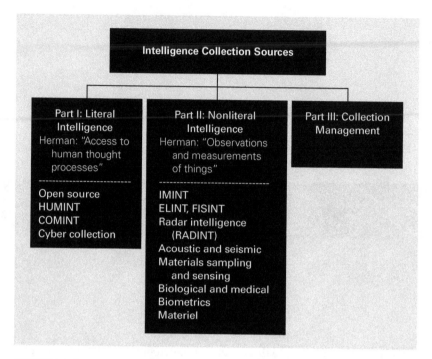

FIGURE 1.1 Book Organization

Analyst Vulnerability. Analysts can challenge the interpretation of communications intelligence (COMINT), human intelligence (HUMINT), cyber collection, or open source, if they have access to the original material (and have language and cultural expertise). As the chapters in Part I indicate, you may have to deal with translator or single-source analyst bias (especially in HUMINT and COMINT). But if the processor or exploiter of nonliteral material makes a judgment, it's difficult to contradict unless you are also an expert in the field. Interpreting a hyperspectral image or an electronic intelligence (ELINT) recording, for example, takes special expertise. Just as you don't read X-rays (unless you're a medical doctor), you don't interpret hyperspectral or synthetic aperture radar imagery. You can't interpret an infrasound recording or a magnetic anomaly detector reading, unless you've had some training. Even optical images, which can be interpreted to some extent, have nuances that are best left to imagery analysts. This inability to independently verify nonliteral evidence causes all-source analysts much angst. Often, analysts are placed in the position of having to accept the conclusions reached by single-source analysts because of their inability to question the validity of the conclusion. They are left unable to spot potential bias or mistakes.

Customer Vulnerability. Customers—those who must take action based on intelligence—have a different vulnerability. Many believe that they can personally analyze raw literal intelligence—HUMINT, COMINT, and open source. These sources are usually considered "soft"—the product's credibility may be open to question. Literal intelligence usually must be translated and interpreted, and mistakes or bias can creep into either part of the process. You also have the possibility of deception, which is more common with literal intelligence. Experienced all-source analysts are trained to deal with these credibility issues. But raw literal intelligence often goes directly to the end users, bypassing the all-source analysts; and because customers are absent training and experience, they are apt to draw poor, even dangerous, conclusions—sometimes by rejecting valid intelligence reporting, sometimes by accepting invalid reporting. On the infrequent occasions when customers get the raw nonliteral intelligence, they have the same problems but usually are a bit more cautious about using the material.

Timeliness. The delineation between literal and nonliteral intelligence has become more significant because of the increasing demand for timely information. Intelligence must be timely, especially when used to support modern military operations. The literal information sources rarely meet this requirement. As Michael Herman notes, customers believe that "textual sources cannot be counted upon, certainly not in near real time."[2] But two of the important nonliteral collection sources used in military operations, imagery intelligence (IMINT) and ELINT, routinely meet the timeliness standard.

Libraries. Literal intelligence reporting is stored in repositories so that it can be searched (usually using keywords). But these repositories are static and relatively small compared with the huge dynamic libraries that characterize nonliteral intelligence. You have to determine what to measure for many specialties in nonliteral intelligence and to what level of detail. You have a set of biometric "fingerprints" for every person you collect on and an extensive set for nuclear materials. Hyperspectral imaging, discussed in Chapter 10, requires massive libraries, and they're quickly out of date. As Chapter 14 explains, every aircraft or tank has a unique sound signature; and you can often identify specific aircraft or vehicles, leading to an even larger library.

For these reasons, along with each requiring different analytical approaches, it makes sense for literal and nonliteral collection to be discussed separately.

Figure 1.2 shows the types of collection covered in this book and identifies the chapter where that type is discussed. The figure also distinguishes the types of literal and nonliteral intelligence.

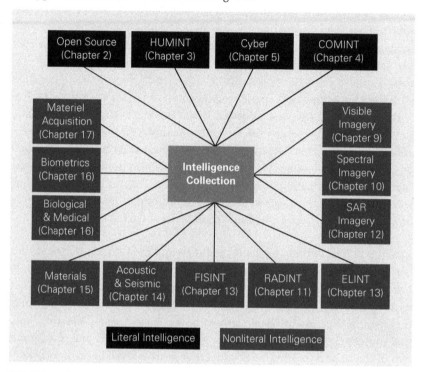

FIGURE 1.2 Taxonomy of Intelligence Collection

Part I: Literal Collection

The key to understanding intelligence collection (or intelligence, for that matter) is to look at it as a complex system and to apply systems methodology in examining it. This methodology characterizes any system in three ways: by its function, process, and structure. Following that methodology, in Part I we look at the literal collection INTs, with a focus on function, process, and structure. Let's look at each of these characteristics in the context of intelligence collection.

FUNCTION

Function determines what a system produces and for whom. In collection that means determining who the customers are, what is produced for them, the purposes that the product serves, and how valuable it is to them. Most chapters in Part I also have a brief discussion of the sources following the function section.

But there is another way to look at the function performed—by the nature of the product and the customer set.

Much intelligence collection is high volume, with automated processing of a mass of material, which then is disseminated widely. Customers and all-source analysts get a great deal of open source, HUMINT, IMINT, and signals intelligence (SIGINT) without having to ask for it.

The other kind is targeted or boutique collection. Think of the contrast between a Wal-Mart and a boutique store such as Tiffany's that caters to a select customer set. Targeted collection is usually expensive, produced in small quantity for a few customers. It requires extensive processing and exploitation.

The collection INTs shown in brown in Figure 1.3 are targeted. Those shown in blue are usually high volume collection but sometimes are targeted. ELINT is an example: it can be either, as we'll see in Chapter 13.

PROCESS

Process, in this book, refers to how information moves through the collection phase to get to the customers. It is often described as the intelligence

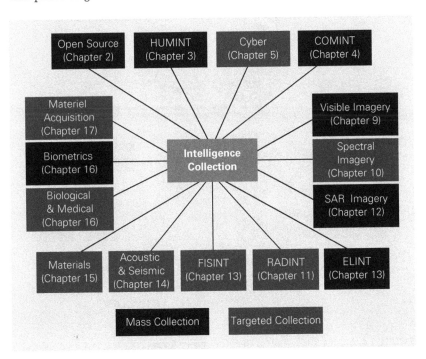

FIGURE 1.3 Mass versus Targeted Collection

cycle, but this is a misnomer; intelligence generally, and collection in particular, does not work as a cycle.

The book *Intelligence Analysis: A Target-Centric Approach* explains in detail why the intelligence process is not a cycle. Most books and courses on intelligence nevertheless continue to view it as a cycle. And collectors have a slightly different view. They tend to view the process as shown in Figure 1.4.

The primary focus of the chapters in this book is on the overall process shown in Figure 1.4. Collectors tend to group it into three distinct stages, as shown in the figure: requirements and tasking are called the front end: the process of deciding what information to go after and what collection means to use. Then you have collection. Following that, processing, exploitation, and dissemination of the intelligence that has been collected are called the back end. In an ideal system, you'd then identify the gaps in knowledge. You then revise the requirements, and the process begins anew.

There's a clue here in the use of the terms front end and back end. It's more reasonable to think of it as a straight line process with a beginning and an end, rather than a cycle. That's how it works in practice. In theory, there should be a connection between dissemination and requirements, forming a cycle. That's how it is shown in most textbooks. But intelligence collectors typically only are responsible for the process from requirements to dissemination. They don't control the step in which new requirements are generated

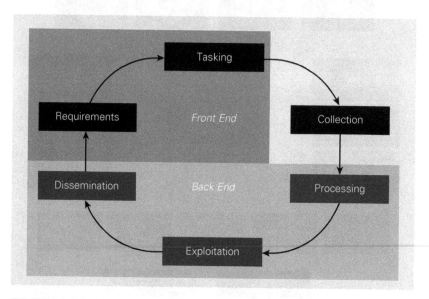

FIGURE 1.4 A Collector's View of the Intelligence Cycle

based on the gaps in knowledge. Someone else has to do it. Usually, that's the all-source analyst, working with the customer.

STRUCTURE

Structure refers to how a system is organized and why. It considers the driving forces that shape the configuration of the system.

When applied to collection, structure is needed to efficiently (that is, in the least costly and most timely way) and effectively (that is, to succeed with minimum risk) obtain useful intelligence. You want a structure that can carry out the process and achieve the function. We're going to spend most of the time on the function and process of collection. We'll talk only in general terms about structure in this book. The collection organizations and programs keep changing and will continue to change, driven by bureaucratic considerations. But the basic processes and functions endure.

All collection structures are compromises, with their attendant problems. We'll discuss those in some detail. The structures vary within each collection discipline, but they have two recurring themes: whether to create a stovepipe or a collaborative structure and how much to centralize versus distributing the collection function.

"Stovepipe" versus Collaborative Structure. Most countries divide collection methods using the INT (short for intelligence) guilds to protect equities—that is, to define the areas of collection responsibility of large collection organizations. In the United States, for example, the National Geospatial-Intelligence Agency (NGA) is responsible for IMINT. SIGINT is a responsibility of the National Security Agency (NSA) in the United States and of the General Communications Headquarters (GCHQ) in the United Kingdom. So INT names are the result of bureaucratic initiatives, not proper INT descriptions. These are what we call the stovepipes. The division used in the United States, and followed to some extent in several countries, is shown in Figure 1.5.

Stovepipe, as noted in the preface, is the term used to describe a structure that is a relatively isolated vertical conduit for intelligence. Stovepipes are common among collection organizations at the national level. They are less so at the tactical military and law enforcement levels. Compartmentation is a key part of the reason for a stovepipe structure. Such compartmentation reduces the risks of disclosures that cause national embarrassment or loss of sources (e.g., the WikiLeaks disclosures during 2010). So intelligence collection organizations use various forms of compartmentation, especially to

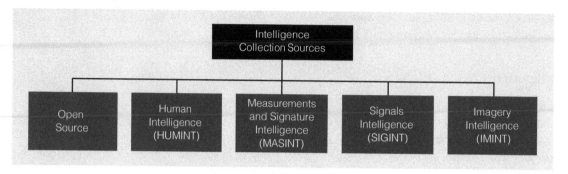

FIGURE 1.5 Stovepipe Structure of Intelligence Collection

protect what are sometimes called their crown jewels—their most sensitive products. This book discusses some of the structures and processes they use to do that.

The taxonomy of intelligence collection described in Figure 1.2 will seem somewhat strange to readers who are familiar with the traditional U.S. division into open source, HUMINT, SIGINT, IMINT (or GEOINT), and measurements and signatures intelligence (MASINT). But the U.S. demarcation, useful as it may be in defining structure, is not useful in studying the function and process of intelligence collection. It leads to careless use of terminology; for example, people often use the term *SIGINT* when they really are describing COMINT. And the other components of collection traditionally included as SIGINT (ELINT and foreign instrumentation signals intelligence [FISINT]) are treated quite differently throughout the tasking, processing, exploitation, and dissemination stages of the collection process.

At the opposite extreme from stovepipes are collaborative units such as fusion centers, which share intelligence freely across collection boundaries.[3] Fusion centers work well at the lower classification levels where protection of sources and methods is not such a critical issue. But the more widely sensitive information is shared, the more likely it is to become openly known. As a simple example, suppose that 99.9 percent of a group can be trusted to protect a secret. By the time the group has grown to 1,000 members, you're down to about a 36-percent chance that it's still a secret.

Centralized versus Decentralized Structure. Below the top-level stovepipe structure shown in Figure 1.5, different collection INTs use different structures; they are discussed in this book. In structuring an organization to collect, process, analyze, and disseminate intelligence, the up-front question is this: Do you create a centralized organization, a decentralized one, or some mix? In answering that question, you have to consider the

- customers and their needs,
- sources of collection, and
- processing requirements.

Let's look at them in turn, recognizing that the three are very much interconnected.

Customers. There are generally considered to be three levels of intelligence, viewed from the customer perspective. Military customers usually demarcate them as strategic, operational, and tactical.[4] Other customers such as policymakers and law enforcement organizations sometimes divide them into two levels: strategic and tactical. It has been suggested that the lines between these levels are blurred to the point that the distinction is no longer useful. University of Maryland Professor William Nolte, a veteran of the COMINT world, has observed that "national and departmental intelligence, military and nonmilitary intelligence, or strategic and tactical intelligence, simply do not exist as separate realities."[5] We'll continue to use them here, though, for the purpose of discussing collection structure.

A major customer consideration concerns the timeliness of the information that is collected. The customer's need for timeliness differs, depending on whether the customer is receiving strategic, operational, or tactical intelligence. Strategic and operational intelligence are usually not time-critical, compared with tactical intelligence; so the structure to support them tends to be centralized.

A decentralized structure is more attractive for supporting tactical intelligence, whether military or law enforcement. It allows the intelligence unit to be responsive to the immediate needs of the tactical organization. Tactical intelligence requires rapid dissemination to a specific group of end users within the theater of operations. The resulting structure has to be predesigned in advance for speed. Some law enforcement (e.g., counternarcotics) groups must deal with the same time-critical pressures. So a decentralized structure has advantages in providing time-sensitive intelligence.

Sources. A centralized organization has substantial advantages when collection must deal with a diversity of sources. Large intelligence organizations such as those of major powers collect worldwide. They make use of aircraft and satellites, overt ground-based sites, seaborne collectors, and covert and clandestine operations. Though collected from different sources, much of this material only makes sense when collated together to produce a more complete picture of a situation. The collation is best done centrally.

The bulk of tactical military intelligence, though, is collected by units (aircraft, ground sites, and ships) deployed in a theater and is most useful to the parent military organization of the collector. Communicating the material from these collection assets to processing and analysis units requires the use of highly secure communications. But even for intelligence services that have modern secure communications worldwide, it makes little sense to send it to a central unit unless the central unit can add value. This, combined with the desire of military units to control their intelligence assets, results in a tension between the military and other (primarily national) users. Military commanders often observe that "if I don't control it, I can't depend on it." The military services are therefore prone to argue that information collected in the field should be classified as operational support information, not intelligence.

Another source consideration is the sensitivity of the information that is collected. While strategic and operational intelligence is usually not time-critical, the source of the information is often very sensitive. Centralized control usually is better at protecting sources and methods.

Processing, Analysis, and Dissemination. Finally, the processing and analysis requirements shape the structure of a collection system. One advantage of centralization is that it can achieve what is often referred to as *critical mass.* Having all the processing, exploitation, and analysis talent in one place helps in planning, standardization, training, and mentoring. A high volume of traffic yields best to centralized processing. And a centralized group has the luxury of doing in-depth exploitation and analysis that is difficult to do in a decentralized structure.

But a common criticism of centralized operations is that they take too long to produce intelligence, analyzing it in detail instead of simply translating and disseminating it. The basis of the problem is that centralized organizations have no competition in getting the information out. Add to this the natural tendency for a single-source analyst to want to fully understand the material before reporting it, and you have a combination that encourages delay where the information is not time-sensitive. An example of this from outside the intelligence world is the history of the Dead Sea Scrolls. The original plan was for a centralized translation of the scrolls (several translators were selected, and each originally was given exclusive rights to translate a section of the scrolls). The original translators were in no hurry (being scholars, they wanted the recognition that comes from analyzing as well as translating) until they suddenly had competition in translating the material.

Decentralization has problems, though, when it comes to collating and sharing information. Decentralization inevitably involves duplication of effort. It also can make information sharing more difficult; competition provides an incentive to hoard the information for advantage. And while competition provides an incentive to get material out quickly, that advantage comes at a price. News organizations have to deal with a similar problem, and their experience illustrates the risk associated with a decentralized organization. News organizations are fast in getting the information out, so as not to be scooped. They all want to beat each other to the punch. The result is that they occasionally get the facts wrong because of the rush to be first. A similar problem occurs when there are multiple competing collection organizations: The rush to be first can easily result in erroneous or at least misleading intelligence reports.

Other Structures. In organizing at the lower levels, we eventually come to an additional question: do you further structure topically, by country, or by source? A team focused on the source is familiar with the special quirks of the source but less familiar with customer needs (since it will have many customers). A topical organization (e.g., counterterrorism, economics, military) has more customer focus but may miss key features of the source. A country or regional suborganization deals best with the translation issue, grouping linguists by language.

Finally, a high volume collection organization that supports many customers typically uses a different structure than a small operation that supports a select customer group. The difference is discussed in the next section.

Part II: Nonliteral Collection

Part II of the book is organized much like Part I. Because it deals with nonliteral collection there is more emphasis on the process. The focus is on explaining how the collection sensors work, and specifically on the back-end process. The reason for this shift is that many of the nonliteral collection systems, their capabilities and limitations, are not well understood by all-source analysts and their customers.

Part II interchangeably uses the terms *nonliteral* and *technical* collection. The word *technical* is not meant to refer to the use of technology. All of the collection disciplines shown in Figure 1.2 rely on technology; COMINT and cyber collection in particular cannot function without sophisticated technologies. As noted earlier, technical collection in this text is defined as the collection, processing, and exploitation of nonliteral information—information in a form not used for human communication.

We begin with an overview of nonliteral (technical) collection systems. We continue with a discussion of sensors and of the fundamental idea of collecting signatures. Signatures are explained in Chapter 6. Because they are mentioned here, a brief definition: **Signatures** refer to the distinctive characteristics of persons, objects, or activities that result from processing of collected intelligence. Most of the signatures collected for intelligence are from the electromagnetic (EM) spectrum (which includes the optical spectrum) and are collected at distances of a few kilometers to thousands of kilometers, using a technique called *remote sensing*. Other signatures such as those from radioactive material are collected at very short ranges. After an overview of how the sensors work, the techniques and systems used for intelligence collection are discussed in depth. This includes a discussion of platforms (aircraft, satellites, ships, and ground sites) that are used to collect signatures for intelligence purposes.

The next several chapters are devoted to discussing how specific systems work and how the results are processed. Technical collection involves using radar, radio frequency receivers, lasers, passive electro-optical devices, nuclear radiation detectors, and seismic or acoustic sensors. These instruments gather measurements (such as radar cross-sections, radiant intensities, or temperatures) to characterize military operations and tactics; to assess missile, aircraft, and propulsion systems performance; to monitor research, development, testing, and production facilities; and to understand cultural and economic activities, environmental effects, and naturally occurring phenomena.

A separate class of sensors operates outside the electromagnetic spectrum. Most of these collection sensors operate at short ranges and sense acoustic, magnetic, or nuclear signatures. These non-RF sensors are discussed in subsequent chapters. The sensor chapters provide specific examples of sensors used in technical collection and discuss the fundamental limitations and trade-offs that are inherent in any technical collection sensor.

Some technical collection does not involve sensors at all. Instead, the signatures are obtained by collecting physical objects and equipment (usually referred to as **materiel**) or samples of substances (usually grouped under the heading of **materials**). These collection specialties are discussed in Chapters 15 through 17.

Nonliteral collection as defined and discussed in this book has different names within intelligence organizations, depending on the organization and the specific field being discussed. Much of it is often called MASINT in the United States and allied countries. The term *MASINT* also encompasses a number of acronyms that identify unique sources, such as

ACOUSTINT (collection of acoustic signals)

IRINT (collection of infrared signals)

LASINT (collection of laser signals)

NUCINT (collection of nuclear debris and radiation)

OPTINT (collection of nonimaging optical intelligence)

RADINT (radar tracking and measurement of aerospace vehicles)

Some classes of technical collection have specific names, such as advanced geospatial intelligence (AGI), electronic intelligence (ELINT), geospatial intelligence (GEOINT), or imagery intelligence (IMINT). These terms are a convenient shorthand, and some of them are used in this book to describe subsets of technical collection. They are widely used in the United States and allied intelligence communities, so the reader needs to understand what they mean. Still, many of them are not helpful and simply promote confusion and overlap of responsibilities, especially in the U.S. intelligence community. As noted earlier, many of these names derive from political and bureaucratic rather than physical considerations.

Terms like AGI and GEOINT are not helpful in describing collection. GEOINT and other terms that have recently come into popular vogue, like *activity-based intelligence*, are in any event not collection INTs. They are forms of all-source analysis, and all intelligence organizations—including national-level, military support, and law enforcement intelligence—do geospatial analysis and activity-based intelligence analysis.

In summary, the United States and many other national intelligence organizations are structured by what we call INTs, which are often used to create what are called stovepipes, but the educational process is ill-served by using these organizational divisions to structure learning. In this book, many of these terms are subsumed under the term technical collection, which has some unifying themes:

- Collection of nonliteral information, as noted previously
- Identification of a signature
- Association of a signature with a person, feature, or object and identification of changes in the state of the person, feature, or object (for example, by geolocating him, her, or it)

It can be argued that the term MASINT covers this definition. But many processes in what are traditionally called SIGINT and IMINT, in fact, involve the measurement of an object or signal and the development of an identifying signature. For example, imagery interpretation often involves both measurement of objects in an image and identifying unique signatures of objects in an image.

Introduction

Part III: Collection Management and Strategy

Part III discusses the management of collection and the development of collection strategies. A number of studies in the United States have investigated collection organizations and addressed the need for better interaction among the different INTs that are covered in this book. The 104th Congress directed a study, "IC21: The Intelligence Community in the 21st Century," that recommended consolidating technical collection and exploitation activities (which include SIGINT, IMINT, and MASINT) into a technical collection agency—identical to the structure defined by the Deputy Director of National Intelligence for Collection.[6] This book does not directly address the merits of such an agency, but the final chapter does focus on the substantial challenges of managing collection across disciplines.

Part III explains how collection can be managed most effectively across disciplines or stovepipes. It deals heavily with the front end—the planning, requirements, and tasking phases. Much of the discussion focuses on the strategy for collection, aiming to make intelligence collection as high as possible in the chain of preferences described below.

The ideal collection strategy is **clandestine**. That is, the opponent never knows that it happened. The reason is that if the opponent knows about it, then the collection has less value. The opponent can take measures to minimize the damage (e.g., by changing operational plans if he suspects that they have been compromised) and to prevent future losses to the same collection effort. There are numerous ways to collect clandestinely, and some of them are covered in this book. You can make a collection device small and conceal it well. If it's large and must be mobile, you can disguise it, for example, in a plumbing service van or a beer truck. If it flies, you can make it very stealthy and quiet.

Failing clandestine collection, the next best thing is for the opponent to be uncertain just what was lost to the collector. The opponent might know that you have agent penetrations or communications intercepts and what your imagers can do. But he may not know where the penetrations are, which communications links are being read, and what your imagery targets are. As much as possible, you want to conceal the mission or purpose of the collection. Finally, in technical collection, it may be that the fact of collection is known, but the capability of the equipment (and what you're getting from it) is unexpected. Having a technology edge helps this.

Next in line of preference is that the collection is resistant to counterintelligence (including destruction, capture, compromise, or denial and deception) if the opponent knows what is being lost and how. A simple example is the surveillance camera that is ubiquitous in banks and many stores. You may know that it's there, but your options for countering it are limited. Against a well-configured set of surveillance cameras, you may be able to conceal your identity but not your activity.

The least desirable case happens when the opponent knows what you are collecting and can do something to counter it. Examples include knowing who your agents are, which of his codes you have broken, where your cyber collection has succeeded, what your imagery targets are, and what you're learning from the imagery. If you ever get to the worst case, you are set up to be deceived and manipulated.

Summary

Intelligence collection divides broadly into two types. One type produces access to human thought processes in the form of *literal* intelligence. One type produces *nonliteral* intelligence based on the observations and measurements of things. We can comprehend literal intelligence without need for special assistance other than language translation. Nonliteral intelligence requires expert processing and exploitation to make it understandable, and even then we often require interpretation assistance from analysts who specialize in that collection discipline.

Intelligence collection is best looked at from a systems point of view; that is, by examining the function, process, and structure of the collection system.

- *Collection function* is concerned with the sources used, what the collection produces, and for whom. Functionally, intelligence collection divides into two major categories. Much of it is high volume, produced for a large customer set, and widely distributed; this could be thought of as mass or volume collection. The other category is targeted or boutique collection, produced in small quantities for a relatively small customer set.

- *Collection process* explains how information moves through the stages of collection to get to the customers (usually all-source intelligence analysts). Collectors view this process as having three stages: the front end, comprising requirements and tasking; collection; and the back end, comprising processing, exploitation, and dissemination (often abbreviated "PED").

- *Collection structure* focuses on the organizational form that is used. At the top level, this usually takes the form of what are called stovepipes, because they are relatively isolated and compartmented conduits for the flow of information. Below that level, the structure may be stovepiped or collegial, and it may take a centralized form, a decentralized form, or some mix. The customers, the nature of the sources, and the processing and exploitation needs all determine which structure works best.

In Part I, the four literal collection systems—open source, HUMINT, COMINT, and cyber—are examined using this systems analysis model.

Part II examines nonliteral (technical) collection systems, most of which rely on remote sensing using some part of the electromagnetic spectrum. Part II takes a similar organizational approach to that used in Part I, with emphasis on how the collection systems work and on the back-end process. Most of these nonliteral collection means are less well known than those described in Part I.

Part III goes into collection management, with a focus on the front end where requirements and gaps in knowledge are translated into a collection strategy and thence into tasking of collection assets.

The ideal collection strategy does not present an obvious threat. That typically means that collection is *unwarned, unconventional,* and *unexpected.* Preferably, collection is clandestine; the opponent never knows that it happened. Failing that, it is desirable for the opponent to be uncertain what secrets were lost to your collection. If the opponent does know what was lost and how, then at least collection should be resistant to counterintelligence (including destruction, capture, compromise, or denial and deception). The worst case occurs when the opponent has all of the knowledge needed to effectively counter collection, such as by denial, deception, and perception management.

NOTES

1. Michael Herman, *Intelligence Services in the Information Age* (New York: Frank Cass Publishers, 2001), 82.
2. Ibid.
3. An explanation of fusion centers and how they operate is in Robert M. Clark, *Intelligence Analysis: A Target-Centric Approach,* 4th ed. (Washington, DC: CQ Press, 2012).
4. JCS Joint Pub 2–0, "Joint Doctrine for Intelligence Support to Operations," Chapter 3.
5. William M. Nolte, "Rethinking War and Intelligence," in *Rethinking the Principles of War,* Anthony D. McIvor, ed. (Annapolis: Naval Institute Press, 2005), 423.
6. U.S. House of Representatives, Permanent Select Committee on Intelligence Staff Study, "IC21: The Intelligence Community in the 21st Century" (June 5, 1996).

2. Open Source Intelligence

Open source is a term used to describe material that is publicly available but is used to produce intelligence. Open source information traditionally meant published material—newspapers, books, and periodicals. As such it formerly was referred to as *literature intelligence (LITINT)*. The term LITINT fell into disuse because it was too narrow; it did not include radio and television broadcasts.

Today open source intelligence covers much more than traditional published sources, and the term *open source intelligence (OSINT)* has become the standard descriptor. It includes media such as newspapers, magazines, radio, television, and computer-based information; professional and academic material from conferences, symposia, professional associations, and academic papers; government reports and official data; and user-generated Web content such as social networking sites, video sharing sites, Twitter, wikis, and blogs. Commercial databases hold vast economic data that are available for the price of a subscription. All fit the open source category, though they are not published in the traditional sense.

Open source collection is defined as the process of finding, selecting, and acquiring information from publicly available sources; translating foreign language material; and analyzing it to produce actionable intelligence. The following sections describe the structure of open source organizations, their sources, and the process of producing open source intelligence.

Function

Open source material is the dominant source of intelligence in volume, and arguably in value as well. In the United States, it's been estimated that 90 percent of what is needed to produce intelligence is found in open source.[1] Its chief value is that, compared with other literal sources such as human intelligence (HUMINT) and communications intelligence (COMINT), it is relatively easy to obtain. It also is valuable for customer organizations (e.g., law enforcement) where lack of clearances constrain access to classified material.

Open source has two major roles in intelligence.

- Its most visible role is as the source for a finished intelligence product. Open source is where the all-source analyst should start, because it's so cheap to get and easy to use. Analysts should not turn to more expensive collection resources until exhausting the potential of OSINT. They should almost never ask collectors to go after things that already are in open source. And they should keep coming back to it as the expensive sources provide new leads. In practice, this does not occur enough because of a perception issue, as discussed in the next section.

- The second role is that of triggering collection or validating collection by another INT such as COMINT or HUMINT; that role is discussed later in this chapter.

PERCEPTIONS OF OPEN SOURCE

Despite its value and the wide availability of open source, there continues to be a debate within governments about open source as a legitimate collection INT. Governmental intelligence, in the view of many, is about discovering secrets. As a result, open source is not well perceived among all-source analysts, and this perception problem hinders its effective use. In 1996, a congressional commission created to study intelligence issues noted that vast amounts of open source information had become readily available, but the intelligence community had been slow in using it.[2]

Nearly a decade later little had changed, according to another commission assembled to assess the intelligence community's failed prewar assessment that Iraq was developing weapons of mass destruction. Open sources "offer vast intelligence possibilities," said the WMD Commission's 2005 report. "Regrettably, all too frequently these 'non-secret' sources are undervalued and underused."[3] The WMD commission went on to observe that analysts "rely too much on secret information and use non-clandestine and public information too little. Non-clandestine sources of information are critical to understanding societal, cultural, and political trends, but they are underutilized."[4]

Though both commissions criticized all-source analysts' inattention to open source, there are at least two explanations why analysts are reluctant to use open source more heavily in finished intelligence:

- Analysts really don't want to admit that something was discovered in open source.[5] In a sense, open source is a threat; after all, anyone can do it without a clearance.
- Many analysts consider secret data collected by covert means to be more meaningful or important than open or unclassified data, and to weigh it more heavily.[6]

This bias against open source has received much criticism. It does have a basis, though: the concept of competitive advantage. In both government and commercial affairs, all players seek a competitive advantage over their opponents. Open source, because it is available to all players, can't provide that competitive advantage. Secret information can do so, and both governmental and competitive intelligence analysts prefer it for that reason.[7]

The perception problem has led some clandestine services (though not, to the author's knowledge, the U.S. service) to report open source material as if it had been collected by an agent. What has happened is that a case officer, pressed to justify his value, created fictitious agents and provided open source material as the agent's reporting. The headquarters offices of some clandestine services keep track of open source publications in their target countries, to ensure that their HUMINT reporting does not duplicate open source reporting.

MAINTAINING GLOBAL AND REGIONAL COVERAGE

Any country having global interests must have current information about possible opportunities or threats to its national interests worldwide. In intelligence terms, it must maintain **global coverage**. And all countries have regional concerns; they must maintain similar databases about nearby countries. In intelligence terms, they must maintain **regional coverage**.

To address these needs, the U.S. intelligence community has developed many variants on what is called a **basic encyclopedia**—which provides intelligence on regions (ports, airfields, military bases, economic intelligence, environmental intelligence, etc.). This intelligence, much of which is unclassified, is also called a **baseline**. Following are two examples; both

Open Source Intelligence

rely primarily on open source intelligence, supplemented by classified sources:

• U.S. military intelligence has long maintained a document called the Basic Encyclopedia (BE). This compendium describes every installation that might be of interest to intelligence agencies and to the operational and planning staff of military commands. The encyclopedia contains basic data on the identification, location, and function of each installation and assigns a unique BE number to each. It can be used to select potential fixed targets for attack and to identify installations (such as public utilities and hospitals) that are not to be attacked. The compendium was originally called the "Bombing Encyclopedia," but the name was changed because the addition of mosques, public utilities, and hospitals might leave a false impression that these were targets for attack.

• The Central Intelligence Agency (CIA) annually publishes the World Factbook, both online[8] and in a classified version. The online version can serve as a regional coverage baseline for almost any country's diplomatic, military, and intelligence services.

Such baselines can be handled by open source and can be kept current by staffers without security clearances. Alternatively, they can be quickly updated when needed rather than being constantly maintained. For example, suppose a country moves into a watch status (because it appears that a crisis is developing there or customer interest has increased). An existing but outdated baseline can quickly be updated with open source material and supplemented with classified material.

SUPPORTING SPECIFIC ANALYTIC PRODUCTS

Almost all finished intelligence products rely on open source—some more than others. Following is a breakdown by the intelligence discipline. Even when a government controls the media, the nuances (what is reported and what isn't reported) can provide valuable insights. That was true before the Internet; it's still true. Social networking adds a whole new dimension, as discussed later in this chapter.

Political. Political analysis draws heavily on open source intelligence. The statements of government leaders tell us much about their attitudes, their personalities (for personality profiling), their intent, and the stresses that may exist within their governments. Their statements always have to be analyzed in context (who they are talking to and what agendas they have, for example) and have to be assessed with a good understanding of the leaders' national and organizational cultures. This is discussed in more detail in the process section.

In assessing political intelligence, one has to be able to distinguish two types of bias: systemic and random bias. A bathroom scale (the old-fashioned spring-controlled kind) has a systemic bias. It will consistently weigh somewhat more or less than the actual weight, and you can calibrate for that bias. It also will have a very small random bias due to the temperature of the spring or how you stand on the scale. This bias is much more difficult to determine and really isn't of interest anyway in the case of a bathroom scale.

Similarly, some TV news stations (Fox News and MSNBC come to mind) are believed to have a political bias. Also, the *New York Times* and the *Wall Street Journal* often have different views on the same news event. These are all systemic biases. You can calibrate for them, that is, take them into account, when interpreting news reports. They also have what we'll call random biases: that is, they occasionally deviate from the party line. Like the bathroom scale, these biases are frequently difficult to identify. Unlike the bathroom scale's random biases, these variances can be of great interest, because they often indicate an agenda behind the news reporting.

Exactly the same thing happens with the media in other countries, and the variances can be of great intelligence significance. Fine nuances in public statements can convey a lot to an experienced political analyst. Minor word changes in a regime-controlled press (e.g., the former Soviet Union or in China today) can signal a policy shift.[9] Political analysts of the Soviet Union, nicknamed "Kremlinologists" in the U.S. intelligence community, once made a living catching these shifts.

Economic. It has been estimated that 95 percent of economic intelligence is derived from open source.[10] Economic analysis relies heavily on the very large databases concerning international trade and national economies that have been assembled by international organizations such as the United Nations. From these and other sources, economic analysts compile statistics about many areas of the economy: agricultural production, trade, raw materials, industrial output, and energy, to name just a few. As with political reporting, small shifts in these statistics can have great intelligence significance.

Economic analysts also depend on macroeconomic models to produce trend assessments about economic sectors, and open source provides the primary feedstock for these models.

The Soviet Union, during the Cold War, made extensive use of open source economic reporting in an unusual way. Kremlin officials did not trust the official reports they received about their own economy. They read carefully, and sometimes acted on, assessments of their economy published in the West by academics and by the CIA. In an interesting twist, the Kremlin's subsequent actions after the leadership read a CIA report obviated the report's main conclusion. The CIA report concluded that the Soviet petroleum industry was facing a serious shortfall. Following the release of the CIA study, the Kremlin directed a major shift in investment spending in favor of the oil and gas industries. Soviet extraction and exploration increased significantly during the late 1970s, and the shortfall never happened.[11]

Military. Military and scientific and technical (S&T) intelligence depend on open source, especially for triggering other collection sources. Open source material is commonly perceived as less useful for military intelligence because the "good" material is classified. In fact, a group of unclassified facts, put together, can be classified. It's often the analysis of the facts that makes the collection classified, as the following example illustrates.

A significant intelligence success during World War II was based on the skillful use of open sources. The Germans maintained effective censorship on open source about war materiel production. But they published their freight tariffs on all goods, including petroleum products. Working from those tariffs, a young U.S. Office of Strategic Services analyst, Walter Levy, conducted geospatial modeling to pinpoint the exact location of the German refineries, which were subsequently targeted by allied bombers.[12]

Military organizations also publish their thinking about strategy and tactics openly. Most military academies publish journals in which professors and students share ideas about military affairs. And senior officers often write articles or books on the same topics. In the 1970 movie *Patton,* General George Patton reads a book on tactics written by his opponent, Field Marshal Erwin Rommel. Patton, in the movie, uses the knowledge to defeat Rommel's forces.

In the case of China, the problem isn't lack of open source about military developments. The Chinese produce great volumes of it. One problem lies in figuring out which material deserves credibility—a topic we'll return to later, in a discussion of source analysis. A second problem is interpreting the material correctly, as the following example illustrates.

The misreading or misinterpretation of open sources can have serious national consequences. In 1965, Lin Biao, then the expected successor to Chairman Mao Zedong, wrote a pamphlet asserting that the countryside of the world (the developing countries) would defeat the cities (the advanced countries). The U.S. leadership concluded that the pamphlet was a Chinese blueprint for supporting subversion around the world, especially in

Indochina. That conclusion factored into President Lyndon Johnson's decision to intervene in Vietnam. A much later examination of the text indicated that Lin Biao actually was arguing almost the opposite: that the conduct of a revolution was the responsibility of the people in that country, to be carried out primarily through their own efforts. Far from indicating a Chinese willingness to intervene, it set limits on Chinese military support.[13]

Other. Many other intelligence disciplines rely heavily on open source. Scientific, technical, and environmental intelligence all make extensive use of open source. An intelligence discipline that has carried various names— social intelligence, psychosocial intelligence, and in military parlance, "human terrain"—relies heavily on open source. It includes information about local culture, customs, religious persuasion, the economic situation, and political attitudes.[14]

Open source has been particularly effective in providing intelligence about terrorists and insurgent groups.[15] These groups depend on the Web, open publications, and radio and television broadcasts to recruit and rally adherents to their causes. The volume of relevant material is so great in the case of terrorists that compendia of terrorism open source intelligence have been generated.[16] The British Broadcasting Company's (BBC) regional monitoring station in Uzbekistan, for example, routinely transcribes broadcasts by Afghan radio stations sympathetic to the Taliban, providing an insight into the thinking of the militant Islamists.[17]

Law enforcement use of open source has increased markedly in the last two decades. The rise in Internet-related crime has led to a corresponding rise in law enforcement use of this open source to identify, track, and apprehend these criminals:

- White-collar criminals make extensive use of the Internet to defraud. Law enforcement uses the same media to identify the perpetrators.
- Social networking sites attract sexual predators and stalkers. Law enforcement makes use of those sites to catch them.
- Many organized criminal groups such as gangs use the Web for communications. Monitoring the communications allows police to selectively target enforcement operations.

Competitive. For competitive intelligence, open source is perhaps the major source, since cyber collection,[18] clandestine HUMINT, and COMINT are problematic, if not illegal, activities for businesses. However, companies have to make a number of government-required filings, and many of these are publicly available. Press releases and trade show literature provide additional insights. Firms such as Barron's and Dow Jones provide extensive financial information about companies to their customers. Credit reporting companies such as Dun & Bradstreet in the United States and Teikoku Databank in Japan can provide additional insights into the financial condition of companies.

Extensive personal information about corporate executives also is openly available. It can provide details about their education, family, cultural roots, and past executive decisions that allow for creating a psychological profile. It can detail their networks and corporate allies.

OTHER USES

In addition to being the feedstock for finished intelligence, OSINT makes a number of major contributions to intelligence. Let's look at a few of them.

Providing Context and Validation. Open source is most valuable when used in conjunction with classified intelligence. Much is learned by comparing government pronouncements in the press to the information gleaned from diplomatic exchanges and clandestine HUMINT. The same is true in the competitive intelligence world. Insights into a company's real plans and intentions often come from comparing press releases to intelligence gained from HUMINT.

Often, when an intelligence collector comes up with something of interest, open source helps to fill in the gaps in knowledge. For example, suppose that imagery has observed a ship at a pier, and the purpose, cargo, or destination of the ship is of some intelligence interest. Open source information such as cargo manifests, held by the maritime insurers at Lloyds of London, can provide answers. Observations of massive population movement can be explained by online postings, for example, Doctors Without Borders reports or UN humanitarian reports.

Providing Plausible Cover. A great advantage of open source is that it can be shared with allies or used for diplomatic confrontations (e.g., in démarches). It has similar value in homeland security because it can be shared with local law enforcement and first responders in general. A major problem, especially in coalition operations, démarches, and law enforcement, is the releasability of classified information. If the information is available in open source, then it can be used as a cover to conceal the fact that sensitive methods (e.g., HUMINT or COMINT) were originally used for the collection.

As an example, suppose that an analyst receives a sensitive HUMINT report indicating that the Iranian government is deploying new antiship cruise missiles in locations that threaten shipping in the Gulf of Oman. The report can't be shared with coalition partners or commercial shippers that use the Straits. But it's highly likely that the deployment will be noticed by locals and will appear in a social network site; or rumors of the deployment might reach Oman and appear as a news article in an Omani newspaper. Ordinarily, an intelligence analyst would not rely much on such a questionable source. But equipped with the knowledge from HUMINT that the reporting is accurate, the analyst can cite the open source to support his conclusions.

Deception and Signaling. Open source often is useful in communicating with an opponent. Obviously, it can be used for deception or to influence an opponent's decisions. A more subtle point is that it can be used to send a signal. The signal can be in a published article such as a newspaper or conveyed orally; the latter type of signal is discussed in the chapter on HUMINT.

Signaling is a common practice in the commercial sector. In business, signals are often conveyed by actions rather than by words. A competitor's price increase or decrease, an acquisition, a new product line, or a major reorganization, among other things, can be a signal of the company's future intentions in the market.

Analyzing signals requires examining the content of the signal, its context, its timing, and its source. Statements made to the press are quite different from statements made through diplomatic channels—the latter usually carry more weight.

Process

We'll talk about the open source process as if it were linear. Like so much of the intelligence business, it really isn't. One jumps from step to step, sometimes backward, sometimes forward. But in a linear order, the major steps are:

1. Planning and identifying sources
2. Collection (locate the good stuff and validate it)
3. Processing (translation)
4. Analysis
5. Dissemination

Let's go through them in that order, recognizing that open source analysts do jump around—sometimes, going back from the analysis step to locate more material or validating while analyzing, for example.

PLANNING AND IDENTIFYING SOURCES

Because of the vast amount of open source that is available, collection has to be planned based on knowledge of what is of intelligence interest. Historically, most open source material came in printed (hard) copy. Today, the most commonly used sources are online. So let's start with what has become the dominant open source: the World Wide Web.

The World Wide Web. The Web has become, in a relatively short time, the largest single repository of open source material. Almost any subject of intelligence interest has extensive coverage on the Web. The quality of material there, however, varies greatly. Much that is misleading or completely false resides on the Web, and analysts must use Web sources with caution. But much valid material also resides on the Web, and the commercial browsers and search engines make searching the material comparatively easy. Overall, the Web has become a useful source for many types of intelligence products.

The Internet as a communications medium falls in an ambiguous category; is it open source, cyber collection, or COMINT? It could be treated as any one of these. In describing the Web as open source, we're talking about material that is accessible with some kind of search engine or on a publicly accessible website. Material that requires extraordinary means (e.g., hacking) to acquire, such as emails, falls into the category of cyber collection. (See Chapter 5 for details.)

Online Databases. A wide variety of online databases can help in open source research. The rapid expansion of global information networks provides analysts with large volumes of organized information that were previously unavailable. Most of these are now available through the World Wide Web, usually by paying a fee for access. The number and availability of these commercial databases is changing rapidly. Premium commercial sources originally included a few such as Factiva, Lexis-Nexis, and Dialog. Today, there are many specialized databases and even a few free general purpose databases such as Wikipedia.

Specialized databases offer some advantages in contrast to the general mass of material available on the Web. They are usually organized by subject for easier searching and often have been checked for validity. For example, one of the more useful sources of technology information for both government and competitive intelligence is in online patent databases. These have consistently proven to be one of the most valuable sources of technology information. For many organizations that perform classified research, patents are the only way to publish their results openly. Jane's (military hardware), Oxford Analytica, and Lloyds of London (shipping) are other examples of specialized databases. There are many others, with new ones popping up all the time. Efficient searches on these may require a librarian or expert in the specialized search.

For material that is not on the Web or otherwise online, specific sources for physical or electronic collection have to be identified. Following is a description of some major sources.

Hard Copy Sources. As previously noted, the traditional open source was hard copy material, primarily books, magazines, and newspapers. Though many of these are now available online, some open source material still is not available through the Web. Hard copy open source literature can be obtained from libraries and from scientists and businesspeople who have frequent dealings with their foreign counterparts. Some newspapers, telephone books, monographs, journals, and technical literature are still available only in hard copy.

Radio and TV. During World War II, both the BBC and the Foreign Broadcast Monitoring Service (the predecessor to the Foreign Broadcast Information System [FBIS]) began monitoring German and Italian radio broadcasts. The BBC effort started in 1939, when the British government asked the BBC to translate and disseminate foreign journal and newspaper articles. Known as BBC monitoring, the operation was set up in an old British mansion in Caversham, near Reading, where it remains today. It collects publicly available material in more than 100 languages, providing the results to civil servants, ministers, and commercial clients.[19] The BBC also reported radio broadcasting of intelligence interest in its *Digest of Foreign Broadcasts.*[20]

The British Secret Service set up a novel and very successful covert operation that made use of BBC monitoring of German radio broadcasts during World War II. A "black radio" station in the United Kingdom was staffed with native German speakers (including anti-Nazi prisoner of war [POW] volunteers). Purporting to be a German Wehrmacht station, it broadcast news for the troops. Interspersed with actual news items were tidbits of distortions and gossip designed to drive a wedge between the Wehrmacht and the Nazi party. The full story is told in Sefton Delmer's book, *Black Boomerang.*[21]

After the war, BBC and FBIS monitoring was expanded to include television broadcasts. TV broadcasts of foreign leaders' speeches proved particularly valuable, and not only for assessing the content. The video also gave analysts an opportunity to assess the physical and mental health of world leaders, a topic discussed in detail in Chapter 16.[22]

Gray Literature. The most useful hard copy documents are those limited-distribution documents and papers known as *gray literature.* This term is applied to limited edition publications that are not available through normal commercial channels. Many research and manufacturing organizations publish controlled reports or closed-circulation journals that contain sensitive or proprietary information. Trade shows and conferences produce similar volumes of limited-distribution literature in the form of papers or conference proceedings.

Some such journals are actually classified. Others are restricted access, so it is a bit of a stretch to call them open source. As an example, back in the Cold War days, U.S. analysts were aware that the Soviet military produced a classified journal called *Military Thought* that contained valuable insights into the leadership's views on warfare. For the most part, analysts were unsuccessful in obtaining copies. The Soviets tightly controlled the circulation of these and other journals.

However, some sensitive journals may be found in public libraries or in private collections due to errors in document control or distribution, and they can often be obtained by clandestine collection (for example, by agents). For example, an intelligence officer picked up a terrorist training manual that was distributed at a public event in Southeast Asia.[23] And some restricted circulation Soviet journals on electronics technology once, for some reason, wound up in a West German university library.[24]

The in-house publications of commercial organizations, even when not restricted, are often more valuable than trade journals; they tend to present more detail on work being carried on within the organization. Conference proceedings, which also fit into the gray literature category, usually have more value than the widely distributed journals and magazines.

The Internet provides an equivalent type of gray literature—websites and chat rooms having password-protected content. Such sites often can have great intelligence value. The challenge, of course, is getting into them—a topic that is discussed in Chapter 5.

Human Sources and Commercial Imagery. Some intelligence organizations consider certain types of HUMINT and IMINT to fall into the category loosely defined as open source. NATO, for example, considers open source as including overt human experts or observers.[25] Nongovernmental organizations (NGOs) such as the International Committee of the Red Cross and Doctors Without Borders fall within this definition. They fall on the border between HUMINT and open source.

Commercial imagery also could be considered to be open source. Large volumes of imagery, for example, are becoming publicly available from commercial imaging satellites. Some such imagery is available for free online, and some is available for a fee. But commercial imagery is dealt with as imaging intelligence in Chapters 9 and 10.

COLLECTION

As noted above, collection has two major steps: locate the good stuff, and validate it.

Locate the Good Stuff. One of the myths about open source, noted in the introduction, is that it's readily available. It may be out there somewhere, but finding the relevant and really good material can be very difficult. We've discussed the challenge of finding gray literature. Social networking sites are readily accessible, but finding the important ones in the great volume of such sites can be a daunting task.

Ironically, one problem of open source intelligence is that it is so abundant; an all-source analyst cannot possibly take advantage of all the available material. In fact, such an analyst cannot even learn about all of the available ways to obtain open source materials. Tracking the data sources is a full-time job. The solution is to turn to experts on research. In governmental intelligence organizations, the open source analyst can fill this role. For others, reference librarians are skilled at finding hard copy materials worldwide and are especially helpful on gray literature. They can help search and retrieve documents from many different databases, including commercial databases. As these databases become available worldwide, almost any country or commercial enterprise should have an excellent research capability available to its analysts.

A persistent problem with online data sources remains this inability to extract relevant information from the mass of data. The all-source analyst inevitably encounters information overload. Both government and commercial development projects continue to work toward the goal of creating a human-computer team that would dramatically improve the capability of people to make inferences in complex, data-intensive domains. Such a team would vastly increase the ability to identify key facts hidden in immense quantities of irrelevant information, to assemble large numbers of disparate facts to reach valid conclusions, and to produce new patterns that assist in further analyses. We can reasonably expect to see steady improvement in the problem of extracting relevant information from the morass. For the present, though, the problem is finding the really good stuff in the mass of available material.[26]

For too long, open source searches have been delegated as just an additional duty for all-source intelligence analysts. This seems to be a short-sighted approach. No one would seriously propose that such analysts be required to collect their own signals or imagery intelligence (though analysts sometimes do so, in the case of commercial imagery). However, that is precisely what we do with open source material.

Librarians and open source analysts can conduct searches far more efficiently; it's their specialty. They already know where the most useful sources are located for a given issue. So they can focus quickly on a current intelligence issue and go to the sources that will have the information needed.[27]

But turning the search problem over to these specialists has its own risk of missing relevant material. All-source analysts understand the subject of the search and can spot nuances that would escape someone without their subject-matter expertise. One compromise solution has been recommended—that intelligence organizations develop a cadre of highly skilled open source analysts and library professionals to work alongside all-source analysts in order to provide tailored OSINT support to the analytical process.[28]

Another challenge is that intelligence organizations must be subtle in conducting Web searches, and open source analysts are skilled at this. Some websites are in effect *trapped* to identify and track unwary visitors, even to reach back and infect their computers. In this environment, protecting sources and methods can be a problem. An Internet search by a known intelligence organization can be noticed and can be a tip-off of targets or of interest. You often have to search anonymously. And all websites are able to track the number of visitors. A sudden surge of interest from a particular country or region (such as the Washington, D.C., area) can be a tip-off to hostile intelligence services that something is amiss.

Validate It. Validity was an easier issue to deal with pre-Internet when you mostly were dealing with established sources for hard copy material. Even electronic databases had a known and trusted source. But even back then, reliability of the information could be a problem.

Today, the continuing problem of reliability, of sorting the true from the false, increases the cost as much as anything. One has to vet the material and analyze it very carefully. Open source is an excellent way for a hostile service to plant misleading material. As noted previously, it's also a good way to send a signal, since it's the only one that an opposing service is certain to receive (other than diplomatic discussions). Some of the standard checks done in validation are to look at the following:

Accuracy. It's often necessary to cross-check against known valid sources, especially against existing finished intelligence. This is usually the job of the all-source analyst, but it sometimes is an appropriate role for the open source analyst.

Credibility and Authenticity. There can be a lot of checks on credibility. Check the URL. What type of domain is it, for example, .com; .org; .edu; .gov; .mil; or country code? Check that it's an appropriate source for the material presented. Check to see if it's a personal page. Independently search on the author's name (sometimes embedded in the website's source code). Check who owns the host server and where it is. Then cross-check to see if the author is located physically near the server. Find out who links to the site. See if the site is in reliable Web directories.

Currency. Old material is not necessarily bad material; but, recently published material is usually of more interest in intelligence. And in any event, it's important to establish a publication date on all material in order to evaluate its significance.

Sponsorship. This will be an important thing to know in checking for bias during the analysis phase.

Note that a failure to pass validity checks does not mean that the information is useless. Even Web pages having questionable validity may have intelligence value. Deception attempts, for example, may not pass validity checks, but the fact that an attempt was made can tell you much about an opponent's intent.

PROCESSING

Processing usually requires translating from a foreign language. The primary process issues here involve getting language expertise, especially in African,

Open Source Intelligence

Arabic, and South Asian languages, and ensuring that the translation is free from bias. Let's look at each of these in turn.

Language Expertise. Intelligence services with global interests never seem to have enough translators. The shortage is especially severe where competence is needed in obscure languages. In the United States, the need to track terrorist activity and the requirements of the Afghan conflict fueled a demand for languages such as Farsi, Pashto, and Dari. The U.S. shortage was summarized in a 2011 report by the Senate Select Committee on Intelligence:

> The Committee found that serious shortfalls persist for languages critical to intelligence agency missions in spite of multiple past and ongoing efforts to improve this capability. While IC agencies have attempted to correct their hiring patterns and increase their language training programs, many still rely heavily on contract linguists, interpreters, and translators for critical languages. Persistent shortfalls in critical languages coupled with the increasing volumes of information available through open source and other means have exacerbated the effects of a national deficit in foreign language capability on intelligence collection and analysis.[29]

A country such as the United States has many residents with native capability in difficult languages such as Arabic and Farsi. But typically these residents were born in countries such as Iraq and Iran or have family living abroad. For them, security clearances are difficult to get. This would seem to be less of a problem for open source analysts than for COMINT analysts, as discussed in Chapter 4. Open source is unclassified, after all. Even so, most intelligence organizations would prefer not to reveal what material they are translating, because it indicates an intelligence interest in specific subjects.

An intelligence service always has the option of turning to the services of its allies for translation help. Where very large volumes of material need to be translated, this may be the only feasible solution. The United States could, for example, ask Kuwait or the United Arab Emirates to take on Arabic translations. This doesn't deal with the clearance issue, though. And it increases the risk that the translation will contain some type of bias, as discussed next.

Translation Bias. Customers of open source reporting tend to assume that translations accurately reflect the meaning of the original. It sometimes happens that the translations do not, and bias is the reason. We have to deal with two types of bias in translating foreign language material. One is good. One is bad. They both can be bad if their existence is not acknowledged and assessed. Let's look at them, one at a time.

Source Bias. This was discussed earlier. Source bias is not a bad thing; in fact, it's good, so long as you know it exists and what the bias is. It helps you to assess incoming information. Knowing the bias of a source helps put the intelligence in perspective or provides insights into what a government or faction is thinking.

- The extensive Chinese official press treatment of the Falun Gong[30] movement indicates much about the level of concern about the threat that the movement presents to the government.
- The Liberation Tigers of Tamil Eelam (known as the "Tamil Tigers") developed a worldwide media network during an insurgency in Sri Lanka that had been going on since the late 1970s. During 2007 to 2008, publications controlled by the group gave clues that the Tigers believed that they were losing. The publications argued that a military solution to the conflict was not possible, in an apparent attempt to build support for a cease-fire and negotiations. The Tigers were eliminated militarily in 2009.

Translator Bias. We want the facts, but the opinions (of the source, not the translator) also have intelligence significance. The trick is to capture the former but not the latter opinions. Translator bias occurs both for translators who are translating their native languages and for translators whose native language is that of their parent service (e.g., English speakers in the United States and United Kingdom).

The difficulty faced by translators for whom English is a second language is this: they understand the nuances of their own language but may have a problem expressing them in English. Furthermore, they often have personal opinions about the message that they are translating, and those personal opinions can slip into the result. It's very hard for a native speaker to overcome a lifetime of cultural inclinations and provide a truly neutral translation.

Translators whose native language is that of their parent organization often have similar difficulties. They may understand the nuances of English, but they can miss the subtle meanings contained within their second language. And their personal views can slip into the translations as well. If you have to translate some material, and the ideas in it are really repugnant or exactly the opposite of your personal beliefs, you're likely to have a tough time getting it right.

Open Source Intelligence

There are solutions to the translator bias problem, but they range from the inadequate to the expensive. Software translation is an inexpensive way to handle large volumes of material, but it's inadequate. It doesn't capture subtleties. Some words or concepts simply don't translate well from one language to another. It's not truly translator bias, but it has the same outcome. Web-based translation software is widely used for translation, but it has the same difficulties in identifying shades of meaning. The Web also contains traps for the unwary, as noted earlier.

Having independent translations of the same material is a more costly way to deal with translator bias. But you have to get translators who don't have the same bias. For example, having an al Qaeda sympathizer for one translator (if you could get one), and an opponent for a duplicate translation, would be the idea. Then you carefully examine the parts where the translations differ. A less expensive alternative to independent translation is to have a peer review by a separate translator. This is the same technique that all-source analysts use to help avoid the bias trap.

An ancillary problem is organizational culture that (consciously or not) encourages translator bias. The translation process has room for mischief, and organizational mindset can cause that mischief. It usually manifests itself in the form of translations that support policies of the translator's parent organization.

- A 2005 U.S. government report entitled *The Military Power of the People's Republic of China* contained an assertion that China "plans to field" anti-satellite systems. The report was based on translations of Chinese open source writings. An independent review of the Chinese original text revealed that the translation completely changed the meaning. The original article simply recommended that China factor international arms control developments into its response to military space competition. The translation said that China will pay "close attention to progress made in military use of space *while actively developing anti-satellite systems*," a statement not found in the original.[31]
- For their part, Chinese translations of U.S. policy statements often reflect a similar bias to support Chinese policy decisions. The Chinese especially are prone to select and quote inflammatory statements made by U.S. officials, even where the official is not in a policy-making position.

The solution is straightforward but difficult to reach in practice: The parent organization of an open source analytic group should not have a vested interest in the material that is being translated.

ANALYSIS

The most valuable part of a translation is often the open source analyst's commentary. A straight translation, without background or context, can be misleading. The open source analyst can be a big help in providing this context; after all, it's the analyst's primary job, and he or she typically has a solid background in the target culture.

If a foreign news article or journal requires no translation (in the case of the United States or United Kingdom, for example, it is written in English), it is important to closely examine the motivations behind the publication. Japanese news reports published in both Japanese and English often differ significantly, and the Japanese version is likely to provide a more accurate picture. The English version is likely to be toned down to make it more palatable to U.S. readers.

The volume of publication on a topic can be an indicator of many things. For commercial firms, it can indicate interest in a technology or concept. Patents, for example, are not always published to protect an invention; sometimes, they are intended to scare the competition or to establish the patentee's professional credentials.

Governments often use volume to sell a message and especially to convey a propaganda message to their people. Repetition of a message can increase its acceptance. Continuing an example cited previously, Chinese government-controlled publications initially orchestrated a campaign against Falun Gong that alleged that the movement was antiprogress and antiscience. When this approach failed to take hold, they switched to other frequently repeated messages: that Falun Gong was in collusion with foreign, anti-China, forces; and that adherents practiced self-immolation. The open source analyst following this trend should note it explicitly in commentary rather than simply translating and reporting.

The purpose of open source analysis, then, is to place the material in context. Two methods of doing this are source analysis and content analysis.

Source Analysis. Source analysis is done to some extent in the validation part of the process. This step involves a thorough assessment of the source's qualifications, official position, and influence. As in other areas of intelligence, the general rule for open source is this: What is said is not as important as who said it. Statements by a head of government typically carry more weight than do those of a head of state. A finance minister's statements on budgetary issues carry more weight than do the same statements made by a minister of the interior.

Open Source
Intelligence

Open source reporting on China provides a compelling example of the need for source analysis. China publishes volumes of material on national security and military affairs. Chinese websites containing sensational claims about weapons have in the past been used as sources to show both capability and intent to take on the West (the United States, especially) militarily. Unless one carefully assesses the source, it is possible to prove almost any point that one wishes to make about China's foreign policy, military capability, or intent. U.S. government analyses of Chinese policies especially have been based on selected quotations of Chinese authors, with the implication that they are influential, but the analyses often fail to provide evidence that they are.[32]

An excellent example of this problem is a Chinese book by two Peoples' Liberation Army (PLA) colonels called *Unrestricted Warfare,* published in 1999. The book was widely read in the West and often cited by some U.S. officials as representative of PLA thinking on how to respond to the revolutionary change in warfare. But the book reportedly was not accepted by the mainstream Chinese military apparatus.[33] Many assessments of Soviet publications during the Cold War fell into a similar trap.

So it is essential to conduct a source assessment as part of the analysis step. Analysts should make the case why they think certain authors and articles are credible and reflect official thinking, and they should identify any uncertainties that may exist about the source. This part of the process also helps in identifying both deception and signaling.

Source analysis also involves looking at patterns over time. Frequently, the author of an open source publication has a prior publication history. Leaders of countries and corporations give many speeches and interviews. Journalists often have written many articles in the past. Analysis often involves comparing the new material to past material and observing changes in the pattern.

Content Analysis. Before discussing what we mean by content analysis, let's define what content analysis is not.

Open source analysis, and content analysis in particular, does not include making *substantive* judgments about the content of the material. That is the role filled by the all-source analyst, who draws on a broad range of sources.

Content analysis, instead, is a pattern research tool. It is used to determine the presence of certain words, concepts, themes, phrases, characters, or sentences within texts or sets of texts. The purpose is to quantify and analyze the presence, meanings, and relationships of the words and concepts. From this, a content analyst can then make inferences about the messages within the material, the author, and the audience.

One underlying assumption of content analysis is that words and phrases mentioned most often are those reflecting important concerns in any communication. Content analysis also can establish underlying motivations or viewpoints. A typical example is that of establishing the political viewpoint of a media source. Content analysis can, for example, identify the systemic bias discussed earlier; for example, it can establish that Fox News has a different political perspective than does MSNBC or CBS. It can also distinguish the viewpoint of the *New York Times* from that of the *Wall Street Journal.*

Some examples of questions that can be answered by content analysis include these:

- What are the antecedents of an article? What does the article tell you about the source? For example, is the source what it is claimed to be? (The *Black Boomerang* radio broadcasts, described earlier, derived much of their effectiveness from the broadcaster's claim to be a German Army radio station.)
- Why was the article written? If it is propaganda, what is its purpose?
- What are the logical consequences (e.g., impact) of the message?
- Does the article deviate from a standard pattern for that culture? If so, why?
- Is the channel or style of publication significant?
- Can any conclusions be drawn about the psychological or emotional state of persons or groups from the article?
- Can the intentions, focus, or communication trends of an individual, group, or institution be inferred from the content?

Some of these questions, obviously, spill over into the realm of the all-source analyst. But the open source analyst often possesses unique insights. A prime example of an open source analyst's value occurred during the Cuban Missile Crisis in 1963. A BBC analyst identified a subtle offer by Soviet leader Nikita Khrushchev to end the crisis peacefully during a Radio Moscow broadcast (an example of the use of open source for signaling).[34] The offer was passed by the BBC to President John F. Kennedy, leading to the famous statement by Secretary of State Dean Rusk that "we're eyeball to eyeball, and I think the other fellow just blinked."

Most Web users routinely do content analysis when they get emails purporting to be from, for example, a bank or a U.S. government agency. Banks and the U.S. government have certain styles of writing that are difficult for an East European criminal group to replicate.

DISSEMINATE

Dissemination is a comparatively easy job with limited-volume classified sources. It's a more serious job with open source. You want to make the vast volume of open source material accessible and searchable. Do you go with a push approach—sending selected material to customers who are believed to have an interest? Or do you use the pull approach—make it available and count on the customers to find it using their search engines? Often, the solution is a combination of push and pull: make the title or abstract of the publication widely available and then translate the material if a specific customer requests it.

Most open source material is made widely available. And because most open source material is unclassified, the natural dissemination medium is the Internet. Governments and corporations may choose to control dissemination by using virtual private networks. NATO, for example, has such a network, the NATO wide area network (WAN), and uses it for open source dissemination. Companies in the business of providing open source, such as Jane's, charge for subscriptions to their services.

There are good reasons not to disseminate some open source product widely. Where the material indicates a sensitive intelligence interest in a topic, it needs to be more carefully protected. And a producer of gray literature often restricts its dissemination. It's a good practice to similarly restrict knowledge of the fact that the gray literature has been acquired and translated by an intelligence service.

The copyright issue also can force some type of control on the product. Governments such as the United States have used a marking such as "Official Use Only" (which is not really a classification) to avoid being accused of copyright infringement. But copyright can become a major problem when the information needs to be shared internationally or with private organizations, for example, with humanitarian assistance organizations.

Governments also face the problem of what to do with sensitive material that appears in open source. A considerable fraction of material in open source is considered to be classified by the affected governments, especially online postings such as those in WikiLeaks.[35] Obviously, just because it is in open source does not mean that it is declassified. Some governments—China, for example—try to counter embarrassing revelations with their own press releases. Others prefer to ignore the offending material. U.S. government employees and their contractors are cautioned to neither confirm nor deny items that appear in the open media.

Most dissemination is to end users (customers) and to all-source analysts. But some dissemination is designed to support other collection INTs. **Tip-off** is a term used by collectors for the process of alerting other parts of an intelligence community about a time-sensitive collection opportunity. Open source frequently provides tip-off, especially to COMINT and HUMINT collectors. Sources of such tip-off include news services and private observers who post messages and photographs about what they have observed. This is an invaluable source for directing collection on fast-developing events, such as the Mideast unrest during early 2011. Obviously, these sources can be misleading or slanted; part of the skill of the open source analyst is explaining the context and describing any bias.

Targeting is similar to tip-off in nature, but it is usually longer term and more deliberate. It includes identifying people and organizations for COMINT and HUMINT targeting and locations for IMINT targeting. The social networking sites—blogs, Facebook, LinkedIn, and similar sites—provide a rich set of material that can be used for targeting. And even if the collector cannot get to a key person directly via social networks, it may be possible to reach the target indirectly through friends or associates who network.

Structure

Open source differs from the other collection INTs in two ways.

- First, anyone can do it. It's been done commercially for years. Small intelligence services, terrorists, and commercial entities all have easy access and make use of it. Open source is readily available to terrorist groups, and we know from their writings that terrorists rely heavily on it. It's the equalizer that allows small intelligence services to compete with the big guys.
- Second, the product needs no special protection. Dissemination, though, can run into copyright issues. And open source translations can reveal an intelligence service's interest in specific topics that the service would rather not disclose.

These two differences shape the way open source organizations are structured and operated. Until the mid-1990s, the structure for open source intelligence was stable. Governments collected and translated foreign media: newspapers, journals, and radio and television broadcasts from target nations. The target media had long track records. The volume and credibility of information in these media were relatively predictable.

In the United States, much of this open source was collected and disseminated by the FBIS. As previously noted, FBIS originated as the Foreign

Broadcast Monitoring Service just prior to World War II. It subsequently became an open source intelligence component of the Central Intelligence Agency's Directorate of Science and Technology. It monitored, translated, and disseminated within the U.S. government openly available news and information from media sources outside the United States. It maintained a number of monitoring stations at locations around the world.

To complement the FBIS effort, several intelligence agencies (including the National Security Agency [NSA], the Defense Intelligence Agency [DIA], and the military service intelligence agencies) over the years have maintained their own separate groups for acquiring and translating open source material that addresses their specific interests. In the United Kingdom, the BBC has a long history of open source collection, filling a role similar to that of FBIS. Many other countries followed suit during the Cold War. East Germany's intelligence organization, the Ministry for State Security, analyzed 1,000 Western magazines and 100 books a month and summarized more than 100 newspapers and 12 hours of West German radio and TV broadcasting daily.[36]

Much has changed since the 1990s. During that time, globalization and the increasing need for government, NGOs, and commercial firms to acquire information across the globe has fueled an industry. Today many firms provide worldwide open source information, forming what has been called a "private-sector intelligence community." Four such firms are U.S. companies Stratfor and Intellibridge and U.K. companies Jane's Information Group and Oxford Analytica.[37] In addition, many firms provide very specialized open source information tailored to commercial firms in sectors such as banking, agriculture, and energy.

Meanwhile, within the U.S. government a number of studies have highlighted the need for a better open source intelligence structure. One such study, the WMD Commission report, recommended a centralized organization responsible for open source collection. The result was that in 2005 the FBIS became the Open Source Center (OSC) located within CIA but under the Director of National Intelligence. The OSC is tasked with the collection and analysis of freely available intelligence.

But due to the overwhelming volume of open source material requiring translation and analysis, many governmental organizations continue to address their specialized needs. Within the United States, the Department of Defense (DoD), Department of Homeland Security (DHS), Drug Enforcement Administration (DEA), and most intelligence community organizations have some type of open source capability. Law enforcement makes extensive use of open source. And thanks to the World Wide Web and online machine translation, almost anyone can function as an open source analyst. The result is that the United States has a hybrid structure for open source—neither centralized nor totally decentralized. Each structure in fact has its advantages:

- The advantages of a centralized arrangement are economy of scale. You can maintain a substantial cadre of analysts in almost any language of interest. You avoid duplicating translations. Also, open source has an advocate when budgets come around.
- The advantages of a more dispersed arrangement are that the many open source analysis centers can serve their parent organizations better. NSA's open source translations, for example, focus on foreign communications systems designs and provide details on their characteristics—a subject of high interest to COMINT collectors.

Decentralized arrangements work so well that open source can be, in effect, a cottage business. Any country, business, or NGO can set up an open source collection and analysis center. It's very inexpensive in comparison with all other collection INTs, making it a great equalizer among intelligence services, NGOs, and international corporations.

Summary

Open source material is perhaps the most widely used source of intelligence; certainly most intelligence production is based on it. Political and economic intelligence rely heavily on open source, as do scientific, technical, and environmental intelligence. Military intelligence does also, especially in combating terrorism and in developing intelligence about what the military calls "human terrain." Law enforcement makes increasing use of open source—the Internet—in combating Internet crime and apprehending sexual predators and stalkers. Being inexpensive and unclassified and requiring no special protection, open source is useful for sharing in coalition operations and for steering classified collection.

Despite its value and its wide use, some writers question whether open source is a legitimate collection INT. As a result, open source suffers from a perception problem among all-source analysts, and the perception problem leads to its misuse (or nonuse). It is often overlooked by government intelligence organizations in favor of classified information. The perception and use problem derives in part from the perception that open source provides no competitive advantage, since anyone can do it.

Open source information has traditionally meant published material that is publicly available—newspapers, books, and magazines. The World Wide Web, including online databases, is the dominant source today. But much valuable material still is available only in hard copy (some newspapers, books, and magazines). Radio and television broadcasts have been a useful intelligence source since World War II, and remain so. Gray literature—material that is unclassified but not widely available—also continues to be important.

The open source process typically has 5 phases:

1. Plan and identify sources. The up-front challenge is to find the really good items in the mass of available material. Often it is necessary to rely on search specialists.

2. Locate the good stuff and validate it. One has to vet the material and analyze it very carefully. Open source is an excellent way for a hostile service to plant misleading material. Validation requires looking at accuracy, credibility, and authenticity of the material, checking how current it is, and identifying the sponsors.

3. Translate. Most sources have some bias, and it is important to know what that is. But sometimes the translators or their parent organizations also have a bias that distorts the meaning of the translation.

4. Analyze. Provide commentary on the source's bias, and motivation for providing the material. Place the material in context via source analysis or content analysis. What is said is not as important as who said it. Content analysis is a pattern research tool that identifies significant deviations from past publications or finds subtle messages in the material.

5. Disseminate. Open source has a very large customer set, and the material has to be made available and searchable. This can be done either by push—sending selected translations to specific customers; or by pull—making all the material available for customers to search and retrieve the items of interest.

Structurally, open source is diversified. Large organizations provide open source translation and analysis support to the U.S. and U.K. intelligence communities (the OSC and BBC, respectively). But worldwide, this is a cottage industry, easily done by small specialized units. The centralized organizations achieve economies of scale; decentralized units provide tailored open source reporting for their parent organizations.

NOTES

1. Susan B. Glaser, "Probing Galaxies of Data for Nuggets," *Washington Post* (November 25, 2005), A35.
2. *Commission on the Roles and Capabilities of the United States Intelligence Community* (1996), Chapter 8, accessed 21 September 2012 at http://www.gpoac cess.gov/int/int012.pdf.

3. "Report of the Commission on the Intelligence Capabilities of the United States Regarding Weapons of Mass Destruction," March 31, 2005, p. 13, accessed 24 September 2012 at http://www.gpo.gov/fdsys/pkg/GPO-WMD/content-detail .html.

4. Ibid.

5. Susan B. Glaser, "Probing Galaxies of Data for Nuggets," *Washington Post,* (November 25, 2005), A35.

6. Rob Johnson, *Analytic Culture in the US Intelligence Community,* Center for the Study of Intelligence (CIA, Washington, DC, 2005), 24.

7. William M. Nolte, "Rethinking War and Intelligence," in *Rethinking the Principles of War,* Anthony D. McIvor, ed. (Naval Institute Press, Annapolis, 2005), 432.

8. The World Factbook is accessible at https://www.cia.gov/library/publications/ the-world-factbook/.

9. Glasser, "Probing Galaxies of Data for Nuggets," A35.

10. Daniel Patrick Moynihan, *Secrecy: The American Experience* (New Haven, CT: Yale University Press, 1998), 227.

11. James Noren, "CIA's Analysis of the Soviet Economy," Chapter 2 in "Watching the Bear: Essays on CIA's Analysis of the Soviet Union" (CIA Center for the Study of Intelligence, 2001), accessed 21 September 2012 at https://www.cia .gov/library/center-for-the-study-of-intelligence/csi-publications/books-and- monographs/watching-the-bear-essays-on-cias-analysis-of-the-soviet-union/ article02.html.

12. Walter Laqueur, *The Uses and Limits of Intelligence* (Somerset, NJ: Transaction Publishers, 1993), 43.

13. Henry Kissinger, *On China* (New York: Penguin Press, 2011), 105.

14. Lt. Col. Jack Marr et al., "Human Terrain Mapping: A Critical First Step in Winning the COIN Fight," *Military Review* (March–April 2008), 18–24.

15. Glasser, "Probing Galaxies of Data for Nuggets," A35.

16. See, for example, the "Terrorism Open Source Intelligence Reports," formerly published weekly for the US military by Interaction Systems Incorporated.

17. Cahal Milmo, "After 70 Years Monitoring the Airwaves, BBC Listening Post Could Be Cut Off," *The Independent* (July 13, 2010), accessed 3 March 2012 at http://www.independent.co.uk/news/media/tv-radio/after-70-years-monitoring- the-airwaves-bbc-listening-post-could-be-cut-off-2025090.html.

18. "Cyber collection" as used here does not include normal Web-based research. Chapter 5 provides a definition of cyber collection.

19. Cahal Milmo, "After 70 Years Monitoring the Airwaves, BBC Listening Post Could Be Cut Off."

20. "OSINT Report 3/2010," International Relations and Security Network, ETH Zurich (October 2010), accessed 21 September 2012 at http://www.isn.ethz.ch/ isn/Digital-Library/ISN-Insights/Detail?lng=en&ots627=fce62fe0–528d-4884– 9cdf-283c282cf0b2&id=122008.

21. Sefton Delmer, *Black Boomerang* (New York: Viking Press, 1962).

22. Gary Thomas, "Spies Track Physical Illnesses of Foreign Leaders" (September 20, 2011), Voice of America, accessed 21 September 2012 at http://www.voanews .com/english/news/usa/Spies-Track-Physical-Illnesses-of-Foreign-Leaders- 130222673.html.

Open Source Intelligence

23. Peter Eisler, "Today's Spies Find Secrets in Plain Sight," *USA Today* (April 1, 2008), accessed 21 September 2012 at http://www.usatoday.comhttp://www.usatoday.com/tech/news/surveillance/2008-03-31-internet-spies_N.htm.

24. Private conversation with CIA senior analyst Norman Davis, 1973.

25. "NATO Open Source Intelligence Handbook" (November 2001), p. 9, accessed 21 September 2012 at http://www.oss.net/dynamaster/file_archive/030201/ca5fb66734f540fbb4f8f6ef759b258c/NATO%20OSINT%20Handbook%20v1.2%20-%20Jan%202002.pdf.

26. Glasser, "Probing Galaxies of Data for Nuggets," A35.

27. "NATO Open Source Intelligence Handbook" (November 2001), 19.

28. Eliot A. Jardines, Testimony before the House Committee on Homeland Security, Subcommittee on Intelligence, Information Sharing, and Terrorism Risk Assessment (June 21, 2005).

29. United States Senate, "Report of the Select Committee on Intelligence, United States Senate, covering the period January 3, 2009 to January 4, 2011." U.S. Government Printing Office (March 17, 2011), p. 26, accessed 21 September 2012 at http://www.intelligence.senate.gov/pdfs/1123.pdf.

30. Falun Gong is a spiritual discipline first introduced in China in 1992 that combines meditation, exercises, and moral philosophy. The Chinese government considers it a threat to the regime; it has suppressed the movement, imprisoning and torturing Falun Gong members.

31. Gregory Kulacki and David Wright, "An Analysis of the March 2005 Report by the U.S. National Air and Space Intelligence Center," Union of Concerned Scientists, 15 September 2005, accessed 21 September 2012 at http://www.ucsusa.org/assets/documents/nwgs/nasic-analysis-final-9-15-05.pdf.

32. Gregory Kulacki, "Statement Following China's January 2007 Anti-Satellite Test," Union of Concerned Scientists (February 2007), accessed 21 September 2012 at http://www.ucsusa.org/assets/documents/nwgs/kulacki-on-chinese-asat-test.pdf.

33. Chen Yali and Eric Hagt, "China Book Shelf," *ChinaSecurity,* #2 (2006), accessed 21 September 2012 at http://www.chinasecurity.us/index.php?option=com_content&view=article&id=253&Itemid=8.

34. Cahal Milmo, "After 70 Years Monitoring the Airwaves, BBC Listening Post Could Be Cut Off."

35. Glasser, "Probing Galaxies of Data for Nuggets," A35.

36. "OSINT Report 3/2010."

37. CIA, "Are You Ready?" (Global Futures Partnership, July 2001), accessed 21 September 2012 at http://www.oss.net/dynamaster/file_archive/090916/6e2588a3d13c9db47d49d9c23b464d79/Are%20You%20Ready.pdf.

3. Human Intelligence

This chapter is about the use of human sources for collection. The term **human intelligence (HUMINT)** is used both to describe intelligence that is collected by human sources and to describe the process of collection. It is frequently done by governments, but a massive amount of HUMINT worldwide is collected by nongovernmental organizations (NGOs) and commercial entities.

Function

HUMINT is concerned with gathering information from people on domestic or foreign topics of intelligence concern. Following is a summary of the HUMINT function for some key mission areas or intelligence disciplines.

MILITARY SUPPORT

HUMINT can give a decisive advantage in military confrontations. It has done so many times throughout history:

- Sir Francis Walsingham's spy network provided him with details about the plans, readiness, and capabilities of the Spanish Armada that helped the English fleet to defeat it in 1588. Information provided by one spy, Anthony Standen, allowed the English to know exactly when the Armada would arrive.

- Prior to World War I, Austria-Hungary's chief of counterespionage, Colonel Alfred Redl, was recruited by Russian intelligence and provided them the Austrian invasion plan for Serbia. The Russians shared the information with Serbia's military command, so that the Serbians were well prepared for the invasion. In addition to providing Austria's military secrets to Russia, Redl provided the Austrian military with erroneous information about Russian military strength and disclosed the identities of Austrian agents in Russia.[1]

- During the Cuban Missile Crisis in 1962, President Kennedy had intelligence provided by KGB Lieutenant Colonel Oleg Penkovsky that the Soviet nuclear arsenal was much smaller than previously thought, that the Soviet missile fueling systems were not fully operational, and that the Soviet missile guidance systems were not yet functional. Armed with this intelligence, Kennedy was able to pursue a more aggressive policy that included a naval quarantine of Cuba.

The Soviets had their HUMINT successes during the Cold War, as well. According to Paul Redmond, "four spy cases alone could have given the Soviet Union a decisive advantage if war had broken out":

- the Walker spy ring provided the KGB with a capability to read the U.S. Navy's encrypted communications;
- the Clyde Conrad spy ring provided details of the U.S. Army's operational plans and communications in Western Europe;
- Robert Hanssen passed to the Soviets U.S. plans for allowing the government to survive a nuclear attack; and
- Aldrich Ames compromised CIA's human sources working in the Soviet Union during the mid-1980s.[2]

HUMINT provides valuable insights to support military strategic and operational planning. But the bulk of HUMINT that is routinely collected and used in wartime is tactical in nature. Prisoner interrogations provide a wealth of material of immediate use about the morale, location, and combat readiness of opposing forces. It's an old technique, but it continues to be successful. During the U.S. Civil War, Union interrogators at Gettysburg were able to determine that they had prisoners from every Confederate division except General Pickett's—leading them to conclude correctly that Pickett, having fresh troops, would lead the attack on the following day.

HUMINT can provide insights into weapons development programs, from concept to production, deployment, and systems operations. It can provide details about research that may lead to technological breakthroughs or about emerging threats.

HUMINT also makes the data collected by communications intelligence (COMINT), imagery intelligence (IMINT), and open source intelligence more comprehensible, and thus more effective, and yields important insights into data collected by technical collection systems. Access to plans, equipment, or technical documentation collected through HUMINT gives an analyst an inside view into weapons capabilities or production techniques that, in turn, supplements data collected from other sources.

POLITICAL AND ECONOMIC SUPPORT

HUMINT is usually the best source of intelligence about a foreign leader's attitudes and decision making. It can provide plans, trade secrets, and indications of political instability or regime changes. HUMINT has long been used to support political and trade negotiations. If you can obtain the opponent's negotiating strategy, then negotiations can usually be resolved very favorably for your side. Usually, the existence of such insider information is kept secret, even long after the event. But in 2010, Helmut Metzner, chief of staff to the German foreign minister, was sacked for providing sensitive political information to U.S. embassy officers. His role was disclosed as a result of the WikiLeaks publication.[3]

COUNTERTERRORISM AND COUNTERNARCOTICS

HUMINT is critical in supporting counterterrorism and counternarcotics operations and in dealing with criminal activity generally. It typically is the best source of a criminal adversary's plans and intentions. It usually is the best method of dealing with illicit networks. HUMINT is especially effective when combined with technical collection.

- The trackdown and killing of drug kingpin Pablo Escobar in 1993 required a synthesis of collection sources. Colombian and U.S. intelligence teams pulled together HUMINT on Escobar's network of associates, financial structure, and pattern of operations. COMINT collection of Escobar's cell phone communications helped focus HUMINT targeting.[4]
- The 2011 raid on Osama bin Laden's compound that resulted in his death was preceded by extensive HUMINT operations and technical surveillance.

Human
Intelligence

The HUMINT involved interrogation of al Qaeda prisoners at Guantanamo Bay, surveillance of bin Laden's courier, and renting a safe house near the Abbottabad compound. This HUMINT led to extensive imagery of the compound provided by the National Geospatial-Intelligence Agency (NGA), along with other technical surveillance measures.[5]

LAW ENFORCEMENT

HUMINT remains one of the primary collection methods used by law enforcement. The FBI and state law enforcement used human sources (informers) for years to great effect against the American Mafia.[6] More recently, human sources have been invaluable in the war on drugs and against domestic terrorists. Many such sources are not recruited agents but volunteers.

DECEPTION AND SIGNALING

The topic of deception and signaling was introduced in Chapter 2. Signals often are conveyed via HUMINT.

Recognizing and interpreting an opponent's signals is one of the more difficult challenges that HUMINT collectors must face. Depending on the situation, signals can be made verbally, by actions or by displays, or by very subtle nuances that depend on the context of the signal.

In negotiations, signals can be both verbal and nonverbal. True signals often are used in place of open declarations, to provide information while preserving the right of deniability. False signals are used to mislead, usually to gain a negotiating advantage.

Signaling between members of the same culture can be subtle, with high success rates of the signal being understood. Two U.S. corporate executives can signal to each other with confidence; they both understand the rules. A U.S. executive and an Indonesian executive would face far greater risks of misunderstanding each other's signals. The cultural differences in signaling can be substantial. Cultures differ in their reliance on verbal and nonverbal signals to communicate their messages.

COMMERCIAL HUMINT

Commercial espionage techniques developed rapidly during the industrial revolution, when Britain had an edge in many manufactures and was the target of the French, Germans, Dutch, and Swedes, who attempted to recruit skilled artisans (with their tools, if possible).[7] Of course Britain returned the favor, targeting technologies where the others had an advantage. The defense often took the form of keeping their employees narrowly focused on a single part of any major process such as steelmaking or industrial chemicals. No one person could give away the whole process.[8]

The Soviet Union later refined this technique. Within Soviet military industries, no single émigré, defector, or spy—unless he was a top level executive—knew very much of the overall picture. Everything was as compartmented as the Soviet system could make it. This system made for great security against HUMINT but at a high price in thwarting adaptability and knowledge sharing among those who needed the information.

HUMINT today is a major source of intelligence information for many commercial organizations, and many governments also use HUMINT for commercial purposes. The challenge for commercial organizations is to collect HUMINT without violating legal or ethical constraints. Most corporations do not use clandestine HUMINT (for example, agents in the employ of their competitors) for ethical reasons. Even where ethics do not constrain corporations, the companies usually try to avoid clandestine HUMINT because of the costs associated with exposure. Two examples illustrate the exposure hazards of clandestine commercial HUMINT:

- In 2000, Oracle Corporation admitted that it had hired an investigator to find documents embarrassing to Microsoft; the tactics used reportedly included covert searches of political organizations in Washington, D.C., and payment to janitors for trashed documents showing improper Microsoft activities.[9]
- In 2001, Procter & Gamble engaged in information collection against rival Unilever that included the technique known informally as "dumpster diving" or TRASHINT—sifting through Unilever's off-property trash for documents. Once exposed, Procter & Gamble reportedly agreed to pay Unilever $10 million as part of a settlement.[10]

Both incidents resulted in damaging media coverage of the offending companies.

Commercial espionage by governments is a completely different matter. Neither ethical nor legal considerations seem to constrain governments. France and Israel have been identified in U.S. congressional reporting as "heavily involved" in economic espionage against the United States.[11] But China has developed commercial espionage into a fine art. The Chinese Ministry of State Security co-opts some of the thousands of students, tourists, business travelers, trade delegations, and scientists who visit the United States and European countries every year. France, in fact, has been both the beneficiary of its espionage against the United States and the victim of espionage by China. French businessmen have fallen prey to entrapments based on compromise, materials theft, false tenders for procurement, and bribes by the Chinese.[12]

THE CHANGING TARGET

During World War II, and then again throughout the Cold War, U.S. and allied HUMINT had the advantage of a known, relatively stable target. Nazi Germany, Japan, and the Soviet Union were difficult targets, but they were *the* targets, and somewhat predictable. It was easier to conduct long-range planning for HUMINT collection.

Since the 1990s, the United States and its Cold War allies have had to deal with a range of complex targets. As a former Director of Central Intelligence (DCI) noted, "We have slain a large dragon. But we live now in a jungle filled with a bewildering variety of poisonous snakes."[13] Added to this is the increasing prevalence of important targets that are networks. Many of these new targets are ethnic/family/clan-based organizations that are especially difficult to penetrate. The U.S. and Commonwealth services must deal with more language and cultural diversity than in the past. They have to staff, train, and equip for many more problem areas than in the Cold War arena.

So the target is constantly changing, and it's difficult for HUMINT to keep up. HUMINT lacks the targeting flexibility that other INTs possess—it is constrained by the source's knowledge and access. It is much more opportunistic. Some of the best sources have been walk-ins. A major shift in the last two decades has been from state to nonstate targets. But HUMINT resources cannot simply be redirected. For these reasons, a surge capability is difficult for HUMINT to create.

At the same time, this new target set has given clandestine services an increasingly important role: that of the enabler of other kinds of collection. Because a clandestine service is present in a target country and knows how to operate there, it can enable many other INTs. COMINT, cyber collection, electronic intelligence (ELINT), foreign instrumentation signals intelligence (FISINT), materials sampling, and acoustic monitoring are examples of collection that can be undertaken with the assistance of a clandestine service.

Process

This section is about **tradecraft**—the techniques that are used to acquire HUMINT, clandestinely or overtly. Clandestine tradecraft is about recruiting and developing good sources and running them effectively. It also includes some more aggressive techniques, such as surreptitious entry to steal files and ciphers.

As noted earlier, human intelligence divides broadly into the two categories of clandestine and overt HUMINT. The two have quite different processes. Clandestine HUMINT operations require a large and complex infrastructure from which to operate, including overseas offices, safe houses, cover legends, and specialized training. In the United States the CIA has been the dominant source of clandestine HUMINT. The U.S. military services also collect HUMINT clandestinely but mostly they do overt collection. HUMINT collection in the competitive intelligence world is largely overt.

The following subsections outline the major HUMINT sources, starting with the familiar clandestine sources but including émigrés, defectors, elicitation, and interrogation sources. The common theme of these sources is that the intelligence is collected by one person interacting with another person to obtain information.

The products of governmental HUMINT activities include embassy officers' assessments, information elicited from contacts, information from paid agents, or documents or equipment clandestinely acquired by purchase or theft. The human sources can be diplomats and defense attachés, international conference attendees, defectors, émigrés, or refugees. (An attaché is a technical expert on the diplomatic staff of his or her country in a foreign capital. An émigré is a person who has permanently left his home country, usually for political or economic reasons.)

Volunteers—cooperating private individuals and organizations—also can supply privileged information that they encounter in the course of their work. Nongovernmental organizations have proliferated in recent years and are increasingly useful sources about foreign developments.

CLANDESTINE COLLECTION

The type of HUMINT that is popularized in books and films is collected clandestinely. When the collector is a governmental organization, it is typically called a clandestine service. Basically, clandestine collection involves case officers (who are employees of a clandestine service) conducting espionage by recruiting and running agents (who are not employees). Usually, though not always, the agents are citizens of the country where they conduct espionage.

Espionage is illegal in all countries. But few countries have really effective counterintelligence services. In most countries, the environment for conducting espionage is therefore relatively benign, and competent services can run operations (though with the risk of occasional embarrassment). Some countries—China, Iran, and Russia, for example—have an extensive internal security apparatus. As a result, they are very hostile environments for clandestine operations. In a select few (North Korea comes to mind), recruiting and running an agent is extremely difficult.

Clandestine HUMINT sources (the classical spies, moles, or agents that one reads about in spy fiction) are possibly the highest cost source for the quantity of information obtained. Therefore, targeting must be done carefully. But clandestine HUMINT may be the best way to determine plans and intentions.

Case officers normally rely on agents, either recruited or volunteers, to provide intelligence. Another category, widely used in law enforcement, is that of an informant: a source that is not controlled and won't accept tasking.

Clandestine operatives also engage in material and materiel acquisition. The intelligence uses of collected material and materiel are discussed in Chapters 15 and 17. Two common techniques for doing the collection, discussed later in this chapter, are theft and the use of front companies.

Clandestine collection normally has three phases: recruiting the agent, running the agent, and ending the relationship. Let's look at them.

The Recruitment Process. The recruitment process involves spotting a potential agent, assessing his potential, and recruiting and vetting him. Recruiting can be convoluted and take years; fast recruitments usually don't turn out well. Each step described below poses challenges and dangers that have to be assessed, so it's usually a very deliberate process.

Spotting. Spotting is all about identifying a potential agent. The usual approach is to observe government officials stationed abroad, looking for evidence that an official is dissatisfied with his country or personal situation, or that he or she might be willing to spy for some other reason. Split loyalties and narcissism, poor parental relationships, a failed marriage, infidelity, or substance abuse all indicate a potential vulnerability to recruitment. Potential agents also may be recommended by prior walk-ins who knew them and believed that they were susceptible to recruitment.[14]

The general characteristics of a good agent are that he or she should

- be willing to spy. Agents acting under duress will want to end the espionage relationship and are likely to lie to the case officer;
- have reasonable access to the information being sought or the location to which access is sought. Some agents might only be required to permit entry

of a technical collection team for the purposes of installing surveillance equipment;

- be a trusted individual. A military officer should be trusted within his unit. A terrorist should be trusted within his cell; and
- have a psychological make-up that can withstand the pressures of espionage.

Social networks now allow spotting by identifying a potential agent's social, economic, and lifestyle preferences. Personal data are becoming more easily accessible via social plug-ins in cross-platform applications (e.g., connecting Facebook and Twitter accounts). Increasingly, gaining access to a single networking site will open up a person's entire social networking universe to exploitation.

Assessing. Some agents go through the full recruitment process. Some bypass the spotting step; these are the **walk-ins**—someone who simply shows up (often at a country's overseas embassy) and volunteers to spy. Many of the most successful spies on both sides of the Cold War were walk-ins. The United States benefited from walk-ins such as Oleg Penkovsky, Ryszard Kuklinski, and Adolf Tolkachev. The Soviets were at least as successful, acquiring walk-ins such as John Walker, Aldrich Ames, and Robert Hanssen.

Whether active recruitment or walk-in, each potential agent has to be assessed; how well does he or she stack up against the characteristics described above? And what motivates the agent? Assessing motivation is very important in being able to interact effectively with an agent. Motivation to spy varies among individuals. The acronym MICE (money, ideology, compromise, ego) has been used as a shortcut to classify a potential agent's motivation, though revenge is often a fifth factor.

Money has been the key motivator for American spies. James Olson, former CIA counterintelligence official, notes that "Americans betrayed their country for many reasons, mostly for money."[15] Walker, Ames, and Hanssen were paid millions of dollars for their spying.

Ideology was a motivating factor on both sides of the Cold War. A number of spies in both the United States and the United Kingdom provided information to the Soviets because of their support for Communism. Defense Intelligence Agency (DIA) analyst Ana Montes and State Department employees Walter and Gwendolyn Myers supported the Castro regime and volunteered to spy for Cuba. None of them were paid substantial sums by the Cuban intelligence service. Many of the Soviet walk-in spies were motivated by hatred of their system, although some were seeking to get out of financial trouble before they were discovered. Ideology was a motivating factor for Ryszard Kuklinski, a colonel in the Polish general staff, who sought out the CIA and volunteered to spy. Kuklinski was outraged by Soviet intent to use Poland to serve Soviet interests. He provided the United States and NATO with the top secret strategic plans and other intelligence about the Warsaw Pact military alliance over a period of nine years.[16]

Compromise implies the use of coercion or blackmail to obtain the agent's cooperation. Compromise has serious disadvantages as motivation, as discussed later. Homosexuality was once considered a vulnerability that could be exploited by compromise, but it is no longer considered so in most societies.[17]

Ego can also be a contributing motivation, although it seldom is the sole motivation for conducting espionage. Apparently, ego was a major factor for Robert Hanssen, who felt a sense of superiority over his fellow FBI agents.[18] Oleg Penkovsky appears to have been motivated in part by ego.

The motivation for becoming an agent is rarely simple and straightforward, though. In most instances, there are multiple motivations at work. Jonathan Pollard tried to sell secrets to several countries, but his motivation in spying for Israel appears to have been largely ideology. Financial pressure initially may have motivated Robert Hanssen, but ego played a large role in his continued activity.

The assessment process also addresses whether the identified candidate has access to the information being sought, or if intended as a long-term penetration, whether he will progress in his career and have access in the future. Some recruitments do not pay dividends for many years. There is also the question of a trade-off with other sources. Can the information being sought be obtained via other means? This would make the candidate superfluous. Recruiting a spy requires a lot of resources and attention by the case officer and the clandestine operations support network. If the information can be obtained or even inferred by other means, that may be the preferred course to follow.

Also in the assessment process, the recruiting organization has to ascertain whether the candidate might be a **dangle.** A dangle is an attractive potential recruit intentionally placed in front of a hostile intelligence service. The idea is for the target service to initiate contact and thus believe it has spotted, developed, and recruited an agent. If the target service swallows the bait and accepts the agent, then the dangle's parent service may learn the identities and vulnerabilities of some of the target's officers, its collection requirements, and tradecraft.[19] Dangles can also be used to pass misinformation to the recruiting organization.

Recruiting. After a completed and favorable assessment, the case officer has to make the pitch to the potential agent. Success here depends on the skill of the case officer. The case officer tries to present an attractive offer that is based on the candidate agent's perceived motivations. He may promise assistance to the candidate in doing something the candidate wants but cannot accomplish himself. The recruitment package might involve obtaining specialized medical treatment for a family member, assistance in obtaining a Western education for children, or money needed for some purpose, such as to purchase a home.

Some recruitments take a long time. Many fail for a variety of reasons— the candidate may simply be opposed to spying, he may want something that can't be provided, or he may impose conditions that are dangerous for the case officer.

Some nations use a "false flag" in recruiting an agent. That is, the case officer represents himself as belonging to one organization but, in fact, belongs to another. Israel's foreign intelligence agency, Mossad, is known for using false flag recruitments of Arab spies. Most Arabs are unwilling to spy for Israel, but many are willing to spy for what they believe to be another Arab country or organization.

Coercion and bribery are other tools of the trade used mostly against the West. The bribery can be subtle. One commentator has observed that "the typical Chinese way is, you help the Chinese, they help you to develop an export business to sell cheap salad bowls to Kmart."[20]

Coercion often takes the form of blackmail for indiscretions or criminal activity. The Soviet Union long had specific hotel rooms in Moscow fully equipped with bugs and cameras to record the activities of foreign visitors and often provided opportunities for the visitor to conduct indiscretions in those rooms. Many of the better hotels in China that cater to foreigners are similarly equipped today.[21] Any resulting compromise can be used as leverage to force people to spy against their countries. But a coerced agent usually is not a good one. He fails the first characteristic of a good agent: willingness to spy. Clayton Lonetree, a Marine guard at the U.S. Embassy in Moscow, was caught in an illicit love affair with a KGB-controlled girlfriend and then coerced into spying for the Soviets. Lonetree eventually turned himself in, consumed with guilt.[22]

Vetting. After a successful recruitment, the next step is to vet the new agent. Vetting primarily is concerned with testing the agent's veracity, for example, spotting dangles. The United States relies on the polygraph in questioning agents about lifestyle, contacts, access to information, and past history, searching for signs of deception in the responses. Many other countries use techniques that predate the polygraph for vetting.

Running the Agent. After the recruitment process is complete, and the new agent is on board, it is time to reap the reward of all that effort. The agent must be provided guidance on what to collect, and the collected material must be communicated back to headquarters, assessed, and reported. Some agents know what is likely to be important to their new masters. One reason that intelligence officers make such good agents is that they usually have a good idea of what is needed. Another reason is that they have some idea of what tradecraft to practice. But almost all agents need some training, especially on conduct of meetings and other communications with their case officers.

The primary challenge, once the training phase is complete, is to maintain secure two-way communication between the agent and the handler. Since the beginning of spy activity, spies have had to communicate their information back to their handlers and to do so clandestinely. The case officer needs to provide instructions to the agent, and the agent needs to provide information (raw intelligence) to the case officer. This can sometimes be done in clandestine meetings between the two, for example, in a bar or on a park bench. Face-to-face meetings are often risky but are essential for assessing, training, resolving issues and problems, making sure that requirements are understood, and changing plans or targets.

Face-to-face meetings are especially risky in countries with sophisticated counterintelligence or security services, for example in countries such as Russia, China, and Iran, so indirect contacts are often the best means of communication. An important job of any counterespionage team is to identify agent communications, whether direct or indirect.

It has been noted that agents are "most vulnerable to being caught not while procuring the information, but when attempting to pass their secrets to a third party."[23] The successes in security surveillance by the KGB's 7th Directorate in Moscow depended on the vulnerability of spies who needed to pass information. Oleg Penkovsky was detected by a KGB surveillance team that was following Janet Chisholm, the wife of a British diplomat, after a tip from a KGB agent in London, George Blake.[24]

Clandestine services have developed a number of techniques to diminish this vulnerability. Two of the oldest techniques are brush passes and dead drops.

Brush passes refer to a general set of techniques where one person directly passes a physical object to another person. Usually this is done in a crowded public place to defeat visual surveillance. The two people pass each other, and may even appear to bump into each other, and an object is passed between the two (or possibly, identical-looking objects such as briefcases or newspapers are swapped).

Dead drops also are used to avoid direct meetings between the agent and his case officer. The location of the dead drop could be a loose brick in a wall, a library book, a hole in a tree, or under a boulder. The dead drop should be located so that it can be serviced (that is, the contents can be picked up) without the pickup being observed by a member of the public or the security forces who may be watching. The case officer or agent also needs some sort of signal to let his counterpart know that the dead drop is loaded for a pickup—for example, a chalk mark on a wall.

One would-be spy, Brian Regan, created a novel type of dead drop. He buried several bags full of classified material in Virginia's Pocahontas State Park. Regan's plan was to sell the locations of the material to the highest bidder. In August 2001, he was arrested as he started to board a plane for Zurich, carrying the addresses of Chinese and Iraqi officials with whom he planned to meet.[25]

Traditional techniques such as brush passes and dead drops have been supplemented by a number of methods that rely on modern communications technology. These methods collectively are referred to as covert communications, or "COVCOM" in the United States.

One of the oldest techniques for covert communication is **steganography**, or secret writing. The traditional approach is to write a message in invisible ink between the visible lines of an apparently innocuous letter. Counterespionage routinely relies on opening suspect correspondence (known in the trade as a "flaps and seals" operation) and testing for secret writing. So secret writing is not commonly used by sophisticated intelligence services. It still finds use in countries where technical methods of communication are not available. During World War II, agents used a sophisticated type of steganography called the microdot: a technique of photographing and reducing a page of text to the size of a pinhead, then making it look like the period at the end of a sentence.

Modern steganography, as discussed in the COMINT chapter, makes use of computer technology. The rise of the Internet has provided many new opportunities for clandestine communications using, for example, Internet cafes. It also has given rise to new types of steganography. In digital steganography, electronic communications place steganographic coding inside of a document file, image file, or program. Media files are ideal for steganographic transmission because of their large size. As a simple example, a sender might start with an innocuous image file and adjust the color of every 100th pixel to correspond to a letter in the alphabet, a change so subtle that someone not specifically looking for it is unlikely to notice it.

Radio provides agents and their handlers with a means of rapid remote communication, sometimes over great distances. In the mid-20th century, high frequency (HF) radio was widely used for agent communications because it could span continents. But radio communications can be intercepted. Several techniques are used to avoid interception. One of the more popular is to send compressed messages in very brief transmissions (known as burst transmissions). Agents also use what are called "low probability of intercept" communications. These include spread spectrum (using a signal that looks like noise to normal receivers) and frequency hopping (moving rapidly from place to place in the radio frequency spectrum to dodge intercept receivers).

In the latter half of the 20th century, many agent communications moved to satellites and cell phones. Satellites provide a more secure means for agents to communicate intelligence and receive instructions. Reportedly, CIA in the 1960s used communications relay satellites, codenamed BIRDBOOK, in low earth orbit to maintain covert communications with agents. However, a disadvantage of such low orbits is that the satellite is in view for only a few minutes during a given pass over an agent's location.[26]

Encryption also is used to protect the contents of messages that might be intercepted, but this requires a more sophisticated support system for the agent. Cryptanalysts formerly could break most codes used by agents. During 1942 through 1945, the United States and the United Kingdom intercepted and gradually decrypted (mostly during the Cold War) Soviet agent communications in an effort known as Project VENONA. Modern cryptography provides codes that are widely available and virtually unbreakable using current technology. But if you can successfully break into agent communications and identify the sources, it is possible to take down entire espionage nets. The arrests and convictions of Julius and Ethel Rosenberg and Alger Hiss, among others, were based largely on VENONA intercepts.[27]

In addition to communications, a number of chores have to be done that fall into the general area of care and feeding. Agents must be provided with equipment for securely collecting and transmitting intelligence—such as miniature cameras, radios, and photocopiers. Agents have to be paid a salary, and the payment must be in such a form that it does not come to the attention of counterintelligence services. Some protection has to be arranged for both the agent and his family in case the operation goes sour.

Exit Strategy. Relationships don't last indefinitely, and the relationship with a human source eventually will end. Sometimes the source's value has diminished or ended. The source's access may have been lost, or the information that he or she can provide is no longer important enough. Perhaps the source no longer is reliable (or perhaps he or she never was). If a clandestine source doesn't die naturally and isn't caught, at some point he or she will need to be retired. The ending of this relationship often is painful for both the source and the handler because of the emotional relationship that develops over time.

Sometimes the source continues to have value, but the risks of being caught have become too great. In such cases, the source usually must be exfiltrated (removed from his native country to a place of safety). Some clandestine services are willing to cut ties with the agent in such cases, but most feel an ethical obligation to extract the agent (along with close family members, if possible) from a dangerous situation. Israeli intelligence, for example, has a history of exfiltrating former agents and collaborators and resettling them in Israel. In 2000, as Israel ended its long occupation of southern Lebanon, it pulled a large number of its Lebanese agents out of Lebanon and resettled them.[28]

Exfiltration of an agent is commonly a more complex undertaking than the Israel/Lebanon example because the operation must be conducted in a hostile country. It usually involves creating false identities, personal documentation, cover legends, and disguise. The cover stories used can be quite elaborate. One of the more elaborately planned exfiltrations did not involve agents, but it illustrates the planning that is involved. In January 1980, CIA successfully extracted six U.S. embassy employees who had been trapped in the Canadian embassy in Tehran after the Iranians seized the U.S. embassy in November 1979. The exfiltration plan required extensive support from the Canadian government (which led to its being referred to as the "Canadian Caper"). Among other things, it required forming a bogus film company, picking a script that involved shooting scenes in Tehran, getting Iranian government approval for the movie, disguising the six embassy employees as actors, providing them with false passports and cover stories, and getting everyone through airport checkpoints.[29] The story has been told in books, a TV movie, and the 2012 movie *Argo*.

SUPPORTING CLANDESTINE COLLECTION

A number of techniques support the clandestine collection of intelligence. Following are some of the important ones.

Cover. HUMINT operatives must travel to foreign countries, and in most cases, they cannot function effectively if their profession is known to the host country. Clandestine services officers, in particular, must conceal their actual role. Some form of cover (e.g., assumed identity) is needed.

There are two types of cover—official and nonofficial. Persons under official cover work in official government positions. The deepest level of cover is nonofficial cover. Such operatives are called NOCs. NOCs are much more difficult for a counterintelligence service to identify but much more vulnerable if identified.

The Soviet Union probably has made the most aggressive use of nonofficial cover, relying on a variant form called an "illegal." An illegal has a false identity and legend. Illegals are selected at a young age and trained extensively before assuming their new identity, usually of a young person who has died without surviving family. They may then be sent abroad, often for many years, even decades, before beginning their espionage careers. Soviet illegals of note include Rudolf Abel (real name: Vilyam Genrikhovich Fisher), who supported the atomic bomb spies in the United States and was caught in 1957, and Gordon Lonsdale (real name: Colon Trofimovich Molody), arrested in the United Kingdom in 1961. Since the collapse of the Soviet Union, Russia has continued to use illegals, though apparently with less success than in the early days of the Cold War. On June 27, 2010, the FBI arrested 11 illegals who had assumed false names and backgrounds—in one case stealing the identity of a dead Canadian. The 11 appear not to have been very successful spies and were exchanged for prisoners held in Russia.[30]

The types of cover used by NOCs vary broadly. Fisher ran a photography studio in New York. Molody's cover was as a jukebox salesman. The 11 Russian illegals arrested in 2010 had such diverse covers as journalists, realtors, a think tank staffer, a financial services representative, an accountant, a travel agent, and a software tester.

Both the CIA and the British SIS (MI-6), among others, make use of NOCs.[31]

All forms of overseas cover are increasingly a problem for all clandestine services. The increased availability of life history data to foreign governments and increasing worldwide availability of technologies such as biometrics exacerbate the cover problem. Crossing borders has become a particularly hazardous event for the undercover officer. With the advent of biometric information, false documents are easier to discover. Furthermore, the ability to investigate the background of a suspicious person has grown rapidly with the Internet. In fact, a person without a cyber footprint is treated with suspicion.

As a result, nonofficial cover is becoming both more necessary and more difficult to maintain, and new types of NOCs have to be created. Nontraditional platforms for agent recruitment also are increasingly necessary, and these cost more to maintain than official cover platforms.[32]

Front Companies. The preceding discussion focuses on cover for individuals. Clandestine services also need cover for organizations that support overseas clandestine activities, for example, for logistics, covert action, and the acquisition of foreign materiel of intelligence interest. These usually involve cover companies and co-opted businesses. Following are some major uses of cover companies, along with specific examples.

Espionage Cover. The Amtorg Trading Corporation was founded in 1924 by the Soviet Union. An American company based in New York, it served as a buying and selling organization in trade between the Soviet Union and the United States until the 1930s. It also provided a convenient cover for a number of Soviet espionage agents.

Covert Operations Support. One of the better known cover businesses, known in the trade as "proprietaries," was Air America: In August 1950, the CIA secretly purchased the assets of Civil Air Transport, an airline that was started in China after World War II by General Claire L. Chennault and Whiting Willauer. Later renamed as Air America, the airline continued to fly commercial routes throughout Asia, acting in every way as a privately owned commercial airline. At the same time, it provided airplanes and crews for secret intelligence operations.[33]

Air America functioned to support a variety of covert operations during the Korean War, during the French conflict with insurgents in Indochina, and later during the Vietnam War. Air America closed down in 1976, shortly after the Vietnam War ended.

Technology and Materiel Acquisition. Many intelligence agencies use the cover of front companies and co-opted businesses for technology and materiel acquisition. Countries such as Russia and China have a long history of targeting Western Europe, the United States, and Japan in particular because of the advanced technology that is available in those countries.

Front companies have several options for obtaining technology and materiel. They often are used to solicit bids for technology or products from legitimate companies. The victim companies often will provide detailed technical knowledge in hopes of being competitive and making sales.[34] The front companies also are useful as transshipment points for purchasing materiel and then making prohibited exports.

In the United States, front companies have the advantage of being "U.S. Persons" under the law; that status constrains the ability of CIA and NSA, for example, in monitoring company activities. Dave Szady, the FBI's chief counterintelligence official, reported in 2005 that the Chinese operated more than 3,000 front companies in the United States. The primary purpose of those companies, he said, is to purchase or steal controlled technologies.[35]

Martin Shih, a U.S. resident, owned several front companies that included Night Vision Technology in San Jose and Queening Hi-Tech in Taiwan. Shih used these cover companies to ship advanced U.S. night vision technology to centers such as the North China Research Institute, which is closely linked to the People's Republic of China (PRC) military. Shih was assisted in the shipments by Philip Cheng, who owned a front company called SPCEK. Cheng reportedly told FBI agents that he and Shih had been working together to transfer night vision technology to the PRC for approximately three years. One technique used by Shih and Cheng reportedly was to provide shipping documents stating that Taiwan was the final destination for the cameras. The cameras then were diverted to China.[36] The Chinese military reportedly was able to reverse engineer the technology and manufacture night vision equipment that is comparable to current U.S. military designs.[37]

Front company ownership or corporate control is relatively difficult to conceal in countries such as the United States and those in Western Europe that have extensive corporate reporting requirements. But ownership can be hidden more easily elsewhere. Iran developed a network of front companies (posing as schools or private laboratories) in Dubai to acquire technology for use in improvised explosive devices (IEDs) in Iraq and for its nuclear program. After Dubai closed down the front companies, Iran set up similar networks in Malaysia.[38]

Surveillance and Countersurveillance. All clandestine services, as part of their tradecraft in both collection and counterespionage, practice the arts of surveillance and countersurveillance.

- Surveillance divides broadly into two forms: the traditional surveillance conducted by humans, usually in public places by observing and eavesdropping, and technical surveillance, which uses the tools of technology—video cameras, audio devices, or communications intercept equipment.
- Countersurveillance, then, is all about detecting and defeating an opposing intelligence service's attempts to conduct surveillance of your

side's espionage operations. Disguise is one of many techniques used to defeat surveillance or in exfiltration. Defeating technical surveillance has a specific name in the business: technical surveillance countermeasures, usually denoted as TSCM.

Surveillance usually requires that you first identify the operatives of the opposing intelligence service—the case officers. These are usually staffers of the opponent's embassy in country. Identifying intelligence officers in an embassy is the FBI's job in the United States and CIA's job overseas. In the United Kingdom, a similar separation exists between MI-5 and MI-6. Domestic surveillance is much easier to do; you control the environment and can get help from local law enforcement and from telecommunications companies. Overseas, your counterespionage officers mostly are operating illegally, so these resources are not as easily available. In some countries, though, liaison (e.g., local law enforcement) can be used to help in surveillance. And telecommunications company employees or law enforcement officials can be recruited as agents to help in surveillance or countersurveillance.

Good surveillance teams go through extensive training and also usually have a number of years of experience in both surveillance and countersurveillance. This is definitely a learned art. The best services in this field also equip their teams with sophisticated high-tech devices to assist in surveillance.

Double Agents and Moles. A major tool of offensive counterespionage is the double agent. A double agent can be a spy who becomes an employee or agent of the target intelligence service or an agent who is turned as a result of discovery and threats (usually of execution) for noncooperation. Double agents are often used to transmit disinformation or to identify other agents as part of counterespionage operations. Their success depends on trust by the organization that they are working against; the organization that they are working for helps build that trust by providing true, but low-value, information to pass along.

The objective of using double agents usually is to control the operations of the foreign intelligence service. One of the best known examples is the success that Cuban intelligence had in discovering and doubling CIA's agents in Cuba—many, if not all of whom in the 1970s and 1980s may have been double agents.

The great fear of any intelligence service is a specific kind of double agent: the **mole**, a trusted insider who provides information to an opposing service. On the flip side, the holy grail of HUMINT is the penetration of a foreign intelligence service—ideally, a double agent who works in the counterintelligence component. The Ames and Hanssen cases illustrate the extensive damage that such double agents can cause.

This fear, in itself, has led many clandestine services to engage in self-inflicted injuries. Counterintelligence chief James Angleton's obsession with finding a mole inside CIA is one well-known example. There is a trade-off between catching a mole and disrupting normal intelligence operations. In the case of Angleton, many observers concluded that the harm he caused to the organization's morale and operations far outweighed any possible benefits from finding a mole (assuming that one existed then).[39] The KGB and its predecessors, both during and after the Stalin era, were similarly obsessed with finding moles and had similar problems. The British MI-5 was torn during much of its Cold War history by searches for moles—a number of which actually existed.[40]

Surreptitious Entry. Clandestine collection of intelligence is often facilitated by surreptitious entry. It can be used to steal or copy information of intelligence value from files or computers or to emplace listening devices or cyber collection devices for continuing collection. Most clandestine services have some capability for surreptitious entry. The Soviet KGB, Israel's Shin Bet, and the FBI all have used surreptitious entry into foreign embassies to copy material, steal codebooks, and implant or service audio devices.[41] The Russians, French, Chinese, and others have been known to surreptitiously enter hotel rooms to examine briefcases and computers left behind by visiting officials and businessmen.

The challenge is first, to not get caught, and second, to leave behind no evidence of surreptitious entry. As a result, clandestine services have developed to a fine art many technical skills associated with successful entry. Lock picking, creating duplicate keys, and defeating combination locks are well-known examples. And the entry does not always involve rooms or safes. The skill called flaps and seals, described earlier, is applied to open and copy mail that may be of intelligence interest, leaving behind no evidence of the opening.[42]

ISSUES IN CLANDESTINE COLLECTION

A number of criticisms of clandestine HUMINT have been discussed in the literature over the years. Some major ones are the following:

- HUMINT is a dirty business. Most clandestine collection techniques are illegal in the host country, after all. Even some overt techniques are. Methods such as torture and assassination clearly are over the line both legally and morally but nevertheless are conducted by some services. In recruiting and running agents you have to "deal with the devil." It's a dirty hands business, and both customers and case officers have to develop a tolerance for unsavory assets such as narcotraffickers and hit men if the job is to be done. One professional in the field observed to me that "we hire people that we wouldn't want working for us." Collection priorities and the national interest have to be balanced against human rights issues. HUMINT organizations then have to deal with the image problem when such assets are recruited and subsequently exposed.

- HUMINT traditionally has a low-tech culture. Both managers and case officers are comfortable with a low-tech approach. The stress is on tradecraft and especially interpersonal skills because of the importance of the bond between case officer and agent. Technical collection systems provide great opportunities, but many HUMINT organizations worldwide have been slow to adopt them.

- The tendency is to avoid risk. HUMINT is naturally a very risky form of intelligence—risks include exposure, political embarrassment, and personal danger. While clandestine HUMINT provides unique insights, it also provides the highest potential for political embarrassment. It relies on humans, with their flaws and biases. And many in a clandestine service's management chain can say *no* to risk-taking.

- HUMINT is regarded as *squishy*. Much like open source, it has the problem of being regarded as soft intelligence. And since it is perceived to be soft, its use by customers may be determined by how well it fits with the customer's views. HUMINT sources are known to mislead due to bias or personal motivations, and some are vehicles for deception operations run by opposing counterintelligence services.

Another major criticism of clandestine collection is that it isn't timely. Customers want quick responses to their requirements; they are accustomed to the rapid response capabilities of IMINT, COMINT, and open sources. They have similar expectations for timely HUMINT. In the case of clandestine HUMINT, intelligence services can't deliver. Clandestine HUMINT is not like COMINT or IMINT; it takes a long time to produce. It also usually requires a long-term investment and a level of patience that most customers lack. For foreign intelligence operations, case officers have to be recruited and trained and often given language training as well.

Sources have to be developed, validated, trained, and positioned. Time is required to develop access once requirements are in hand, and customers seldom recognize this fact.

Compared with the other INTs, HUMINT also takes more time to collect due to the need to contact the source, even when that source has already been developed (that is, recruited). Furthermore, the tight security that must surround and protect the clandestine source means that substantial time delays will exist from the time the source finds out about something until the information reaches an intelligence analyst. Fast communication of perishable data is important in crisis or wartime, but speed tends to increase the risk that the source will be exposed.

And the available sources may not have the answer. HUMINT by its nature cannot always be on target. Collectors have to provide their best shot by working with the sources they have. There are ways to deal with this; information that is not available from one source may be available from another source or from piecing together several sources. But again, that takes time.

Finally, HUMINT management has to deal with a problem that is common in other collection systems as well: the temptation to inflate intelligence reports. After all, a collector's job depends on providing useful intelligence. Sometimes, especially in HUMINT, the temptation leads to exaggerating or falsifying reports. A highly regarded case officer of the Israeli Mossad, Yehudi Gill, was arrested in 1997 and subsequently sentenced to five years in prison for doing just that. When his highly placed Syrian agent ceased to provide valuable intelligence, Gill simply made it up. Some of his falsified reporting about Syrian military developments almost led to a needless military confrontation between Israel and Syria.[43]

OVERT COLLECTION

Despite the media attention to clandestine operations, most HUMINT is in fact collected overtly. Following are some of the most common techniques.

Elicitation. Elicitation is the practice of obtaining information about a topic from conversations, preferably without the source knowing what is happening. Elicitation is widely practiced in gatherings of diplomats and military attachés and in the commercial sector during business executives' social hours and sales conventions. In fact, elicitation may be the most valuable tool of a successful diplomat. Because diplomats are all aware of the game, the information that is elicited may be tainted, but diplomatic gatherings are also valuable avenues for sending signals. In the business world as well, executives use meetings to signal competitors informally about their intentions, especially where use of more formal channels would violate antitrust law.

Making direct contact with knowledgeable sources in their home country or organization is often difficult, and the setting can be unfavorable for elicitation. However, these sources often discuss their work at international conferences and during visits with other professionals. Elicitation is an effective tactic to use at such professional gatherings, particularly where economists, trade specialists, scientists, or engineers convene to present papers. These professionals are a valuable source of HUMINT, and the greater their egos, the more information—and the more valuable information—they are likely to impart. They are connected to other professionals in their home countries and in their organizations. Analysts, where they possess the appropriate credentials, often attend such meetings and do their own collection by elicitation.

Diplomats have a long-standing tradition of collecting intelligence through elicitation, and the rules of diplomatic immunity ensure that they cannot be prosecuted as spies. In fact, most diplomats are careful to distinguish the information that they collect and analyze from intelligence; they do not consider themselves to be spies. Nevertheless, the information contained in embassy cables is an important source of intelligence, as revealed in the 2010 WikiLeaks incident.

One of the most respected U.S. intelligence officers, Allen Dulles, did much of his early intelligence work as a diplomat. Dulles graduated from Princeton University and in 1916 entered the diplomatic service. In his posts in several European countries during World War I, much of Dulles's work involved gathering intelligence information. His record as an intelligence officer is well known. In his diplomatic role, however, he unknowingly missed an opportunity that could have changed history. While serving in Switzerland, Dulles reviewed and rejected Vladimir Lenin's application for a visa to visit the United States, passing up the opportunity to personally meet with Lenin.

The diplomatic staff in an embassy often is thought of as dealing primarily with political and economic issues. But most embassy staffs also have military attachés, who have the job of collecting military intelligence. U.S. organizations such as the FBI and DEA often have staff in place responsible for liaison on law enforcement issues and for collecting counterterrorism and counternarcotics intelligence. The U.S. Department of Agriculture representative collects information that, though usually not considered intelligence, has much the same impact.

Reportedly, 80 percent of the work of the U.S. Defense HUMINT Service, which manages the military attaché corps, is devoted to overt collection, for example, collecting publicly available information, attending scientific and professional conferences, and interviewing persons who have had access to information of interest.[44]

The challenge in getting information from an elicitation source is to ask the right questions. Experts have advantages in elicitation because of their knowledge of the subject matter and because the elicitation appears to be a natural part of their interaction with other experts. Experts, however, bring their biases to the process.

Part of the fine art of elicitation is careful staging—that is, selecting the right setting and timing for posing questions and sometimes providing inducements. The Chinese, for example, are masters at staging for collecting information through inducement. They reportedly "roll out the red carpet for American scientists visiting China, hoping to nudge them into revealing secrets."[45] The most common practice is to employ a technique that is carefully designed to leave visitors exhausted and off guard. It starts with a hectic day of tourism, followed by an evening cocktail reception. After a few drinks, the visitor is approached by a graduate student seeking research assistance, usually on a topic that the visitor had previously been unwilling to discuss. The Chinese approach is one of subtlety; they steal secrets only when necessary, preferring to persuade foreign visitors to give them up voluntarily.[46]

A variant of elicitation is the use of *sampling techniques,* which could be thought of as group elicitation. Sampling techniques are best known for their use in public opinion polls. They are valuable sources for creating a human terrain model. When analysts need to know something about a large group of people (such as the attitudes on Middle East issues among the Arab population), they do not undertake the difficult or impractical task of surveying each member of the group. Instead analysts make estimates based on a small subset of the population. Sampling theory provides strategies for picking an optimum sampling method and estimating the error in the result.

Another variation of elicitation is to trade for information, much as the liaison services do. While Peter Schwartz was at Royal Dutch Shell, he made regular use of scenarios as a medium of exchange by presenting talks on the scenarios to selected groups—for example, insights on airline fuel futures to airline executives. In return, he received information from the executives on airline planning that he could use to refine his scenarios.[47]

Plant Visits. Visits to a manufacturing plant or other facility are a time-tested way to obtain intelligence. The Chinese had a monopoly on porcelain manufacturing until the early 1700s, when a Jesuit priest visited the Chinese royal porcelain factory and obtained the secrets of porcelain manufacturing for the French—who in turn lost the secret to a British industrial spy. Nearly a century later, Britain lost its edge in cotton manufacturing when a wealthy Bostonian named Francis Cabot Lowell visited English and Scottish textile mills, memorized the designs and floor layouts, and duplicated them in Waltham, Massachusetts.[48]

During the Cold War, plant visits often were used for obtaining advanced technology for military use. The Soviets, and later the Chinese, made numerous visits to U.S. industrial facilities in attempts, often successful, to acquire advanced military and civilian technologies.

Liaison. National intelligence organizations find it expedient to establish liaison relationships with intelligence and law enforcement groups in other countries, sometimes even when official relationships between the two countries are cool. CIA, prior to 2001, reportedly had liaison relations with some 400 foreign security, police, and intelligence organizations.[49] The number undoubtedly is larger today, as the requirements for counterterrorism intelligence have greatly expanded the need to conduct intelligence liaison. Commercial (competitive intelligence) groups have their own liaison networks with governments, NGOs, and other corporations to share information about such things as terrorist threats to corporate executives abroad and product counterfeiting.

The nature and closeness of the liaison relationship are critically dependent on the level of mutual trust and confidence between the two organizations and in turn, on their respective reputations for discretion and security. As Michael Herman observed, "National reputations for good or bad security are crucial elements in international intelligence standing."[50] During the cold war, the United States and other countries were reluctant to share information with West German intelligence, fearing that it had been penetrated by the East Germans (which turned out to be the case).

Intelligence liaison also is not uncommon among governmental and nongovernmental groups. Nongovernmental organizations provide many opportunities for government or commercial firms to conduct liaison for intelligence gathering. Two historical examples are the World War II liaison set up by the U.S. Office of Naval Intelligence with Mafia groups for counterespionage operations using dock workers' unions and by the Office of Strategic Services for subsequent operations against the Fascist government in Sicily. Mafia chief "Lucky" Luciano was released from prison, reportedly for his assistance in counterintelligence and to help with the Sicilian operation.[51]

The ethics of the Mafia liaison have been hotly debated over the years, and many intelligence officers argue that intelligence groups should not cooperate with criminal organizations. Their reservations are often summed up with the adage "If you go to bed with dogs, expect to wake up with fleas." The contrary argument is that one should use a nonjudgmental approach when choosing liaisons—if they can help more than they hurt, use them.

Liaison has a number of risks, one being the issue of false corroboration. It is not uncommon for several intelligence services to unwittingly use the same agent. (After all, if one service will pay you for what you know, others may be willing to do so.) When the agent's information is shared among intelligence services through liaison, it will seem to come to the analyst from different sources—the liaison service and the analyst's own HUMINT service. As a result, a single agent's information will be given added credibility that it does not deserve.

Liaison reports have a special credibility problem because the liaison service has its own agenda. The United States and other countries make use of liaison services. But they have to continually be aware of the potential bias of the second party collector.

Another problem with liaison is that you have to rely on the liaison service to check out the source's credentials (vetting the source, as discussed earlier). Beginning in 2000, Germany's Federal Intelligence Service, the BND, provided the United States with intelligence about Iraq's alleged biological warfare (BW) program from a human source codenamed "Curveball." In this case, the Germans themselves apparently were suspicious of the source but did not allow U.S. intelligence officers to interview him. U.S. analysts nevertheless relied heavily on Curveball's information in reaching an erroneous judgment that Iraq had an active BW program in 2002.[52]

Liaison with neutral or unfriendly powers comes with additional risks. You cannot be certain what friendly services will do with the intelligence you provide. Things are even less certain with neutral or unfriendly services. During the 16th century, under the reign of Sultan Suleiman the Magnificent, the Ottoman Empire developed a competent intelligence service by relying on liaison with Venice's diplomatic and HUMINT services. But the Venetians in turn used the relationship to report to European governments on the character and activities of the Sultan.[53] Sweden, while pursuing a policy of nonalignment, had liaison with both Nazi and Allied intelligence services during World War II and with Western powers (primarily Britain and the United States) during the Cold War.[54] The outcome benefited both Sweden and its liaison partners; but for both sides, the risk that the Swedes would also help the opponents made for strained relationships. In a later phase of the Cold War, the United States shared intelligence with China during the brief Chinese invasion of Vietnam in 1979.[55]

The collapse of the Muammar Qaddafi government in Libya during 2011 resulted in the publication of Libyan intelligence files. The files reportedly indicated that Qaddafi's intelligence service had liaison relationships with MI-6 and CIA.[56]

Liaison relations with neutral or adversarial governments usually involve some form of quid pro quo that may not be worth the consequences. A repressive regime that is hiding terrorists might be willing to sell out the terrorists in exchange for intelligence about its domestic opposition. For many governments, that is too high a price for intelligence. But it has been observed that liaison relationships between adversaries can exist for long periods of time. Israeli intelligence reportedly has long-term relationships with the intelligence services of several Arab states.[57] Reportedly, U.S. intelligence had liaison relationships with Syria after 9/11 because of Syria's interest in not being perceived as supporting the attacks.[58] The intelligence that is provided in these circumstances has to be viewed with great caution and at least cross-checked against other sources. There is a substantial risk that the liaison service will manipulate the intelligence it provides, to benefit its own interests.

While liaison is listed here under the heading of overt collection, it can be overtly or clandestinely conducted. Some liaison relationships are extremely sensitive and must be handled clandestinely. Examples include liaison where two countries officially have chilly diplomatic relations or where the liaison relationship would cause problems for either party with a third country if known.

Two-sided liaison relationships commonly involve trading information. But sometimes the exchange is of information for something else of value to one side. Instead of information, one side may get hardware for intelligence collection (e.g., to improve the quality of intelligence it provides to the other side). Sometimes, intelligence is exchanged for diplomatic or commercial favors.

The result is that two-sided liaison sometimes appears to be an unequal exchange. The Italians tended to share intelligence with the Germans during World War II but not vice versa.[59] The KGB's liaison with East European services during the Cold War tended to benefit the Soviet Union more than it did East European governments. In such cases, though, the primary beneficiary has provided something of value—military support to its partners, in the case of Nazi Germany and the Soviet Union.

Multisided liaison tends to be more overt. This kind of liaison has become more common, driven by a shift from threats to nations to transnational threats, where many countries have a common interest (in countering piracy, narcotics trafficking, and terrorism, for example). The benefit of liaison, and especially multisided liaison, is that intelligence ceases to be a zero-sum game. One state's gain in knowledge no longer is simply another state's loss of its secrets; two or more states receive the benefit.

Interrogation. Interrogation might best be described as elicitation in a controlled setting. The difference is that the interrogator has physical custody and some control over the fate of the source—who usually is a prisoner charged with a crime, a prisoner of war, an émigré, or a defector. The specific tactics used depend on the interrogator's degree of control and the willingness of the detainee to cooperate. Émigrés and defectors usually evince the greatest willingness to cooperate.

Émigrés and Defectors. Government intelligence routinely makes use of émigrés and defectors. Émigrés have departed a country legally, but in some countries would not have been allowed to leave if they had information of significant intelligence value. Defectors have departed the country illegally and often have information of value.

However, both émigrés and defectors have voluntarily left their native lands, usually for economic or political reasons. As a consequence, their objectivity on such issues is in question, and their information must be carefully screened. As with elicitation sources, asking the right question is important; defectors in particular want to please their new friends, and they tend to give answers that do that.

Corporate (competitive) intelligence routinely makes use of a different type of émigré or defector—one who formerly worked for the competition—to get information about trade secrets such as marketing strategies, costs, and proprietary processes. Corporate émigrés and defectors typically have the same problems with objectivity as do governmental defectors. They also often carry the added baggage of former employment agreements and legal issues that the traditional émigré or defector is not forced to carry. Additionally, when changing corporate loyalties within a country, a corporate émigré or defector cannot expect governmental protection if accused of stealing trade secrets. Internationally, however, such protection may be available.

- During 1993 and 1994 the international automobile industry was the stage for the dramatic defection of J. Ignacio Lopez de Arriortua and six other senior managers from General Motors (GM) to Volkswagenwerk AG. Lopez and his colleagues apparently took a number of sensitive GM documents with them, as any defector should do if he wishes to increase his value to his new organization. Lopez was accused of masterminding the theft of more than 20 boxes of documents on research, planning, manufacturing, and sales when he left GM to become a Volkswagen executive in 1993. The German government followed the time-honored tradition of providing governmental protection for defectors; they at first refused to prosecute Lopez, and a subsequent prosecution was dropped. Volkswagenwerk AG eventually paid GM damages in a civil suit. A U.S. grand jury subsequently indicted Lopez for fraud and transportation of stolen documents, but Spain's High Court refused to extradite him.[60] Corporate defectors to a country having less cordial relations with the United States would likely gain more protection, as would the company they defected to.

• Gary Min worked as a research chemist for DuPont for 10 years before accepting a job with DuPont competitor Victrex, a U.K. company, in October 2005. Between August and December of that year, Min downloaded 22,000 sensitive documents from DuPont files. His Victrex-owned notebook computer was seized on February 8, 2006, while he was at a meeting with Victrex officials in Geneva. The confiscated computer, containing some of the downloaded documents, was given to the FBI. Victrex, tipped off by DuPont officials, assisted in Min's arrest. Min subsequently pleaded guilty to trying to steal $400 million worth of company trade secrets and was sentenced to 18 months in jail.[61]

As these two examples suggest, what has been called "the insider threat" tends to follow a certain pattern. Most thefts of proprietary and confidential information are made by current employees. Furthermore, the thefts appear to occur between the time when an employee has made the decision to leave the company and the time when the employee actually leaves.[62]

Prisoners and Detainees. Military and law enforcement officials have the substantial advantage of conducting HUMINT in a controlled situation. Prisoners and detainees can be coerced or cut deals for information. Intelligence about the opposing forces, their positions, intent, and morale all can be obtained from prisoners of war. Law enforcement officers obtain information about the location of physical and financial assets and the identities of criminal network leadership from prisoners. The interrogations of al Qaeda prisoners at Guantanamo Bay have been controversial, but the detainees reportedly provided key pieces of information that ultimately led to the location and death of Osama bin Laden.[63]

Chapter 2 described the Black Boomerang operation during World War II, where the British operated radio stations that purported to be German military news stations. The news reports described actual events that were remarkably detailed, with subtle additions that were calculated to cause splits between the German military and the Nazi party. This black propaganda operation made a novel use of prisoner-based intelligence. A major source of the material came from interrogations, from conversations among German prisoners of war (POWs) that were captured by microphones conveniently hidden in POW recreational areas, and from personal details pulled from letters that German POWs sent to their families.[64] Some German POWs, unhappy with the Nazis, also volunteered to help with the broadcasts.

There are legal restraints, in most Western countries, on the degree of coercion that can be used in interrogation of prisoners and detainees. These restraints, or the lack thereof, became a political issue as a result of U.S. actions in Iraq. The most notorious events in Iraq were the interrogations and abuse at the Abu Ghraib prison that occurred in 2004. Partly in response to publicity about such abuses and the role that physicians played in them, the American Medical Association has declared that it is unethical for physicians to participate in interrogation of prisoners by the military or law enforcement agencies.

Current U.S. restrictions on interrogation prohibit any form of physical pain. Interrogators may not use waterboarding. They may not use hypothermia or treatment which will lead to heat injury. They cannot perform mock executions. They may not deprive detainees of necessary food, water, or medical care. And they may not use dogs in any aspect of interrogations.

Legal and ethical issues aside, many argue that pain, coercion, and threats are unlikely to elicit good information from a subject. One study of the subject has concluded that "the scientific community has never established that coercive interrogation methods are an effective means of obtaining reliable intelligence information."[65] Instead, many experienced interrogators argue that a softer approach has proven to be effective. Professor of Medicine and Bioethics Steven Miles observed that "effective interrogation seeks to build rapport, articulate common interests, exploit a subject's jealousy of comrades, or offer in exchange for information something the prisoner sees as being in his or her interest."[66]

A number of tougher or more deceptive interrogation techniques have proved to be effective without being coercive. Law enforcement has long used the good-cop/bad-cop routine, and it works in other arenas as well.

Especially effective is the false flag scenario that makes detainees think they're under the control of another country or organization than they actually are. Another technique that can be effective, isolation from other prisoners, is prohibited under the Geneva Accords for prisoners of war but is usable against non-POW detainees.

Structure

HUMINT differs from most other collection INTs in that it is so eclectic. As with open source, any person is capable of collecting HUMINT, and many do so. For governments and commercial entities, this presents a difficult structural problem. How do you effectively organize to collect and disseminate HUMINT with this vast number of potential collectors?

Furthermore, both governmental and nongovernmental HUMINT have a very large customer set. These customer needs force the acquisition of a diverse set of HUMINT sources. Policy customer needs differ from military support needs, and the sources used differ significantly. As a result, most governmental HUMINT is divided structurally in three basic ways: clandestine versus overt, foreign versus domestic, and military versus nonmilitary.

CLANDESTINE VERSUS OVERT HUMINT

Most governments operate a clandestine service, and it goes under many names: CIA's National Clandestine Service (NCS), the UK's Secret Intelligence Service (SIS, popularly known as MI-6), and Russia's Sluzhba Vneshney Razvedki (SVR, the successor to the KGB). Whatever the name, a clandestine service does many other things besides secretly exploiting agents for the purpose of collecting intelligence (that is, clandestine HUMINT collection). It typically is responsible for a range of foreign clandestine intelligence operations including espionage, counterespionage, covert action, and related foreign liaison activities. For example, a clandestine service

- works in liaison with other governmental services (domestic and foreign) to run all types of operations;
- taps telephones and installs listening devices;
- breaks into or otherwise gains access to the contents of secured facilities, safes, and computers;

Human Intelligence

- steals, compromises, and influences foreign cryptographic capabilities so as to make them exploitable by COMINT;
- protects its operations and defends the government from other intelligence services by engaging in a variety of counterespionage activities, including the aggressive use of double agents and penetrations of foreign services;
- clandestinely emplaces and services signals intelligence (SIGINT) and measurements and signatures intelligence (MASINT) sensors; and
- uses techniques and access to run programs to influence foreign governments and developments in what are called *covert actions.*[67]

The unifying aspect of these activities is not some connection to HUMINT; rather, they are highly diverse but interdependent activities that are best conducted by a clandestine service.[68]

So, not all of the activities of a clandestine service involve HUMINT collection. The converse is true. Not all government-collected HUMINT is collected by clandestine services. Diplomatic services have long engaged in HUMINT, both openly and clandestinely. Law enforcement organizations do the same.

Overt HUMINT is collected largely to serve departmental needs, though it may be widely shared across a government. Most, if not all, diplomatic services collect intelligence overtly, though they don't refer to it as intelligence. Many other governmental agencies want their own HUMINT. The U.S. State Department provides reporting that looks very much like HUMINT; and departments such as Treasury, Commerce, and Agriculture all have attachés in foreign countries with the assignment of providing similar reporting. Mostly, these organizations don't engage in clandestine HUMINT, relying instead on elicitation.

In contrast to this decentralized structure for overt HUMINT, clandestine HUMINT is usually tightly controlled by a single organization. Otherwise, as with any set of compartmented efforts going after the same target, multiple clandestine HUMINT services can trip over each other—two services trying to recruit or elicit information from the same asset would be an extreme example, or having one service recruit an asset and another (supposedly friendly) service request that the local police arrest the same asset. It happens!

FOREIGN VERSUS DOMESTIC INTELLIGENCE

Ethical and legal restrictions often force separate structures within HUMINT. Primarily, this concerns the problem of separating domestic from foreign intelligence. The United Kingdom maintains separate domestic (MI-5) and foreign (MI-6) intelligence services. Russia separates its Federal Security Service (FSB) from the SVR. Israel has the Mossad for foreign intelligence and the General Security Service (Shin Bet) for domestic and counterintelligence.[69] The United States traditionally has separated the two, with the CIA being responsible for foreign intelligence and the FBI taking the lead on domestic intelligence.

Some countries combine domestic and foreign intelligence in one organization. China's Ministry of State Security, for example, has both an internal and an external mission. Such a combination has some advantages: persons of intelligence interest are less likely to be lost when moving from a foreign to a domestic location (or vice versa) if their movements are under the cognizance of a single agency. This was identified as a problem in postmortems of the 9/11 attacks. Subsequently, in 2005, a National Clandestine Service was created with authority to coordinate foreign HUMINT operations of other agencies such as the FBI and DIA. The NCS, which reports to the Director of the CIA, is comprised of collection management officers, operations officers (case officers), paramilitary operations officers, and support personnel. But the domestic/foreign organizational separation was maintained; the NCS continues to focus outside U.S. borders, and the FBI continues to focus on domestic issues, with a requirement that the two collaborate closely.

Since 2005, the U.S. distinction between foreign and domestic intelligence officially has been blurred; it's now all supposed to fall under the umbrella of national intelligence. However, things aren't quite as simple as that in the world of HUMINT collection. Within the United States, HUMINT collection remains a responsibility of several national agencies.

To illustrate, consider the stated mission of the FBI's Directorate of Intelligence, which is to penetrate transnational networks including terrorist organizations, foreign intelligence services, those that seek to proliferate weapons of mass destruction, and criminal enterprises. There appears to be at least an overlap of responsibility with the Department of Homeland Security in counterterrorism, with the DEA in counternarcotics, and with local law enforcement in countering criminal enterprises. Stresses have developed, for example, between the FBI and the New York Police Department (NYPD) in the area of HUMINT collection. The NYPD's Intelligence Division has sent detectives (functioning as HUMINT collectors in the law enforcement arena) outside state borders and to foreign countries such as India, angering the FBI leadership.[70]

The United States is not unique in dealing with such stresses. The U.K. Security Service, known as MI-5, is responsible for "protecting the United

Kingdom against threats to national security from espionage, terrorism and sabotage, from the activities of agents of foreign powers, and from actions intended to overthrow or undermine parliamentary democracy by political, industrial or violent means." But inevitably there is overlap between MI-5's mission and that of local law enforcement.

Both national and local law enforcement units also deal with the clandestine versus overt division of HUMINT. Undercover police officers operate in many localities, while other police officers collect HUMINT overtly as part of their routine patrols or in interrogating detainees. The FBI used clandestine agents for years to penetrate and monitor the activities of the Ku Klux Klan.

MILITARY VERSUS NONMILITARY HUMINT

If they have the resources to do so, countries tend to separate their military from nonmilitary HUMINT collection. Russia long has kept the KGB (now SVR) separate from the military's intelligence service, the Glavnoye Razvedyvatel'noye Upravleniye (GRU). The Second Department of the Chinese People's Liberation Army General Staff has a responsibility for HUMINT that is separate from that of China's Ministry of State Security. The Military Intelligence Branch (AMAN), part of the Israeli Defense Forces, provides military intelligence that is separate from Mossad.[71]

However, all clandestine services that collect foreign intelligence provide HUMINT about military matters, especially where it supports national-level decision making. This overlap raises a number of problems, such as duplication of effort and competition for funding.

Within military intelligence, two additional divisions exist that have to be accommodated organizationally. First, national-level military intelligence requirements are quite different from those at the field level. Military services rely on diplomatic reporting from attachés for national (strategic) intelligence. Combat units in a theater of operation usually have field HUMINT units that gather tactical intelligence from sources such as prisoner interrogation and clandestine HUMINT.

From the time that the United States was founded, American military services have conducted both kinds of HUMINT. The War and Navy departments, and later the Department of Defense, all developed HUMINT capabilities to support their operations. At the national level, these operations were handled primarily by military attachés reporting to their respective services. In 1965, this operation was centralized within the Defense

Attaché System, which brought all the military service attachés together within DIA.[72]

The second division that has to be considered is that between overt and clandestine HUMINT. All of today's U.S. military services and combat commands have established organizations to recruit spies and debrief individuals of interest in order to gather information about foreign weapons systems, doctrine, and other matters of interest to military officials. The significance attached to clandestine HUMINT operations has varied among the services and within some of the services over time. From 1966 to 1977, the Navy operated a clandestine collection unit, designated the Naval Field Operations Support Group and known as Task Force 157. The Army maintained a consistently high level of interest in HUMINT throughout the Cold War. From 1981 to 1989, the U.S. Army's Intelligence Support Activity provided clandestine HUMINT and conducted covert operations to support military operations.[73]

The current U.S. military clandestine HUMINT structure dates from 1995, when the Defense HUMINT Service (DHS) was created within DIA. DHS absorbed the HUMINT efforts of the services. The Army vigorously opposed the move because it had the most to lose. The reorganization was intended to reduce the cost of four separate military HUMINT organizations and to improve collaboration in military HUMINT. At the same time, overt and clandestine HUMINT were combined within one organization: DHS also assumed responsibility for the Defense Attaché System and consequently for the overt collection of information for military customers.[74]

COMMERCIAL

Most competitive intelligence units are organized to rely on corporate employees for HUMINT. Some multinational companies have set up structures that encourage large numbers of their employees to collect and report competitive intelligence worldwide. A few of the more aggressive companies use independent consultants for HUMINT. The practice of using independent consultants has its risks; some will use practices that are considered unethical, such as obtaining intelligence under false pretenses (posing as purchasing agents, for example).

Clandestine HUMINT by one firm against another is illegal in most countries. Some companies nevertheless collect clandestine HUMINT, ignoring the legal issue. And some governments collect clandestine HUMINT from commercial firms—France and China being notable examples.

STRUCTURE OF CLANDESTINE HUMINT

Clandestine HUMINT organizations tend to have a different organizational structure than do overt HUMINT collectors, for a number of reasons. Clandestine HUMINT operates with different tradecraft and under different legal restrictions than does overt HUMINT. The skills needed to recruit and run a spy differ from those needed for elicitation of conference attendees or for interrogation of detainees. The support structure for clandestine operations is much more complex than that for overt HUMINT.

As noted earlier, almost any person can collect HUMINT. Some intelligence services (the United States and United Kingdom come to mind) prefer to be highly selective about, and protective of, their clandestine sources. They have a centralized organization, where headquarters controls the hiring and running of agents and the norm is to take responsibility for the agents' welfare, including compensation for their services. Control of clandestine operations is also centralized; the usual approach is to have one person (such as a CIA chief of station or an SVR *Rezident,* the Russian equivalent) in a country approve all clandestine operations there, but even that becomes a problem in transnational operations. The centralized structure has been criticized as becoming, over time, too bureaucratic, unimaginative, and stuck in traditional ways of doing things.[75]

Some services, in contrast, opt for a distributed and more laissez-faire structure, accepting the increased risks in order to extend their capabilities. These services either prefer not to rely on paid agents or supplement paid agents with volunteers.

- Mossad, with a relatively small service, relies heavily on its *sayanim* (derived from a Hebrew word meaning *to help*), a group of tens of thousands of volunteers worldwide. The sayanim feed Mossad information or provide operational support such as passports, automobile loans, buildings for surveillance, emergency funds, and medical assistance.[76]
- The Chinese Ministry of State Security operates with few paid agents but relies on an extensive network of students, travelers, and citizens abroad of Chinese descent. Most of these are volunteers or engage in espionage in return for something that China can offer (such as good treatment for the agent's family in China or business opportunities tied to China's booming economy.)[77] The Chinese approach has both advantages and drawbacks. It provides a great deal of incoming raw intelligence, but much of it is low grade, and some of it is misleading. A lot of resources have to be allocated just to collating the incoming intelligence. The job that Chinese intelligence faces in assessing the volume of incoming raw intelligence has

to be a massive one, with consequent risks of being taken in by a deception operation.

Below the top level, clandestine HUMINT has to establish a substructure. It would be desirable to divide by mission, but that can be hard. Counterterrorism, counternarcotics, and military operations support, for example, often overlap.

Most common is a regional division (e.g., Russia, China, sub-Saharan Africa). But on high-priority transnational issues, it may be essential to organize specific mission-focused units, for example, against terrorism or weapons of mass destruction (WMD) proliferation. So the resulting structure can be a hybrid. No matter what subdivision is selected, some cross-unit collaboration is necessary. Subunits might focus, for example, on political, military, and economic issues, but a given HUMINT source may be able to provide intelligence across all these disciplines.

Summary

Humint = recruiting

The traditional HUMINT as depicted in spy novels is collected clandestinely. Such HUMINT at the national level is usually carried out by intelligence officers known as *case officers* who work for a clandestine service. Case officers normally make use of agents, either recruited or volunteers (known as walk-ins), who operate under the service's control. National and local law enforcement also collect clandestine HUMINT, normally by using informants: sources that are not controlled and often won't accept tasking.

A clandestine service has many other responsibilities in addition to clandestine collection. The unifying aspect of these activities is not some connection to HUMINT; rather, they are highly diverse but interdependent activities that are best conducted by a clandestine service. They include liaison, covert action, and counterintelligence. So not all of the activities of a clandestine service involve HUMINT collection. The converse is also true. Not all government-collected HUMINT is collected by clandestine services. Diplomatic services have long engaged in HUMINT, both openly and clandestinely. Law enforcement organizations do the same.

In addition to spies (agents), HUMINT is collected from liaison contacts, émigrés, defectors, detainees, and travelers—sometimes clandestinely, sometimes overtly.

- Defectors have departed their home country illegally and are more likely to have information of value than émigrés, who depart legally.

- Diplomats have a long history of collecting intelligence, usually overtly or via liaison with their counterparts. Military, law enforcement, and agricultural attachés, for example, collect specialized intelligence for their parent agencies—though they may not call it intelligence. Liaison provides many benefits but carries risks that the liaison partner will use the relationship for perception management, will engage in unsavory activities, or will demand an unacceptable quid pro quo.

- Interrogation of prisoners and detainees has the advantage that you have control of the source and can offer inducements to get information.

- Travelers to other countries and students abroad are potential sources for elicitation when they return. Use of such travelers for commercial espionage has been practiced for centuries. Governments wishing to acquire advanced technology, such as China, have developed such espionage to a fine art.

Clandestine HUMINT collection, being illegal in most countries, has an elaborate process to protect the sources (agents) from exposure and to defend against counterintelligence. The process has three major stages—recruitment, running the agent, and ending the relationship. Recruitment involves

- spotting, or identifying a potential agent—one who is willing to spy, has access to the desired information, is trusted by his organization, and can handle the pressure of espionage;

- assessing the motivation for spying—usually money, ideology, compromise (coercion or blackmail), ego, or revenge;

- recruiting, or making the pitch, which is sometimes done under a false flag—pretending to represent a country or organization that the source regards favorably (Coercion is used by countries such as Russia and China, but coerced agents usually are less effective because they operate under duress); and

- vetting, which is essential in ensuring that the source is legitimate, for example, and not a dangle by a hostile service.

Running the agent requires guiding the collection effort and getting the collected material back to headquarters. Support to the agent, or care and feeding, requires that the case officer provide espionage equipment, funds, and cover. The primary challenges in this stage involve clandestine communication with the agent and acquiring the agent's information using techniques such as dead drops and brush passes.

All clandestine relationships end eventually, and the end stage has to be planned for. The agent may leave voluntarily or be retired or may have to be exfiltrated because the risk of exposure has become too great.

Clandestine HUMINT operatives operate in foreign countries under some form of cover. There are two types of cover—official and nonofficial. The deepest level of cover is nonofficial cover. Such operatives are called NOCs by the CIA and British SIS, and "Illegals" by the Russians. Increasingly, it is difficult to maintain either type of cover because of biometric identification and the wide availability of biographic data on the Internet.

Major intelligence services make use of front companies, known as proprietaries, for espionage cover, support to covert operations, and acquiring technology, equipment, and industrial know-how.

Clandestine services conduct a number of operations that fall into the category loosely called tradecraft. Surveillance and countersurveillance are two of these. Surveillance involves either human observation or technical operations (audio or video collection). Countersurveillance, as the name implies, is aimed at defeating an opposing intelligence service's surveillance attempts. A third tradecraft operation, surreptitious entry, involves gaining access to locked rooms and safes, to computers, or to mail (an area of tradecraft called flaps and seals). The goal is to (1) not get caught in the act and (2) leave no evidence of the act behind.

An intelligence service very much wants to have double agents (an opponent's agents who have been turned) or moles (agents emplaced in a hostile service) working for them. And every clandestine service greatly fears having their own agents turned or moles within their own service. A major function of counterintelligence lies in recruiting the former and identifying the latter.

The major part of HUMINT is collected overtly rather than clandestinely, mostly using one of these techniques:

Elicitation is the practice of obtaining information about a topic from conversations, preferably without the source knowing what is happening. Elicitation is widely practiced in gatherings of diplomats and military attachés and in the commercial sector. It requires selecting the right setting, timing the questions properly, and asking the right questions. Sampling techniques are also used, much as is done in public opinion polling.

Plant visits to obtain intelligence about manufacturing techniques and technology have a long history; their use increased significantly during the Cold War.

Liaison relationships are mostly bilateral and involve sharing intelligence, often in exchange for equipment or diplomatic or commercial favors. Multilateral relationships have become increasingly important in dealing with issues such as terrorism and weapons proliferation.

Human Intelligence

Interrogation is used to obtain information from prisoners and detainees. Coercive interrogations, including some of what are called "enhanced interrogation" techniques, have given interrogation a bad name. But there is a rich set of techniques available to persuade or mislead prisoners and detainees into cooperating and providing intelligence without resorting to the questionable techniques.

HUMINT is collected by many organizations from many sources and for many purposes. As a result, there are many different structures, potential for overlapping collection, and intelligence sharing issues in HUMINT. Legal restrictions or the nature of collection often require separating foreign from domestic collection, as is done in the United States, the United Kingdom, Russia, and Israel. But countries such as China combine the two in order to better track people as they move into and out of the country. Because the military is the biggest single customer, most countries have a separate organization to handle it and further subdivide military HUMINT into national and tactical levels. Homeland security and local law enforcement have continuing issues about where the boundary is. Multinational corporations collect HUMINT for commercial purposes, sometimes sharing the product with government organizations.

NOTES

1. Richard Grenier, "Colonel Redl: The Man Behind the Screen Myth," *New York Times* (October 13, 1985), accessed 21 September 2012 at http://www .nytimes.com/1985/10/13/movies/colonel-redl-the-man-behind-the-screen-myth.html.
2. P. Redmond, "The Challenges of Counterintelligence." Chapter 33 in L. Johnson (ed.), *The Oxford Handbook of National Security Intelligence* (Oxford: Oxford University Press, 2010), 541.
3. Ian Traynor, "WikiLeaks Cables Claim First Scalp as German Minister's Aide is Sacked," *The Guardian* (December 3, 2010), accessed 21 September 2012 at http://www.guardian.co.uk/media/2010/dec/03/wikileaks-first-scalp-german-aide.
4. Mark Bowden, *Killing Pablo* (Atlantic Monthly Press, 2001).
5. "Timeline: The Intelligence Hunt Leading to Bin Laden," *BBC News South Asia* (May 6, 2011), accessed 21 September 2012 at http://www.bbc.co.uk/news/world-south-asia-13279283.
6. Clarence Walker, "A Special Investigative Report: American Mafia Recruits Sicilian Mafia," in *American Mafia.com* (August 2004), accessed 21 September 2012 at http://www.americanmafia.com/Feature_Articles_272.html.
7. David S. Landes, *The Wealth and Poverty of Nations* (New York: W. W. Norton and Company, 1998), 276.
8. Ibid., 279.
9. Ibid.

10. Arthur Weiss, "How Far Can Primary Research Go?" *Competitive Intelligence Magazine* (November–December 2001), 18.

11. "France, Israel Cited in CIA Espionage Study," *Los Angeles Times* (August 15, 1996), accessed 21 September 2012 at http://articles.latimes.com/1996-08-15/business/fi-34524_1_economic-espionage.

12. Henry Samuel, "Chinese Use Honeytraps to Spy on French Companies, Intelligence Report Claims," *Telegraph* (February 2, 2011).

13. Douglas F. Garthoff, "Directors of Central Intelligence as Leaders of the US Intelligence Community, 1946–2005" (2007), Chapter 12, accessed 21 September 2012 at https://www.cia.gov/library/center-for-the-study-of-intelligence/csi-publications/books-and-monographs/directors-of-central-intelligence-as-leaders-of-the-u-s-intelligence-community/chapter_12.htm.

14. R. Wallace and H. K. Melton, *Spycraft: The Secret History of the CIA's Spytechs, from Communism to al-Qaeda* (New York: Dutton, 2008), 365.

15. James Olson, *The Ten Commandments of Counterintelligence,* Center for the Study of Intelligence (2007), p. 242. Accessed 21 September 2012 at https://www.cia.gov/library/center-for-the-study-of-intelligence/csi-publications/csi-studies/studies/fall_winter_2001/article08.html.

16. Benjamin Weiser, *A Secret Life* (New York: Public Affairs, 2004).

17. James Olson, *The Ten Commandments of Counterintelligence.*

18. D. Wise, *Spy: The Inside Story of How the FBI's Robert Hanssen Betrayed America* (New York: Random House, 2002), 270–281.

19. John Ehrman, "What Are We Talking About When We Talk About Counterintelligence?" Center for the Study of Intelligence, *Studies in Intelligence,* Vol. 53, No. 2 (2009), 18, accessed 21 September 2012 at https://www.cia.gov/library/center-for-the-study-of-intelligence/csi-publications/csi-studies/studies/v0153n02/toward-a-theory-of-ci.html.

20. Wise, *Spy: The Inside Story of How the FBI's Robert Hanssen Betrayed America*, 12.

21. Ibid., 14.

22. M. Beardon and J. Risen, *The Main Enemy: The Inside Story of the CIA's Final Showdown with the KGB* (New York: Random House, 2003), 198–202.

23. R. Wallace and H. K. R. Melton, *Spycraft,* 420.

24. Ibid., 31.

25. Yudhijit Bhattacharjee, "Tale of a Would-be Spy, Buried Treasure, and Uncrackable Code," *Wired* (January 25, 2010), accessed 21 September 2012 at http://www.wired.com/magazine/2010/01/ff_hideandseek/4/.

26. R. Wallace and H. K. R. Melton, *Spycraft: The Secret History of the CIA's Spytechs, from Communism to al-Qaeda,* 421–441.

27. Robert L. Benson, "The Venona Story," NSA/CSS Historical Publications, accessed 24 September 2011 at http://web.archive.org/web/20060614231955/http://www.nsa.gov/publications/publi00039.cfm.

28. Shlomo Shpiro, "Speak No Evil," in Jan Goldman (ed.), *Ethics of Spying,* Volume 2 (Lanham, MD: The Scarecrow Press, 2010), 63.

29. Antonio J. Mendez, "A Classic Case of Deception," CIA *Studies in Intelligence,* (Winter 1999/2000), accessed 25 September 2011 at https://www.cia.gov/library/center-for-the-study-of-intelligence/csi-publications/csi-studies/studies/winter99-00/art1.html.

30. Peter Baker, "Swap Idea Emerged Early in Case of Russia Agents," *New York Times* (July 9, 2010), accessed 21 September 2012 at http://www.nytimes.com/2010/07/10/world/europe/10russia.html?ref=russianspyring2010&pagewanted=2.

31. Nicholas Anderson, *NOC: Non-official Cover: British Secret Operations* (London, UK: Enigma Books, 2009).

32. "A Tide Turns," *The Economist* (July 21, 2010), accessed 21 September 2012 at http://www.economist.com/node/16590867/.

33. William M. Leary, "About Air America," accessed 21 September 2012 at http://www.air-america.org/About/History.shtml.

34. E. M. Roche, *Corporate Spy: Industrial Espionage and Counterintelligence in the Multinational Enterprise* (New York: Barraclough, 2008), 131–135.

35. P. Devenny, "China's Secret War," FrontPageMagazine.com (March 31, 2005), accessed 21 September 2012 at http://archive.frontpagemag.com/Printable.aspx?ArtId=9146.

36. Henry K. Lee, "Cupertino Man Gets 2 Years for Exporting Military Technology to China," *San Francisco Chronicle* (December 5, 2007), accessed 21 September 2012 at http://articles.sfgate.com/2007-12-05/bay-area/17273210_1_china-homeland-security-affidavit.

37. P. Devenny, "China's Secret War."

38. Joby Warrick, "Iran Using Fronts to Get Bomb Parts from US," *Washington Post* (January 11, 2009), A01.

39. See, for example, Tom Mangold, *Cold Warrior: James Jesus Angleton—CIA's Master Spy Hunter* (New York: Simon & Schuster, 1991).

40. See Peter Wright, *Spycatcher* (New York: Viking Penguin, 1987), for details on the search for moles within MI-5 and MI-6.

41. Christopher Andrew and Vasili Mitrokhin, *The World Was Going Our Way* (Cambridge, MA: Perseus Books, 2005), 225.

42. Wallace and Melton, *Spycraft*, 208–213.

43. Shlomo Shpiro, "Speak No Evil," 61–62.

44. *Commission on the Roles and Capabilities of the United States Intelligence Community* (1996), Chapter 10, accessed 21 September 2012 at http://www.gpoaccess.gov/int/int014.pdf.

45. D. Wise, *Spy: The Inside Story of How the FBI's Robert Hanssen Betrayed America*, 13.

46. Ibid.

47. Peter Schwartz, *The Art of the Long View* (New York: Doubleday, 1991), 78.

48. Brian Champion, "A Review of Selected Cases of Industrial Espionage and Economic Spying, 1568–1945," *Intelligence and National Security*, v. 13, no. 2 (1998), 123–143.

49. Gregory F. Treverton, *Reshaping National Intelligence for an Age of Information* (Cambridge, MA: Cambridge University Press, 2001), 137.

50. Michael Herman, *Intelligence Power in Peace and War* (Cambridge, UK: Cambridge University Press, 1996), 211.

51. Richard Eels and Peter Nehemkis, *Corporate Intelligence and Espionage* (Old Tappan, NJ: Macmillan, 1984), 59; Charles D. Ameringer, *U.S. Foreign Intelligence* (Lanham, MD: Lexington Books, 1990), 170.

52. "Report of the Commission on the Intelligence Capabilities of the United States Regarding Weapons of Mass Destruction" (March 31, 2005), 80, accessed at http://www.gpo.gov/fdsys/pkg/GPO-WMD/content-detail.html.

53. Lord Kinross, *The Ottoman Centuries* (New York: William Morrow, 1971), 175.

54. Wilhelm Agrell, "Sweden and the Dilemmas of Neutral Intelligence Liaison," *Journal of Strategic Studies* (August 2006), 633–651.

55. Henry Kissinger, *On China* (New York: Penguin Press, 2011), 360.

56. Rod Nordland, "Files Note Close CIA Ties to Qaddafi Spy Unit," *New York Times* (September 3, 2011).

57. Jennifer E. Sims, "Foreign Intelligence Liaison: Devils, Deals, and Details," *International Journal of Intelligence & Counter Intelligence,* Vol. 19, No. 2 (Summer 2006), 195–217.

58. Ibid.

59. Ben Macintyre, *Operation Mincemeat* (New York: Harmony Books, 2010), 253.

60. Emma Daly, "Spain Court Refuses to Extradite Man G.M. Says Took Its Secrets," *New York Times* (June 20, 2001), accessed 21 September 2012 at http://www.nytimes.com/2001/06/20/business/spain-court-refuses-to-extradite-man-gm-says-took-its-secrets.html?ref=joseignaciolopezdearriortua.

61. Larry Greenemeier, "Massive Insider Breach at DuPont," *Information Week* (February 15, 2007), accessed 21 September 2012 at http://www.informationweek.com/news/197006474.

62. Ibid.

63. Marc A. Thiessen, "Punishing the Heroes," *Pittsburgh Post-Gazette* (May 6, 2011), accessed 21 September 2012 at http://www.post-gazette.com/pg/11126/1144413-109-0.stm?cmpid=news.xml.

64. Sefton Delmer, *Black Boomerang* (New York: Viking Press, 1962).

65. Intelligence Science Board, *Educing Information: Interrogation: Science and Art,* National Defense Intelligence College Press (2006), 130.

66. Steven Miles, "Torture and the Medical Profession," in *Ethics of Spying,* Vol. 2, Jan Goldman, ed. (Lanham, MD: Scarecrow Press, 2010), 183.

67. U.S. Congress, "IC21: The Intelligence Community in the 21st Century" (June 5, 1996), Chapter 9, accessed 21 September 2012 at http://www.gpo.gov/fdsys/pkg/GPO-IC21/content-detail.html.

68. Ibid.

69. Shlomo Shpiro, "Speak No Evil," 60.

70. Jeff Stein, "NYPD Intelligence Making FBI Blue," *Washington Post* (April 26, 2010), accessed 21 September 2012 at http://voices.washingtonpost.com/spy-talk/2010/04/nypd_intelligence_making_fbi_b.html.

71. Ibid.

72. *Commission on the Roles and Capabilities of the United States Intelligence Community,* Chapter 10.

73. Ibid.

74. Ibid.

75. Richard L. Russell, "The Weakest Link," in *Rethinking the Principles of War,* Anthony D. McIvor, ed. (Annapolis, MD: Naval Institute Press, 2005), 471.

76. Gordon Thomas, "Mossad's License to Kill," *Telegraph* (February 17, 2010), accessed 21 September 2012 at http://www.telegraph.co.uk/news/worldnews/middleeast/israel/7254807/Mossads-licence-to-kill.html.

77. Wise, *Spy: The Inside Story of How the FBI's Robert Hanssen Betrayed America,* 12–13.

4. Communications Intelligence

Communications intelligence, or COMINT, is the interception, processing, and reporting of an opponent's communications. The National Security Agency (NSA) defines COMINT as "technical and intelligence information derived from foreign communications by other than their intended recipient."[1] (Law enforcement organizations would undoubtedly drop the word *foreign* from this definition.) Communications in this definition includes voice and data communications, facsimile, video, and any other deliberate transmission of information. Internet transmissions are a form of communication, but their collection and analysis is treated in Chapters 2 and 5.

COMINT in the most general sense long predates the development of telecommunications. The intercept and analysis of semaphore (signal flag) communications and American Indian smoke signals was common centuries ago. And governments routinely have intercepted foreign government communications for decades. Today COMINT is a large-scale activity providing customers with intelligence on diplomatic, military, economic, and scientific developments internationally, as well as supporting law enforcement efforts domestically.

Function

The functions served by COMINT—that is, the targets—have changed steadily and expanded significantly throughout the last century. Throughout the first half century, the primary targets were military and diplomatic communications. Beginning about midcentury, world trade grew rapidly and the collection of economic intelligence became important. At about the same time, COMINT also began providing information about scientific and technical developments. Late in the 20th century, narcotics trafficking, money laundering, and organized crime became important targets. During the first decade of this century, international terrorism became the preeminent target.

At the strategic level, COMINT collection, like human intelligence (HUMINT) collection, can provide insights into plans and intentions. It can contribute information about people, organizations, financial transactions, equipment, facilities, procedures, schedules, budgets, operations, testing, deployment, and environmental conditions. COMINT gives insights about personal and organizational relationships. It reveals details about sensitive or classified programs. In the past, COMINT seldom provided much detail because it dealt primarily with brief conversations. This is no longer the case, as large volumes of material are now transmitted by data communications or facsimile.

COMINT, for example, reportedly provided the critical element in identifying Libya's Rabta chemical plant as a producer of chemical warfare (CW) agents. In 1998, a toxic waste spill occurred at the plant. According to a report prepared by the U.S. Congress's Office of Technology Assessment, Libyan officials placed emergency phone calls to Imhausen-Chemie, the West German firm that had designed the plant. Frantic to get advice on cleaning up and repairing the plant, the Libyans discussed the problem at length with the Germans—confirming that the plant was in fact producing CW and that the German firm knew that fact.[2]

Targets of COMINT for strategic intelligence include government leadership, research and development organizations, test facilities, criminal enterprises, economic activities (such as international funds transfers), participants in test and operational activities, and executive policy discussions. For example, the history of U.S. cryptanalysts breaking the Japanese diplomatic cipher (the "Purple Code") prior to World War II is well known. Less well known is that a Soviet cryptanalyst, one year later, also broke the code. This success gave Moscow a strategic advantage during the war; it made clear that Japan would not attack the Soviet Union, allowing Stalin to shift half of his Far Eastern military forces west to fight the Germans.[3]

In between strategic and tactical intelligence, COMINT can support operational planning. It has had a number of successes in wartime. During World War II, the United States scored its Midway victory over the Japanese navy largely because U.S. cryptanalysts had cracked the Japanese naval codes and were able to identify Midway as the Japanese target. In Europe, the British success at breaking the German ENIGMA cipher codes contributed to several World War II successes, including the Normandy landing.[4]

COMINT also can provide operational support in the nonmilitary arena, for example, in supporting negotiations. Soon after the United States sat down in Washington with other naval powers in 1921 to negotiate a naval armaments treaty, it acquired a substantial advantage. The American "Black Chamber" (the Cipher Bureau, the forerunner of NSA), under Herbert Yardley, was monitoring the delegates' communications. Yardley's team broke the cipher used by Japanese participants. The American negotiators then were able to get the minimum possible deal the Japanese had indicated they would accept, absent which the Japanese would have left the conference.[5]

Encryption technology has outpaced cryptanalysis in the decades since World War II, and it would be very difficult, if not impossible, to repeat the Allied successes of that war. The lessons of the war were learned by all countries, and most cryptanalysis successes now come from communications operator mistakes. Of course, a large amount of military and civilian radio traffic remains unencrypted, but almost all sensitive military communications are encrypted, and the trend is to encrypt highly sensitive civilian communications.

Most tactical COMINT is conducted by the world's military services. They conduct COMINT using trained linguists to monitor the mobile radio communications of opposing forces. Military COMINT is used extensively against air-to-ground, ground-to-ground, and naval communications.

Law enforcement groups also rely heavily on COMINT to support ongoing operations and to defeat illicit networks generally. The track down of Pablo Escobar, mentioned in Chapter 3, is a typical example of this heavy reliance on tactical COMINT.

As with the collection systems discussed in previous chapters, COMINT provides finished intelligence and also provides support to other intelligence collectors. For example, it provides tip-off of upcoming events for imagery intelligence (IMINT) targeting. It identifies potential recruitment prospects for HUMINT case officers and can be very helpful in vetting sources.

Process

There are several steps involved in COMINT collection. The process almost always starts with targeting, followed by obtaining access and collecting the information from the communications link. Then comes what is commonly referred to as the back end: processing, analysis, and finally, dissemination of the raw intelligence. Let's go through these steps, one at a time.

TARGETING

Up front, a COMINT organization must select and prioritize the collection targets. There are many potential sources of COMINT. In fact, there are simply too many sources to try and collect them all. If it is used to communicate literal information electronically or audibly, it can be a source for COMINT. The problem often becomes deciding which source, out of the large number potentially accessible, to go after. Often the answer is to select the source that can most readily satisfy intelligence needs, considering the difficulty and risk associated with intercepting it and translating the collected material into useful intelligence. Following is a summary of some of the most used sources and the types of intelligence that can be derived from them. The sensors used to collect from radio frequency (RF) COMINT sources are discussed in Chapter 13.

Microphones and Audio Transmitters. Microphone-and-wire is an old technology but still widely used by some intelligence services. It is cheap, reliable, and long lasting. Unfortunately, it is also relatively easy for counterintelligence units to find. It has long been used in law enforcement and counterintelligence.

The audio transmitter, popularly known as the "bug," also has been useful for decades. Because it transmits a radio signal rather than using a wire, it is simpler to emplace than the microphone-and-wire. It also is cheap and requires no great technical skill to use, so it is particularly popular among the less sophisticated intelligence organizations and in industrial espionage. The audio transmitter typically uses low radiated power to avoid detection, has its own power supply (unless it can tap into the building power system), and is small enough to be effectively concealed. Increasingly, bugs can provide video as well as audio.

Advancing technologies in miniaturization, power sources, and transmission techniques have made the audio/video transmitter more effective and harder to find. Burst transmissions (very short, usually one second or less, radio signals), spread spectrum (typically signals that look like noise), and other techniques are available to reduce the probability of detecting these bugs. More sophisticated bugs use difficult-to-detect infrared transmission. Remote command and control techniques have been employed to switch transmitters on and off, reducing the probability of detection and conserving battery life.

Remote Acoustic Monitoring. Where an intelligence service cannot gain access to a facility for a microphone-and-wire or audio transmitter installation, it can sometimes use one of several remote acoustic monitoring techniques. All such techniques depend on the ability of structural or emplaced objects in a room to pick up sound and vibrate mechanically.

The sensor that does this is a specialized type of microphone called the **geophone**. The geophone picks up mechanical vibrations directly from the building structure and transmits the audio out of a facility by wire or a radio transmitter. Whether the vibrations are from voice or machine noise, the geophone can effectively receive sound from several rooms away. Typically, the geophone is placed in a structural beam that runs into the area to be monitored. The vibrations from conversations in the room travel along the structural beam and are picked up by the geophone.

Fluidics, a method to surreptitiously collect audio information, exploits the way in which acoustic energy travels with relatively low loss in liquids, or in gases if channeled. Thus, if a water pipe picks up acoustic energy, the audio signal will travel long distances within the pipe and can be picked up by a microphone or geophone remotely. Electrical conduit or air ducts will also propagate audio over substantial distances. The old-style audio headsets that passengers once used in commercial airliners used hollow tubes that took advantage of this channeling effect in an air conduit.

Since the 1940s, a technique called **radio frequency flooding** of installations has been used for intelligence collection. The flooding signals usually operate in the microwave range and are used to collect information remotely, much as a radar senses its target. Flooding depends on the fact that objects, especially metal ones, vibrate slightly in response to audio in a room. A beam of microwave energy striking the metal object will be reflected from it with some weak modulation imposed by the audio vibrations. If the reflected energy can be collected and demodulated, conversations in the area can be monitored. Innocuous signals such as those emanating from a television or radio station can be used successfully to flood an installation.

Perhaps the best known instance of radio frequency flooding was that conducted by the Soviets against the U.S. Embassy in Moscow early in the

Cold War. The Soviets presented the U.S. ambassador with the great seal of the United States, which he subsequently used as décor in his study. The Soviets had concealed a passive sound pickup device in the seal. During George F. Kennan's ambassadorship in 1952, a routine security check discovered that the seal contained a metal strip that would vibrate slightly in response to sounds within the room. The Soviets illuminated the Great Seal with a strong RF signal from a nearby location, and the metal strip radiated a return signal that was modulated by any sounds in the ambassador's office.[6]

Laser radar techniques have been used to exploit audio vibrations from windows or similar fixtures within an office since the 1960s. The principle is the same as for radio frequency flooding. An infrared laser (which is invisible to the human eye) can be aimed at an office window from distances ranging up to hundreds of yards. If the proper infrared band is selected for the laser, the window glass will reflect the energy. Conversations inside the office will cause the windowpane to vibrate slightly, and these audio vibrations will modulate the reflected laser energy. An optical receiver located near the laser transmitter can then pick up the backscattered energy, demodulate it, and recover the audio. The technology to use such laser devices is now widely available.[7]

Telephone Surveillance. Let's take a brief look at telephones—wired telephones, mobile phones that once resided only in moving vehicles, and today's cell phones, which communicate via a network of cell towers. The technologies used to communicate by telephone have changed, and the intercept systems have changed to keep up with them.

Fixed telephones are perceived as almost archaic today. But they still are widely used and a target of COMINT. One long-used approach is to monitor the telephone of interest through a tap. The tap can be placed somewhere on the line connecting the phone to a switching center. Sometimes due to faulty design or because it has been modified to do so, a telephone handset will pick up conversations in the area even when turned off (or for older handsets, resting in its cradle).

Telephone conversations also can be intercepted in bulk by COMINT equipment if the equipment is properly positioned to collect either the cable or microwave point-to-point transmissions from the telephone company's trunk lines. The obvious challenge with such intercepts on civil systems is the sheer quantity of conversations. COMINT processors can become swamped—especially so, if the language must be translated. Some means of specific telephone recognition must be found to allow selection of the conversations of interest. Ideally, telephone numbers of intelligence interest can be identified in advance. Failing that, it often is necessary to resort to identifying keywords in conversations.

Tactical COMINT in military units often has relied on field telephone conversations. In static warfare (that is, trench warfare), these telephones used wires laid on the ground across a battlefield. During World War I and again in the Korean War, it was found that such telephone conversations could be intercepted by what was essentially a wire buried in the ground near enemy positions and connected to headphones. The technique was called "ground return intercept."

Mobile telephones (today, primarily cell telephones) have largely replaced the fixed telephone in civil use. One of the better known COMINT operations during the Cold War involved intercepting the mobile phones that equipped the Kremlin leadership's limousines. The intercepts, operated from listening posts in the U.S. and British Moscow embassies, provided extensive details on Kremlin decision-making processes and the personalities and vulnerabilities of Soviet leaders. The value of these intercepts dropped dramatically after columnist Jack Anderson revealed their existence in the *Washington Post* in September 1971.[8]

Today, cellular telephone networks are an easy target for COMINT. An individual device or an entire cell tower can be targeted.[9] Interception can be done near the phone itself, near the tower, or at the routing center.

Cell phone networks today are encrypted, but most current encryption provides little protection. The most popular cell phone encryption worldwide is Global System for Mobile communications, or GSM. GSM encryption can be broken routinely and not just by government COMINT services. Commercially available intercept kits can crack wireless GSM encryption on these phones, at a modest price of about $2,000. The kits mimic cell phone tower base stations to take control of a cell phone. They then defeat the encryption, and according to one expert in the field, "take your call and manage it just like [it] was the cell tower, forwarding it on through the rest of the network."[10]

Cell phones are mobile, but they can still be located and tracked—a big advantage in surveillance of a target. Almost all cell phones carry GPS that provides their precise location; failing that, an intercept operator also can identify the cell tower being used or use direction-finding equipment to locate the cell phone's position. Revisiting the case of drug kingpin Pablo Escobar yet again, Colombian police found Escobar in the city of Medellin by using U.S.-provided direction-finding equipment against his cell phone.[11]

Cell telephones are heavily used by terrorists and by narcotraffickers. The numerous successes against both by military and law enforcement units have led to these cell phone users taking a number of defensive measures. Techniques such as brief calls and code words, discussed later, have been used defensively but with mixed success at best. Escobar, for example, knew of the risk of intercept and kept his calls brief to avoid exactly the outcome that he experienced.

One favored approach for governments in collecting telephone conversations is to locate the intercept sites in a protected building within a foreign country—typically an embassy or consulate. From such locations, microwave tower communications often can be intercepted; cell phone conversations and two-way radios such as police radios can be intercepted routinely. During the Cold War, the Soviets maintained as many as five such sites in the Washington area and another four in New York.[12]

Push-to-Talk. COMINT units have long targeted what are called push-to-talk communications. They are called push-to-talk because, like a citizens' band (CB) radio, you cannot listen and talk simultaneously. You must push the transmit button to communicate and release it to listen. Many radios used by military forces for air-to-ground and ground-to-ground tactical communications are push-to-talk. During World War II, the U.S. Army relied on handheld radios, called walkie-talkies, for tactical ground communications. These radios were targets for both German and Japanese field COMINT units. More modern push-to-talk radios have proved to be profitable targets for intelligence collection by field-deployed signals intelligence (SIGINT) units in the fighting in Iraq and Afghanistan. Especially in an urban counterinsurgency environment, short-range (line-of-sight) wireless communications are common. They typically use either handheld push-to-talk radios or cell phones.[13]

The use of code talkers to preserve the secrecy of tactical push-to-talk communications is widely known because of the 2002 movie *Windtalkers*. The movie is based on U.S. Marine use of Navajo Indians as radio operators in the Pacific theater during World War II. Navajo is not a written language, and few outsiders understood it. The Japanese never cracked the code. Less well known is that code talking originated during the closing days of World War I, when the U.S. Army used Choctaw Indians for the same purpose on telephone lines that were suspected of having been tapped by the Germans.[14]

Underwater Sound. Naval tactical communications to submarines use underwater sound. This allows the submarine to receive communications without surfacing. Since the U.S. Navy developed its first underwater telephone, nicknamed "Gertrude," in 1945, most submarines worldwide have been equipped with similar devices. These telephones only function at relatively short ranges, but they can be intercepted by other submarines or sonobuoys.[15]

High Frequency Communications. One of the earliest and most significant successes of high frequency (HF) COMINT came at the Battle of Tannenberg, late in August 1914, during the opening moves of World War I. The Russian First and Second Armies were advancing through Eastern Prussia toward the German Eighth Army. Communications among the Russian headquarters were handled by high frequency radio (which can be received over a wide geographic region), and some of these communications were not enciphered. On the night of August 25, German radio units intercepted messages that gave the deployment and missions of the two Russian armies. Over the next few days, further intercepted messages gave away the strength, positions, and movements of the Russian armies. It quickly became apparent to the German commanders that General Samsonov's Second Army was being placed in an exposed position near the German town of Tannenberg, and that Russian General Rennenkampf's First Army was not in a position to provide support if Samsonov's army was attacked.

General von Hindenberg, commander of the German Eighth Army, positioned his entire force for an attack on the Russian Second Army. On August 26 he began the attack, and over the next three days he deployed his units in response to Russian countermoves, being forewarned by additional intercepts of Russian radiograms. The result was a spectacular German victory; the Russian Second Army was decimated, General Samsonov committed suicide, and the eastern front ultimately settled into a stalemate.[16]

During World War II, COMINT was used extensively to monitor the long-range HF communications of ships and submarines. Large direction-finding antennas allowed both sides to locate seaborne units and track their movements.

Satellite communications largely replaced HF for long-distance communications in the latter part of the 20th century. But HF enjoyed a resurgence for tactical use during the Vietnam War. The U.S. Army found that a technique called Near Vertical Incidence Skywave (NVIS) could provide reliable communications over short ranges, even over mountainous terrain. The signal is sent almost vertically and bounces off the ionosphere and back to receivers within a few hundred kilometers. Because the signal did not propagate to long ranges, NVIS provided some security; COMINT units could only intercept the signal at locations relatively close to the transmitter (on the order of a few hundred kilometers, depending on the operating frequency and ionospheric conditions).

High-Capacity Communications Systems. A number of communications systems carry a large volume of traffic. For years, this load was carried by microwave radio relay communications and by buried coaxial cables (including submarine cables). Satellite communications began to pick up some of this volume during the latter part of the 20th century, and today, most of the volume is carried by fiber-optic cable. These media all carry a diverse set of traffic. The mix typically includes television, telephone, fax, data links, private voice, video, and data.

Microwave Radio Relay. Microwave point-to-point communications use metal towers with fixed antennas. The towers must be within line of sight of each other, so they are separated by about 20 miles (depending on the terrain). The antennas transmit a narrow beam to the next tower; it usually is intercepted by placing the intercept antenna either somewhere in the narrow main beam or close to a relay tower. Fiber optics has replaced relay towers in many areas, and those towers have been repurposed for cell phone communications. But radio relay is still used in many parts of the world, especially in mountainous terrain where laying fiber-optic cable would be difficult.

Satellite Communications. Much international telephone and data traffic is carried by communications satellites, and a number of systems have been orbited to serve solely domestic needs. This traffic can be intercepted by many unintended recipients. Satellites carry a large volume of news and business telephone conversations, making them valuable targets for political and economic intelligence. Military communications also are carried by satellites, but typically they are encrypted.

Any country can buy a communications satellite ground station and use it for intercept. Such activity for commercial intelligence purposes is likely to increase in the future, though it is illegal under international law. A number of governments routinely intercept satellite communications, sifting it for information of value—including information that will permit their own companies to compete in international markets.

During the Cold War, the Soviet Union had a number of sites capable of intercepting international communications. The best known was one installed at Lourdes, Cuba. It has been described as "the most sophisticated Soviet collection facility outside the Soviet Union itself." It could monitor sensitive U.S. maritime, military, and space communications as well as telephone conversations within the United States.[17]

France reportedly has developed a network of COMINT stations that systematically eavesdrop on satellite communications worldwide. Monitoring stations are said to exist in French Guiana, in the city of Domme in southwestern France, and in New Caledonia.[18] A number of other countries operate satellite COMINT sites. Israel maintains a major COMINT base at Urim, in the Negev. The base reportedly collects against Intelsat satellites, maritime communications via Inmarsat, and numerous regional satellites operated by Arab countries.[19] Even the relatively small Swiss intelligence service operates a three-site network, called Onyx, to monitor international civil and military communications.[20]

Cable. Like microwave relay or satellite communications, cable carries a high volume of traffic. But it can be more difficult to intercept (since some form of physical access is necessary; the cable signals cannot be intercepted remotely with antennas). One easy way to tap into cable traffic, however, is at a transfer point. The United States did so for some years, under a program called Operation SHAMROCK. Rather than go through the difficult task of tapping a cable, though, NSA did so very simply by obtaining the traffic directly from three international cable companies located in the United States.[21]

The United States and other countries have had some success in tapping into undersea cable communications, according to the literature. In the early 1970s, the U.S. government learned of the existence of an undersea cable running parallel to the Kuril Islands chain, connecting the major Soviet naval bases at Vladivostok and Petropavlovsk. A program nicknamed IVY BELLS was established to tap into the cable.

In 1981, however, the program halted abruptly after Western satellites photographed a small fleet of Russian warships gathered over the exact location of the listening device. The operation had been betrayed to the KGB in January 1980 by Robert Pelton.[22]

Israel's COMINT organization, known as Unit 8200, apparently has a similar operation ongoing in the Eastern Mediterranean. Unit 8200 reportedly taps undersea cables that link Israel to Europe via Sicily.[23] A number of other countries in the Middle East and North Africa use undersea cables in the area; these cables also would likely be of interest to the Israelis.

Cable traffic originally was carried by copper coaxial cable, very similar in design to the coaxial cables used in home television sets. Because it transmitted a radio frequency signal, it could be collected without actually breaking into the cable sheath.

Its replacement in most areas is fiber-optic cable, which presents much more of an intercept challenge. Actually, there are two major challenges. First, a fiber-optic cable has many fibers in it, each carrying a large volume

Communications Intelligence

of traffic. You have to select fibers that carry interesting information and select the specific material within each fiber. Second, the wide bandwidth of optical fiber makes it impractical to download all of the communications for subsequent processing.

Before you can make that selection, though, you have to get access to the fiber. A fiber cable that runs for some distance will have repeater boxes along its length to amplify the transmitted signal.

Targeting Priorities. Because there are so many choices for COMINT targeting, you have to identify the sources that the priority intelligence targets are likely to use and concentrate on those.

- Terrorist units formerly used cell phones extensively, until the consequences of being intercepted became too severe. They still use cell phones, though carefully. And they make use of the Internet.
- National policymakers and diplomatic officials use telephones, satellite, and cable (including undersea cable) to communicate. But this traffic is mostly encrypted.
- Senior military officers use much the same means as national policy officials. Field units rely extensively on radio communications including push-to-talk radios. Most of the strategic-level traffic is encrypted, as are some field radios.
- International business uses the Internet, satellite, and cable. Increasingly, business relies on encryption for transmitting sensitive corporate information.
- Criminal organizations are targeted using telephone taps, bugs, and cell phone collection.

The targeting trade-off is to balance difficulty or risk versus importance. For example, a HUMINT-enabled collection, such as by a fiber-optic cable tap, is both difficult and risky. Therefore, it should only be attempted when the potential payoff for success is high. Satellite communications and push-to-talk radios, in contrast, are easy to collect and very low risk. So they can be targeted for even low-priority requirements.

ACCESS

After targeting, you have to get access to the communications link. COMINT requires some form of access to the desired communications medium so that communications can be collected. This can be a very easy process. Air-to-ground (push-to-talk) communications and traditional HF communications are readily intercepted over a wide area. Microwave point-to-point communications require being close to a transmission tower or somewhere in the main beam of the link. Some signals are more difficult to acquire because they are deliberately made difficult to intercept (for example, by spreading the frequency bandwidth to an extent that intercept receivers cannot match or transmitting a very weak signal, just sufficient for the intended receiver). These are called **low probability of intercept (LPI)** communications. Others require unusual, expensive, or intrusive methods to gain access. Cable and wired telephone communications, for example, often require a physical tap. The different means of access were discussed in the previous section.

COLLECTION

Collection involves two steps: acquiring information from the communications after access (usually referred to as interception) and passing that information on to a location where it can be processed. Typically, though, there is a critical filtering step here. A bulk communications link (such as fiber-optic cable or satellite communications) contains mostly traffic that has little or no intelligence value. Therefore, many signals will be acquired that must be discarded; there simply isn't enough bandwidth to send all of the material to the processing center. This is usually done by conducting a survey soon after obtaining access to the link. The survey identifies the important material, and everything else is discarded during the ensuing collection step. For example, a survey of a fiber-optic cable tap would identify and subsequently discard television signals. Periodically, another survey would be conducted of the tap to ensure that no material of value was being missed.[24]

For wireless communications—especially cell telephones and push-to-talk radios—an important part of collection is geolocating the source. A number of geolocation techniques are used in RF COMINT; they are discussed in detail in Chapter 13.

PROCESSING

After collection, the material must be processed. Processing is the conversion of collected information into a form suitable for analysis, or sometimes for the direct dissemination of intelligence, either automatically or under human supervision. If the material is coming from a single channel that is known to be important, then this is relatively easy to do.

But before the collected material proceeds further in processing, it must go through another filtering step. Even though the volume of material at this

Communications
Intelligence

point has shrunk dramatically from that initially collected, the remaining material would choke the system if not filtered further. For high-volume communications, and sometimes even for single channel communications, the processing challenge is to identify from the mass of incoming material the relatively small fraction that is of intelligence interest. One technique for doing the paring is to program the processing systems to detect words and phone numbers of interest.[25] This is, at best, an imperfect step in the process. Material of intelligence value inevitably winds up in what is sometimes referred to as "bit heaven"—discarded because it is not recognized as having value.

The material that survives this severe filtering step then must be categorized, prioritized, and routed to analysts for detailed exploitation. The first step typically is to convert the material into a standard format and attach message or signal related information; for example, the telephone numbers of the parties to a telephone conversation would be attached so that they can be used for phone number searches later on.

A number of other processing techniques then are used to further narrow the incoming volume to manageable size. A few of these are:

- Processors must extract traffic from the bulk channels and place it in categories for further processing. Three broad categories of interest have typically been used: voice grade channels, which normally carry telephone conversations; fax communications; and data (including message traffic). These three need to be separated, because they will subsequently undergo different types of processing.

- Word spotting is often used to identify possible communications of interest. Most COMINT libraries contain names of persons, places, or things of intelligence interest, and the appearance of these words in a message causes the message to be tagged for further processing.

- Speech recognition systems do much the same thing, by automatically selecting telephone communications of intelligence interest when the speaker uses certain key words.[26]

Finally, if the material is encrypted, it must be forwarded to a group that specializes in doing cryptanalysis, discussed next.

Cryptanalysis. There are basically two ways for a COMINT unit to decrypt an encrypted message. The more difficult way is to have skilled cryptanalysts, aided by powerful computers, break the code. The easy way is to have someone (usually a HUMINT operative) steal the ciphers. Russia has a long history of conducting very good COMINT by the simple expedient of stealing ciphers. Tsarist Russia's intelligence service, the Okhrana, is regarded as having had the best code breakers in the world in its time, chiefly by virtue of its efforts at purchasing or stealing codes and ciphers. Its replacement in the Soviet regime, the OGPU (later KGB), continued the tradition with at least equal skill.[27]

Cryptanalysis is the most sophisticated and difficult stage of processing. It has always been an arcane art and remains so even in these days of computer-based cryptanalysis. It is very expensive in its use of both human and computer resources, so the source has to be determined to be of significant value in order for resources to be committed to breaking the code.

Until a period shortly after World War II, only military, intelligence, and diplomatic communications were encrypted, so breaking these codes could be assumed to have intelligence value. Most such codes could be broken through some combination of theft of the keys, hard work by cryptanalysts, mistakes made by the sender, and luck.

The encryption technique most commonly used in this time frame was the one-time pad, in which words are converted to numbers and then the numbers changed by an additive key. The key is called a one-time pad because, if it is kept secret and only used once, the resulting encrypted message is unbreakable. It randomly shifts each character in a message to a different character, based on the corresponding character in a key (the pad).

But compromise (e.g., via theft of the pad) or its misuse has resulted in numerous cryptanalysis successes over the years. The spectacular U.S. and U.K. cryptanalytic success codenamed VENONA that was mentioned in Chapter 3 was a result of one-time pad misuse. During and immediately after World War II, a number of Soviet intelligence and diplomatic messages were sent with reused one-time pads, allowing U.S. cryptanalysts to decrypt the messages. This led to the exposure of a number of Soviet agents in the United States and the United Kingdom.[28]

Cryptanalysis often depends on the fact that certain words tend to appear in official communications, especially in military communications. One way to counter simple cryptanalysis, then, is to pad the text with irrelevant text. During World War II, the U.S. Navy routinely added such text padding at the beginning and at the end of encrypted communications, leading to one of the most noted misunderstandings of an official message during that war.

During the naval battle of Leyte Gulf, Admiral William Halsey's task force 34 was drawn off in pursuit of a Japanese decoy force, leaving a critical gap in the Leyte Gulf defenses. The Pacific Fleet Commander in Chief, Admiral Chester Nimitz, transmitted a message to Halsey that read (after decryption): "TURKEY TROTS TO WATER GG FROM CINCPAC ACTION COM THIRD

FLEET INFO COMINCH CTF SEVENTY-SEVEN X WHERE IS RPT WHERE IS TASK FORCE THIRTY FOUR RR THE WORLD WONDERS."[29]

The beginning (before GG) and the end (after RR) text was padding and should have been removed before Halsey saw the message. It wasn't. Halsey apparently was well-read enough to know that the latter padding, "the world wonders," evokes the lines of Alfred Lord Tennyson's poem, *The Charge of the Light Brigade*. Taking that final sentence to be a deliberate insult, Halsey, as the story goes, went into a fit of rage.

The digital computer allowed encryption to become widely available. The computer can generate and use keys for encryption—some of which are vulnerable to computer-based cryptanalysis, the better ones of which are almost invulnerable to being broken. Since then, many governments have struggled to deal with the resulting proliferation of encryption. Governments want to protect their security services' capability to decipher COMINT. At the same time, they want to protect their industries against eavesdroppers trying to obtain commercial intelligence. But how do you protect your commercial segment while keeping criminal elements and terrorists from using the same cryptography? If you're the head of a SIGINT organization, you want to break everyone else's code but let no one break your code or the codes of the organizations that you're protecting. It's a tough trade-off.

Also, independent groups eventually are going to develop their own "unbreakable" codes. The alternative would be to make widely available some codes that could be broken only by government agencies—even though some governments would use that capability to help their own industries against competitors. The governments then could keep more sophisticated encryption technology for their own use—which is exactly what they try to do.

But governments move slowly. It takes time to shift government policies and put the structure in place to make them work. That gives a big advantage to individuals and small groups in this Internet age; these small entities are quick to adapt and are technically savvy. For some time, the code makers have been winning against the code breakers. Encryption technology has been outpacing cryptanalysis. A recurring problem is the need to control the access to "unbreakable" codes by terrorists and narcotraffickers.

Another method used by terrorists and narcotraffickers to avoid the detection of compromising information is steganography. Steganography was introduced in the HUMINT chapter as secret writing; it is more broadly defined as the art and science of hiding information by embedding messages within other, seemingly innocent messages. Modern steganography hides messages inside computer files. It works by replacing bits of useless or unused data in graphics, audio, text, or HTML files. The message often is embedded in a map or a photograph. A digital image of a landscape, for example, might hold a communiqué or a map. A digital song file might contain blueprints of a targeted building.[30] Unless the COMINT processor has some idea that digital steganography is embedded in a specific file, it can be very difficult to find.

Language Translation. Much of the material handled by any COMINT service will be, for that service, in a foreign language. So the final processing step usually is language translation.

COMINT translation has the same challenge as in open source, only more so because of clearance issues. Native speakers can be used in open source translation, but the security clearance restrictions constrain their use in COMINT translation. After 9/11 and the ensuing conflict in Afghanistan, the U.S. and allied COMINT communities found themselves critically short of translators for the principal languages spoken there: Pashto, Dari, Uzbek, and Turkmen. Reportedly, NSA had only two or three translators who could handle those languages.[31]

This is a continuing problem for any COMINT service that must provide global coverage. A crisis can break out anywhere, and the translators for the local languages can't be stockpiled for possible future use. Because of the security clearance issue, COMINT translators usually are not native speakers. That drawback has not been serious for tactical military COMINT, where the traffic is usually simple to understand. However, it can be a serious problem for strategic COMINT, where nuances in the translation can be critical.

The chief constraint on COMINT use today is that it is labor-intensive, relying as it does on trained linguists. Eventually, machine translation of speech may help to ease this bottleneck, primarily in screening communications to find the most important ones for a detailed look by a human translator.

ANALYSIS

After translation, the next phase in the processing is a detailed look by analysts. The analysis phase requires placing the material in context (using collateral sources and past intercepts of the same source) and adding the analyst's commentary. The nature of the customer and time constraints shape the depth of analysis that is given to the material. Tactical material usually has to go on a fast track, and the sources and customers are well known, so the process is automated and the material may receive little or no analysis at all.

Most COMINT analysis concerns accurately assessing the content of the communications. As a starting point, the analyst often has to identify and deal with concealment and deception. When using cell phones or the Internet, targets may talk around a topic, often by using prearranged code. The 9/11 attackers communicated openly and disseminated information using prearranged code words. For instance, the "faculty of urban planning" meant the World Trade Center, and the Pentagon was referred to as the "faculty of fine arts." Mohammed Atta's final message to the 18 other terrorists who conducted the 9/11 attacks read, in code: "The semester begins in three more weeks. We've obtained 19 confirmations for studies in the faculty of law, the faculty of urban planning, the faculty of fine arts, and the faculty of engineering."[32] The number 19, of course, referred to the number of cell members who were to board the four aircraft.

Customers often object to this analysis step, arguing that it slows the dissemination process. But for strategic COMINT, bypassing the analysis is a major mistake. Raw COMINT can be misleading.

Prime Minister Winston Churchill, reading Field Marshal Erwin Rommel's decrypted cables during World War II, concluded that the Germans were desperately short of supplies in North Africa. Basing his interpretation on this raw COMINT traffic, Churchill pressed his generals to take the offensive against Rommel. Churchill did not realize what his own intelligence analysts could have readily told him: Rommel consistently exaggerated his shortages in order to bolster his demands for supplies and reinforcements.[33]

More recently, Secretary of State Colin Powell used three NSA intercepts during his 2003 UN presentation to "prove" the U.S. contention that Iraq was concealing its possession of weapons of mass destruction (WMD). All three intercepts were ambiguous. One discussed "modified vehicles" that supposedly were used in WMD development. A second intercept allegedly involved an order to "clean out" an ammunition depot. The third was an order to "remove the expression 'nerve agents' wherever it comes up in the wireless instructions." Subsequent evidence showed that all three intercepts were connected with the Iraqi attempts to purge evidence about their *past* WMD programs, in a futile attempt to avoid giving the United States a cause to invade.[34] Had the ambiguous intercepts been collated with other COMINT and collateral sources, it is likely that their actual meaning could have been determined before the Powell presentation.

So raw COMINT, as the above examples illustrate, can be misinterpreted by its customers. But the COMINT analysis step can also introduce distortions in the message. In practice, the translator is also the analyst, and therein exists a potential for bias. Analysts want to have their material read and used. They know that interesting or provocative material is more likely to be read and used. So a natural tendency is to exaggerate the importance of their reporting, and even veteran COMINT analysts can fall into this trap.

The preceding material has discussed content analysis. But two analytic techniques are not concerned with content. They are signature analysis and traffic analysis; both are usable even on encrypted communications.

Signature Analysis. A very important part of COMINT is concerned with signatures, which are discussed in more detail in Part II of this book. No two communications systems are exactly identical, and the knowledge of what communications system is being used by a particular person or organization often has intelligence value. With telephone communications, the signature may come directly from the call itself: the number dialed on a telephone call or the calling line identification that appears on your cell phone to identify the person making the call.

When the communication doesn't carry identifying data, the identity of the equipment operator can sometimes be ascertained using biometrics techniques such as voiceprints (discussed later in this book). The technique is quite old; in the Middle Ages, when COMINT usually meant intercepting and reading letters, handwriting analysis was sometimes used to identify the author. When Morse code telegraphy was in wide use from the late 1800s through World War II, a code operator could recognize another operator by his characteristic pattern of keying the code, known as his "fist." It was an early form of biometric identification.

Modern communications technologies have made the identification process more precise, though more technically challenging to execute. Two apparently identical cell phones will differ slightly in the signals they transmit—perhaps in frequency, signal stability, or the emissions of spurious signals.[35] Two optical fibers will have fine-grained differences in the signals they transmit. If these differences can be measured, then a unique signature can be established for each piece of communications equipment.

Furthermore, consumer electronics are providing more unique signatures that can be associated with an individual. As these devices infiltrate our personal and professional lives—Wi-Fi, Bluetooth, BlackBerrys, iPads, smart watches, and GPS devices—we are increasing the number of possible RF signatures that together can create a unique pattern. By passively monitoring the signatures generated by a person's devices, a statistical correlation can be drawn not only to infer the identity of the person but also to track the person.[36]

Traffic Analysis. Traffic analysis is a method of obtaining intelligence from what are called "externals," that is, from the characteristics of the communications signal, without looking at the information content. It is especially useful when message content is not available, for example, when encryption is used. The externals can be used, for example, to determine the location and movement of a communications emitter. But traffic analysis can do much more, and it is especially effective when combined with signature analysis.

The usual objective of traffic analysis is to build a model of a communications network (or a network of associates) by observing communications patterns. Traffic analysts look at these calling patterns to identify networks of personal or official associations. Traffic analysis is commonly used in assessing military communications and traffic within criminal cartels. Some examples of judgments that can be made based on communications patterns are

- frequent communications from one node can tell the traffic analyst who's in charge or the control station of a network;
- correlating who talks when can indicate which stations are active in connection with events;
- frequent communications often indicate that an operation is in the planning stage;
- no communication can indicate either no activity, or that the planning stage is complete; or
- rapid, short communications are often connected with negotiations.

Traffic analysis can be countered, to some extent, by techniques such as inserting dummy traffic in the network.

DISSEMINATION

COMINT dissemination involves (1) getting the material to the right customers, on time, so that it can be used, and (2) protecting the source. The most time-sensitive and important COMINT is that associated with a developing crisis such as an attack or the loss of a ship or aircraft. NSA has long had a capability to provide fast-response reporting of COMINT associated with a crisis. The formal structure for doing this is called the CRITIC system.[37]

The tagging process discussed earlier helps in getting the material to the right customers. Dissemination is largely by cable, and tags, topic words, or keywords in the cable help end users to search for relevant COMINT traffic.

Battlefield Dissemination. With large armies in the field, getting the COMINT reporting to the right level has long been a problem, especially in a fast-moving combat situation. The U.S. military, during the 2003 invasion of Iraq, found it possible to get intercepts to army and corps commanders expeditiously. It proved more of a problem to get the intercepts to division commanders and their subordinates—though when the information could be gotten to division and battalion commanders, it often was instrumental in avoiding ambushes and identifying opportunities for attack.[38] Part of the problem lies in getting the secure communications capability down to lower levels in the field. Another part is the necessity to protect the source, discussed next.

Protecting the Source. Tactical COMINT is mostly useful to smaller military or law enforcement units—such as the division or battalion commanders noted above. It has to be quickly disseminated at a low level of classification. Strategic and operational traffic is usually more sensitive and requires more analysis; it usually receives a higher classification as well. Some COMINT material is so valuable that the source must be protected at all costs; the fact of successful decryption, for instance. The Ultra COMINT, based on the decryption of Germany's Enigma machine traffic during World War II, is an example. Ultra was protected by dissemination procedures such as hand carrying the decrypted material to military commanders, sometimes not even sharing it with the commanders' intelligence officers. Additional protections involved restricting the actions that commanders could take based on the traffic. For example, Axis shipping and submarines could not be attacked based solely on Ultra; some cover story (such as a reconnaissance flight or a fictitious spy) had to be created to explain the attacks.[39]

As was the case with Ultra, exceptionally sensitive material usually has special code words, and only a limited set of people have the code word access. COMINT managers have to deal with the trade-off of getting the information to customers without risking loss of the source. There are good reasons for such protection. Valuable sources have been lost as a result of careless use of COMINT by customers. As noted earlier, the U.S. ability to read Soviet leaders' mobile radio traffic was lost after being disclosed by newspaper columnist Jack Anderson in 1971.[40] Reportedly, Osama bin Laden stopped using his cell telephone after a 1998 article in the *Washington Times* disclosed that the United States was monitoring it.

Tip-off. COMINT plays a critical role in providing tip-off to other collection means. It often provides the first clue that something of intelligence interest is about to happen. HUMINT, IMINT, and other SIGINT can then be tasked against the upcoming event. Events about to occur—a missile test, a ship

Communications
Intelligence

about to leave port, a military unit movement, an upcoming narcotics shipment—all can be tipped off by COMINT.

Sharing and Liaison Relationships. Many communications sources have intelligence value, and any large COMINT service will routinely collect far more material than it can process. One obvious solution is to share the workload: to divide up the collection, processing, and analysis. One could, for example, have a central COMINT service handle the strategic communications traffic and have military units deal with most of the tactical traffic.

On a broader scale, friendly countries can share the COMINT workload through liaison relationships. Such resource sharing provides substantial advantages. Some countries have better access to specific targets, especially to internal targets, than your own. Partners can handle part of the load and may have translators in the more difficult languages that you don't have.

So, as with HUMINT, liaison relationships are important in COMINT. The United States has been very aggressive in working with other countries in such liaison. The United States has had formal liaison relations with the United Kingdom, Canada, Australia, and New Zealand that date back to World War II.[41] This so-called "Five Eyes" relationship is an exception to the normal pattern of bilateral relationships. Bilateral relationships are usually preferred because the problems caused by intelligence sharing increase rapidly in multilateral arrangements. Bilateral U.S. liaison relations with Norway, Denmark, and Sweden provided valuable signals intelligence in the early years of the Cold War. The geographic location of these three countries close to the northwestern border of the Soviet Union gave them unique advantages in signals collection.[42] The Soviets had their own COMINT liaison; they worked closely with Cuba and their East European partners. Cuba provided them with particular COMINT advantages because of its geographic proximity to the United States.

Liaison usually relies on the parties having a long-term common interest, for example, in combating terrorism. Some allies have special interests—the United Kingdom obviously is more focused on European affairs than Australia, which is more focused on Asian affairs. These two countries have a vested interest in taking responsibility for those respective parts of the COMINT processing and exploitation load. Absent that common interest, though, it can be difficult to get liaison cooperation. A country with businesses that are profiting from gray arms traffic likely won't help in combating such traffic, for example.

Obviously, sharing has its risks. There is always a possible concern about liaison partners spying on each other. This has not been a problem with the

Five Eyes partners; basically, they don't spy on each other. But as the counterintelligence people point out, there are no friendly intelligence services, only intelligence services of friendly countries. And the Soviet KGB did spy on its East European allies.

A more serious problem is that other intelligence services can have moles from unfriendly countries. Sharing then results in loss of sources. Even absent the mole, the other service can have breaches in security, as the following example illustrates.

In World War II, German General Erwin Rommel was called the "Desert Fox" for his repeated tactical victories over the British in North Africa. His successes were helped by knowing exactly what the British were going to do, allowing him to time his counterstrokes for maximum effect. His source was American Army Colonel Bonner Frank Fellers, liaison to the British forces. Fellers's communications were being intercepted and read by the Germans. His messages were sent by radio, encrypted in the Black Code of the U.S. State Department. The details of this code were stolen in a burglary of the U.S. Embassy in Italy by Italian spies in September 1941; the code was also broken by German cryptanalysts, who read the Black Code messages Fellers sent from Cairo and provided them immediately to Rommel.[43]

Another concern is the possibility that a sharing partner can turn on you. That happened subsequent to the Iranian revolution in 1978, and the United States lost some sources and methods then. Chances are that the Five Eyes partners won't turn on each other, but they do have different goals. And the problem would be worse for the United States in sharing with countries such as Saudi Arabia; they could help with COMINT, but you'd have to be concerned about them shaping any intercepts to further their own goals.

Another problem in sharing is that your connections with one country can sour your connections with another. A country wishing to share with both Pakistan and India, or with both Israel and Egypt, would have a problem diplomatically because of their history of mutual hostility. The solution is to make some liaisons highly classified to avoid offending other countries.

Structure

The Introduction discussed two general ways to structure collection: stove-pipe versus collaborative and either centralized, decentralized, or a mix. We see all of these in the world of COMINT.

STOVEPIPE VERSUS COLLABORATIVE

The major distinction here is the sensitivity of the information that is collected. The sources of strategic and operational COMINT often are very sensitive. They may, for example, depend on success in breaking an encryption scheme. Such COMINT often requires a high level of protection from unauthorized disclosure, and distribution is limited to a relatively small group of users. The stovepipe accommodates this protection need.

In contrast, tactical COMINT usually is disseminated to a large number of end users, but it normally does not need the same high level of protection. A collaborative structure works well here.

CENTRALIZED

A centralized COMINT organization is widely used for supporting strategic and operational intelligence; the product is usually not time-critical. It also has substantial advantages when COMINT must deal with a diversity of sources. Because it can call on this diversity of available sources, a central COMINT group has advantages in dealing with deception.

A high volume of traffic yields best to centralized processing. And breaking ciphers requires a skilled cadre of cryptanalysts, plus very powerful computers, all of which are best placed in a single center.

A centralized COMINT organization, though, usually exercises exclusive control over the product. That may be good for protecting sources and methods but bad if the organization adopts the Dead Sea Scrolls mentality (discussed in Chapter 1) of hoarding the information for analytic advantage.

DECENTRALIZED

The decentralized structure has definite advantages. As noted in Chapter 1, hoarding is a nonissue. No one agency is allowed to exercise complete control over the COMINT product. Also, COMINT units that are part of military and law enforcement organizations are likely to be very much aware of and responsive to their customer needs.

For these reasons, most military services try to keep their COMINT capabilities separate from a central service. As an example, Soviet COMINT was more organizationally split than either U.S. or U.K. COMINT during the Cold War. The KGB had responsibility for diplomatic and other civilian traffic. The GRU had responsibility for military COMINT. An attempt to create a single COMINT organization early in the Cold War failed, apparently in a round of KGB–Ministry of Defense infighting.[44] This pattern continued after the KGB was dismantled in 1991; the COMINT role was assumed by a combination of former KGB departments and was renamed the Federal Agency of Government Communications and Information (FAPSI). FAPSI ceased to exist in March 2003, being reincorporated into the KGB's domestic intelligence successor, the Federal Security Service (FSB). Throughout, though, the GRU continued to retain the military COMINT role.

For much the same reason of responsiveness to the special needs of customers, CIA maintained its own COMINT unit for many years. Entitled Division D, it specialized in collecting international radio telephone communications and conducting intercept operations overseas to serve clandestine operations and counterintelligence needs.[45]

Law enforcement COMINT typically is decentralized for the same reasons. It also is decentralized because it mostly is focused on individual cases and often collects time-sensitive information. Most such COMINT is targeted on a single cell phone or audio device (e.g., a bug).

A MIX

The structure of a large COMINT organization has to accommodate many classes of users with differing needs, and the result usually is a mix that is at least partly decentralized. In particular, the structure that supports tactical COMINT has to be predesigned for speed. This means setting up in advance a system for identifying critical communications, intercepting and translating them, and getting the product to the field units while it still has intelligence value. Field-deployed units are typically set up to do this, but at the same time, they need to get it from national-level collectors that may be located a world away—thus, a mix.

Furthermore, due to the increasing communications volume, any COMINT organization, no matter how large, will be stretched to collect, process, and analyze all of the material that its customers want to have. This overload is made worse by the problem that all intelligence has: Current or tactical intelligence consumes all available resources if you allow it to do so. Inevitably, other organizations have to pick up the slack. For example, NSA's inability to commit resources to counternarcotics in the Western hemisphere reportedly forced the Drug Enforcement Administration to pick up this COMINT mission.[46]

The usual solution is to put COMINT exploitation and analysis near the customers for tactical and law enforcement needs. That was done in the Iraq/Afghanistan theaters for the military and in the Drug Enforcement Administration (DEA) example for counternarcotics COMINT. However, the product often has to go to a widely dispersed customer set, as with counter-terrorism and counternarcotics intelligence. It then makes sense to centralize for wide distribution. Even then, it often is possible to decentralize in another way, sharing the processing load through liaison with other national COMINT services, as discussed earlier.

The U.S. and British COMINT services have followed this structural pattern—a mix—that has become more pronounced in recent years. The military role, in both COMINT collection and analysis, increased dramatically during the Iraq and Afghanistan conflicts.

COMMERCIAL COMINT

The structure of commercial COMINT organizations is shaped by another consideration—legality—that drives it to be centralized and tightly compartmented. COMINT is traditionally considered the province of governments and is generally illegal when conducted by a private entity. But COMINT collection equipment is readily available in the commercial market worldwide. Companies offer equipment and services that can eavesdrop on cell phone calls and tap into fiber-optic cable, for example. The equipment then can search, filter, and index the vast quantity of data obtained through this surveillance.[47] The best commercial units are not cheap, but they rival the best units that government COMINT organizations can supply. As a result, an increasing number of countries use COMINT for economic and political intelligence, targeting especially satellite communications, and some business enterprises do so as well.

So legal or no, COMINT to serve the purposes of business exists. It is hard to tell how widespread the practice is. Commercial COMINT units tend to be small and their product closely held because of its illegal status. In some cases, the communications intercept job is outsourced to trusted specialists who operate in a secret world.

Summary

COMINT is the interception, processing, analysis, and reporting of an opponent's communications. It includes not only bugs and the traditional microphone-and-wire but also advanced technology to collect voice, data, and facsimile communications. COMINT is now a large-scale activity providing customers with intelligence on diplomatic, military, economic, and scientific developments internationally, as well as supporting law enforcement efforts domestically. It provides insight into the plans and intentions of governments, military forces, and criminals. It tracks the movements and funding of terrorists and narcotraffickers. And it cues collection by other collection disciplines, especially HUMINT and IMINT.

The COMINT process starts with a targeting phase. Up front, a COMINT organization must select and prioritize the collection targets. There are simply too many sources to try and collect them all. You have to select the sources that the priority intelligence targets use. Targeting requires that you balance the difficulty or risk of collection versus the importance of the material.

The expansion of all forms of communication in the last 50 years has resulted in a proliferation of potential targets for COMINT. They divide into low capacity or single channel (usually, a single voice communication on a dedicated communications link) and high capacity or multichannel (typically, hundreds or thousands of independent voice, data, or video communications on a communications link). These two types of sources have to be treated differently in planning for collection and targeting (the front end) and in the processing, exploitation, and dissemination phase (the back end).

Microphone-and-wire intercept is an old technology, but it is still widely used by some intelligence services. It is cheap and reliable. Unfortunately, it is also relatively easy for counterintelligence units to find. Some microphone types rely on structural or emplaced objects in a building to pick up sound and transmit it through a part of the building structure.

The audio transmitter or bug also has been a useful collector for decades. Because it transmits a radio signal rather than using a wire, it is simpler to emplace than the mike-and-wire. Also, it is cheap and requires no great technical skill, so it is popular among the less sophisticated intelligence organizations and in industrial espionage.

Telephone surveillance in the past relied on identifying the telephone of intelligence interest and placing a wiretap on it. Most telephone surveillance today focuses on cell phone traffic because it is the preferred communications medium of criminal groups and terrorists. Unencrypted cellular telephone networks are an easy target for COMINT, and even encryption provides no great level of protection. Cell phones are mobile, but they can still be located and tracked. An individual cell phone or an entire cell tower can be targeted. Interception can be done near the phone itself, near the tower, or at the routing center.

Military services conduct the bulk of COMINT efforts worldwide using trained linguists to monitor the mobile radio communications of opposing forces. COMINT that supports ongoing operations, known as tactical COMINT, also is used heavily in law enforcement work and in countering illicit networks generally. Military communications in particular rely heavily on radio. HF radio was the original target, and it is still in use today. Line-of-sight radio, called push-to-talk, is used in military air-to-ground communications. Both types can be intercepted over large areas.

High-capacity or multichannel communications carry a large volume of material of intelligence interest:

• Microwave radio relay systems transmit a narrow beam from tower to tower, requiring collection either close to a tower or by locating an intercept antenna somewhere in the narrow main beam.

• Satellite communications carry both domestic and international telephone and data traffic and video. Many countries have intercept sites dedicated to exploiting this traffic.

• Metal and fiber-optic cables have replaced microwave radio relay in many areas and are used both undersea and in landlines. Such cables require a physical tap to intercept the communications. Fiber-optic cable increasingly is used because it provides very wide bandwidth, allowing high-volume communications with good security.

After targeting, you have to get access to the communications link. COMINT requires some form of access to the desired communications medium so that communications can be collected.

Collection involves two steps: acquiring information from the communications after access (usually referred to as interception) and passing that information on to a location where it can be processed. Typically, though, there is a critical filtering step here to reduce the volume of material to a manageable level.

Processing bulk communications intercepts requires that extensive additional filtering be done up front to discard the material having no intelligence value. The material that survives this severe filtering step then must be categorized, prioritized, and routed to analysts for detailed exploitation and analysis.

If the material is encrypted, the next step is cryptanalysis—breaking the encryption. The easy way to break encryption is to in some way steal the ciphers or encryption keys—a job for HUMINT. The hard way is to apply the brute force approach, using powerful computers that process the encrypted text to identify the key.

In most cases, the final step before analysis is language translation. For intelligence services having worldwide interests, having enough translators in the languages of interest is a continuing problem. Ensuring an accurate translation can also be a problem.

In the analysis stage, the material is examined for content and context. Keyword searches are frequently used to identify important communications. Defenses against keyword searches include talking around a subject or using metaphorical language. In addition to looking at content, analysts make use of what are sometimes called externals:

- Traffic analysis may be used to identify key stations in a network, and the pattern of network communications can sometimes provide intelligence about pending operations even if the material is encrypted.
- Signature analysis can be used to identify and track targets. Such analysis makes use of the fact that no two communications systems are exactly identical, and the system operators sometimes have unique patterns.

COMINT dissemination involves (1) getting the material to the right customers, on time, so that it can be used, and (2) protecting the source. In the case of ongoing military operations, it often proves difficult to get the material to lower command levels. If the material is especially sensitive, it will require additional source protection. For example, constraints may be placed on the military's ability to take actions based on the material.

The volume and nature of communications that are collected tend to shape the structure of COMINT organizations. A high volume of traffic, many sources and many customers, a requirement to decrypt, and no pressing need for timeliness—all argue for a large centralized COMINT organization. Where collection is small scale, timeliness is important, and COMINT must be responsive to needs of specific organizations, the tendency is to decentralize.

Strategic and operational COMINT is usually not time-critical but often requires extensive and specialized processing and analysis. Furthermore, the product is often sensitive, so it has to be tightly controlled and disseminated to selected customers. These considerations drive the centralization of processing and analysis, even though the collection may be done worldwide.

Tactical military COMINT, in contrast, requires rapid dissemination to a specific group of end users within the theater of operations. The resulting structure that supports tactical COMINT has to be predesigned for speed. The material is typically not tightly compartmented. This means setting up in advance a decentralized system for identifying critical communications, intercepting and translating them, and getting the product to customers in the field units while it still has intelligence value. The resulting structure often is a mix of centralized and decentralized COMINT operations. Law enforcement COMINT also is usually decentralized, because it is operated at a local level and focused on very specific targets.

NOTES

1. National Security Council Intelligence Directive No. 6, National Security Council of the United States (17 February 1972, first issued in 1952).
2. U.S. Congress, *Technologies Underlying Weapons of Mass Destruction*, OTA-BfP-ISC-115 (Washington, DC: U.S. Government Printing Office, December 1993) 43.
3. Christopher Andrew and Vasili Mitrokhin, *The Sword and the Shield* (New York: Perseus Books, 1999), 95.
4. F. W. Winterbotham, *The Ultra Secret* (New York: Dell, 1974).
5. NSA/CSS, "Pearl Harbor Review—The Black Chamber," accessed 21 September 2012 at http://www.nsa.gov/about/cryptologic_heritage/center_crypt_history/pearl_harbor_review/black_chamber.shtml.
6. John Wingfield, *Bugging* (London: Robert Hale Ltd., 1984), 21–22.
7. "Laser Microphone" (December 22, 2007), accessed 23 September 2012 at www.bobjunior.com/project/laser-microphone/.
8. John M. McConnell, "The Evolution of Intelligence and the Public Policy Debate on Encryption," Seminar on Intelligence, Command and Control, Center of Information Policy Research (Cambridge, MA: Harvard University School of Government, January 1997), 151.
9. "Wireless Eavesdropping—Not Just for Intelligence Peeps Anymore," *Infosecurity* (November 12, 2010), accessed 21 September 2012 at http://www.infosecurity-magazine.com/view/13953/wireless-eavesdropping-not-just-for-intelligence-peeps-anymore.
10. Ibid.
11. Mark Bowden, "A 15-Month Manhunt Ends in a Hail of Bullets," *Philadelphia Inquirer* (December 17, 2000).
12. Andrew and Mitrokhin, *The Sword and the Shield*, 344.
13. Matthew M. Aid, *The Secret Sentry* (New York: Bloomsbury Press, 2009), 266–267.
14. "Chocktaw Code Talkers of WWI," accessed 21 September 2012 at https://pantherfile.uwm.edu/michael/www/choctaw/code.htm.
15. A. Quazi and W. Konrad, "Underwater Acoustic Communications," *IEEE Communications Magazine* (March 1982), 24–29.
16. For more information, see Wilhelm Flicke, *War Secrets in the Ether* (Laguna Hills, CA: Aegean Park Press, 1994), 4–12.
17. Dino Brugioni, *Eyeball to Eyeball: The Inside Story of the Cuban Missile Crisis* (New York: Random House, 1990), 560.
18. Ibid.
19. Nicky Hager, "Israel's Omniscient Ears," *Le Monde diplomatique* (September 4, 2010).

20. Swiss Federal Department of Defense (September 6, 2007) (in French) accessed 21 September 2012 at Project ONYX réalisé : la Délégation des Commissions de gestion et l'Autorité de contrôle indépendante contrôlent sa conformité au droit.

21. L. Britt Snider, "Recollections from the Church Committee's Investigation of NSA," *CSI Studies in Intelligence* (Winter 1999–2000), accessed 21 September 2012 at https://www.cia.gov/library/center-for-the-study-of-intelligence/csi-pub lications/csi-studies/studies/winter99–00/art4.html.

22. Sherry Sontag and Christopher Drew, *Blind Man's Bluff* (New York: HarperCollins, 1998), 98.

23. Hager, "Israel's Omniscient Ears."

24. Duncan Campbell, "Interception Capabilities 2000," A report to the Director General for Research of the European Parliament, April 1999, accessed 21 September 2012 at http://www.fas.org/irp/eprint/ic2000/ic2000.htm.

25. Hager, "Israel's Omniscient Ears."

26. Ibid.

27. Andrew and Mitrokhin, *The Sword and the Shield,* 43–45.

28. Ibid., 143.

29. James D. Fornfischer, *The Last Stand of the Tin Can Sailors* (New York: Bantam Dell, 2004), 213.

30. United States Institute of Peace, "Terror on the Internet: Questions and Answers," accessed 21 September 2012 at http://www.usip.org/publications-tools/terror-internet/terror-internet-questions-and-answers.

31. Aid, *The Secret Sentry,* 220.

32. United States Institute of Peace, "Terror on the Internet: Questions and Answers."

33. Michael Herman, *Intelligence Power in Peace and War* (Cambridge, MA: Cambridge University Press, 1996), 96.

34. Aid, *The Secret Sentry,* 243–244.

35. U.S. Federal Highway Administration, "Assessment of Automated Data Collection Technologies for Calculation of Commercial Motor Vehicle Border Crossing Travel Time Delay" (April 2002), accessed 21 September 2012 at http://ops.fhwa.dot.gov/freight/freight_analysis/auto_tech/sect_2a.htm.

36. George Spafford, "Underlying Patterns Can Reveal Information Security Targets," SearchSecurity.com, accessed 21 September 2012 at http://searchsecurity.tech target.com/news/article/0,289142,sid14_gci1193714,00.html.

37. NSA, "Cryptologic Almanac 50th Anniversary Series: The Formation of NSOC," accessed 2 October 2011 at http://www.nsa.gov/public_info/_files/crypto_ almanac_50th/the_formation_of_nsoc.pdf.

38. Aid, *The Secret Sentry,* 258–262.

39. F. W. Winterbotham, *The Ultra Secret: The Inside Story of Operation Ultra* (Bletchley Park and Enigma, London: Orion Books Ltd, 1974).

40. Aid, *The Secret Sentry,* 152.

41. Duncan Campbell, "Interception Capabilities 2000."

42. Matthew M. Aid, "In the Right Place at the Right Time: US Signals Intelligence Relations with Scandinavia, 1945–1960," *Journal of Strategic Studies,* Vol. 29, No. 4 (August 2006), 575–605.

43. HistoryNet.com, "Intercepted Communications for Field Marshal Erwin Rommel," accessed 21 September 2012 at http://www.historynet.com/intercepted-communications-for-field-marshal-erwin-rommel.htm.

44. Andrew and Mitrokhin, *The Sword and the Shield,* 337.

45. CIA, "Family Jewels" declassified document (May 16, 1973), 544–546, accessed 21 September 2012 at http://www.gwu.edu/~nsarchiv/NSAEBB/NSAEBB222/family_jewels_full_ocr.pdf.

46. Aid, *The Secret Sentry,* 305.

47. Shaun Waterman, "Surveillance Tools: Not Just for Spies Now," *Washington Times* (December 5, 2011), accessed 21 September 2012 at http://www.washingtontimes.com/news/2011/dec/5/surveillance-tools-not-just-for-spies-anymore/.

5. Cyber Collection

Collection that is undertaken against an information processing system or network does not fit under any of the traditional INTs. It typically has some connection with human intelligence (HUMINT), because it is often an extension of the technical collection efforts carried out by HUMINT operatives. Cyber collection also resembles communications intelligence (COMINT), especially when collection from data communications networks is involved. Collection against publicly available information processing systems such as the World Wide Web falls into the category of open source. This chapter focuses on collection against protected systems, though the Web often is a channel for such collection.

Most articles about cyber collection, or hacking, are written from the defense point of view and are consequently pessimistic and full of warnings. This chapter takes a more optimistic perspective because it takes the point of view of the attacker. A basic rule of strategic conflict is that *the offense always wins.* That rule applies especially in cyber collection. As in other areas of strategic conflict, the attacker has the advantage. The defense must defend against all possible forms of attack. The attacker just needs to find the weakest point and attack it. The attacker has time working for him; patience and persistence are the keys to success. As former hacker Dustin Dykes has noted, "The security systems have to win every time; the hacker only has to win once."[1] The best that the defender can do is to make a collection effort more difficult and expensive or slow it down. Winning in the long term is not an option.

Attackers are helped in their efforts by the mindset of the defenders, by the complexity of computer networks, and occasionally by simple human error:

- Mindset. Network administrators and network defenders find it difficult to think like attackers.[2] The defenders naturally want to believe that they have a secure system. The cyber collectors know better. The motto of the hacker is, "If there is a flaw in the security, we'll find it."[3] Computer security programs tend to focus on vulnerability, because vulnerabilities are easier to assess than threats. Governments and private companies find it difficult to view the targets—computers, networks, and databases—as the attackers do. Because of a lack of threat knowledge, companies and countries devote valuable resources to nonexistent threats simply because they are looking at the whole realm of the possible. And because the defenders have not done threat assessments from the attackers' viewpoints, defenders don't devote enough resources to areas under attack.

- Complexity. Large software programs and large networks always have more vulnerabilities than do smaller, less complex ones. Furthermore, new vulnerabilities appear every day, which is why time favors the attacker. The continual changing of system hardware and system and applications software; the frequent installation of patches and upgrades; the introduction of new features such as instant messaging, Internet relay chat, and Bluetooth— all provide a steady stream of new opportunities for attack. Every modification to the system creates a potential vulnerability. The constant changes form what Kevin Mitnick, a former hacker and now computer security expert, calls a "target-rich environment."[4]

- Human Error. Intelligence collection in general thrives on an opponent's mistakes, and cyber networks offer many opportunities for mistakes that make the system vulnerable. Poor configuration control of networks is common. Devices are improperly connected to the network.

Up to this point, we've been using the word *attack* to mean hacking a computer or network for any purpose. But this chapter is *not* about cyber activities known variously as information operations, cyber operations, or computer network attack (CNA). CNA operations are conducted by military forces and hackers with the intent to degrade, disrupt, deny, or deceive. The effects of CNA typically are readily observed. Instead, we're talking about *collection* operations where the computer or network continues to function normally. In the remainder of the chapter, *attack* means CNA; we'll use *collection* or *espionage* to describe cyber collection.

There are two general types of cyber collection: computer network exploitation, or CNE, and direct or indirect exploitation of a single computer or an intranet (a privately maintained computer network that requires access authorization). The following sections describe some commonly used techniques for exploiting both networks and single computers in intelligence. Because this is a rapidly changing and highly technical field, these descriptions are of necessity cursory.

Function

This section deals with the targets of cyber collection and the benefits that accrue to the collector.

For technically advanced countries such as Russia, China, Israel, and France, operations aimed at networks and computers may have become the most productive source of intelligence. One reason is the sheer volume and diversity of useful information that is available on computers. This includes not only information of direct intelligence value, such as military posture, plans, and economic data, but also information that can help in targeting other collection assets. Personnel data, for instance, can be acquired by targeting online employment search sites. The resumes on these sites often give details about classified programs and provide personal details that assist in the targeting of individuals for COMINT operations or for recruitment as HUMINT sources.[5] Much of this falls into the realm of open source, but some materials require sophisticated CNE to acquire.

Another reason for the rising importance of cyber collection is the relatively low risk involved in obtaining it. The U.S. National Counterintelligence Executive reportedly has posed this question: "If you can exfiltrate massive amounts of information electronically from another continent, why risk running a spy?" Dr. James A. Lewis, director of the Technology and Public Policy Program at the Center for Strategic and International Studies, has put it succinctly:

> There is little or no consequence for malicious cyber activities that do not involve the use of force. So while countries are very cautious in using cyber techniques for attack, they feel very little constraint in using cyber techniques for espionage or crime. Crime, even if state sponsored, does not justify a military response. Countries do not go to war over spying. For these reasons, the immediate threat in cyberspace involves espionage and crime.[6]

Cyber
Collection

The proliferation of computer capabilities around the world, and the development of commercial computer espionage capabilities, has resulted in the rapid expansion of computer network exploitation by governments, industrial spies, and hackers. Commercial computer espionage has continued to increase during this decade, and it has become difficult to distinguish such efforts from national security targeting. Many groups are interested in collecting commercial information, including competitors, hostile intelligence services, organized crime groups, and pranksters or hackers. Increasingly, these intelligence efforts are sponsored by governmental rather than nongovernmental groups. The intelligence services mostly acquire information; the criminals steal resources and extort money; the hackers do all of those things and disrupt information systems as well.

Much of the publicity about cyber operations (both CNA and CNE) concerns attempts by foreign entities (governments, companies, criminal enterprises, and freelance hackers) to conduct espionage or theft against U.S. targets. But the bulk of CNE and CNA worldwide probably is conducted against non-U.S. companies and foreign governments and is far less visible. Both the governments and private corporations don't want to publicize their failures—assuming that they've discovered them.

If it's on a computer somewhere and is of intelligence interest to a country, or to a commercial or a criminal enterprise, it's a target for cyber collection. And most information of intelligence interest exists on a computer somewhere. The specific targets depend on the country or organizational interests. Many countries will target political intelligence about neighboring countries and economic intelligence about trading partners. Israel likely focuses on terrorist groups and Arab governments. For China, Taiwan would be high on the list, along with dissident groups such as Falun Gong. For many countries and companies, the proprietary information held by foreign companies can provide a commercial advantage or enable a technological leap forward. Industrial espionage is popular among advanced countries, in part because it presents a relatively soft target for cyber collection and in part because of the economic benefits of success.

To illustrate the vulnerability of even relatively sophisticated countries to cyber collection, let's consider three states that are often considered to be hard targets for intelligence: China, Iran, and North Korea.

China is often cited in the U.S. trade press and congressional hearings as a major cyber threat. And the United States is certainly an important target for China. But according to a retired senior U.S. Navy officer in the signals intelligence field, Russia, France, Israel, and Taiwan conduct the most cyber espionage against the United States, at least partly for economic reasons.[7]

Furthermore, China itself appears to be a major victim of cyber attacks and cyber espionage. According to Microsoft, China is "at the top of the list (of browser-based attacks) because the software developers there are not as disciplined in writing code with security in mind and the huge market is an attractive target for malware writers."[8]

Beijing's government networks are not immune to cyber collection, either. In fact, they may be more vulnerable than U.S. government networks. Several Chinese government networks, including sensitive defense institutes, have been hacked by a U.S. security expert who specializes in penetrating Chinese computer networks. The expert also found that Chinese webcams, computer routing switches, and Internet telephones had vulnerabilities; many of them were on networks used by the Chinese military. These vulnerabilities would allow a collector to turn the webcams into surveillance devices and to use the telephones for COMINT.[9] The spiritual group Falun Gong, which has been a target for repression, appears to be both a victim of CNE and CNA by the government and an instigator of cyber attacks on the government.[10]

Iran has been a target of highly publicized attacks and is a target for cyber collection as well. During 2009 and 2010, Iran's Natanz nuclear facility reportedly was infected with a destructive malware called Stuxnet (discussed later). During 2011, a variant of that malware called Duqu (named for a *Star Wars* villain) was discovered. Duqu exploited a vulnerability of Microsoft Word and appears to have been aimed at highly specific targets in Iran and Sudan. In contrast to the attack design of Stuxnet, Duqu apparently was designed purely for cyber collection against specific targets in those countries.[11]

North Korea, despite its obsession with security, is another example of a state vulnerable to CNE. Only a few thousand North Koreans can access the World Wide Web. For the rest, the only Web access is to Kwangmyong, the nationwide intranet established around 2000 by the Korea Computer Center in Pyongyang. Kwangmyong connects universities, libraries, cybercafés, and other institutions with websites and email.[12] But it is at least as vulnerable to CNE as the Web, and the fact that it is an intranet tends to give its users a false sense of security. The North Koreans who have access to both the Web and Kwangmyong can (intentionally or unintentionally) create a path for exfiltration of data taken from computers on the intranet.

Less developed countries are even easier targets for cyber espionage than these three. Their governments are generally less sophisticated in cyber defense, and more cyber sophisticated countries probably exploit their technological advantage to routinely obtain political, economic, and military intelligence from the Internet, intranets, and stand-alone devices, much as

Cyber
Collection

they exploit their edge in COMINT. The less developed countries are also targets for another reason. Their governments and their commercial enterprises provide soft entry points for collection about third party governments that are hard targets. For example, a Western European government, no matter how secure its cyber systems, might lose sensitive details about its diplomatic dealings with a country in sub-Saharan Africa, thanks to the weak cyber protections in the latter's computer network.

Process

Cyber collection is aimed at a rich and rapidly growing set of hardware and software targets, the major categories being

- computers and intranets with Internet connection, including tablets and smart phones;
- intranets that aren't connected to the Internet, such as military networks; and
- stand-alone machines (that connect to no network of any kind).

This section looks at the process for cyber collection against each of these.

COMPUTER NETWORK EXPLOITATION

There are numerous ways to exploit target networks. Collectors must first gain access to the target network, have tools to exploit it, and remove any evidence of the operation. Collectors can exploit a vulnerability that occurs in the network or is presented by the supply chain. They can masquerade as an authorized user or use human assets to gain physical access to the network. Once they gain access, they usually leave behind a software implant called a **backdoor**. The implants communicate back to the controlling organization, allowing collectors to acquire data from the network. The process can be summed up in five steps:

- Target selection is the first phase of targeted collection. Information on potential targets is compiled from a variety of public sources, including social and professional networking sites, conference proceedings, academic papers, and project information, in order to generate a profile of the target.
- Passive network analysis and mapping involves nonintrusive probing of the target network, confirms the presence of network devices, and maps their connectivity. During this step, the probers conduct analysis to

understand the network from fragments of evidence about it and then create a model of the system, much as intelligence analysts do.

- Vulnerability scanning makes contact with the target network and its components using publicly available keys. Vulnerability scanning can be done both on and off the Internet, and it uses many of the tools that are used by top-tier hackers. It involves a wide range of specialized techniques such as pinging and port scanning.

- Exploitation is the step widely known as hacking. The collector conducts a survey, establishes access to the target system, and installs software implants for future access. Most such implants, as noted earlier, are called *backdoors*—a form of software code that allows unauthorized access to a computer or network, ideally while remaining undetected.

- Sustained collection uses the backdoor to obtain useful intelligence information from the computer or network through continuing access.

In the second and third steps—network analysis and mapping and vulnerability scanning—the main criterion for success is to be unnoticed. The scanner, in particular, has to be invisible to various types of intrusion detection systems or **sniffers**—software programs or human administrators checking access or searching for intruders. These increasingly pose risks for the collector; formerly the presence of a sniffer was relatively easy to detect, but newer forms of sniffer software are much less visible. Once the collector has alerted the defender, access to the network becomes very difficult to achieve.

The next two steps, exploitation and sustained collection, require the collector to install the backdoor and keep its presence concealed. The backdoor (sometimes referred to as a trapdoor) permits easy continuing access to a computer's software or operating system. Systems development staff install legitimate backdoors to bypass security routines. This allows them to enter the system at any time to run tests, upgrade systems, or fix problems. Normally, these legitimate backdoors are eliminated when the system becomes operational. However, backdoors may be left open by mistake or by intention to permit continuing maintenance.

The most exciting backdoor known existed only in the movies decades ago. The plot of *WarGames* (1983) centers on a high school–aged hacker discovering a backdoor that allows him access to the North American Aerospace Defense Command's strategic defense software. Believing that he has stumbled on a sophisticated new computer game, he begins to make moves that almost provoke World War III.

The backdoor is perhaps the primary tool used by collectors for industrial computer espionage. In poorly defended systems, a backdoor can give unlimited access to data in the system. Valuable corporate proprietary information has been acquired time and again from competitors through backdoors.[13]

It is also possible to proceed directly from target selection to exploitation. This can happen when the target receives an email that appears to come from a trusted source—an acquaintance or someone within the same organization. The email might ask the target to open an attachment; Adobe PDFs, images, and Microsoft Office files are commonly used. When the file is opened by the vulnerable program on the victim's computer (such as Excel, PowerPoint, Word, or Adobe Acrobat), a backdoor program executes and the computer has been compromised. At the same time, a seemingly normal file or image appears on the target's computer screen, so that the recipient has no reason to suspect that something is amiss. Emails are widely used for exploitation because it is possible to identify an employee's trusted relationships and professional networks by looking at his or her email patterns.[14]

Alternatively, the email may direct the target to a website that contains the backdoor, with much the same outcome. Such a website is called a **drive-by download site**. It typically relies on vulnerabilities in web browsers and browser add-ons. Users with vulnerable computers can be infected with malware simply by visiting such a website, even without attempting to download anything.[15]

Sustained collection then begins when the target's compromised computer sends a beacon signal to the collector's server. This check-in or beaconing activity is designed to blend in with normal web traffic. The compromised computer sends its IP address and operating system information and then receives and executes a set of commands giving the collector full control of the user's system. The collector can then acquire files from the computer, email or send data from the computer, or force the compromised computer to download additional malware. From there, the collector can use the infected computer to exploit the victim's contacts or other computers on the target network.[16]

Sustained collection makes use of a number of tools that are known in the business as *exploits*. An **exploit** takes advantage of software vulnerabilities to infect, disrupt, or take control of a computer without the user's consent and preferably without the user's knowledge. Exploits take advantage of vulnerabilities in operating systems, web browsers, applications, or other software components.[17] The preferred target of exploits changes constantly as vulnerabilities are found and corrected in all of these targets. For example, exploitation of the Adobe Flash Player had been quite low until 2011, when it suddenly became a major target. Adobe provided patches and updates throughout 2012 to eliminate the vulnerabilities, only to encounter new versions of malware as hackers went after the patched versions and even moved to place Trojans (discussed below) on mobile versions of Flash Player.[18]

Four of the most widely known exploits are Trojan horses (usually abbreviated "Trojans"), worms, rootkits, and keystroke loggers.

- A **Trojan horse** is a seemingly innocent program that conceals its primary purpose. The purpose is to exfiltrate data from the target computer system. Operating systems software and almost any applications software package—screen savers, spreadsheets, word processors, database managers—could be Trojan horses. A simple Trojan in a word processor might, for example, make a copy of all files that the word processor saves and store the copies in a location where the horse's master can access them later. Another simple Trojan horse, once activated, waits until the user attempts to log off. It then simulates a real logoff while keeping the user online. When the user next attempts to log on, the Trojan captures the user's password for its master and simulates a logon.

- A **worm** can do many of the things that a Trojan does and can also do such things as install a backdoor. But in contrast to the Trojan, the worm is designed to be completely concealed instead of masquerading as an innocent program. Hackers have used worms to instruct a bank computer to transfer money to an illicit account. Worms also are used to transmit controlled data to unauthorized recipients; this is how they are used in cyber collection.

- A **rootkit** is software code designed to take control of a computer while avoiding detection. The term comes from the expression in the Unix operating system for fundamental control of a computer (*root access*). The equivalent in Microsoft Windows is termed *administrator access*. The rootkit is often concealed within a Trojan.

- **Keystroke loggers**, or keyloggers, can be hardware or software based. Their general purpose is to capture and record keystrokes. For cyber collection, they specifically are intended to capture passwords and encryption keys. Hardware keyloggers often are mounted in keyboards, requiring access to the keyboard at some point—though the advent of wireless keyboards has provided the option for collectors to collect keystrokes by monitoring the wireless signal from nearby. Software keyloggers usually are implanted in the computer's operating system.

While all of these exploits can be used for cyber espionage, they are most effective when they are used against a *zero-day* vulnerability. Also called a

zero-hour or *day zero* vulnerability, this is an application vulnerability that is unknown to defenders or the software developer. It derives its name from that time (called the zero hour or zero day) when the software developer first becomes aware of the vulnerability. Until that moment of awareness, the developer obviously cannot develop a security fix or distribute it to users of the software. Zero-day exploits (the software that uses a security gap to carry out an intrusion) are highly valued by hackers and cyber espionage units because they cannot be effectively defended against—at least not until sometime after zero day arrives.[19]

Collection via the Web requires more than the deployment of these exploits. The cyber espionage organization must control the exploits and use them to obtain the desired information while maintaining the secrecy, or at least the deniability, of the operation. Often, this is done by a device called a **botnet**. The controller of a botnet is usually referred to as a command-and-control (C&C) server. It issues instructions to the botnet, which directs the activities of infected computers (referred to as zombies) through communication channels such as Internet Relay Chat or HTTP. The botnet's command-and-control server can't be easily shut down because it's hard to determine its real location.

Figure 5.1 shows the sources (distribution sites) of malware infections worldwide logged by Microsoft security monitoring systems during the fourth quarter of 2011.[20] The graphic, taken alone, does not tell the full story; many of the sites are intermediaries, the actual attack being launched from another site, usually in another country. Canada and the Middle East, for example, are more likely transit points for attacks rather than being sources.

Comparing the attack site distribution with the locations of malware infections (Figure 5.2) reinforces a point made earlier in this chapter: Countries lacking a high level of cyber expertise are generally more vulnerable to malware.

When a hacker enters a system, as the following examples illustrate, the victim usually cannot identify the real source or purpose of the intrusion.

In 1999 and 2000, unidentified hackers downloaded scores of "sensitive but unclassified" internal documents from computers in the Department of Defense and in the Los Alamos and Lawrence Livermore labs. The effort was traced to a foreign country whose officials denied being involved, but the intrusions suddenly stopped.[21]

During 2008 to 2009, a team of Canadian cyber security experts investigated a centrally controlled and organized cyber espionage network. This network primarily targeted computer networks in India, the Offices of the Dalai Lama, and the United Nations. The espionage network made use of

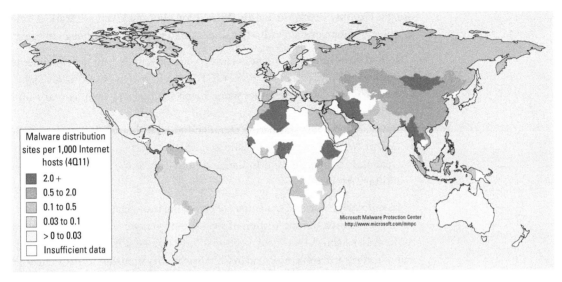

FIGURE 5.1 Malware Distribution Sites during the Second Quarter of 2011

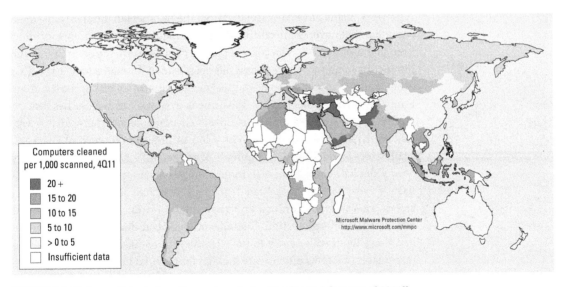

FIGURE 5.2 Malware Detected on Computers during the Second Quarter of 2011[22]

numerous cloud computing systems and free web hosting services to conceal the sources of the collection effort. But the exfiltrated data reflected a pattern of targeting specific systems based on user profiles pulled from social networking platforms and social media systems that included Twitter,

Google Groups, Blogspot, Baidu Blogs, blog.com, and Yahoo! Mail. A few samples of the material exfiltrated illustrate the range of espionage interest:

- Indian government diplomatic correspondence, including two documents marked "SECRET," six as "RESTRICTED," and five as "CONFIDENTIAL"
- 1,500 letters sent from the Dalai Lama's office between January and November 2009
- Detailed personal information about an Indian military intelligence officer
- Documentation of Indian missile and artillery systems
- Academic papers on Sino-Indian and Sino-Taiwanese issues and Chinese military exports

In spite of the detailed evidence collected, the investigators could not determine the identity and motivation of the espionage network. The investigators could only establish that the collection effort originated from a group of command-and-control servers located in China, primarily from the city of Chengdu.[23]

DIRECT ACCESS TO A COMPUTER OR INTRANET

A network that is physically isolated from the Internet (an intranet) or a single computer that never connects to the Internet requires a different type of effort from that used in CNE. The collector has to gain access to the computer or the intranet in some way. Once access has been gained through a network jack or cable, a utility closet, or some similar device, almost anything can be done. From the defense point of view, the game is over and the defense has lost.

One of the simplest targets is a personal notebook computer that is carried on trips or to conferences. With a few minutes of uninterrupted access, a collector can download the contents of a notebook's hard drive. Computers or any devices containing electronic storage—separate hard drives or USB flash drives, for example—can legally be searched when they are taken across international borders, and they often are. Encrypting the material does not provide protection. Customs officials can demand the encryption key, deny the traveler entry to their country, or confiscate the computer. In many cases, customs officials are looking for terrorist material, pornography, or hate literature, but countries that have a reputation for commercial espionage also are likely to make intelligence use of the material acquired.

Gaining entry to a notebook computer provides the collector with one-time access. But if it is expected that the notebook will later be connected to an intranet, the collector can place a backdoor in the computer.

In cases where computers and intranets never leave a secure facility, and where remote access is not possible, it is necessary to use field operations to access networks. This category encompasses deployment of any CNE tool through physical access or proximity. In intelligence, these are called HUMINT-enabled operations; in the world of hackers, they are usually referred to as *social engineering*.[24] They encompass such classical HUMINT techniques as gaining access under false pretenses, bribery or recruitment of trusted personnel in a facility, and surreptitious entry. They can be as crude as leaving infected memory sticks in the facility's parking lot, in hopes that someone will pick them up and plug them into the network.[25] HUMINT-enabled operations are often facilitated by human error or carelessness, and complex intranets are particularly susceptible to both.

Even physical access to areas outside a protected area can help in either direct access or CNE. The TRASHINT (dumpster diving) technique mentioned earlier is sometimes a prelude to cyber attack or exploitation. One can often obtain network information, system architecture, and passwords from trash.

Wireless devices are an especially attractive target for espionage, either against the device itself or against a computer or intranet that it connects to. As one example of many, exploits that affect the Android mobile operating system published by Google and the Open Handset Alliance were observed to increase dramatically beginning in 2011.[26] Many computers connected to otherwise secure intranets are equipped with wireless devices, for example, for wireless keyboards or mice or for communicating with wireless printers. Unless the wireless capability is disabled, this represents a vulnerable point for entry to the intranet.

Products to support cyber espionage against wireless devices are available worldwide. Gamma International, a U.K.-based firm, provides one of many such tools. Called Finfisher, it can be used to enter wireless networks, smart phones, computers, and cell phones or to intercept Skype communications and obtain encryption passwords. One of its features is the ability to send a fake iTunes update to targets to infect their computers with the company's surveillance software. The company offered to sell Finfisher to Hosni Mubarak's secret police in Egypt, prior to Mubarak's overthrow by protesters during 2011.[27]

Another technique that works especially well against wireless devices is to introduce vulnerabilities when a company provides the inevitable patch to its software. The growth of tablet computers and other mobile devices makes downloadable apps a useful vehicle for malware delivery as well.

Following are a few examples of how cyber collection has worked in practice.

THE AGENT.BTZ INFECTION

An infected USB flash drive inserted into a Defense Department (DoD) laptop computer in 2008 was claimed to cause "a significant compromise" of the DoD classified computer networks. The flash drive's exploit, subsequently named Agent.btz, moved onto a network run by the U.S. Central Command.[28] Once that network became infected, any thumb drive used on the machine acquired a copy of the malware, ready for propagation to other computers and networks. Possibly as a consequence, the exploit subsequently infected two classified networks as well as some unclassified ones. The Secret Internet Protocol Router Network (SIPRNet), which the Defense and State departments use to transmit material of no higher than Secret classification, was infected. Agent.btz also infected the Joint Worldwide Intelligence Communications System (JWICS), which carries material classified Top Secret.[29]

The compromise received a great deal of publicity. DoD claimed that it was the most significant breach to U.S. military computers in history. The code had been used before by Russian hackers, leading DoD authorities to claim that a Russian intelligence service was behind the effort.[30] But the circumstances surrounding the Agent.btz incident make this seem unlikely. To conduct cyber collection, the malware would have had to communicate with a command-and-control computer for instructions on what files to remove and how to transmit them. But SIPRNet and JWICS have at best very limited (and closely monitored) connection to the public Internet. Without that connection, an intruder would have had no way of exploiting the access provided by Agent.btz. In fact, the intruder wouldn't even have been able to determine that Agent.btz had found its way into the CENTCOM network.

The subsequent removal of Agent.btz was an expensive and time-consuming process. But the exploit itself was relatively crude by the standards of a sophisticated foreign intelligence service, especially the absence of an adequate exfiltration mechanism, noted above. The following examples illustrate what a CNE exploit should look like.

STUXNET

In contrast to the Agent.btz exploit, Stuxnet illustrates the type of precision attack that is most effective in both CNA and CNE. Stuxnet was a worm designed to infect and disable a specific type of computer performing a specific task. The target, investigators believe, was the computer controlling the isotope separation centrifuges in Iran's Natanz uranium enrichment facility.

Stuxnet was used in a sustained and directed attack, conducted over a 10-month period beginning in 2009. Reportedly, at least three versions of the program were written and introduced during that time period. Investigators found that the first version had been completed just 12 hours before the first successful infection in June 2009. One attack, in April 2010, exploited a zero-day vulnerability in Windows-based computers.

Once introduced, the Stuxnet worm infected all Windows-based industrial control computers it found while searching for specific equipment made by the Siemens Corporation. Upon finding its target, the worm was programmed to damage a uranium centrifuge array by repeatedly speeding it up, while at the same time hiding its attack from the control computers by sending false information to displays that monitored the system.[31]

The attack appears to have been at least partially successful. International inspectors visiting Natanz in late 2009 found that almost 1,000 gas centrifuges had been taken offline. Investigators therefore speculated that the attack disabled some part of the Natanz complex.

How the complex became infected has been a matter of speculation, because there are several possible ways the worm could have been introduced. A classified site like Natanz probably is not connected directly to the Internet. The attacker could have infected industrial organizations that would be likely to share information, and therefore the malware, with Natanz. An infected email sent to one of the Natanz operators could have carried the worm. Or a USB flash drive carrying the worm could have been provided to one of the operators.[32]

A sophisticated and targeted worm such as Stuxnet would need to be tested to ensure that it would succeed against its target, preferably without causing damage to unintended targets. Stuxnet recorded information on the location and type of each computer it infected, indicating a concern about protecting unintended targets.[33] Israel reportedly built an elaborate test facility at their Dimona nuclear weapons development center. The facility contained a replica array of the Natanz Iranian uranium enrichment plant.[34] Such a test site would have been necessary for the design of the attack software.

While Stuxnet was an attack malware, it indicates the state of the art in CNE. Stuxnet operated by fingerprinting any computer system it infiltrated to determine whether it was the precise machine the malware was looking for. If not, it left the computer alone.[35] The Duqu program that was associated with Stuxnet could gain access to a specific computer on a network, acquire classified or proprietary information from it, manipulate the defense system so that everything appeared to be operating normally, and exfiltrate the data via the operator's apparently secure mechanisms for placing data on the infected computer or network.[36]

FLAME

During 2012, malware was discovered that appears to have targeted Microsoft Windows computers in the Middle East for intelligence purposes. Called

Cyber Collection

Flame, it reportedly had been operating for five years in these countries.[37] Flame is more powerful and flexible than Stuxnet and has a number of features that illustrate the level of sophistication and precise targeting that is possible today in cyber collection:

- Flame incorporates five distinct encryption algorithms and exotic data storage formats both to avoid detection and to conceal its purpose.
- It does not spread itself automatically, doing so only when directed by a controlling entity (the command-and-control server).
- It allows the controlling entity to add new malware at any time for targeted collection.
- It enables the controlling entity to remotely change settings on a computer, gather data and document files, turn on the computer microphone to record conversations, log keystrokes, take screen shots, and copy instant messaging chats.[38]

Flame is the most sophisticated piece of malware discovered to date, far more complex than Duqu. It functions as a backdoor and a Trojan. It also has wormlike features, so that it can replicate itself in a local network and on removable media if it is instructed to do so by its controller. Flame's sophistication earned it the "Epic Ownage" award from the 2012 Black Hat convention—the equivalent, among cyber security experts, of an Oscar.[39] (So far, no one has come forward to accept the award.) Figure 5.3 shows the locations and the number of computers found by Kaspersky Lab to be infected by Flame.[40] The infections found in Israel and the West Bank are not distinguished in the Kaspersky data, but based on the overall infection pattern, they most likely are concentrated in the Palestinian regions of the West Bank.

GAUSS

During 2012, Kaspersky Lab identified a new cyber collection toolkit that appears to have been created by the same government that developed and deployed Flame. Called Gauss, it has many similarities to Flame: their architecture, module structures, and method of communicating with command-and-control servers are strikingly similar. The owners of the Gauss command-and-control server shut it down shortly after Kaspersky Lab announced its discovery.

Gauss is an example of a highly targeted intelligence collector. It infected personal computers (PCs) primarily located in Lebanon and stole browser history, passwords, and access credentials for online banking systems and

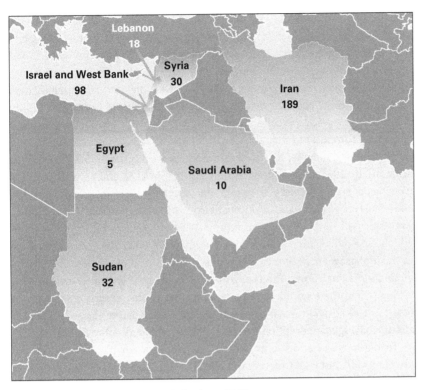

FIGURE 5.3 Geography of Flame Infections, 2012

payment websites from its targets. Kaspersky Lab identified more than 2,500 infections and estimated that the total infections numbered in the tens of thousands.

Based on the Kaspersky analysis, it appears that the targeting was intended to collect intelligence about financial transactions. The targets included a number of Lebanese banks including the Bank of Beirut, EBLF, BlomBank, ByblosBank, FransaBank, and Credit Libanais. Gauss also targeted specific Citibank and PayPal accounts.[41]

SUPPLY CHAIN CONTAMINATION

The concept of embedding malicious things in some desirable object is ancient. It comes, in fact, from Greek mythology. Throughout nine years of war with the city-state of Troy, the Greeks were unable to break into the city. On the advice of the Greek hero Odysseus, they built a massive wooden statue of a horse ostensibly as an offering. The Greek fleet then sailed away and the Trojans celebrated victory by bringing the horse into the city. What they also brought into the city was a cadre of Greek warriors who waited inside the hollowed-out horse until dark, then exited, and opened Troy's gates to the Greek army. So many cyber exploits today carry the name Trojan horse (or simply Trojan). And as with the original Trojan horse, the supply chain today provides excellent opportunities for inserting something malicious into computer systems.

The Soviets successfully used this stratagem against the U.S. embassy in Moscow. In 1984, typewriters being used in the U.S. embassy in Moscow were discovered to have been bugged. The microelectronic bugs were inserted while the typewriters were in shipment to the Moscow embassy. The machines were shipped to the Soviet Union by a Western European shipping firm in which the Soviet Union had a controlling interest. Once the typewriters were in the embassy, according to one report, "Each press of a key transmitted a distinctive signal down the typewriter's power cable and into the building wiring. Computers could then reconstruct the cables exactly as they were typed . . . the Soviets were able to intercept cables before they were coded, circumventing an encryption system that is considered unbreakable."[42]

Technology has allowed us to hide malware in many places, and the supply chain (all the way from component manufacturer to end user) is a very attractive place. Anyone in the supply chain before sale has the access necessary for inserting malware in a computer or other electronic device. Such embedded malware is very difficult to detect, and most purchasers do not have the resources to check for such modifications.

Even better than getting access to a target's computer is to manufacture the computer. The hardware can be modified in ways that are not readily detectable but that allow an intelligence service to gain continuing entry into the computer or communications system. Targeted components can be add-ons that are preinstalled by the computer manufacturer before the computer is sold. A user may not even use the vulnerable add-on or be aware that it is installed.[43] Malware inserted in a computer before sale can call home after being activated, exfiltrate sensitive data, allow remote control of the computer, and insert Trojan horses and worms. Such backdoors are not limited to software installed on the computer. Hardware components such as embedded radio frequency identification (RFID) chips and flash memory can be the sources of such malware.

Much of the hardware that goes into computers and telecommunications systems sold worldwide is now made in countries such as China. In July 2011, in testimony before the House of Representatives' Oversight and

Government Reform Committee, a senior Department of Homeland Security official testified that electronics sold in the United States are being pre-loaded with spyware, malware, and security-compromising components. The principal source of the malware is believed to be China.[44]

It is also possible to conceal the origin of the equipment to facilitate its acceptance. In 2008, the Federal Bureau of Investigation (FBI) seized $3.5 billion worth of counterfeit communications equipment that was made in China. Because the fakes appeared to have been manufactured by Cisco, a U.S. company, they had been purchased by the U.S. military. The equipment easily could have contained hidden backdoors, though there is no evidence that this particular shipment did.[45] The following example, though, illustrates a case where the backdoors were in place at the point of sale.

During 2011, Microsoft researchers purchased 20 brand-new desktop and laptop computers in selected cities in China. Four of the 20 machines had counterfeit versions of Microsoft Windows that were infected with malware. The malware had a number of features that would make it useful for either cyber espionage or CNA:

- It would allow a remote controller to operate the computer's microphone and video camera.
- An included keylogger could capture all the user's keystrokes.
- The malware could be spread to uninfected computers via USB drives.
- Its main feature was the Nitol virus, which is used to steal personal information and uses an infected computer as a zombie to carry out distributed denial of service attacks that flood websites with traffic and make them unreachable. Nitol also provides a backdoor so that additional malware can be loaded onto the infected machine whenever it is connected to the Internet.

Computers infected with the Nitol virus were controlled through an Internet domain called 3322.org, which had previously been linked to malicious activity. Microsoft, after obtaining a court order in September 2012, took control of the domain and blocked its operation.[46]

COLLECTING EMANATIONS

If a computer or network is not connected to the Internet and if physical access is out of the question, it may be possible to obtain intelligence using short-range sensors to exploit equipment emanations. If a computer or an intranet component emits compromising electromagnetic signals, sensors placed close by can recover information being processed. Electronic and

Cyber Collection

magnetic signals can radiate from the area both in space and through power lines or other conducting paths. Collection of keystroke emanations from wireless keyboards was previously noted, but even a conventional wired keyboard can emit a compromising signal.

These types of technical collection efforts are difficult to detect. They are a capability of sophisticated adversaries and require extensive HUMINT support. The U.S. government's attempts to improve protection against the collection of emanations some years back spawned a sizable industry known as TEMPEST. TEMPEST technology uses shielding and other electronic design techniques to reduce radiated electromagnetic signals that might be picked up by clandestine collectors.

Structure

A structural debate exists within the United States and other countries, having to do with the nature of cyber operations generally. Computer network exploitation and computer network attack overlap, in much the same way that electronic warfare and signals intelligence (SIGINT) overlap. The same capabilities are used for both CNE and CNA. Both require some way of getting into the target network or computer. Very similar malware is used for both, the difference being in what the malware does after it is introduced into the target network or computer. Furthermore, defense against both CNE and CNA employs many of the same skills. So one view is that all offense (CNE and CNA) and cyber defense should be housed within the same organization.

The United Kingdom appears at the moment to have such a centralized structure. The Government Communications Headquarters (GCHQ), the British COMINT organization, has the assignment to defend against cybercrime and cyber espionage. It also probably has the cyber offense role as well (CNE and CNA). But there are plans to separate criminal from other cyber activity, by putting cybercrime in the new National Crime Agency.[47] So the United Kingdom may be moving toward the same division of responsibilities that the United States has, as discussed below.

Within the United States, the assignment of cyber responsibilities is complex and is likely to remain so. The Defense Department has a responsibility for CNE and CNA against opposing military forces and for cyber defense against such forces. To carry out that responsibility, during 2010 it put in place the U.S. Cyber Command under the Strategic Command (STRATCOM), with the Director of the National Security Agency (NSA) as the commanding officer. Each service has a component within the Cyber Command: the 24th Air Force, Army Forces Cyber Command, Navy's 10th Fleet, and Marine Forces Cyber Command.

But a division of responsibility exists between military and civilian cyber operations in the United States. In April 2011, General Keith Alexander, Director of NSA, identified his major concern in a speech in which he said that "my mission as commander of U.S. Cyber Command is to defend the military networks . . . I do not have the authority to look at what's going on in other government sectors, nor what would happen in critical [U.S.] infrastructure. That right now falls to DHS." Department of Homeland Security (DHS) Secretary Janet Napolitano responded in a speech in which she made the point that "at DHS, we believe cyberspace is fundamentally a civilian space."[48]

The major fault line in U.S. cyber responsibilities, though, is the domestic/foreign divide. Within both domestic and foreign networks, the responsibility for cyber collection remains unclear. Domestically, the FBI, Drug Enforcement Administration (DEA), and local police forces share responsibility for collection against organized crime. Overseas, the military departments, Central Intelligence Agency (CIA), and NSA all have intelligence collection responsibilities. To further complicate matters, a target of cyber collection may have both domestic and foreign components and use multiple networks that cross many international (including U.S.) boundaries. At present, the rules of engagement for cyber collection are still being worked out.[49] Because substantial budget dollars ride on the decisions, the debate is likely to continue for some time. And as the earlier example of Microsoft's collecting infected computers illustrates, the commercial sector has a role to play as well.

The Chinese framework for cyber collection provides a contrast to the U.K. and U.S. structures. And it appears to be an analogue to the Chinese approach to HUMINT: deploy large numbers of collectors against large numbers of targets, discarding subtlety in favor of volume. A complex collaborative relationship exists among Chinese hackers, industrial enterprises, and the Chinese government. The government recruits from among the Chinese hacker community, and consulting relationships exist between hackers and security services. Both the government and industrial enterprises engaged in cyber espionage get custom malware from the hacker community.[50]

As it did with HUMINT, China must find a way to make use of the cyber intelligence that it obtains. Because it conducts so many successful cyber collections, the Chinese problem lies in collating the mass of intelligence that they collect. That would seem to be a problem any intelligence service would like to have—until it actually must deal with it.

Cyber
Collection

Cyber collection shares a structural feature with HUMINT and open source: many people can do it—witness the large number of freelance hackers and the number of China-based collection attempts. But the best of these people are incredibly good; they give their employers a huge edge in collection. If you select at random a group of experienced software programmers, according to experts in the field, the best in the group will be between 10 and 28 times more effective than the mediocre ones.[51] Assuming that this ratio translates over to the hacker world, the best in the cyber collection business should be far better than the average.

The U.S. media provides almost daily hyperbole about the West being "stolen blind" by cyber espionage, especially by China. The real threat may be quite different. One informal survey of cyber collection professionals indicated that they believe China deploys large numbers of aggressive and highly visible cyber collectors, but Russia uses more skilled and professional ones. The best in the business, according to this group, are the NSA and Britain's GCHQ.[52] In cyber collection, as in HUMINT, visibility is not necessarily an indicator of success.

COLLECTION AGAINST CYBERCRIME

Cyber tools are used by a number of criminal organizations both to acquire wealth and to protect their operations from cyber collection by law enforcement. As a result, organized crime presents a particularly difficult target for cyber collection. As noted earlier, the best cyber operators are far above the average, and organized crime can afford to hire the best both for offense and for defense. Against this formidable foe, a number of governmental and commercial organizations do cyber collection within the United States and internationally.

Within the United States, the National White Collar Crime Center, known as NW3C, provides support to law enforcement in preventing and investigating high-tech crime—which includes cybercrime. The support includes training, investigative support, and research.

The FBI has a major role in countering cybercrime and operates the Internet Crime Complaint Center. In 2008, the FBI shut down an online criminal enterprise that had more than 2,500 people involved in buying and selling stolen financial information that included credit card data and login information.[53]

Internationally, liaison and cooperation are essential in countering cybercrime. During 2008, for example, the FBI and Egyptian law enforcement authorities closed down a transnational crime ring that specialized in cyber operations for identity theft and money laundering.[54] Unfortunately, cyber criminals tend to be located in states where government cooperation to track the perpetrators is unlikely—Nigeria and Belarus, for example.

COLLECTION AGAINST COMMERCIAL ENTERPRISES

The focus of much cyber collection by governments is against commercial enterprises, for stealing proprietary information and technology. But specialized equipment and secret techniques that until recently were the exclusive preserve of government and military cyber organizations now are available from many companies worldwide. The companies noted in Chapter 4 as providing COMINT equipment also provide equipment and software to monitor Internet activity. A Chinese company reportedly offers software that can crack the security on any Hotmail or Gmail account.[55]

Summary

Cyber collection is not about what is variously called information operations, cyber operations, or computer network attack—those activities that involve attacks on computers and networks to degrade, disrupt, deny, or deceive. Cyber collection is about operations in which the computer or network continues to function normally. It divides into two basic types: computer network exploitation, also known as remote access collection, and direct access operations. Cyber collection also is not about searching the Internet, which was covered in Chapter 2. Instead, it is about collection against protected systems, though the World Wide Web often is a channel for such collection.

Cyber collection is a valuable source of sensitive intelligence for many countries, and it is a profitable enterprise for many criminal groups as well. Both use techniques that are widely known as hacking to obtain intelligence from computers and data networks. Cyber collection is popular, in part, because of the sheer volume of useful information that is available on computers. It is attractive also because there is relatively little risk involved in obtaining it.

The discussions of cyber collection and cyber attack in the literature take the view of the defense and consequently are pessimistic. When viewed from the collector's perspective, the picture is much brighter. As in other areas of strategic conflict, the attacker (here, the collector) has the advantage. The defense must defend against all possible forms of attack. The collector

Cyber
Collection

need only select one vulnerability. And the collector has time working for him.

Collectors are helped in this process by the mindset of the defenders and by the complexity of computer networks: Complexity equates to vulnerability. Hardware and software changes, patches, and upgrades, along with poor configuration control, all open vulnerabilities that collectors can exploit.

Cyber collectors have to get either electronic or physical access to the target computer or network, have tools to exploit it, and remove any evidence of the operation. There are typically five steps in the process:

1. *Target selection.* The purpose here is to generate a profile of the target to determine the most profitable targets for collection.

2. *Passive network analysis and mapping.* The objective is to create a detailed model of the target without being noticed.

3. *Vulnerability scanning.* Collectors can exploit a vulnerability that occurs in the network or is presented by the supply chain. They can masquerade as an authorized user or use human assets to gain physical access to the target network.

4. *Exploitation.* Once the collector gains access, he or she usually leaves behind some form of software implant, often called an *exploit* or a *backdoor,* to allow continued access.

5. *Sustained collection.* The collector obtains useful intelligence information from the computer or network through continued access using the exploit.

An isolated network or computer requires physical access, usually HUMINT-enabled. In the hacker trade, this is known as social engineering: using false pretenses, bribery, or recruitment of trusted personnel in a facility. In some cases, surreptitious entry may be required. Even a few seconds inside a secure facility can be all that is needed. HUMINT-enabled operations often are aided by human error or carelessness, and complex intranets are particularly susceptible to human error and carelessness. The supply chain for computers and communications equipment provides another route for surreptitious introduction of malware.

The structure of cyber collection is not settled, because it does not fit neatly into existing stovepipes. It typically has some connection with HUMINT, because it is often an extension of the technical collection efforts carried out by HUMINT operatives. Cyber collection also resembles COMINT, especially when collection from data communications networks is involved. And it overlaps with computer network attack, since it uses the same tools and expertise. To add to the complexity, at the U.S. border a division of responsibility exists, with law enforcement organizations having internal responsibilities and national intelligence organizations operating externally. Finally, many entities—governmental units, organized crime, and lone-wolf hackers—do cyber collection against governments, criminals, and commercial enterprises.

NOTES

1. Quoted in Kevin D. Mitnick and William L. Simon, *The Art of Intrusion* (Indianapolis, IN: Wiley, 2005), 115.
2. Ibid., 43.
3. Ibid.
4. Ibid., 62.
5. Kevin G. Coleman, "Cyber Espionage Targets Sensitive Data" (December 29, 2008), accessed 21 September 2012 at http://sip-trunking.tmcnet.com/topics/security/articles/47927-cyber-espionage-targets-sensitive-data.htm.
6. James A. Lewis, Center for Strategic and International Studies, Testimony before the House of Representatives Committee on Oversight and Government Reform Subcommittee on National Security, Homeland Defense and Foreign Operations on "Cybersecurity: Assessing the Immediate Threat to the United States" (May 25, 2011), accessed 21 September 2012 at http://csis.org/files/ts110525_lewis.pdf.
7. Seymour M. Hersh, "The Online Threat," *The New Yorker* (November 1, 2010), 44–55.
8. Elinor Mills, "Microsoft: Trojans Are Huge and China Is Tops in Browser Exploits," accessed 21 September 2012 at http://news.cnet.com/8301-1009_3-10080428-83.html.
9. Shaun Waterman, "Chinese Databases Exposed To hackers," *Washington Times* (April 26, 2011), accessed 21 September 2012 at http://www.washingtontimes.com/news/2011/apr/26/chinese-databases-exposed-to-hackers/.
10. Ellen Nakashima and William Wan, "Chinese Denials about Cyberattacks Undermined by Video Clip," *Washington Post,* (August 4, 2011), accessed 21 September 2012 at http://www.washingtonpost.com/world/national-security/state-media-video-candidly-depicts-chinas-developing-cyber-weaponry/2011/08/22/gIQAqyWkbJ_story.html.
11. R. M. Schneiderman, "New Computer Malware May Presage Another Cyberattack, Potentially on Iran," *The Daily Beast* (November 16, 2011), accessed 21 September 2012 at http://www.thedailybeast.com/articles/2011/11/16/new-computer-worm-may-presage-another-cyber-attack-potentially-on-iran.html.
12. Sangwon Yoon, "Is the Inter-Korean Conflict Going Cyber?" *Al Jazeera* (June 24, 2011), accessed 21 September 2012 at http://www.aljazeera.com/indepth/features/2011/06/20116206572748130.html.
13. John McAfee and Colin Haynes, *Computer Viruses, Worms, Data Diddlers, Killer Programs, and Other Threats to Your System* (New York: St. Martin's Press, 1989), 79.
14. Bryan Krekel, "Capability of the People's Republic of China to Conduct Cyber Warfare and Computer Network Exploitation," Northrup Grumman Corporation

Cyber
Collection

(October 9, 2009), accessed 21 September 2012 at http://www. uscc. gov/research papers/2009/NorthropGrumman_PRC_Cyber_Paper_FINAL_Approved %20Report_16Oct2009. pdf.

15. *Microsoft Security Intelligence Report,* Vol. 12, accessed 16 September 2012 at http://www.microsoft.com/security/sir/default. aspx.

16. Joint Report JR03-2010, "Shadows in the Cloud: Investigating Cyber Espionage 2. 0," Joint report of the Information Warfare Monitor and Shadowserver Foundation (April 6, 2010), accessed 21 September 2012 http://www.scribd .com/doc/29435784/SHADOWS-IN-THE-CLOUD-Investigating-Cyber-Espionage-2-0.

17. *Microsoft Security Intelligence Report,* Vol. 12.

18. Ben Weitzenkorn, "Adobe Flash Player Hit by Hackers on Both Ends," *Security News Daily,* accessed 21 September 2012 at http://www.securitynewsdaily .com/2191-adobe-flash-player-iphone-android.html.

19. *Microsoft Security Intelligence Report,* Vol 12.

20. Ibid.

21. Association of Foreign Intelligence Officers (AFIO) Weekly Intelligence Note 36-02 (September 9, 2002), available from the association by contacting afio@ afio.com.

22. Ibid.

23. JU03–2010, "Shadows in the Cloud."

24. Mitnick and Simon, *The Art of Intrusion,* Chapter 10.

25. "War in the Fifth Domain," *The Economist* (July 1, 2010), accessed 21 September 2012 at http://www.economist.com/node/16478792?story_id=16478792.

26. *Microsoft Security Intelligence Report,* Vol. 12.

27. Kim Zetter, "Spy Firm Videos Show How to Hack WiFi, Skype, and Email," *Wired* (December 8, 2011), accessed 21 September 2012 at http://www.wired .com/threatlevel/2011/12/spy-firm-videos/.

28. William J. Lynn III, "Defending a New Domain," *Foreign Affairs* (September/ October 2010), accessed 21 September 2012 at http://www.foreignaffairs.com/ articles/66552/william-j-lynn-iii/defending-a-new-domain.

29. Ellen Nakashima, "A Cyber-Spy Is Halted, but Not a Debate," *Washington Post* (December 9, 2011), 1.

30. Lisa Daniel, "Lynn Outlines Cyber Threats, Defensive Measures," American Forces Press Service (August 25, 2010), accessed 21 September 2012 at http:// www.defense.gov/news/newsarticle.aspx?id=60600.

31. John Markoff, "Malware Aimed at Iran Hit Five Sites, Report Says," *New York Times* (February 11, 2011), accessed 21 September 2012 at http://www. nytimes .com/2011/02/13/science/13stuxnet.html.

32. Ibid.

33. Ibid.

34. William J. Broad, John Markoff, and David E. Sanger, "Israeli Test on Worm Called Crucial in Iran Nuclear Delay," *New York Times* (January 15, 2011), accessed 21 September 2012 at http://www.nytimes.com/2011/01/16/world/ middleeast/16stuxnet.html?_r=1&pagewanted=all.

35. Mark Clayton, "Stuxnet Malware Is 'Weapon' Out to Destroy . . . Iran's Bushehr Nuclear Plant?" *Christian Science Monitor* (September 22, 2010).

36. Ibid.

37. Damien McElroy and Christopher Williams, "Flame: World's Most Complex Computer Virus Exposed," *Telegraph* (May 29, 2012), accessed 29 May 2012 at http://www.telegraph.co.uk/news/worldnews/middleeast/iran/9295938/Flame-worlds-most-complex-computer-virus-exposed.html.

38. Ibid.

39. Leyden, "Flame Worm's Makers Fail to Collect Epic Ownage Award."

40. Figure created by the author from data provided by Kaspersky Lab, accessed 4 October 2012 at http://www.kaspersky.com/threats.

41. Kaspersky Lab, "Kaspersky Lab Discovers 'Gauss'—A New Complex Cyber-Threat Designed to Monitor Online Banking Accounts" (August 9, 2012), accessed 4 October 2012 at http://www.kaspersky.com/about/news/virus/2012/Kaspersky_Lab_and_ITU_Discover_Gauss_A_New_Complex_Cyber_Threat_Designed_to_Monitor_Online_Banking_Accounts.

42. Robert Gillette, "Sophisticated New Devices: KGB Eavesdropping Pervasive, Persistent," *Los Angeles Times* (April 13, 1987), accessed 21 September 2012 at http://articles.latimes.com/1987-04-13/news/mn-504_1_bugging-devices/3.

43. *Microsoft Security Intelligence Report,* Vol 12.

44. "U.S. Invokes Cold War Powers in Hunt for Chinese Telecom Spyware," *Bloomberg News* (November 30, 2011), accessed 21 September 2012 at http://business.financialpost.com/2011/11/30/u-s-invokes-cold-war-powers-in-hunt-for-chinese-telecom-spyware/.

45. Jeffrey R. Jones and Mark A. Thomas, "Cyber Espionage: What's the Big Deal?" *Defense Intelligence Journal,* Vol. 1, No. 1 (2009), 96.

46. Angela Moscaritolo, "Microsoft Finds Malware Pre-loaded on PCs in China," *PC Magazine* (September 14, 2012), accessed 16 September 2012 at http://www.pcmag.com/article2/0,2817,2409730,00. asp.

47. Jack Clark, "GCHQ to Take Hub Role in UK Cybersecurity," ZDNet UK (November 25, 2011), accessed 21 September 2012 at http://www.zdnet.co.uk/news/security/2011/11/25/gchq-to-take-hub-role-in-uk-cybersecurity-40094512/.

48. Nakashima, "A Cyber-Spy Is Halted, but Not a Debate."

49. Ibid.

50. Krekel, "Capability of the People's Republic of China to Conduct Cyber Warfare and Computer Network Exploitation."

51. See, e.g., Fred Brooks, *The Mythical Man-Month;* and Robert L. Glass, *Facts and Fallacies of Software Engineering* (Boston, MA: Addison-Wesley, 2002).

52. "War in the fifth domain."

53. Benjamin L. Cardin, "We're All at Risk from Cyber Attack," *Baltimore Sun* (December 15, 2010), accessed 21 September 2012 at http://articles.baltimoresun.com/2010-12-14/news/bs-ed-cybersecurity-20101214_1_cyber-criminals-cyber-crime-transnational-crime.

54. Ibid.

55. Shaun Waterman, "Surveillance Tools: Not Just for Spies Now," *Washington Times* (December 5, 2011), accessed 21 September 2012 at http://www.washingtontimes.com/news/2011/dec/5/surveillance-tools-not-just-for-spies-anymore/.

Cyber
Collection

6. Overview of Nonliteral Collection

Nonliteral collection, as explained in Chapter 1, describes types of technical intelligence that require specialized expertise in order to transform raw data into easily understandable information for customers. After collection, the intelligence must be processed to obtain a measurable signature or other information about the object. The processed information must be exploited. Finally, the results must be provided to the customer and retained for future use. Note that we sometimes collect a physical object and sometimes just measure the signature from an object or an area.

The organization of the chapters in Part II is intended to facilitate learning about the various types of nonliteral collection. This chapter introduces, in very general and nontechnical terms, the three parts of a technical collection *system;* that is, the function, process, and structure of the system, comparing and contrasting how they change from one technical stovepipe to another. Nonliteral collection relies heavily on sensors that reside on platforms (such as ships, satellites, and aircraft). Chapters 7 and 8 provide a general discussion of these sensors and platforms, primarily those used in remote sensing.

Chapters 9 through 17 go into more detail on individual collection systems, focusing on features that characterize that collection INT. The intent is for every reader to gain an appreciation and understanding of the intelligence potential of each INT. At the same time, the material in the sources and process sections of several of these chapters tends to be more technical and designed for those who want a bit deeper understanding of the topic. Part III, Chapter 18, shifts gears to discuss the management of all collection efforts (both literal and nonliteral) in an intelligence community of enormous complexity.

Function

Technical collection represents perhaps the largest asymmetric edge that technologically advanced countries such as the United States and its allies have in the intelligence business. Other countries can do as well or even better in the collection disciplines covered in Part I. Many countries do well in human intelligence (HUMINT), taking advantage of the relatively open societies in the United States and Europe. Most countries have similar access to open source collection—the openly available material that includes the Internet. Many countries collect communications intelligence (COMINT). And cyber collection is a cottage industry. But technical collection requires a sophisticated technological infrastructure. Increasingly, major powers are making the investment in satellite-based imaging systems, but most do not yet invest in the wide *range* of technical collection assets that the United States uses.[1]

Technical collection has three generic functions, all interrelated. It supports other functions, but these three are common to almost all the collection discussed in Part II.

SITUATIONAL AWARENESS

At all governmental levels, leaders need to be aware of developing international situations that affect the decisions they must make. Law enforcement officials and private sector executives have a similar need for intelligence that falls under the general heading of situational awareness. Military services have a name for it: they call it battlespace awareness. For a power with regional or global interests such as the United States or China, this includes monitoring activity on the earth's surface, undersea and underground, in the air, and in space.

Technical collection systems provide much situational awareness in the form of imagery, radar, and electronic intelligence. They provide intelligence on topics as diverse as terrain mapping; detecting movement and physical changes within a geographical area; illicit activity such as narcotics and gray arms shipments; threats posed by air, space, and ballistic missile systems; illegal immigration; and international trade activity. Battlefield commanders rely on technical collection to monitor the activity of friendly and hostile forces within the battlespace. Fleet commanders rely on it for monitoring activity on open oceans and in littoral areas. Law enforcement and immigration officials rely on it for monitoring all kinds of illicit traffic.

A major part of providing situational awareness is the indications and warning (I&W) function: Technical collection has provided warnings of imminent military actions, mass migrations, or disease outbreaks, for example.

LOCATING AND TRACKING A TARGET

On intelligence subjects as diverse as terrorism, narcotics traffic, weapons proliferation, and gray arms traffic, it often is important to identify a specific target (ship, aircraft, ground vehicle, or person) and track its movement or activities. Many of the technical collection systems discussed in Part II are capable of doing that. Using its signature, commanders can distinguish specific items of an opponent's military equipment on the battlefield for highly selective tracking of movement and for targeting. Signatures obtained via technical collection are used to identify and track nuclear, chemical, biological, and advanced conventional weapon systems.

CHARACTERIZING A TARGET

Characterizing the target can have many meanings. It can mean identifying people of intelligence interest and assessing their physical condition and behavior. It can mean assessing the significance of activities. It includes determining the purpose and output of a production plant and assessing an underground or unidentified structure. Collection techniques like multispectral thermal imaging (discussed in Chapter 10) provide valuable insights for identifying trace gaseous emissions, such as those produced by nuclear or chemical weapons whether in production, storage, or employment. Signatures are used to characterize environmental features that have intelligence value—including surface temperatures, water quality, material composition, and pollutants.[2]

Technical collection provides the details needed to assess weapons performance for dealing with issues like weapons proliferation, arms control, and treaty compliance. Collection can determine the dimensions and other features of an object such as a tank, missile, or warhead to help identify specific models or types.[3] Signatures collected before, during, and after a test event (for example a ballistic missile test or a nuclear detonation) are useful in interpreting the test results. Such collection relies on target identification from a safe distance based on target features that are difficult to conceal, such as rocket plumes and the biological or molecular composition of chemicals and biological agents. It is also valuable for overcoming an opponent's denial efforts (e.g., camouflage). Technical collection can render many modern concealment and camouflage methods ineffective.

Process

The generic technical collection process is shown in Figure 6.1 (which is another version of Chapter 1's Figure 1.4). It typically has a front end, where collection planning is done; followed by collection and a back end, where the collected material is turned into raw intelligence.

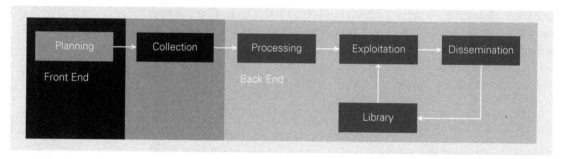

FIGURE 6.1 The Technical Collection Structure and Process

PLANNING

Many collectors refer to the step prior to collection as tasking or targeting. But tasking and targeting don't adequately describe what happens in every collection effort. Planning is a more general term, though even it doesn't fully describe the actions that are taken. The planning phase typically includes identifying requirements, analyzing the target(s), developing a collection strategy, and tasking specific collectors. The planning segment of the process is discussed in detail in Chapter 18 for all of collection, both literal and nonliteral, and includes the challenge of planning across collection INTS.

COLLECTION

Collection usually requires deploying equipment or applying existing assets against the targets of interest that were identified in the planning stage. Most technical collection makes use of remote sensing in some specific part of the electromagnetic (EM) spectrum. The spectrum is described in terms of frequency or wavelength and typically is thought of as having two parts: the radio frequency (RF) spectrum and the optical spectrum, which are discussed in Chapter 7.

But a number of important collection programs involve neither the EM spectrum nor remote sensing. Seismic sensing (Chapter 14) is an example of remote sensing that does not involve the EM spectrum. Many other types of sensing, such as acoustic sensing (Chapter 14), magnetic sensing (Chapter 15), and biometric sensing (Chapter 16) function only at short ranges. Materials sampling or physical acquisition is done in a few cases. Material samples are collected for detailed analysis, discussed in Chapter 15. An opponent's or competitor's equipment (materiel) may be acquired for exploitation, discussed in Chapter 17.

PROCESSING

The processing, exploitation, and analysis of literal intelligence discussed in Part I can be difficult and demanding. But, with the possible exception of cyber collection, customers can at least understand how it is done. That is not the case with much of nonliteral collection. Processing of the technical collection product borders on the arcane. In fact, the main difference between technical or nonliteral collection and the literal collection discussed in Part I lies in the processing and exploitation phases.

Processing of technical collection is about locating, identifying, or characterizing an object, person, or event of intelligence interest, usually by extracting a signature. Recall from Chapter 1 that signatures are created from the measurement of the strength, intensity, or state of some physical or chemical entity over space, time, and/or frequency. Measurements can be made, for example, of an object's dimensions, temperature, signal strength, or atmospheric pressure, all of which are physical quantities. For example, imagery of a tank, an aircraft, or a ship produces a signature: a characteristic shape, dimensions, and features that identify it. The sound of that tank, aircraft, or ship in operation creates another type of signature—an acoustic signature. Such signatures are used by today's smart weapons systems to detect and positively identify surface targets, sometimes even while a weapon is in flight.[4] But intelligence collection is needed beforehand to obtain the characteristic signature of the target.

The most numerous signatures that are collected in intelligence come from remote sensing, using sensors that operate in some part of the electromagnetic spectrum. Such sensors are introduced in Chapter 7, and specific details about them are addressed in Chapters 9 through 13.

A wide range of signatures that are collected from materials, from events, and from humans do not involve electromagnetic sensing. The collection, processing, and exploitation methods used are discussed in some detail in Chapters 14 and 15. Most such signature collection does not involve remote sensing (with one important exception, that of underwater and underground acoustic sensing). So non-EM signature collection typically is done at very short ranges.

Fingerprints, voiceprints, DNA, and facial features exemplify another type of signature; they all provide signatures that identify a specific person. A number of such signatures are used to identify persons and to track their movements. Fingerprints are signatures based on the intensity (darkness) of coloration in a two-dimensional space. They have been used for decades to identify individuals. More recently, techniques such as biometrics have been used for the same purpose. To identify individuals, forensic scientists measure the bonds in the 13 parts of the DNA molecule that vary from person to person and use the data to create a DNA profile of that individual (sometimes called a DNA fingerprint). There is a negligible chance that another person has the same DNA profile for these 13 DNA regions (except for cases such as identical twins).

Another type of signature is a chemical signature, which measures the presence (and often the quantity) of chemical compounds or elements in a sample. Nuclear and chemical measurements produce signatures that are used in treaty monitoring and weapons proliferation intelligence. Trace measurements of krypton-85, a radioactive gas, are a signature that plutonium-239 (a fissionable material used in nuclear weapons) is being produced at a facility. Traces of phosphorus oxychloride in an industrial effluent can be a signature that indicates chemical warfare agent production.

EXPLOITATION

Exploitation uses the signatures to identify patterns and establish the significance of the material that has been collected. It is often referred to as single-source analysis (though it may draw on many collateral sources). So we have imagery analysts and COMINT analysts, radar analysts and telemetry analysts, among others.

In order to be usable for intelligence purposes, as noted earlier, a signature must be associated with a person, place, object, or process. That is a key function performed during the exploitation phase. Often in intelligence, collectors want to locate a specific person, object, or event in space and time, and the signature is used for this purpose.

As discussed above, the processing phase of technical collection generally produces *signatures*. Exploitation and analysis, either of a single source or of several sources, generally identifies *patterns* that have intelligence significance. This is a simplistic view, and there are exceptions to it, but it is a useful starting point for discussing the process in the chapters that follow. It is worthwhile to distinguish between signatures and patterns, since the two concepts often overlap and the distinction can be subtle at times. To illustrate the difference between a signature and a pattern, consider an intelligence example of recent significance: the identification of Osama bin Laden's hiding place.

Figure 6.2 shows a drawing of the compound formerly occupied by Osama bin Laden in Abbottabad, Pakistan.[5] This drawing, and the image from which it was created, show a combination of signatures that are readily recognized. There are high privacy fences, a few buildings, gates, and communications satellite antennas, each of which has a distinct signature. But the layout of these features creates a pattern that has intelligence significance. The unusually high walls, many gates, and privacy measures indicate an excessive concern with security and an attempt to confuse and delay would-be invaders.

It can be difficult to distinguish the difference between a pattern and a signature, and there is a certain amount of overlap between the two in practice. But the Abbottabad example illustrates how things usually work

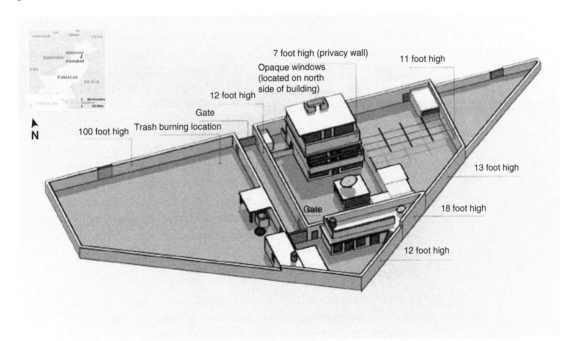

FIGURE 6.2 Osama bin Laden Compound in Abbottabad, Pakistan

out. The processing phase provided a number of signatures. An imagery analyst in the exploitation phase, familiar with how residential compounds in that region typically are laid out, could recognize the unusual pattern that the combined signatures produced.

Following are some additional examples to illustrate the difference between signatures and patterns in intelligence.

- A sniper killing of a victim in a public place, using a .223 caliber rifle, would constitute a signature. Repeated sniper attacks in public places using a .223 caliber rifle on randomly selected victims over a period of time would constitute a pattern of operations of a criminal—in law enforcement terms, a *modus operandi.* (This specific pattern will be familiar to some readers. It describes the Beltway sniper attacks that occurred in the Washington, D.C., metropolitan area during three weeks in October 2002.)
- A biological sample taken from dead chickens is found to contain a signature—that of the H5N1 (avian flu) virus. Subsequent medical sampling in the region discovers the presence of the virus in a number of humans in the region; *that* constitutes a pattern.
- The wake of a small boat traveling at high speed is a signature that can be detected visually or by radar, sometimes even when the craft itself cannot be detected. A series of those signatures, taken over time, creates a pattern of boat movement that can indicate something about the captain's intent. For example, it could be a movement pattern associated with illicit narcotics traffic.
- Chapter 4 contained a discussion of the unique COMINT signatures associated with cell phones and Wi-Fi devices that can be used to identify and track a person. The resulting details about the movement of that person constitute a pattern.

Signatures are usually the products of multiple measurements collected over time and under changing circumstances. They often reflect dynamic changes in a target or event. For example, the radar, infrared (IR), and acoustic characteristics of an aircraft in flight will change predictably as the attitude, power level, and flight configuration of the aircraft change. These signatures can be used to identify specific targets or events or discriminate among them when they are again encountered.

DISSEMINATION

The results of the exploitation are disseminated to users. Some dissemination is to all-source analysts, some to end-user customers, and some to single-source analysts in other collection stovepipes. As is true with literal intelligence, the classification of the material may limit dissemination and in some cases result in needed intelligence not getting to the end user. For very sensitive material, a number of techniques must be applied to protect the sources and methods during dissemination. Also, dissemination is quite different for the product of mass collection than for targeted or boutique intelligence. All these differences are discussed in the following chapters for specific INTs.

LIBRARIES

A major continuing task in technical intelligence is the maintenance of signature databases. Many collection systems can obtain signatures in real time (within seconds). But detecting a signature is insufficient; one needs to be able to identify that signature and usually to associate it with a person, object, event, or location.[6] Technical collection has very limited value unless one can associate the signatures or patterns with a specific person, type of activity, or class of objects.

The database that permits this association has a specific name, as illustrated in Figure 6.1. It is called a library, and a great many of them exist in the world of technical collection. In contrast to most Part I collection, a signature or pattern library usually is an essential part of the process.

When a new signature is identified, a library allows it to be associated with a specific person, phenomenon, object, or class of objects. During the exploitation phase, existing libraries are searched to identify the signature. After the processing and exploitation phases, the newly collected signature may be added to the existing library as part of the dissemination step. The result creates signatures that are stored in a library, usually to be retrieved in another round of exploitation on another day. This is a well-established process: The FBI's fingerprint library has operated this way for more than a century.

For a technical collection system to make rapid and accurate identification on the battlefield, these libraries have to be current, readily available, and easily searched.[7] Signature identification often must be performed in real or near real time, particularly to support tactical operations. And the libraries have to provide the signatures at the needed level of fidelity. This is a continuing challenge, and it's not getting easier as collection technology advances. Many existing signature databases are out of date, since they contain data recorded by older, much lower fidelity sensors.

Structure

Chapter 1 described the structure of intelligence collection at the national level. The structural breakout shown in Figure 1.5 is a fairly common one among national governments. The United Kingdom, France, Russia, and several other countries all have a similar top-level division, usually placing technical collection organizations within their military departments (as the United States does).

But within any large collection organization focused on a specific INT, subordinate structures are needed to support collection from a specific source or class of sources. Within a national-level imagery intelligence (IMINT) organization, for example, there typically will be subunits that collect and process only visible optical imagery; or only spectral imagery; or only radar imagery. The usual pattern is the stovepipe that was discussed in the Preface and that is structured to follow the process shown in Figure 6.1.

So, the nature of the process shapes the structure. But the customers and the sources shape it as well. Chapter 1 discussed the difference between mass collection and boutique collection. The specific structural design used in technical collection usually depends on whether the collection is mass or boutique. A mass collection system that supports many customers has to be automated as much as possible, especially when the intelligence produced is time-critical. Boutique collection typically is aimed at specific targets; it usually requires more up-front planning, and the processing and exploitation are usually more time-consuming, labor-intensive, and expensive. The structure, again, reflects that difference. It determines, for example, where to locate the processing, exploitation, and dissemination systems. Where time is critical, these assets may be located on board a ship, in an aircraft, or on the ground close to the battlefield. Where special processing and exploitation expertise is required and timeliness is not so critical, they are located centrally, often far from the point of collection. Collection results that are to be widely disseminated also tend to be processed centrally if timeliness is not a factor.

Prior to the Cold War, very little use was made of technical collection by national-level customers. Military aircraft conducted photo and electronic intelligence (ELINT) reconnaissance flights to support military operations in the theater. That all changed in the United States when a need arose for detailed knowledge of strategic targets located in the Soviet Union and the People's Republic of China. Coverage of these targets initially was provided by U-2s operated by the Central Intelligence Agency (CIA), and the processing and exploitation was handled centrally. That led to a central U.S. organization to handle strategic imagery. Later, the need to support strategic planning and treaty monitoring drove the centralization of other technical collection, processing, and exploitation programs that are discussed in Part II. Strategic intelligence to support a broad range of topics—weapons acquisition, treaty monitoring, warning of disease outbreaks, and energy shortages—all these, and many more, became important in the last half of the 20th century.

Concern for protecting sources and methods can shape structure and vice versa. Clandestine technical intelligence operations tend to more closely resemble sensitive HUMINT and COMINT. National-level customers typically want to protect the competitive advantage that intelligence gives them, so centralized processing and exploitation are combined with limited dissemination of clandestine technical intelligence. In contrast, tactical military ELINT and IMINT usually require little protection and must be disseminated quickly to a large set of customers, so they rely on a decentralized structure. Law enforcement in the United States already has a highly decentralized structure. Because intelligence has to be shared among a number of agencies at the national, state, and local levels, these agencies of necessity take a more flexible approach to sources and methods.

Summary

Technical or nonliteral collection finds wide uses in intelligence. It is used, among other things, to identify and track persons and vehicles, assess industrial processes, monitor treaty compliance, target smart weapons, defeat camouflage, and interpret weapons test results. Technical collection can be described as having three generic functions, all interrelated, though it supports other functions as well:

- *Situational awareness,* that is, the knowledge of developing situations that affect national, law enforcement, or commercial leaders' decision making. Military organizations call it battlespace awareness. It includes indications and warning.
- *Locating and tracking a target,* which becomes important in countering terrorist and criminal activities and illicit weapons of mass destruction (WMD) or gray arms traffic.
- *Characterizing a target,* for example, identifying and assessing people, activities, weaponry, industrial plants, and underground facilities.

The major steps in the process are shown in Figure 6.1, which also describes the way collection is structured: It is a linear process.

To repeat Michael Herman's comment from the Introduction, technical (nonliteral) intelligence is about "observations and measurements of things" that have intelligence significance. The process to do that begins with planning collection against specific targets of intelligence interest. A collection strategy, discussed in Chapter 18, is needed. Then comes collection—applying the available collection assets against the targets. Most nonliteral collection is done by sensors operating in some part of the EM spectrum, but some valuable intelligence is collected by non-EM sensors or by physical access. In fact, a wide range of signatures are collected from materials, equipment, processes, and humans but do not involve EM sensing. Technical collection, for example, is used to obtain acoustic, nuclear, chemical, biological, and biometric signatures.

The processing and exploitation of collected material mostly involves identifying a signature or pattern, tying it to a specific target, associating it with other targets and events, and monitoring target movements. Most technical collection, then, requires obtaining and analyzing nonliteral information in the form of signatures. A signature is created by measuring the strength, intensity, or state of some physical or chemical entity, over space, time, frequency, or all three.

The analysis of signatures often results in the identification of a pattern that has intelligence value. In order to be useful for intelligence, the signature also has to be associated with a person, object, or process. This includes locating the signature (and therefore the person, object, or process) in space and time. The result of that process is disseminated as raw intelligence, to eventually be incorporated into all-source intelligence.

An essential component of technical collection is the signature library that associates signatures with a specific person, object, or process. Increasingly, these signatures need to be accessed by military and law enforcement operational units in real time.

The structure of technical collection units is shaped by the nature of the sources and customers (mass collection, with many targets and many customers, has to rely on automated systems for the back end; boutique collection with few sources and a select customer set tends to have a more deliberate, time-intensive, and expensive back end). A need to protect sources and methods forces a more centralized and stovepiped structure.

NOTES

1. Mark M. Lowenthal, *Intelligence: From Secrets to Policy,* 4th ed. (Washington, DC: CQ Press, 2009), 69–73, 90–101.
2. J. J. Szymanski and P. G. Weber, "Multispectral Thermal Imager: Mission and Applications Overview," *IEEE Transactions on Geoscience and Remote Sensing,* Vol. 43, No. 9 (September 2005), 1943–1949; Jeffrey L. Hylden, "Remote Sensing of Chemical Plumes (17)," Pacific Northwest National Laboratory, April 2001, www.technet.pnl.gov/sensors/macro/projects/es4remchem.html.

3. John L. Morris, "The Nature and Applications of Measurement and Signature Intelligence," *American Intelligence Journal,* Vol. 19, No. 3 & 4 (1999–2000), 81–84.

4. Don Atkins and George Crawford, "Reprogramming Brilliant Weapons: A New Role for MASINT," *American Intelligence Journal,* Vol. 17, No. 3 & 4 (1997), 45–46.

5. U.S. Department of Defense public domain image, acquired 26 September 2012 at https://www.google.com/search?q=U.S.+Department+of+Defense+drawing+of+bin+Laden's+compound+in+Abbottabad,+Pakistan&hl=en&prmd=imvns&tbm=isch&tbo=u&source=univ&sa=X&ei=MUBjUOfeM02E9QTr40HwCg&ved=0CC8QsAQ&biw=936&bih=800.

6. Zachary Lum, "The Measure of MASINT," *Journal of Electronic Defense* (August 1998), 43.

7. Steven M. Bergman, "The Utility of Hyperspectral Data to Detect and Discriminate Actual and Decoy Target Vehicles," Naval Postgraduate School, Monterey, CA (December 1996), xiii–xv.

7. Collection Sensors

Much of nonliteral intelligence collection is done by sensors. The bulk of such collection is done by electromagnetic (EM) sensors, which are covered in detail in Chapters 9 through 13. Acoustic sensors are discussed in Chapter 14, and nuclear radiation sensors in Chapter 15. One area of literal collection—radio frequency communications intelligence (RF COMINT)—is also done by sensors, as discussed in Chapter 4. In order to fully understand these later chapters, you need this introductory overview of sensors.

First, there's nothing mysterious about sensors. We all come equipped with four very important ones. Our eyes are very sensitive to a specific frequency band (known as the visible band) in the optical part of the electromagnetic spectrum. Our ears are sensitive to sounds in a specific band of the acoustic spectrum. We have used our eyes and ears to collect intelligence since before the time of recorded history. Over the years, inventors have created a number of electromagnetic and acoustic sensors to aid our eyes and ears as intelligence collectors. One of the earliest such devices was the telescope, used for intelligence collection during the 1600s. (There is a reason that the original telescope was called a "spy-glass.") Today we have a rich set of sensors that support intelligence collection.

Second, all sensors collect signatures that are used to identify or classify targets of intelligence interest. Continuing the simplistic example above, our senses collect and recognize a very large set of signatures. Our ears, for example, easily distinguish the opening four notes of Beethoven's 5th Symphony from the opening notes of a Beatles song. The acoustic signatures are quite different.

Most sensors receive and process energy from some part of either the electromagnetic or the acoustic spectrum. All of the sensors used to collect intelligence have these things in common with our eyes and ears:

- They have a definite region of *coverage*.
- Within that region of coverage, they have some level of *resolution* that allows them to distinguish targets of interest.

The performance of any sensor, and its value in intelligence, is determined by its coverage and resolution in four performance categories:

1. Spatial
2. Spectral
3. Intensity
4. Temporal

We'll come back to these in a moment. In the meanwhile, we usually characterize sensors in two ways: by their mode of operation (either active or passive) and by their effective range. (Some can function at great distances from their targets; others operate only at very short ranges.) Before going further, let's look at both characteristics in detail.

ACTIVE VERSUS PASSIVE SENSORS

Sensors divide into two general classes: active and passive. Our eyes and ears are passive sensors; they receive only. Bats and dolphins have active sensors—they rely on transmitting sound and receiving the reflected sound to locate targets.

Active sensors such as radars and active sonars transmit a signal and then interpret the signals that are reflected off the target. Passive sensors exploit natural emissions or man-made signals or use an alternative illumination source, such as the sun. Most passive sensors operate in the microwave or optical bands. Each class and frequency band has unique advantages and disadvantages. And each class encompasses several specific sensor types, each of which has advantages and disadvantages.

REMOTE VERSUS CLOSE-IN SENSING

Some sensors used in intelligence can operate at very long ranges, and their use is called remote sensing. Others are designed to function in the immediate vicinity of their targets, and their use is often referred to as close-in sensing. One might think that our natural senses function only close-in, but we can hear the sound of thunder from a lightning strike many miles away, and we can view objects in the night sky that are many light-years away.

Remote sensing is important in intelligence because EM waves can be collected at great distances, depending on such factors as the strength of the signal, the noise entering the sensor, and the sensor's sensitivity. When mounted on satellites or aircraft, EM sensors can obtain information about the earth's surface or activity on or near the earth's surface at very long ranges. A great deal of this remote sensing is done for civil applications—environmental and resource management studies, weather forecasting, and so forth. In intelligence, remote sensing from air or space focuses on mapping the earth, characterizing objects on it, and locating and tracking the movement of man-made objects. It also includes the reverse—observing the movement of airborne or spaceborne objects (aircraft, ballistic missiles, or satellites) from the earth's surface.

But EM waves also can be sensed well at short distances. At short ranges, EM sensors find many intelligence uses because they can sense very weak signals, including unintentional emissions. The challenge often is to get the sensor into close proximity without being discovered.

Most acoustic sensors, and all nuclear radiation sensors, function only at very short ranges. But acoustic signals can be sensed at remote distances under certain conditions. For example, some acoustic signals can travel through the earth or water and be sensed at distances of hundreds or even thousands of kilometers. These signals also can have intelligence value, and they are discussed in Chapter 14.

Performance Categories of Electromagnetic Sensors

The remainder of this chapter and the next few focus on EM sensing. We'll start by looking at the four sensor performance categories noted earlier—spatial, spectral, intensity, and temporal.

SPATIAL SENSING

Spatial sensing allows us to locate an object and, by spatial measurements of its size and shape, to identify specific objects. Our eyes do this routinely, locating and identifying objects and people in our immediate vicinity.

Collection Sensors

Cameras produce an image that permits an imagery interpreter to identify objects of intelligence interest and to measure the objects' dimensions—provided that the interpreter knows the scale of the image. The original film cameras have been replaced by **electro-optical (EO) imagers**, which are discussed in Chapter 9. The EO imagers used in intelligence are basically sophisticated versions of the digital cameras now widely available. EO imagers and **synthetic aperture radars (SARs)**, discussed in Chapter 12, can both geolocate objects and measure their dimensions.

Coverage. All sensors are able to look at a defined volume of space. Radio frequency sensors have a defined beamwidth. Optical sensors have a defined field of view. Beamwidth or field of view is determined by the size of the aperture and by the frequency of the transmitted or received signal. The antenna in a cell phone has extremely broad beamwidth, because the tower signal can come from any direction. But a dish antenna used to receive satellite TV has a relatively narrow beamwidth and must be aimed exactly at the broadcast satellite. Our eyes have a fairly wide field of view. A telescope has a much larger aperture than our eyes, giving it a relatively narrow field of view.

It is especially desirable in imaging to obtain spatial coverage over a wide area, and there are two ways to do this. The first approach is to image one small area at a time, and so over time to build up a complete picture of a large region. The second approach is to image the entire region nearly simultaneously. The latter method is very difficult to do, but it has special value in intelligence, and imagery analysts call it **synoptic coverage**.

Resolution. The ability of a sensor to separate two objects spatially is known as **spatial resolution**. Our vision allows us to identify a person by facial recognition at close range. At some distance, the face becomes blurred. Our eyes no longer can resolve enough features to identify the person.

Resolution is measured differently depending on whether or not the sensor is obtaining an image. The term **resolution cell** is used to define spatial resolution in all forms of imagery and in radar, but the meaning in imagery is somewhat different than the meaning in radar. The basic meaning, in all cases, is this: two separate targets located in the same resolution cell cannot be told apart.

• Radar conducts measurements in three dimensions. Conventional nonimaging radar is used to locate a target in a volume of space, so the term **radar resolution cell** is used. Such a cell has two parts: angular resolution (which describes the limit on a radar's ability to distinguish targets in azimuth and elevation) and range resolution (which describes the limit on ability to distinguish targets in distance from the radar). The resulting radar resolution cell is therefore a volume of space.

- In imagery, whether optical, radiometric, or radar, the resolution cell refers to the size of the target area that corresponds to a single pixel in an image. Stated another way, spatial resolution is a means of specifying the ability to visually resolve objects in the scene. The length of one side of a resolution cell is called the **ground sample distance (GSD)** in earth imaging. For an image having a 2-meter GSD, a resolution cell in the image is 2 meters square. The greater the GSD or the size of the resolution cell, the poorer the spatial resolution and the more difficult it becomes to resolve and recognize objects on the ground. Good spatial resolution—the ability of the sensor to distinguish small objects—allows the identification of specific vehicles, for example. With poor resolution, the objects are blurred or indistinguishable.

Images where only large features are visible are said to have coarse or low resolution. In fine or high-resolution images, small objects can be detected. Intelligence sensors, for example, are designed to view as much detail as possible and therefore have very fine spatial resolution. Commercial satellites provide imagery with resolutions varying from less than 1 meter up to several kilometers.

The accuracy with which a sensor can resolve a target's location becomes important when the target is to be attacked by precision weaponry. In general, optical imagery provides the most accurate location of a target because the location of known objects in the image can be used to estimate the location of a target. The location of the imaging platform when the image is taken can be important for obtaining spatial accuracy, and the global positioning system (GPS) is used extensively to determine the exact location of sensor platforms. The French SPOT imaging satellite, for example, has a spatial accuracy on the order of 30 meters.[1] Spatial accuracy is harder to achieve in signals intelligence (SIGINT), where the term **geolocation accuracy** is used to describe the sensor's performance.

Spatial measurement accuracy is also important in identifying the visual signatures of objects. A given missile, for example, has a unique set of dimensions at some level of measurement accuracy. If a sensor can only measure those dimensions to within 1 meter, then it is unlikely that the missile signature can be uniquely identified. A sensor that can measure those dimensions to within a millimeter is likely to come up with a unique signature that will distinguish it from all other missiles of the same type.

Collection
Sensors

SPECTRAL SENSING

Before going into the characteristics of spectral sensing, let's briefly look at the two major parts of the EM spectrum in which these sensors function—the RF and optical spectrums.

The RF Spectrum. Figure 7.1 shows the part of the radio frequency spectrum that is used for remote sensing in intelligence. The RF spectrum continues into lower frequencies (off the left side of the figure), but intelligence collectors are primarily concerned with the part of the spectrum shown here. Note that the spectrum is divided into named bands; these will be discussed in later chapters. The spectrum also continues upward in frequency (to the right), but the continuation is the optical spectrum, discussed next.

Signatures are collected in the RF spectrum in two ways: by passive sensors that collect RF energy *emitted by* the target and by active or passive sensors

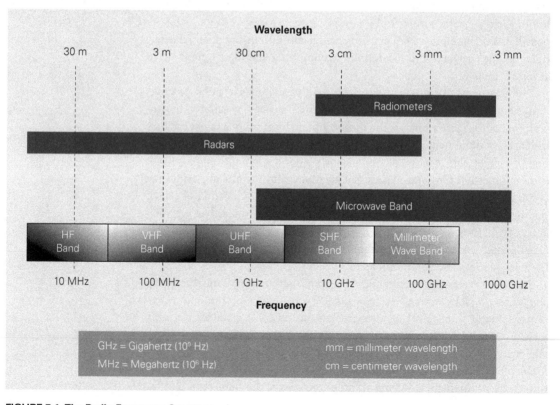

FIGURE 7.1 The Radio Frequency Spectrum

that collect RF energy *reflected from* the target. Passive RF sensors collect a wide range of natural and man-made emissions, including

- intentional emissions, such as communications and radar signals;
- RF emissions incidental to human activity, such as auto ignition noise;
- natural emissions, such as lightning discharges (which are not usually of intelligence interest, being basically noise); and
- thermally generated emissions (which also are noise, but are used in imaging).

Most of the reflected RF energy collection is done by radars, which transmit in fairly narrow bands within the RF spectrum. Radars are discussed in Chapters 11 and 12. In a few cases, reflected RF collection is done without a radar transmitter, and these special cases are discussed in Chapter 13.

The Optical Spectrum. Figure 7.2 is a continuation of the spectrum from Figure 7.1 to higher frequencies (shorter wavelengths). This part of the EM spectrum is called the optical spectrum; the sensors used here are fundamentally different from those used in the RF spectrum.

In the optical spectrum, it is customary to refer to a part of the spectrum by wavelength (usually in micrometers, commonly called *microns* and abbreviated μm) rather than by frequency; the frequency numbers are so large as to be cumbersome and are described in terms that are difficult to comprehend, such as terahertz and pentahertz.

The optical spectrum is represented in Figure 7.2 as being composed of energy bands, each having its own name or designation. The band boundaries shown in the figure are commonly used, but there is no accepted standard either for the number of bands or for their boundaries. Astronomers, for example, divide the infrared band into three very broad bands (near, mid, and far infrared) extending from 0.7 to 350 microns.[2] The definitions shown in Figure 7.2 are used throughout this book, since they are most convenient for discussing intelligence applications.

Typically, optical sensing for intelligence purposes makes use of energy in a wavelength range from the ultraviolet to the infrared portions of the electromagnetic spectrum. Most optical sensors function in some specific band within this region from the ultraviolet through the long wavelength infrared (LWIR). Note that the visible part of the spectrum, extending from about 0.4 μm to about 0.75 μm where the eye and most sensors function, occupies only a small fraction of the overall optical spectrum.

As Figure 7.2 indicates, the optical spectrum also is divided into two regions based on the nature of the signature obtained. Within these two regions are specific bands that have distinct signature characteristics.

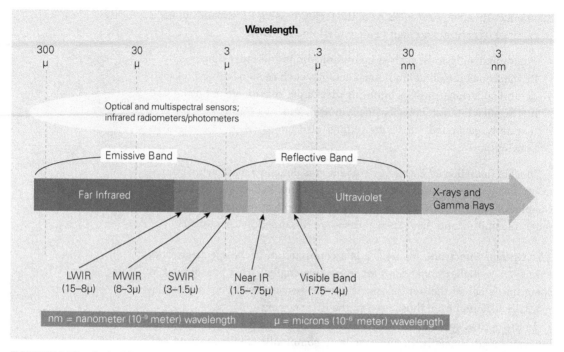

FIGURE 7.2 The Optical Spectrum

- The **reflective band** comprises the ultraviolet (UV), visible, near-infrared (NIR), and short wavelength infrared (SWIR) bands. These bands are called reflective because sensors operating in them normally work in daytime only, sensing energy reflected from the sun. The NIR and SWIR bands are therefore known as the reflected infrared bands because they rely on the infrared part of the solar radiation reflected by the earth's surface. Some night vision goggles operate in the NIR band using an IR illuminator. Though the NIR band is called reflective, there also are important emissions in this band that have intelligence significance. For example, sensors in the NIR band can detect rocket plumes, ship lights, or factory lights at night to signal that the factory is operating.

- The **emissive band** extends from mid-wavelength infrared (MWIR) through LWIR into the far IR band. In contrast to the reflective band, sensors in this band do not depend directly on the sun's illumination. Within the emissive band, the MWIR and LWIR bands are often called the thermal infrared bands. Sensors in this band depend on the fact that all objects above absolute zero emit energy somewhere in the emissive band; the hotter the object, the more energy emitted and the shorter the wavelength.

Coverage. All sensors cover a defined part of the EM spectrum. RF sensors have a defined bandwidth. Optical sensors have a defined spectral coverage. The sensor has not been designed that can cover the entire electromagnetic spectrum. Radio receivers are used in the RF band to detect radio waves; detectors are used in the optical band. As one moves upward in the RF band, different receiver types and antennas are needed. As one moves across the optical band, different detector types are required. It's all EM energy, but the energy behaves differently and must be detected differently. Our eyes, for example, are limited to seeing in the visible spectrum. A reindeer's eyes can see in the ultraviolet spectrum, something human eyes cannot do.

Resolution. The ability of a sensor to distinguish among energies of varying frequencies or wavelengths emitted by or reflected from a target is known as **spectral resolution**. The amount of information that can be derived from a sensor increases as a function of spectral resolution, as does the level of information available to the collector. High spectral resolution is important for intelligence purposes in both the RF and optical bands.

In the visible spectrum, panchromatic (black-and-white) imagery allows one to simply detect objects. As images of the same scene are added from different parts of the spectrum—for example, red, green, blue, and near IR— the analyst can make more detailed assessments of the object. Adding still more images of the scene from the IR spectrum allows greatly detailed assessments—for example, identification of a specific gas being discharged from a smokestack.

The simplest type of spectral sensing device is a **spectroscope**, an optical device that splits incoming light according to its wavelength. A prism is the simplest type of spectroscope. A **spectrometer** is a spectroscope that also measures the intensity of light over different wavelengths in the electromagnetic spectrum (from gamma rays and X-rays into the far infrared). It typically is used in intelligence to identify materials (for example, chemical effluents or factory emissions). Imaging spectrometers are the most useful type in intelligence because they obtain an image of an area while measuring the spectral characteristics of each object in the image. Chapter 10 discusses the collection of intelligence using imaging spectrometers.

Spectral resolution in the RF band is called **frequency resolution**. It allows a passive sensor such as an electronic intelligence (ELINT) sensor (discussed in Chapter 13) to distinguish among possible emitters of a signal—to identify a certain type of radar system, for example. Higher frequency resolution might allow the same ELINT sensor to identify the specific transmitter. A radar receiver with high spectral resolution can determine the movement of a target by measuring the Doppler effect.[3] Within the RF band, the device used to obtain spectral resolution is called a **spectrum analyzer**.

Spectral accuracy—the measure of the accuracy with which a sensor can determine the frequency or wavelength of a signal—is important in SIGINT and in spectral and radar imaging. Fine grain measurements of the signal spectrum are used to identify specific emitters, discussed in Chapter 13. In optical sensing, spectral accuracy determines, for example, whether a chemical compound can be identified. Some types of spectral imaging that are discussed in Chapter 10 provide such accuracy; some don't.

INTENSITY SENSING

Measurements can be taken of the intensity of energy received (called a radiometric measurement). All electromagnetic signals must have some minimum level of intensity in order for a sensor to detect the signal; this is known as a detection threshold. But not all sensors measure the intensity of the signal. Following are some that do.

Radiometers are passive sensors that receive, record, and measure the intensity of electromagnetic energy that is emitted from objects. The term is commonly used to refer to sensors in the microwave and millimeter wave bands, but it also is used to refer to infrared sensors. Optical radiometers are also called **photometers**. A photometer measures the intensity of incoming light in some part of the optical spectrum. An **imaging radiometer** obtains both the spatial and intensity signatures of an object. It forms, in effect, a radiometric map. Imaging radiometers operate mostly in the thermal IR and microwave bands.

Radar is an acronym, derived from the term Radio Detection And Ranging. Radar systems are active sensors that provide their own source of electromagnetic energy. Most radars emit microwave radiation in a series of pulses from an antenna, while the antenna moves its main beam to search a volume of space. When the energy reaches a target, some of the energy is reflected back toward the sensor. This backscattered microwave radiation is detected, measured, and timed. The time required for the energy to travel to the target and return to the sensor determines the distance or range to the target. A radar therefore obtains both spatial and intensity signatures—spatial, by measuring the round-trip travel time for a pulse and the direction in which the radar antenna's main beam was pointing when the pulse was transmitted; intensity, by measuring the strength of the returned signal.

Because radar provides its own energy source, it can produce images day or night. Microwave radar is able to penetrate through clouds and most rain, making it an all-weather sensor. Radars also operate in the millimeter wave bands and in the optical bands using lasers as the transmitters, but weather adversely affects these bands.

Coverage. All sensors have a range of intensity that they can receive; the range is defined by two thresholds. The lower threshold is a point below which incoming EM energy is considered noise and above which it is considered a signal. An incoming signal that is too weak falls below this threshold and cannot be detected, like a weak radio station that is overwhelmed by static. The upper threshold is the point where the signal is too strong, so that it saturates the receiver or, at some level of intensity, burns it out. The operating range of intensity for a sensor lies between these two extremes of detectability and saturation and is called the sensor's **dynamic range**. The idea of dynamic range is familiar to anyone who has listened to a cheap audio system. If the volume control is set too low, the very soft notes of music disappear; if the volume control is set too high, the loud sounds become distorted. Our eyes have a dynamic range as well. As the available light level decreases, we lose first the ability to see colors; finally we lose the ability to see anything at all. At the opposite extreme, vision can be overwhelmed by very intense light, and again we lose the ability to see.

For intelligence collection, the lower detection threshold needs to be as low as possible because signals are often very weak, for two reasons. First, the sensor often must be located far from the signal source. Second, even when the sensor can be located close to the source, the signals themselves are often very weak. The limitation on lowering a sensor's lower threshold is noise from external or internal sources. As the threshold is lowered, more and more noise spikes or interfering signals appear above the threshold and are mistaken for the desired signal. These spikes are referred to as false alarms. As an example, an optical sensor could in theory detect a single photon—the smallest possible quantity of light—from a target of interest. But the sensor would also detect a large number of photons from objects near the target, and noise within the sensor itself would make it almost impossible to identify the one photon coming from the target.

Depending on the application, threshold can be lowered to allow more of these false alarms, known also as false positives—noise that is mistaken for a desired signal. Alternatively, if the threshold is raised, the risk increases of getting more false negatives—desired signals that are discarded as noise. There are several techniques for lowering the threshold (reducing the false negatives) while not increasing the false positives. One is to use several sensors simultaneously and compare the received signals. Another is to use one sensor but to repeatedly collect the signal over time to eliminate false positives.

Resolution. Often called **radiometric resolution**, intensity resolution is a measure of the difference in signal intensity that can be detected and recorded by a sensor. The finer the radiometric resolution of a sensor, the more sensitive it is to detecting small differences in reflected or emitted energy. A sensor with a high radiometric resolution will recognize very subtle variations in energy at a given frequency or wavelength, such as the difference between two types of trees or the presence of camouflage in an image.

The degree to which a sensor can resolve differences in intensity is important in determining the power output of a source. An infrared sensor can detect the emissions of hot gases from a power plant. But the temperature of the emissions, derived from the intensity measurements of the IR signal, can indicate how much power the plant is generating. In ELINT, the strength of the signal collected from a radar can be used to determine the radar's output power. In radar, the strength of a radar return can be used to tell something about the target. A large metal target such as a Boeing 747 typically will have a strong return signal; at the same range, a small remotely piloted vehicle made of plastic and fabric will have a very weak return signal.

TEMPORAL SENSING

Most sensors collect signatures over a period of time, and intelligence is very much concerned with the changes in those signatures over time. Changes in the spatial measurement of an object often indicate target motion; changes in the spectral or intensity measurements usually result from target activity, and specific changes may constitute a signature that indicates a certain type of activity. For example:

• When a nuclear reactor is operating, the heat causes a shift to higher frequencies in the infrared spectrum of energy emitted from the reactor building, and the intensity of infrared radiation increases as well.

• When a radar changes operating modes, the change often is observed as a change in the spectral signature (a frequency or bandwidth change) or as a change in signal intensity.

Measurements in the time dimension allow **change detection**, a key concept that is revisited in several later chapters. Change detection is a powerful tool in intelligence. Increases in thermal infrared emissions from aircraft engines indicate that the aircraft has recently been in operation; similar increases from ships tell us that the ship is about to get under way.[4] Road and surface building construction, changes in rock and soil composition, and excavations all can be observed as changes in imagery over time. Digital processing of successive images can subtract the features that have not changed between images, allowing an imagery analyst to identify the features that have changed.[5] Radar offers even more sensitive means for observing small changes and is discussed in Chapter 12.

Coverage. In intelligence, the ultimate wish would be to have **surveillance**, defined as the continuous or near-continuous observation of a target area. For many sensors and the platforms that carry them, currently the best that can be obtained is **reconnaissance**, defined as periodic observation. The choice between the two usually involves trade-offs in other types of coverage or in resolution, which is discussed next. For example:

- An emplaced sensor, such as a surveillance camera focused on a street, can provide continuous coverage (assuming some illumination source at night and excluding times when vision is blocked by fog). But such a camera can only cover a very small geographical area.
- An aircraft can provide continuous coverage of a much larger area but only for a relatively short time by loitering; it eventually must return to base for refueling.
- A low earth orbit satellite, discussed in the next chapter, can observe an even larger area, but it can only cover a given spot on earth for about 8 to 10 minutes. It can only do reconnaissance, not surveillance. Also, because its sensor is typically farther from the target than the aircraft sensor, its resolution suffers by comparison.
- A geostationary satellite, also discussed in the next chapter, can provide surveillance of a large area of earth, but its distance from earth lessens the ability of its sensors to detect weak signals.

Resolution. Resolution refers to measuring the span of time between collection events, and it can have different meanings. It can refer to the time that elapses before a collection asset can sense a target for a second time (often called the **revisit time**).

- A video camera offers good temporal resolution; it constantly refreshes the scene it views, so it revisits a scene many times per second. In effect, it conducts surveillance of an area.
- An RF receiver used in SIGINT tunes rapidly through a band, often revisiting a particular frequency several times per second. The antenna,

however, may have to be aimed at a different volume of space periodically to cover other targets of interest.

- An air or space search radar scans through a specific region of space as slowly as once every 10 seconds and as rapidly as several times per second.
- A typical imaging satellite at low altitude might circle the earth 14 to 16 times a day. Its temporal resolution, or revisit time, would be about 90 minutes—the length of time before it can again look at a particular target.

Temporal resolution also can refer to separating two closely spaced events in a signature. Our eyes, for example, have an upper limit on temporal resolution. A video display refreshes itself about 60 times per second (60 Hz). Because our eyes can't resolve separate images at that rate, the pictures flow smoothly together. At around 15 Hz, our eyes can detect separate images, and we perceive a jerky motion in the display.

A radar signature can change very rapidly as the radar changes operating modes. An ELINT receiver that is monitoring the radar must be able to detect these changes. An optical sensor that monitors for nuclear blast detection must be able to identify the unique pattern of two light bursts in rapid succession that characterizes a nuclear burst.

The measurement accuracy of a signal's arrival time at a sensor is known as temporal accuracy, which is important in obtaining spatial accuracy. For images taken from an aircraft or satellite, the timing of the image is important because the platform is moving constantly. Timing the imaging event to within a second is adequate for many purposes. In contrast, for systems that receive radio frequency signals (for example, for radar and ELINT), the timing must be far more accurate and measured to a high level of precision. Timing the arrival of a signal is critical in geolocating the source. A radar measures range by accurately and precisely determining the time between transmitting a pulse and receiving an echo from the target. As discussed in Chapter 13, geolocating an emitter depends on accurately and precisely measuring the arrival time of the signal at different points. The GPS, in addition to geolocating a platform, provides a timing reference that intelligence sensors can use to precisely determine the time when an image is taken or a signal arrives.

Trade-Offs in Sensor Design and Usage

A perfect sensor would look in all directions continuously, across the entire spectrum, with no limit on its resolution or sensitivity. All its measurements, moreover, would be accurate. Stated another way, it would have perfect spatial, spectral, intensity, and temporal coverage and would resolve all of these to any desired level of detail and desired degree of accuracy.

Of course, such a sensor does not exist. All sensors are the result of compromises. This section discusses the performance characteristics that have to be traded off, with some of the major trade-offs discussed in the following section.

RESOLUTION VERSUS COVERAGE TRADE-OFFS

When we began to use telescopes some 400 years ago, we quickly discovered a limitation of that sensor: it gives substantially better resolution on objects, but your field of view shrinks accordingly. The better the resolution, the worse the spatial coverage. We've had to deal with that trade-off in sensors ever since.

Intelligence collectors want to obtain the greatest possible coverage—spectral, spatial, radiometric/intensity, and temporal—with the highest possible resolution from their sensors:

- Coverage allows them to collect as many target signatures as possible, not missing important ones.
- Resolution allows them to better discriminate between similar signatures that come from different targets.

So, global synoptic coverage with high resolution is desired in all four performance categories. The trend is for improvements to occur in all these categories as technology advances. However, at any given level of technology, improvements in one category usually come at a cost in some other category. Consequently, all sensor designs are compromises.

The main choice, though, is usually between resolution (spatial, spectral, intensity, or temporal) and coverage. Imaging sensors can cover a large area of the earth quickly. They can do this because they can have a very wide swath width, allowing the sensor to search a wide area in one pass. But in doing so, they must choose between swath width and spatial resolution. Generally speaking, the finer the resolution, the less total ground area can be seen. Good resolution is essential for detecting observables on the surface. However, sensors that have wide swath widths generally have poor spatial resolution, and sensors with good resolution usually have small swath widths. As an example, a NOAA-18 weather satellite sensor covers a large swath of the earth (more than 1,500 km across), but its best resolution is on the order of 15 km—sufficient for obtaining global temperature maps but not useful for most intelligence purposes. In comparison, current imaging satellites, such as France's SPOT and Israel's Ofeq satellites, have swath widths measured in a few kilometers but with spatial resolution on the order of 1 meter.[6]

Similar constraints and concessions exist for passive RF sensors. A larger antenna aperture allows the RF sensor more sensitivity and also permits it to better separate objects in space. But the result is a narrower beamwidth, so the spatial coverage suffers. For SIGINT sensors, wide bandwidth (spectral coverage) is desirable. But either the detectability of weak signals (intensity coverage) or the revisit time to a specific frequency (temporal coverage) has to suffer as the spectral coverage increases.

Another type of accommodation occurs when the operating profile of a sensor platform is changed. An aircraft or satellite can be moved farther away from the target area to provide better spatial coverage, but resolution inevitably becomes worse.

RESOLUTION TRADE-OFFS

Trade-offs also have to be made among the four types of resolution—spatial, spectral, intensity, and temporal—in the design of a sensor. Improving one type of resolution always costs resolution in one of the other three types. For example, to achieve high spatial resolution, an optical sensor has to have a small pixel size, discussed in Chapter 9. However, this reduces the total amount of energy that a pixel receives. The result is reduced radiometric (intensity) resolution—the ability to detect fine energy differences. To increase the amount of energy detected (and thus, the radiometric resolution) without reducing spatial resolution, the wavelength range would have to be expanded. But this would reduce the spectral resolution of the sensor.

Sensor Suites

There are two basic ways to overcome the constraints discussed above. Both involve using multiple sensors.

One can deploy a number of platforms (satellites, ships, aircraft, or ground sites, all of which are discussed in Chapter 8), each carrying a sensor, to provide better spatial, spectral, radiometric, or temporal coverage. For example, Chapter 8 describes how a number of satellites can be placed in orbit to provide global coverage; the required number increases at lower satellite altitudes.

One can also put multiple sensors on a single platform, each sensor optimized for a specific purpose so that they complement each other. One sensor might provide high spatial resolution, another might provide excellent spectral resolution, and a third might provide a broad area of coverage. The continuing advances in sensor technology have provided smaller and lighter sensor packages that make it easier to put multiple sensors on a single airborne or spaceborne platform. Because of the tendency to stovepipe collection, most countries tend to put only one type of sensor (such as SIGINT or IMINT) on a satellite platform. This has some advantages—systems engineering is simpler. The orbit can be optimized for the sensor; typically, SIGINT and IMINT sensors have different preferred orbits.

Where it can be done, though, the advantages of a platform that can collect two or more types of intelligence, such as IMINT and SIGINT, are apparent. One can get simultaneous collection of both types of intelligence from a target at the same time, and a lot more can be learned about what is happening at the target. An example of a multisensor platform discussed in Chapter 8 is the Global Hawk unmanned aerial vehicle. It carries both an imaging radar and an optical imager that complement each other very well: the imaging radar can function in spite of clouds or fog and has good spatial coverage; the optical imager can obtain images having high spatial resolution. India also has taken the approach of putting multiple sensors on one platform. Their Communication-Centric Satellite is an example. It is being designed as an intelligence collection satellite with both SAR imagery collection and COMINT collection capabilities. The satellite is scheduled to launch in 2014.[7]

Obviously, the two techniques (deploying a number of platforms or putting multiple sensors on a single platform) can be combined by putting multiple sensors on multiple platforms. The Maui space surveillance site, also discussed in Chapter 8, has a number of optical sensors housed in separate domes. Some provide excellent spatial coverage and are used for sky searches, while others provide excellent spatial resolution and are used for obtaining images of satellites. Within a single dome, several sensors may use the same optics—some for obtaining high radiometric resolution, others for obtaining high spectral resolution.

Another example of multiple sensors on multiple platforms is the satellite constellation that was operated by the European Space Agency (ESA). ESA launched ERS-1 in 1991 and ERS-2 in 1995. The two satellites were designed to complement each other in spatial and temporal coverage. Each satellite carried a combination of four (ERS-1) or five (ERS-2) sensors, including a synthetic aperture radar and an infrared radiometer.[8] Both satellites are now defunct.

Signatures

All of the sensors in this chapter collect measurements that after processing result in specific signatures. The signatures then are exploited and analyzed to produce raw intelligence about the sensors' targets. The bulk of sensors used in intelligence operate in some part of the electromagnetic spectrum. A few sensors do not. Two examples, touched on in this chapter and described in later chapters, are sensors that produce acoustic and radiological signatures.

EM SIGNATURES

An electromagnetic signature is created by the interaction of EM energy with matter (material solids, liquids, and gases), as illustrated in Figure 7.3. EM sensors function by receiving either emitted or reflected energy. When a wave of EM energy from a source such as the sun or a radar transmitter interacts with matter, the incoming (incident) radiation can be reflected, refracted, scattered, transmitted, or absorbed. EM energy striking a rough object (such as a rock or bare earth) or a diffuse object (such as a cloud of water vapor) is scattered in many directions or absorbed. Some energy also may pass through the object. Energy striking a smooth reflective object, such as a metal plate, will mostly be reflected.

Furthermore, objects emit EM energy both naturally and as a result of human actions, as suggested in Figure 7.4. All matter (solids, liquids, and gases) at temperatures above absolute zero emit energy, mostly in the thermal (infrared) regions of the spectrum, as discussed in Chapter 10. Lightning strikes and auroras generate very strong RF and optical signals. Radioactive substances emit gamma rays.

Man-made objects emit EM energy both intentionally and unintentionally. Communications equipment, radar, and building lights all intentionally emit RF or optical energy to serve our purposes. But a wide range of man-made objects also unintentionally emit EM energy as a consequence of their functioning—like the truck in Figure 7.4, which emits RF noise from its spark plugs and infrared energy from its hot engine. As discussed throughout this book, these natural and artificial emissions create a signature that can have intelligence use for locating the vehicle, identifying it, and tracking it as it moves.

Both emitted and reflected RF signals provide signatures that allow intelligence analysts to draw conclusions about the targets from which the signals were emitted or reflected. These signatures are discussed in some detail in Chapters 11 through 13.

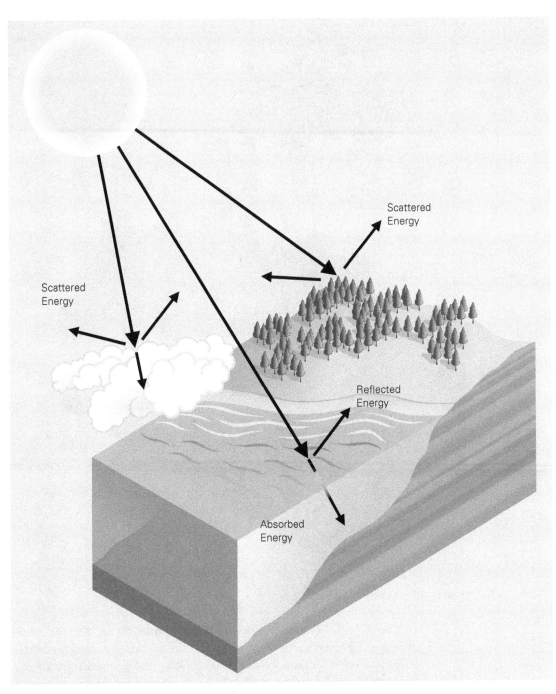

Scattered
Energy

Scattered
Energy

Reflected
Energy

Absorbed
Energy

FIGURE 7.3 The Interaction of EM Energy with Matter

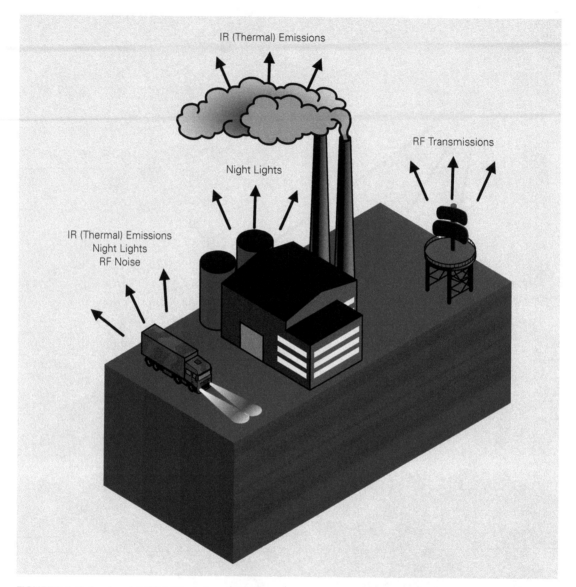

FIGURE 7.4 Natural and Artificial Emission of EM Energy

The utility of remote EM sensing derives from the fact that when EM energy is reflected and/or emitted from solid, liquid, or gaseous materials, it is modified by those materials. This modified energy constitutes a signature that is unique to the material. Emitted and reflected radiant energy can thus be used to obtain a signature that is unique to a particular material or object.

Many signatures of intelligence importance in the optical band are spectral signatures. The interaction of EM energy with matter can cause the emission of energy in specific parts of the spectrum shown in Figure 7.2; this resulting signature will be unique to the matter that emits the energy. Spectral signatures therefore can be used to identify individual materials, alone or in mixtures.

A key component of an EM signature is the polarization of the electromagnetic wave. All electromagnetic waves, RF or optical, are polarized, meaning that the electric field vibrates in some direction. Polarization is an important concept in intelligence because it can be used to obtain unique signatures in both radar and optical imaging as well as in ELINT. The concept is introduced and explained here, and it will be revisited frequently throughout the remainder of Part II.

Radio frequency signals that are deliberately transmitted have a definite polarization and can be defined as one of three types. The wave can be linearly polarized, meaning that the electric field vibrates back and forth in a straight line. It can be circularly polarized, so that to an observer the incoming electric field seems to spin like the second hand of a clock (but far faster). Or it can be elliptically polarized, so that the electric field spins, but the electric field vector is stronger in one direction.

In addition to these three polarization types, the polarization has many possible orientations. A linearly polarized wave may vibrate up and down (vertically polarized), side to side (horizontally polarized), or at some angle in between. The type of polarization and the orientation can be used to tell something about the emitter.

Naturally emitted EM waves have a different type of polarization than deliberately transmitted waves. They are likely to be randomly polarized, meaning that the polarization changes constantly in random fashion. The best-known example is sunlight. The exception is sunlight that bounces off a flat surface—water, for example. The reflected light is horizontally polarized (and we perceive it as glare). Sunglasses can be designed to pass only vertically polarized light, filtering out the horizontally polarized glare. They do this because they have many fine vertical lines that pass vertically polarized light and eliminate horizontally polarized light. To determine the effectiveness of your sunglasses, hold them slightly in front of you and look at a bright reflective surface through the lenses; then, keeping your eyes on the surface through the lens, rotate the lens 90 degrees. The reflective surface should become brighter, as the lens passes rather than filters the horizontally polarized reflected light.

Polarimetry is the measurement of the polarization of EM energy, and a polarimeter is used to make these measurements. Optical polarimetry is often called **ellipsometry**. It is extensively used in astronomy to characterize distant stars and galaxies. In intelligence, this measurement when used with radar is called radar polarimetry, discussed later.

ACOUSTIC SIGNATURES

Acoustic signatures are collected in the spectrum that includes audible sound (above 20 Hz) and infrasound (below 20 Hz and usually not detectable by the human ear). These signatures are covered in detail in Chapter 14.

RADIOLOGICAL SIGNATURES

Radiological signatures are created by emissions from radioactive material, in the form of alpha and beta particles and gamma rays. These signatures are covered in detail in Chapter 15.

Summary

Most nonliteral intelligence collection is done by sensors. The bulk of such collection is done by EM sensors, but acoustic and nuclear radiation sensors also are widely used. COMINT collection also makes use of both EM and acoustic sensors.

Sensors can be active or passive. Active sensors (radars) transmit a signal and then interpret the signals that are reflected off the target. Passive sensors exploit natural emissions, man-made signals, or energy reflected from the target, usually reflected solar illumination. EM sensors can be either active or passive. Acoustic and nuclear radiation sensors are almost all passive.

Some sensors used in intelligence can operate at very long ranges, and their use is called *remote sensing*. Others are designed to function in the immediate vicinity of their targets, and their use is often referred to as *close-in sensing*.

All sensors can collect *signatures* that are used to identify or classify targets of intelligence interest. Some objects radiate energy either naturally or as the result of human actions, and that creates a signature. All objects reflect, absorb, or scatter energy that hits them, and the nature of this interaction also creates a signature. Most such energy, again, comes from some part of the EM spectrum. It divides broadly into two regions—the radio frequency spectrum and the optical spectrum. The sensors used, and the phenomena sensed, differ significantly in these two regions.

All of the sensors used to collect intelligence have these things in common: They have a definite region of *coverage*, and within that region of coverage, they have some level of *resolution* that allows them to distinguish targets of interest. The performance of any sensor, and its value in intelligence, are determined by its coverage and resolution in four performance categories: spatial, spectral, intensity, and temporal.

• The coverage performance of a sensor is determined by its coverage in these four categories. No sensor can cover the entire EM spectrum. Sensors can observe only a defined volume of space at any instant. Two thresholds limit a sensor's ability to detect a range of intensities—detectability of weak signals and saturation caused by strong signals; these thresholds define the sensor's dynamic range. Continuous temporal coverage (surveillance) is possible, but many sensors can only conduct reconnaissance, defined as periodic revisits to the target.

• The resolution performance of a sensor defines its ability to distinguish separate features in a signature, whether spatial, intensity, spectral, or temporal. It includes separating targets spatially, for example, in an image. Resolving fine details in signature intensities can help, for example, to detect camouflage in an image. Spectral resolution allows a sensor to distinguish among energies of varying wavelengths emitted by or reflected from a target. Temporal resolution can mean revisit time between looks at a target or it can mean separating two closely spaced events in a signature.

The accuracy of signature measurement is also an important performance characteristic; it establishes the uniqueness of the signature. Spatial accuracy can mean accuracy in locating a target or in measuring its dimensions. Intensity accuracy is important for determining the power output of a source such as a radar. Spectral accuracy permits identifying specific emitters of an RF signal or identifying specific chemical compounds. Temporal accuracy is needed for accurate geolocation of a target and for identifying specific signatures.

A perfect sensor would look in all directions continuously, across the entire spectrum, with no limit on its resolution or sensitivity. All its measurements, moreover, would be accurate. Stated another way, it would have perfect spectral, spatial, intensity, and temporal coverage and could resolve all of these to any desired level of detail and any desired degree of accuracy. Such a sensor doesn't exist. All sensors are the result of compromises or trade-offs in coverage, resolution, and accuracy. Within each of these, the sensor also has to compromise between spatial, spectral, intensity, and temporal performance. In general, improving any one of these results in degraded performance for another.

The solution for many intelligence collectors is to use a suite of sensors on a single or multiple platforms, where each sensor is optimized for a specific performance area and where the sensors complement each other.

A key signature component of an EM wave is the wave's polarization. All electromagnetic waves, RF or optical, are polarized, meaning that the electric field vibrates in some direction. Polarization is an important concept in intelligence because polarization can be used to obtain unique signatures in both the radio frequency and the optical regions of the EM spectrum.

NOTES

1. Satellite Imaging Corporation, "Spot-5 Satellite Sensor," accessed 22 September 2012 at http://www.satimagingcorp.com/satellite-sensors/spot-5.html.
2. NASA definition of near, mid, and far infrared bands (2009), accessed 22 September 2012 at http://www.ipac.caltech.edu/Outreach/Edu/Regions/irregions.html.
3. Doppler effect, or Doppler shift, refers to a change in the observed frequency of an acoustic or electromagnetic signal emitted by or reflected from a moving object, when the object and the observer are in motion relative to each other.
4. Joe Lees and Robert Mott, "Change Detection for More Actionable Intelligence," *Spectroscopy* (January 1, 2006), accessed 22 September 2012 at http://www.spectroscopyonline.com/spectroscopy/article/articleDetail.jsp?id=285288.
5. Ibid.
6. Satellite Imaging Corporation, "Spot-5 Satellite Sensor," Barbara Opall-Rome, "Israel Declares Ofeq-9 Reconnaissance Satellite Operational," *Space News* (June 22, 2010), accessed 22 September 2012 at http://spacenews.com/launch/100622-israel-launches-spy-satellite.html.
7. Kerur Bhargavi, "India's Spy in the Sky by 2014," *DNA India* (February 10, 2010).
8. European Space Agency, "ERS Overview" (updated August 17, 2011), accessed 22 September 2012 at www.esa.int/esaEO/SEMGWH2VQUD_index_0_m.html.

8. Collection Platforms

This chapter focuses primarily on the use of collection platforms for remote sensing, since most technical collection is done that way.

As we discussed in Chapter 7, remote sensing has a long history. Sensing space objects from earth, for example, dates back to antiquity, even before Galileo invented the telescope. The reverse, sensing the earth's surface, has been of intelligence interest for centuries. The French were the first to use manned balloons for aerial reconnaissance in 1794, during their conflict with Austria. This reconnaissance contributed to the French victory by providing a way for the French to observe the makeup and activities of their enemies. The French experiment involved two themes that recur in all collection platforms:

- *Getting the intelligence from the collection platform to those who need it.* For the French, this involved a balloonist either sending flag signals or putting a written message in a sandbag fitted with rings and sliding it down the tether cable.
- *Protecting the platform from hostile action.* The French used two widely separated tether cables to reduce the chance that the enemy would end the reconnaissance by cutting the cable so that the balloon drifted away.

Since then, remote sensing has evolved to include an extensive array of sophisticated instruments that collect information from a variety of platforms. In fact, if it can fly, float, travel through space, or move along the ground, it is potentially a platform for intelligence collection. It doesn't even have to move if it is in the right location. Aircraft, satellites, ships, submarines, and ground platforms all are used for collecting intelligence. But the two problems—getting the intelligence from the platform to the customer and protecting the platform from discovery or attack—persist today.

Remote sensing platforms can be used in intelligence for surveillance or reconnaissance. The difference between the two is the dwell time on the target area; surveillance is defined as continuous dwell, while reconnaissance is a dwell for a relatively short period of time, even a snapshot. Since low earth orbit satellites can see a given spot on earth for only a few minutes at a time, this platform can only be used for reconnaissance. All other platforms discussed in this chapter—aircraft, ships, submarines, and ground stations—can be used for either surveillance or reconnaissance.

Since the resolution and accuracy of sensors improve as the sensor gets closer to the target, it is desirable to place the collection platform as close to the target as possible. And that is possible when collectors are only interested in collecting data from targets at a fixed location. For example, video surveillance cameras can be positioned to focus on entryways to monitor specific areas and can obtain enough resolution to identify people. Banks, hospitals, malls, and convenience stores have used video surveillance routinely for years. At distances of 1 meter or less, the iris and retinal scan instruments discussed in Chapter 16 can provide very precise (and accurate) recognition of individuals.

When the sensor is moved closer to a target area, the potential coverage area shrinks. Most targets of intelligence interest, and especially people, are mobile. To continue the surveillance camera example, a single camera can identify individuals but cannot track their movements outside the immediate area. The United Kingdom achieves some tracking capability in public areas by simply using more cameras—nearly 2 million of them—but even that doesn't ensure tracking of an individual.

As noted in the previous chapter, all sensors have to deal with this trade-off problem of coverage versus accuracy and resolution. So intelligence services like to use a wide range of platforms; some platforms can get close to the target for high accuracy and resolution, and some offer wide area coverage.

The discussion of platforms begins with those that routinely provide global coverage: satellites.

Satellites

Satellites provide the bulk of the remote sensing used today in intelligence. A satellite can be used for observing the earth's surface or for observing other satellites. Satellites have unique characteristics that make them particularly useful for intelligence collection. One of the major advantages is that a reconnaissance satellite can legally overfly any country while obtaining intelligence information. An aircraft or **unmanned aerial vehicle (UAV)** cannot. Another advantage is that satellites are used for many purposes that have nothing to do with intelligence. Satellites do earth resources sensing and provide communications for commercial, military, and nonmilitary governmental purposes. Therefore, it can be difficult for opponents to identify those satellites that are collecting intelligence.

Many countries have launched reconnaissance satellites since the first launches in 1960; Russia, China, the United States, France, Germany, Japan, India, and Israel all have reconnaissance satellites in orbit. The total number of launches over the years probably is in the hundreds. Satellites have a lifetime of only a few years, and there have been a number of launch failures, especially in the early years.

Satellites used for intelligence purposes customarily are referred to in the United States as overhead collection assets. The term additionally could be applied to aircraft, which also collect imagery and signals intelligence (SIGINT) from overhead (and some writers do include aircraft in the definition). But over the years the term *overhead collection* has acquired an understood meaning: collection from satellites.[1] Another term for satellite collection that will be revisited in this book is the euphemism **national technical means (NTM)**, which is still used occasionally. The term had its origin in the Limited Test Ban Treaty of 1963, where the signatories used it in agreeing that they would not interfere with each other's satellite collection capability. At the time, both sides wanted to protect that capability but did not want to admit publicly that they were spying from satellites.

The two most important things to understand about satellites are (1) how different orbits function, and their relative advantages in intelligence collection; and (2) the constraints imposed by the space environment.

ORBITS

The path followed by a satellite is referred to as its *orbit*. Satellites are constrained to move in defined orbits. They cannot hover over a point on the earth (and thus provide surveillance) except in a geosynchronous orbit, as discussed below. In all other orbits, satellites move with respect to the earth and can provide reconnaissance. This can be an advantage in geolocating targets using radio frequency (RF) sensing, discussed in Chapter 13.

Satellite orbits are matched to the capability and objective of the sensors the satellites carry. The type of sensor carried and the mission of the satellite determine the type of orbit chosen. Orbit selection can vary in terms of altitude (satellite height above the earth's surface), orientation, and movement relative to the earth. Four general classes of orbits are commonly used to collect intelligence. Figure 8.1 illustrates the four.

• A **low earth orbit** (LEO) satellite orbits between 200 and 1,500 km above the earth's surface. Earth imaging satellites and some SIGINT satellites typically use this orbit, since closeness to the target is most important. Satellites in LEO circle the earth in about 90 minutes.

• A **medium earth orbit** (MEO) satellite typically orbits at 10,000 to 20,000 km above the earth. At these altitudes, satellites need some protection from the high-energy particles in the Van Allen radiation belts that are discussed later in the chapter. A major intelligence advantage of the MEO satellite is survivability: it is more difficult for opponents to locate and attack

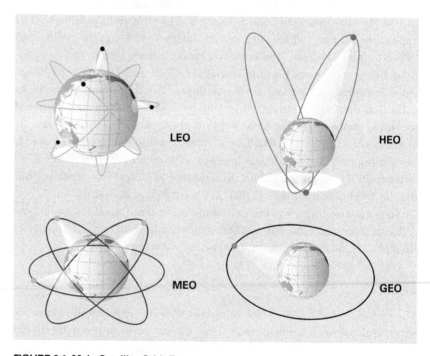

FIGURE 8.1 Main Satellite Orbit Types

during wartime than LEO satellites, and the orbit provides better sensing capabilities than the GEO or HEO satellites (see below) can deliver.

• A **highly elliptical orbit** (HEO) satellite is placed in an orbit in such a way that it will spend the greatest amount of time over a specific area of the planet. Thus, if a HEO satellite is launched to provide communications or collect intelligence in the arctic region, its orbit would be configured so that it spends the bulk of its time in orbit above these latitudes. The **apogee** (highest altitude) is typically around 35,000 km, and the **perigee** (lowest altitude) is typically around 500 km.

• A **geostationary** (GEO) satellite orbits the earth in an equatorial orbit at an altitude of 35,800 km, where its rotational period is equal to that of the earth's rotation (24 hours). The result is that the geostationary satellite turns with the earth and remains over the same fixed point of the planet at all times. The fixed nature of a geostationary satellite with respect to a given point on the earth allows the satellite to conduct surveillance, observing and collecting information continuously over a specific area.

Figure 8.2 illustrates a side view comparison of these four orbit types, drawn to scale. Note that the MEO orbits are shown as two distinct orbit

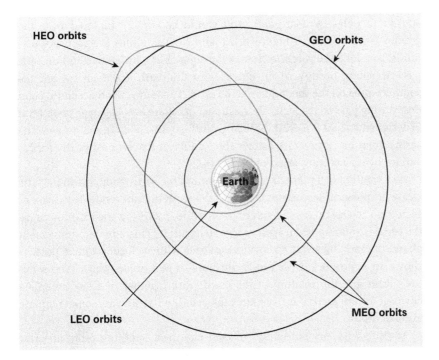

FIGURE 8.2 Side View of Orbit Types

altitudes. The reason for this separation is explained in the discussion on the space environment, later in this chapter.

All these satellite orbits have a specific **inclination** that is measured in degrees. A satellite's inclination describes the angle of the orbit measured from the equatorial plane.

- A GEO satellite, for example, must move at the same speed as the earth's rotation in order to maintain its fixed position over the earth. Therefore, it has approximately a zero degree inclination, so that it travels over the equator eastward (in the direction of the earth's rotation).
- Satellites in a **polar orbit** have a 90-degree inclination; they cross the equator moving directly north or south and cross over the poles. Figure 8.3 shows a satellite in a polar orbit.[2]
- Satellites having more than 90 degrees inclination are in a **retrograde orbit**; they move in the opposite direction from the earth's rotation. The most extreme example of a retrograde orbit is that of a 180-degree inclination satellite (which moves along the equator westward).

It is important in many intelligence applications to have global coverage, which is usually supplied by a LEO satellite in a **near-polar orbit**—so named for the inclination of the orbit relative to a line running between the north and south poles. A near-polar orbit would be slightly inclined from the ground track shown in Figure 8.3. Many LEO satellites are in near-polar orbits, in which the satellite crosses the equator at a different point on each pass, traveling northward on one side of the earth and then toward the southern pole on the second half of its orbit. These are called **ascending** and **descending passes**, respectively, as shown in Figure 8.3. The near-polar orbit is designed so that the orbit (basically north-south), in conjunction with the earth's rotation (west-east), allows the satellite to cover most of the earth's surface over a certain period of time.

As a satellite in a polar orbit moves around the earth from pole to pole, its east-west position would not change if the earth did not rotate. However, as seen from the earth, it seems that the satellite is shifting westward because the earth is rotating (from west to east) beneath it. This apparent movement allows the satellite swath to cover a new area with each consecutive pass, as shown in Figure 8.4 (which also illustrates a retrograde orbit).[3] The satellite's orbit and the rotation of the earth work together to allow complete coverage of the earth's surface after the satellite has finished one complete cycle of orbits.

Starting with any randomly selected pass in a satellite's orbit, an **orbit cycle** is completed when the satellite retraces its path, passing over the same point on the earth's surface directly below the satellite (called the

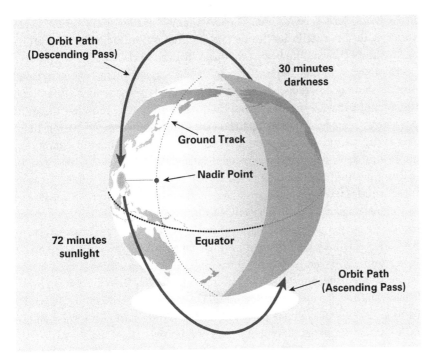

FIGURE 8.3 Geometry of a Polar Orbit

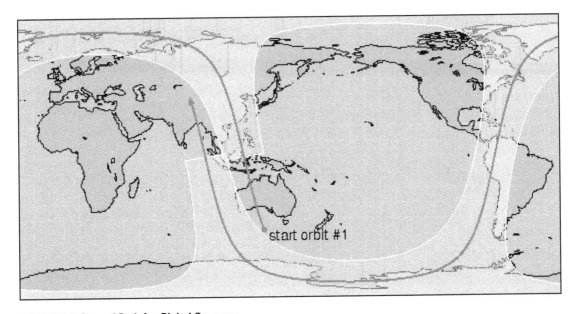

FIGURE 8.4 Ground Path for Global Coverage

nadir point) for a second time. The exact length of time of the orbital cycle varies with the satellite's altitude and inclination. In Figure 8.5, 14 orbits occur before the satellite begins to repeat its orbit cycle.

The interval of time required for the satellite to complete its orbit cycle is not the same as the revisit period. Using steerable sensors, a satellite-borne instrument can view an area away from its nadir before and after the orbit passes over a target, thus making the revisit time less than the orbit cycle time. The revisit period is an important consideration for a number of monitoring applications, especially when frequent imaging is required (for example, to monitor a rapidly developing crisis situation). In near-polar orbits, areas at high latitudes will be imaged more frequently than the equatorial zone due to the increasing overlap in adjacent swaths as the orbit paths come closer together near the poles, as illustrated in Figure 8.5.[4] For this reason, reconnaissance satellites may operate at lower inclinations, providing increased lower latitude coverage but no polar region coverage. An example is the Israeli series of reconnaissance satellites called Ofeq (Hebrew for *horizon*). These satellites have a retrograde orbit at 144 degrees inclination, phased so as to give optimal daylight coverage of the Middle East. An Ofeq satellite makes a half-dozen or so daylight passes per day over Israel and the surrounding countries, whereas U.S. and Russian imaging satellites only get one or two passes per day over the same area from their higher inclination orbits.[5]

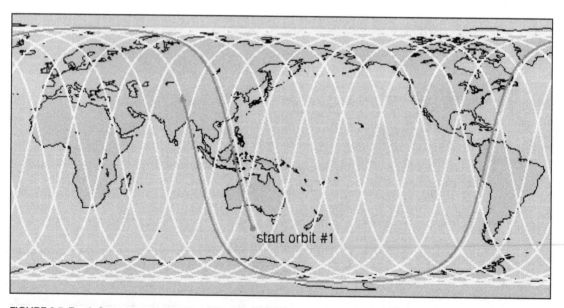

start orbit #1

FIGURE 8.5 Earth Coverage of a Sun-Synchronous Orbit

The discussion to this point has been about coverage of the earth by a single satellite. And, as noted, a single LEO satellite can cover the entire earth about twice per day. To get more frequent coverage, more satellites have to be deployed. In intelligence, it is highly desirable to have synoptic coverage, that is, to leave no important target area unmonitored. But doing this takes a lot of satellites. Figure 8.6 illustrates the coverage problem for a hypothetical constellation of satellites in a circular orbit at 4,000 km altitude, 90 degrees inclination (that is, a polar orbit), where the coverage is defined such that the minimum angle of elevation from the target to the satellite (known as the **grazing angle**) is 20 degrees.[6] Note that it takes more than 12 satellites to obtain continuous coverage at the equator, while a two-satellite constellation has very large gaps of more than two hours between coverage passes. At higher latitudes, fewer satellites are required because the satellites pass a given point at high latitudes more frequently than they pass a given point at the equator, as noted previously.

SATELLITES AS IMAGING PLATFORMS

Satellites have the advantage of being able to collect imagery more quickly over a larger area than airborne systems and to provide a predictable viewing geometry. The coverage may not be as frequent as that of an airborne platform, but—depending on the orbit, the viewing geometry, and the geographic area of interest—a single LEO satellite typically has a revisit period of less than two hours.

One specific orbit—the **sun-synchronous orbit**—is widely used for intelligence collection of optical imagery. A sun-synchronous orbit is so named

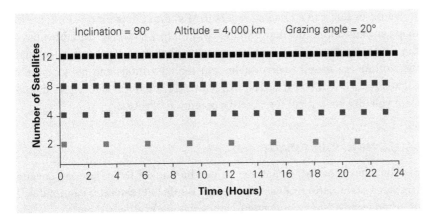

FIGURE 8.6 Equatorial Coverage for Different Satellite Constellations

because the satellite's orbit moves westward with the sun's apparent movement. As a result, the satellite passes over a given point on the earth at approximately the same time every day.

At LEO altitudes, a sun-synchronous orbit is approximately 98 degrees. In terms we've discussed earlier, that means the satellite orbit is both retrograde and near-polar. For the example shown in Figure 8.5, the satellite might cross the equator 28 times a day, crossing northward (ascending pass) at 3:00 a.m. local time and crossing southward (descending pass) at 3:00 p.m. local time.

A sun-synchronous orbit usually has the ascending pass on the shadowed side of the earth, while the descending pass is on the sunlit side, as illustrated in Figure 8.3. Imaging sensors that collect reflected solar energy only image the surface on the sunlit side, when solar illumination is available. In contrast, active sensors that provide their own illumination (synthetic aperture radars, or SARs) or passive sensors that record emitted (for example, thermal) radiation can also image the surface on the shadowed side of the earth.

Because satellites in a sun-synchronous orbit collect images at about the same local time each day, the lighting conditions in an image remain about the same from day to day. It is important for imagery interpretation that the light conditions are about the same in successive images of a target. This allows the imagery analyst to detect even slight changes that have intelligence significance—changes in the signature of an object such as a tank, factory, or radar. Typically, the time of day of the overpass is selected to help in interpretation. The best time to collect imagery is during either the mid-morning or midafternoon. At those times, the shadows from objects such as towers, vehicles, and buildings are available and of sufficient length to aid in imagery analysis.[7]

Satellites that carry imaging radars (SARs) don't depend on sunlight, so they can have any orbit that provides good target coverage. Satellites have the advantage, compared with the aircraft platforms discussed later, that their orbits are usually very stable, and their positions can be accurately calculated. As will be discussed in Chapter 12, platform stability and constant velocity are critical for effective operation of SARs.

SATELLITES AS SIGINT PLATFORMS

Satellites have several advantages for conducting SIGINT. They can cover a large area of the earth in a very short time. While LEO satellites cannot dwell on a target area, their movement across the earth allows them to quickly geolocate the source of a signal. GEO satellites can dwell on a target area indefinitely, and HEO satellites can have a relatively long dwell (on the order of 10 hours) near apogee. The disadvantage of both GEO and HEO satellites is that, being relatively far from their targets, they require large antennas and even then cannot readily pick up weak signals.

THE SPACE ENVIRONMENT

It is stating the obvious to note that space is a hostile environment. Humans venture into space only after donning protective clothing and equipment. Satellites also require extensive protection; some possible orbits encounter such a hostile environment that they are not used.

In all orbits, satellites face the threats posed by penetrating objects, such as micrometeoroids and space debris. In some orbits, satellites also must deal with high-energy charged particles, radiation, and hot and cold plasmas (a plasma is an ionized gas; if the gas particles are moving very rapidly, and thus have a high energy level, the plasma is described as hot).

The radiation belts, known as the **Van Allen radiation belts**, encircle the earth and contain particles trapped in the earth's magnetic field. The more dangerous inner belt contains highly energetic protons. The weaker and less stable outer belt contains energetic electrons. The radiation in these belts can degrade electronic components, especially the sensors onboard a satellite. Sensors designed to sense photons or radio waves also respond to energetic particles passing through them. The effect over time is a gradual degradation until the onboard devices finally fail. Another problem caused by both energetic particles and the hot plasma in the earth's magnetosphere is internal charging—the buildup of an electrostatic charge on the spacecraft that can cause onboard electronics to fail.

Furthermore, the radiation belts are not uniform, and they possess unique features that have to be considered in designing orbits for collection platforms. One of the best known of these features is the South Atlantic Anomaly, a region in space above the South Atlantic Ocean where the earth's magnetic field is weakest. As a result, the region is characterized by high-energy protons and electrons that disrupt the functioning of the charge-coupled devices used in imaging satellites.[8] As recently as 2012, an intelligence satellite—the USAF's Space Based Surveillance Satellite—was dealing with electronics disruptions due to the South Atlantic Anomaly.[9]

Figure 8.7 illustrates the four orbit types discussed earlier. Note that the two MEO orbits are designed to avoid both radiation belts (as is the LEO orbital regime). HEO orbits, however, move through both radiation belts, so satellites in these orbits need additional shielding from radiation effects.

Collection
Platforms

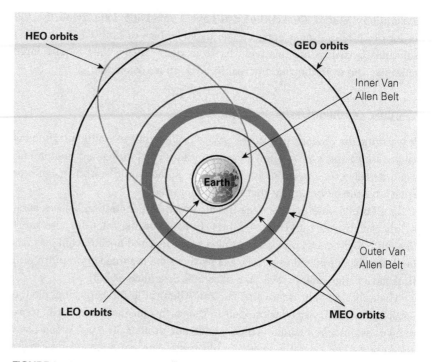

FIGURE 8.7 Van Allen Radiation Belts

Another hazard of the space environment is the combination of space debris, micrometeoroids, and dust that can damage or destroy a satellite. Space debris is an increasing threat as more satellites are placed in orbit along with launch-related debris. Ground-based optical and radar systems can monitor the near-earth space environment to warn against objects above about 1 cm in diameter. But at the high collision speeds of orbital objects, a much smaller micrometeoroid can do substantial damage.

Space debris has become much more of a problem for LEO satellites in recent years, largely as a result of two events. On January 11, 2007, China conducted an antisatellite weapons test that created a massive debris cloud at LEO altitudes. On February 10, 2009, a Russian satellite collided with the Iridium 33 commercial satellite, creating an even greater debris cloud.[10]

While the earth's shadow isn't a hazard like those discussed above, it does cause problems for some spacecraft. A typical LEO satellite spends close to one-third of its time in darkness. Since most satellites rely primarily on solar cells for power, this means that the LEO craft has only about two-thirds of the power that is available to a HEO or GEO satellite.

Aircraft and UAVs

Airborne platforms have a number of advantages—flexibility, ability to surveil an area, and ability to get close to the target. Getting close to the target can be a particular advantage when using optical sensors, which cannot see through clouds. Unlike a spaceborne optical sensor, an airborne sensor may be able to get close enough to the target to be below the cloud cover. Furthermore, the airborne optical sensor offers a dramatic improvement in image quality compared with a spaceborne sensor. Commercial spaceborne sensors such as GeoEye have demonstrated a resolution of 1.3 feet per pixel (resolution cells and pixels are discussed in Chapter 9). Commercially available aerial photography has demonstrated the ability to provide imagery with a resolution of 1.5 inches per pixel—a tenfold improvement in image quality.[11]

When developing and testing new collection sensors, airborne platforms have many advantages over satellites. They can serve as testbeds for new designs and be brought back to the ground after each flight so that the problems can be corrected. The sensors are accessible for maintenance on a regular basis. If the sensor design needs modification, it can be readily done. But once a sensor is launched on a satellite, none of these things can be done—except at great expense. For these reasons, sensors intended for eventual satellite use often are first tested on aircraft. Finally, because of the harsh space environment discussed previously, spaceborne sensors must be certified as "space qualified"—meaning that they must pass much more stringent environmental testing than airborne sensors.

Airborne platforms have two significant disadvantages. First, they cannot legally overfly what intelligence organizations describe as "denied areas" (areas where overflight is prohibited by international law). Second, aircraft are vulnerable to counter-air weaponry. (While satellites are susceptible to the emerging threat of antisatellite weapons, such an attack on another country's satellite in peacetime would violate international law.) The vulnerability issue has increasingly led to the use of UAVs in place of manned aircraft. UAVs are just as vulnerable as aircraft to attack, but the loss of a UAV does not mean the loss of a pilot. UAVs typically have a smaller radar and optical signature, which provides them some protection from being detected. But power for radar sensors may be limited on aircraft and even more so on UAVs.

As sensor carriers, airborne platforms have additional drawbacks. Some sensors cannot tolerate vibration or turbulence. Imaging radars, for example, have special problems on aircraft. SAR imagery is affected by aircraft motion variations and by weather conditions. In order to avoid image artifacts or geometric positioning errors due to random variations in aircraft motion, the

FIGURE 8.8 Global Hawk UAV

SAR must compensate with sophisticated geolocation equipment and advanced image processing, discussed in Chapter 12.[12] Generally, these are able to correct for all but the most severe variations in motion, such as significant air turbulence.[13]

Although airborne radar systems are susceptible to such platform motion problems, they have the flexibility to collect data from different look angles and look directions. They can adjust the imaging geometry for the particular terrain being imaged. They can acquire imagery from more than one look direction and so can obtain intelligence information that would be difficult for a satellite-borne radar (for example, by looking into an open hangar door). An airborne radar can collect data anywhere and at any time, as long as weather and flying conditions are suitable.

A current example of an airborne platform is the Global Hawk UAV, shown in Figure 8.8. It provides military commanders with near-real-time, high-resolution intelligence, surveillance, and reconnaissance imagery. Global Hawk carries an electro-optical imager (discussed in Chapter 9) and a synthetic aperture radar (discussed in Chapter 12).

Global Hawk can range as far as 12,000 nautical miles at altitudes up to 65,000 feet (19,812 meters), flying at speeds approaching 340 knots for as long as 35 hours. During a typical mission, the aircraft can fly 1,200 miles to an area of interest and orbit the target area for 24 hours. It has been used to provide battlefield surveillance in places like Iraq and Afghanistan, and it also provided strategic intelligence.

Global Hawk is a relatively large, long-range UAV. While it has performance advantages over smaller UAVs, it is relatively expensive. The trend is toward the proliferation of small, short-range UAVs. Small UAVs are increasingly being used for battlefield intelligence and law enforcement intelligence. They commonly are the size of model airplanes, and their size is decreasing. UAVs currently under development are dragonfly sized and carry video cameras that can be used for intelligence collection.[14]

Aerostats

Satellites, aircraft, and UAVs all have one major disadvantage: Single platforms are unable to perform continuous surveillance of a target area over a period of days. (The one exception is the geostationary satellite.) The **aerostat**, a lighter-than-air vehicle that can remain stationary in the air (including blimps, dirigibles, and tethered balloons), can do that. Most aerostats are tethered, but free-flying aerostats (usually called airships) are able to either maintain position for extended periods or move around as the mission requirements dictate. The U.S. military has used tethered aerostats for surveillance in Iraq.[15]

Aerostats can carry radar, optical, or SIGINT sensors, or any combination. Since the 1980s, the U.S. Air Force (USAF) has operated tethered aerostats, nicknamed "Fat Alberts" after a 1970s cartoon character. The aerostats provide radar coverage of the U.S. southern border to detect drug-smuggling aircraft.[16] The standard tactic for the smugglers is to fly below ground radar coverage; ground-based radars have very short ranges (about 10 kilometers) against low-flying aircraft. An aerostat-borne radar can extend this detection range to hundreds of kilometers.

The United States is developing a high-altitude unmanned airship for surveillance and intelligence use. This new airship would reportedly be capable of operating at 65,000 feet altitude and staying aloft for 10 years. Using its onboard radar or other sensors at that altitude, the airship would be able to monitor targets of intelligence interest over a region the size of Iraq.[17] At 65,000 feet altitude, the airship would be above the jet stream and therefore more capable of remaining in one area for an extended time.[18]

Ships and Submarines

Ships are advantageous for remote sensing in that they have longer loiter times and more power than aircraft or satellites. However, as with the vibrations of airborne platforms, a ship's instability can limit the performance of onboard sensors, especially in rough seas.

A current example of a ship used as an intelligence collection platform is Norway's *Marjata,* shown in Figure 8.9. The ship is operated by the Norwegian Intelligence service and is considered to be one of the most sophisticated intelligence collection ships in existence. Its main role reportedly is surveillance of Russian submarine activity in the north. It operates close to the Russian border.[19]

FIGURE 8.9 Norwegian Intelligence Collector *Marjata*[23]

The ship has an unusual hull shape, with a number of characteristics that make it an excellent intelligence collector. Its narrow front and wide beam make it a very stable surveillance platform even in the rough weather of the Arctic. It also has a large internal bay devoted to computing and analyzing the collected data; and an onboard capability to do technical analysis of collected signals.[20]

The ship's design illustrates one of the challenges of collecting SIGINT from ships or submarines: These systems can only collect out to the line of sight. To extend the line of sight and consequently the detection range, the antennas are placed as high up as possible. The design also demonstrates another feature that is common to SIGINT ships: Many of the SIGINT antennas are hidden to conceal their collection capabilities, in this case by radomes—the ball-shaped structures located around the central mast.[21]

The challenge of getting better detection range in shipborne SIGINT can be solved, to some extent, by operating a tethered aerostat platform, as previously discussed, from a ship. Beginning in the late 1980s, the U.S. Army and the U.S. Coast Guard began operating a small fleet of leased commercial vessels with tethered aerostats to detect and monitor boats and airplanes suspected of drug smuggling. The aerostats carried radars that functioned in much the same way as the "Fat Albert" radars discussed earlier.[22]

Submarines have an advantage over ships in their ability to conduct clandestine intelligence collection. They are often able to approach another naval vessel, foreign port, or naval test area without detection and, by raising a periscope or periscope-mounted antenna above the water surface, collect visual or signals intelligence. Submarines also can collect underwater acoustic signals or deploy leave-behind sensors. During the 1982 Falklands war between the United Kingdom and Argentina, Britain deployed five of its nuclear attack submarines about 20 kilometers off the Argentine coast. The boats had been fitted with passive detection devices that could detect Argentine radio and radar transmissions. The submarines used these devices to track Argentine ships by their radar transmissions. The submarines also monitored radio traffic from Argentine air bases onshore. When radio traffic indicated the launch of an air strike, the submarines were able to transmit a warning to the task force commander via satellite link in time to alert the combat air patrol. This early warning gave the British fleet about 45 minutes to prepare for the Argentine air raids. The British submarines for the most part were able to operate undetected by staying submerged with only the SIGINT antennas above the sea surface. Some of them were occasionally detected and attacked, but none were damaged.[24]

Ground Sites

Ground sites are used for remote sensing of aircraft, ballistic missiles, and satellites. Radar and optical sensors can be used both for locating these objects spatially and for collecting signature measurements for object identification. Some ground-based platforms used in intelligence are mobile or portable, but some very important ones are large fixed sites that therefore have the disadvantage of having a fixed coverage area. Offsetting this disadvantage, fixed sites are very stable platforms with precisely known locations (in order to precisely locate something, you have to know precisely where you are). Ground sites are used for air and space surveillance, surface surveillance, and close-in clandestine collection, all discussed below. They also find intelligence use in acoustic and seismic sensing, discussed in Chapter 14.

AIR AND SPACE SURVEILLANCE SYSTEMS

An important intelligence use of ground sites is for air and space situational awareness. Air surveillance is routinely done by thousands of radars worldwide, only a few of which are collecting intelligence. Space surveillance is done at only a few sites, and they include some important intelligence collectors. Two examples of such sites are the Cobra Dane radar, discussed in Chapter 11, and the Maui Space Surveillance System, discussed below.

Figure 8.10 shows the Maui Space Surveillance System, an optical site that combines operational satellite tracking facilities with a research and development facility. It is located at the 10,000-foot summit of Haleakala Mountain on the island of Maui, Hawaii. The mountaintop location is well suited for both astronomical telescopes and optical facilities used for space surveillance. The high elevation means that the site is usually above cloud cover, and it also reduces the distortion in viewing caused by the atmosphere.

The telescopes at Maui track man-made objects to GEO altitudes and beyond, and they collect optical signatures to use for space object identification. The

FIGURE 8.10 Maui Space Surveillance System

site has several telescopes that accommodate a wide variety of sensor systems, including imaging systems, photometers, infrared radiometers, and low-light-level video systems, all of which are discussed in subsequent chapters.[25]

SURFACE SURVEILLANCE

Surface surveillance radars have been used by military forces since World War II for battle space awareness. They are used to detect and recognize moving targets such as people, vehicles, watercraft, and low-flying rotary wing aircraft. Such radars have been used for intelligence collection in urban warfare; border, airport, and nuclear facility security; observing terrorist and narcotrafficker movements; and monitoring activity of opposing forces on the battlefield.[26]

Radars and SIGINT systems that scan the skies, such as space surveillance radars and most air defense radars, have no special requirement to be situated high above the ground. But radars and SIGINT systems that must scan the earth's surface or detect low-flying aircraft need as much altitude as possible. As with the SIGINT ship in Figure 8.9 and the aerostat radars previously discussed, increased height equals increased detection range. Aerostats often are impractical for use in battlefield areas, as they are easy targets for opposing counter-air systems. The solution has been to develop battlefield surveillance systems that can raise their antennas when operating. The BUR radar built by the European firm EADS and shown in Figure 8.11 illustrates the use of this design approach in a radar designed to detect low-flying aircraft and helicopters.[27]

The BUR illustrates another advantage of battlefield surveillance radars—they have to be mobile, both to move with the front and to avoid being targeted for attack—a point that is revisited in Chapter 13.

CLOSE-IN CLANDESTINE COLLECTION

Modern electronics technology allows us to fit almost any of the passive sensors discussed in this book into a small package that can be clandestinely emplaced near a target of interest. Electro-magnetic and acoustic sensors are now sufficiently small and rugged that they can be deployed in large numbers and operate for extended periods without maintenance. Such devices can be disguised as innocuous objects or concealed and located near hostile borders or in controlled spaces within countries.

One of the earliest such devices that has been openly acknowledged is the Igloo White sensor that was deployed along the Ho Chi Minh trail during the Vietnam War. Approximately 20,000 of these sensors were dropped from aircraft, and some were deployed by special oper-

FIGURE 8.11 Battlefield Surveillance Radar

ations ground forces. The sensors monitored acoustic and seismic signals from the North Vietnamese trucks and troops on the trail and tracked their movements.[28]

A modern example of such a sensor is the Steel Rattler. This is a camou-flaged hand-emplaced acoustic sensor with a thermal imager that can detect, classify, and identify ground vehicles by their acoustic or thermal signa-tures. Its primary target has been the vehicles that carry mobile missiles, called transporter-erector-launchers (TELs). An air-launched version of the acoustic sensor, called Steel Eagle, was developed in 1998. Steel Eagle is dropped by aircraft such as the F-15, F-16, and F/A-18, so that the impact buries it in the ground as shown in Figure 8.12.[29]

Summary

Technical intelligence relies on an extensive array of sophisticated instru-ments that collect information from a variety of platforms—satellites, air-craft and UAVs, aerostats, ships, submarines, and ground stations. Collection platforms must be protected so that they can survive in a hostile environment. Where possible, it is also desirable to make them clandestine, to allow them to collect intelligence without the opponent being aware of the collection.

Remote sensing platforms can be used in intelligence for surveillance or reconnaissance. The difference between the two is the dwell time on the

FIGURE 8.12 Steel Eagle Acoustic Sensor[30]

target area; surveillance is defined as continuous dwell, while reconnaissance is a dwell for a relatively short period of time, even a snapshot.

Some platforms operate close to their intended target, providing high resolution and accuracy but sacrificing spatial coverage. Some operate at great distances to obtain spatial coverage or to protect the platform from hostile action but sacrifice resolution and accuracy to do so.

Satellites carry sensors that provide most of today's technical intelligence. A satellite can be used for observing the earth or for observing other satellites. Satellites have several unique characteristics that make them particularly useful. One of the major advantages in intelligence is that a satellite can legally overfly any country to get intelligence information. An aircraft or UAV cannot.

Satellites used for intelligence purposes are customarily referred to as overhead collection assets. The term could be applied as well to aircraft, which also collect imagery and signals intelligence from overhead. But over the years, the term *overhead collection* has acquired an understood meaning: collection from satellites.

Satellites operate in four types of orbits. Closest to the earth are the LEO satellites that can complete a single orbit in less than two hours; they function at altitudes below 1,500 km. Most imaging satellites and some SIGINT satellites use this orbit. MEO satellites, at altitudes between 10,000 and 20,000 km, are more survivable because they are more difficult to locate and attack in wartime. HEO satellites have an apogee near 35,000 km and a perigee near 500 km and normally are used to provide medium-term reconnaissance of high latitude and polar regions. GEO satellites appear to remain at a fixed point above the earth at 35,800 km and are useful for continuous surveillance of about one-third of the earth's surface.

LEO satellites used for intelligence collection usually follow near-polar orbits, wherein the ground track moves westward during each succeeding pass in a retrograde orbit to provide global coverage. Imaging satellites frequently use a retrograde orbit that is sun-synchronous, meaning that the satellite crosses the equator at the same local (sun) time each day.

Aircraft and UAVs are heavily used for electronic reconnaissance, where they can operate near (but usually not overfly) hostile territory. UAVs have the additional advantage that they do not have an onboard pilot, so when necessary they can conduct imaging operations over hostile territory. Fuel constraints limit the time they can remain in the target area. In contrast, aerostats (unmanned balloons) have the advantage of very long loiter times and can conduct imagery, radar, or SIGINT surveillance of a given area.

Ships have an advantage for remote sensing in that they have longer loiter times and more power available than do aircraft or satellites. However, a ship's instability can limit the performance of onboard sensors, especially in rough seas. Submarines have additional advantages in their ability to conduct clandestine intelligence collection. They are often able to approach another naval vessel, foreign port, or test area without detection, and by raising a periscope or periscope-mounted antenna above the water surface, collect visual or signals intelligence.

Ground sites range in size from very large fixed facilities used for radar and optical surveillance of space and ballistic missile activity, to the mobile battlefield surveillance radars and SIGINT systems and the unattended sensors or small clandestine devices used for close-in sensing.

NOTES

1. Albert D. Wheelon, "Technology and Intelligence," *Technology in Society,* Vol. 26 (April–August 2004), 245–255.

2. Figure accessed 22 September 2012 from www.centennialofflight.gov/essay/Dictionary/SUN_SYNCH_ORBIT/DI155.htm.

3. Figure accessed 22 September 2012 from www.newmediastudio.org/DataDiscovery/Hurr_ED_Center/Satellites_and_Sensors/Polar_Orbits/Polar_Orbits.html.

4. Ibid.

5. Barbara Opall-Rome, "Israel Declares Ofeq-9 Reconnaissance Satellite Operational," *Space News,* (June 22, 2010), accessed 22 September 2012 at http://spacenews.com/launch/100622-israel-launches-spy-satellite.html.

6. Figure derived from U.S. Patent 5931417, "Non-geostationary orbit satellite constellation for continuous coverage of northern latitudes above 25° and its extension to global coverage tailored to the distribution of populated land masses on earth" (August 3, 1999).

7. Canada Centre for Remote Sensing, "Tutorial: Fundamentals of Remote Sensing Image Interpretation & Analysis," accessed 22 September 2012 at www.ccrs.nrcan.gc.ca/resource/tutor/fundam/chapter4/02_e.php.

8. Sharma Jayant, Grant H. Stokes, Curt von Braun, George Zollinger, and Andrew J. Wiseman, "Toward Operational Space-Based Space Surveillance," *Lincoln Laboratory Journal,* Vol. 13, No. 2 (2002), 328.

9. Andrea Shalal-Esa, "U.S. Air Force Begins Using Boeing Surveillance Satellite," Reuters (August 20, 2012), accessed 13 October 2012 at http://news.yahoo.com/u-air-force-begins-using-boeing-surveillance-satellite-003010197-sector.html.

10. Paul Marks, "Satellite Collision 'More Powerful than China's ASAT Test,'" *New Scientist* (February 13, 2009), accessed 22 September 2012 at www.newscientist.com/article/dn16604-satellite-collision-more-powerful-than-chinas-asat-test.html.

11. Eric Lai, "In Satellite Photo Resolution Race, Who's Winning?" *Computerworld* (October 24, 2008), accessed 22 September 2012 at www.computerworld.com/action/article.do?command=viewArticleBasic&articleId=9118079&intsrc=hm_list.

12. Zheng Liwen, Lv Xiaolei, and Xing Mengdao, "Imaging Method of UAV High Squint SAR," *Heifei Leida Kexue Yu Jishu* (December 1, 2007), 431.

13. Canada Centre for Remote Sensing, "Tutorial: Fundamentals of Microwave Remote Sensing" (January 29, 2008), accessed 22 September 2012 at www.ccrs.nrcan.gc.ca/resource/tutor/fundam/chapter3/09_e.php.

14. "The Fly's a Spy," *The Economist* (November 1, 2007), accessed 22 September 2012 at www.economist.com/displaystory.cfm?story_id=10059596.

15. Julian E. Barnes, "Spy Blimp: Air Force Planning Giant Airship," *Chicago Tribune* (March 13, 2009).

16. U.S. Air Force, "Tethered Aerostat Radar System," U.S. Air Force Fact Sheet (August 2007), accessed 22 September 2012 at www.af.mil/information/factsheets/factsheet.asp?id=3507.

17. Barnes, "Spy Blimp."

18. "U.S. Army's $150m 'Super-blimp' High-Altitude Airship in Crash Landing Just Hours after Launch," *MailOnline* (July 28, 2011), accessed 22 September 2012 at http://www.dailymail.co.uk/news/article-2019454/US-Armys-150m-super-blimp-high-altitude-airship-crash-landing-hours-launch.html.

19. Military-today.com, "Marjata Intelligence Collection Ship," accessed 26 September 2012 at http://www.military-today.com/navy/marjata.htm.

20. Ibid.

21. Ibid.

22. U.S. General Accounting Office, Report #GAO/NSIAD-93-213 (September 10, 1993), accessed 22 September 2012 at http://www.dtic.mil/cgi-bin/GetTRDoc? AD=ADA271225&Location=U2&doc=GetTRDoc.pdf.

23. Photograph by Peter John Acklam (July 4, 2011), used with permission, accessed 3 October 2012 at http://en.wikipedia.org/wiki/File:FS_Marjata_in_Kirkenes.JPG.

24. "The Falklands Radio Line," Strategy Page (December 4, 2007), accessed 22 September 2012 at http://www.strategypage.com/htmw/htsub/articles/20071204 .aspx.

25. "Air Force Maui Optical & Supercomputing Site," U.S. Air Force, www.maui .afmc.af.mil/. Photo from NASA, Johnson Space Center, Orbital Debris Program Office (Photo gallery), accessed 22 September 2012 at www.orbitaldebris.jsc.nasa .gov/photogallery/photogallery.html.

26. Lav Varshney, "Ground Surveillance Radars and Military Intelligence," Syracuse Research Corporation (December 30, 2002), accessed 26 September 2012 at http://www.mit.edu/~lrv/cornell/publications/Ground%20Surveillance%20 Radars%20and%20Military%20Intelligence.pdf.

27. "Germany Orders New AESA Battlefield Radars," *Defense Industry Daily* (May 19, 2009), accessed 26 September 2012 at http://www.defenseindustrydaily.com/ germany-orders-new-aesa-battlefield-radars-02452/.

28. John T. Correll, "Igloo White," *Air Force Magazine,* Vol. 87, No. 11 (November 2004), accessed 22 September 2012 at http://www.airforce-magazine.com/ MagazineArchive/Pages/2004/November%202004/1104igloo.aspx.

29. Kevin T. Malone, Loren Riblett, and Thomas Essenmacher, "Acoustic/Seismic Identifications, Imaging, and Communications in Steel Rattler," Sandia National Laboratories, published in *SPIE,* Vol. 3081, 158–165, accessed 19 July 2012 at http://lib.semi.ac.cn:8080/tsh/dzzy/wsqk/SPIE/v013081/3081-158.pdf.

30. U.S. DoD public domain image from "Steel Eagle/Argus Program Overview" (November 21, 2002), accessed 26 September 2012 at http://www.google.com/url ?sa=t&rct=j&q=&esrc=s&source=web&cd=5&ved=0CD0QFjAE&url=http%3A%2 F%2Fwww.acq.osd.mil%2Fdpap%2Fabout%2FPEOSYSCOM2002%2Fpresent ations%2FTechTransferPanel-ARGUS-WinstonCampbell-Snyder.ppt&ei=TcxkU LqaKYL08gTKmICAAw&usg=AFQjCNH6NuStXAKz0f58iIYKufgNx616Ig.

9. Optical Imaging

This chapter discusses optical imaging, which is an important source of intelligence for military forces. In the past few decades, it has become important for nonmilitary uses such as national policy making and earth resources management. In recent years, as imagery from space has become commercially available, optical images also have been used for intelligence by nongovernmental organizations (NGOs), commercial firms, and terrorists. Most such imaging is conducted during the day, because it is the traditional visible imaging and depends on the sun for illumination. But useful intelligence can be gained from visible imaging at night to detect lights from human activity.

Optical imaging systems also can image outside the visible band and can provide what are called spectral signatures. Such sensors can function in any part of the optical spectrum introduced in Chapter 7 and displayed in Figure 7.2. This chapter, though, focuses on sensors that create images in the visible part of the spectrum that extends from about 0.4 μm to about 0.75 μm—that being the best known and the most heavily used part of the optical spectrum for intelligence purposes.

Chapter 10 expands on the material introduced here and discusses the use of special-purpose sensors that operate in different bands of the optical spectrum. Some of these sensors produce a single image in a nonvisible band. Some produce a set of images, each image being at a different wavelength in the spectrum. A few produce no image, only sensing the intensity of energy received in some part of the spectrum. All of these measurements and images have become important sources of intelligence in recent years.

Function

EARTH IMAGING

Electro-optical imagers are useful in intelligence because they can cover large areas of the earth's surface, with spatial resolutions sufficient for obtaining useful signatures and performing imagery interpretation. They provide a target signature in the form of a target's location plus identifying features (that is, features that allow the identification of a type of terrain, building, aircraft, or ship). A particular pattern of building and equipment layouts might identify a complex, for example, as a weapons test range or a nuclear fuel reprocessing plant. Recall that the pattern is not a signature. As discussed in Chapter 6, the pattern identification is the result of analysis of a combination of signatures (building and equipment layouts).

Continuous imaging (that is, surveillance) also can provide information about target movements. Ground-based and airborne video cameras are increasingly being used by both law enforcement and military units for conducting surveillance of developing situations on the ground or at sea. Unmanned aerial vehicles (UAVs) and aerostats provide excellent platforms for these steerable video cameras. For intelligence purposes, such airborne surveillance allows analysts to establish connections between known and unknown targets, determine the time history of those connections, and identify new targets. Airborne video is effective in tracking terrorist or insurgent movements, dealing with weapons proliferation, and monitoring activity at borders and ports.[1]

SPACE SURVEILLANCE

The preceding section discussed the use of optical sensors in creating images of the earth's surface or of objects of interest. A second major function of optical sensors is supporting *space situational awareness*. In combination with the radar sensors discussed in Chapter 11, optical sensors provide details about the location and movement of objects in orbit around the earth and details that help to identify the objects. With the increasing trend toward both military and civilian uses of space, it has become important for all countries to be aware of what is in orbit and the potential threats to their national interests from other countries' space systems. To do that, optical sensing is used to help identify objects in space, understand their missions, and, ultimately, determine if they have hostile intent.

Space situational awareness is also important to both military and civilian users of space because of the large number of objects—both operational satellites and space junk—in orbit. Because of the increasing potential for collisions (which create more space junk), major spacefaring nations maintain catalogs of space object orbital parameters for collision warning. In the United States, the space surveillance network uses both optical and radar sensors to maintain a space catalog and to support collision avoidance.

The main advantage of optical systems is their relative cost effectiveness in searching for and tracking satellites that are in highly elliptical (HEO) and geostationary (GEO) orbits. While it is possible to use radar to track satellites at GEO altitudes, such radars are extremely expensive because of the necessary specialized high-power equipment and their high power consumption. Optical tracking systems, on the other hand, cost less per unit than radars. Their low cost and ease of use make optical systems attractive to third world countries wishing to develop a space surveillance capability.

Optical systems also are valuable for concealing the fact of intelligence collection. Whereas an opponent's satellite can detect that it is being tracked by radar, it cannot detect that it is being tracked by a passive optical system. Since the sun usually is being used as an illuminator, the optical site does not give away its location or mission in performing its observations.

Process

The preceding section described the importance of optical imaging of the earth from airborne and spaceborne platforms and of optical surveillance of satellites from the earth. There are significant differences in the processes used for each, as discussed in this section.

PLANNING

Collection planning is done quite differently for airborne imaging than for spaceborne imaging. Aircraft and UAV flights are planned on an individual basis to meet specific needs (usually military or law enforcement operations).

Flight routes are planned in advance, but they can be altered in flight to collect against high interest targets that suddenly become available.

Which of these platforms (manned aircraft, UAV, aerostat, or satellite) is used for collection depends on the location and nature of the target and on the type of imagery required. Imaging of denied areas must typically be done by satellites, which have global access. If the collection organization has control of the airspace, then aircraft, UAVs, and aerostats may be used and have the advantage of being able to loiter over an area to conduct surveillance—something that imaging satellites cannot do. Aerostats are particularly useful for their long-duration loitering capability, where video surveillance is usually preferable to still images.

For imaging satellites, the orbit is set and only small changes are possible. Imaging satellites operate in low earth (LEO) orbits to get the best possible resolution, which means that the satellite cannot dwell for long on a target of interest. Within the field of regard, the satellite can image any location. But the best quality imagery comes from directly beneath the satellite (nadir), and image quality steadily worsens further from nadir. So it is desirable to plan images as close to nadir as possible.

Typically, the satellite is tasked in advance, and changes to the target set are not made on an ad hoc basis except in crisis situations. Optical imaging of the earth usually is planned against three general target classes: specific targets in specific locations (known as point targets); a specific geographic region (called a directed search area); or a river, road, or railroad (referred to as a line of communication). Targets have to be ranked according to some priority system. The required image quality has to be taken into account, along with any special constraints such as collection geometry.

Optical sensing of satellites from earth has both similarities and differences from optical imaging of earth from space. In both cases, cloud conditions determine whether intelligence collection can be done. Collection in both cases also has to be timed to take advantage of target visibility and lighting conditions. When imaging the earth's surface, we usually want to choose a time when shadows are present to aid in interpreting imagery. When looking at satellites, we ideally would like to have the ground site in darkness while the sun illuminates the satellite (a situation called the **terminator condition**). The major difference is that imaging of earth from space is done by reconnaissance; the imaging satellite cannot dwell on a target for long. Satellites, though, can be observed continuously when clouds and lighting conditions permit. So planning is designed to allocate resources among three missions: maintaining the space catalog of satellites, searching for new satellites, and monitoring new satellites that are discovered, in order to determine their missions.

COLLECTION

The most widely used type of imagery in intelligence is panchromatic (black-and-white) imagery of the earth's surface within the visible spectrum and collected by a manned aircraft, UAV, or satellite platform. Such imagery depends on the presence of an illuminator such as the sun, as discussed in Chapter 7. This imagery is described as reflective sensing or reflective imaging because it relies on the reflection of energy from the target. Handheld cameras, for example, do reflective imaging; in low light levels, a flash attachment provides the illuminating energy.

We'll first explain how an optical sensor works, then look at the geometry for earth imaging, and finish by explaining the different types of imaging sensors.

How Optical Systems Work. Optical imaging systems are usually called electro-optical imagers because the incoming optical signal hits a detector array, where it is converted to an electrical signal for transmission and storage. They are, for all practical purposes, telescopes with digital cameras attached. All optical systems discussed in this chapter and Chapter 10 operate as illustrated in Figure 9.1, which shows the basic function of a telescope. At the left, light from two distant objects arrives at the telescope from two slightly different directions. Because of the relatively great distance to the objects, the light rays from each object are essentially parallel when they arrive at the telescope. The optics focus the incoming energy from a light source at a point on what is called the **focal plane**. Two dimensions of a telescope (or of any optical system) define its performance: the size of the aperture and the focal length.

Aperture. The light from each object is collected by a circular opening, or aperture, having diameter D; in this example, a lens of diameter D focuses the light into images of the two objects at the focal plane. (Sensors used for remote sensing in intelligence mostly use a concave mirror to do the focusing instead of a lens, because lenses become very heavy as the aperture size increases.) As the diameter increases, the amount of light that can be collected also increases, and therefore the sensor's sensitivity increases. The amount of light collected by a circular sensor is proportional to D^2.

Focal Length. The focal length, F, of the sensor is defined by the distance between the aperture and the focal plane.

The above discussion assumes a perfect optical system. The resolving power (or resolution) of a telescope is a measure of its ability to distinguish fine detail in an image of a source. Optical aberrations due to the telescope design or flaws in the manufacture and alignment of optical components can degrade the resolving power, as does peering through the earth's turbulent atmosphere. However, even if a telescope is optically perfect and is operated in a vacuum, there is still a fundamental lower limit to the resolving power it can achieve. The limit is related to the distance *s* in Figure 9.1. If *s* is too small, the two images overlap and cannot be resolved.

To get the best possible image that the optics will permit, the image in the focal plane needs to have as much spatial resolution as possible. What this means is that the separation *s* between the two sources at the focal plane must be sufficient to detect both sources.

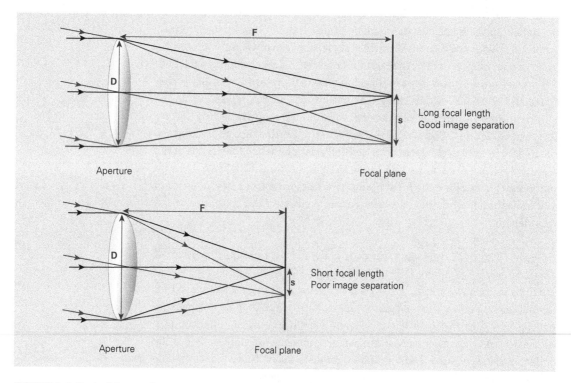

FIGURE 9.1 Optical Sensor Components

To keep *s* as large as possible, the optical sensor must have a large focal ratio, known to photographers as the **f number**. This is defined as the ratio of the focal length of the telescope to its diameter, that is, f = F/D. The idea is illustrated in Figure 9.1. As the focal plane is moved away from the lens, the focal length F increases and makes the separation *s* larger. The f number increases, image separation is better, and the telescope has better resolution.

Better separation, though, comes at a price. The trade-off for larger f is that while resolution improves (better image quality), there is less light on each pixel. A camera using an f number of f16 produces a better quality image than it does when using f2 but at the price of 64 times less light on each pixel. Anyone who has used a zoom lens on a film camera may have noticed this effect; the image becomes darker as you zoom in and the f number increases. (This effect is hard to see in a digital camera; the electronics compensate for the decreased light.)

Increasing the focal length also decreases the field of view. The telescope can resolve objects better, but it sees a smaller area at any given distance. Figure 9.2 illustrates this constraint. To appreciate this difference, suppose you are looking at a scene through a cardboard tube that is 1 inch in diameter and 1 inch long (f = 1). You would be able to see a great deal of the scene. Now replace that tube with one that is 1 inch in diameter but 20 inches long (f = 20). Very little of the scene would be visible, as the field of view has been significantly narrowed.

One way to compensate for the decreased light on each pixel is to increase the lens diameter to admit more light (while increasing the focal length to improve resolution). To illustrate how this has developed over time:

- The National Reconnaissance Office's (NRO's) 1960s vintage Corona satellite had a 24-inch focal length and a 6.8-inch diameter lens, producing an f number (F/D) of 3.5.[2] The small focal length gave it a wide field of view and wide area coverage, but its resolution was poor.
- By the late 1960s, the Gambit (KH-8) satellite had achieved a resolution of less than 2 feet with its 43.5-inch aperture, 175-inch focal length camera, giving an f number of 4.09.[3]
- The Hexagon (KH-9) satellite, operated during the 1970s and 1980s, did not match the resolution of the KH-8; its camera had a 20-inch aperture and focal length of 60 inches, giving it an f of 3.0 and a best image resolution of 2 to 3 feet. But it could cover a much larger area than the KH-8.[4]
- The optical sensor in the GeoEye-1 satellite (launched in 2007) has a 13.3-meter focal length and 1.1-meter diameter aperture, giving a much better f number (F/D) of 12.[5] The long focal length gives a good resolution, but the field of view is very narrow and its images cover a relatively small area.

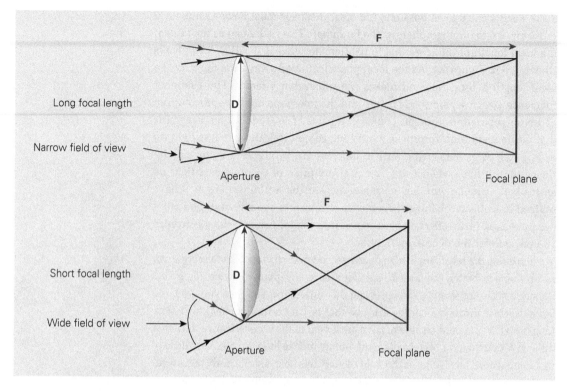

FIGURE 9.2 Effect of Focal Length on Field of View

The other way to compensate for the decreased light on each pixel is to improve the sensitivity of the detector. In old cameras, this sensing unit was photographic film. Film cameras that required high resolution or needed to function at low light levels used a more sensitive film known as high-speed film; it produced good photographs at higher f numbers. In modern cameras and intelligence sensors, the detector is a flat matrix of tiny light-sensitive solid-state devices called a focal plane array (so called because it is placed at the point where the telescope optics focus incoming light energy—the focal plane in Figure 9.1). Most such sensors use a charge-coupled device (CCD) for the focal plane array. Current generation CCDs are much more sensitive than the highest speed film. For comparison, the NRO's Corona camera used high-speed film and provided an image resolution of 8 to 10 feet.[6] The digital camera in the GeoEye-1 satellite, with its better f number and more sensitive CCD detectors, is able to produce images with 0.41-meter resolution.[7] GeoEye-2, completed in 2013, has an even better f number and still more sensitive detectors, giving it a resolution of 0.34 meters.[8]

If the focal plane array detects visible light, it requires no special cooling. And such devices are relatively cheap to build. But, increasingly, optical sensors used in intelligence and earth resources sensing operate in both the infrared and the visible parts of the spectrum. At the lower frequency (longer wavelength) part of the infrared spectrum, the detectors in the focal plane array must be cooled in order to make them more sensitive. Cooled focal plane arrays are much harder to build and more expensive.

Imaging Geometry and Imaging Platforms. Having detailed the basics of an optical system in the discussion above, this section covers the basics of imaging with optics. The distance between the target being imaged and the type of platform plays a large role in determining the detail of information obtained and the total area imaged by the sensor. Sensors located far away from their targets typically can view a larger area, but they cannot provide as much detail when compared with sensors that are close to the target. Figure 9.3 illustrates the field of regard, which is the limit of what an intelligence collection satellite might see. The field of regard is the total area that a collection platform is capable of seeing by pointing the sensor.

There are some basic differences between what a sensor can see of the earth when on an intelligence collection satellite (such as the NRO's Gambit or Hexagon, or Israel's Ofeq)[9] versus when that same sensor is on an airplane. A satellite can see a large part of the earth's surface; an aircraft much less. The collection satellite potentially can observe a sector anywhere in a whole province or country at a given moment, but its sensor cannot distinguish fine details. In contrast, a UAV-mounted camera could read the license plate on an auto or recognize an individual when the UAV overflies an installation at low altitude. But the low altitude limits the field of regard; so the camera could only view the immediate area around the installation.

The detail that can be seen in an image depends on the sensor's spatial resolution (that is, the size of the smallest possible feature that can be detected). Spatial resolution of passive sensors (the special case of radar sensors will be discussed later) depends in part on the sensor's field of view (FOV). The FOV is the angular cone of visibility of the sensor, measured in degrees, as shown in Figure 9.3. It determines the surface area that is seen from a given altitude at one moment in time. The size of the area viewed is determined by the FOV

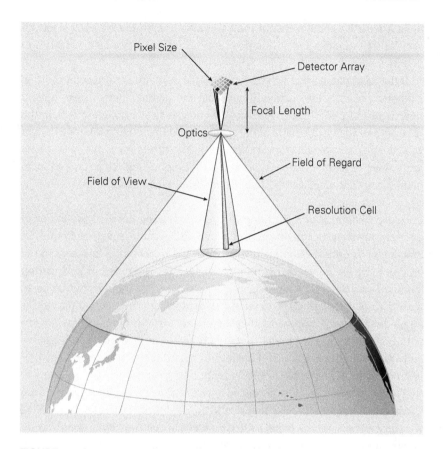

FIGURE 9.3 Sensor Field of View and Field of Regard

and the distance between the ground and the sensor—the farther the sensor is from the earth, the larger the area that is viewed.

Aircraft as optical imaging platforms have the advantage of getting close to the target for better resolution. But when they must overfly hostile territory, they are vulnerable to attack. So optical imaging aircraft generally are designed to be either high flying (such as the U-2) to avoid air defenses or very low flying, to be undetectable by most radars, and in either case, preferably very fast. Imaging aircraft have mostly been replaced by UAVs, which have the advantages of being cheaper to operate and do not risk a pilot.

Figure 9.3 illustrates two other important concepts—that of the resolution cell and the pixel. Most remote sensing images are composed of a matrix of picture elements, or pixels, which are the smallest units of an image. In a digital camera—and most electro-optical sensors used in intelligence are digital cameras—a pixel is defined by the size of the detector elements in the camera. Image pixels are normally square and represent a certain area on an image.

Each detector element receives light energy from a defined ground area that is called the resolution cell. A ground object can be detected if its size is equal to or larger than the resolution cell. If the object is smaller, it may not be detectable; the detector will average the brightness of all features in that resolution cell. Smaller objects can sometimes be detected if their reflectance is so strong as to dominate within their resolution cell.

As an example, if a spaceborne optical sensor has a spatial resolution of 10 meters, then when an image from that sensor is displayed at full resolution, each pixel represents an area of 10 meters by 10 meters on the ground. In this case the pixel size and resolution are the same.

So, the pixel size and resolution correspond; a camera's resolution cannot be better than the pixel size. However, it is possible to display an image with a pixel size different from the resolution. Satellite images of the earth often have their pixels averaged to represent larger areas, although the original spatial resolution of the sensor that collected the imagery remains the same.

Black-and-white cameras show the intensity of visible light in a pixel; color cameras also give some indication of wavelength in the pixel, but they do not measure the intensity of different wavelengths.

Imaging Sensors. Three types of collection sensors are used for imaging the earth's surface from aircraft: UAVs, aerostats, and satellites. Figure 9.4 shows a comparison of these three types. The following sections discuss how they are used.

Cross-Track Scanners. Also known as optical-mechanical or whiskbroom scanners, the cross-track scanner uses a scanning mirror that projects the image of a single surface resolution element (in effect, a pixel) onto a single detector. A cross-track scanner images the earth, back and forth in a series of lines perpendicular to the direction of platform movement, as shown in Figure 9.4. Each line is scanned from one side of the sensor to the other, using a rotating mirror. As the platform moves forward, successive scans build up a two-dimensional image of the earth's surface.

The instantaneous field of view (IFOV) is the angular region seen by a single detector in the sensor (shown as the small black region in Figure 9.3).

Optical Imaging

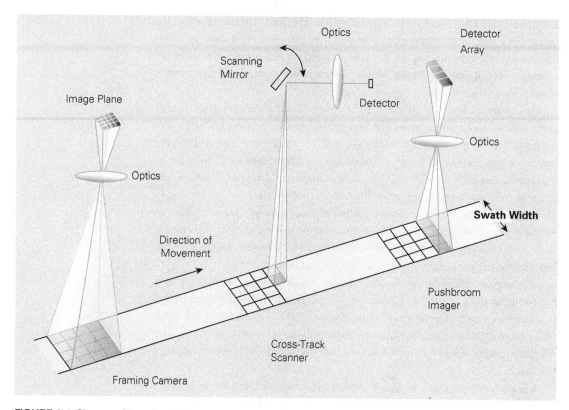

FIGURE 9.4 Classes of Imaging Systems

The IFOV of the sensor and the altitude of the platform determine the ground resolution cell viewed and, thus, the spatial resolution. The angular field of view is determined by the sweep of the mirror, measured in degrees, and that angle determines the width of the imaged swath. Airborne scanners typically sweep large angles (90 to 120 degrees). Satellites, because of their higher altitude, need only to sweep fairly small angles (10 to 20 degrees) to cover a broad region. Because the distance from the sensor to the target increases toward the edges of the swath, the ground resolution cells consequently become larger and the images become distorted at the edges.

The cross-track scanner is a simple design; therefore, it is easier and cheaper to put on a satellite than the two types discussed next. But the length of time that the sensor sees a ground resolution cell as the rotating mirror scans (called the dwell time) is generally quite short. The result is that the cross-track scanner has relatively poor sensitivity and, therefore, poor spectral and intensity resolution.

Pushbroom Imagers. Instead of a scanning mirror, some imaging systems use a linear array of detectors located at the focal plane of the image, which moves along in the flight track direction as indicated in Figure 9.4. The forward motion of the platform allows the imager to receive optical energy from successive strips of the earth and to build up a two-dimensional image, perpendicular to the flight direction.

These systems are called pushbroom imagers because the motion of the detector array resembles the bristles of a broom being pushed along a floor. Each individual detector at any instant measures the energy for a single ground resolution cell. The size of the detectors therefore determines the pixel size and, in turn, the spatial resolution of the system. A current example of a pushbroom imager used in intelligence is the one carried on the French Pleiades imagery satellite. The use of pushbroom imaging allows Pleiades to have a relatively wide swath width of 20 kilometers, while obtaining a resolution of 0.5 meters.[10]

Framing Cameras. The most widely used sensor in remote sensing today is the framing camera, shown on the left side of Figure 9.4. This sensor will be familiar to most readers, since most cameras, including smartphone cameras and video cameras, are framing cameras. It uses conventional camera optics and an array of detectors located in the focal plane. The framing cameras originally installed on aircraft and reconnaissance spacecraft such as the Corona (KH-4), Gambit (KH-8), and Hexagon (KH-9) used photographic film, but almost all framing cameras now used in intelligence rely on a detector array of CCDs. The more detectors in the array, the smaller each detector becomes and the better the imagery resolution becomes. But, as noted earlier, there is a trade-off: a smaller detector has less light striking it, and consequently, the sensitivity becomes worse.

An example of a current framing camera design is that carried by the Global Hawk UAV. It has a 10-inch reflecting telescope that provides common optics for two framing cameras—one operating in the visible band and one in the infrared band (3.6 to 5 microns). At its best resolution (called the spot collection mode), the camera can collect 1,900 frames a day with frame size 2 by 2 kilometers. It can locate targets to within a 20-meter circular error of probability (meaning that 50 percent of target locations will be accurate to within 20 meters). The camera can also operate in a wide area search mode, covering a swath up to 10 kilometers wide at lower resolution.[11]

Each type of imaging system shown in Figure 9.4 has distinct advantages and disadvantages. The framing camera provides an image that covers a

Optical
Imaging

large area in one snapshot, but it requires technologically sophisticated planar arrays of small, sensitive detectors. The cross-track scanner can use a single very simple detector, but its overall sensitivity suffers because it spends little dwell time in each of the cells shown in Figure 9.4. The push-broom imager is a compromise—it allows more dwell time in each cell than the scanner and is less complex than the framing camera.

Framing cameras and pushbroom imagers are probably the most commonly used imaging systems today. Which one works best depends on the mission requirements. If the system must map very large areas of the earth, then the pushbroom imager is probably the best bet. Spectral imagers, discussed in Chapter 10, also tend to use pushbroom imagers because a separate linear array of detectors is used for each spectral band. If the system is intended to take a series of images of known target areas, then the framing camera is better; it can provide the most detailed image of the target area because of its higher sensitivity.

Video. If continuous surveillance of an area is desired, then a framing camera can be operated in video mode—giving up the ability to search a large area in favor of monitoring activity in a specific area. Many UAVs carry framing cameras that operate much like smartphone cameras—you can choose either to collect single images or to run the camera continuously to collect a video of the scene.

In typical airborne video surveillance activity, the platform constantly monitors an area and feeds data to the ground for real-time analysis. Most cameras used in video surveillance today have a field of view that is fairly small in order for the camera to have good resolution, which is needed for a good identification of the target and to establish a target signature. The challenge often is to track moving targets over an extended period of time. As the target moves around in the scene, it will sometimes be hidden by buildings or trees. The target has to be reacquired when it emerges. Increasingly this requires automated tracking of the target, followed by using its signature to automatically reacquire the target when it emerges from cover.[12]

Newer video surveillance designs can view a wide area at high resolution. The concept is to use multiple cameras and to optically merge the separate images to provide both a wide field of view and high spatial resolution. Such sensors, with a capability to view in both the visible and infrared spectrum, offer the possibility of nonstop surveillance. One such sensor has demonstrated the capability to provide continuous, real-time video imagery of an area the size of a small city with a resolution fine enough to track 8,000 moving objects in its field of view.[13]

Space Surveillance. Optical sensors that look from the earth out into space function in the same way as airborne or spaceborne sensors that look down at earth. They all use the same type of source: a telescope backed by an array of sensitive light detectors. But the telescopes used for space situational awareness are typically much larger and more capable. The field of regard is the hemisphere limited by the horizon; the field of view is determined by the telescope design but typically is very narrow because of the need to detect very small objects.

Optical sensor performance for space sensing is controlled by the same factors as for earth sensing: Performance is determined primarily by the size of the optics. In general, larger apertures provide better performance. But performance is measured differently. The important factor is the visual magnitude that the sensor can detect.

Visual magnitude (m_v) is a measure of the relative brightness of an object. A higher m_v equates to a dimmer object. The brightest stars have a visual magnitude near 1. The dimmest stars that can be seen by the unaided eye have magnitude 6. Satellites have a highly variable m_v; their reflectivity changes depending on how much of the satellite is visible (the aspect ratio) and the material of the visible portion. A typical GEO satellite has a visual magnitude of between 11 and 13—about the magnitude of the moons of Mars. GEO satellites can be detected and tracked with telescope apertures on the order of 0.5- to 1-meter diameter.

Ground-Based Space Surveillance. Most optical sensing systems do not have their own dedicated transmitters. Instead, they generally use the sun as their transmitter. (This is perhaps the single most significant difference between optical and radar operation against satellites.) Using the sun as the transmitter allows optical systems to operate at shorter wavelengths, but it also makes them dependent on favorable lighting and weather conditions. When used for detecting and tracking satellites, optical sites have to satisfy two conditions:

- First, the ground site normally must be in darkness while the sun illuminates the target (the terminator condition described previously). But LEO satellites may have almost half their orbit in earth's shadow, making it possible to track them optically only during several hours before sunrise and after sunset when the terminator condition is satisfied. A LEO satellite may overfly an optical site many times each day, but opportunities for optical tracking may only occur many days apart. For certain satellites, such as sun-synchronous satellites, favorable lighting conditions may not occur for several months at a time. HEO and GEO satellites make better targets since they remain illuminated during much of the night.

• Second, the ground site must have favorable atmospheric conditions. The inability to operate during adverse weather is a severe limitation for optical sensors. Clouds, fog, and haze severely reduce an optical system's ability to function, while the same conditions have little effect on radars. The best locations for clear, dark skies are typically at higher elevations. Geographic locations less subject to adverse atmospheric effects and light pollution also are desirable.

Though the terminator condition is optimum for optical sensing, passive daytime sensing is possible. LEO satellites have been tracked during daylight hours using visible light filters and narrow field of view optics. The filters pass only specific light wavelengths and reject all others, significantly reducing light from sources other than the satellite. The infrared signature of a satellite viewed against the cold background of space has also been used to track satellites during the day.

Optical tracking systems are rarely used to track LEO spacecraft because the high orbital velocity of the satellite limits the observation period by the optical sensor. They are, however, used to track space objects in GEO or HEO orbits; these orbits permit long observation periods during favorable lighting conditions.

The primary U.S. ground-based optical sensor for obtaining tracks on space objects is the ground-based electro-optical deep space surveillance (GEODSS) system. The GEODSS sensor is an electronically enhanced telescope that uses low-light television cameras. Sensor data can be stored for analysis locally or transmitted in near real time to the Space Surveillance Center for analysis, if required. The sensors provide tracking that is accurate enough to maintain a space object catalog, including satellites in GEO orbits. The sensors operate only during clear weather at night.

Each GEODSS site has three telescopes, each facing a different section of the sky. As the satellites cross the sky, the telescopes take rapid electronic snapshots, showing up on the operator's console as tiny streaks. Computers then measure these streaks and use the data to figure the current position of a satellite in its orbit. Star images, which remain fixed, are used as reference or calibration points for each of the three telescopes. There are three GEODSS sites, located at Socorro, New Mexico; Diego Garcia, in the Indian Ocean (shown in Figure 9.5); and Maui, Hawaii.[14] The Maui GEODSS site is part of the Maui Space Surveillance System that was discussed briefly in Chapter 8.

FIGURE 9.5 Diego Garcia GEODSS Site[15]

Space-Based Space Surveillance. While most optical tracking and imaging of satellites is done from ground-based sites, the trend is to do space-based optical surveillance of space targets. Space-based surveillance of satellites has several advantages. The effects of weather and the atmosphere are eliminated. There are more opportunities for getting sun illumination of the target satellite. Images can be obtained at closer ranges to provide better resolution.

Both satellites and reentry vehicles can be tracked and imaged from space. The U.S. Air Force (USAF) Space-Based Visible Sensor, for example, was designed to track both types of vehicles. Its sensor suite includes a visible sensor in the 300 to 900 micron band along with sensors that function in the long-wave infrared and ultraviolet bands.[16] Searches in the infrared (IR) region are easier to do (there is no problem of atmospheric windows).

The challenges of space-based surveillance of space lie in selecting the right orbits for the telescope and the right target areas for search. Because telescopes have a relatively small FOV, wide area search for LEO, medium earth orbit (MEO), and HEO satellites is difficult. Using a telescope with a wide field of view makes it easier to search for and acquire the target. However, a telescope's tracking accuracy suffers when it has a wide FOV. Several solutions to this problem exist. Attaching a small, wide FOV finder telescope to a larger, narrow FOV tracking telescope is one method. Another solution uses a separate acquisition telescope. GEO satellites operate in a more constrained region, so GEO search is possible with narrow FOV telescopes.[17]

On occasion, an imaging satellite will fly close enough to another satellite to obtain a high-resolution picture of it. This technique is called *satellite-to-satellite* imaging or *sat-squared* imaging.[18] Figure 9.6 illustrates how well such imaging can work. On April 15, 2012, the French space agency CNES used its Pleiades Earth observation satellite to capture an image of the European Space Agency's Envisat satellite. At a distance of about 100 kilometers, Envisat's main body, solar panel, and radar antenna are clearly visible in the figure.[19]

PROCESSING

Today, most remote sensing data are recorded in digital format. So almost all image interpretation and analysis requires digital processing. Digital image processing typically entails formatting and correcting the data, digital

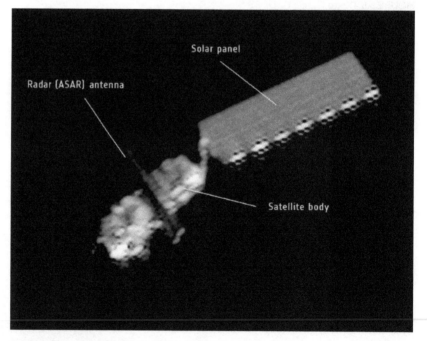

FIGURE 9.6 Satellite-to-Satellite Image of Envisat

Image of Envisat courtesy of *Space.com*.

enhancement to permit better visual interpretation, and sometimes auto-mated classification of targets and features—all done entirely by computer. In order to process remote sensing imagery digitally, the data have to be recorded in an appropriate digital form. Several commercially available soft-ware systems have been developed specifically for such image processing and analysis.

To get an image that is useful for intelligence, at least two processing functions have to be carried out: preprocessing and image enhancement.

Preprocessing involves making radiometric or geometric corrections to the image before the information of intelligence value is extracted.

- Radiometric corrections involve correcting the data for sensor irregu-larities, eliminating unwanted sensor or atmospheric noise, and ensuring that the image accurately represents the amount of optical energy that the sensor received.
- Geometric corrections involve correcting for geometric distortions that are created as the sensor looks at different angles from the vertical and then converting the target locations to actual coordinates (latitude and lon-gitude) on the earth's surface.

Image enhancement improves the appearance of the imagery, helping in the visual interpretation and analysis stages. This functions much like the redeye or blur removal feature of some digital cameras. Three types of enhancement are frequently used to help interpret imagery: contrast enhancement, spatial filtering, and edge enhancement.

- Contrast enhancement involves increasing the tonal distinction between various features in a scene so that the features are more prominent.
- Spatial filtering is used to enhance (or suppress) specific spatial pat-terns in an image to emphasize the interesting parts and eliminate the unin-teresting parts of the image. One might, for example, gray out all of the buildings in a large city except the ones of intelligence interest, so that the latter stand out prominently from the rest.
- Edge enhancement is commonly used in processing images for intel-ligence. Features of interest to the imagery analyst often have sharp straight edges that are not common in natural features, and edge enhancement high-lights these features.[20]

Think of image enhancement as being like using Photoshop to edit a facial photo, with the opposite objective. Instead of eliminating the wrinkles

Optical
Imaging

and blemishes, we want to make them stand out more clearly so they can be analyzed.

IMAGE EXPLOITATION AND ANALYSIS

After processing, exploitation is the next step in converting imagery into intelligence. This conversion is done by trained experts who were formerly known as photo interpreters. The advent of digital imagery and the increasing complexity of the exploitation process led to a name change for these professionals. They are now generally called imagery analysts, or geospatial intelligence (GEOINT) analysts in the United States.

An image of any region of the earth will contain many different signatures. And imagery analysis often relies on identifying a unique signature within that set. Most liquid natural gas tanker ships, for example, have above-deck gas storage domes that uniquely identify the ship as a tanker. Many facilities, such as nuclear power plants, possess unique signatures because of the functions that must be performed at the facility—reactor cooling structures, for example. Imagery analysts become adept over time at quickly recognizing these features.

After a signature has been identified and characterized, imagery analysts use several specialized techniques to convert it into intelligence. As a simple example, during the Suez crisis in 1956, the National Photographic Interpretation Center (NPIC) developed a technique they called "tentology"—counting the number of tents in the field at Cyprus and multiplying by the number of troops assigned to each tent, thereby coming up with a count on the number of British troops in Cyprus.[21]

The history of Libya's chemical warfare plant at Rabta, which dates from 1984, provides an example of how imagery exploitation and analysis works in practice as well. This plant was mentioned briefly in Chapter 4. According to a report by the U.S. Office of Technology Assessment,

> Libyan government officials adamantly insisted that the Rabta facility was a pharmaceutical plant, designated Pharma-150. Yet the factory was unusually large by the standards of the pharmaceutical industry and was ringed by high fences and 40-foot sand revetments—seemingly excessive security for an ordinary chemical plant. Since the production facility was completely enclosed inside a warehouse-like structure, overhead photography revealed nothing about the process equipment inside, but the plant's oversized air-filtration system suggested that it was intended for the production of toxic chemicals.

It was not until August 1988, however, that the CIA obtained more solid evidence that the Rabta plant was engaged in CW agent production. Following a partial test run of the production process, an accidental spill occurred as highly toxic wastes were being transferred for disposal outside the plant. The resulting cloud of fumes killed a pack of wild desert dogs in the vicinity of the plant. Their bodies, detected by satellite, indicated that the plant was producing chemicals of warfare toxicity.[22]

Imagery analysis also has to deal with the problem of denial and deception, which is increasing as more countries orbit imaging satellites. A subsequent attempted deception at the Rabta plant provides an example. According to the Office of Technology Assessment report, the Rabta plant was believed to have been destroyed by fire on March 13, 1990. But the French SPOT-1 satellite photographed the facility on March 18, and it appeared to be intact. The Libyans had created the illusion of a major fire for overhead imagery by painting scorch marks on the building roof and burning several truckloads of old tires to produce black smoke. The Libyans also had sent ambulances to the area to help maintain the deception.[23]

Stereoscopic Imagery. Another valuable tool in imagery analysis is to use stereoscopic imagery. Soon after aerial photography began to be used in intelligence, it became apparent that an imagery analyst could obtain more useful detail from a three-dimensional (3-D) image than from the two-dimensional (2-D) image provided by conventional photography. To create a 3-D illusion of depth in a photograph, a **stereograph**—a combination of two photographs of the same scene taken from slightly different angles—must be created using a stereo camera. At short ranges, this can be done by a camera with dual lenses. In aerial or satellite photography, stereographs are created by taking two successive images of the same ground area with suitable spacing; the two images are called a stereo pair. The slightly different perspectives of the two images mimic stereoscopic vision. One angle records the scene from the perspective of a viewer's left eye and the other from the perspective of the right eye. Stereographic imagery can efficiently display the distribution of the physical, biological, and cultural components of a given landscape. Natural and man-made features all have different identifying signatures that are more readily recognized in 3-D than in 2-D imagery.

During World War II, many countries began to obtain 3-D imagery using stereographs in aerial reconnaissance. Camouflaged weapons and structures were difficult to see in conventional aerial photographs, but aerial stereographs enabled military personnel to see through the camouflage and recognize hidden features that only stereoscopic vision could reveal. Stereo imaging was a capability of the Gambit (KH-8) satellite.[24]

To appear as a single 3-D image, the two stereograph pictures must be placed side by side and viewed through a **stereoscope**, a device that simultaneously presents the left photograph to the viewer's left eye and the right photograph to the right eye. The stereoscope consists of two lenses that can be adjusted along a slide bar to be as far apart as the viewer's eyes; the lenses are placed in a raised mount (on collapsible legs) that is positioned about six inches above the central region of the stereo pair. The brain receives each image separately and integrates them into a single 3-D image. The stereoscope has been largely replaced by modern digital imagery and signal processing; most stereographs are now created and displayed electronically.

Imagery Interpretation Scales. The value of the signature obtained in a given image is critically dependent on the quality of the image. Imagery analysts rely on some type of imagery interpretation scale to tell them how useful an image might be for identifying unique signatures and patterns.

For decades the U.S. intelligence community has used the National Imagery Interpretability Rating Scale (NIIRS) to quantify the interpretability or usefulness of imagery. The NIIRS is intended to provide an objective standard for image quality; the term *image quality* can mean different things to imagery analysts than to optical engineers. In practice, imagery analysts found that simple physical image quality metrics, such as image scale or resolution, did not adequately predict image interpretability. More complex metrics were tried but were too confusing to use. NIIRS ratings, in contrast, were found to provide a good shorthand description of the information that can be extracted from a given image. Table 9.1 is a summary version of the U.S. imagery rating, or NIIRS, scale.[25]

For a given optical system, the NIIRS values get higher as the collector gets closer to the target. To illustrate typical NIIRS performance, the Global Hawk UAV can deliver NIIRS 6 visible imagery at its normal operating altitude in its wide area search mode. The infrared sensor at the same altitude can deliver NIIRS 5 imagery.[26]

Analysis Example: The Arab Spring. The bulk of earth imagery intelligence is derived from government-owned systems. Increasingly, though, imagery from commercial satellites such as GeoEye is being used by intelligence agencies.[27] The quality of such imagery has improved to the point that it is very useful for intelligence and not just for governments. It can be used

TABLE 9.1 Description of NIIRS Rating Scale

NIIRS value	Description and Examples
0	Interpretability of the imagery is precluded by obscuration, degradation, or very poor resolution.
1	Detect a medium-sized port facility or distinguish between taxiways and runways at a large airfield.
2	Detect large hangars at airfields or large buildings (for example, hospitals, factories, and warehouses).
3	Identify the wing configuration (for example, straight, swept, or delta) of large aircraft. Identify a large surface ship by type (for example, cruiser, auxiliary ship, or noncombatant/merchant). Detect trains or strings of standard rolling stock on railroad tracks (not individual cars).
4	Identify large fighters by type. Detect an open missile silo door. Identify individual tracks, rail pairs, control towers, and switching points in rail yards.
5	Distinguish between aircraft by the presence of refueling equipment (for example, pedestal and wing pod). Identify radar as vehicle-mounted or trailer-mounted. Identify air surveillance radars on ships. Identify individual rail cars by type (for example, gondola, flat, or box) and/or locomotives by type (for example, steam or diesel).
6	Distinguish between models of small/medium helicopters. Identify the spare tire on a medium-sized truck. Identify automobiles as sedans or station wagons.
7	Identify fittings and fairings on a fighter-sized aircraft. Detect details of the silo door hinging mechanism on launch silos and launch control silos. Identify individual rail ties.
8	Identify the rivet lines on bomber aircraft. Identify a handheld surface-to-air missile. Detect winch cables on deck-mounted cranes. Identify windshield wipers on a vehicle.
9	Differentiate cross-slot from single slot heads on aircraft skin panel fasteners. Identify vehicle registration numbers on trucks. Identify screws and bolts on missile components. Detect individual spikes in railroad ties.

Optical Imaging

by NGOs, corporate entities, or even private citizens to produce useful intelligence, as the following example illustrates.

Beginning in February 2011, many parts of the Middle East and North Africa were disrupted with the advent of what became known as the "Arab Spring." The Arab Spring began in Tunisia and spread from there. A popular revolt developed against the Qaddafi regime in Libya, and the ensuing conflict caused large numbers of Libyans to flee the country.

Figure 9.7 is a GeoEye image of the main border crossing between Libya and neighboring Tunisia at Ras Ajdir, Libya, early in the conflict. The image was taken on March 3, 2011. It illustrates the sort of intelligence that is needed by governments and by NGOs that must respond to refugee crises. Imagery analysts at IHS Jane's concluded that several thousand displaced

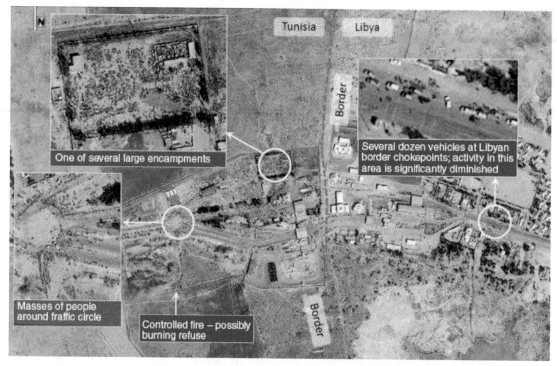

FIGURE 9.7 Displaced Libyans in Tunisia in 2011

Satellite image by GeoEye. Analysis performed by IHS Jane's.

Libyans were gathered in open or makeshift camps on the Tunisian side. On the Libyan side, the analysts noted that cross-border traffic had been suspended and that choke points had been set up to control or block traffic.[28] As the conflict continued and spread to other countries, GeoEye and other commercial imagers provided invaluable unclassified intelligence that could be used in U.N. debates, multinational policy and military planning, and NGO relief efforts.

Unfortunately, imagery exploitation and analysis remains the bottleneck in the imagery world. Image processing, to a large extent, can be automated. Exploitation cannot. It requires the attention of an imagery analyst who can examine the imagery and put it in context. The problem is especially severe for imagery that supports ongoing military operations. In a 2010 report, the Government Accountability Office (GAO) told Congress that the capability to gather imagery intelligence (IMINT) is outpacing U.S. ability to transmit the data to ground stations and is overwhelming the available imagery analysts. The problem is particularly severe for UAVs; the GAO noted that only about half of all the imagery collected by a single Predator UAV is capable of being exploited and observed:

> The military services and defense agencies face long-standing challenges with processing, exploiting, and disseminating data from numerous intelligence, surveillance, and reconnaissance (ISR) systems—including manned and unmanned airborne, space-borne, maritime, and terrestrial systems—that play critical roles in support of current military operations.[29]

Space Surveillance Processing and Exploitation. We said earlier that space surveillance has three missions: to discover new satellites in orbit, to obtain and update the orbital information on all satellites, and to identify the missions of satellites. We'll look at processing and exploitation for each mission in turn.

Search for New Satellites. Occasionally, optical systems must conduct searches to detect new satellites and to reacquire tracking on satellites that have been lost. Optical search for satellites is done by using a telescope drive. The drive moves the telescope across the sky at the same rate that the stars appear to move. This keeps the distant stars in the same positions in the field of view. As the telescope slowly moves, its camera takes very rapid electronic snapshots of the field of view. Star images, which remain fixed, are electronically erased. Satellites, however, do not remain fixed, and their movements show up as tiny streaks that can be viewed on a console screen. In the processing phase, computers measure these streaks and use the data to determine the position and calculate the orbit of a satellite.[30]

Searches for satellites in GEO, or near the apogee of HEO, require a different approach since satellites in these orbits show apparent movement very slowly. A process of elimination is typically used. Star catalogs are used to account for the stars in the field of view, while space object catalogs are used to account for known satellites, thus leaving only new or moved satellites. Another approach that is used to detect GEO satellites is to turn off the telescope drive. A GEO satellite or debris then appears as a point, with the stars appearing as streaks.

Obtaining Orbital Parameters. In order to keep track of satellites and predict their future locations, we need the orbital parameters, which are called

orbital elements or the element set. These are determined by tracking the satellite. One way to get angular tracking of satellites is to measure the location of the satellite among stars at various points along the satellite's track. Since the reference stars' positions are known, the angular position of the satellite and its orbit can be calculated. The process is much the same as for search; the telescope moves to keep the stars apparently stationary, and times and positions of the satellite are compared with known stars and the position of the satellite is determined. Alternatively, it is possible to track very dim objects by moving the telescope to follow the tracked object, so that the object's image remains stationary on the detector. The long exposure times allow the detector to collect additional light. The problem is that the trajectory of the target satellite must be known in advance in order to move the telescope with the satellite's trajectory.

We'd like to get both angle and range tracking of satellites. Passive optical systems can do angular tracking but cannot directly measure the range to a target like radars can. Radar systems measure the round-trip transmission time to a target to determine the range. But an optical system using the sun as its illuminator has no reference starting time from which to determine range. A network of optical systems can obtain range, though, by using the angle of arrival technique to be discussed for radio frequency (RF) systems in Chapter 13. If several sites simultaneously track an object, triangulation on the object will yield its range.

Alternatively, an active optical system can be used to obtain range. A laser can function as both an illuminator and radar transmitter. Laser rangefinders use light in the same way radars use radio waves to measure the round-trip transmission time to an object to determine its range.

Object Identification. Space object identification (SOI) requires a number of specialized processing techniques. Optical SOI systems may be either passive or active. Passive optical SOI systems use the sun's illumination to provide optical signature information. Active optical SOI systems, as previously noted, rely on a laser to illuminate the target. A laser illuminator has several advantages when compared with using only the sun. First, the laser can be used for both day and night operations. Second, it can obtain the object's spin rate from the Doppler signature. Third, it can provide better imaging than is possible using only passive illumination.

Perhaps the most useful optical technique for space object identification is to obtain an optical image of the object. The Air Force Maui Optical Station has an imaging capability: the Advanced Electro-Optical System (AEOS) Imaging Sensor. With its 3.67-meter aperture, AEOS is the largest

U.S. optical telescope designed for tracking satellites. The 75-ton telescope points and tracks very accurately for deep space tracking, yet is fast enough to track both low-earth satellites and missiles. Its sophisticated sensors include an adaptive optics system, radiometer, spectrograph, and long-wave infrared imager, providing a variety of signatures that help in object identification.[31]

DISSEMINATION

The dissemination of visible imagery long has been driven by a demand for speed. The intelligence conveyed in imagery is perishable, especially in crises and in tactical military and law enforcement operations. But all customers, from the U.S. president on down, want the imagery as quickly as they can get it.

When the imagery product came from photographic film, *quickly* meant days or even weeks, as noted earlier. The wide use of digital imaging reduced that time to hours, then to minutes. Today, video imagery is available to all customers in real time, which is one of the reasons it is so attractive. But some imagery must be exploited and analyzed to produce intelligence, and the presence of a human (the imagery analyst) in the process means that there is a lower limit to the time for dissemination—perhaps minutes to hours.

Classification of the imagery product is another dissemination issue that has been largely resolved. Many customers (most law enforcement officers and foreign nationals, for example) have no security clearance. So the imagery needs to have the lowest possible classification, preferably unclassified. If the means for obtaining the imagery do not need to be kept secret, this is not a problem. For example, aircraft and UAVs are widely known as vehicles that collect imagery, so the material can be released at an unclassified or at most secret level. And commercial satellite imagery is unclassified.

On the other hand, when special capabilities are used to collect the imagery or unique features of the imagery must be protected, a high classification and very limited distribution are required, based on a pressing need to know. This means that some entities in the very large customer set for visible imagery (such as foreign partners) will not have access to the material at all.

Imagery Libraries. Panchromatic imagery is limited because only spatial measurement (height, length, width, and shape) can be made on panchromatic images. Some indication of intensity is present because bright objects will appear white in the image and dim objects will appear black. Therefore, a crude sort of signature can be obtained, but the resulting signature libraries are fairly simple. These libraries have been compiled over many years in the form of what were called photo interpreter keys—books that contained images of, for example, specific types of tanks, airplanes, ships, and buildings.[32] Such libraries now are called imagery analysis keys.

An example of a signature library data set is one based on *cratology*, which is defined as the study of the function of shipping crates observed in photography. The size and configuration of a shipping crate often will indicate what is inside. Imagery analysts over the years have developed substantial libraries of information on weapons crates down to the size of ammunition boxes. Using the libraries, an analyst can identify the type of ammunition or artillery shells by measuring the box used to ship them.[33] Protrusions from the crates for toolboxes, rotors, or similar clues help identify specific contents of the crates.[34]

Cratology has been used for many years to identify movements of military hardware. An early example of cratology success occurred at the beginning of the Cuban Missile Crisis in 1962. On September 28, imagery analysts observed crates on the deck of a Soviet ship bound for Cuba; the crates were uniquely designed to ship IL-28 medium bombers. This report, along with reports of ballistic missiles being stationed in Cuba, led to a U-2 flight in October that brought back pictures of the ballistic missile sites under construction.[35]

Press reports claim that during August 2006 a U.S. reconnaissance satellite observed crates being loaded onto an Iranian transport aircraft near Tehran. Based on the dimensions of the crates, U.S. intelligence analysts reportedly concluded that Iranian C-802 Noor antiship cruise missiles were being loaded onto the aircraft. According to the press report, the identification set off a chain of diplomatic action that kept the missiles from being delivered to Hezbollah guerrillas who were fighting Israeli forces in Lebanon.[36]

Space Catalogs. Most countries that maintain space surveillance systems also maintain a catalog of space objects—both those of intelligence significance and of debris. These libraries have a specific name; they are called space object catalogs or space catalogs. France, the United States, Russia, and the European Space Agency, for example, all have their own space catalogs. These catalogs quickly go out of date and have to be maintained. In the United States, updates are handled by the Space Surveillance Network. About 20,000 objects are maintained in the U.S. catalog.

Structure

Optical imaging of the earth's surface is organizationally fragmented, based in part on the different missions that it supports and based in part on the diversity of the customer set. The type of collection platform used also affects the organizational structure that is adopted. Following is a general summary of the structural breakout.

Prior to the Cold War, very little use was made of imagery by national-level customers. Military aircraft conducted photo reconnaissance flights to support military operations in the theater. That situation changed during the Cold War. As noted in Chapter 6, the need for national-level, detailed knowledge of strategic targets in the Soviet Union and the PRC, along with the sensitive nature of U-2 collection, drove the United States to centralize the processing and exploitation of imagery acquired by U-2 aircraft.

With the shift to satellite-borne imaging systems, the national structure remained centralized to handle the large-area coverage and high volume. The early Corona imaging satellite used film cameras, with the film returned to earth days or even weeks after the images had been taken. The delay was frustrating for policymakers, who often needed current information about developing crises around the world. The move to electro-optical sensors speeded the processing and allowed a capability for imagery to be sent directly to many customers. The resulting competition for limited collection assets required a central prioritization system, discussed in Chapter 18.

The U.S. pattern of a central organization for handling national requirements is followed in other countries that employ imaging satellites. Optical imagery to support national requirements usually is centralized in an organization that provides imagery products for a wide range of policymakers and military customers. In the United States, the National Geospatial-Intelligence Agency (NGA) has this responsibility.

Aircraft and UAV imagery coverage may sometimes be done at the national level, but military forces are the primary customers for this imagery. Military tactical imagery support typically is organic; that is, it is handled by airborne reconnaissance platforms (aircraft and UAVs) in the theater of operation. Processing and exploitation centers are located in the theater, and the imagery is distributed to units in the theater. Law enforcement organizations have a similar structure.

Commercial companies such as France's Spot Image operate the Système Pour l'Observation de la Terre (SPOT), a constellation of imagery satellites, and sell the product. GeoEye, Inc., a U.S. company, sells satellite imagery to companies such as Microsoft and Google, and to government entities such as NGA.

Optical
Imaging

The mission of tracking and identifying space objects (to include satellites, space debris, and ballistic missile reentry vehicles) from the earth's surface is typically given to the military. The United States has two such military organizations with different space sensing missions. The Space Surveillance Network under the U.S. Strategic Command is responsible for satellites and space debris. The U.S. Missile Defense Agency has its own system for detecting and tracking ballistic missiles in flight. Russia's Space Surveillance System is part of the Air and Space Defense Forces, a branch of Russia's Armed Forces. Europe has its European Space Agency with a planned European space surveillance system. But individual European countries maintain separate systems to support national needs. France has its own space surveillance system, and Germany has its Space Situational Awareness Center.

Summary

Optical imaging systems are usually called electro-optical imagers, because the incoming optical signal hits a detector array, where it is converted to an electrical signal for transmission and storage. Electro-optical imagers are attractive because they can cover large areas of the earth's surface, with spatial resolutions that are sufficient for obtaining useful signatures and doing imagery interpretation.

Optical sensors are, for all practical purposes, telescopes with cameras attached. The optics focus the incoming energy at a point called the focal point. Two dimensions of a telescope (or of any optical system) define its performance: the size of the aperture and the focal length. In order to resolve separate targets, it is necessary to make the ratio of focal length to aperture diameter (the f number) as large as possible. The trade-off is that increasing the f number both narrows the sensor's field of view and decreases its sensitivity.

An electro-optical imager uses an array of sensitive detectors located in the focal plane that detects incoming light from the entire field of view. The goal is to make the detectors as small as possible (to improve resolution) and as sensitive as possible (to detect weak signals). Each detector collects light energy from a specific resolution cell in the target area, and that light creates one pixel in the resulting image.

Three types of EO imagers are widely used. Simplest is the cross-track scanner, which uses a scanning mirror to focus the light energy from each resolution cell onto a single detector and scans through all of the resolution cells in the field of view. Because it spends little time staring at any part of the target area, its sensitivity is poor. A pushbroom imager uses a linear array of detectors to sweep the target area as the platform moves, giving it better sensitivity than a cross-track scanner. Most complex and most common is the framing camera, which uses a detector array to provide the best sensitivity of the three.

In order to get an image that is useful for intelligence, at least two processing functions have to be carried out. The first is preprocessing: radiometric corrections are made to eliminate noise and to accurately represent the intensity of features in the image, and geometric corrections are done to remove image distortions. The second is image enhancement, to improve the appearance of the imagery to assist in visual interpretation and analysis by enhancing contrast and enhancing specific spatial patterns such as edges. Processing also can involve using false color in order to display image features that are not in the visible spectrum.

Image exploitation and analysis relies on identifying a unique signature in the image. One example is cratology, the discipline of identifying the contents of a crate by its physical measurements. Exploitation is helped by the use of stereo imagery, created by imaging a target area from two different angles to obtain a 3-D image.

Ground-based optical sensing of satellites relies on large telescopes, usually located on mountaintops to avoid cloud cover and reduce atmospheric distortion. Their purpose is to either track a satellite to determine its orbit or to identify the satellite. A satellite often can be identified by its unique signature—a combination of the satellite's orbit, its shape, and its reflectivity characteristics.

Space-based optical sensors can obtain high-resolution images of satellites to aid identification, because the atmosphere is not a factor and the image can be obtained at closer ranges than is possible with ground-based imaging.

NOTES

1. Katie Walter, "Surveillance on the Fly," *Science and Technology Review* (October 2006), Lawrence Livermore National Laboratory, accessed 22 September 2012 at www.llnl.gov/str/Oct06/Pennington.html.

2. National Reconnaissance Office, "Corona Fact Sheet," accessed 14 September 2012 at http://www.nro.gov/history/csnr/corona/factsheet.html.

3. National Reconnaissance Office, "Gambit 3 (KH-8) Fact Sheet," accessed 14 September 2012 at http://www.nro.gov/history/csnr/gambhex/Docs/GAM_3_Fact_sheet.pdf.

4. National Reconnaissance Office, "Hexagon (KH-9) Fact Sheet," accessed 14 September 2012 at http://www.nro.gov/history/csnr/gambhex/Docs/Hex_fact_sheet.pdf.

5. Satellite Imaging Corporation, "GeoEye-1 Satellite Sensor," accessed 14 September 2012 at http://www.satimagingcorp.com/satellite-sensors/geoeye-1.html.

6. National Reconnaissance Office, "Corona Fact Sheet," accessed 14 September 2012 at http://www.nro.gov/history/csnr/corona/factsheet.html.

7. Satellite Imaging Corporation, "GeoEye-1 Satellite Sensor," accessed 14 September 2012 at http://www.satimagingcorp.com/satellite-sensors/geoeye-1.html.

8. Satellite Imaging Corporation, "About GeoEye-2," accessed 29 September 2012 at http://launch.geoeye.com/LaunchSite/about/Default.aspx.

9. Both SPOT and Ofeq are acknowledged to be intelligence collectors by the French (http://www.spotimage.fr/web/en/1803-defence-intelligence-security.php) and the Israelis (http://www.haaretz.com/hasen/spages/869771.html), respectively, accessed 22 September 2012.

10. Jean-Luc Lamard, Catherine Gaudin-Delrieu, David Valentini, Christophe Renard, Thierry Tournier, and Jean-Marc Laherrere, "Design of the High Resolution Optical Instrument for the Pleiades HR Earth Observation Satellites," *Proceedings of the 5th International Conference on Space Optics* (Tolouse, France, March 30–April 2, 2004), 149–156, accessed 22 September 2012 at http://articles.adsabs.harvard.edu//full/2004ESASP.554.149L/0000149.000.html.

11. Airforce-technology.com, "RQ-4A/B Global Hawk High-Altitude, Long-Endurance, Unmanned Reconnaissance Aircraft, USA," accessed 22 September 2012 at http://www.airforce-technology.com/Projects/rq4-global-hawk-uav/.

12. Pablo O. Arambel, Jeffrey Silver, and Matthew Antone, "Signature-Aided Air-to-Ground Video Tracking," *Conference Proceedings of the 9th International Conference on Information Fusion* (Florence, Italy, July 10–13, 2006).

13. Walter, "Surveillance on the Fly."

14. USAF, "Ground-Based Electro-optical Deep Space Surveillance," Fact Sheet, accessed 22 September 2012 at http://www.af.mil/information/factsheets/factsheet.asp?id=170.

15. USAF Photo, accessed 25 September 2012 at http://www.af.mil/shared/media/photodb/photos/060501-F-0000S-003.jpg.

16. Jayant Sharma, Grant H. Stokes, Curt von Braun, George Zollinger, and Andrew J. Wiseman, "Toward Operational Space-Based Space Surveillance," *Lincoln Laboratory Journal*, Vol. 13, No. 2 (2002), 309–334.

17. Estrella Olmedo, Noelia Sanchez-Ortiz, and Mercedes Ramos-Lerate, "Orbits and Pointing Strategies for Space Based Telescopes Into an European Space Surveillance System," Proceedings of the 5th European Conference on Space Debris (April 2009).

18. FAS Space Policy Project, accessed 22 September 2012 at www.fas.org/spp/military/program/track/index.html.

19. Tariq Malik, "Huge, Mysteriously Silent Satellite Spotted by Another Spacecraft," *Space.com* (April 20, 2012), accessed 26 September 2012 at http://www.space.com/15369-mysteriously-silent-envisat-satellite-space-photos.html.

20. Helen Anderson, "Edge Detection for Object Recognition in Aerial Photographs," University of Pennsylvania Department of Computer and Information Science Technical Report No. MS-CIS-87-14, 1987, accessed 22 September 2012 at http://repository.upenn.edu/cgi/viewcontent.cgi?article=1634&context=cis_reports.

21. Dino Brugioni, *Eyeball to Eyeball: The Inside Story of the Cuban Missile Crisis* (New York: Random House, 1990), 33.

22. U.S. Congress, *Technologies Underlying Weapons of Mass Destruction,* OTA-BfP-ISC-115 (Washington, DC: U.S. Government Printing Office, December 1993), 42–43

23. Ibid., 44.

24. National Reconnaissance Office, "Gambit 3 (KH-8) Fact Sheet," accessed 14 September 2012 at http://www.nro.gov/history/csnr/gambhex/Docs/GAM_3_Fact_sheet.pdf.

25. John M. Irvine, "National Imagery Interpretability Rating Scale (NIIRS): Overview and Methodology," in Wallace G. Fishell, ed., *Proceedings of SPIE,* 3128, *Airborne Reconnaissance XXI* (November 21, 1997), 93–103.

26. Rand Corporation, "Exploring Advanced Technologies for the Future Combat Systems Program," Chapter 2 (2002), accessed 22 September 2012 at http://www.rand.org/content/dam/rand/pubs/monograph_reports/MR1332/MR1332.ch2.pdf.

27. Richard A. Best Jr., "Imagery Intelligence: Issues for Congress," *CRS Report for Congress: 20* (April 12, 2002).

28. GeoEye, "Analysis Report: Activity on the Libyan/Tunisia Border Using GeoEye-1 Imagery," Image taken on 3 March 2011, accessed 1 October 2012 at http://www.geoeye.com/CorpSite/assets/docs/gallery/Libya_Border_GeoEye_Imagery_IHS_Janes_Analysis_Mar2011.pdf.

29. Anthony L. Kimery, "IMINT Processing Problems Impact War on Terror," *HSToday* (April 26, 2010), accessed 22 September 2012 at http://www.hstoday.us/blogs/the-kimery-report/blog/imint-processing-problems-impact-war-on-terror/4961ddab3a70e6883667bafe91fc0c0d.html.

30. FAS Space Policy Project, accessed 22 September 2012 at www.fas.org/spp/military/program/track/geodss.htm.

31. USAF, "Air Force Maui Optical and Supercomputing Site (AMOS)" (April 30, 2012), accessed 22 September 2012 at http://www.kirtland.af.mil/library/factsheets/factsheet.asp?id=16930.

32. Melissa Kelly, John E. Estes, and Kevin A. Knight, "Image Interpretation Keys for Validation of Global Land-Cover Data Sets," *Journal of the American Society for Photogrammetry and Remote Sensing,* Vol. 65, No. 9 (September 1999), 1041–1050.

33. Thaxter L. Goodell, "Cratology Pays Off," CIA Center for the Study of Intelligence, *Studies in Intelligence* Vol. 8, No. 4 (Fall 1964), 1–10.

34. Dino Brugioni, *Eyeball to Eyeball: The Inside Story of the Cuban Missile Crisis* (New York: Random House, 1990), 73.

35. Ibid.

36. John Diamond, "Trained Eye Can See Right Through Box of Weapons," *USA Today,* (August 17, 2006), accessed 22 September 2012 at www.usatoday.com/news/world/2006-08-17-missiles-iran_x.htm.

Optical Imaging

10. Radiometric and Spectral Imaging

Most images that are used in intelligence are collected in the visible band, as discussed in Chapter 9. But imaging outside that band, especially ultraviolet and infrared imaging, can provide much useful intelligence that does not appear in visible imagery. As an example from the natural world: We noted in Chapter 7 that reindeer can see ultraviolet (UV) light. Their eyes evolved to have that capability for a reason. Lichen, animal fur, and urine absorb UV light, while snow reflects it strongly. So their UV vision allows the reindeer to see dark areas against the snow to find their next meal (lichen) while avoiding being the next meal for wolves by spotting the furry wolves and areas where the wolves have marked their territory. Simplistic as that example may seem, radiometric and spectral imaging do similar things for us in intelligence. That is the subject of this chapter.

Let's begin with some important definitions.

- **Radiometric imagers** do two things that are useful in intelligence. They create an image of a scene at the frequency where the radiometer operates (which could be somewhere in the microwave, infrared (IR), visible, or UV bands); and they measure the intensity, or brightness, of objects at that frequency or wavelength.
- **Spectral imagers** are just a set of imaging radiometers, each operating at a different wavelength. So they create many simultaneous images of a

scene, all appearing somewhat different because they all feature different wavelengths.

As a simple example, suppose you look at the same scene through, in succession, a red, blue, and green glass. The images all will appear identical *except* that some features will appear brighter through one glass than another. Trees and grass will appear brightest when seen though the green glass, while the sky will appear darker. The converse happens when you view the scene through the blue glass. If your eyes could see the same scene through a glass that only let infrared or ultraviolet light through, the features would again have different brightness.

Function

Intelligence has used radiometric sensing and imaging for decades. Spectral imaging is a newer technology, and new intelligence applications keep appearing as the technology is improved.

RADIOMETRIC IMAGING

A radiometric image will show different features of intelligence interest depending on the frequency or wavelength at which the imager operates. In the visible, UV, and near IR bands, the imager mostly depends on reflected energy from the sun. That's why it is called the reflective band. In the longer wavelength (lower frequency) IR bands, the imager measures the intensity of energy emitted by objects (which is why it's called the emissive band). The hotter the object, the more energy it emits and the shorter the wavelength at which it emits most strongly. For example:

- Radiometric imagers detect and track ground vehicles, ships, aircraft, satellites, and reentry vehicles in the emissive band. They can measure the hot spots on these targets and get some indications of their missions and operational status.
- Spaceborne infrared sensors routinely detect and geolocate explosions or track ballistic missiles and space launch vehicles. That capability is used both for intelligence and to provide warning of a missile attack. Since the 1960s, the U.S. military has operated its Defense Support Program (DSP) satellites, using a technique called **Overhead Persistent Infrared (OPIR)**, to detect ballistic missile launches or atmospheric nuclear explosions.

Thermal imaging is the term for radiometric imaging that is done in the emissive band. It can be done either day or night, because the radiation is emitted rather than reflected. It is used for a variety of intelligence applications. In military reconnaissance, it is used to detect tanks, trucks, and aircraft on the ground and ships at sea—all of which, when operating or having recently operated, are hotter than their surroundings. During the Gulf War (Operation Desert Storm, 1990 to 1991), U.S. forces routinely determined the status of Iraqi military equipment by monitoring heat emissions using thermal imaging.

Nuclear plant activity and many industrial processes produce thermal patterns that can be monitored for intelligence purposes.[1] Some countries have also tested the use of infrared imagery to remotely track submerged submarines. The technique depends on the tendency of water displaced by the submarine to rise to the surface, creating a wake that has a different temperature from the surrounding ocean and therefore can be detected by infrared sensors.[2]

SPECTRAL IMAGING

Even more intelligence can be gained by creating images of a target area in many nonvisible bands as well as the visible spectrum, thereby creating a composite picture of the target area. We use such composite images to identify targets of interest and to characterize the targets based on measurements of the energy received from them. Military forces may later use these infrared signatures that have been identified and catalogued to attack the targets.

Spectral imaging has a number of other intelligence applications. It is useful for studying the rock structures of the earth, determining mineral composition, and assessing mining operations and underground facilities construction. Bathymetry (the study of sea bottom composition and topography) is useful for maritime intelligence. Knowledge of ocean depths is used to identify shipping channels and for a number of military applications.

It is highly desirable in object identification to be able to determine the materials that the target is made of, detect degradation of the surface, identify hidden payloads, resolve anomalies, and classify and identify the target. Spectral imaging has demonstrated the ability to do all of these things. Spectral analysis of reentry vehicles, for example, allows analysts to identify the surface materials of the reentry vehicle.[3]

Spectral imagers have substantial advantages in intelligence because they make an opponent's denial and deception (using camouflage, for example) very difficult. Buried roadside bombs and tunnel entrances are more readily detected in spectral imagery.

Radiometric and Spectral Imaging

Spectral imaging also has many nonintelligence uses. It is used extensively in environmental studies, including agriculture and geology. In agriculture, healthy vegetation can be distinguished from stressed, or dying, vegetation. This capability is useful in intelligence support to drug eradication efforts, as healthy coca or opium poppy crops can be distinguished in multispectral imaging from crops that have been damaged by herbicides.

Process

PLANNING

Planning for radiometric imaging depends on how the product is to be used. Radiometers are used for many purposes, both operational and intelligence. Spaceborne devices such as OPIR imagers and bhangmeters, discussed later, simply monitor a region of the earth for activity of interest and record measurements when the activity occurs. So no special mission planning is necessary. Radiometric imaging of battlespace and oceans from airborne platforms requires much the same sort of planning as is done for the airborne optical imaging discussed in Chapter 9.

Planning for spectral imaging also is very similar to the planning for optical imaging that was discussed in Chapter 9. The same platforms are used. The major difference is that spectral imaging requires more labor-intensive processing and exploitation, so targets are carefully prioritized in advance.

COLLECTION

Chapter 7 included an introductory overview of the electromagnetic (EM) spectrum. This section revisits the spectrum in detail in order to clarify how radiometric and spectral images are collected. To begin with, it is important to understand the types of intelligence information that can be collected in each part of the spectrum by radiometric sensors. The source is EM energy that is emitted or reflected in some part of the spectrum—primarily of the optical spectrum, but radiometric imaging can be done in the microwave spectrum as well.

The Optical Spectrum. Starting in the millimeter wave band and moving up in frequency toward the optical spectrum, increasingly the atmosphere affects the propagation of EM waves. Figure 10.1 illustrates the absorption that occurs across the EM spectrum. Above the green shaded area in the figure, the atmosphere effectively blocks the passage of EM energy. Below the shaded area, the energy passes through with little loss. In the shaded region, the losses may or may not allow a sensor to obtain a readable signal.

At any time, a given spectral sensor will only observe a small part of the overall spectrum shown in Figure 10.1. The sensor is designed only to collect radiation within a specific bandwidth or set of narrow bands for a specific purpose. Chapters 7 and 9 discussed the division of the optical spectrum into two major regions—reflective and emissive. Solids and liquids are usually examined in the reflective spectral region from about 0.5 μm to about 2.5 μm. A source of radiant energy—typically the sun—is necessary to produce spectra in this reflective spectral region. The emissive region, which is found at longer wavelengths, is more typically used to examine gases.

The infrared part of the spectrum is subdivided into smaller sections, as discussed in Chapter 7. Again, there are no standard divisions. Following are some of the commonly used ways to define divisions:

- Some band definitions characterize the type of signature obtained; an example is the division into emissive versus reflective signatures, as previously discussed. Finer distinctions are sometimes made among types of target signatures—characterizing fires and hot missile exhausts, for example, versus characterizing thermal radiation from a tank engine.
- Some definitions separate the infrared spectrum by the presence of atmospheric windows—the regions where the atmosphere is transparent, as indicated in Figure 10.1.
- Some definitions are based on the sensitivity of IR detectors. Different detectors work well in different parts of the band. For example, silicon detectors are sensitive in the visible band and in the IR band to about 1 micron, while indium gallium arsenide detector sensitivity starts around 1 micron and ends between 1.7 and 2.6 microns.

While there is no widely accepted way to define the infrared bands, a frequently used scheme is outlined below and used throughout this book.

Near-Infrared (NIR). The NIR band is closest to visible light and extends from 0.75 μm to 1.5 μm in wavelength. Night vision devices work in this band. The longer wavelengths in the NIR band reflect uniquely from minerals, crops, and vegetation and moist surfaces; different tree types can be distinguished, for example. The 0.76 to 0.9 μm part of the band is useful for shoreline mapping. The band is used in imaging to counter the effectiveness of camouflage; poorly designed camouflage reflects differently than the surrounding vegetation. Image intensifiers are commonly used in this part of

Radiometric and Spectral Imaging

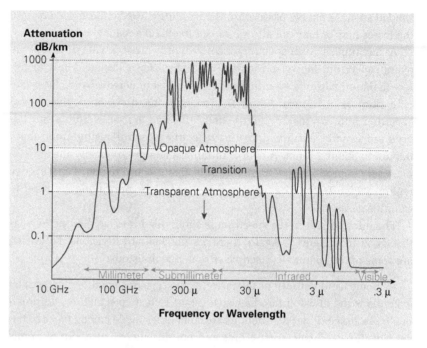

FIGURE 10.1 Atmospheric Attenuation of EM Waves

the spectrum up to about 1 micron; an image intensifier amplifies the weak incoming NIR signal to provide a viewable image in low-light conditions.

Short Wavelength Infrared (SWIR). The short wavelength infrared band extends from 1.5 μm to 3 μm. Sensors in this band are used to detect the presence of water and for vegetation analysis; oil on water can be discriminated and the moisture content of soil and vegetation can be determined. SWIR signals can penetrate clouds to a limited extent.

Although the SWIR band is considered as being in the reflective part of the IR band, it is used to detect a class of emissions that have intelligence significance. The hot exhausts of ballistic missiles during the boost phase of flight emit a strong signature in this band; explosions also create an SWIR band signature. The overhead persistent infrared sensors discussed in Chapter 9 tend to function in this band for characterizing missiles in boost phase and to determine the type of munitions causing an explosion.

Mid-Wavelength Infrared (MWIR). The mid-wavelength infrared band, also known as intermediate infrared (IIR), extends from 3 μm to 8 μm. It is a transition band that produces emissive signatures, with a few reflective signatures of importance. Solar reflectance from bright objects (such as metal-roofed buildings) is significant in this band. In guided missile technology, this is the heat-seeking region in which the sensors carried by passive IR homing missiles are designed to work. The missiles home in on the IR signature of the target aircraft, typically the jet engine exhaust plume. This region is also used to characterize the temperature of objects on the earth's surface. It also is used to characterize some gaseous effluents. When heated by the sun, gases produce spectra in the MWIR region, about 2.5 to 6 μm.[4] An atmospheric window exists in this band between 3 and 5 μm.

Long Wavelength Infrared (LWIR). The long wavelength infrared band is a major atmospheric window extending from 8 μm to 15 μm. The region near 10 microns is often called the thermal imaging region because objects near room temperature emit more strongly in this region. LWIR sensors use this signature to obtain a completely passive image of the earth based on thermal emissions only, and they require no external light or thermal source such as the sun. This is the primary band used to characterize gaseous effluents for intelligence purposes. Many production processes create signatures in this band. Forward-looking infrared (FLIR) systems that are mounted on vehicles and aircraft also use this area of the spectrum to view the surrounding region during darkness. Detectors used in this band generally must be cooled to obtain acceptable sensitivity. This band is sometimes also called the far infrared, but many definitions treat this as a separate band, as discussed next.

Far Infrared. The far infrared band extends above the 15-μm wavelength to the millimeter wave range. For overhead imaging purposes, the cutoff is around 30 μm, since the atmosphere is opaque at longer wavelengths.

Radiometric Imaging. Chapter 9 discussed visible imaging, mostly of reflected energy from the sun. Radiometric imaging can use reflected energy, though mostly it relies on receiving natural energy emissions from warm targets. When it relies on energy emitted in the infrared or microwave bands, it is specifically called thermal imaging. When such radiometric images are produced in several spectral bands, the result is spectral imaging, discussed in the next section.

   Recall that all objects at temperatures above absolute zero emit EM energy. As the target becomes hotter, both the strength and frequency of emissions increase; very hot objects (a lamp filament or a rocket exhaust, for example) radiate in the visible range. Anyone who has seen a heater filament being

Radiometric and Spectral Imaging

heated to red-hot temperatures has observed the phenomenon of spectral radiation as a function of temperature. If heated beyond red-hot it becomes white-hot and, if it does not melt first, it becomes blue-hot. Vehicles or factories that are in use tend to radiate more strongly and at higher frequencies than when idle. The presence of such hot spots on a vehicle or building allows conclusions to be made about the nature and status of that vehicle or the use of that building.

Different objects radiate differently. Rock, earth, seawater, and vegetation all have different emission patterns, known as emissivities. The concept of emissivity is important in understanding the infrared emissions of objects. Black objects, for example, absorb energy far more rapidly than white objects, as any owner of a black automobile knows. Black objects also radiate energy more rapidly than white objects. A perfect emitter is called a blackbody. Emissivity is a property of an object that describes how its thermal emissions deviate from the ideal of a blackbody. Two objects at the same physical temperature will not appear to be the same temperature to an infrared sensor if they have differing emissivities.

These three facts—that all objects at temperatures above absolute zero radiate electromagnetic energy, that energy strength and frequency increase as temperature increases, and that different objects radiate differently—are the basis for radiometric imaging.

Radiometric sensors take advantage of the emissivity phenomenon to obtain information about ships, aircraft, missiles, structures, and the environment (the natural background). These passive sensors receive and record the electromagnetic energy that objects naturally emit. The radiometer records the natural energy that is emitted in the infrared or microwave bands by heated objects.

As noted above, radiometers can operate in either the microwave or optical bands. This chapter is primarily about radiometric imaging in the optical part of the spectrum, because that is the imaging that finds the widest use in intelligence. But microwave radiometry relies on the same thermal emissions as optical radiometry; the chief difference is in the sensor design. So this chapter includes microwave radiometry as well.

Microwave Radiometers. The microwave radiometer records the natural energy that is emitted in the RF band by heated objects. As with IR radiometers, the warmer the object, the more energy it radiates. A good microwave radiometer has an intensity resolution of 1 degree Celsius (that is, it can sense temperature changes of 1 degree Celsius). However, microwave radiometers have a comparatively slower search rate compared with IR radiometers. They typically must view the target for a long period of time because much less energy is emitted in the microwave band.

Microwave radiometers normally use cross-track scanning, as shown in Figure 9.4, but an antenna is used in place of optics. In place of a detector, microwave radiometers mostly use a very sensitive RF receiver, while detectors are increasingly being used in the millimeter wave part of the band.

While microwave radiometers have poorer spatial resolution than IR radiometers, they have a substantial advantage for intelligence use. IR radiometers cannot penetrate clouds, haze, fog, or precipitation. Microwave radiometers can—though their performance is degraded by precipitation. Many microwave radiometers are designed to receive millimeter wave energy, which provides better resolution than lower frequency band radiometers. As illustrated in Figure 10.2, though, the image still is not as good as a visual image.[5]

In Figure 10.2, one can observe that darker objects in the visible image tend to be lighter in the radiometric image and the converse. This is a characteristic of radiometry: darker objects tend to both absorb and emit energy more strongly than do light objects, so they show up more brightly.

FIGURE 10.2 Comparison of Radiometric and Visible Imagery

Infrared Radiometers. Infrared imaging radiometers that detect emitted energy are called thermal imagers. Remote sensing of energy emitted from the earth's surface in the thermal infrared (3 μm to 15 μm) band is different from the sensing of reflected energy. Thermal sensors essentially measure the surface temperature and thermal properties of targets. They use photo detectors that typically are cooled to temperatures close to absolute zero in order to avoid the noise created by their own thermal emissions.

Hot objects radiate in the infrared bands, as noted previously. Imaging of ground- and sea-based, airborne, and spaceborne targets in these bands is routinely done for the purpose of target identification and assessment. Such infrared sensing is best done at night, when the background is typically cooler and hot objects stand out. Figure 10.3 shows an infrared image of the U.S. space shuttle made during shuttle mission STS-96, taken in the MWIR band. The nose and forward parts of the wings show the intense heat experienced by the shuttle during reentry.[6]

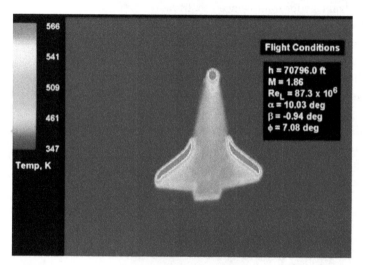

FIGURE 10.3 Infrared Image of the Space Shuttle

Imagery that portrays relative temperature differences across the image is sufficient for most intelligence applications. Actual temperature measurements can be made, but they require accurate calibration and measurement of the temperature references and detailed knowledge of the emissivity of the target, geometric distortions, and radiometric effects. If actual temperature is needed, the sensor makes use of an internal temperature reference. Comparing the detected radiation to the reference allows the imagery analyst to establish the absolute temperature of an object in the image.

Thermal imaging is usually done in two specific regions where the atmosphere is transparent to IR: 3 to 5 μm (MWIR) and 8 to 14 μm (LWIR). In these IR regions, though, detectors are not as sensitive as visible light detectors. So thermal imagers have to use larger pixels in order to get enough energy for detection, and spatial resolution is worse than the same image in the visible band.

Several specialized radiometric sensors are used in intelligence for collecting against specific targets. Following is a discussion of three such collectors: OPIR sensors, bhangmeters, and polarimetric imagers.

OPIR Sensors. An important radiometric sensing technique in intelligence is called OPIR sensing, which uses a planar array or scanning system similar to those depicted in Chapter 9 (Figure 9.4) to detect and track intense emissions of IR energy over a large area of the earth. The purpose is to detect, locate, and characterize events of intelligence significance—primarily large explosions and missile launches. For example, using OPIR, explosions in the upper atmosphere and near space can be detected and identified as nuclear with great confidence for yields above about a kiloton.[7] This sensing technique was previously called overhead nonimaging infrared (ONIR), a term that did not adequately describe the result. Figure 10.4 illustrates the OPIR signature obtained from a HEO satellite of a Delta IV launch on November 4, 2006.[8] The launch vehicle itself is not visible in the picture, but the intense IR plume is clearly visible. As the figure shows, the product of OPIR is an image, though not a high-resolution image.

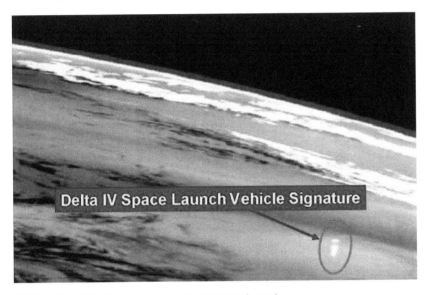

FIGURE 10.4 OPIR Collection of Delta IV Rocket Launch

For many years, the DSP satellite was the primary sensor for OPIR collection. It has been replaced by the Space-Based Infrared System (SBIRS). Figure 10.5 shows an artist's conception of the SBIRS satellite.[9] Satellites like this rely on IR to detect and report ballistic missile launches and other infrared events having intelligence significance. SBIRS reportedly has higher sensitivity and can more accurately estimate the missile location, launch point, and impact point than did the DSP satellites. SBIRS has been certified by NGA as a technical intelligence collector.[10]

In 2009, France launched its own version of the SBIRS satellite, called Spirale. It is a demonstration system, designed to test the concept of a future

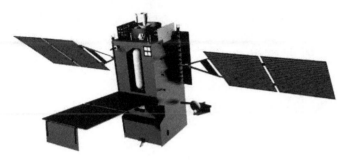

FIGURE 10.5 SBIRS Satellite

space-based operational system for providing the French with an early warning of a missile attack. Two Spirale satellites, launched into a HEO orbit, are collecting imagery in several infrared bands.[11]

Bhangmeters. A few radiometers measure target signature changes over time, looking for unique signatures that have intelligence significance. One such specialized radiometer is the bhangmeter. It has very good temporal resolution and records light fluctuations with a time resolution of less than a millisecond. It has a specific purpose: detecting atmospheric nuclear explosions. The name *bhangmeter* originated with some of the early skeptics who did not believe such sensing was possible. *Bhang* is a variation of Indian hemp that is smoked for its hallucinogenic impact; skeptics suspected that anyone who believed such an approach was feasible must have been smoking bhang.

All atmospheric nuclear explosions produce a unique, readily detectable signature: an extremely short and intense flash, followed by a second much longer and less intense burst of light. The initial flash typically lasts 1 millisecond. The following light burst takes up to several seconds to develop, depending on the size of the explosion, and lasts a comparable period of time.

The U.S. Vela satellites dating from the 1960s carried bhangmeters and other sensors designed to detect nuclear explosions. Controversy about a possible Israeli or South African nuclear test brought notoriety to the program. On September 22, 1979, the bhangmeter on a Vela satellite detected the characteristic double flash of an atmospheric nuclear explosion, apparently over the Indian Ocean or South Atlantic. The characteristics of the bhangmeter signature indicated that it was a low-kiloton explosion (approximately 3 kt). The onboard bhangmeters were not true imaging sensors and could not perform geolocation. However, the test event was later localized by hydroacoustic data to the Indian Ocean, in the vicinity of South Africa's Prince Edward Island.[12]

The detection raised the possibility that some nation—particularly South Africa or Israel, or the two in collaboration—had conducted a covert test. A U.S. presidentially appointed panel in 1980 examined the evidence and concluded that the signature did not result from a nuclear test. Many U.S. government officials and scientists have disagreed with the findings of the presidential panel,[13] and the controversy still remains unresolved.

Polarimetric Imagers. Radiometry is usually thought of as measuring the intensity of electromagnetic energy emitted by an object (or received within one pixel), but it can also involve measuring the polarization of the received signal. In the optical band, such measurements are usually called polarimetry; in the RF band, the term *polarimetric radiometry* is commonly used.

Polarimetric imaging measures the polarization of energy in each pixel of an image. This measurement allows an imagery analyst to distinguish between different materials in the image more effectively than simply measuring the intensities.

Natural light, such as light from the sun, has random polarization (as discussed in Chapter 7) and is called unpolarized light. When such light is scattered from a rough surface—and most natural surfaces are rough—the light may be weakly and unpredictably polarized. In contrast, when the light is reflected from a relatively smooth surface—and man-made objects often have smooth parts—the light acquires a strong polarization, as Figure 10.6 illustrates. Recall from Chapter 7 that a polarized wave can be linearly polarized, circularly polarized, or some polarization in between (called elliptical polarization). In polarimetric imaging, two linear polarizations—horizontal and vertical—are usually measured.

Polarimetric imaging is useful for penetrating shadows and for detecting weak signatures or camouflaged targets, which can be important in intelligence. The U.S. Naval Research Laboratory has demonstrated the effectiveness of polarimetric imaging for these purposes in tactical reconnaissance.[14]

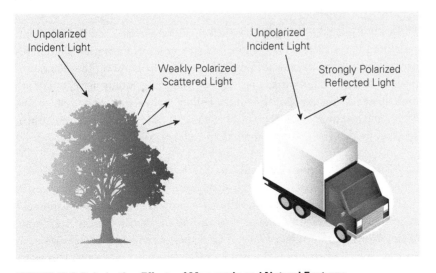

FIGURE 10.6 Polarization Effects of Man-made and Natural Features

Contrast enhancement techniques, discussed in Chapter 9, can improve contrast in shadowed regions. Polarimetric imagery is an improved form of contrast enhancement because it provides four distinct images, each containing different contrast information from the others.[15] The four images can be exploited together to obtain more details about shadowed or camouflaged objects.

Microwave radiometers also can use polarimetry for special purposes. Measuring the polarization of microwave energy emitted from the sea surface, for example, allows one to determine wind direction. Since 2003, the WindSat radiometer on the U.S. Defense Department's Coriolis satellite has been making such wind measurements.[16]

Spectral Imaging. A spectral image can be thought of as many images of the same scene, each created at a different wavelength. Imaging an object at different wavelengths allows intelligence analysts to identify unique spectral signatures of targets. More such images provide more spectral information. The result is a better defined spectral signature and a more accurate identification of materials in the images.

Spectral signatures, as noted in Chapter 7, depend upon the interactions of radiant energy and various materials (solids, liquids, and gases) through processes of scattering, absorption, reflection, and emission. Reflected or emitted radiation is affected by the absorption, reflection, and emissive properties of different materials. Understanding the various interactions allows imagery analysts to identify materials in the image. Spectral interactions typically result in spectral signatures that are uniquely related to the materials involved.

Spectral imaging of the earth's surface is done from aircraft, UAVs, and satellites. Three classes of spectral imagers are currently used for intelligence and earth resources sensing; the division is based on the number of distinct spectral bands that they collect. Most commonly used today are **multispectral images (MSI)**, which collect between 2 and 100 bands. **Hyperspectral images (HSI)** collect between 100 and 1,000 bands, and **ultraspectral images (USI)** collect more than 1,000 bands.

Multispectral Imaging. Spectral imaging is commonly done by a device called the imaging spectrometer; it also is called a **multispectral scanner**. A multispectral scanner uses either the cross-track scanner or the pushbroom imager, as described in Chapter 9, with one major difference: A separate detector or separate linear array of detectors is required to measure each spectral band or channel. During the scan, the energy detected by each separate detector or linear array of detectors is sampled electronically and digitally recorded. Each of these two sensor designs has advantages and disadvantages.

The rotating mirror design of the cross-track scanner is simpler to design and use and is easier to calibrate. But the length of time the instantaneous field of view (IFOV) sees a ground resolution cell as the rotating mirror scans (the dwell time) is quite short, and so the spectral, spatial, and radiometric resolution are relatively poor.

The pushbroom scanner with linear arrays of detectors, combined with the pushbroom motion, allows each detector in an array to measure the energy from each ground resolution cell for a longer period of time (longer dwell time) compared with the cross-track scanner. This allows more energy to be detected and improves the radiometric resolution. The increased dwell time also allows using smaller IFOVs and narrower bandwidths for each detector. The result is finer spatial and spectral resolution without losing radiometric resolution. But the detectors must be calibrated so that the measurements are consistent.

The framing camera would provide the best dwell time if it could be used in spectral imaging. But one would need a separate pixel frame for each spectral band, and that quickly becomes unwieldy to build.

A large number of multispectral imagers are flying today on aircraft and in satellites. They support military operations, other government purposes, commercial interests, and of course—intelligence. Most satellites, such as GeoEye-1 and France's SPOT 5, image in four spectral bands (red, blue, green, and Near IR). Some produce more images. NASA's Landsat 7 satellite has 7 bands, one of which is LWIR. The Worldview 2 satellite, launched in 2009, has eight multispectral bands (visible and NIR).

Multispectral sensors have relatively poor spectral resolution. This limits material detection because many of the fine-grain features have been eliminated in the resulting image. However, although specific materials cannot be identified, it is possible to differentiate between materials. It is easy to tell that some materials are different because the spectral signatures are different—even in five bands. To obtain the higher resolution needed to identify specific materials, it is necessary to use HSI or USI.

Hyperspectral and Ultraspectral Imaging. HSI and USI imagers have the same basic design as MSI imagers but are more complex. They collect hundreds or thousands of simultaneous images in very narrow spectral bands, giving them very high spectral resolution. That allows them to discriminate between different targets based on their spectral response in each of these narrow bands.

Radiometric and Spectral Imaging

HSI and USI images therefore contain far more spectral information than MSI images, making them much more information-rich but also more difficult to process and analyze. They have the potential to provide details about an intelligence target that simply cannot be achieved with conventional or MSI imagery. For example, high spectral resolution in the LWIR band is necessary for the detection, location, identification, and characterization of gases. However, processing and analyzing HSI and USI data is a difficult and time-consuming process, often requiring custom software and very expensive expert labor.

So acquiring more wavelength bands, and then processing them in separate images, allows better identification of the target. As Figure 10.7 indicates, increasing the number of spectral bands allows a progression from detecting a target, to classifying it, and then to identifying a specific object or gas. How this is done is discussed in the section on processing and exploitation. Here, as in other areas, one encounters a trade-off: MSI imagers have less spectral resolution but typically cover large geographical areas. Commercial and civil MSI satellites such as Landsat, Ikonos, and Quickbird provide extensive area coverage, at relatively low spectral and geographical resolution. HSI satellites provide limited area coverage with good spectral resolution.

The attractiveness of the HSI technique resulted in a rush to deploy operational HSI systems to support coalition operations in Afghanistan. One such system reportedly was deployed on the U.S. TacSat 3, launched in May 2009.[17]

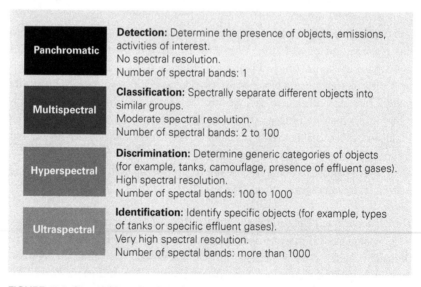

FIGURE 10.7 Spectral Imaging Resolution and Levels of Information Obtained

A number of hyperspectral sensors have been deployed on aircraft. Most are designed to provide coverage in the visible, NIR, and SWIR bands for earth resources sensing. Typical is the NASA/JPL Airborne Visible/Infrared Imaging System sensor, which collects 224 contiguous spectral bands between 0.4 and 2.5 microns from aircraft platforms.[18]

Airborne hyperspectral imagers also operate in the MWIR and LWIR bands. These sensors are specifically designed to detect gaseous effluents or objects of intelligence significance. One is the Airborne Hyperspectral Imager, an LWIR hyperspectral imager that collects narrow-band images from 7.5 to 11.5 microns in 256 spectral bands. This sensor was originally designed to detect the presence of buried land mines, relying on the change in infrared absorption features of disturbed soil. This sensor also has been used to detect gas releases and to classify mineral types.[19]

A few hyperspectral sensors have been carried on satellites. In 2000, NASA launched the Earth Observing-1 (EO-1) Advanced Land Imager satellite carrying the Hyperion sensor. Hyperion is a high-resolution hyperspectral imager capable of collecting 220 spectral bands (from 0.4 to 2.5 μm) with a 30-meter spatial resolution. The instrument images a 7.5 km by 100 km land area per image and provides detailed spectral mapping across all 220 channels with high radiometric accuracy.[20]

Germany is developing a hyperspectral imaging satellite for earth resources sensing that also could have intelligence uses. The EnMAP satellite is being designed to image in approximately 250 narrow spectral channels, 136 of which would be in the SWIR band and 96 in the NIR band. The satellite, planned for launch in 2015, would use pushbroom imaging spectrometers having a spatial resolution of 30 meters within a 30-kilometer-wide swath.[21]

Spectral imaging of space objects also is done for intelligence purposes. The Advanced Electro-Optical System (AEOS) sensor described in Chapter 9 also has a spectral imaging feature. AEOS has demonstrated the capability to do hyperspectral imaging of satellites.[22]

Ultraspectral sensing is characterized by even higher spectral resolution and narrower bandwidths than HSI. Ultraspectral sensors are still being developed and tested.

PROCESSING

After it has been collected, radiometric or spectral imagery has to go through the three phases of processing, exploitation, and analysis so that users can make sense of the signatures that have been collected.

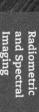

Radiometric and Spectral Imaging

The processing discussed in Chapter 9 for imagery has to be done for radiometric processing and is an initial step before the spectral processing begins. For example, geometric corrections are used to accurately fit the image to a map of the target area. The raw data have to be adjusted using radiometric (intensity) and spectral calibrations prior to exploitation. In order to be useful, the signatures or images also must be corrected for the effects of the atmosphere on the reflected or emitted radiant energy as it travels between the ground target and the collector.

Calibration is important in spectral imaging for the same reason as in the commercial world: People would not want to purchase a digital camera if they could not be assured that the colors in the scene would be faithfully reproduced in the image, and they would generally be displeased if the image were much brighter or darker than expected. Calibration is necessary to ensure faithful reproduction of image intensity and spectral characteristics.

The next step involves a series of image transformations—operations similar in concept to those for image enhancement that were discussed in Chapter 9. The processing is considerably more complex for spectral signatures. Unlike image enhancement operations, which are normally applied only to a single channel of data at a time, spectral image transformations involve combined processing of data from multiple spectral bands. The images have to be manipulated to combine and transform the original bands into new images that better display or highlight certain features in the scene.

The processing of imagery that includes nonvisible bands presents special challenges. A camera may be able to obtain images in the nonvisible part of the spectrum, but our unaided eyes cannot see those parts. Therefore, a major challenge of such imagery is to somehow represent the nonvisible part in the visible spectrum so that it can be exploited and analyzed. The solution is to use *false color*. A commonly used technique, for an image that must include the near infrared band, is to shift all colors in wavelength approximately 0.15 microns to a higher-frequency (shorter wavelength) part of the spectrum. The result is that a green object is depicted as blue, a red object as green, and an infrared reflection as red. Blue objects cannot be depicted and appear black. Another technique is shown in Figure 10.8, a false color image taken by NASA's Terra satellite.[23] This image of a copper mine in southeastern Arizona was created by combining the visible green, near infrared, and short wave infrared band images. The copper deposits, which reflect strongly in the near infrared band, show as a bright blue. The moist areas in the southern part of the image reflect strongly in both of the infrared bands and show as purple. While false color allows an imagery analyst to analyze the image, customers of intelligence do not like it as much as visible imagery since it is harder to understand the image without training.

A spectral image can be thought of as many images of the same scene, each created at a different wavelength. Figure 10.9 illustrates how the overall images are formed and how a signature is created for each pixel in a hyperspectral image.[24] Three different pixels are selected: one of water, one of soil, and one of vegetation. As the figure illustrates, each pixel has a unique spectral signature of intensity versus wavelength.

FIGURE 10.8 False Color Image

The signatures shown in this figure are called **spectral response curves** because the images were taken in the reflective part of the band. *Response* means that they characterize the reflectance of features or targets over the wavelengths in this part of the band. The curves are usually referred to as **spectral emissivity curves** at wavelengths longer than 2.5 microns because they are caused by thermal emissions from the feature or target, rather than reflected energy.

Multispectral, hyperspectral, and ultraspectral images are all processed in much the same fashion. But multispectral imaging has a relatively coarse spectral resolution. As a result, the signatures of different objects are often similar. If a multispectral imager were used to produce Figure 10.9, the trees, earth, and water pixels all would have different response curves, as they do in the figure. But more specific classes (such as different clay types or different types of trees) could not be distinguished. Two similar objects cannot be differentiated unless their signatures contain many more wavelengths than in this example. This means that a sensor with higher spectral resolution is required. Spectral resolution, as noted earlier, describes the ability of a sensor to define fine wavelength intervals. The finer the spectral resolution, the narrower the range of wavelengths included in a particular channel or band.

Hyperspectral and ultraspectral imagers provide this high-spectral resolution by acquiring many more images simultaneously in many narrow, contiguous spectral bands. Each pixel in a scene has an associated spectrum that is substantially more detailed. As a result, hyperspectral and ultraspectral data offer a more detailed examination of a scene than multispectral data, which are collected in broad, widely separated bands.

Radiometric and Spectral Imaging

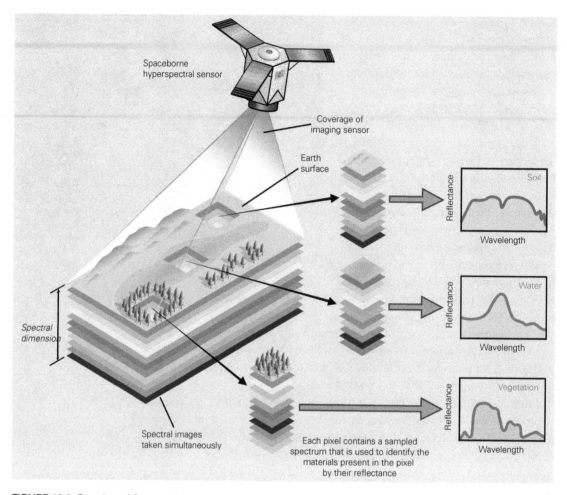

FIGURE 10.9 Creation of Spectral Images

For intelligence purposes, the major advantage of hyperspectral imaging occurs in the emissive (MWIR and LWIR) region, especially in detecting, characterizing, and identifying effluent gases. Gases in the emissive region tend to have very narrow, sharply defined spectral features. In contrast to the relatively smooth curves for solid matter shown in Figure 10.9, gas signatures in these bands are jagged, with many sharp peaks and valleys as shown in Figure 10.10.

EXPLOITATION AND ANALYSIS

After processing, the imagery is exploited and analyzed. Radiometric imaging is done in a single band, so exploitation and analysis are comparatively

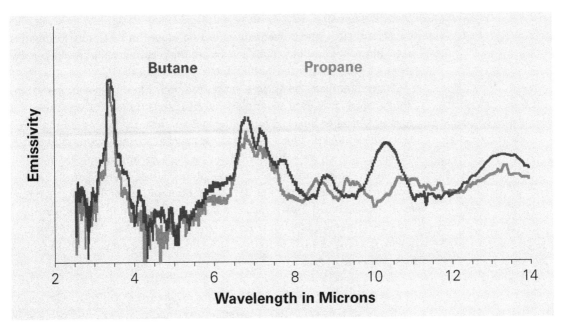

FIGURE 10.10 Spectral Signatures of Two Gas Pixels in a Hyperspectral Image

simpler than is the case for spectral imaging. Both make use of the techniques of anomaly detection and target identification, discussed below.

First, the raw spectral data have to go through a sophisticated exploitation process in order to translate the spectral signature from each pixel into a form useful to an analyst. Exploitation depends heavily on computer algorithms that examine spectral information in each pixel to identify and, in some cases, quantify materials—including gases—present in the scene. The spectra are then compared with available signatures in a spectral library (discussed in the next section) for identification.

Next, the different classes of features and details in a spectral image have to be distinguished by comparing their spectral signatures over different wavelength ranges. Exploitation is a complex process, but it is well suited to automated processing techniques. Multispectral, hyperspectral, and ultraspectral images are processed in much the same way, but the signatures produced and the information that can be extracted are different.

A standard exploitation technique in searching large geographical areas is called anomaly detection. Anomaly detection is commonly used when nothing is known about the scene under surveillance, but collectors are looking for anything that might be out of place (for example, a vehicle partially concealed in a forest or an oil or chemical spill in an otherwise uncontaminated area). Anomaly detection algorithms flag any suspicious areas in a scene and pass those cues to an imagery analyst, a spectral analysis system, or another sensor for a more detailed look.[25]

Target identification is, in a sense, the opposite of anomaly detection. This technique is used when the analyst is looking for the signature of a specific object or material of intelligence interest. In the case of the OPIR sensor described previously, the analyst may be looking for a missile plume or the flash from an explosion. Spectral imagery analysts might look for specific chemical effluents in a gas plume when investigating possible weapons of mass destruction (WMD) production or performing environmental monitoring. The targets, and the processes used for target identification, are different depending on whether a radiometric, MSI, HSI, or USI sensor is being used. The following sections discuss some of these targets and processes.

Target Identification for Multispectral Signatures. Different classes of materials such as water and vegetation can usually be separated using very broad wavelength ranges in the visible and near-infrared regions. Multispectral imaging is quite capable of doing this. In addition, MSI from the infrared regions can discriminate features invisible to the naked eye. Specific land features become obvious to the trained analyst. For example, oil-bearing rock appears different from rock having no oil content. Underground structures appear different from the naturally occurring ground surface. Heat generation facilities stand out prominently, as do other mechanical heat producers like aircraft and tank engines. Natural substances like vegetation produce their own unique signatures, as well.[26]

Healthy vegetation appears green in the visible spectrum because it contains chlorophyll, which absorbs blue and red light waves. Stressed vegetation (for example, vegetation with inadequate water or recently cut brush for camouflage) has less chlorophyll and therefore absorbs less of the blue and red light waves, so it appears different when viewed with multispectral sensors. Many countries apply this process to determine healthy crop rotations, assess deforestation around the globe, and obtain information for archaeology and urban analysis.[27] Military and law enforcement organizations use multispectral imagery to reveal marijuana crops cultivated under forested canopies because marijuana leaves reflect a different color of green than the surrounding vegetation. Even commercially available visible imagery has been used successfully to identify marijuana fields, and MSI can do such identification more readily than visible imagery.[28]

Target Identification for Hyperspectral and Ultraspectral Signatures.
Hyperspectral and ultraspectral signatures are more challenging to analyze
than the MSI signatures described above, as far more detail is contained in
the signature. We would like to be able to identify the materials in every
pixel in a scene. But doing so would require that we create representative
spectral signatures for every known material. A database holding all these
spectra would probably contain millions of spectral signatures.

Furthermore, downloading all of the data from a scene and processing it
would be a massive undertaking, especially from a satellite. Fortunately,
most of the pixels in a scene are not of intelligence interest—trees, rocks,
pastureland, water, and so forth. An easier approach is to have the onboard
processor discard the uninteresting data and select only the few points that
appear interesting. That is, the processor filters the data against a target spectrum of interest. All pixels whose spectra match the target spectrum (to a
specified level of confidence) are marked as potential targets.[29]

This easier approach runs into a major snag, though. It assumes that the
pixels containing the target are pure, that is, the target material fills the
entire pixel and is not mixed with any background material. That seldom
happens. A hyperspectral or ultraspectral image pixel will typically have
more than one material present in it. The result will be a composite spectrum for that pixel—that is, a combination of the spectra of each individual material present. The composite spectrum has to be resolved into its
individual components, assuming that the spectrum of each pure component is present in the spectral library. For example, a gas plume may be
transparent, so any pixel containing the plume will be a mixture of
the plume and the ground beneath it. The pixel spectra in this case will
not resemble the target spectrum unless the background material can
somehow be suppressed.[30]

The objective of target identification is to determine the materials present
in the target scene. For example, an analyst tasked with assessing the chemical warfare (CW) potential of a production facility within a target country
would need to address the following questions about the facility:

- What does the facility produce?
- What process is being used?
- What is the production capacity and rate?
- What is the current facility status?

Detailed hyperspectral signatures can resolve the first question, provided
a sufficient number of materials can be identified from the spectral data set
to allow identification of the process taking place. In order to identify the

Radiometric
and Spectral
Imaging

process, the analyst needs access to a library of signatures associated with the different processes for the production of the CW agents.

Determining the production capacity and rate usually requires repeated collection from the target facility. The production processes are usually not continuous, as plants typically produce chemicals in batches. As a result, effluents may not be expelled continuously. There may be periods of apparent inactivity for maintenance or other purposes. Establishing the current facility status may require multiple collection passes for the same reasons.

For the proliferation or arms control analyst, the final step in exploiting a hyperspectral data set is to determine what all this means. Answering the four questions outlined above requires more than simply exploiting hyperspectral data. The analyst must often pull in information from other sources and disciplines. Plant modeling and process simulation may be required in difficult cases.

DISSEMINATION

Dissemination of radiometric sensing products tends to be limited to specific customers. OPIR monitoring, for example, is intended to provide early warning of a missile launch and to identify atmospheric nuclear weapons tests, so missile defense and treaty monitoring organizations are customers for the product.

Dissemination of spectral imagery is much like that for visible imagery, but the customer set is substantially smaller and quick dissemination, at least currently, is not an option. The processing and exploitation simply take time.

Spectral Libraries. To identify a material in the analysis phase as discussed above, an analyst has to have access to a spectral library. Exploitation and analysis of spectral signatures are not possible without a library of signatures. Such a library has to include each of the signatures shown in Figure 10.10, for example. A library that is useful for intelligence analysis would include a large number of minerals, organic and volatile compounds, vegetation, and man-made materials.

Many spectral libraries are openly available, and they can be useful for assessing vegetation, geology, and common materials. The spectra for camouflage, military metals, and other materials of intelligence significance are typically kept in classified libraries.

But these signatures alone are not sufficient. In Figure 10.9, for example, analysts might need to distinguish different types of soil or vegetation or to distinguish pollution in the water. These will all have different spectral signatures, and even the same object will have different signatures at different temperatures. So to adequately exploit hyperspectral data, the libraries have to be very large to begin with, and they are constantly expanded. The existing multispectral libraries do not give the detail needed for hyperspectral exploitation.

Getting good hyperspectral signatures is a slow process. Furthermore, getting good signatures on materials of importance for intelligence can be especially challenging. For example, special facilities are needed to get signature data for toxic substances such as nerve agents.

The creation of a spectral library follows the process illustrated in Figure 10.9. For each pixel, an intensity measurement is made at each wavelength (each spectral channel). The result is a set of intensity measurements like that shown in Figure 10.10. These are tagged, in this case as butane and propane signatures, and retained in the library.

A library of such pixels has to be at the proper spectral resolution, but the proper resolution varies across the spectral band. Signatures behave quite differently in the reflective and emissive bands. Material signatures in the reflective region, as in Figure 10.9, tend to exhibit broad features that generally change very slowly with wavelength. In contrast, the signature can vary rapidly with wavelength in the emissive region, as in Figure 10.10. This complex structure has to be captured for the library. The trick is to get enough spectral resolution in each part of the band—but not too much; greater spectral resolution than needed adds to the size of the spectral data set but does not add to the information content.

Spectral signatures also have to be characterized in some way so that they can be searched when placed in a library. One method is to use a three-step characterization. First, one describes the general shape of the signature. Second, a coarse measurement is made of the major features embedded in the signature. Third, a technique called feature analysis captures fine detail about all the significant features in the signature, such as position in the spectrum, width, depth, and asymmetry.

The results of the signature characterization then are used to group signatures into a hierarchical structure. An unknown spectrum is identified by comparing it with a very general class of signatures and then with increasingly smaller and more tightly clustered groups of signatures. In this way, analysts can search a large database to identify the spectral signature most similar to that of the pixel.[31]

Each pixel in a hyperspectral image will have a spectrum that exhibits features like those shown in Figure 10.10. A very large amount of data is contained in a single pixel, and a massive amount of data is contained in a hyperspectral image. A hyperspectral image can be represented in the form of a three-dimensional data set called a **data cube**. The top of a data cube is

Radiometric
and Spectral
Imaging

one of the images of a region. The depth dimension represents wavelength. An example of a data cube is illustrated in Figure 10.11, which shows a 240-image cube.[32] The radiometric intensity of any given pixel at any given wavelength is represented by a color code. The top-level image sometimes appears as it would to the eye, but in Figure 10.11 it is a false color image. The layers behind it indicate intensities at increasingly long wavelengths in the infrared bands. The spectral signature of one pixel (marked with a line on the cube) is shown on the right.

 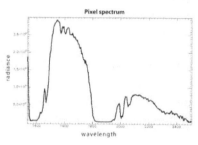

FIGURE 10.11 A Hyperspectral Data Cube

Structure

A number of military, intelligence, and civilian organizations conduct radiometric and spectral imaging to support their customers. So all steps in the collection process are fragmented. The structure is similar to that for optical imaging, but the customer set is much narrower, and time usually is not as critical.

As with visible imaging, spectral sensing and imaging is conducted to serve civilian, military, intelligence, and other governmental purposes. In the United States, both NOAA and NASA, as well as all the military services, conduct radiometric or spectral imaging. Law enforcement organizations increasingly are making use of the capability.

Summary

Radiometric and spectral imaging are used in intelligence for many of the same purposes as the visible imagers discussed in Chapter 9. But the signatures they produce give additional insights about their targets. While the images can be produced in both the reflective (including visible) and emissive parts of the spectrum, some of the most useful intelligence is produced in the emissive part, where thermal imaging is done.

Radiometric imaging produces a single image centered on a wavelength somewhere in the optical or microwave spectrum. The features that can be extracted from the image depend on the wavelength selected. For reflective imaging:

- In the visible part of the spectrum, three bands often are imaged separately—red, blue, and green. Each band can highlight different features or objects in the image.
- The NIR band is the fourth common band; it is closest to visible light and extends from 0.75 to 1.5 μm in wavelength. Night vision devices work in this band. The longer wavelengths in the NIR band reflect uniquely from minerals, crops and vegetation, and moist surfaces.
- The SWIR band extends from 1.5 to 3 μm. Images in this band are used to detect the presence of water and for vegetation analysis based on reflective signatures.

Thermal imagers are used in both the microwave and infrared parts of the spectrum. They create images that rely on heat-generated emissions from the target. Infrared radiometers have better resolution than microwave radiometers, but they cannot see through clouds as the latter can. Space-based infrared radiometers are used to detect ballistic missile launches and atmospheric nuclear detonations. Two of the thermal bands find extensive intelligence use:

- The MWIR band, extending from 3 to 8 μm, is a transition band that produces both emissive and reflective signatures. This is the heat-seeking region in which the sensors carried by passive IR homing missiles are designed to work.
- The LWIR band is a major atmospheric window extending from 8 to 15 μm. The region near 10 microns is often called the thermal imaging region, because objects near room temperature emit more strongly in this region. LWIR sensors use this signature to obtain a completely passive image of the earth based on thermal emissions only. This is the primary band used to characterize gaseous effluents for intelligence purposes.

Radiometers can measure the polarization as well as the intensity of a signal, and this measurement frequently has intelligence value: Light reflected from a smooth surface such as a vehicle or aircraft runway will be strongly polarized, but light from natural features is randomly polarized.

Radiometric and Spectral Imaging

Spectral imaging produces a set of simultaneous images of the same scene, each at a different wavelength. Any single pixel in the scene therefore will have a spectral signature of intensity versus wavelength that can be used to identify the material or object in that pixel.

Imaging in a single spectral band creates the simplest type of optical image: a panchromatic image. But it conveys no spectral information. The various wavelengths of the visible spectrum are not individually distinguished, and only the overall reflectance in the entire visible portion is recorded. The same thing is true for radiometric imaging in the IR and microwave bands. The image records variations in intensity, but not variations in intensity across the spectrum. Spectral imaging, in contrast, records intensity variations and therefore can provide a rich set of signatures.

Spectral imaging involves simultaneously acquiring a number of images at different electromagnetic wavelengths within these bands. Imaging an object at different wavelengths allows intelligence analysts to identify unique spectral signatures of targets. The more the wavelength bands that are separately acquired and processed in separate images, the more is the information that can be obtained about targets in the images. Increasing the number of spectral bands allows one to progress from detecting a target, to classifying it, to identifying a specific object or gas. MSI is most commonly used today and is collected from aircraft and satellite platforms. HSI and USI provide far more spectral information than does MSI, making them much more information rich but also more difficult to process and analyze.

The first step in processing spectral information is to calibrate the raw data from the sensor. Other corrections, such as radiometric and spectral calibrations, must also be applied to the data set. The raw data must be geo-rectified—that is, accurately fit to a map of the target area. In order to be useful, collected spectral signatures also must be corrected for the effects of the atmosphere on the reflected or emitted radiant energy as it travels between the ground target and the collector. The next processing step is image transformation, which takes nonvisible bands and translates them to the visible, usually through the use of false color. Image transformation also highlights features of intelligence interest.

In the exploitation phase, the different classes of features and details in an image are distinguished by comparing their responses over distinct wavelength ranges. To do this, an analyst has to have access to a spectral library. Exploitation and analysis of spectral signatures is not possible without a library of such signatures. A library that is useful for intelligence analysis would include a large number of minerals, organic and volatile compounds, vegetation, and man-made materials. The spectra for camouflage, military metals, CW agents, and other materials of intelligence significance are typically kept in classified libraries.

NOTES

1. Alfred J. Garrett, Robert J. Kurzeja, B. Lance O'Steen, Matthew J. Parker, Malcolm M. Pendergast, and Eliel Villa-Aleman, "Post-launch Validation of Multispectral Thermal Imager (MTI) Data and Algorithms," U.S. Department of Energy Report No. WSRC-MS-99-00423 (1999).

2. Guo Yan, Wang Jiangan, and He Yingzhou, "Detecting the Thermal Track of Submarines by Infrared Imagery," *Wuhan Haijun Gongcheng Xueyuan Xuebao* (June 1, 2002), 89.

3. John A. Adam, "Peacekeeping by Technical Means," *IEEE Spectrum,* (July 1986), 42–80.

4. Alfred J. Garrett, Robert J. Kurzeja, B. Lance O'Steen, Matthew J. Parker, Malcolm M. Pendergast, and Eliel Villa-Aleman, "Post-launch Validation of Multispectral Thermal Imager (MTI) Data and Algorithms," U.S. Department of Energy Report No. WSRC-MS-99-00423 (1999).

5. M. R. Fetterman, J. Grata, G. Jubic, W. L. Kiser, Jr., and A. Visnansky, "Simulation, Acquisition and Analysis of Passive Millimeter-Wave Images in Remote Sensing Applications," Opt. Express 16, 20503–20515 (2008), accessed 23 September 2012 at http://www.researchgate.net/publication/23640558_Simulation_acquisition_and_analysis_of_passive_millimeter-wave_images_in_remote_sensing_applications.

6. Daniel W. Banks, Robert C. Blanchard, and Geoffrey M. Miller, "Mobile Aerial Tracking and Imaging System (MATrIS) for Aeronautical Research," NASA/TM-2004-212852 (August 2004).

7. National Academy of Sciences, *Technical Issues Related to the Comprehensive Nuclear Test Ban Treaty* (Washington, DC: National Academies Press, 2002).

8. USAF Briefing, "Infrared Space Systems Wing: Contributions to Transforming Space" (November 6, 2007), accessed 22 September 2011 at www.californiaspaceauthority.org/conference2007/images/presentations/071106-1000b-McMurry.pdf.

9. Image accessed 3 October 2012 at http://commons.wikimedia.org/wiki/File:SBIRS-GEO_2.jpg.

10. USAF, "Infrared Space Systems Directorate," accessed 23 September 2012 at http://www.losangeles.af.mil/library/factsheets/factsheet.asp?id=5330.

11. "France Accepts Spirale Early Warning System Demonstrator," *Defense Technology News* (May 20, 2009), accessed 23 September 2012 at www.defencetalk.com/france-spirale-space-early-warning-system-19033/.

12. Carey Sublette, "Report on the 1979 Vela Incident" (September 1, 2001), accessed 23 September 2012 at http://nuclearweaponarchive.org/Safrica/Vela.html.

13. The National Security Archive, "The Vela Incident: Nuclear Test or Meteoroid?" (May 5, 2006), accessed 23 September 2012 at www.gwu.edu/~nsarchiv/NSAEBB/NSAEBB190/index.htm.

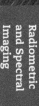

Radiometric and Spectral Imaging

14. Rulon Mayer, Richard Priest, Christopher Stellman, Geoffrey Hazel, Alan Schaum, Jonathon Schuler, and Michael Hess, "Detection of Camouflaged Targets in Cluttered Backgrounds Using Fusion of Near Simultaneous Spectral and Polarimetric Imaging," Naval Research Laboratory Report (August 8, 2000).

15. Michael J. Duggin, "Factors Controlling the Manual and Automated Extraction of Image Information Using Imaging Polarimetry," *Proceedings of SPIE*, Vol. 382, No. 85, accessed 23 September 2012 at http://www.deepdyve.com/lp/spie/factors-controlling-the-manual-and-automated-extraction-of-image-2ua10wr8HM/1.

16. Karen St. Germain, Peter Gaiser, and Mustufa Bahrain, "Polarimetric Radiometry and Ocean Surface Wind Vector: From Windsat to CMIS," accessed 23 September 2012 at www.ursi.org/Proceedings/ProcGA05/pdf/F10.2(01469).pdf.

17. Lewis Page, "New Prototype US Spy Satellite Rushed into Active Use," *Space* (June 11, 2010), accessed 23 September 2012 at http://www.theregister.co.uk/2010/06/11/artemis_goes_active/.

18. Jet Propulsion Laboratory, "AVIRIS Airborne Visible/Infrared Imaging Spectrometer," accessed 23 September 2012 at http://aviris.jpl.nasa.gov/.

19. Paul G. Lucey, Tim J. Williams, Michael E. Winter, and Edwin M. Winter, "Two Years of Operations of AHI: A LWIR Hyperspectral Imager," *Proceedings of SPIE*, 4030, No. 31–40, accessed 23 September 2012 at http://proceedings.spiedigitallibrary.org/proceeding.aspx?articleid=903351.

20. *Space Daily*, "EO-1 Offers First Hyperspectral Imager" (January 17, 2001), accessed 23 September 2012 at www.spacedaily.com/news/eo-sats-01b.html.

21. "EnMAP—Germany's Hyperspectral Satellite for Earth Observation," German Aerospace Center, accessed 30 September 2012 at http://www.dlr.de/dlr/en/desktopdefault.aspx/tabid-10379/567_read-421/.

22. Robert Plemmons, Wake Forest University, "Tensor Methods for Space Object Identification Using Hyperspectral Data," Slides 30–36, accessed 23 September 2012 at http://www.cs.cornell.edu/cv/TenWork/Slides/Plemmons.pdf.

23. NASA Image of the Day, posted November 8, 2007. A public domain image, accessed 23 September 2012 at http://earthobservatory.nasa.gov/IOTD/view.php?id=8196.

24. Gary A. Shaw and Hsiao-hua K. Burke, "Spectral Imaging for Remote Sensing," Lincoln Laboratory Journal, Vol. 14, No. 1 (2003), 4, accessed 30 September 2012 at http://www.ll.mit.edu/publications/journal/pdf/vol14_no1/14_1remotesensing.pdf.

25. Edward Ashton, Brian Fianagan, and Sherry Olson, "Analyzing Hyperspectral Data," *The Edge* (MITRE Corporation publication), (September 1999), Vol. 3, No. 3, 1, accessed 23 September 2012 at www.mitre.org/news/the_edge/september_99/first.html.

26. W. F. Belokon, M. A. Emmons, W. H. Fowler, B. A. Gilson, G. Hernandez, A. J. Johnson, M. D. Keister, J. W. McMillan, M. A. Noderer, E. J. Tullos, and K. E. White, *Multispectral Imagery Reference Guide* (Fairfax, VA: Logicon Geodynamics, Inc., 1997), 2–8.

27. Belokon et al., 2–5, 6.

28. Associated Press, "Swiss Police Spy Marijuana Field with Google Earth" (January 29, 2009), accessed 23 September 2012 at http://www.highbeam.com/doc/1A1-D960T7180.html.

29. Lewis Page, "New Prototype US Spy Satellite Rushed into Active Use," *Space*, (June 11, 2010), accessed 23 September 2012 at http://www.theregister.co.uk/2010/06/11/artemis_goes_active/.

30. Ashton, Fianagan, and Olson, "Analyzing Hyperspectral Data."

31. Ibid.

32. Centre for Integrated Petroleum Research, "Virtual Outcrop Geology" (2012), accessed 30 September 2012 at http://org.uib.no/cipr/Project/VOG/hyperspectral.htm.

11. Radar

Radar has entered our lives and become ubiquitous over the last six decades. We encounter it in media weather reports and on the highway (in the form of speed traps). Radar helps keep us safe when we fly, and in the future it appears that it will help protect us when we drive. Originally developed for military purposes, it now has many civil applications. And it is used continuously to provide intelligence, which is the subject of this chapter and the next.

Chapter 7 categorized sensors as either active or passive. Chapter 9 examined passive imaging in the visible part of the spectrum, followed by passive radiometric and spectral imaging in Chapter 10. We now begin to focus on active sensing, which usually is done by radar. This chapter is about the many applications of conventional radars (that is, those that do not use synthetic aperture techniques). It also sets the stage for a discussion of synthetic aperture radar (SAR) in Chapter 12.

In contrast to the passive sensors discussed in the two previous chapters, radars produce their own illumination energy. This feature gives radars some advantages in intelligence collection. For example, they operate day or night, not needing the sun to reflect energy from a target. Radars that operate in the microwave band can function in most weather conditions. Unlike optical sensors, they are unaffected by clouds.

Function

The first radars were put into operation for air defense—that is, to provide warning of approaching hostile aircraft. These were the Chain Home radars that the British built in the late 1930s. During World War II they provided early warning and subsequent tracking of German bombers as the aircraft crossed the English Channel, giving the British fighters time to get in position to meet the Germans.

The United States began building radars at about the same time as the British, but their first radar use in combat was less than successful. An Army Air Corps radar located at Opana Point, Hawaii, detected the approaching Japanese attack force on December 7, 1941. But the attackers were mistakenly identified as a scheduled flight of B-17s from the United States and no warning was given. During the course of the war, shipborne and ground-based radar repeatedly gave the Americans and British a combat edge against German, Italian, and Japanese ships and aircraft. Airborne radars that could search the ocean's surface later in the war made life difficult for German submariners. Some authors have credited radar as being the invention that won World War II because of all these successes.

Radars today have a wide range of civil and military applications. Most radars are used to locate a target and track its movement. Examples include commercial air traffic radars, naval ship surface and air search radars, and air defense radars. Surface-based radars are used to search the sky (or the surface, at relatively short ranges) and track targets such as ships, aircraft, and satellites. Most airborne and spaceborne radars are used to map the earth's surface or to detect and track ships and heavy ground vehicles such as tanks and missile launchers. Airborne radars also search the sky for weather or other aircraft. Radars can be placed on almost any platform. They range in size from the towering over-the-horizon (OTH) radars discussed in this chapter to small devices that can be carried in a backpack or mounted on an automobile.

In short, radar is used for a number of purposes, most of which have nothing to do with intelligence. If radar data are used for immediate operational purposes and quickly discarded, then it is considered operational information, not intelligence. Air traffic control radars and ship and aircraft navigational radars fall into the operations category; the information they collect has little value later.

Sometimes, though, radar information is collected and retained for its value beyond the moment. It may be useful for scientific research. It may be intelligence. It may be provided by a radar that normally supports operations—an air or missile defense radar, for example. Most radar intelligence is in fact provided by radars that also have operational missions. For example, the test flights of new aircraft and unmanned aerial vehicle (UAV) designs sometimes are monitored by air defense radars and the results used by scientific and technical (S&T) intelligence centers in systems evaluation.

Very few radars have only an intelligence function. OTH radars have been deployed to monitor air traffic and ballistic missile launches in denied areas for intelligence. The Cobra Dane and Cobra Judy radars described in this chapter monitor the reentry stage of ballistic missile testing—though even those two radars also have operational missions. (The term *Cobra* occurs on occasion as part of the name of a U.S. intelligence collector. It does not refer to a snake; it's an acronym meaning "Collection By Remote Assets.")

Clearly, the distinction between operational military use and intelligence use can be difficult to draw, and the two uses often overlap. For example, radar tracks of a hostile aircraft or ship usually have little value after the mission is over, as noted earlier. However, if the aircraft or ship is a new version, not previously seen, then the radar tracking data are likely to contain valuable intelligence information about the performance of the ship or aircraft, and the intensity of the radar return might tell something about the use of antiradar (stealth) technology. The following are some general rules of thumb concerning radar use:

- Searching for and tracking aircraft or ships is mostly operations but can also be intelligence.
- Searching for and tracking ballistic missile reentry vehicles (R/Vs) that are being used in conflict is operations, but the same tracking of R/Vs that another country is testing is intelligence.
- Searching for and tracking another country's satellites is operations when the information is used to avoid satellite collisions or to target the satellite for attack. The same information, when used to determine the satellite's mission, is intelligence.
- Imaging the earth's surface can be scientific research, operations, or intelligence, depending on how the data are used.

As an example of the last rule of thumb, the Joint Surveillance and Target Attack Radar System (JSTARS) aircraft carries an imaging radar that provides details about targets moving in the scene. The movement information could be used for targeting moving vehicles such as tanks and trucks in combat situations and so would be considered operations. However, information about such movements could also be used to get a general picture of enemy intentions, and so would have intelligence value. Clearly, there is overlap between the two: The same radar can be used for both operations and intelligence collection simultaneously.

Process

PLANNING

Much radar surveillance is carried on routinely; ocean, battlefield, or space surveillance is typically a 24/7 effort. Ground-based, shipborne, and aerostat search radars usually conduct such surveillance; they monitor all activity in their fields of view continuously. Aircraft, UAV, and spaceborne radar collection usually require mission planning with specific targets in mind.

Some planning for intelligence collection using radar is ad hoc, based on indications that a weapons test is imminent, for example. Search and imaging radars may be specifically targeted on an area of intelligence interest, such as a region where a crisis is developing. Or target tracking radars may be aimed at specific targets based on a tip-off that the target is of interest. Object identification and imaging radars also usually are targeted on specific items of intelligence interest.

COLLECTION

Most intelligence collection using radar involves air surveillance, surface (land and ocean) surveillance, space surveillance, and tracking and characterizing reentry vehicles. Following an introductory section on radar operating bands and how radar works, we'll look at some radars that have been used to collect intelligence in the various frequency bands.

Radar Frequency Bands. Most radars operate in designated blocks of frequency bands within the radio frequency (RF) spectrum that was discussed in Chapter 7. The International Telecommunication Union (ITU) has assigned specific frequency blocks for radar throughout the very high frequency (VHF), ultra high frequency (UHF), and microwave bands. The U.S. military and the Institute of Electrical and Electronics Engineers (IEEE) have assigned much broader frequency bands to the same designators, as Table 11.1 illustrates. However, the ITU bands more precisely describe where radars actually operate throughout most of the world. U.S. radars normally

TABLE 11.1 Radar Frequency Bands

Radar Band Designation	International Telecommunication Union Frequency Bands	IEEE and Military Frequency Bands
HF	—	3–30 MHz
VHF	138–144 MHz; 216–225 MHz	30–300 MHz
UHF	420–450 MHz; 890–942 MHz	300–1000 MHz
L	1215–1400 MHz	1–2 GHz
S	2.3–2.5 GHz; 2.7–3.7 GHz	2–4 GHz
C	5.250–5.925 GHz	4–8 GHz
X	8.50–10.68 GHz	8–12 GHz
K_u	13.4–14.0 GHz; 15.7–17.7 GHz	12–18 GHz
K	24.05–24.25 GHz; 24.65–24.75 GHz	18–27 GHz
K_a	33.4–36.0 GHz	27–40 GHz
V	59.0–64.0 GHz	40–75 GHz
W	76.0–81.0 GHz; 92.0–100.0 GHz	75–110 GHz

operate within the ITU designated frequencies. A few countries, such as Russia, operate radars outside the ITU bands, so the broader band IEEE and military designators have some utility.

Laser radars work in the optical spectrum and do not have designated bands within that part of the spectrum.

How a Radar Works. At its most basic, a radar consists of a transmitter, antenna, receiver, signal processor, and display. Most radars use the same antenna for transmission and reception of signals.

The radar transmitter generates EM waves that radiate from an antenna that illuminates the air or space with radio waves. Any target that enters this space, such as an aircraft, scatters a small portion of this radio energy back to the receiving antenna. This returned signal is amplified by an electronic amplifier, processed, and displayed for a radar operator. Once detected, the object's position, distance (range), and bearing can be measured. As radio waves travel at a known constant velocity (the speed of light—300,000 kilometers per second or 186,000 miles per second), the range may be found by measuring the time it takes for a radio wave to travel from the transmitter to the object and back to the receiver. For example, if the range were 186 miles, the time for the round trip would be $(2 \times 186)/186,000 =$ two-thousandths of a second, or 2,000 microseconds. Most radars are pulsed, meaning that the radiation is not continuous but is emitted as a succession of short bursts, each lasting a few microseconds. An electronic timer measures the time delay between pulse transmission and the returned signal and calculates the target range. Azimuth, elevation, and range to the target determine the target's position. The radar thereby provides the precise location of the target and, based on target movement between pulses, predicts the future position of the target.

Modern radar receivers digitize the returned signal, transforming it into a series of bits that can be processed in several different ways to extract information about the target signature. These digital receivers allow the detection of weak target returns and the determination of target position, movement, and configuration. The receivers allow the radar to operate in different modes; depending on the nature of information desired about the target, the radar can change its pulse shape and modulation, transmitting the pulses in different directions and at different pulse repetition rates. The digital receiver processes all the received data and automatically extracts the desired information.

Radars also identify moving targets and measure their velocity by observing the Doppler shift in frequency when RF energy is reflected from a moving target. The Doppler shift is an important part of the target signature. It is used in many ways in technical collection and is essential to the functioning of imaging radar, to be explained in Chapter 12.

To meet the demands of precisely tracking targets and searching for additional targets, radar antennas have evolved into new configurations. Most older radars continue to use some variant of the familiar parabolic antenna, which shapes the RF energy into a beam. However, the parabolic antenna must be mechanically moved to detect or track a target, and it can track only one target at a time.

New radars increasingly use phased array antennas instead of parabolic antennas. Rather than move the antenna mechanically, the phased array steers radar energy electronically. In a phased array, there are many thousands of small antenna elements placed on a flat structure. If the signals from the separate elements all occur at the same time and in phase, they form a radar beam where the beam direction is perpendicular to the array face. To detect objects that do not lie directly in front of the array face, devices that shift the phase of the signal reaching the antenna elements are used. These phase shifters change the direction in which RF energy leaves or enters the antenna and thereby control the direction of the main beam.

Since phased array radars have several thousand antenna elements, multiple beams can be formed in rapid sequence or even at the same time. Thus, a phased array radar is capable of simultaneously tracking several hundred targets; a computer calculates the proper target measurements for each of these beams. Phased array radars have advantages. They are inherently multifunction and they can both search for and track many different objects at the same time. They were slow to be adopted because they were considerably more expensive than parabolic dish antennas to build and maintain, but the cost of building and maintaining them has come down enough to make them the preferred design for new radars.

For highly precise tracking of ballistic missiles and satellites, interferometric radars are sometimes used. In an interferometer design, several comparatively small antennas are deployed in the pattern of an L or X on the ground; one or more of the antennas transmits a signal at the target, and the return signal from the target is received by all the antennas. By comparing the phase differences in the return signal among the antennas, the radar can accurately determine the azimuth and elevation to the satellite or R/V and provide accurate trajectory or orbital parameters.

Operating Modes. Most radars are optimized for one of the collection modes discussed below. All of these modes are used to collect intelligence.

Search radars transmit a beam that is scanned across a volume of space to detect targets. The beam blankets the volume with radar energy. Airport surveillance radars and many air defense radars are of this type: the beam from the radar is rotated so that it scans 360 degrees in azimuth to monitor air traffic in the immediate area. Chapter 8 provided an illustration of the type. The surveillance radar shown in Figure 8.11 is an example of a search radar designed to monitor air activity over a battlefield.

Long-range search radars, such as those used in ballistic missile defense (BMD) and space surveillance, usually require large phased array antennas and high power, and they tend to operate in the lower radar frequency bands (VHF and lower UHF bands). The U.S. PAVE PAWS radar; the FPS-85 radar at Eglin AFB, Florida, that is described in this chapter; and the Russian Dnepr and Dar'yal radars are examples of search radars. One of their missions is to detect previously unknown targets so that the targets can be tracked and identified.

Tracking radars keep the beam on a target (usually a target detected by a search radar) to follow or track the target throughout the radar's volume of coverage. Tracking radars are used to establish where a target is and where it is going. When tracking a satellite, this is known as establishing the satellite's orbital elements. Tracking radars can use either phased array or dish antennas and usually operate at higher microwave frequencies. Phased arrays are useful for both search and track. One of their advantages, noted earlier, is that they can simultaneously track many targets—a particularly important advantage in space surveillance. For all antenna types, the accuracy of tracking is limited by the antenna beamwidth; narrow beamwidths are better.

Object identification radars obtain a unique signature from a target such as a satellite, aircraft, ship, or vehicle. That signature is used to identify the target's mission or purpose. Such use of radar to identify and characterize objects is part of a subfield of measurements and signatures intelligence (MASINT) called radar intelligence (RADINT). RADINT targets include satellites, missiles, ships, aircraft, and battlefield vehicles.

An object identification radar can do many things, depending on its design. It can image the target, determine its radar cross-section, identify and discriminate among targets, precisely measure components, determine the motion of the target or its components, and measure the target's radar reflectance and absorption characteristics. Radar returns can be used, for example, to reconstruct the trajectories of missiles and convey the details and configuration of the missile reentry vehicle itself.[1]

A specific type of object identification radar called **space object identification (SOI)** radar uses a combination of techniques to obtain information about satellites, reentry vehicles, and space debris. Such radars rely on three techniques for object identification:

- target movement (trajectory or orbital parameters) and changes in movement;
- radar cross-section (RCS) and variations in RCS with time; and
- radar imaging.

Imaging radars create a picture of the target. Some aircraft radars create an electronic map of the earth's surface that is used for navigation. Some imaging radars are specifically designed to create high-resolution images of the earth's surface or of specific objects. Earth imaging radars, known as synthetic aperture radars (SARs), are discussed in detail in Chapter 12. This chapter examines some radars that are used to create images of objects.

Multifunction radars can function in two or more of the modes discussed above. Fighter aircraft radars, for example, are multifunction radars; they can track an aircraft while simultaneously searching for other aircraft in the area. The Cobra Dane radar is another example of a multifunction radar. It can search for targets, track them, and obtain target measurements by changing its mode of operation.

Vibrometry is a radar technique that finds frequent intelligence use. It depends on remotely sensing vibrations from a target. A coherent radar (one that maintains a constant phase) illuminates the target area; the radar receiver extracts the Doppler shift backscattered from the target to obtain a signature.

Microwave vibrometers have been used to collect communications intelligence (COMINT) for decades. The concept is to transmit a strong coherent EM signal at a nearby target (on the order of a few hundred meters away). The target then reradiates the signal, modulated by the slight vibrations (usually acoustic vibrations) that it experiences. The reradiated signal is then recovered by a receiver antenna and demodulated to recover the acoustic signal. This technique was introduced in Chapter 4 and described as RF flooding there. It has been used to recover audio, as it did in the story of the U.S. ambassador's great seal. Chapter 4 also described how lasers use the same technique to exploit audio vibrations from windows or similar fixtures within a building for COMINT purposes.

Vibrometry can also be used to obtain nonliteral information about a target, the target area, or activity in the area. Vibrometry is used for target identification, for example; it can identify the unique signature created by RF signals reflected from moving parts of a target. It can sense vibrations from the surface of a building or the ground above an underground facility to identify processes going on in the facility or machines that are operating in the facility. The acoustic signatures generated by machinery often uniquely identify the machine, and both the machine identity and its pattern of operation over time can provide valuable intelligence insights. Lasers can be used for many of the same purposes—for example, to detect machine noise or a helicopter blade's rotation rate. Laser radar vibrometry was used to identify a helicopter at 5-kilometer range in the 1980s.[2]

Instead of transmitting an RF signal at the target area, one can use intentional RF radiation from a source near the target to obtain signatures. A radar or radio mounted on an aircraft, for example, will have its signal modulated by the aircraft propellers or jet turbine blades. The modulation, though weak, can provide both the aircraft type and identification of the specific aircraft. Innocuous signals such as those emanating from a television or radio station also can be used successfully to flood an installation or target.

Over-the-Horizon Radar. Radars divide generally into two classes, based on their operating geometry: OTH radars that can see targets beyond line-of-sight, and radars that are limited to line-of-sight operation.

OTH radar operates in or near the high frequency (HF) band, where radio waves are reflected from the ionosphere—the phenomenon that allows international radio broadcasts to be received from stations thousands of miles away. Conventional radars operate at line of sight, meaning that they cannot see targets close to the earth's surface at long distances.[3] In contrast, OTH radars bounce signals off the ionosphere to see around the earth's curvature, making it possible to conduct radar surveillance of otherwise inaccessible regions at ranges of 1,000 kilometers or more. They can monitor both aircraft and ship movements. But such radars are expensive to build and tricky to operate. They depend on the ionosphere, which is a continuously changing reflector. The operating band is very noisy; the band has many interfering signals, and a high frequency radar has no reserved frequencies (as Table 11.1 indicates). The radar gets intense clutter from the backscattered ground return, from which the desired signal has to be separated. These problems require the design of a radar with a very large antenna, very high power, and sophisticated signal processing. Two such radars that the United States has used for intelligence are Cobra Mist and the Air Force's FPS-118 (OTH-B).

The FPS-95 OTH radar, codenamed Cobra Mist, was built on the English North Sea Coast in the late 1960s to monitor air and missile activity in Eastern Europe and the western areas of the Soviet Union. Cobra Mist was expected to detect and track aircraft in flight over the western part of the Soviet Union and the Warsaw Pact countries and monitor missile launches from the Soviet Union's Northern Fleet Missile Test Center at Plesetsk. The radar operated in the frequency range from 6 to 40 MHz.

Cobra Mist was one of the largest, most powerful, and most sophisticated OTH radars of its time, and the OTH radar community expected it to set new standards for performance and capability. It was designed to detect and track aircraft movements and missile launches at ranges of 500 to 2,000 nautical miles, corresponding to one bounce off the ionosphere. A searchlight mode was provided for high-priority targets whose approximate locations were known *a priori*. These targets could include single aircraft, compact formations of aircraft, or missile launches.

The key to this radar's performance, as with any OTH radar, was to separate target returns from the strong ground clutter.[4] However, the detection performance of the radar was spoiled from the beginning by noise that appeared at all ranges where ground clutter was present. The sophisticated signal processors were unable to separate targets from what became known as "clutter-related noise."

Experiments performed at the site failed to uncover the source of the noise. The noise appeared to be associated with imaging of land areas and not of sea surfaces. The possibility of electronic countermeasures was considered and not ruled out. After many attempts to locate the source of the noise and correct the problem, the radar program was terminated in June 1973 and the equipment removed from the site or allowed to deteriorate. The cause of the noise is still unknown.[5]

OTH-B, the U.S. Air Force's over-the-horizon-backscatter air defense radar system, was the largest radar system in the world in terms of earth coverage. Six OTH-B radars were built over a 25-year period starting in 1970 and deployed to monitor aircraft traffic approaching the United States. Three radars located in Maine monitored traffic over the north and south Atlantic Ocean and the Caribbean Sea. Three radars located in Oregon and California monitored traffic over the North and South Pacific Ocean.

However, the OTH-B program suffered from an accident of timing. The Cold War ended shortly after the radars were deployed. The three OTH radars on the West Coast were mothballed. The three radars in Maine were redirected to counternarcotics surveillance—specifically, to detect aircraft approaching the United States across the Gulf of Mexico. The OTH-B tracking data were transmitted directly to Department of Defense (DoD) and civilian law enforcement agencies that were responsible for counternarcotics operations. The East Coast radars formally ceased operations in October 1997.[6]

Despite the challenges of making OTH radars work, they continue to be used both to support operations and to collect intelligence. The reason is that a single OTH radar can surveil a very large area of the earth. Figure 11.1 illustrates the point; it shows the breadth of area coverage that OTH-B provided.

At closer ranges, but still beyond the visible horizon, radars also can be designed to operate as **surface-wave radars**. Customarily, such radars are used to detect and track oceangoing ships or low-flying aircraft at ranges up to a few hundred kilometers. Though they are called OTH radars, these radars do not bounce their signals off the ionosphere. Instead, the radar energy travels along the sea surface, is reflected from obstacles such as ships, and returns to the receiver antenna. Australia has deployed one such radar, called the Surface-wave Extended Coastal Area Radar (SECAR), in northern Australia. SECAR makes use of separate transmission and reception sites and is designed to provide coastal surveillance, economic asset protection, smuggling deterrence, weather/storm monitoring, illegal immigration monitoring, and seaborne traffic control.[7]

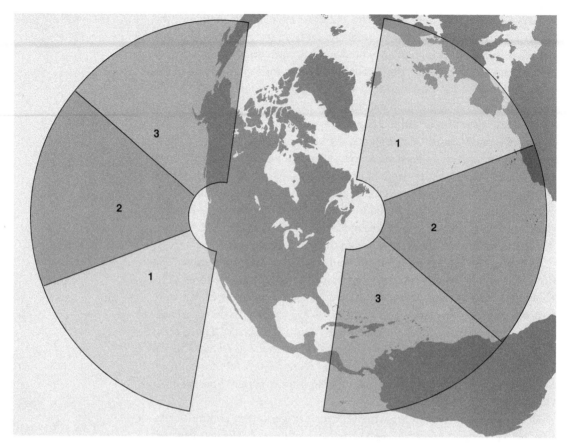

FIGURE 11.1 OTH-B Radar Coverage

Most radars operate at frequencies higher than HF and, because they cannot see targets below the horizon, are called line-of-sight radars. Following is a discussion of the main line-of-sight radar operating bands, with some examples of radars used for intelligence that operate in the VHF and higher-frequency bands. This is an illustrative list of such radars and does not include all radars used for intelligence collection.

VHF. Radars operating in the two standard VHF bands (138 to 144 and 216 to 225 MHz) are usually designed for long-range search. Formerly these bands were used for airspace search, but now the most common application of VHF radars—at least in intelligence—is for ballistic missile and satellite detection and tracking. These ground-based radars typically use large antennas (though smaller than those used in the HF band). A major disadvantage is that, like the HF band, the VHF band is quite crowded with other signals and generally very noisy.

The French Graves is an example of a VHF radar used in intelligence. It was specifically designed for space surveillance. It has a novel design: a **bistatic radar**, meaning that the transmitter and receiver are spatially separated. The Graves transmitter is located near the Dijon Air Base in eastern France. The receiver is located on the Albion Plateau in southern France, some 400 kilometers away. The transmitter electronically scans a volume of space continuously using a VHF signal. The receiver scans the same volume of space, detecting satellites and estimating the satellite velocity and direction from the Doppler shifted return. The radar reportedly can detect objects in orbit at an altitude of between 400 and 1,000 km.

The Graves radar became operational in November 2005. Since then, it has been keeping a database of some 2,000 satellites up to date. According to the French, Graves has tracked a few dozen sensitive satellites for which the United States does not publish orbital elements. The French have threatened to publish the orbital elements about the U.S. satellites as a negotiating tool; they object to the U.S. practice of including orbital data on sensitive French satellites in the U.S. space catalog.[8]

UHF. The UHF radar bands (420 to 450 and 890 to 942 MHz) are used to operate radars similar in design and purpose to those in the VHF band. The UHF band, though, encounters less noise and interference. The UHF band is defined as extending from 300 to 3,000 MHz, which technically includes the radar L and S bands that are discussed below. However, by convention the term *UHF radar* only is used to denote a radar operating in the 420 to 450 and 890 to 942 MHz bands.

Figure 11.2 is a picture of the FPS-85 radar, located in Florida.[9] It is an example of a radar dedicated to perform space surveillance, which includes searching for, detecting, tracking, and reporting objects in space. The FPS-85 operates at 442 MHz.

FIGURE 11.2 FPS-85 Radar

This radar was built in 1961. It was developed as a scientific experiment, because it was the first phased array radar of such size and power. Destroyed by fire in 1965, the facility was rebuilt and has operated continuously day and night since 1969.

The FPS-85 is well-suited for space surveillance. Its location and its main beam boresight at 180 degrees in azimuth (due south) and 45 degrees elevation angle above the horizon allow it to achieve excellent coverage of space.[10]

The radar has a database of more than 7,000 satellites and space debris, and it tracks these objects as they enter the radar's coverage area. It makes about 20,000 observations each day and relays the time, elevation, azimuth, range, and range rate data on each object to the North American Aerospace Defense Command (NORAD) facility at Cheyenne Mountain, Colorado. It can observe deep-space objects out to the range of geosynchronous orbiting satellites—up to 37,500 kilometers—and can track 200 near-earth targets simultaneously.

Note that the FPS-85 has two antennas, one for transmitting and one for receiving. This does not make it a bistatic radar like the Graves radar discussed previously. A bistatic radar has its antennas separated by a distance comparable to the distance from the radar to its targets, usually on the order of several hundred kilometers. The use of two antennas in the FPS-85 simplifies the RF hardware design and allows the radar to both search and track more efficiently.

L Band. The 1215 to 1400 MHz band is heavily used worldwide for air surveillance, and intelligence uses include tracking aircraft of interest (e.g., those carrying illicit cargo). It also finds intelligence uses for ballistic missile and satellite detection and tracking. It is a good compromise band: high enough in frequency to avoid the noise and interference effects of lower frequencies but low enough that high-power search radars can be built at a reasonable cost.

The Cobra Dane radar is an example of such an intelligence collection sensor. It was built in 1977 on the island of Shemya, Alaska. The radar's primary mission is to track and collect signature data on foreign intercontinental ballistic missiles (ICBMs) and submarine-launched ballistic missiles (SLBMs). That signature data supports treaty monitoring and technical assessments of foreign ICBM performance. Cobra Dane also has an operational mission; it provides early warning for missiles that would impact the continental United States.[11]

Cobra Dane is a phased array radar, as shown in Figure 11.3, operating in the 1215 to 1400 MHz band. It uses a narrow bandwidth signal for target acquisition and tracking and uses a wide bandwidth (200 MHz) signal for signature analysis of ballistic missile reentry vehicles.[12]

Cobra Dane can also detect, track, and catalog satellites and obtain signature data on them. But it has limitations in handling that mission because of the trade-off problem discussed in Chapter 7. The radar was built to acquire, accurately track, and obtain detailed signature data on ballistic missile reentry vehicles impacting on Russia's Kamchatka peninsula and the North Pacific. That requirement led to designing radar with a fixed orientation (that is, a fixed boresight)

FIGURE 11.3 Cobra Dane Radar

toward Kamchatka. As a result, its spatial coverage is less satisfactory for satellite tracking. Its location and orientation prevent it from seeing satellites in some orbits. Only satellites with inclinations between 55 and 125 degrees can be tracked.[13] The FPS-85, in contrast, is well positioned to obtain orbital information about satellites in almost all orbits.

S Band. The two S bands (2.3 to 2.5 and 2.7 to 3.7 GHz) are used for both air and naval search radars and target-tracking radars. These radars tend to have smaller antennas than L band radars, so they are often mobile. Both mobile ground-based and shipboard radars make use of the band.

An example of such a radar used primarily for intelligence is the Cobra Judy radar. The two Cobra Judy radars (S and X bands) are mounted on a ship, the USNS *Observation Island.* The ship's primary mission is to collect detailed radar signature data on strategic ballistic missiles to verify compliance with international arms control treaties. A secondary mission is to collect data for U.S. missile development and theater missile defense systems testing. It monitors and collects data on foreign ballistic missile tests, complementing the Cobra Dane radar.[14]

The *Observation Island* is one of the oldest active ships in the U.S. Navy; it originally was a merchant ship when launched in 1953. It is to be replaced in 2014 by the USNS *Howard O. Lorenzen,* shown in Figure 11.4. The new ship carries the Cobra King radar, which transmits in both the S and X bands (making it what we call a dual-band radar). The S band Cobra King radar will use a phased array antenna mounted on a rotating turret so that it can search

FIGURE 11.4 USNS *Howard O. Lorenzen*[15]

for, detect, and track multiple targets simultaneously.[16] Cobra Judy will be allowed to retire, and Cobra King will presumably pick up and carry on the same missions.

C Band. Radars in the 5.25 to 5.925 MHz band typically are designed to provide very precise tracking. Radars in this band also are commonly used for fire control (that is, to target ships or aircraft for attack).

ALCOR, a satellite and ballistic missile tracking radar, is one of three space surveillance radars located at Kwajalein Island in the South Pacific. The other two radars are the ARPA Long-range Tracking and Identification Radar (ALTAIR) and the Target Resolution and Discrimination Experiment (TRADEX). ALCOR is a high-power, narrow-beam tracking radar. It uses a narrowband (6-MHz bandwidth) pulse for tracking targets and a wideband (512-MHz bandwidth) pulse for obtaining images of targets. The wideband waveform provides a range resolution of approximately 0.5 meters. These high-resolution data, coupled with advanced radar signal processing, allow it to generate satellite images. The images are used to identify and characterize space objects and to assess spacecraft health and mission status.[17]

X Band. The 8.5 to 10.68 GHz band, like the C band, has traditionally been used for precision tracking radars. It was not considered a good band for long-range searches because the typical radar antenna in this band has been rather small (on the order of 1 meter to a few meters in size), and getting the high power needed for long-range search was not easy.

Newer radars have overcome this obstacle. And some new radar designs in this band can do it all: search, track, and get detailed signature data. An example is the sea-based X band radar shown in Figure 11.5. It is a floating, self-propelled, mobile radar station designed to operate in high winds and heavy seas. It is part of the U.S. government's ballistic missile defense system. The radar can detect and track ballistic missiles and satellites at long ranges. Its operation at X band, around 10 GHz, allows it to transmit a wide bandwidth signal, obtain high resolution of tracked

FIGURE 11.5 The X Band Radar at Sea

objects, and consequently obtain very detailed signatures. The signatures enable the radar to discriminate an R/V from decoys, the rocket body, and debris.[18]

The X band radar was designed to be mobile to allow mission flexibility. As noted earlier in the examples of the Cobra Dane and FPS-85, these two radars have a fixed location and antenna orientation that is advantageous for their design missions, but their spatial coverage is also fixed. Cobra Dane, for example, can cover Russian missile tests but is not well positioned to cover North Korean missile tests. The X band radar could collect against either.

Laser Radars. Laser radars operate much like microwave radars. The radar transmits pulses of laser light and detects energy reflected from the target. As with all radars, the time required for the energy to reach the target and return to the sensor determines the distance between the two. Unlike RF band radars, laser radars cannot penetrate clouds. But the laser radar has two big advantages:

- its beam is very narrow, so that it can illuminate an extremely small surface (on the order of 1 centimeter diameter at short ranges, less than 1 meter at aircraft-to-ground distances); and
- it can transmit very short pulses and measure distance to a high degree of precision.

The narrow beam and short pulses allow laser radars to produce three-dimensional images. And they are able to do so without using the SAR techniques discussed in Chapter 12. They can measure the dimensions of features (such as forest canopy or building height relative to the ground surface).

One of laser radar's most important intelligence uses is for defeating camouflage or forest canopy. The laser takes many measurements of the same target area so that it in effect finds holes in the covering material. It therefore is able to penetrate through the camouflage mesh to obtain a return from the object inside. Using this technique, laser radars have demonstrated a capability to provide three-dimensional (3-D) imagery of military vehicles concealed under foliage or camouflage. The images are of sufficient quality for analysts to perform object classification and identification.[19] Figure 11.6 illustrates an example of the visible image of a tank concealed by camouflage netting (on the left) and a laser image of the same tank (on the right).[20]

FIGURE 11.6 Laser Radar Image of a Tank under Camouflage Netting

An important intelligence application of laser radar is in exploiting the phenomenon of fluorescence. Some targets fluoresce, or emit energy, when they are struck by light energy. This is not a simple reflection of the incident radiation. In practice, a laser illuminates the target with a specific wavelength of radiation. A sensor carried with the laser is capable of detecting multiple wavelengths of fluoresced radiation. When the target is irradiated, it absorbs the laser energy; its molecules, atoms, or ions are excited and emit energy at longer wavelengths. The emission of longer wavelength radiation is then measured by the sensor, and the wavelength of the emitted radiation provides a characteristic signature of the target material. The technique relies on much the same spectral sensing process that was discussed in Chapter 10.

Laser radars also are used to identify materials at a distance. Many chemical and biological agents, and spoil from excavations, have characteristic fluorescence spectra when exposed to ultraviolet (UV) and visible light, so UV or visible lasers are used for fluorescence sensing. For intelligence usage, UV light has an obvious advantage in such roles: It is not visible to the human eye, so UV illuminators are less likely to be detected (we're not concerned about the reindeer). Rare earth elements and some heavy atom elements such as uranium can fluoresce efficiently. In daytime, the fluorescence is difficult to detect because of the strong reflection of normal sunlight, but special filters can be used to block out the visible sunlight and pass the fluorescence. Sensors have demonstrated the ability to detect pollutants such as oil slicks on the ocean using laser-induced fluorescence.[21]

Finally, laser radar is useful for tracking space objects, because it does not depend on having the proper lighting conditions and target geometry that is described in Chapter 9. Figure 11.7 shows an example of such a radar; the Russian Sazhen-M has two telescopes. One is the laser transmitter; the other receives the return signal.

PROCESSING AND EXPLOITATION

Processing and exploitation of radar data for intelligence purposes usually are intended to provide the location of a target of interest over time, that is, tracking. This tracking information provides a type of pattern.

- For aircraft, the pattern is geospatial; the aircraft's location and flight track can tell something about its mission, for example, hostile intent or illicit arms or narcotics traffic. Speed and altitude of the aircraft also can help to identify its mission.
- For ballistic missiles, the pattern is the reentry vehicle's trajectory. The trajectory allows the radar to identify the R/V target. Also, the radar can identify R/V maneuvers during reentry (such maneuvers usually are designed to avoid antimissile defenses or to improve warhead accuracy).

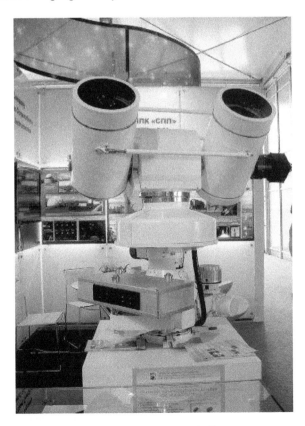

FIGURE 11.7 The Sazhen-M Laser Radar[22]

- For satellites, the pattern is the satellite's orbital parameters. The orbital parameters help to determine the satellite's mission. A historical record of an object's orbital behavior can be used to determine what is normal versus unusual behavior. A satellite will sometimes maneuver in order to correct for drift or drag, and these maneuvers provide additional intelligence about the satellite's mission and operational status.

Target movement is a relatively easy way for a radar to provide some identification of the target. It is particularly important in collecting information about ballistic missile tests. A ballistic missile R/V has a ballistic coefficient, or **beta**. Beta is a number based on the weight, drag, and cross-section. Vehicles with a high beta are usually smooth and slender, and they have little drag; they zip through the upper atmosphere without decelerating much and slow down only when reaching the thick lower atmosphere. Vehicles with a low beta do most of their slowing down in the upper atmosphere. Radar decoys that may accompany an R/V are typically lighter than reentry vehicles, and so they are more affected by the atmosphere. Finally, as noted above, some reentry vehicles can maneuver, either to improve accuracy or to avoid BMD defenses, and intelligence customers want to know whether an R/V is capable of maneuvering.

For satellites, target movement also can tell a great deal, for much the same reasons. A heavy satellite in near-earth orbit is slowed less by atmospheric drag than a light item of debris. The movement of a satellite out of its predicted orbit can indicate its operational status and its intentions. Satellites can be moved by thrusters, for example, to avoid attack or to escape surveillance.

Processing and exploitation has a second major intelligence purpose: to identify a target, and in some cases, to measure certain features of the target.

A radar can measure the RCS of an aircraft, a satellite, or R/V, and the RCS will vary over time. A periodic variation in RCS may indicate that the target is tumbling or maneuvering. Some variations can indicate that the target is changing its orientation, for example, that an onboard antenna is being moved.

Imaging radars are also used to identify airborne and spaceborne objects. But most search and tracking radars lack the resolution needed to provide useful imagery of these targets. Object identification radars have the necessary resolution and use it to identify radar returns from different parts of an aircraft, a satellite, or an R/V, creating a signature. Each target reflects radar energy in a unique radiation pattern or radar cross-section (signature) that is a function of the shape and material properties of the target and the radar-to-target geometry. Different types of objects produce different but definable signatures that can be measured to determine shape and size and used to identify and classify targets of interest.

For example, a satellite is composed of several interconnected objects, each of which scatters radar energy back toward the radar. At certain orientations of the satellite relative to the radar, the arms that interconnect these centers also strongly reflect radar energy back toward the radar. Furthermore, each major scattering center, in turn, is composed of several smaller scattering centers, which can be separated (resolved) by a high-resolution radar.

Imaging radar techniques attempt to resolve these scattering centers with the highest possible resolution, so that the scattering centers form a detailed image of the satellite. Some object identification techniques also attempt to observe motion of the centers (for example, the reorientation movement of antennas or solar panels). The combination of imagery and observation of component movements can reveal a great deal about the mission and operations of the aircraft, satellite, or R/V.

By recording the range and magnitude of the energy reflected from all parts of a target as it passes by, a two-dimensional image of the surface can be produced. Figure 11.8 shows the radar image of a cone-shaped reentry vehicle, as compared with the actual shape of the vehicle.[23]

Conventional long-range search radars cannot provide images. They have a wide beamwidth (on the order of hundreds of meters) at satellite ranges, so that the scattering centers cannot be resolved in azimuth; normal radar pulse

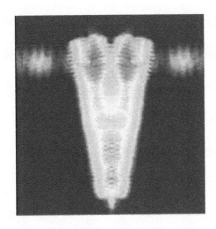

Reentry Vehicle-Radar Image

Reentry Vehicle Shape

FIGURE 11.8 Radar Image of a Reentry Vehicle

widths are on the order of tens to hundreds of meters, so that the scattering centers cannot be resolved in range. The target appears to such radars as a single large scattering center.

In contrast, an object identification radar uses very wide bandwidth, giving a pulse that can effectively separate scattering centers that are less than 1 meter apart in range. A technique called range-Doppler processing can then be used to obtain good azimuth resolution. In particular, a technique called **inverse synthetic aperture radar (ISAR)** can be used to create an array that is effectively thousands of meters long in the direction of travel of the satellite or aircraft; such an array has a very narrow beamwidth along the direction of travel, so that scattering centers can be resolved in azimuth. The technique follows the same principle used by the airborne and spaceborne SARs discussed in Chapter 12, except that the radar is stationary and the target moves, instead of the reverse (which is why it is called *inverse* SAR). The U.S. Haystack radar in Massachusetts and the German tracking and imaging radar (TIRA) in Wachtberg, Germany, are examples of object identification radars that have an ISAR capability.

The combination of high-range resolution and high azimuth resolution can be used to generate a radar image.[24] Figure 11.9 shows a radar image of the Envisat satellite. Compare this with the optical image of Envisat that is shown in Chapter 9 (Figure 9.6). As the figure suggests, radar imaging is not as easily understood as optical imaging. The image requires interpretation and an understanding of how satellites or aircraft are designed. The image was produced by the TIRA radar on April 10, 2012.[25]

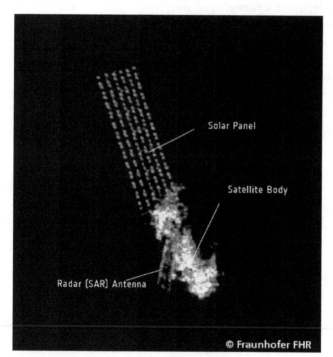

© Fraunhofer FHR

FIGURE 11.9 Radar Image of Envisat

Image of Envisat courtesy of *Space.com* and Fraunhofer FHR.

DISSEMINATION

As previously noted, some radar intelligence is collected continuously and routinely disseminated to a large customer set; orbital elements of satellites, for example. Battlefield, air, and ocean surveillance products are also widely disseminated. But radar also is used for *boutique* or targeted intelligence collection against, for example, missile tests and aircraft involved in smuggling or gray arms traffic. This targeted collection product receives a more limited dissemination.

The use of optical systems to maintain a space catalog was discussed in Chapter 10. Space surveillance radars are the primary tool used to maintain the catalog for low earth orbit (LEO) satellites. Object identification radars also rely on a set of RCS signatures and images to use when assessing new satellite, aircraft, or ship targets.

Structure

Most of the radars that support intelligence collection are owned and operated by military or law enforcement units and are used primarily for operational purposes. All U.S. military services operate radars that have a primary operational function but sometimes serve intelligence purposes. Air, ocean, and space surveillance radars all have on occasion seen such dual use.

Law enforcement units operate radars for air, ground, and ocean surveillance—primarily for countering narcotics traffic and illegal immigration, and in some regions, for dealing with gray arms traffic. These radars also directly support operations and are controlled by operational units, but they also provide intelligence as a second mission.

Summary

Radars have a wide range of civil and military applications. Most radars are used to geolocate a target and track its movement. Airborne and spaceborne radars also are used to map the earth's surface, detecting and tracking targets of interest on the surface; or in the case of airborne radars, to search the sky for weather or for other aircraft. Radar, therefore, is used for a number of purposes, most of which have nothing to do with intelligence. The general rule is that if the radar data have enduring value beyond the immediate demands of the mission, it is either intelligence or research data. If it has no such enduring value, it is usually operational data.

Radars usually are optimized to perform one of four functions. Search radars transmit a beam that is scanned across a volume of space to detect targets. Tracking radars keep the beam on a target (usually a target detected by a search radar) to follow or track the target throughout the radar's volume of coverage. Imaging radars create a picture of the target, but the images produced by conventional RF band radars have poor resolution. Object identification radars measure the physical characteristics of an airborne or spaceborne target in order to obtain intelligence details about the target. Multifunction radars perform two or more of these functions. Radars also can obtain unique target signatures that have intelligence value—vibrometry signatures, for example. In vibrometry, a coherent radar illuminates the target or target area; the Doppler shift backscattered from the target provides a signature that has intelligence value.

Radars for space and missile surveillance are designed to perform one or more of three functions: search for ballistic missiles, reentry vehicles, or space objects (satellites or space debris); precisely track such objects; and identify them. Each function requires a somewhat different radar design, although radars can be built to perform all three functions by compromising functionality. Phased array radars are commonly used because they can perform multiple functions and track multiple targets simultaneously.

Most radars operate in designated blocks of frequency bands, and radars use these operating bands for specific intelligence purposes:

- OTH radars operate in or near the HF band; they bounce signals off the ionosphere to see around the earth's curvature, making it possible to conduct radar surveillance of otherwise inaccessible regions. They have the advantage of monitoring targets that are moving at substantial distances inside a country or on the ocean and providing almost continuous surveillance at ranges on the order of thousands of kilometers.
- VHF and UHF radars are used for space surveillance.
- L band radars find wide use for monitoring air activity and are used also to monitor ballistic missile testing.
- S and C band radars provide precise tracking of aircraft, missiles, and satellites. In addition to a tracking role, C and X band radars also are used to obtain imagery of these targets.
- Laser radars have the advantage of using a much narrower beam and more precise range measurement capability than microwave radars. These advantages allow laser radars to create 3-D images. They also allow laser radars to do two things that are of intelligence interest: to see through forest canopy and camouflage netting and to track satellites with high accuracy.

NOTES

1. US Army Field Manual FM 2-0, "Intelligence," Chapter 9 (May 17, 2004).
2. *U.S. Army Communications-Electronics Command Annual Historical Review* (October 1, 1985–September 30, 1986), 200.

3. The Chain Home radar operated in the HF band, because the British could build high-power transmitters only in that band at the time. But it operated as a conventional line-of-sight radar, not as an OTH radar.

4. Any radar that observes the earth's surface must deal with clutter—unwanted signals returned from the ground or water surface. The clutter return often is strong enough to conceal the targets of interest. Radars also encounter clutter from weather phenomena such as rain.

5. E. N. Fowle, E. L. Key, R. I. Millar, and R. H. Sear, "The Enigma of the AN/FPS-95 OTH Radar," accessed 23 September 2012 at www.cufon.org/cufon/cobramst .htm.

6. USAF Fact Sheet: "Over the Horizon Backscatter Radar: East and West," accessed 23 September 2012 at www.acc.af.mil/library/factsheets/factsheet_print.asp? fsID=3863&page=1.

7. Australian Government Department of Defence, "Radar Surface-Wave Extended Coastal Area (SECAR), accessed 23 September 2012 at http://www.defence.gov .au/teamaustralia/radar_surface-wave_extended_coastal_area_(SECAR).htm.

8. Peter B. de Selding, "French Say 'Non' to U.S. Disclosure of Secret Satellites," Space.com (June 8, 2007), accessed 2 October 2012 at www.space.com/3913- french-disclosure-secret-satellites.html.

9. Photo courtesy of the U.S. Air Force.

10. J. Mark Major, "Upgrading the Nation's Largest Space Surveillance Radar," www .space.com/3913-french-disclosure-secret-satellites.htmlwww.swri.edu/3PUBS/ BROCHURE/D10/survrad/survrad.HTM.

11. "Missile Defense: Additional Knowledge Needed in Developing System for Intercepting Long-Range Missiles," U.S. General Accounting Office [GAO-03- 600] (August 2003), Photo from www.DefenseImagery.mil (photographer, Sgt. Robert S. Thompson).

12. National Security Space Road Map, "Cobra Dane" (1998), accessed 23 September 2012 at www.wslfweb.org/docs/roadmap/irm/internet/surwarn/init/html/cobradan .htm.

13. E. G. Stansbery, "Growth in the Number of SSN Tracked Orbital Objects," NASA Report presented at the 55th International Astronautical Congress of the International Astronautical Federation, the International Academy of Astronautics, and the International Institute of Space Law (Vancouver, British Columbia, October 4–8, 2004), accessed 22 September 2012 at http://ntrs.nasa.gov/archive/ nasa/casi.ntrs.nasa.gov/20060022013_2006009640.pdf.

14. Raytheon Corporation, "Cobra Judy Radar System," accessed 22 September 2012 at www.raytheon.com/capabilities/products/cobra_judy/.

15. U.S. Navy, "USNS Howard O. Lorenzen (T-AGM-25)," public domain photo accessed 28 September 2012 at http://www.navsource.org/archives/09/53/5325 .htm.

16. Richard Scott, "Cobra Judy Replacement Starts Trials," *Jane's Defense & Security Intelligence & Analysis* (July 31, 2012), accessed 28 September 2012 at http:// www.janes.com/products/janes/defence-security-report.aspx?id=1065970069.

17. "The ARPA Lincoln C-Band Observables Radar (ALCOR)," accessed 23 September 2012 at www.smdc.army.mil/KWAJ/RangeInst/ALCOR.html.

18. GlobalSecurity.org, "Sea-Based X-Band (SBX) Radar," accessed 23 September 2012 at www.globalsecurity.org/space/systems/sbx.htm.

19. Richard M. Marino and William R. Davis Jr., "Jigsaw: A Foliage-Penetrating 3D Imaging Laser Radar System," *Lincoln Laboratory Journal,* Vol. 15, No. 1 (2005), 23.

20. Photo from Alfred B. Gschwendtner and William E. Keicher, "Development of Coherent Laser Radar at Lincoln Laboratory," *Lincoln Laboratory Journal,* Vol. 12, No. 2 (2000), 393.

21. T. Sato, Y. Suzuki, H. Kashiwagi, M. Nanjo, and Y. Kakui, "A Method for Remote Detection of Oil Spills Using Laser-Excited Raman Backscattering and Backscattered Fluorescence," *IEEE Journal of Oceanic Engineering,* Vol. 3, No. 1 (January 1978), 1–4.

22. Photograph by Elen Schurova, used with permission, accessed 26 October 2012 at http://www.flickr.com/photos/elschurova/6065690244/sizes/1/in/photostream/.

23. Daniel R. Martenow, "Reentry Vehicle Analysis," CIA, *Studies in Intelligence* (Summer 1968), figure taken from Kevin M. Cuomo, Jean E. Piou, and Joseph T. Mayhan, "Ultra-Wideband Coherent Processing," *Lincoln Laboratory Journal,* Vol. 10, No. 2 (1997), 203.

24. Nicholas L. Johnson, "U.S. Space Surveillance," paper presented at World Space Congress (Washington, DC, September 1, 1992).

25. Tariq Malik, "Huge, Mysteriously Silent Satellite Spotted by Another Space-craft," *Space.com* (April 20, 2012), accessed 26 September, 2012 at http://www.space.com/15369-mysteriously-silent-envisat-satellite-space-photos.html.

12. Synthetic Aperture Radar

Chapters 9 and 10 discussed passive imaging that relies on the sun as an illuminator or on emissions from the target. In contrast, from Chapter 11 we know that radar imagery uses active sensing and for that reason has some substantial advantages, as discussed below.

We also know from Chapter 11 that a conventional radar can create an image as it scans the earth's surface. Airborne and shipborne search radars routinely provide an image of the surrounding area that is useful for navigation. The problem is that conventional radars (even those operating in the microwave band) cannot produce imagery with much detail—though the laser radars discussed in Chapter 11 can do so. Microwave radar images, though, have poor resolution because the pixels are quite large (on the order of hundreds of meters, depending on the radar's pulse width and on distance from the radar).

Such is not the case with synthetic aperture radar (SAR). For this and other reasons discussed below, when *imaging radar* in intelligence is discussed, the reference usually is to SAR, which is definitely not a conventional radar.

Function

A SAR is one of the most complex remote sensors to build and operate. But it is the most important one used in intelligence. SAR images have a number of advantages when compared with optical imaging:

- SARs can provide high-resolution images at night and under most weather and cloud conditions.
- SARs acquire their images by observing sideways from the SAR platform; this means they can look into openings in buildings, sheds, and tunnels.
- SAR imagery is capable of characterizing the ground texture, vegetation, sea surface, snow, and ice in detail. It can even note slight changes in these over time.

SAR imagery also can be combined with visible, infrared, or hyperspectral imagery to produce unique insights about a target that are not possible with any one imagery type alone. Following are some of the important intelligence applications of SARs.

TERRAIN MAPPING AND CHARACTERIZATION

Optical imagers can provide maps, but because they do not measure range to the target, they don't do well at determining terrain elevation. SARs do measure range, so they can provide precise topography of the target area. Furthermore, SARs can characterize terrain, identifying soil and moisture conditions that might affect military force movements. They do this by measuring the radar backscatter from the target area; moist soil, sand, rocky areas, and bogs all have different signatures that can be identified.

CHANGE DETECTION

One of the major advantages of SAR is its ability to detect changes in a scene over time. Change detection is an application to which SAR is particularly well suited. Examples of surface changes that can be observed include vehicle tracks, crops growing or being harvested, and soil excavation. Changes in the terrain surface due to underground construction also can be observed by change detection. The underground excavation results in both vertical settlement and a horizontal straining that is detectable.[1]

FOLIAGE AND CAMOUFLAGE PENETRATION

SARs can penetrate numerous materials or surfaces that would normally hide equipment or facilities (for example, canvas tents and most wooden sheds become transparent to radar). An application of SAR that has obvious intelligence uses is foliage penetration. Chapter 11 discussed the use of laser radars to find holes in foliage and to image hidden targets. SARs can do the same thing without the need to find holes, depending on the

SAR operating frequency. Most SARs operate in the higher microwave bands—C and X bands—because target resolution improves as frequency increases. But radars in these frequency bands do not penetrate foliage well, and their penetration capabilities get worse as frequency increases. However, SARS can also be built to operate in the UHF, or even in the VHF bands. At these lower frequencies SARs can effectively image objects concealed in dense foliage, even objects located underneath the forest canopy.[2] They also penetrate into dry earth for short distances to detect buried objects such as land mines.[3,4]

IDENTIFYING TARGETS AND TRACKING MOVING TARGETS

SARs can identify and classify targets of intelligence interest—ships, aircraft, and military vehicles.[5] The higher the SAR's resolution, the more detail it can obtain about a target.

SARs also have a capability to detect target motion. This capability can be used to create an image that highlights moving targets in an area. This feature is commonly called **moving target indicator (MTI)** or ground moving target indicator (GMTI). The term *MTI* is more often used because it is a more accurate description. MTI can be used to detect aircraft, helicopter, or ship movements, as well as ground vehicular movement. If the MTI SAR operates in the very high frequency (VHF) or ultra high frequency (UHF) range, as noted above, it also can locate and track moving targets that are concealed in foliage.[6]

Process

PLANNING

Because a SAR uses substantial power when transmitting, and because such power is limited onboard a satellite, spaceborne SARs don't operate continuously. Collection usually must be planned in advance to look at specific targets or target regions of interest, with an eye to conserving power. Airborne (including unmanned aerial vehicle, or UAV) SARs aren't so severely power-limited and are more likely to be operated continuously.

Tasking of spaceborne SARs also is constrained because the orbit is more or less fixed. Imaging of specific targets has to be timed so that the targets are in the proper geometry (off to the side of the satellite and located somewhere between the maximum and minimum range). Airborne SARs have more flexibility; they can select a flight pattern that puts targets within the proper geometry.

FIGURE 12.1 Airborne SAR Image of the Pentagon

Planning also must take into account the compromise between area coverage and resolution, discussed in Chapter 7. Strip map mode provides better coverage. Spot imaging mode provides better resolution. In addition, for many SARs it is necessary to choose between an MTI mode of operation and an imaging mode.

COLLECTION

Synthetic aperture radar's specialty is creating a high-resolution image of a target area on the earth's surface from a satellite, aircraft, or UAV, based on the microwave energy backscattered from a target area. A SAR image is a map of the intensity of this energy that is backscattered from points in the scene. Brighter image pixels correspond to points of higher backscatter return. Figure 12.1 illustrates the effect, in a radar image of the Pentagon taken from an airborne SAR.[7] A number of points on the building, especially the building edges, are very strong radar reflectors and show up as bright returns.

How a SAR Works. Good image resolution is critical to intelligence value. An imagery analyst can provide more accurate intelligence from more detailed signatures. Trucks can be distinguished from tanks and bombers from transport aircraft, given sufficient resolution. In general, the SAR's performance in target detection and classification depends on good image resolution. Applications discussed later in this chapter, such as change detection, depend on it.

A SAR has to have good resolution in both range (in the direction of the SAR beam) and azimuth (perpendicular to the radar beam) in order to form a high-resolution image. Each requires a completely different technique to accomplish this. When researchers first were looking at the use of radar to create images in the early 1950s, they faced two problems:

- First, in order to get enough energy in a pulse to detect small targets, they had to transmit very long pulses, which gave very poor range resolution—on the order of kilometers, where less than a meter was needed.

- Second, the beam from an antenna spreads out with distance, so that a one-degree-wide beam is one kilometer wide at 60-kilometer range—meaning that the azimuth resolution is one kilometer, far short of the goal of less than one meter.

Obtaining Range Resolution. Solving the first problem was relatively easy. For conventional radars, range resolution depends on the duration of the transmitted pulse (called pulse width). A one-nanosecond pulse (one-billionth of a second) has a range resolution of approximately one foot, which provides very good range resolution. But a one-nanosecond pulse has very little energy in it, so the backscattered signal from most targets will be difficult for the radar receiver to detect. A longer pulse, say, one microsecond, would provide 1,000 times as much energy, which gives a more detectable backscattered signal. But a one-microsecond pulse has a range resolution of about 1,000 feet, which is totally unacceptable for intelligence applications. The challenge is to illuminate the target with a one-microsecond (or longer) pulse but to obtain the range resolution of a one-nanosecond pulse.

The solution was to create a pulse that has long duration but is electrically short, using a technique called **pulse compression**. Most SARs do this using a pulse that is frequency modulated (FM), called a **chirped pulse**: its frequency smoothly changes over the duration of the pulse, as shown in Figure 12.2. A pulse like the one shown contains many frequencies and, thus, has a wide frequency bandwidth. Consequently, it can be processed to give the range resolution of a much shorter pulse having the same bandwidth. The result is that you get the energy of a long pulse combined with the resolution of a short pulse. Using this technique, many radars (both

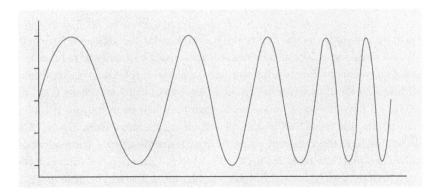

FIGURE 12.2 **Frequency Change in a Chirped Pulse**

conventional and SAR) have demonstrated 1.8-GHz transmit bandwidths (corresponding to a range resolution of 0.1 meter) while having ample energy to detect small targets.

Obtaining Azimuth Resolution. Solving the second problem—azimuth resolution—was not so easy. It meant creating a very long antenna. Physically, this was not possible. An antenna capable of giving one-meter azimuth resolution would have to be about as long as its distance from the target, on the order of a few hundred kilometers. Obviously, such an antenna cannot be carried on an aircraft or satellite *if* a standard phased array radar design is used—specifically, if all the elements of the antenna array transmit a pulse at the same time. The solution lay in recognizing that (1) the antenna did not need a large *physical* aperture if it could have a large *electrical* aperture; and (2) you could get a large electrical aperture simply by not requiring that the pulses from the antenna elements be transmitted at the same time. That is, you transmit a pulse from a small antenna; move the antenna a short distance, transmit another pulse; move again and transmit again; and so on. You then store all of the returning echoes from each pulse and process them to get the effect of an antenna that is as long as the distance moved by the small antenna throughout the process—typically hundreds of kilometers long. The key to the success of SAR was this recognition that the pulses did not have to be transmitted at the same time, so long as they were transmitted *coherently*—as explained below.

Of course, even fast-moving satellites take some time to travel hundreds of kilometers, and it takes far longer if the SAR is carried on an aircraft or a UAV. Changes in the target area and changes in the aspect angle seen by the radar during this imaging time cause some distortions in the resulting image, as discussed later.

Forming the SAR Image. Synthetic aperture radar imaging is a two-step process of data acquisition and coherent processing of a series of radar range echoes to recover a fine resolution image of a scene. A SAR works by transmitting a series of *coherent* pulses at a target area; coherent means that the pulses all have the same phase, as though they had been transmitted as a continuous sine wave that is shut on and off to generate pulses. Figure 12.3 illustrates how the coherent pulse train is transmitted in a succession of pulses at equal time intervals $(t_1, t_2, \ldots, t_n)$ as the aircraft or satellite moves. For a SAR to work, it is essential that all the pulses that will be used to form an image be transmitted coherently and that the radar retain a memory of the exact frequency and phase of the transmitted signal.

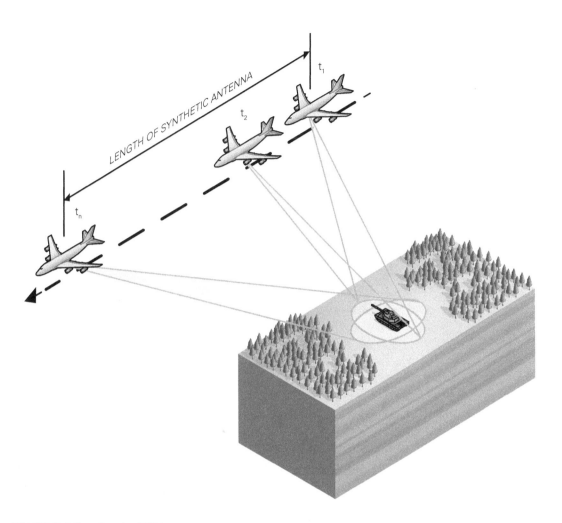

FIGURE 12.3 Forming the SAR Image

When a backscattered signal returns, the receiver measures the intensity of the return and compares the backscattered signal frequency and phase with that of the transmitted signal. Slight shifts in frequency (phase differences) are noted, and these signal intensity and phase differences are recorded. This record, collected over many pulses, is called phase history data (PHD). This intensity and spectral information, collected over time, is used to create a target image.

To help understand how the SAR can precisely locate a small target within the large ground footprint shown in Figure 12.3, it helps to understand how Doppler shift works. If you were an observer in the aircraft shown in the figure, at time t_1 you would see targets in the highlighted ground area moving toward you; the radar would measure a higher frequency return than it transmitted (positive Doppler shift). At time t_2, you would see the target area moving more slowly toward you than before, and the radar would measure a decreasing Doppler shift. Later, the Doppler shift would go to zero as you passed the target area. Then as you reached time t_n in the figure, the target area would appear to be receding, and the radar would measure a negative Doppler shift.

The SAR uses this perception of relative motion to place targets in the azimuth or cross-range direction. Targets located at different points in the target area will have different Doppler histories. The radar receiver captures all these returns and their associated Doppler shifts, and subsequent processing of the phase history data provides the desired high azimuth resolution on each target in the scene. Because of this reliance on the Doppler shift to get azimuth resolution, a SAR cannot image well from directly overhead.

Most of us have experienced the Doppler shift, or Doppler effect, in sound waves. The sound heard from a rapidly moving vehicle such as an airplane, or the horn on a passing train, drops to a lower key as the vehicle passes by. The Doppler effect works the same way in both sound and electromagnetic waves and, in fact, can be used for imaging in both cases. Ultrasound imaging for medical diagnosis relies on the Doppler effect both to image inside the body and to measure blood flow in the image.

Spotlight and Strip Map Imaging. SARs can operate either as spotlight or as strip map imagers. Either mode can be used, depending on the trade-off that is made between the level of resolution needed and the desired area of coverage.

In spotlight mode, the entire spacecraft is rotated into the direction of the target to increase the integration time and, therefore, the in-track resolution. To get the best resolution, a SAR is operated in spotlight mode, where data are collected from a single patch of terrain. As the SAR platform moves past the scene, the radar beam is continuously adjusted so that it always points to the same area of the ground. The SAR image resolution improves (that is, the distance between distinct pixels becomes smaller) as the total collection time on the patch of ground increases. Thus, the longer the collection time, the better the resolution because the movement of the spacecraft in effect creates a longer antenna.

The image in Figure 12.3 shows an example of spotlight imaging geometry. During the SAR platform movement, the antenna is steered so as to

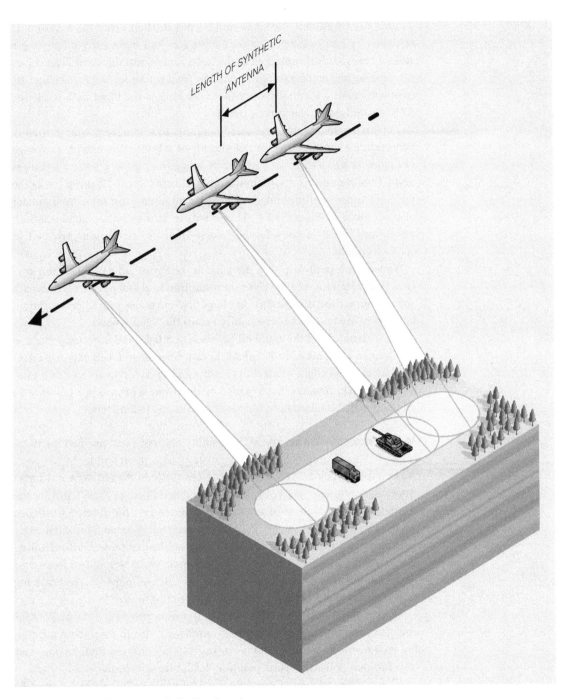

LENGTH OF SYNTHETIC ANTENNA

Synthetic
Aperture Radar

FIGURE 12.4 Spotlight versus Strip Map Imaging

continually illuminate the same ground patch. High azimuth resolution is achieved by using an antenna of modest size and coherently processing a series of range echoes obtained as the radar moves past the scene. The coherent processing combines the information from the series of range echoes to, in effect, create a synthetic array that is as long as the flight path while the SAR is spotlighting the ground patch.

For strip map imaging, the antenna points in a fixed direction (normally perpendicular to the direction of aircraft or satellite movement, as shown in Figure 12.4). In this case, the effective length of the synthetic aperture is much less than in the spotlight example. It turns out to be the same as the width of the area illuminated on the ground at any instant—the diameter of one circle in Figure 12.4. This aperture still provides good azimuth resolution, but it is considerably worse than the resolution provided in spotlight mode.

The advantage of strip map imaging, as the figure indicates, is that it covers a much larger area. One gives up resolution to get area coverage. As with any remote sensor, the goal is to get large area coverage with high resolution, but improving one of these generally makes the other worse.

An illustration of the trade-off between spotlight and strip map mode is the German radar satellite TerraSAR-X, described later. It can obtain 1-meter resolution in spotlight mode, but it is limited to covering an area of 5 kilometers by 10 kilometers. In strip map mode, the area of coverage grows to 30 kilometers by 50 kilometers, but resolution drops to 3 meters.[8]

Moving Target Indicator. The MTI capability has been demonstrated in a number of SARs and used both for combat operations support and for intelligence. An example is the AN/APY-3 radar carried by the Joint Surveillance and Target Attack Radar System (JSTARS) aircraft, a modified Boeing 707. JSTARS has the capability to obtain images of moving targets and can tell the difference between wheeled and tracked vehicles. JSTARS can even tell whether a potential target moving down a road is a tank or a jeep—a capability that proved critical during the Gulf War of 1990 to 1991. During that war, JSTARS was able to locate and track high-value targets such as Scud missile launchers, convoys, river crossing sites, logistics sites, assembly areas, and Iraqi retreat routes.[9]

During the conflict in Afghanistan, the airborne MTI role of JSTARS changed from tracking major military units (as it did in Iraq) to monitoring the movement of small groups of insurgents, identifying their origins and travel routes, and supporting planning for future operations.[10]

Global Hawk is another example of a SAR having MTI capability. In addition to its electro-optical and infrared sensors (discussed in Chapter 9), the Global Hawk carries a synthetic aperture radar that can image an area the size of Illinois (40,000 nautical square miles) in just 24 hours. Through satellite and ground systems, the imagery can be relayed in near real time to battlefield commanders. The radar operates at X band with a 600-MHz bandwidth and 3.5-kilowatt peak power. It has flexibility, being able to select different modes depending on the type of intelligence needed:

- A wide-area MTI capability is used to detect moving targets within a radius of 100 kilometers.
- The combined SAR-MTI strip mode provides 1-meter resolution over a swath 37 kilometers wide at ranges from 20 to 110 kilometers.
- For target identification, a spot mode can provide 0.3-meter resolution over 10 square kilometers—a useful capability for ocean surveillance.[11]

Polarimetric SAR. Chapter 10 introduced polarimetry and described its uses in optical imaging. SARs can also use polarimetry to obtain signatures that have intelligence value.

SAR images are generated by sending and receiving microwave pulses. The microwaves are generally transmitted as either horizontally or vertically polarized electromagnetic waves. In older SAR designs, the radar could only receive the same polarization that it transmitted. Most current SARs transmit and receive multiple polarizations (and are referred to as *polarimetric SARs*) because they provide additional details about targets that single-polarization SARs do not provide. A polarimetric SAR is better at target identification and classification, for example.

Polarimetric SAR is of value for nonintelligence topics such as monitoring crops, soil moisture, forests, snow cover, sea ice, and sea conditions. It is used for geological mapping. Some of these applications also are relevant in intelligence.

An early example of a polarimetric SAR is the SIR-C radar that was carried on the space shuttle *Endeavor* in April and October 1994. The SIR-C was actually three radars, one operating at L band, the second at C band, and the third at X band. The L band and C band antennas could measure both horizontal and vertical polarizations.

The polarimetric data from the two shuttle flights provided detailed information about the surface geometric structure, vegetation cover, and subsurface features.[12] Subsequent processing of the data showed that the SIR-C radar had the ability to obtain very high resolution images of ships at sea, sufficient for identifying specific ships.[13] Germany's TerraSAR-X and Israel's TECSAR are examples of currently operational satellites that carry polarimetric SARs.

Platform Choice for SAR. Both airborne and spaceborne platforms carry SARs. Depending on the tactical situation and the intended use of the imagery, there are trade-offs between the two types of platforms. For either platform, though, a significant advantage of using a SAR is that the spatial resolution is not heavily dependent on range to the target. Thus, one can get very good resolution from both platform types. Each platform has its advantages, though.

• Aircraft can get the SAR closer to a target and generally can transmit more power than spaceborne radars. Airborne SARs can therefore detect smaller targets, enabling them to generate more detailed (finer grain) imagery.

• Spaceborne radars have a better imaging geometry because they operate at much higher altitudes than airborne radars. At altitudes of several hundred kilometers, spaceborne radars can image the same swath widths as airborne radars but over a much narrower range of incidence angles, typically ranging from 5 to 15 degrees, as illustrated in Figure 12.5. This geometry provides for more uniform illumination and makes imagery interpretation easier. Artifacts such as layover and shadowing, discussed later, are less of a problem with spaceborne SAR imagery.

An example of the current state of the art in SAR collection for reconnaissance applications is Germany's SAR-Lupe satellite, an artist's conception of which is shown in Figure 12.6.[14] The first of five SAR-Lupe satellites was launched in December 2006, and the fifth was launched in June 2008. The five satellites operate in three 500-kilometer orbits in planes roughly 60 degrees apart. The radar operates in X band at a center frequency of 9.65 GHz. The SAR-Lupe's average power consumption is about 250 watts, and its expected life is 10 years.

The SAR-Lupe has performance characteristics that make it an excellent intelligence collection sensor. Its three-meter-diameter dish antenna, the back of which is shown in the figure, reportedly provides a resolution of about 0.5 meter over a frame size of 5.5 km on a side in the spotlight mode where, as previously noted, the satellite rotates to keep the dish pointed at a single target. Resolution is about 1 meter over a frame size of 8 kilometers by 60 kilometers in the strip map mode, where the satellite maintains a fixed orientation over the earth and the radar image is formed simply by the satellite's motion along its orbit. The radar is able to image a given area of earth once every 10 hours or less.[15]

As with visible and spectral imagery, commercial SAR imagery is becoming increasingly important in intelligence. It has special advantages for the military in coalition operations, because the imagery can be shared freely with allies. The imagery typically does not have the high resolution of dedicated intelligence SARs such as SAR-Lupe, but the resolution is adequate for applications such as wide area ocean search and tracking of naval vessels. Since 2008, the U.S. Sixth Fleet has been using commercial SAR imagery to provide

FIGURE 12.5 Swath Width and Incidence Angle in Airborne and Spaceborne SARs

FIGURE 12.6 Artist's Concept of Germany's SAR-Lupe Spacecraft

near-real-time situational awareness. Because the imagery is unclassified, it doesn't require special handling when being shared within the fleet, and it can be shared with allied vessels. *Near real time* in this context means typically between 25 and 55 minutes from image collection until an image arrives at a ship and 90 minutes until an exploited image is available.[16]

PROCESSING, EXPLOITATION, AND ANALYSIS

Processing and exploitation is an important part of all technical collection. But it is especially important that it be done well for SAR imagery, because of the complexity of the raw data that is collected and the presence of imagery artifacts that must be dealt with in the imagery analysis phase.

Automated image processing is required to transform the stored pulse returns from each pixel (the phase history data) into a recognizable image. The chain of processing is as follows:

Phase history data are collected and processed to form a *complex image*, which is then further processed to form a *detected image*.

The task of the image processor is to combine all of the returns received from a given area to produce a focused image. The SAR processing algorithms are very sophisticated because they must account for a steadily changing scene as the radar moves; individual targets scatter energy differently at different aspect angles between the target and radar.

SAR data are collected by rapid pulsing over a period of several seconds. During this period the angle between the SAR antenna and the ground is changing. The initial processing of phase history data is done using the assumption that the intensity of return from each point in the scene is the same for each pulse. The following processing assumptions are made:

- Flat terrain
- Stationary targets
- Constant radar cross-section (RCS) throughout the collection time frame
- Quiet microwave environment (no interference)

Both natural and artificial features in the scene typically violate one or more of the above assumptions. The result is a set of imagery distortions called *artifacts* that imagery analysts must deal with. Each of these artifacts will be discussed in turn.

The Nonflat Terrain. The assumption of flat terrain is violated most of the time. Very few land areas are completely flat. Mountains and vertical structures create two artifacts in a SAR image: **shadowing** and **layover**. More complex structures can create apparent targets downrange from the complex structure, as discussed below.

Shadowing is fairly easy to understand because it is much like the shadows created by the sun. Shadowing occurs in the downrange direction from targets elevated above the surrounding terrain, such as mountains and buildings. The shadowed region appears as a black area in the SAR image because no signal was returned from that region of the scene. Figure 12.7 illustrates how shadowing works; the area behind the building is in shadow, and objects located in that area cannot be observed.

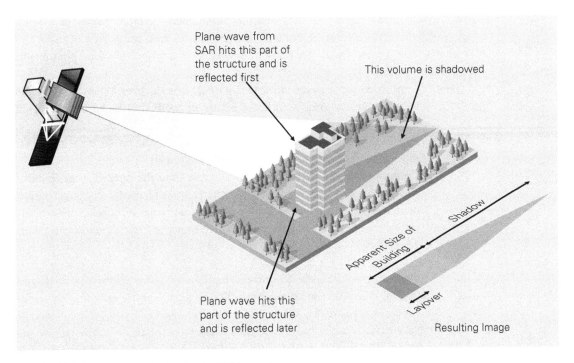

FIGURE 12.7 Layover and Shadowing in SAR Imagery

Elevated targets also produce layover toward the SAR flight track, also illustrated in Figure 12.7. Layover occurs because a SAR puts all scene points that are at the same range into the same range cell in the image. In Figure 12.7, the radar pulse hits the building top first, because it is closer to the radar. Because of the flat earth assumption, when the imagery is processed, the return from the top of the building is placed closer to the radar, while the return from the bottom of the building is placed at its correct flat earth position. Tall structures thus appear to lay over on top of the ground on the near-range side of the target.

Both the shadowing and layover effects show up in the SAR image of the Pentagon in Figure 12.1. The airborne SAR was located south of the building, looking north; the shadowing effect is clearly displayed on the northeast and north sides, and a layover effect can be seen in a bright line offset from the building parallel to the southwest side.

The extent of layover depends on grazing angle and the height of the elevated target. In Figure 12.7, if the SAR were at a lower elevation angle (lower grazing angle), then the difference in time between the pulse hitting the top of the building and the bottom would be less, and the layover would be smaller.

Image interpretation is complicated in layover regions due to the overlap of the elevated structure with features on the near-range side of the structure. Layover will also cause a distortion of any topographic variations in the scene.

Multibounce creates the opposite effect from layover. When a SAR looks at an urban area or a complex structure or cavity, the backscattered signal does not necessarily return directly to the radar. Multibounce signatures can appear in SAR imagery for complex targets where the microwaves reflect off more than one point before returning to the sensor.

Because the multibounce path is longer than the normal single bounce backscatter, the SAR distorts the target shape and places the target multibounce signature downrange from the actual target location. For complex targets, there can be several multibounce signatures corresponding to different paths.

Nonstationary Targets. The processing of SAR phase history data assumes that all targets in the scene are stationary for the entire time that the radar illuminates the scene. When this is not the case, such as for moving targets, an artifact is produced in the SAR image. As the target moves across the scene, it creates an artifact due to improper focusing. The phenomenon is much the same as when a camera with slow shutter speed takes a picture of a fast-moving object. The object will be blurred in the picture because, while

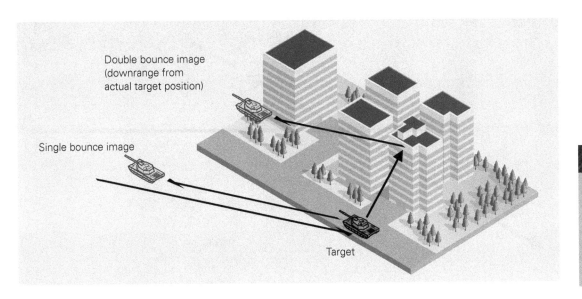

Double bounce image
(downrange from
actual target position)

Single bounce image

Target

FIGURE 12.8 SAR Multibounce Phenomena

the shutter is open, the object occupies several different locations in the image frame. It is the same with a SAR and a moving target: While the SAR is transmitting its pulses to form an image, the target is moving through several pixels in the image frame.

The artifact resulting from target movement depends on the nature of the movement; some of the most common are target displacement, smearing, and target distortions. Which artifact occurs is determined by the geometry between the SAR platform and the target and the motion of the two with respect to each other. Following is a description of two common artifacts due to target movement.

Target displacement is the result of target movement toward or away from the SAR. As Figure 12.9 shows, if the target (in the figure, a tank) is moving toward the SAR platform, then the target image is shifted in the direction of the SAR platform movement. If the target is moving away from the SAR, the shift is in the opposite direction.

Smearing results from changes in target velocity. Suppose the targets in Figure 12.9 were not moving at a constant velocity but instead were accelerating or decelerating toward or away from the SAR. This acceleration or deceleration causes a constantly changing displacement when the image is formed. Instead of a simple displaced image as shown in the figure, the result is a smeared image of the target parallel to the direction of SAR movement (called the azimuth direction). The changing target speed causes the

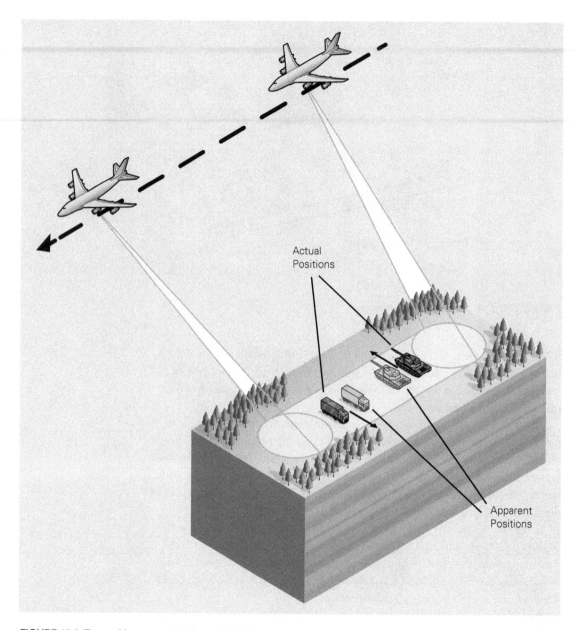

FIGURE 12.9 Target Movement Artifacts in SAR Imagery

shift to vary during the collection interval. This variation generates the azimuth smear. The shape of the smear depends on grazing angle and squint, as well as the target motion.

Azimuth motion also causes smearing in the azimuth direction. If the target is moving at a constant velocity in the azimuth direction, the smear will be linear. In contrast, if the target is accelerating or decelerating, the smear will have a curved shape.

Smearing is often exploited to infer information about the motion of a target; however, in many cases the smearing can obscure or distract from targets of interest. A processing technique called smear reduction is used to clean up the SAR image by removing smearing.

Another form of smearing is caused by objects that stay in a fixed position but that rotate or vibrate. They cause a distorted return that appears in the SAR image as a spatially repeating (periodic) signature. These signatures are often too faint to be seen in SAR data. However, for systems with large vibrating or rotating metallic parts the signal can be exploited. Rotating helicopter blades or large fan blades associated with cooling towers usually appear in a SAR image as a distorted target. The distortion usually shows up as pairs of echoes that are displaced azimuthally on either side of the target, the distance from the target indicating the speed of rotation or vibration. A vibrating earth or vibrating building will produce a similar distortion, but the returned signal generally will be too weak to show up in the SAR image.[17]

Nonconstant RCS. Processing also makes the assumption that RCS remains constant while the image is being created. A perfectly round sphere has a constant RCS, no matter from what direction it is illuminated. Nothing else does. Few, if any, spheres are present in a typical SAR scene; most of the objects in the scene will have a changing RCS as the SAR-to-target geometry changes. The resulting bright spots in the SAR image (where the RCS of objects becomes suddenly very large) are called glint. For example, edges that are perpendicular to the SAR beam will return a higher signal leading to bright image pixels, or glint. Some curved surfaces can create bright streaks along the curved edge. This effect is especially noticeable from power lines or telephone wires.

Flat surfaces can vary greatly in RCS. A common example is a flat metallic rooftop that becomes very bright when the SAR beam is perpendicular to it at some point in the collection period. If this is strong enough it can lead to receiver saturation. The target seems expanded on the image, a phenomenon called image *blooming*. As with smear reduction, glint reduction techniques are used to clean up a SAR image by removing this artifact.

The Unquiet Microwave Environment. The imaging capability of a SAR can be seriously limited or denied by an interference signal in the SAR operating frequency band. Such interference can be deliberate (jamming) or due to radio frequency interference occurring in the SAR frequency band. The way an interfering signal looks in the SAR imagery depends on the type of interference; it typically is a streak in range, in azimuth, or in both, sometimes resulting in a bright cross centered on the interfering transmitter.[18]

Synthetic aperture radars are highly flexible; they can collect or process data in a number of ways that have intelligence value. The following sections discuss a few of these.

Change Detection. The advantages of change detection were introduced earlier. Three techniques are used for change detection: incoherent change detection, coherent change detection, and SAR interferometry. The first two techniques require repeat passes, separated in time by hours, days, weeks, or even years, wherein the SAR looks at the same target area at approximately the same azimuth and elevation. Figure 12.10 illustrates the

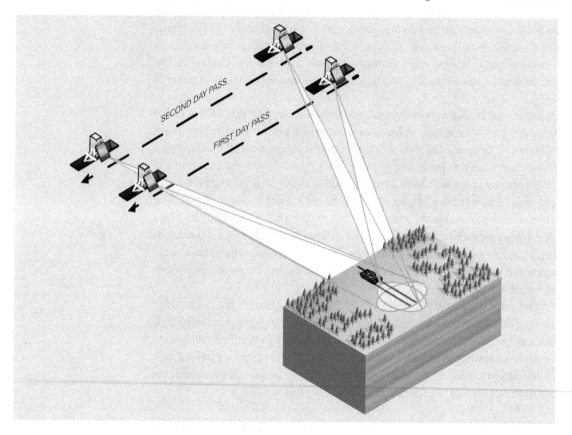

FIGURE 12.10 Geometry for Repeat Pass Imaging

repeat pass case. The third technique, SAR interferometry, can be done in a single pass but requires two separate receive antennas located on the same platform.

Incoherent change detection identifies changes in a scene by comparing the intensity of energy backscattered from individual pixels between successive passes. Significant changes in local regions (for example, due to a truck, ship, or tank being present in one image but not in the next) will show up as significant changes in the backscattered energy intensity. The technique can also be used to detect changes in soil or vegetation moisture content or surface roughness.

Coherent change detection (CCD) requires a more sophisticated level of signal processing but can detect very subtle scene changes.[19] These change images provide valuable intelligence by revealing information like traffic patterns, type of traffic, and terrain maps of critical areas where tunnels may be in use, such as in Afghanistan.[20] CCD can provide signatures that indicate not only that traffic has occurred in the area but that a certain type of traffic has occurred.[21] Germany's TerraSAR-X and SAR-Lupe are two examples of operational radars that can perform coherent change detection.

Coherent change detection relies on, in effect, overlaying two radar images to produce a picture of what changed in the time between the two images. It does this by measuring and storing both the intensity and phase (phase history data) of each image pixel—in contrast to incoherent change detection, where only intensity is measured. On a subsequent pass, intensity and phase are again measured. Very slight changes in the surface—fractions of an inch—are detected as phase changes in the phase history data. Of course, the return from vegetation will usually change between the passes due to growth or to wind, and the ground may change due to natural causes such as rain. These changes also show up in CCD imagery.

CCD is affected by what is called *image decorrelation* or *baseline decorrelation*. If there is a significant difference in the imaging geometry between the primary and repeat pass collection, the two images will not correlate (that is, coherence will be lost). To avoid decorrelation, the collector tries to use exactly the same flight paths in the two passes. When the paths are identical or nearly so, any intensity or phase differences between the image pair can be attributed to changes in the scene. In practice, however, it is very difficult to fly the same flight track due to inaccuracies in the platform navigation information. This is particularly true in airborne systems where the effects of wind and turbulence can result in significant flight track offsets. The resulting decorrelation has to be dealt with in processing.[22]

SAR interferometry, also known as interferometric SAR, requires acquiring images using two independent receive antennas located on the same moving platform. The two images are then processed to identify and exploit differences in the intensity and phase of the image pair. Depending on how the two receive antennas are deployed on the platform and how they are operated, two different types of intelligence information can be obtained.[23]

One approach is to use SAR interferometry to detect moving targets in the scene. To do this, the two receive antennas are located side-by-side on the platform. As the platform moves, the front antenna receives the backscattered return from a target area. A few milliseconds later, the rear antenna is in the exact position that the front antenna had occupied, and at that exact time it receives the backscattered return *from the next pulse* of the same target area. Because the target geometry is identical for the two received pulses, any change in the return intensity or phase must be caused by movement in the target area. All the unchanged backscatter return can be eliminated, and only slow moving targets in the scene will remain.[24] The technique may also be used for mapping ocean currents.

The other approach is to use SAR interferometry for terrain mapping. One way to do this is to have the satellite carry two receive antennas, located one above the other. The difference here is that both antennas receive and process the same backscattered pulse simultaneously. Because the two antennas view the scene with slightly different imaging geometries, changes in terrain features can be measured precisely.

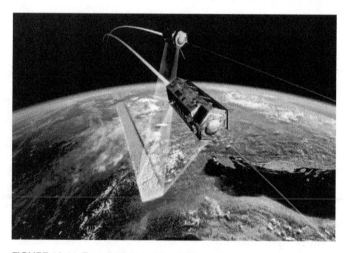

FIGURE 12.11 TerraSAR-X and TanDEM-X

Another technique is to use two satellites, flying in formation, each carrying a SAR and imaging the same target area. The German TerraSAR-X and its almost identical twin, the TanDEM-X, illustrate how SAR interferometry works using two satellites. The two satellites fly in close formation (between 200 meters and a few kilometers apart) and simultaneously image the same region, as illustrated in Figure 12.11.[25] The combined PHD is processed to give a three dimensional (3-D) image of the earth's surface, so that detailed terrain maps can be created. The technique is similar to the use of stereoscopy in visible imaging. The product, a digital 3-D image of the earth, is sold commercially but has obvious intelligence uses. The pair can also do polarimetric imaging.[26]

SAR interferometry can potentially provide highly accurate measurements of terrain elevation.[27] SAR interferometry is used to generate topographic maps, map surface deformation, monitor landslides, measure the velocity of objects, determine the structure and composition of vegetation, and, as noted above, detect change.

Two-color multiview (or multicolor multiview, where more than two images are compared) is the best technique for displaying small changes in SAR imagery between images taken days, weeks, or even years apart. The technique shows in one-color objects that were in the first image but have left the scene in the second image. Objects that have arrived in the scene since the first image are shown in a second color. Changes in position of vehicles, fences, coastlines, or buildings under construction are easily identified using two-color multiview from image pairs collected weeks to years apart.[28]

Polarimetric Processing and Exploitation. When a polarized pulse strikes a target and is reflected back toward the radar, the polarization is changed by the reflecting surface. Typically, the reflected signal contains a combination of horizontal and vertical polarizations, which is described as elliptically polarized. The relative amount of horizontal and vertical polarization in the return depends on the structure, reflectivity, shape, orientation, and roughness of the reflecting surface. Therefore, measuring the returned polarization from an object can provide additional information about the object. This measurement is the basis of the process of polarimetry.

SAR polarimetry involves acquiring, processing, and analyzing the polarization of the signal backscattered from the target area. In polarimetry, this backscattered signal is processed to determine scattering mechanisms, or the fingerprint, of the surface materials. A SAR can operate in four different ways to obtain this polarization information. The backscattered signal from a given target will be different for each of these scenarios:

- Transmitting and receiving the same polarization—the conventional approach
- Transmitting one polarization and receiving the opposite (known as cross-polarization)
- Transmitting one polarization and receiving both
- Transmitting and receiving both polarizations (a SAR that does this is called fully polarimetric)

For example, backscatter from a rough surface generally results in a single polarization coming back to the receiving antenna. In contrast, backscatter from trees is diffuse and contains a mix of polarizations, because the radar wave interacts with the trunks, branches, and leaves of the canopy. These properties of such a complex surface can be determined by a fully polarimetric SAR.

SAR Imaging over Water. Over water, SAR sensors observe only the ocean's surface; unlike ground returns, there is almost no water penetration. A completely smooth water surface or biological and man-made slicks (such as oil slicks) return very little energy to the radar and appear to be black in the resulting image. The sea surface, though, is seldom smooth, and backscatter from a rough sea surface produces a return that can be measured and analyzed. For example, though radar energy doesn't significantly penetrate into seawater, SAR measurements can indirectly provide information about water depth—often a critical piece of intelligence for naval operations. Ocean waves display different patterns in a SAR image as the waves move from deep to shallow water.

Polarimetric SAR has some special advantages in SAR imaging over water. The water surface returns very little horizontally polarized energy to the radar. But objects in the water return both polarizations. As a result, the horizontally polarized backscatter often will highlight small, pointlike targets such as mines floating in the water.

Figure 12.12 illustrates some of the features that can be obtained by imaging the open ocean. This is a SAR image taken by the Spaceborne Imaging Radar on the space shuttle *Endeavor* in 1994. It demonstrates some of the richness of SAR capabilities because it includes multiple frequencies and multiple polarizations. The image is actually a combination of three different radar images, and three colors are used to distinguish them. The L band radar images are shown in red for horizontal polarization and blue for vertical polarization. The horizontally polarized C band radar image is shown in green. The combination of the red and blue images creates the purple color effect. The line in the lower left shows the stern wake of a ship; it is about 28 kilometers long. The length of the wake indicates that

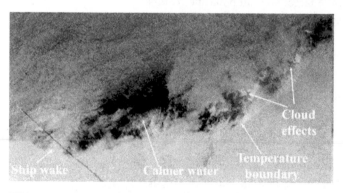

FIGURE 12.12 SAR Image of the North Atlantic

the ship is probably discharging oil, which makes the wake last longer and causes it to stand out in the image. A fairly sharp temperature boundary, probably a front, extends across the image and separates two water masses having different temperatures. The different water temperatures cause two different wind patterns that are creating two different wave patterns. The light green area in the lower part of the image is rougher water with more wind. The purple area is calmer water with less wind. The dark patches are smooth areas of low wind, probably caused by clouds along the front, and the bright green patches are likely due to ice crystals in the clouds that strongly reflect the C band radar waves.[29]

Moving Target Indicator. As discussed earlier, moving objects create distortions and artifacts in a SAR image. But moving targets clearly can be of high intelligence interest, so instead of eliminating the blurs and displacements created by moving targets, there is information to be gained by singling out those movements for detailed analysis. Two techniques are commonly used to detect moving targets: SAR interferometry, discussed earlier, and measuring the Doppler shift.

MTI relies on the Doppler shift in order to detect and track moving targets at long ranges. The JSTARS radar is an example. The antenna can be tilted to either side of the aircraft, where it has a 120-degree field of view covering nearly 50,000 square kilometers. It is capable of simultaneously tracking 600 targets within a 250-kilometer range. The radar can track any moving objects of vehicle size. In addition to being able to simultaneously detect, locate, and track large numbers of ground vehicles, the JSTARS radar has a limited capability to detect helicopters, rotating antennas, and slow-moving fixed-wing aircraft.

Figure 12.13 illustrates the type of display that a JSTARS radar can produce.[30] It shows the lines of retreating Iraqi forces during the first Gulf War (Desert Storm) on February 28, 1991—an image that has become known as

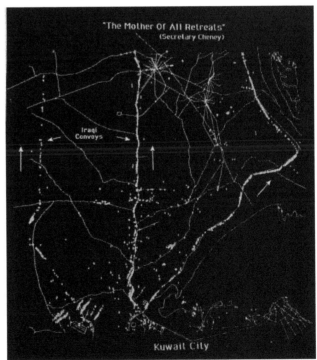

FIGURE 12.13 JSTARS MTI Image of Iraqi Retreat, 1991

"The Mother of All Retreats," in mimicry of Saddam Hussein's boast that this would be "The Mother of All Battles."

The figure illustrates another important capability that MTI can offer for intelligence. It allows the imagery analyst to extract road map information and to assess traffic flows. Once roads have been mapped and normal traffic flows have been established, the analyst is well positioned to identify priority targets and to identify changes in traffic that have intelligence significance (for example, the traffic increase that would presage a major military operation or, in this case, a major retreat). In this figure, fleeing convoys of Iraqis can be readily seen on three roads.[31]

After the material has been processed and exploited, and after analysis has extracted as much useful intelligence as possible, the imagery product has to be disseminated.

DISSEMINATION

Visible imagery often is disseminated directly to end users who usually can understand it unaided, though some features may require assistance from imagery analysts. It is not so simple for radar imagery. It has to be annotated and explained by a qualified imagery analyst. A number of the artifacts discussed in this chapter—layover, shadowing, target displacement, and distortion, among others—can mislead the image viewer.

Battlefield SAR images usually are disseminated at a relatively low classification (no higher than Secret) and ideally can be shared with coalition partners. Special SAR collection or exploitation techniques may require a higher classification and more limited distribution to protect sources and methods.

As with optical imagery (visible and spectral), libraries are needed for imagery interpretation. These libraries are more complex than the imagery analysis keys used with visible imagery, because the signature of a given target will be different depending on the radar operating frequency and the combination of polarizations used.

Structure

The SAR imagery structure is shaped by the nature of the customer, the collection platform, and whether the collection is clandestine or overt.

Like visible and spectral imaging, imagery to support national requirements usually is centralized in an organization that provides imagery products for a wide range of policymakers and military customers. Aircraft and UAV imagery coverage may sometimes be done at the national level, but military forces are the primary customers of this imagery. Military tactical imagery support typically is organic; that is, it is handled by airborne reconnaissance platforms (aircraft and UAVs) in the theater of operation.

While SAR imagery collection for intelligence usually is done by a national level organization that also does visible imaging, the processing and exploitation is completely different than that for visible imagery. So a separate suborganization is likely to be used.

Overt collection is done by many governmental and commercial organizations. Military, other governmental, and commercial organizations have all made use of SAR imagery from NASA in the past. Airborne and satellite imagery from sources such as TerraSAR-X is sold commercially.

Summary

A conventional radar can create an image as it scans the earth's surface, as noted in Chapter 11. Airborne search radars do this routinely, but the image has poor resolution because the pixels are quite large and become larger with increasing distance from the radar. Such is not the case with a SAR.

A SAR creates a high-resolution image of the target area based on the radio frequency energy backscattered from a target area. A SAR image is a map of the intensity of this energy that is backscattered from points in the scene. Brighter image pixels correspond to points of higher backscatter return.

A SAR differs from a conventional radar in that it synthesizes a long antenna using a sequence of pulses. Longer antennas produce better resolution images in the azimuth direction. To form what is effectively a long antenna, the radar transmits pulses coherently and retains a memory of the exact frequency and phase of the transmitted signal. When a backscattered signal returns, the radar measures the intensity of the return and compares the backscattered signal frequency with that of the transmitted signal. Slight differences in frequency, or phase differences, are noted, and these signal intensity and phase differences are recorded. This record, collected over many pulses, is called phase history data and is used to create the long synthetic antenna.

To get good range resolution, a SAR transmits what is effectively a very short pulse by using a very wide bandwidth signal. Most SARs use a long pulse that is frequency modulated (FM), called a *chirped pulse:* its frequency smoothly increases or decreases over the duration of the pulse. It thus has a wide frequency bandwidth, and in processing it can give the range resolution of a much shorter pulse having the same bandwidth.

The initial processing of phase history data is done using the assumption that the intensity of return from each point in the scene is the same for each pulse. This requires four processing assumptions to be made: that the terrain is flat, the targets are stationary and have a constant radar cross section, and the radio frequency environment is quiet. Both natural and artificial features in the scene typically violate one or more of the above assumptions, so additional interpretation and analysis has to be done to correct for the resulting artifacts in the image:

- Because the terrain is not flat, shadowing hides the region behind mountains and buildings, and layover causes the top of a structure to appear closer to the radar than it should be.
- Target movement causes the target to be smeared or displaced, or both, in the resulting image.
- Unless the target is a perfect sphere, its radar cross section will change during the imaging process, causing streaks and image distortion.
- Unintentional radio frequency interference or deliberate jamming will usually create streaks in the resulting image.

SARs can also use polarimetry to obtain signatures that have intelligence value. They do this by transmitting at least one polarization and receiving two polarizations. A SAR that both transmits and receives two polarizations (forming four possible combinations of transmit and receive polarization) is called fully polarimetric. When the polarized pulse strikes a target and is reflected back toward the radar, the polarization is changed by the reflecting surface. The relative amount of horizontal and vertical polarization in the return depends on the structure, reflectivity, shape, orientation, and roughness of the reflecting surface. So measuring the returned polarization from an object can provide additional information about the object.

One of the major advantages of SAR is its ability to detect changes in a scene over time by making successive passes and imaging the same scene from the same SAR location. Change detection can identify objects that have entered or left the scene between imaging passes and can also observe new vehicle tracks, crops growing or being harvested, soil excavation, and changes in the terrain surface due to underground construction.

SARs operating in the VHF or low UHF bands can image objects concealed in foliage. These SARs can also penetrate into dry earth for short distances.

SARs also can be operated in a special mode called Moving Target Indicator (MTI) or Ground Moving Target Indicator (GMTI) that is designed to enhance the detectability of target motion. MTI mode can be used to monitor aircraft, helicopter, or ship movements as well as tracking ground vehicular movement.

NOTES

1. J. Happer, "Characterization of Underground Facilities," JASON Report JSR-97-155 (April 1999), accessed 23 September 2012 at http://www.gwu.edu/~nsarchiv/NSAEBB/NSAEBB372/docs/Underground-JASON.pdf.
2. Merrill Skolnik, ed., *Radar Handbook,* 3rd ed. (New York: McGraw-Hill, 2008), 17.33–17.34.
3. L. Carin, R. Kapoor, and C. E. Baum, "Polarimetric SAR Imaging of Buried Landmines," *IEEE Transactions on Geoscience and Remote Sensing,* Vol. 36, No. 6 (November 1998), 1985–1988.
4. David J. Daniels, *Ground Penetrating Radar,* (London, UK: The Institution of Engineering and Technology, 2004), 5.
5. Dai Dahai, Wang Xuesong, Xiao Shunping, Wu Xiaofang, and Chen Siwei, "Development Trends of PolSAR System and Technology," *Heifei Leida Kexue Yu Jishu* (February 1, 2008), 15.
6. Zhou Hong, Huang Xiaotao, Chang Yulin, and Zhou Zhimin, "Ground Moving Target Detection in Single-Channel UWB SAR Using Change Detection Based on Sub-aperture Images," *Heifei Leida Kexue Yu Jishu* (February 1, 2008), 23.
7. Sandia National Laboratory, accessed 23 September 2012 at www.thespacereview.com/article/790/1.
8. S. Buckreuss, R. Werninghaus, and W. Pitz, "The German Satellite Mission TerraSAR-X," *IEEE Radar Conference 2008,* (May 26–30, 2008), INSPEC Accession No. 10425846, 306.
9. USAF Factsheet, "E-8C Joint Stars," accessed 23 September 2012 at http://www.af.mil/information/factsheets/factsheet.asp?id=100.
10. Rebecca Grant, "JSTARS Wars," *Air Force Magazine* (November 2009), accessed 5 September 2012 at http://www.airforce-magazine.com/MagazineArchive/Pages/2009/November%202009/1109jstars.aspx.
11. U.S. Air Force, "RQ-4 Global Hawk" (January 27, 2012), accessed 23 September 2012 at http://www.af.mil/information/factsheets/factsheet.asp?id=13225.
12. Jet Propulsion Laboratory, "JPL Imaging Radar," accessed 23 September 2012 at http://southport.jpl.nasa.gov/.
13. D. Pastina, P. Lombardo, A. Farina, and P. Daddi, "Super-Resolution of Polarimetric SAR Imaging," *Signal Processing,* Vol. 83, No. 8 (August 2003).
14. OHB System, "SAR-Lupe," accessed 23 September 2012 at https://www.ohb-system.de/sar-lupe-english.html.
15. OHB System, "SAR-Lupe."
16. Commander Richard J. Schgallis, "Commercial Space for Maritime Awareness," *Geospatial Intelligence Forum,* Vol. 8, No. 2 (March 2010), 12–13.
17. Skolnik, *Radar Handbook,* 17.25–17.27.

18. Ibid., 24.49–24.51.

19. Mark Preiss and Nicholas J. S. Stacy, "Coherent Change Detection: Theoretical Description and Experimental Results," Australian Department of Defense, DSTO-TR-1851 (August 2006), accessed 23 September 2012 at http://www.dtic .mil/cgi-bin/GetTRDoc?AD=ADA458753.

20. John L. Morris, "The Nature and Applications of Measurement and Signature Intelligence," *American Intelligence Journal,* Vol. 19, Nos. 3 & 4 (1999–2000), 81–84.

21. Preiss and Stacy, "Coherent Change Detection."

22. Ibid.

23. Sun Xilong, Yu Anxi, and Liang Diannong, "Analysis of Error Propagation in Inteferometric SAR," *Heifei Leida Kexue Yu Jishu* (February 1, 2008), 35.

24. Ibid.

25. NASA, "TanDEM-X," accessed 23 September 2012 at http://ilrs.gsfc.nasa.gov/ satellite_missions/list_of_satellites/tand_general.html.

26. Space Daily, "German Radar Satellite TanDEM-X Launched Successfully" (June 22, 2010), accessed 23 September 2012 at http://www.spacedaily.com/reports/ German_Radar_Satellite_TanDEM_X_Launched_Successfully_999.html.

27. Skolnik, *Radar Handbook,* 17.30–17.33.

28. John W. Ives, "Army Vision 2010: Integrating Measurement and Signature Intelligence" (April 9, 2002), accessed 23 September 2012 at http://www.dtic .mil/cgi-bin/GetTRDoc?AD=ADA400786.

29. NASA, "North Atlantic Ocean," accessed 23 September 2012 at http://southport .jpl.nasa.gov/pio/sr11/sirc/naocn.html.

30. Public domain photograph from the U.S. Air Force, available at http://acute.ath .cx/link/motherof.jpg.

31. M. Ulmke and W. Koch, "Road Map Extraction Using GMTI Tracking," *Conference Proceedings of the 9th International Conference on Information Fusion,* Florence, Italy (July 10–13, 2006).

13. Passive RF

This chapter is about the collection, processing, and analysis of emissions in the RF spectrum that have intelligence value. The collection part relies on passive radio frequency (RF) sensors, which are carried on all of the types of collection platforms discussed in Chapter 8: aircraft, satellites, UAVs, aerostats, ships, submarines, and ground sites. These sensors collect and process four basic types of RF emissions for four different purposes. Three of those types are discussed in this chapter. The four are

- communications signals, collected as communications intelligence (COMINT) (Chapter 4);
- radar signals, collected as electronic intelligence (ELINT);
- telemetry signals, collected as foreign instrumentation signals intelligence (FISINT); and
- intentional and unintentional emissions that are collected as RF measurements and signatures intelligence (MASINT).

COMINT was treated separately in Chapter 4 for two reasons. First, the COMINT product is literal, so it logically fits in Part I. Second, not all COMINT is collected by passive RF sensing. COMINT relies heavily on RF, but it also uses other collection means, audio collection and fiber-optic cable being two of the most important.

Any discussion of passive RF collection has to deal with terminology that can confuse the reader. Most books would title this chapter "Signals Intelligence (SIGINT)" and would discuss the collection of signals. The first three types listed above—COMINT, ELINT, and FISINT—are the generally accepted components of SIGINT. But the term *SIGINT* causes some difficulty, for the following reasons:

Not all SIGINT is passive RF. As noted above, much COMINT collection does not rely on passive RF signals.

Not all passive RF is SIGINT. A number of intentional and unintentional emissions have intelligence value but do not fall into any of the traditional SIGINT categories, though they are collected by the same sensors. Technically, they aren't signals at all. Collectively, they are referred to as RF MASINT.

So the terminology can be confusing, even more so because common practice is to say *SIGINT* when the speaker really means *COMINT*. In this chapter, we'll make frequent use of the terms *SIGINT* and *signal* even when discussing RF MASINT, as a matter of convenience. But you should keep in mind that RF MASINT is different. And while the chapter focuses on non-COMINT signals intelligence, the collection systems, the platforms, and geolocation all are also important for RF COMINT.

After an overview of the functions performed by ELINT, FISINT, and RF MASINT, this chapter discusses the process: how passive RF collection works. It then goes into one of the most important applications of RF sensors in intelligence—that of geolocation. In some cases, it may be critically important to geolocate the source of the signal. In others, the source is already known, and the contents of the signal itself are important.

While all passive RF collection uses much the same collection means, these subdisciplines have significantly different processes. So separate process subsections treat ELINT, FISINT, and RF MASINT applications.

Function

Passive RF collection is important for identifying, geolocating, and assessing the performance of systems that radiate RF energy. The military relies on it for targeting and for determining the threat posed by weapons systems.

ELECTRONIC INTELLIGENCE (ELINT)

Electronic intelligence refers to the information extracted through the collection, processing, exploitation, and analysis of signals transmitted by radars, beacons, jammers, missile guidance systems, and altimeters. Because most ELINT is conducted against radars, the following discussion assumes that the target is a radar.

The acronym ELINT may be unfamiliar to some, but ELINT is widely collected around the world. The radar detector that some motorists use to detect police radar is an ELINT sensor. The proliferation of radars worldwide has made ELINT collection and analysis an essential part of planning for any military operation and increasingly important in law enforcement. Airborne, spaceborne, seaborne, and ground-based radars must be identified and located continuously to support such operations. For a country such as the United States that has worldwide interests, this is a massive undertaking.

ELINT to support these operations divides broadly into two classes: operational and technical, as illustrated in Figure 13.1 and discussed in the following sections. Both types have a common end goal—support to countermeasures against the radar or against the platform carrying the radar—but they use different techniques to get there, and they have different time frames to meet their customer needs.

Operational ELINT. Most of electronic intelligence is devoted to the intercept and analysis of radar signals in order to locate radars, identify them, determine their operational status, and track their movements. This type of ELINT is generally referred to as operational ELINT and is often abbreviated as OPELINT.

The military intelligence product of operational ELINT is called the radar order of battle. Military forces determine an opponent's radar order of battle in order to deny information to those radars or destroy them in conflict.

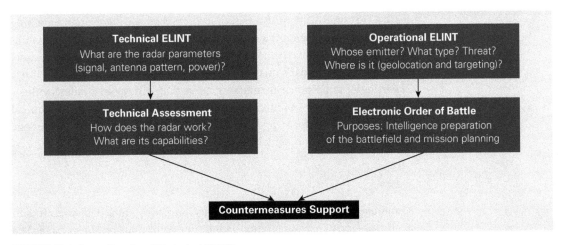

FIGURE 13.1 Operational and Technical ELINT

Operational ELINT proved to be of great value in recent Mideast conflicts, where the U.S. Air Force and Navy both conducted large-scale operational ELINT in support of combat missions.

Operational ELINT is primarily of interest to military field commanders and increasingly to law enforcement officers for tactical intelligence. A ship, aircraft, or surface-to-air missile unit can often be tracked best by continuously pinpointing the location of a radar that it carries. Operational ELINT is used extensively in modern warfare to locate targets for air attack and to locate threat radars so that attacking aircraft can avoid or defeat the defenses that the radars control. Highly accurate geolocation of these emitters is critical for targeting highly accurate munitions.

On the modern battlefield, a radar that stays in one place, transmitting a recognizable signal at high power continuously on a single frequency, is likely to quickly become a smoking pile of rubble. The development of sophisticated ELINT systems that can precisely geolocate radar signals, combined with the advent of highly precise ("smart") munitions, has changed the shape of battle. Battlefield threat radars (those that control air defenses) have become highly mobile; they are on the air for brief periods, only when necessary, and they are prone to relocate quickly after going on the air (a technique known as shoot and scoot). This places a premium on very fast geolocation and fast transmission of the collected intelligence to combat units.

Technical ELINT. Technical ELINT is used to assess a radar's capabilities and performance, to determine the level of technology used in building the radar, and to find weaknesses in the radar to help electronic warfare designers defeat it. It involves either the measurement of radar signal characteristics to a very high order of accuracy or measurements to determine something about a radar's operation that will reveal its detection and tracking capabilities. The primary objective is to obtain technical parameters that will allow assessment of the radar's mission, targets, performance, and vulnerabilities. Of particular importance are measurements that will reveal a radar's vulnerability to electronic countermeasures, as Figure 13.1 suggests. Technical ELINT also has strategic goals of assessing a country's level of technology and preventing technological surprise.

FISINT

A number of platforms used for military purposes—missiles, aircraft, and satellites—carry instrumentation to monitor conditions on the vehicle. The instrumentation measures such things as velocity, pressures, temperatures, and subsystems performance. There are two situations where it is necessary to transmit the instrumentation readings to a ground station for analysis: missile and aircraft testing and satellite status monitoring. Such RF transmissions are called telemetry.

Missiles that are undergoing testing carry instruments called transducers that continuously obtain instrument readings and transmit (telemeter) them to the ground station for later laboratory analysis. Telemetry is used in missile testing because it usually is not possible to recover an onboard recorder and analyze it later. And in the event of a catastrophic failure, the telemetry often will indicate what went wrong. Ballistic and cruise missiles carry telemetry systems only during their test phases; operational missiles do not carry telemetry.

Aircraft and unmanned aerial vehicles (UAVs) that are being tested usually can be recovered intact, unlike missiles. But even in those tests, the instrumentation readings are telemetered. In the event of catastrophic failure, again, the onboard recorder isn't likely to survive.

Almost all satellites must carry a means for receiving communications from the ground (command signals or command uplink) and a means for transmitting information about the satellite status to the ground (telemetry or telemetry downlink). Both the command uplink and the telemetry downlink can be intercepted and analyzed to obtain information about the satellite's location and status.

Because telemetry involves the deliberate transmission of information, its interception could be considered a part of COMINT. But because it is nonliteral information and because it transmits measurements, telemetry intercept logically fits as part of technical collection. As such, it is referred to in the U.S. Intelligence Community as FISINT.

RF MASINT

Several categories of RF emissions are of intelligence value but, as noted at the beginning of this chapter, their collection is not called SIGINT even though they usually are collected by SIGINT systems. The difference is that these emissions are not intended to transmit a signal. As noted earlier, they customarily are referred to as RF MASINT. Some of these RF emissions are deliberate, but most are not. A variety of events can cause such emissions of RF energy. One of the most important, for intelligence purposes, is the electromagnetic pulse that is created by a nuclear detonation.

Electromagnetic Pulse. The electromagnetic pulse (EMP) effect was first observed in the original testing of high-altitude airburst nuclear weapons.

Such airbursts produce a very short, intense RF energy pulse. The pulse then propagates in all directions from its source. The electromagnetic pulse is, in effect, an RF shock wave. The pulse can produce transient voltages of thousands of volts on electrical conductors such as wires or exposed parts of printed circuit boards.

Satellites carrying EMP sensors have been in orbit for decades because of their value in identifying nuclear weapons tests. During the suspected South African or Israeli nuclear test incident that was described in Chapter 10, the EMP sensor carried on the Vela satellite was not operational. As a result, no independent confirming EMP signature could be obtained, helping to cast doubt on whether a nuclear test had actually occurred.[1]

RF Damage Weapons. The discovery that a nuclear-detonation-caused EMP could disrupt or destroy electronic equipment led to the creation of a class of weapons to create a similar effect and accomplish the same result without the need to detonate a nuclear device. These weapons generate a very short, intense energy pulse producing a transient surge of thousands of volts that kills or disrupts semiconductor devices. They can disable unshielded electronic devices, including practically any modern electronic device within the effective range of the weapon. Their targets typically are electronic systems, such as aircraft or guided missile sensors, tactical computers, and artillery fuses. Intelligence has a role in detecting the testing of these RF damage devices so that suitable countermeasures can be taken (primarily shielding sensitive electronics to protect them from damaging pulse power levels).

Unintentional Emissions. A wide variety of equipment radiates RF as part of its normal functioning, including internal combustion engines, electrical generators, and switches. The emissions can be used to identify and geolocate motor vehicles or ships, though at relatively short ranges. Specific pieces of equipment can often be identified by their RF signatures. The functions being performed within a factory building and the rates of production, for example, can sometimes be determined by monitoring the RF emission patterns.

GEOLOCATION

Pinpointing the location of a target is called geolocation in the collection business. Geolocation is often thought of as locating the target on the surface of the earth or ocean; the definition of the term *geolocation* implies that the target is located on the globe. Most geolocation does, in fact, involve locating surface targets. But for intelligence purposes, geolocation includes locating targets under the earth or ocean, in the air, or out in space. For moving targets, such as vehicles, ships, aircraft, missiles, and satellites, geolocation may have to be done repeatedly in order to track the target's movement. Conventional search radars routinely perform geolocation and tracking of aircraft, ships, and satellites. Military forces geolocate opposing units using a number of techniques, some of which are intelligence and some of which are operations.

In addition to collecting a signal, ELINT and FISINT operations attempt to precisely locate the source of the signal. RF COMINT also is often concerned with locating the source of the communications transmission. The key performance parameter here is geolocation accuracy. Geolocation using optical and radar imaging was discussed in Chapters 9 and 12. Both optical and radar imagery allow very accurate geolocation, either by geometric computations based on the sensor's known location and pointing angles or by reference to an already geolocated object in the image. This chapter focuses on geolocation of targets for intelligence purposes using passive RF sensing, which can approach but cannot match the geolocation accuracy of optical and radar imaging. In contrast to geolocation via imaging, RF geolocation depends on the target emitting a signal. But RF systems can search a very large area at speeds that imaging systems cannot match.

Process

The passive RF collection process, in general, requires that one intercept and collect the signal, identify the signal as having intelligence interest, associate it with a specific emitter or identify the source, geolocate it, process and analyze it to extract useful intelligence, and report the findings. Let's go through these steps for the different targets previously described.

PLANNING

Not surprisingly, the planning for passive RF collection differs according to the intended purpose. ELINT, FISINT, and RF MASINT planning are discussed below.

ELINT. The objective of OPELINT planning is to collect and geolocate all possible signals of interest in an area. Depending on the collection platform, this can be a routine matter or require advance planning. For satellites such as the ELISA collector discussed below, OPELINT is much like a vacuum cleaner operation. If the signal is present, the satellite will collect it. It may take multiple passes, but sooner or later the satellite will be in a position to pick up the signal. For collection from airborne and seaborne platforms, more planning usually is needed to get the platform in a favorable location.

Technical ELINT is tasked against specific targets or target areas (for example, test ranges). Again, the collection platform can be any of those discussed in Chapter 8, and a single collector can collect both operational and technical ELINT. The ELINT collector may have advance knowledge of a radar of interest, so targeting can be specific.

Planning also has to take into account the need to share target information. Where possible, ELINT collection should be set up to cue, and be cued by, other collection assets—especially imagery collectors. When there are indications that a new signal exists (for example, from open source, imagery intelligence [IMINT] or human intelligence [HUMINT]), a target search can be made. But an important part of routine ELINT collection is the search for new signals.

FISINT. Instrumentation signals associated with missile and aircraft testing are associated with specific test ranges, so collection usually requires tip-off of an impending test. Satellite telemetry is usually available for extended time periods, so planning for FISINT against satellites can be done more systematically.

RF MASINT. Planning for collection against nonnuclear weapons tests— nonnuclear EMP, RF damage weapons, or rail guns—has a common problem. Such tests are not likely to occur very often, and the collection system would therefore need to conduct surveillance, possibly at close range, to be sure of monitoring the test. This places a premium on identifying likely test ranges.

Planning for detecting a nuclear EMP signal is simpler. Atmospheric detonations create a strong signal, and it can be identified by satellites that are equipped with the proper sensor. Monitoring for such detections can go on 24/7, as in the Vela satellite example.

Planning for other unintentional emissions centers on identifying the target or target area, deciding what signatures should be collected, and deploying sensors to make the collection. Clandestine HUMINT operations often are necessary for the deployment, and planning has to include provisions for exfiltrating and analyzing the collected signals.

COLLECTION

The passive RF sensors used in intelligence generally are a combination of an antenna, receiver, and signal processor. Some such systems have human operators working directly with the sensor and so may have display and storage systems. Remotely operated sensors, such as those on satellites, usually transmit collected signal information to a ground site. But an antenna and a receiver are the minimum requirements for all such sensors. The sensor's performance is determined almost solely by the design and performance of the antenna and the receiver.

The same system can be applied to collecting any of the three major types of SIGINT: COMINT, discussed in Chapter 4; or ELINT or FISINT, discussed in this chapter. It can also collect RF MASINT. RF collection systems sometimes are optimized to collect only one of these signal types. An ELINT system carried on a UAV would likely be designed to collect only OPELINT in the battlefield area. A clandestine sensor emplaced near a test range might be designed only for FISINT collection at selected frequencies. Other RF collectors might need to collect everything in a wide range of frequencies and signal strengths. Satellites are expensive to build and operate, so they tend to carry very flexible systems that can handle multiple missions and signal types.

So an RF collection system design typically is based on (1) the nature of the target signals to be collected, (2) the requirements for geolocating the signals, and (3) the nature of the collection platform. Each of these design factors is discussed in the next three sections.

Target Signal Trade-Offs. Passive RF collection systems are designed differently from the ones used in communications and radar. A radar or communications receiver is designed to receive and process a specific signal at a specific frequency or set of frequencies. Most passive RF collection systems do not have this luxury; they must receive and process a wide range of signal types over a wide frequency band. Furthermore, they must be able to measure a number of signal parameters. These requirements dictate that any system will be a compromise design that depends on its intended use.

Different designs address the different problems posed by trying to collect everything that is needed from the target signal while maintaining the necessary time, frequency, and spatial coverage. The same three issues discussed in Chapter 7—coverage, resolution, and accuracy—also apply here. As usual, compromises must be made among

- Total bandwidth range (spectral coverage)[2]
- Instantaneous frequency bandwidth—how wide a frequency band can be intercepted at one time (spectral coverage)
- Frequency and time measurement accuracy

- Frequency and time resolution—over how small a band of frequency or time can different signals be distinguished without loss of information
- Sensitivity—what is the smallest signal energy that can be detected (intensity coverage)
- Dynamic range—what is the range of signal energies that can be detected simultaneously (intensity coverage)
- Geolocation capability

No one type of system does all of these things well. The nature of the expected target signals determines which of these characteristics is emphasized in system selection and design. Different designs have been optimized to perform well for specific purposes. Both the receiver and the antenna have to be designed to fit their intended usage.

As an example, the trade-offs in the design of collection antennas are size, gain, beamwidth, and tracking requirements. For high gain, which is desirable since it allows the system to detect weaker signals, the antenna size is large and the beamwidth is narrow. However, high-gain antennas have reduced angular coverage; the performance advantages of the narrow beam (selectivity and sensitivity) must be balanced against the need to cover large areas. A wideband receiver needs to use a highly directional antenna in a dense signal environment to identify and classify complex signals. To cover larger areas it is necessary to mechanically scan the antenna, use multiple antennas, or use a single antenna such as a phased array that generates multiple beams.

The solution, in general, is to use a collection of antennas, receivers, and signal processors of different types working together. One receiver, for example, may be designed to search for and acquire new signals. Another receiver might be used to closely examine signals of interest that are detected by the search receiver. A special processor might then be accessed to measure the signal parameters, such as pulse width and pulse repetition frequency (PRF).[3] The technique is another example of using sensor suites. Using a combination of complementary sensors, when a single sensor does not meet the mission requirements, was discussed in Chapter 7.

Following are some of the specific targets of RF collection and the nature of the systems that work well in collecting such signals.

Narrowband Signals. Narrow bandwidth signals are relatively easy to find in the spectrum and are especially easy when they operate on a fixed frequency. Telemetry signals fit in this class. The challenge is that the signals of interest often are very weak. Because sensitivity is therefore important, collection often makes use of highly sensitive receivers such as superheterodyne receivers and the largest practical antennas for the platform. Alternatively, one can sometimes locate the collection system in close proximity to the target. For close-in work, where a clandestinely emplaced sensor is located near the target signal, the antenna has to be small and easily concealed. Such antennas can be not much more than a short wire or a patch antenna like those used in cell phones.

Wide Instantaneous Bandwidth Signals. Target radars usually have strong signals, but some newer ones can use very wide bandwidths (up to 1 GHz or higher), so wide instantaneous bandwidth is more important for both operational and technical ELINT receivers. Some RF MASINT emissions—those associated with EMP and RF damage–are wideband. The types of receivers and antennas used for collecting wide instantaneous bandwidth signals are discussed in the section below on new signal search.

Low Probability of Intercept (LPI) Signals. Radars continue to be developed that are hard for ELINT systems to collect. A major class of such radars is called low probability of intercept (LPI) radars. Such radars use any one of several techniques to make the radar harder to intercept or harder to locate if intercepted. The simplest such technique is emission control by reducing the transmitted power to the minimum possible level. Some radars transmit each pulse on a different frequency (a technique called frequency hopping) to avoid interception or to defeat the ELINT system's processing capability. Other LPI radars transmit wide bandwidth noise-like signals to hide their presence from ELINT. Radars can even mimic benign signals (such as airport surveillance radars or television stations) to avoid attack.

LPI signals often have to be collected at long range. That requires a combination of weak signal collection capability (high-gain antennas and sensitive receivers) and wide instantaneous bandwidth receivers.

The most advanced LPI radars are relatively new and very difficult for even the best ELINT systems to detect. Called active electronically scanned arrays or AESA, these radars depend on phased arrays and sophisticated electronics to deceive ELINT systems. They have been described as "shape-shifting electronic chameleons with lightning reflexes and highly developed brains that dispatch [ELINT systems] with ease."[4]

New Signal Search. The search for new and unidentified signals is a priority for any RF collection system, but it is especially important in ELINT because these can indicate the presence of new threat radars. Search systems depend on the ability to search through a large part of the RF spectrum very rapidly, so as not to miss what may be a very short duration signal and to do so at the highest possible sensitivity. Again, no one type of receiver can do all types of new signal search. If the target is wideband signals, one might use RF radiometers that can detect the presence of wideband signals but cannot measure signal parameters. Alternatively, crystal video receivers (which are relatively insensitive) can be used at short ranges. Where the search is for frequency hoppers, an instantaneous frequency measurement (IFM) receiver may be preferred; it has good dynamic range and sensitivity. Where the target is a weak signal, especially in a dense signal environment, a microscan (a rapidly scanning type of superheterodyne) receiver may work best.

One of the better general purpose receivers for new signal search is the acousto-optical receiver (which uses the incoming electrical signal to modulate a light wave traveling through glass). It combines good frequency resolution and wide instantaneous bandwidth. It also works very well against a frequency hopper and is one of the preferred receivers for ELINT.

New signal search antennas also must cover a very broad frequency band. Although specific radar bands are identified in Table 11.1, radar signals can appear anywhere in the microwave spectrum. Some antennas are called **frequency-independent antennas** because of their wide bandwidth. They come in a variety of shapes—flat spirals, conical spirals, and log-periodic antennas, which look vaguely like the traditional rooftop-mounted home TV antennas.

Geolocation. A number of different techniques can be used to obtain the location of an RF energy source. The three most widely used are angle of arrival, time difference of arrival, and frequency difference of arrival. RF tagging can be used to create an RF source for geolocation.

Angle of Arrival. The oldest passive RF geolocation technique is to determine the direction of signal arrival. Because electromagnetic waves from a transmitter travel in a straight line, the direction of arrival of the signal is the direction in which the signal source lies.

These traditional direction-finding (DF) systems use two or more sensors working together. Each direction-finding sensor in the system produces a direction-of-arrival estimate for an intercepted signal. An estimated emitter position can be calculated from the intersection of the individual directions of arrival.

Figure 13.2 illustrates how this works for geolocating a cell phone. Each cell tower has an angle-of-arrival sensing capability for all cell phones in its area. The three towers in the figure each determine the angle from which the

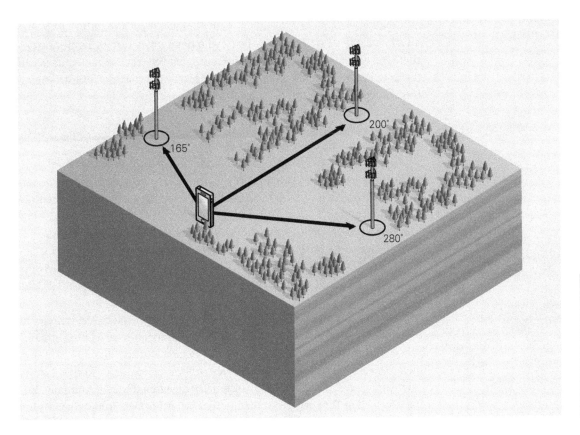

FIGURE 13.2 Using Angle of Arrival to Locate a Cell Phone

phone transmissions are coming, as indicated. Because the tower positions are fixed and well known, it is easy to make the calculation of the phone's location, a process called triangulation. The same technique is used by SIGINT equipment to locate radar signals and communications transmissions from aircraft, ships, satellites, and ground stations.

The accuracy of DF geolocation is limited in two ways.

• No antenna can measure direction of arrival perfectly. All antennas have a definite beamwidth that causes the intersection of the beams to be an area of the earth's surface, not the single point shown in Figure 13.2. Even the best equipment used in SIGINT stations cannot measure angle of arrival to much better than one degree.

• Direction finding makes the assumption that the signal comes in a straight line from transmitter to receiver antenna. That often isn't the case in an urban environment. The signal may bounce off several buildings before arriving at the SIGINT antenna—a phenomenon called multipath propagation. The effect of multipath propagation is that the receiving antenna (a cell tower in Figure 13.2) estimates the signal as coming from the building that it last bounced off, resulting in a geolocation error.

Three antenna types are used to determine angle of arrival: spinners, phased arrays, and interferometers.

A spinner is a single small antenna that is used for direction finding by moving the antenna rapidly (usually spinning it to provide 360 degrees azimuth coverage) and noting the direction the antenna is pointing when the signal is strongest.

Phased arrays were introduced in Chapter 11. Some arrays are specifically designed for geolocating targets in SIGINT because they allow instantaneous coverage of a spatial sector. One widely used array in SIGINT is the circularly disposed antenna array (CDAA), known commonly as the Wullenweber.

The Wullenweber is a large circular antenna array used by the military to triangulate high frequency (HF) radio signals for radio navigation, intelligence gathering, and search and rescue. Because of its immense size and huge circular reflecting screen, the antenna is colloquially known as the "elephant cage." The CDAA was originally developed by the Germans during World War II to receive transmissions from German submarines in the North Atlantic and to determine the general locations of the submarines. The name "Wullenweber" was the cover term they used to identify their CDAA research and development program.[5] Two CDAAs, such as the one shown in Figure 13.3,[6] located sufficiently far apart can geolocate an HF emitter at ranges of thousands of kilometers, using the fact that HF signals reflect off the earth's ionosphere. The geolocation is not very accurate. It depends on the state of the ionosphere and on the accuracy of angular measurement; accuracies are in the tens of kilometers.

Interferometers are sensors that receive EM energy over two or more different paths and deduce information from the coherent interference between the received signals. They determine the direction of arrival by measuring the phase difference of arrival of an RF signal at two or more antenna elements. These antenna elements are physically separated in space by some portion of a wavelength, and the phase difference recorded at the individual elements determines the direction of arrival. So an interferometer is just a phased array with wider spacing. The simplest interferometer consists of a pair of directional antennas that are tuned to receive radio emissions from a source in a desired RF

FIGURE 13.3 AN/FLR-9 CDAA Located Near Augsburg, Germany

band. The signal phases from the two receivers are then compared to determine the direction of arrival of the wave front from the signal. The direction of arrival of the wave front determines the direction to the target radio emitter.

Time Difference of Arrival. Cell towers have a more accurate way to geolocate a signal than DF, and it is extensively used by ELINT systems to geolocate radars also. It depends on the fact that signals travel at a defined velocity—acoustic signals at the speed of sound, electromagnetic (EM) signals (including optical signals) at the speed of light. This speed can be used to geolocate the source of a signal. The speed of travel differs in different media, which can be a problem for acoustic signals. But for all practical purposes, the speed of radio waves is the speed of light. Radars, as noted in Chapter 11, determine the distance to a target by measuring the time delay for the round trip of a pulse. Cell towers can do the same, by pinging—sending out a signal to a cell phone—and measuring the time it takes to receive a response ping from the phone. The measurement determines distance (though again, multipath can be a problem because it introduces a time delay).

SIGINT systems do not transmit, so they cannot directly measure the travel time of a signal from an emitter. They instead make use of an indirect technique for geolocating a target, called **multilateration**. It is also known as hyperbolic positioning. It is the process of locating an object by computing the time difference of arrival (TDOA) of a signal at different locations. Multilateration is commonly used in surveillance applications to accurately locate an aircraft, vehicle, or stationary emitter by measuring TDOA of a signal from the emitter at three or more receiver sites.[7] The technique also works with acoustic signals, which we will discuss in Chapter 14.

A pulse from an emitter will arrive at different times at two spatially separated receiver sites. The TDOA is a result of the different distances of each receiver from the platform. The problem is that for given locations of the two receivers, a large series of emitter locations would give the same measurement of TDOA. For two receivers at known locations, the TDOA geolocates an emitter on a curved surface called a hyperboloid (which is why the name hyperbolic positioning is used). The receivers do not need to know the absolute time at which the pulse was transmitted; only the time difference is needed.[8]

Suppose now that the SIGINT collection system has a third receiver at a different location, and it also can intercept the signal. This makes a second and third TDOA measurement available, as Figure 13.4 indicates. A comparison of the three time differences of signal arrival at the three sensors defines a curve in space; the emitter must be somewhere on this curve. If the emitter is on the earth's surface, the geolocation problem is easily solved: The emitter is located where the curve touches the earth's surface. If the emitter is known to be somewhere above the earth, a fourth sensor would be needed to precisely locate it on the curve.[9]

Multilateration can be far more accurate for locating an object than techniques such as angle of arrival. One can measure time more accurately than one can form a very narrow beam for simple direction finding. The accuracy of multilateration is a function of several variables, including

- the geometry of the receiver(s) and transmitter(s),
- the timing accuracy of the receiver system,
- the accuracy of the synchronization of the receiving sites (this can be degraded by unknown propagation effects),
- the bandwidth of the emitted pulse(s), and
- uncertainties in the locations of the receivers.[10]

TDOA has been the technology of choice for high-accuracy location systems since the advent of radar. The global positioning system (GPS) is TDOA

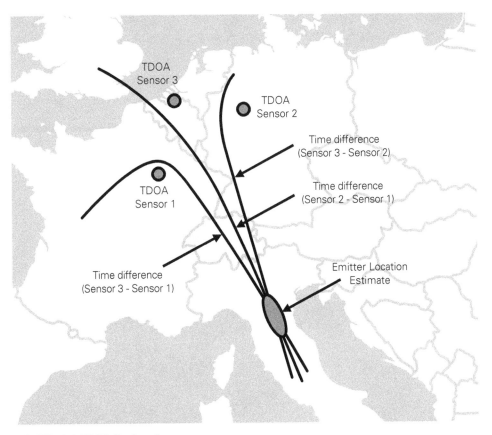

FIGURE 13.4 TDOA Geolocation

based, as are most of the systems proposed for locating emitters. TDOA systems operate by placing location receivers at multiple sites geographically dispersed in a wide area; each of the sites has an accurate timing source. When a signal is transmitted from a mobile device, its signal reception is time-stamped at all antenna sites. The differences in time stamps are then combined to produce the intersecting hyperbolic lines previously discussed.[11] Note in the figure that the emitter location estimate is not shown as a point; instead, it is shown as an ellipse, called an error ellipse in the geolocation trade. The error ellipse indicates the geographical region in which the emitter most likely is located.[12]

An example of a modern TDOA system is the VERA-E, an ELINT system produced by the Czech Republic. Its method of operation is shown in Figure 13.5, and most ground-based TDOA ELINT systems operate in the same

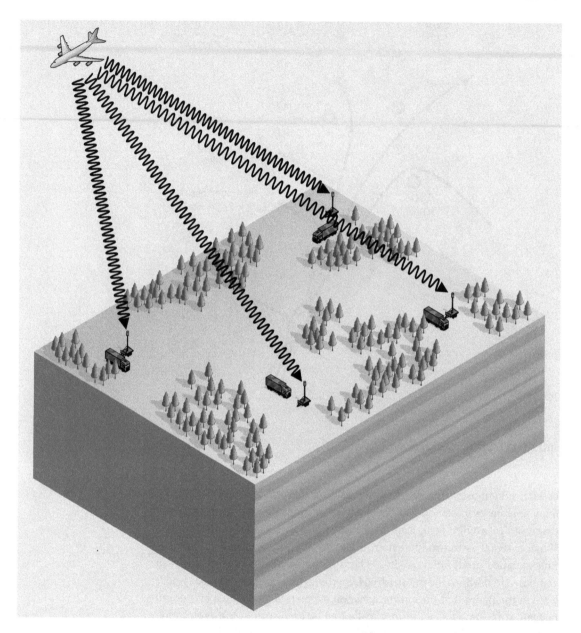

FIGURE 13.5 Use of TDOA to Locate Aircraft

manner. Vera-E uses either three or four receivers, separated by 10 to 25 kilometers. Three receivers provide the location of a target on a map; four receivers can also provide target altitude. VERA-E can only detect and track pulsed emissions, due to the requirement to measure the time of arrival of pulses for TDOA. The receivers operate in the frequency range of 1 to 18 GHz. Position accuracy is stated as 20 meters in azimuth and 200 meters in range at a target distance of 150 kilometers. VERA-E also uses fingerprinting techniques to identify targets. The system can automatically track up to 200 targets simultaneously.[13]

The VERA-E requires four receivers to determine target altitude because the TDOAs among four receivers define a unique point in space, whereas TDOAs among three receivers define a curve, as discussed previously. But it is possible for a single receiver to determine a target's altitude, as discussed later.

Frequency Difference of Arrival. The third technique for geolocation, frequency difference of arrival (FDOA), depends on the fact that signals emitted or received by moving targets have an associated Doppler shift that can be used to determine target location or speed of movement. FDOA is a technique similar to TDOA in that an estimate is made for the location of a radio emitter based on observations from several points. It differs from TDOA in that the FDOA observation points must be in relative motion with respect to each other or with respect to the emitter. (It can also be used for estimating one's own position based on observations of multiple emitters.[14])

This relative motion results in different Doppler shift observations of the emitter at each location. The emitter location can then be estimated with knowledge of the receiver locations and velocities and the observed relative Doppler shifts between pairs of receivers. The accuracy of the location estimate is related to the bandwidth of the emitter's signal, the signal-to-noise ratio (SNR) at each observation point, and the geometry and velocities of the emitter and the receiver locations.[15] A disadvantage of FDOA is that large amounts of data must be moved between observation points or to a central location to do the processing that is necessary to estimate the Doppler shift.

Figure 13.6 illustrates how FDOA works. Three receivers moving from left to right in the figure are attempting to geolocate a stationary emitter. Sensor 1 observes negative Doppler shift because it is moving away from the emitter. Sensor 2 observes zero Doppler shift because it is broadside to the emitter (no relative movement between the two). Sensor 3 observes positive Doppler shift because it is moving toward the emitter. By comparing the frequencies observed by sensors 1 and 3, a SIGINT processor can determine that the emitter lies somewhere on the curve shown. Comparing the frequency observed at sensor 2 with the other two frequencies, the processor

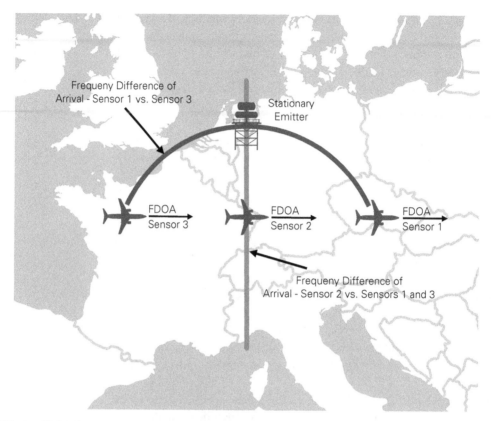

FIGURE 13.6 FDOA Geolocation from Three Moving Receivers

can determine that the emitter is located on the line broadside to sensor 2. The intersection of these three lines determines the location of the emitter. Note that there is an inherent ambiguity in this geolocation; an emitter located on the opposite side of sensor 2 at the same distance would give the same FDOA measurements.

Figure 13.6 suggests another problem with FDOA by noting that the emitter must be stationary. Of course, many emitters of intelligence interest are not stationary; a moving emitter will result in an invalid location unless the ELINT processing system applies some sort of correction. This is the same phenomenon that was discussed in the previous chapter: A moving target causes geolocation error for both SARs and ELINT systems by changing the Doppler shift. However, either by adding additional FDOA sensors or by watching the change in FDOA over time, the ELINT system can make the necessary correction.

Geolocation Accuracy. As noted earlier, the accuracy of geolocation is very important in intelligence support to military and law enforcement operations, and considerable effort goes into improving this accuracy during the processing step.

Geolocation processing must somehow deal with multipath signals. Both angle-of-arrival and TDOA systems are affected by urban multipath. Multipath reception distorts the shape of the signal and the time delay, causing the TDOA system difficulty in accurately determining the point in the signal to be measured by all receivers.[16] As a result, multipath has been generally found to be the single largest contribution to error in a TDOA system. The first signal received at an antenna arrives from the most direct path from the transmitter to the receiving antenna. Typically, especially in an urban environment, additional copies of the signal are received from hundreds of nanoseconds to tens of microseconds later, overlapping the first signal. These copies arrive from reflections occurring off of natural or man-made reflective surfaces in the area, such as hills, buildings, bridges, cars, or even dense woods.[17] The signal processor has to correct for these additional spurious signals.

A fairly straightforward technique for improving geolocation accuracy is to simply use more geolocation assets against a target. For example, to reduce errors in the measurement of the time of arrival of pulses for TDOA, the collector can add more receivers at dispersed locations. Four receivers will provide six hyperboloids, five receivers will provide 10 hyperboloids, and so forth. With perfect measurements, all the hyperboloids would intersect at a single point. In practice, the surfaces rarely intersect because of various errors—which is why the result always is an error ellipse. But the TDOA of multiple transmitted pulses from the emitter can be averaged to improve accuracy.[18]

Another method for improving accuracy is to combine some of the techniques discussed above. More accurate geolocation results when geolocation techniques are combined. TDOA and FDOA are sometimes used together to improve location accuracy, and the resulting estimates are somewhat independent.[19] Angle of arrival can be combined with either to help resolve ambiguities in the target location.[20] For example, if in Figure 13.4 only receivers 1 and 2 were operating, then any emitter could only be geolocated to the curve on the earth that is shown in the figure and labeled "Time difference" (sensor 2 to sensor 1). But if either receiver also could obtain an angle of arrival, the location of the emitter on the curve could be established.

A completely different technique for improving accuracy is to get some help from an emitter in the target area that has a precisely known location.

TDOA and FDOA accuracy can be greatly improved by using a reference signal transmitter, known as a reference emitter or reference beacon. The reference emitter can be, for example, a radar in the target area, the position of which is already known, or a GPS-equipped beacon that has been emplaced in the target area to act as a reference emitter. When a new signal in the target area must be geolocated, the geolocation system receives both the reference emitter signal and the new signal and uses some comparison techniques in its signal processors to reduce the geolocation error.[21]

RF Tagging and Tracking. RF tags are widely used in intelligence and law enforcement. Their purpose is to provide a unique identifier for an object that can be sensed at a distance and used to track the object's movement. A well-known example is the use of RF tags to track stolen automobiles. These tags, which typically include a GPS receiver that tracks the automobile's position, are concealed in the automobile to discourage theft. If a tagged auto is stolen, police can pinpoint its location by receiving the tag's RF signal.

The widest use of RF tagging, though, is in the commercial sector. The simplest and most commonly used type of RF tag is the radio frequency identification (RFID) tag. These tags are extensively used in the retail business and supply chains to track the movement of goods.

An RFID tag is a microchip combined with an antenna in a compact package; the packaging is structured to allow the RFID tag to be attached to an object to be tracked. A computer chip is attached to an antenna, and they are often referred to together as an RFID tag. Data stored on the chip transmits wirelessly through the antenna to an RFID reader or scanning device that operates on the same frequency as the antenna. The tag's antenna picks up signals from an RFID reader or scanner and then returns the signal, usually with some additional data (like a unique serial number or other customized information).

RFID devices can be active or passive:

- Passive RFID tags get their power from the RFID reader. When an RFID reader is directed at a passive RFID tag that is tuned to the reader frequency, the reader sends an EM signal to the tag. The energy received by the tag effectively is used to power its response to the reader. Passive RFID usually requires a reader to be within a foot of the chip, but, depending on the frequency, it can be read from up to 20 feet away.

- Active RFID tags have a battery that provides power to transmit data on the chip, and it can transmit data to very long distances. Some active tags contain replaceable batteries for years of use; others are sealed units, designed essentially as throwaways. Some active tags are connected to an external power source.[22]

RFID tags can be very small. Passive tags can be the size of a large rice grain. Active devices are typically larger—the size of a small paperback book. For intelligence uses, the tags have even been placed in personal objects, such as a walking stick that was provided to Osman Ato, a Somali arms importer. The tag allowed a U.S. Delta Force team to capture Ato in Mogadishu.[23]

Cell phones are, in effect, RFID tags and can be tracked by several techniques. The phones do not have to be in use. They simply have to be turned on. One technique compares the strength of the signal received by nearby cell phone towers to obtain an approximate position of the phone. Much higher accuracy is possible for phones equipped with a GPS receiver. Cell phones using the popular standard global system for mobile communications (GSM) that are GPS equipped can be located to within 10 meters in Europe and to within 25 meters in the United States, South America, and Canada.[24]

The Department of Homeland Security's Marine Asset Tag Tracking System (MATTS) is an example of an active tag that has intelligence applications. It consists of a miniature sensor, data logging computer, radio transceiver, and GPS tracking system integrated into a compact and inexpensive box, about the size of a deck of cards. Affixed to a shipping container, the tag reportedly can transmit through shipboard communications systems, even if the container is placed deep below deck. The tag's signal jumps from container to container until it finds a path it can use. The MATTS box stores its location history and reports it back when in range (up to 1 kilometer) of an Internet-equipped ship, container terminal, or cell phone tower. At any point in a container's journey, the container's location history can be examined, and if anything has gone amiss, authorities are alerted to inspect that particular container.[25]

Platform Trade-Offs. RF collection sensors are designed to function on specific platform types. In fact, it is the nature of the platform that shapes the design of the receiver and of the antenna. Receivers for ground-based and shipboard collection can be very sophisticated, with collocated processing and exploitation. The receivers therefore can have high sensitivity and have maintenance support readily available. Receivers and antennas on satellites, in contrast, have to be rugged and designed for a wide range of signals, since they can't be maintained or redesigned once they're in orbit. Airborne sensors fall somewhere in between these extremes. And clandestinely emplaced antenna/receiver combinations typically have to be very compact, designed to fit in with their surroundings, with a communications link to a remote listening post.

Ground-based antennas can be quite large because they rest on a very stable platform. In contrast, an antenna system on board a ship is limited in its size by pointing and tracking requirements because it must dynamically correct for heading changes, pitch, and roll. This limits the shipboard SIGINT dish antenna diameter to the 5 to 6 meter range. Larger shipboard antennas are possible, but they are difficult to build and operate. Shipboard phased arrays can use electronic steering to compensate for the ship's yaw, pitch, and roll.

ELINT Collection. ELINT collection is done from many different platforms. But increasingly, satellites are used, because they can routinely access targets worldwide. Several countries operate ELINT satellites, primarily to provide order of battle intelligence for their militaries. Russia has its Tselina series of satellites, and China reportedly has several ELINT satellites in orbit.[26]

An example of an OPELINT satellite is the French Electronic Intelligence by Satellite (ELISA), launched in December 2011 and shown in Figure 13.7. ELISA is the latest in a series of French SIGINT satellites (the previous ones were called Cerise, Clementine, and ESSAIM). ELISA comprises a constellation of four satellites, located a few kilometers apart in space. Each satellite receives and records incoming radar pulses and transmits the pulse data to a ground station. The ground station then combines the received signals to geolocate radars using one of the geolocation techniques discussed in this chapter.[27]

Each type of ELINT platform has its own advantages and limitations. Satellites provide good earth coverage. At the other extreme, weak signals often require close proximity collection, which satellites cannot do against ground-based targets. In between the two extremes, UAVs, aircraft, and ship- or ground-based systems (used to collect against surface targets, satellites, and aircraft) have a role. Global Hawk, the VERA-E, and the Norwegian ship *Marjata* are all previously discussed examples of ELINT collection platforms.

Technical ELINT collection typically concentrates on signals that already have been identified and on evolutionary modifications

FIGURE 13.7 The ELISA ELINT Satellites

to these signals. However, the highest priority signals for ELINT collection are always new and unidentified signals because they presumably represent the most advanced capability. Newly developed radars tend to radiate only for short periods in tests and only during times when it is believed that hostile intercept potential is at a minimum. Therefore, short duration intercepts are the best that can be expected for such radars. Most antiship cruise missiles, for example, carry a target acquisition and homing radar to guide the missile into the target. Typical of this class is the French Exocet, an antiship cruise missile, equipped with an X band acquisition and homing radar.[28] Technical ELINT on cruise missile radars is of critical importance in developing countermeasures, especially those needed for ship defensive systems.

Close behind in importance is identifying new and unusual modes of operating existing radars. Some radars, for example, have what is called wartime reserve modes that are supposed to be concealed until needed in wartime—so that the radar will be less susceptible to countermeasures. These wartime modes must be identified if countermeasures against them are to be planned.

Geolocation is an important capability for all RF SIGINT and especially so for operational ELINT. Geolocation equipment such as VERA-E can be located on the ground to locate and track aircraft or satellites. Shipborne equipment can locate and track aircraft, satellites, antiship missiles, or other ships. But geolocation is most effective for locating and tracking surface targets when collection is done above the earth's surface, for example, on aircraft, satellites, or UAVs.[29] Airborne and spaceborne platforms offer a better coverage of the earth's surface than ground sites or ships. The disadvantage of airborne and spaceborne sensors is that their accuracy can be no better than their knowledge of their location when collecting the signals. So it's important for collectors to time-stamp collection events and to keep a log of the platform's position at those times.

FISINT Collection. Telemetry signals are typically very weak. So FIS collection is either done at standoff distances using a large antenna and sensitive receiver or by clandestine collection close in to a test range. But telemetry signals operate on fixed frequencies that are usually well known, so searching for new signals doesn't have to be done often.

RF MASINT Collection

Electromagnetic Pulse. Collection to identify atmospheric nuclear tests worldwide typically is done by satellites. The United States employs EMP sensors on its GPS constellation. The constellation provides total earth surveillance, 24/7.

RF Damage Weapons. Collection of these weapons tests poses a number of challenges. EMP-like weapons have a low frequency pulse that has very wide bandwidth. Some RF damage weapons operate with comparatively narrow bandwidths, in the microwave region above 4 GHz. Tests of all such weapons are not conducted frequently and usually would be timed to avoid the known presence of an opponent's collectors. The consequence is that collection against RF damage device tests is unlikely unless one is able to conduct continuous broadband surveillance of likely test ranges, preferably from a location close to the suspected test range.

Unintended Emissions. A wide range of unintended RF emissions can be intercepted, interpreted, and analyzed. Sensors placed near an installation often can recover information of intelligence value from the equipment inside—sometimes literal, sometimes nonliteral. Collection of unintended emissions from vehicles also is possible, depending on the type of emission. During the Vietnam War, a "Black Crow" sensor called the ASD-5 was carried aboard AC-130 gunships. It reportedly detected the emissions produced by the ignition system of trucks on the Ho Chi Minh trail at distances up to 10 miles.[30]

PROCESSING, EXPLOITATION, AND ANALYSIS

ELINT, FISINT, and RF MASINT are all handled differently in the processing, exploitation, and analysis phases. The differences are discussed in the following sections.

ELINT. Both operational and technical ELINT processing must deal with the challenge of a dense signal environment. Spaceborne SIGINT systems typically observe a large portion of the earth's surface. Airborne systems cover a smaller portion of the surface, but the coverage still is in the thousands of square kilometers. In either case, the result is that the system sees a dense signal environment. In the case of ELINT, for example, many pulses are coming into the ELINT receiver continuously. The environment becomes even denser if the receiver has a wide bandwidth, as ELINT systems typically do.

In order to handle this environment, processing typically depends on the collector putting the pulses in digital form as they arrive. Once digitized, the signals can be processed in many different ways, depending on what information is desired about the signal. Next, the ELINT signal processor must assign each incoming pulse to a specific radar.[31] The desired information then can be extracted and displayed in different ways depending on how it is to be used. In most cases, the ELINT system also must geolocate the radar; geolocation techniques were discussed earlier in this chapter.

OPELINT. Operational ELINT processing and exploitation must first identify the radars that are of special interest, specifically threat radars in a battlefield environment. This requires characterizing the signal and locating its source. Typically, this needs to be done quickly, and the results must be disseminated quickly.

The first step is a matter of signal sorting. Assigning incoming pulses to a specific radar requires classifying and sorting the radar pulses according to signal parameters such as radio frequency, pulse width, and pulse repetition frequency. Signal separation using RF as a sorting parameter has been used quite successfully; however, many different emitters are likely to use the same RF band. For most ELINT environments, the second most useful sorting parameter is the PRF.[32] To sort these signals, ELINT processors rely on a technique called **pulse train deinterleaving**. Pulse train deinterleaving relies on the fact that for radars having a fixed PRF, the pulses will arrive at a constant rate, and a constant rate sequence is easy to identify.[33] Radar designers are aware of this technique, of course, and modern radars often make this signal sorting process more difficult by constantly changing their PRF.

The signal processor then must perform a number of functions that vary depending on the type of intelligence being collected. After the signals have been sorted, they must be identified as coming from a specific type of emitter, assuming that the emitter has previously been collected and analyzed. If the emitter is of a new type, then technical ELINT processing (discussed later) is used to analyze the signal parameters. If the emitter has an electronic signature that is recognized (for example, in an existing signals catalog), then operational ELINT processing techniques are usually employed (for example, to geolocate the emitter and to uniquely identify it for future reference).

A wide range of signal processing techniques are used in ELINT, again, depending on the functions to be performed. Processing of OPELINT is relatively simple, compared with technical ELINT. The main concerns are to identify the signal from an existing ELINT library, determine its status, geolocate it, and get the intelligence out to customers quickly. These considerations tend to drive OPELINT collection and analysis to be done in-theater by tactical collection systems, but strategic systems such as overhead collection are used if the results can be provided to customers in a timely fashion. The emphasis is on the identification and geolocation of specific emitters. As a result, OPELINT displays often are spatial—that is, a map display with specific signals or equipment identifiers named and located on the map.

Operational ELINT can do more than just identify a radar by type. It can also use fine-grain signatures of radar signals to identify and track specific radars. This technique is called **specific emitter identification** or fingerprinting. Just as no two fingerprints are identical, no two radars have identical signal parameters, even though they may be physically identical otherwise. The technique normally requires good technical ELINT to first obtain a very detailed target signature.

Technical ELINT. Technical ELINT requires a two-step process: First, ELINT collectors must obtain a detailed signature of the radar; second, ELINT analysts must conduct a detailed assessment of that signature to obtain performance information. The typical signature comprises three distinct elements: signal parameters, antenna pattern, and power. These three together permit analysts to estimate detection performance.

For technical ELINT, the emphasis usually is on precise measurements of frequency and modulation characteristics. Technical ELINT tends to make use of some type of spectrum analyzer, which typically shows a plot of signal strength versus frequency. The analyzer provides a visual signature that describes the signal bandwidth and modulation, power, and other signal parameters.

Signal Parameter Measurements. The traditional radar signal parameter measurements used in ELINT are the radar's frequency, pulse duration, PRF or pulse repetition interval (PRI), main beam scan pattern, and bandwidth. Frequency and pulse duration help establish the radar's detection range. The PRF or PRI determines the radar's maximum unambiguous range. The radar's main beam scan pattern helps to identify the purpose and modes of radar operation as the radar goes through its functions of search and tracking targets. The radar's bandwidth determines its range resolution.

Radars, when first developed, transmitted a simple unmodulated pulse. Modern radars can be very complex, so they have a number of pulse parameters that need to be measured. They have become much more sophisticated over time. They now modulate the pulse in many ways, either to improve radar performance or to defeat hostile ELINT. The radars may be modulated in frequency, a technique known as **linear frequency modulation (LFM)**. They may be modulated by changing phase, a modulation that is called phase coding. Each pulse may jump randomly to a different frequency, the technique discussed earlier as frequency hopping. The radar signal may look like a burst of noise due to spread spectrum coding. All these techniques, and more, make the job of the technical ELINT collector and the analyst considerably more challenging than it used to be.

Antenna Pattern Measurements. The total radio frequency power fed to a radar antenna is essentially determined by the type of power tube or solid-state device used in the transmitter, the characteristics of the pulses, and the losses by attenuation in the system. The function of the antenna is to concentrate this power in the desired direction, and its ability to do so is called antenna gain. The relative distribution of the energy in all directions is called the antenna radiation pattern. This antenna pattern and the level of power radiated are critical parameters in establishing the performance of the radar. These parameters need to be accurately measured for intelligence and electronic countermeasures (ECM) purposes.

The accurate and comprehensive measurement of a radar antenna pattern is a tedious process, even for the radar's designer. It is a tougher problem for the ELINT analyst because ELINT collection is not usually done under favorable conditions. On a radar test range, the range engineers control the test environment, and they usually strive to make that environment unfavorable for ELINT collectors. Moreover, the patterns seen on the test ranges are not always the ones observed in operational use because environmental and ground effects at the site can make significant changes in the pattern.

Power Measurements. The objectives of ELINT power-pattern measurements are to obtain precise data on the maximum beam power, total radiated power, antenna gain, and variation in gain (side and back lobe distribution) around the antenna. This requires the use of an airborne or spaceborne measuring platform. In theory, the ELINT approach is the same as that used on the antenna test range; the power density is measured and then converted to radiated power on the basis of the known geometry between the radar antenna and the collection system. In practice, the ELINT operation has all the problems encountered on the test range plus an additional one intrinsic to intelligence collection: The target radars are not cooperative. They may not radiate when the ELINT system is searching for them, and they may not radiate in the direction of the ELINT receiver. These handicaps increase the number of potential sources of error that must be eliminated, minimized, or calibrated.

FISINT. Complex and expensive systems such as missiles and satellites have a large number of instrument readings to transmit. It is impractical to devote a separate transmission link to each reading. Telemetry systems therefore combine the signals from the readings in a process called multiplexing for transmission using a single transmitter. Each signal occupies a channel in the multiplex system. At the receiver, the channels are separated (demultiplexed) and sent to separate displays or recorders.

Some telemetry systems, especially older ones, multiplex by allocating a different part of the radio frequency spectrum to each signal; this technique is known as **frequency division multiplexing**. A more complex, but increasingly popular, approach is **time division multiplexing**, where each signal periodically gets to use the entire frequency bandwidth of the transmitter for a short time interval.

Interpretation of intercepted telemetry is difficult, in part because of what is called the scaling problem. The engineers running the instrumentation know the scales for the readings they receive and which channels of telemetry come from which instrument. The intercepting party must often infer both the nature of the instrument and the scale of the readings from external evidence—correlating the readings with external events such as aircraft or missile altitude or speed.

Merely to have made a few key identifications brings a considerable intelligence benefit, because the telemetry analyst can then relate a current launch to earlier ones and decide whether the launch is one of a series. Also, the comparison of telemetry with previous launches might indicate the test of a new vehicle or a new model of a known missile. Given a fair sample of powered-flight telemetry, an analyst can usually say whether a launch vehicle is liquid- or solid-fueled, whether it has a single burning stage or multiple stages, and what ratio of payload to total weight it probably has. The analyst can do this by looking for characteristic signatures in the different telemetry channels. For example, the velocity profile of a ballistic missile has a characteristic signature: Velocity increases steadily with time as the missile accelerates and then flattens when the motor cuts off. A multiple-stage missile then again increases its velocity when the second stage motor kicks in. These acceleration patterns create a unique signature in the telemetry.

Telemetry can be denied to an opponent by encryption, and digital telemetry that is typically sent by time division multiplexing is particularly amenable to encryption. Encryption denies the collector information on what are called **telemetry internals** (that is, the values of the readings themselves). Encryption therefore forces the collector to rely on what are called **telemetry externals** (that is, changes in the signal due to the flight profile of the vehicle), which provide information about aspects of the vehicle's performance.[34] Using externals, the flight profile can be measured using the multipath technique described later in this chapter.

A Missile Launch Sequence. An example from ballistic missile test telemetry illustrates how FISINT exploitation and analysis works in general.

At some point in the ballistic missile launch sequence, the umbilical cable that links the missile to the launch pad is disconnected. From then on, information about the missile's performance has to be communicated to ground stations by telemetry.

During the missile's flight it transmits telemetry signals to ground stations along its flight path. These signals are relayed to a control center, where all of the measurements being made on board the missile are recorded. The intended recipients of telemetry in the ground station have a telemetry channel assignment key. This key identifies which part of the signal is associated with which kind of measurement, a list of calibrations, and conversion factors for translating a given telemetry value into units of acceleration, pressure, temperature, flow rate, or some other variable.

The telemetry can be intercepted and analyzed by an intelligence service. But initially, the intelligence analyst does not have the channel assignment key. The analyst therefore must identify the channels before making use of the measurements. But certain basic measurements are required on any flight. The propulsion system will always have a measurement of acceleration and one of thrust chamber pressure. Missile attitude, velocity, and acceleration all will be measured and telemetered. Knowing what the readings look like for one's own ballistic missile telemetry allows an analyst to search the intercepted telemetry for similar readings.

So the first step for the analyst is to prepare a probable channel assignment key. He or she then applies the laws of physics and past missile design practice to check the key's validity. A trace suspected of being an acceleration measurement, for example, can be checked against either a theoretical or actual plot of acceleration versus time. After identifying the acceleration, the analyst can make use of the fact that the force producing the acceleration (the rocket thrust) is proportional to the pressure in the thrust chamber. Minor changes in the acceleration record will appear in the thrust chamber pressure and can be used to identify the thrust chamber pressure channel.

If a good sample of telemetry is available, then it is possible to identify all the major measurements. The sample must include a major flight transition period such as engine shutdown. During shutdown, for example, several components on the missile act or react in different ways and with different time periods, creating unique signatures in the telemetry.

One of the most valuable measurements concerns the acceleration of the missile. Assuming that the telemetry is intercepted before first-stage burnout, the trace looks like the example shown in Figure 13.8. One can observe two main burning stages, with the first shutdown occurring at 100 seconds.

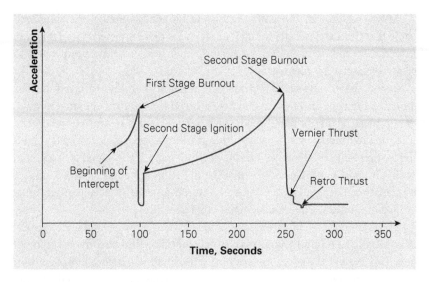

FIGURE 13.8 Typical Missile Acceleration History

The missile then coasts for five seconds until the second stage ignites, and that stage burns for an additional 145 seconds to shutdown. The low plateau in the record after second-stage shutdown indicates that small auxiliary rocket engines used for fine regulation of burnout velocity (vernier engines) operated for 10 seconds after main-engine cutoff. The short negative jump at 270 seconds is caused by the firing of retrorockets to separate the rocket body from the payload.[35]

Using Multipath TDOA to Determine Target Altitude. We've previously talked about multipath as a problem in receiving and geolocating a signal. As noted earlier, it is an especially serious problem in urban environments because the signal can bounce off buildings several times before arriving at the receiver antenna.

But multipath reception can be very useful in FISINT. It can determine the height of an RF emitter such as a missile or aircraft. The difference between time of arrival of a direct signal and a signal reflected from the earth's surface can be used, with some knowledge of the geometry involved, to estimate the height of the emitter, as Figure 13.9 illustrates. The technique can be quite accurate if the reflective surface is smooth (for example, over water), so that specular (mirror-like) reflection is received. It becomes less accurate as the reflection surface becomes rougher; the reflection becomes smeared by a rough surface, so that diffuse reflection occurs. The result is that the signal at the receiver is smeared in time, and it becomes harder to pick out the exact arrival time of the reflected signal.[36]

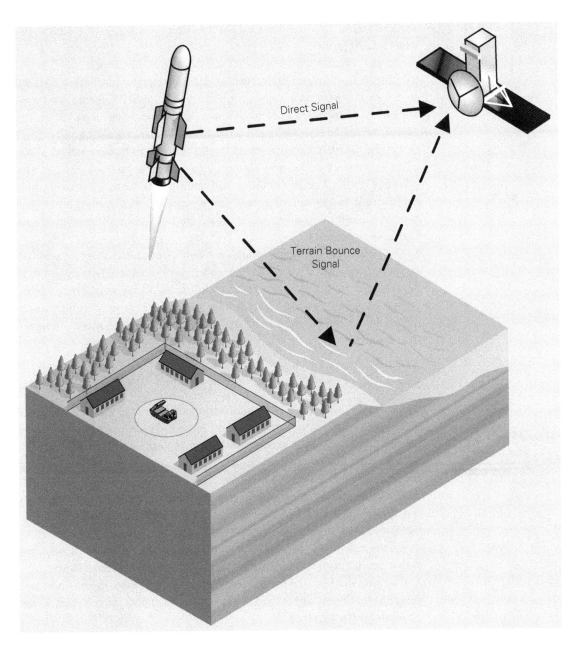

FIGURE 13.9 Use of Multipath Reception to Determine Target Altitude

In tracking an aircraft or a missile using multipath, the TDOA from multipath gives target altitude; the Doppler profile indicates the target movement speed over time. The combination, possibly with the inclusion of angle-of-arrival information, enables intelligence analysts to establish the target's flight profile.[37]

RF MASINT. Atmospheric nuclear testing is very rare; there have been no such tests since China's last atmospheric test in 1980. RF damage and non-nuclear EMP tests are very uncommon, and processing depends on the specific signal. In the case of nuclear EMP, the signal processing and exploitation will identify the location of the test (based on time of arrival of the pulse at various collectors) and provide estimates of burst height and weapons yield. For RF damage and nonnuclear EMP, processing and exploitation is needed to assess the weapons performance. Frequency bandwidth and peak power of the signal are two important measurements that have to be made.

Most unintended emissions are very weak, but sensitive equipment can detect the signals and locate the emitter or use the characteristic signature of the emission to identify the target. In addition to highly sensitive receiving equipment, analysts need highly sophisticated signal processing equipment to deal with unintentional radiation signals and derive useful intelligence from them.

DISSEMINATION

Operational ELINT requires rapid dissemination of the location and identity of targets that have intelligence interest. Technical ELINT usually has a more deliberate dissemination process, and the reporting is usually quite detailed. Because the reporting is used for countermeasures development, it goes to government planners and to hardware developers.

The results of technical ELINT also are used to update an ELINT parameter library. The United States maintains a number of libraries of ELINT signals—one example is called the ELINT parameters list (EPL). If the objective is to track a specific emitter, then the signal parameters that are unique to that emitter need to be identified and placed in a temporary library.

Dissemination of FIS reporting customarily is limited to scientific and technical (S&T) intelligence centers that are responsible for assessing weapons systems performance.

Libraries are a critical part of the FIS process. Once the telemetry channels have been identified with specific onboard sensors, they will be the same in future satellite operations or tests of that missile or aircraft. So telemetry analysts will maintain cheat sheets—keys identifying the purpose of each channel.

The product of battlefield unintended emissions typically is used for operational purposes (locating and destroying targets) rather than for intelligence. Clandestinely collecting unintended emissions for nonmilitary purposes is usually tightly compartmented, and dissemination is limited.

A library of EMP signatures from nuclear tests exists and could be used to evaluate any new atmospheric nuclear test. Signatures for various types of nonnuclear EMP and RF damage weapons also are available. The characteristic RF signatures for vehicles such as tanks and missile transporter-erector-launchers have been measured as well.

Structure

National-level collectors, military field units, and law enforcement organizations all collect OPELINT to serve military and law enforcement customers. The military support fits the definition of mass collection discussed previously. Law enforcement OPELINT collection is more targeted and usually serves immediate tactical rather than intelligence purposes.

Technical ELINT, FISINT, and unintentional radiation all fit the definition of boutique collection. They typically are organizationally separate from OPELINT, being types of targeted collection that support specific intelligence customers.

FISINT and RF MASINT often have the collection phase organizationally separated from the processing, exploitation, and analysis phases. That separation occurs because the same collection systems that are used for ELINT often can collect FISINT and RF MASINT as well. Though processing and exploitation could be handled by the collectors, it usually is better handled by an S&T intelligence center that has specialists in the weapons systems of concern.

Summary

Passive RF sensors used in intelligence usually are called SIGINT collectors and are used to produce RF COMINT, ELINT, and FISINT. Passive sensors also are used to collect RF MASINT.

ELINT includes information extracted through the collection, processing, exploitation, and analysis of signals transmitted by radars, beacons, jammers, missile guidance systems, and altimeters. Most ELINT is conducted against radars and divides broadly into two types: operational and technical.

Passive RF

Operational ELINT involves the intercept and analysis of radar signals in order to locate radars, identify them, and determine their operational status. The product of operational ELINT is called radar order of battle and is used mostly for planning and executing military operations.

Technical ELINT is used to assess a radar's capabilities and performance, to determine the level of technology used in building the radar, and to find weaknesses in the radar to help electronic warfare designers defeat it. It involves either the measurement of radar signal characteristics to a very high order of accuracy or measurements to determine something about a radar's operation that will reveal its detection and tracking capabilities. The highest priority signals for ELINT collection are always new and unidentified signals.

FISINT includes the interception and interpretation of telemetry that is transmitted during missile and aircraft testing. Telemetry can be encrypted to deny the collector information on what are called telemetry internals— the values of the telemetry readings. Encryption forces the collector to rely on what are called telemetry externals—changes in the telemetry signal due to changes in the target's flight profile.

RF MASINT captures and exploits unintentional emissions of radio frequency energy from internal combustion engines, electrical generators, and switches. These emissions are typically weak, but sensitive RF receivers can detect the signals and locate the emitter or use the characteristic signature of the emission to identify the target. RF MASINT also includes collection that is targeted on EMP and RF damage devices.

The two critical components of a SIGINT system are the antennas and receivers. Both involve trade-offs. Antennas would ideally have high gain and cover a large spatial volume with wide frequency bandwidth. Improving any one of these three tends to degrade performance in another. Receivers must trade off among sensitivity, bandwidth, ability to collect many signals simultaneously, dynamic range, resolution, and measurement accuracy. A number of receiver designs exist to optimize one or more of these qualities. As a result, SIGINT systems often use a mix of different antennas and receivers, each designed to collect a specific class of signals.

One of the most valuable contributions of SIGINT sensors is in geolocating and tracking emitters of intelligence interest. The oldest passive RF geolocation technique is DF, which determines the angle of signal arrival. Because electromagnetic waves from a transmitter travel in a straight line, the direction of arrival of the signal is the direction in which the transmitter lies. Spinner antennas, phased arrays, and interferometers can determine the angle of arrival. Two such antennas, well separated, can locate a target on the earth. Three can locate a target in the air or in space.

Another technique for geolocating a radar signal depends on the fact that EM signals travel at the speed of light. This speed can be used to geolocate the source of a signal by measuring the time difference of arrival at widely separated receivers. It is critical to be able to identify specific pulses from the radar for TDOA to work.

A third technique for geolocation depends on the fact that signals emitted or received by moving targets have an associated Doppler shift that can be used to determine target location or speed of movement. Frequency difference of arrival is a technique similar to TDOA in that one estimates the location of a radio emitter based on observations from widely separated points. It differs from TDOA in that the FDOA observation points must be in relative motion with respect to each other or with respect to the emitter.

A fourth geolocation technique requires the presence of an RF tag on the target. These tags are often concealed to prevent removal. They typically include a GPS receiver that determines the target's location and transmits the information to a remote receiver.

Because geolocation accuracy is of high importance, a number of techniques are used to improve it. Geolocation errors can be reduced by using additional SIGINT collectors above the minimum necessary to geolocate the target signal. Another method for improving accuracy is to combine several geolocation techniques; TDOA and FDOA are sometimes used together to improve location accuracy. Angle-of-arrival information can be combined with either to help resolve ambiguities in the target location.

NOTES

1. Carey Sublette, "Report on the 1979 Vela Incident" (September 1, 2001), accessed 23 September 2012 at http://nuclearweaponarchive.org/Safrica/Vela.html.
2. P. Hyberg, "Spread Spectrum Radar Principles and Ways of Jamming It," (Swedish) Defense Research Institute (December 1980).
3. David Adamy, *EW 101: A First Course in Electronic Warfare* (Boston, MA: Artech House, 2001), 59.
4. Barry Manz, "Is EW Ready for AESA (and Vice Versa)?," *The Journal of Electronic Defense* (Washington, DC, September 2012), 31.
5. Michael R. Morris, "Wullenweber Antenna Arrays," accessed 23 September 2012 at www.navycthistory.com/WullenweberArticle.txt.
6. Photo from www.navycthistory.com/craig_rudy_various.html, accessed 23 September 2012, used with permission.
7. Li Tao, Jiang Wenli, and Zhou Yiyu, "TDOA Location with High PRF Signals Based on Three Satellites," *Chengdu Dianzi Xinxi Duikang Jishu* (July 1, 2004), 7.

8. Ibid.

9. Pan Qinge, Yan Meng, and Liao Guisheng, "Joint Location by Time Difference of Arrival and Frequency Difference of Arrival at Multiple Stations," *Heifei Leida Kexue Yu Jishu* (December 1, 2005).

10. Huai-Jing Du and Jim P. Y. Lee, "Simulation of Multi-platform Geolocation Using a Hybrid TDOA/AOA Method," Technical memo, Defence R&D Canada TM 2004–256 (December 2004), accessed 23 September 2012 at http://pubs.drdc .gc.ca/PDFS/unc33/p523132.pdf.

11. Louis A. Stilp, **"Time Difference of Arrival Technology for Locating Narrowband Cellular Signals,"** *Proceedings of SPIE,* 2602 No. 134–144 (1996).

12. Li Tao, Jiang Wenli, and Zhou Yiyu, "TDOA Location with High PRF Signals Based on Three Satellites," 7.

13. ERA Radar Technology, "VERA-E," accessed 23 September 2012 at http://www .radiolokatory.cz/pdf/vera-e.pdf.

14. Pan Qinge, Yan Meng, and Liao Guisheng, "Joint Location by Time Difference of Arrival and Frequency Difference of Arrival at Multiple Stations."

15. K. C. Ho and Y. T. Chan, "Geolocation of a Known Altitude Object from TDOA and FDOA Measurements," *IEEE Transactions on Aerospace and Electronic Systems,* Vol. 33, No. 3 (July 1997), 770–783.

16. Ibid.

17. Ibid.

18. Huai-Jing Du and Jim P. Y. Lee, "Simulation of Multi-platform Geolocation Using a Hybrid TDOA/AOA Method."

19. Pan Qinge, Yan Meng, and Liao Guisheng, "Joint Location by Time Difference of Arrival and Frequency Difference of Arrival at Multiple Stations."

20. Huai-Jing Du and Jim P. Y. Lee, "Simulation of Multi-platform Geolocation Using a Hybrid TDOA/AOA Method."

21. Layne D. Lommen, David O. Edewaard, and Henry E. Halladay, "Reference Beacon Methods and Apparatus for TDOA/FDOA Geolocation," USPTO Application No. 20070236389 (October 10, 2007).

22. Technovelgy.com, "RFID Tags,"accessed 23 September 2012 at www.tech novelgy.com/ct/Technology-Article.asp?ArtNum=50.

23. Jeffrey T. Richelson, *The U.S. Intelligence Community,* 5th ed. (Boulder, CO: Westview Press, 2008), 25.

24. GpsSpying.com, "Mobile Phone Tracking System via the GPS-TRACK Satellite Network," accessed 23 September 2012 at http://www.gpsspying.com/.

25. Department of Homeland Security, "When Your Ship Comes In" (July 2007), accessed 23 September 2012 at http://www.dhs.gov/when-your-ship-comes.

26. Ian Easton and Mark A. Stokes, "China's Electronic Intelligence (ELINT) Satellite Developments," Project 2049 Institute, February 23, 2011, accessed 13 September 2012 at http://project2049.net/documents/china_electronic_intelligence_ elint_satellite_developments_easton_stokes.pdf.

27. CNES report, "Mapping Radar Stations from Space," accessed 13 September 2012 at www.cnes.fr/web/CNES-en/5940-elisa.php.

28. Federation of American Scientists, "Exocet AM39/mm.40," accessed 13 September 2012 at www.fas.org/man/dod-101/sys/missile/row/exocet.htm.

29. Nickens Okello, "Emitter Geolocation with Multiple UAVs," *Proceedings of the 9th International Conference on Information Fusion* (Florence, Italy, July 10–13, 2006).

30. Jeffrey P. Rhodes, "The Machines of Special Ops," *Air Force Magazine* (August 1988), accessed 28 August 2012 at http://www.airforce-magazine.com/Magazine Archive/Pages/1988/August%201988/0888sof.aspx.

31. Adamy, *EW 101,* 112–120.

32. Richard G. Wiley, *ELINT: The Interception and Analysis of Radar Signals* (Boston, MA: Artech House, 2006), Chapter 13.

33. Adamy, *EW 101,* 82.

34. Angelo Codevilla, *Informing Statecraft* (New York: The Free Press, 1992), 122.

35. David S. Brandwein, "Telemetry Analysis," accessed 13 September 2012 at https://www.cia.gov/library/center-for-the-study-of-intelligence/kent-csi/v018n04/html/v08i4a03p_0001.htm.

36. Yang Shihai, Hu Weidong, Wan Jianwei, and Zhou Liangzhu, "Radar Detection of Low Altitude Target in Multipath," *Beijing Dianzi yu Xinxi Xuebao* (April 1, 2002), 492.

37. Ibid.

14. Acoustic and Seismic Sensing

The previous chapters have focused on electromagnetic (EM) sensing, which was defined to include radio frequency (RF) sensing in frequencies up through the millimeter wave band and optical sensing in wavelengths from infrared through ultraviolet.

Signatures of intelligence value are also collected in the acoustic spectrum in the audible (above 20 Hz) and infrasound (below 20 Hz) parts of the spectrum. Typically, this collection depends on the unintentional emission of sound waves created by some kind of disturbance.

- Some acoustic sensors detect sound traveling through the atmosphere or in the ground near the surface and therefore function only at comparatively short ranges (a few meters to a few kilometers). The intelligence product of such collection is usually called ACOUSTINT. The term seismic sensing is usually applied to detecting sound that travels through the earth.

- Acoustic intelligence derived from underwater sound is usually called ACINT. ACINT relies on a class of acoustic sensors that detect sound in water. Sound travels much better in water than in air. Underwater sound created by ships and submarines can be detected at distances of several hundred kilometers.

- A special category of seismic sensing is called teleseismic sensing. The product is sometimes referred to as geophysical intelligence, though that term is also often used to include ACOUSTINT and ACINT. Teleseismic sensing involves the collection, processing, and exploitation of infrasound that travels deep in the earth. Depending on the strength of the source, such infrasound can be detected at distances of thousands of kilometers.

Function

Acoustic sensors are used both in military operations and in intelligence to identify and track ships, submarines, land vehicles, and airborne platforms. They can locate these targets and determine their speed and direction of motion based on sound transmitted through the air or earth. Such sensors can be readily deployed and disguised in all types of terrain.[1] Most of the sensing of sound in air or underground finds tactical military or law enforcement use because detection only can be made at short ranges. Border control, for example, makes use of the sensing of earth vibrations due to footsteps.

Underwater sound sensing also often is done at short ranges for tactical naval purposes. But underwater sound can also be detected at very long ranges, so naval intelligence organizations have used acoustic systems for years to identify and track submarines in open ocean areas.

Seismic sensing has been used to detect and characterize explosions, including nuclear device testing. These infrasound waves can travel intercontinental distances underground or underwater, and their collection and analysis support monitoring of nuclear test ban treaties.

Process

PLANNING

Short-range acoustic sensing or seismic sensing requires some advance planning. In the case of monitoring vehicle or foot traffic, the sensors must be emplaced close to likely areas of movement. Sonar and sonobouys have to be deployed close to likely ship or submarine traffic areas—often at choke points such as straits. Clandestine collection sensors emplaced in denied areas should be designed to fit in their environment and to have a low probability of discovery.

Long-range acoustic and seismic sensing is more of a 24/7 operation, with arrays of acoustic sensors monitoring continuously for signatures of intelligence or operational interest.

COLLECTION

Acoustic collection works best under conditions where sound carries well over large distances, as sound does underwater and infrasound does in the earth under certain conditions. For example, the use of passive sonar to obtain the signatures of submarines and to locate them is well known. The submarine's turbines, propellers, and other onboard machinery generate acoustic noise that can be detected and used for identification at ranges of many kilometers in water.

But sensing often is done at very short ranges for intelligence purposes. Figure 14.1 illustrates the general ranges at which sound and infrasound sensing are carried out at different sound and infrasound frequencies. Following is a discussion of some of the types of signatures that are encountered and how they are used.

Acoustic and Seismic Sensing. The sensing of atmospheric sound for military purposes has a long history, but until World War I it relied on the use of our unaided ears. World War I saw the first deployment of acoustic sensors on the battlefield—their purpose was to locate enemy artillery by triangulating on the sound of cannon fire.[2]

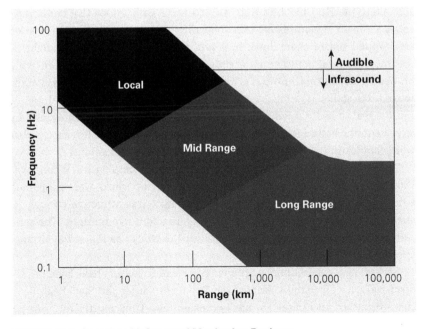

FIGURE 14.1 Sound and Infrasound Monitoring Regimes

Since then, battlefield intelligence has made increasing use of short-range sound or infrasound collection. Land and air vehicles such as trucks, tanks, helicopters, and unmanned aerial vehicles (UAVs) typically have a continuous acoustic power spectrum that extends across the audible range. Many such vehicles also show distinct narrow-band acoustic signatures (for example, from the noise of a gasoline or diesel engine and the sound of rotating tires or tank treads).

Most of these acoustic signatures are only detectable at short ranges, on the order of a few kilometers or less. But the launches of large ballistic missiles can be detected by acoustic or infrasound detection at greater distances. The acoustic signature from a Scud missile launch was successfully measured at a range of 27 kilometers in the frequency band between 1 Hz and 25 Hz.[3]

Under favorable atmospheric conditions, sound will propagate in the air for relatively long distances. Usually, this happens when a temperature inversion exists near the ground (that is, when temperature increases with altitude, instead of the normal decrease). Sound also will propagate farther over water or downwind.

Many of the techniques currently used for acoustic and seismic collection on the battlefield were developed in the previously discussed Igloo White program during the Vietnam War. U.S. aircraft dropped several types of sensors along the Ho Chi Minh trail, all equipped with radios that communicated acoustic signatures back to specially equipped aircraft. One type of air-dropped sensor came down on a camouflaged parachute and caught in the trees, where it could monitor sound in the area. A seismic sensor (with no parachute) buried into the ground due to impact. The antenna, which looked like stalks of weeds, was the only part showing above ground. Many sensors had to be dropped, because not all of them landed favorably, and in any event, the batteries only lasted for a few weeks. Igloo White sensors also were clandestinely deployed by ground teams in some locations.

The sensors tracked the direction and speed of passing truck convoys. From those data, it was easy to determine where the trucks were going and when they were likely to get there. If the target was attractive enough to attack, strike aircraft could be on the scene in about five minutes. The sensors continuously updated the location of the trucks as the strike aircraft approached.[4]

Several new generations of acoustic and seismic sensors have been developed and used since the Vietnam War. The Steel Rattler and Steel Eagle sensors, discussed in Chapter 8, are two examples. They mostly rely on the same techniques used in Vietnam: air drops or ground emplacement and concealment to avoid discovery once in place.

Most acoustic sensors are simply microphones optimized to work in a specific environment (air, underground, underwater) and in a specific part of the acoustic spectrum shown in Figure 14.1. Typically, an array of microphones, rather than a single microphone, is used to permit geolocation. Figure 14.2 shows an example of such an array for acoustic monitoring, used to detect and track low-flying aircraft.[5]

Seismic sensing is the detection and measurement of sound waves that travel through the earth. A seismic signal or wave is created by earth vibration. Both man-made and natural activity can cause earth vibration; the vibration may be slight (a man walking on the earth or sound impact on the earth from an aircraft flying overhead) or very strong (an earthquake or large underground explosion).

FIGURE 14.2 **Array of Acoustic Sensors**

Most seismic sensing uses a device called the geophone—a type of microphone optimized to operate underground and sense in the infrasound and low-frequency sound regions. Figure 14.3 shows the design. Sound and infrasound waves striking the cylinder cause it to move with respect to the magnet that it surrounds. The movement induces an electric current in the wire coil on the cylinder.

Geophones are simple but highly sensitive devices for detecting ground motion; they have been used by seismologists and geophysicists for decades. They find wide use in the oil and gas exploration industry. However, a geophone is typically only used for higher frequency (4 Hz to 400 Hz) seismic sensing, generally at relatively short ranges. Its performance is poor at the very low frequencies (below 1 Hz) that characterize the long-range teleseismic signals discussed later.

Recent technology advances have produced seismic sensors that are more capable for intelligence use than the geophone. Micro electromechanical systems (MEMs) technology has provided both seismic and acoustic sensors that are compact and highly sensitive.[6] Another such sensor uses a fiber-optic cable buried about 18 inches underground. Earth movement will cause slight bends in the cable, and these bends change the amount of laser light that is backscattered from the cable. Computer algorithms then are used to locate and identify the source of the vibration or earth movement.

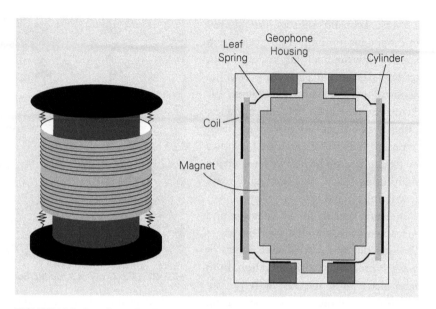

FIGURE 14.3 Geophone Design

The sensor can identify foot traffic and specific vehicles and track their movements.[7]

Much seismic sensing is done at short ranges, usually to support military operations. Following is a discussion of some intelligence applications of seismic sensing.

Monitoring of Foot and Vehicle Traffic. At short ranges, seismic sensors can detect and often identify specific types of foot or vehicle traffic. Their use for battlefield intelligence in the 1960s during the Vietnam War was described earlier. The geophones on the Ho Chi Minh trail relayed data and information to a command center, where analysts converted the data into targeting information for use by combat units.[8]

Monitoring of Buildings and Underground Facilities. Geophones can monitor activity in nearby buildings or underground facilities. The greatest intelligence value from this specialized microphone occurs when the geophone can be placed directly in the building structure—in a wall, structural beam, electrical conduit, or air duct. The geophone picks up mechanical vibrations directly from the building structure and transmits them out of the facility via wire or secure wireless communication. The technique depends on the ability of structural objects in a room to pick up sound (such as voice and machine noise) and mechanically vibrate. Geophones therefore can be used to obtain acoustic signatures that have intelligence value. Their use to obtain communications intelligence (COMINT) from speech that occurs in the building was discussed in Chapter 4.

If it is not possible to emplace a geophone within a building or underground facility, an array of widely spaced geophones in the vicinity of the building can be used both to locate the source of a sound and to identify the device producing the sound. It is well known that all mechanical devices, such as motors and gears, emit acoustic signals. It is possible to identify an acoustic source based on its signal spectrum. The spectral range of many building and underground activities and of machinery is in the range of 10 to 250 Hz.

Acoustic Imaging. Acoustic imaging in intelligence uses much the same phenomena that doctors use to create ultrasound images of the human body. Such imaging already is done in exploration seismology, where explosions or vibrating machines at the earth's surface create waves that reflect or refract off deep structures. A geophone array collects the reflected signals so that an image of geological formations can be created. Such active sensing is obvious to those in the area, so this is unlikely to be useful for intelligence purposes. But it may be possible to clandestinely image underground facilities based on the passive monitoring of acoustic emissions from both stationary and moving equipment within such facilities. The technique requires a good understanding of the geology in the area. An array of passive sensors can then coherently sum the data received to obtain an image of the source that is similar to the image formation process used in seismic exploration.[9]

Underwater Acoustics. Surface ships and submarines emit high levels of underwater noise that can be detected and tracked at ranges of many kilometers. This specialized area of unintentional emissions intelligence is often called ACINT, as noted earlier. Sound generally propagates farther in water than in air and about five times faster in water than in air. Underwater noise is generated by several sources:

- Machinery vibration, which dominates at low speed
- Water flow over the vessel's hull, which becomes more important at vessel speeds above about 10 knots
- Propeller rotation, which generates a signal at the blade turning rate
- Propeller cavitation, which occurs when a high propeller speed creates bubbles in the water
- Crew activity

Acoustic and Seismic Sensing

Underwater sound is collected by a passive device called a **hydrophone** (essentially a microphone that is designed to operate most effectively underwater). Hydrophones are used for both short-range (sonar) and long-range sensing.

Sonar (sound navigation and ranging) is a well-known technology; it has been used by sea creatures for communication and object detection for millions of years. During World War I, the need to detect submarines resulted in major advances in both active and passive sonar technology. Hydrophones subsequently were mounted on ships and submarines. Sonobuoys, first developed by the British in 1944, could be dropped by an aircraft to remotely identify and track submarines. A sonobuoy is simply a hydrophone attached to a flotation device (buoy); the buoy carries a radio transmitter that transmits a received sound signature to the aircraft.

The signature shown in Figure 14.8 was collected at a relatively short range, as many acoustic signatures are. But acoustic signals also travel to great distances in oceans within a natural waveguide, sometimes called a sound channel. The sound channel is a layer in the oceans, about 1 kilometer deep, that is somewhat isolated from the ocean layers above and below. Once in the channel, sound tends to stay in it and travel long distances without significant amounts getting to the surface. Sound created at the surface (from ships and waves) does not easily get into the sound channel. But low-frequency sound generated by submarines readily enters the sound channel and can be detected at long ranges.

The operational challenge in underwater acoustics is to detect the signature of a ship or submarine in a very difficult environment. Underneath the surface, the sea is a noisy environment. This background noise can make it difficult to receive an acoustic signal. For example, the signal can be disrupted or even blocked by changes in water temperature as the signal travels. Other factors, including variations in depth, salinity, and the nature of the seabed, also affect the propagation of sound under water. In relatively shallow water such as that of the Baltic and North Seas, acoustic propagation is a very complex process, and signatures are often very difficult to obtain. But because underwater sound can propagate in so many different modes, it is possible to collect signatures at both short and long ranges using a combination of sensors.

In the mid-1950s, the U.S. Navy took advantage of the sound channel, installing an underwater surveillance system to track submarines at long distances. The **sound surveillance system (SOSUS)** is a multibillion-dollar network of hydrophone arrays mounted on the seafloor throughout the Atlantic and Pacific oceans. These hydrophone arrays listen to the low-frequency sounds in the sound channel, record them, and transmit the data via undersea cables back to shore stations for analysis. A hydrophone array obtains high sensitivity in the same way that a radio-frequency phased array does. It adds the signals from the desired direction while subtracting signals from other directions. The array is steered electronically by adding the signals received from each hydrophone in a specific time sequence.

A hydrophone array can also be towed behind a ship or submarine instead of being fixed to the ocean bottom. Most commonly, such an array of hydrophones is towed in a line behind a vessel, but two- or three-dimensional arrays are also used. The **integrated undersea surveillance system (IUSS)**, which incorporates SOSUS, also includes mobile acoustic arrays that cue operations of tactical antisubmarine warfare forces. IUSS provides the U.S. Navy with its primary means of detecting and identifying foreign submarines in the open ocean.[10]

Figure 14.4 illustrates how a hydrophone array works.[11] The sound from a submarine arrives at each hydrophone at different times, depending on the direction from the array to the submarine. Processing the signals allows the direction to be determined. As the figure suggests, acoustic processing involves dealing with seconds (or fractions thereof) in the time scale; this contrasts to radar and electronic intelligence (ELINT) signal processing, where time differences are measured to nanoseconds.

Teleseismic Sensing. A teleseismic signal is the term used to describe a seismic signal that is created by a strong disturbance and is recorded far from its source. For detecting the lower infrasonic frequencies of teleseismic signals, a seismometer is used.[12] Like the geophone, the seismometer is a type of accelerometer, but it functions in a lower-frequency range. It typically operates over a broad bandwidth (for example, .01 to 50 Hz) and has a high dynamic range (that is, it is sensitive to a wide range of signal intensities).

Two types of events generally can be detected at very long ranges: earthquakes and underground explosions. The primary intelligence concern is the detection and analysis of underground explosions, especially those related to nuclear weapons testing.

Underground explosions can be reliably detected and can be identified at yields of 0.1 kiloton (100 tons of TNT equivalent) in hard rock if conducted anywhere in Europe, Asia, North Africa, or North America. In some locations of interest, such as Novaya Zemlya in Russia, detection of a 0.01-kiloton (10 tons) explosion is possible. Depending on the medium in which the explosion occurs, the signature could vary by a factor of 100; water-saturated soil gives a strong signature, while loose dry soil gives a very weak signature. Underwater explosions provide the strongest signatures;

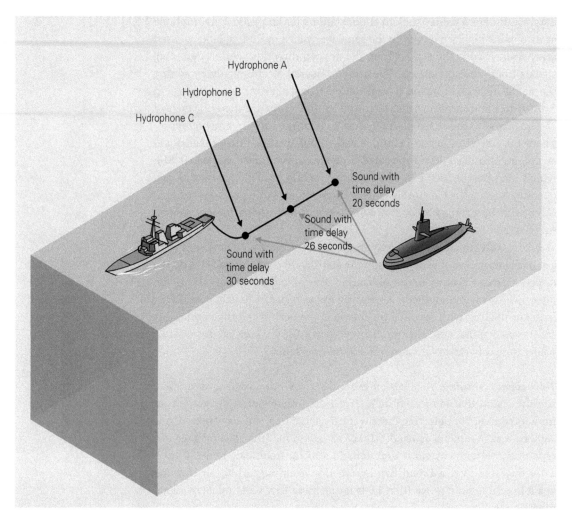

FIGURE 14.4 Towed Hydrophone Array

they can be reliably detected and identified at yields down to 0.001 kiloton (1 ton) or even lower.[13]

The two basic approaches to sensing underground (or underwater) explosions are to sense midrange seismic waves or long-range seismic waves, as Figure 14.5 indicates. The difference in range is due to differences in the way that the waves propagate through the earth. Seismic signals are traditionally called either teleseismic waves or regional waves, depending on the distance at which they are observed. Seismic waves propagate either as

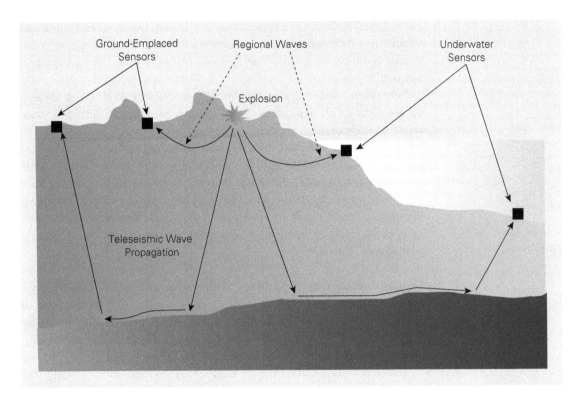

FIGURE 14.5 Seismic Wave Sensing Paths

teleseismic waves through the earth's deep interior, emerging at distances greater than about 1,500 kilometers, or as regional waves (which are similar to the ripples on the surface of a pond). Because teleseismic waves propagate with little loss over ranges from 2,000 to 9,000 kilometers, they are suited to monitoring a large country from stations deployed outside that country's borders. Teleseismic waves were the basis of most U.S. monitoring of foreign nuclear tests prior to the 1990s.[14]

In the decade following the August 1949 Soviet nuclear test, the United States established a system for infrasound detection and deployed a network of seismic stations to monitor underground testing. Over the years, the Soviet Union conducted a number of tests at known testing areas, and these were relatively easy to identify.

The first Soviet underground test was detected in 1961 in an area some 40 nautical miles south of the atmospheric nuclear test site located at Semipalatinsk, in Kazakhstan. Prior to this event, the area in question was not a known test site. However, the area in which the event occurred was not an earthquake zone, was located close to a known test area, and contained sizable mountains suitable for underground testing. The intelligence community therefore concluded that this was indeed a probable underground test site.[15]

Teleseismic sensing can also detect nonnuclear explosions at long ranges. Very small explosions in the deep oceans can be detected thousands of kilometers away. Such explosions create a unique pulse in the recorded signal, caused by the gases that briefly expand and then contract around the explosion. Because acoustic waves also transform into seismic waves when they strike the ocean bottom, the oceans can be effectively monitored by a combination of underwater acoustic and seismic networks. Monitoring sound waves in the oceans is a well-developed discipline, primarily as a result of the creation of acoustic systems to detect submarines as discussed earlier.[16]

Geolocating Acoustic and Seismic Sources. Two techniques are commonly used to geolocate an acoustic or seismic source: measuring the direction of arrival and measuring the time difference of arrival. Both depend on having at least two widely separated sensors to do the geolocation, and both resemble the geolocation techniques used for RF signal geolocation.

The technique of measuring the angle of arrival dates back to World War I, as noted earlier. Several European countries developed acoustic arrays to measure the direction of arrival of sound from artillery fire.[17] Two such arrays that were well separated could triangulate on the source of the sound, much as angle of arrival measurement does for RF signals intelligence. The technique works for atmospheric, underwater, and underground sound geolocation.

The second geolocation method depends on accurate measurement of the time of arrival of the sound again at widely spaced sensors. The time delays measured by such a sensor array allow one to triangulate on the source and pinpoint the location of the noise. The technique is very similar to the time difference of arrival (TDOA) method discussed in Chapter 13, with one very important difference. As noted earlier, the speed of EM signals can be assumed to be the speed of light; it is not as simple with sound waves.

The problem is that the velocity of underground sound propagation varies greatly. In soil, it typically is 500 meters per second; in solid rock it is 5,000 meters per second. Even in the atmosphere, the speed of sound varies, though not as much as in the earth. Underwater sound speed is the most predictable, around 1,500 meters per second, but it also varies, increasing with increasing pressure, temperature, and salinity.

So, identifying the source of a sound based on time of arrival can be a challenge. Furthermore, it is difficult to determine the depth in the earth or ocean of a sound source using a sensor array that is located near the surface. To obtain a source depth, the array must be run down a vertical borehole in the earth or deployed vertically in the ocean.

PROCESSING AND EXPLOITATION

Battlefield Acoustics. A number of identification techniques are being developed to support what is sometimes called battlefield acoustics, emphasizing processing and exploitation of acoustic or seismic signatures at frequencies higher than 10 Hz. But these same techniques can be used for short-range intelligence collection throughout the acoustic spectrum between a fraction of a Hz and a few hundred Hz.

Processing and exploitation depend on being able to pull the signature of interest out of the other sounds in the atmosphere or earth. In the desert,

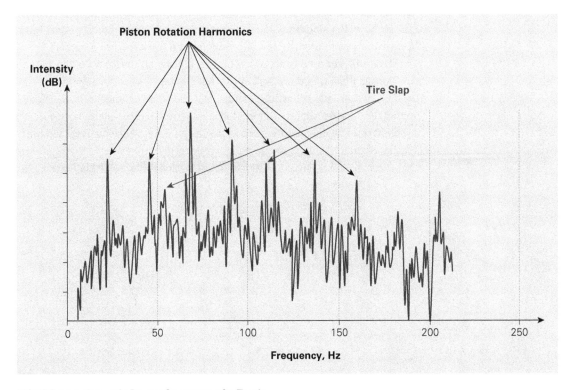

FIGURE 14.6 Acoustic Power Spectrum of a Truck

this may not be a serious problem, but in the jungle or in an urban area, it can be difficult. The challenge in processing and analyzing the Igloo White acoustic signatures was not in detecting the people and the trucks on the Ho Chi Minh trail; it was in separating out the false alarms generated by wind, rain, thunder, earth tremors, and animals.[18]

Processing relies heavily on spectral analysis to separate signatures of intelligence interest from this clutter. Figure 14.6 shows the acoustic signature of a large truck along with a background of other noise sources.[19] It contains significant power in the acoustic spectrum from above 200 Hz down to about 25 Hz. There are distinct narrowband features at harmonic frequencies representing the rotary motion of the engine's cylinders and the periodic slap of slightly asymmetric tires as they roll along the ground. Narrowband features such as these can be used in signal-processing algorithms to enhance detectability and allow identification of the vehicle type.

In the case of moving vehicles with sharp acoustic spikes like those shown in Figure 14.6, one can use the Doppler shift of one or more of these features to obtain a radial velocity measurement. With multiple sonic detectors at different locations, the vehicle's direction of travel and range can be estimated. Furthermore, the amount of detail present in the signature could permit intelligence analysts to identify specific vehicles and track their movements.[20]

Figure 14.7 shows a comparison of acoustic signatures for a Boeing 747, an A-7 Corsair fighter, and a Black Hawk helicopter. In general, each type of jet engine has a unique acoustic signature, but the same jet engine, in a different aircraft, will have a slightly different signature due to differences in the aircraft structure or in engine maintenance, allowing an intelligence analyst to identify specific aircraft. Helicopters are even easier to identify. Note in the figure the characteristic spiked signature associated with helicopter rotor blades.[21]

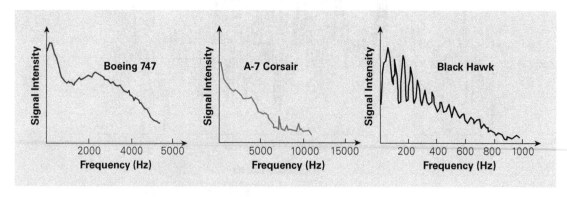

FIGURE 14.7 Comparison of Aircraft and Helicopter Acoustic Signatures

Underwater Acoustics. Ship (including submarine) identification relies on analysis of the sound produced when the ship is under way, especially the vibration produced by its main and auxiliary engines and the sound produced by the propeller revolving. The combination of these noises comprises the ship's acoustic signature. Each ship theoretically has its own unique acoustic signature, a sort of sonic fingerprint similar to those discussed earlier for aircraft and vehicles. These sonic signatures can be used for identification purposes. The identification is made by comparing the signal, recorded by means of hydrophones, with a previously recorded signature. Once a library of such signatures has been developed, subsequent collection and analysis of a signature can provide valuable information regarding vessel classification, identification, activities, and capability.

Ships of identical design, built by the same shipyard, may have almost identical characteristics and thus very similar acoustic signatures. But by using fine-grain measurements of the signatures, an intelligence analyst can differentiate the two ships. The problem is that a ship's acoustic signature changes over time and under different conditions. When a ship's load changes, so does its draft; this changes the acoustic signature. The ship's signature also changes as a result of age, damage, and ship modifications. Some experts believe that the acoustic signature should be measured and recorded every six months to make reliable identification possible.[22]

The spectrogram in Figure 14.8 shows the acoustic signature of the large National Oceanic and Atmospheric Administration (NOAA) ship *Ronald H. Brown* as it approached a hydrophone site in the equatorial Pacific Ocean. The horizontal, continuous, yellow-colored lines, or bands of noise, are created by the rotation of the propeller blades. In the figure, strong lines occur at 21, 35, and 42 Hz. The military routinely uses the characteristics of these blade lines to identify ship characteristics and class, and often individual vessels.[23]

Seismic and Teleseismic Intelligence. Because there are so many seismic events, and because the main objective of seismic intelligence is to detect nuclear testing, the first step is to use the signature information to screen events (that is, to confirm that an event either is particularly suspicious or appears not to have features associated with a nuclear explosion).

- Events are initially screened based on their location. Earthquakes are very rare in most regions of the world—across most of Russia, for example. Any seismic signal from such a region will get careful scrutiny.

Acoustic and Seismic Sensing

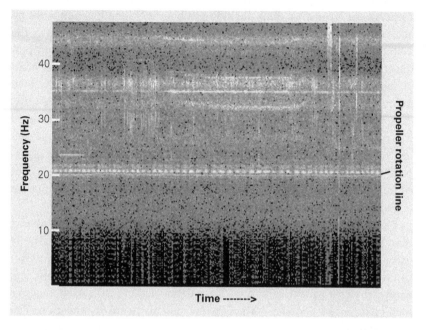

FIGURE 14.8 Spectrogram of a Surface Ship

• Events are then screened based on their depth. For example, an event may have its depth estimated with high confidence as 50 kilometers below the surface. It is highly unlikely that a nuclear detonation would occur below 10 kilometers depth, so such an event would be screened out.

• If the event appears to occur at a shallow depth in a region not known for earthquakes, the next step is to closely examine the signature. This requires a signature library based on past events. In an area where earthquakes are common (such as in much of China), an archive of the earthquake signatures is gradually being built up by monitoring stations.[24] As a result, there exists a large population of previous earthquake signatures against which to compare the signals of a new event.

One signature problem that is not easily solved is that of distinguishing chemical from nuclear explosions. The two have identical seismic signatures. Seismic sensing alone therefore cannot distinguish between them. Large chemical explosions are frequently connected with canal and dam construction. But if the yield is large enough (tens of kilotons or more), there is no question of an explosion's nuclear nature. For lower-yield explosions, some collateral evidence has to be brought to bear to sort out the ambiguity.[25]

Once the detections from a seismic event have been associated and an accurate location estimate has been obtained, the next step in monitoring is that of event identification. This requires close analysis of the event signature and comparison with the signatures in a signature library.

Regional waves are of several types, all propagating only at shallow depths (less than 100 kilometers). These waves typically do not propagate to teleseismic distances. They are affected by the geology of the earth's crust and uppermost mantle; this geology varies greatly around the globe. As a result, regional waves are more complex and harder to interpret than teleseismic waves. Regional wave intensities recorded up to about 1,200 kilometers from a shallow source are typically greater than teleseismic wave intensities recorded at distances greater than 1,800 kilometers. Teleseismic signals from sub-kiloton explosions are often too weak to be detected, but regional signals from such explosions are detectable.[26]

Between 1961 and 1989, the Soviets conducted 340 underground nuclear tests at their Semipalatinsk test site. These tests were mostly detected at the time by Western seismologists using teleseismic signals. After the breakup of the Soviet Union, archives of regional signals from Central Asia became openly available. An investigation of those signals revealed 26 additional nuclear explosions at Semipalatinsk, most of them sub-kiloton, that had not been recognized using teleseismic signals.[27]

Because seismic sensors have very low detection thresholds, a large number of seismic events are detected and analyzed each year. More than 7,000 earthquakes occur worldwide with magnitudes greater than or equal to 4, and about 60,000 with magnitudes greater than or equal to 3, in a year.[28] The challenge is to sort through the tens of thousands of signals collected by the network each day and to collate all the signals that are associated with the same seismic source. The directional sensing capabilities of the International Monitoring System (IMS) stations help in this process of sorting out real signals from false alarms.

A seismic event anywhere in the vicinity of Semipalatinsk was, and still is, presumed to be a nuclear test unless shown otherwise. The same is true of Novaya Zemlya, where the Soviets are known to have conducted five underground nuclear tests, the first in 1964. Seismic events detected at Novaya Zemlya always receive close intelligence scrutiny because of the site's past history of atmospheric testing, the relative lack of seismic activity in the area, and the presence of sizable mountain peaks suitable for underground testing. The Soviets confirmed the site's use as a test area by detonating there, in the fall of 1966, their largest underground nuclear test of about 1 megaton.[29]

The regional waves, as noted earlier, are of different types. The main two types are called **P waves** and **S waves**. P (for pressure) waves are compressional waves, similar to sound waves in the air. S (for shear) waves are transverse

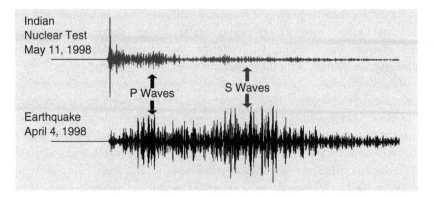

FIGURE 14.9 Comparison of Earthquake and Indian Nuclear Test Seismograms

waves; that is, they move from side to side or up and down, like waves on the sea surface. Because underground explosions compress the surrounding earth, they radiate seismic P waves efficiently. In contrast, earthquakes result from sliding or rupture along a buried fault surface and therefore create the transverse motions of S waves. Explosions will create strong P waves and weak S waves, while earthquakes will create weak P waves and strong S waves. P waves can be identified because they travel faster and are therefore the first to arrive at the monitoring stations.

Signature analysis therefore relies on a comparison of the intensity ratio between different types of seismic waves, using the P waves and S waves to distinguish between explosions and earthquakes.[30] Figure 14.9 shows how significant the difference can be. At the top of the figure is the seismic signature taken from India's nuclear test of May 11, 1998. The signature was recorded at a monitoring station at Nilore, Pakistan. At the bottom is an earthquake measured at the same station. The differences in the P and S waves from the two events are clearly seen.[31]

DISSEMINATION

Battlefield acoustics typically are used for operational rather than intelligence purposes, and so dissemination is very rapid and directly to combat units. The products from Steel Rattler and Steel Eagle sensors described in Chapter 8 exemplify the approach. Information acquired by Steel Rattler in the field is transmitted in small packets by a built-in low-power satellite communication system. Steel Rattler uses advanced acoustic and seismic detection algorithms to categorize and identify various heavy vehicles down to the number of cylinders in the engine. The resulting analysis is compared against an onboard library of known vehicles and a statistical match is determined. Several sensors working together can track the vehicle movement. [32]

The importance of obtaining good signature libraries for EM sensing was discussed in preceding chapters. Acoustic and seismic signature exploitation for intelligence also depends on having good signature libraries. But separate libraries are maintained for each of the major sensor types in this chapter. In the United States, the Army maintains battlefield acoustic and seismic signature libraries. The Navy maintains the underwater acoustic signatures. And the International Monitoring System (IMS) Data Center, discussed below, maintains a teleseismic signature library.

Structure

Because the primary purpose of underwater sound sensing is to identify and locate ships and submarines, this is considered a naval mission, and that is where it is organizationally placed.

The U.S. Navy reportedly uses specially configured attack submarines to obtain the acoustic signatures of foreign submarines. The program reportedly began in 1959, targeted on obtaining a signature library of Soviet submarines. After the end of the Cold War, the Navy program was expanded to include obtaining the acoustic signatures of all potential threat submarines worldwide. After 9/11, cargo vessels entering the United States became a matter of concern because of the possibility that a ship could be used in a terrorist attack. The result was an expansion of the signature library to include more than 120,000 merchant ships.[33]

Battlefield acoustic and seismic collection is done mostly by army field units. In the United States, the signatures are forwarded to the Army's National Ground Intelligence Center for library maintenance.

As a requirement of the Comprehensive Nuclear Test Ban Treaty in 1966, the IMS was set up to incorporate a network of infrasound, hydrophone, and radionuclide sensors worldwide. A typical IMS seismographic array consists of between 5 and 30 sensors spaced over several square kilometers and operated with a central recording system. These arrays can detect very weak signals, reduce the effects of noise, and estimate the directions from which signals are arriving at the station by interpreting the time sequence at which the signals reach individual sensors. Some 50 of these monitoring sites around the world continuously send data in near-real time by satellite to the IMS International Data Center.[34] Using this network of in situ sensors deployed around the globe, signal analysts can locate the source of an explosion by comparing the time of arrival of the signal at each sensor.

Acoustic and Seismic Sensing

Summary

Sound and infrasound sensing, called geophysical intelligence, involves the collection, processing, and exploitation of environmental disturbances transmitted through or over the earth at audible (above 20 Hz) or infrasound (below 20 Hz) frequencies. Such collection works best under conditions where sound carries well over large distances, as sound does underwater and infrasound does in the earth under certain conditions. Sensors that detect low-frequency sound (infrasound) are an exception to the rule that non-EM sensors have short detection ranges. Depending on the strength of the source, such sound can be detected at distances of thousands of kilometers.

But acoustic sensing often is done at very short ranges for intelligence purposes. Battlefield intelligence increasingly makes use of short-range sound or infrasound collection. Land and air vehicles such as trucks, tanks, helicopters, and UAVs typically have a continuous acoustic power spectrum that extends from a few hundred Hz down to a few tens of Hz. Many such vehicles also have distinct narrow-band acoustic signatures that allow vehicle identification.

Surface ships and submarines emit high levels of underwater noise that can be detected and tracked by hydrophones at ranges of many kilometers. This specialized area of unintentional emissions intelligence is often called ACINT. The operational challenge in underwater acoustics is to detect the signature of a ship or submarine in the noisy ocean environment. For long-range sensing up to thousands of kilometers, long arrays of hydrophones are used.

Closely related to underwater acoustic sensing is seismic sensing, the detection and measurement of seismic waves that travel through the earth. A seismic signal or wave is created by earth vibration. Both man-made and natural activity can cause earth vibration; the vibration may be slight (a man walking on the earth or sound impact on the earth from an aircraft flying overhead) or very strong (an earthquake or large underground explosion).

A teleseismic signal is the result of a seismic movement, usually initiated by a strong disturbance in the earth that is recorded far from its source. Explosions and earthquakes cause such disturbances. Explosions create a different teleseismic signature than earthquakes, so the two can be distinguished. But teleseismic means alone cannot distinguish between chemical and nuclear explosions unless the explosion yield is too large to be chemical; the signatures are otherwise identical. At intermediate ranges between teleseismic sensing and short-range seismic sensing, midrange or regional waves can be sensed to detect and characterize explosions.

NOTES

1. B. Kaushik and Don Nance, "A Review of the Role of Acoustic Sensors in the Modern Battlefield," paper presented at the 11th AIAA/CEAS Aeroacoustics Conference (May 23–25, 2005), accessed 28 August 2012 at https://ccse.lbl.gov/people/kaushik/papers/AIAA_Monterey.pdf.

2. Ibid.

3. Christopher Stubbs, "Tactical Infrasound," JASON Report JSR-03-520, The MITRE Corporation (May 9, 2005).

4. John T. Correll, "Igloo White," *Air Force Magazine* (November 2004), Vol. 87, No. 11, accessed 23 September 2012 at http://www.airforce-magazine.com/MagazineArchive/Pages/2004/November%202004/1104igloo.aspx.

5. Tien Pham and Leng Sim, "Acoustic Detection and Tracking of Small, Low-Flying Threat Aircraft," U.S. Army Research Laboratory, accessed 28 September 2012 at http://projects.mindtel.com/2005/SDSU.Ge01600.Sensor_Networks/sensornets.refs/2003.%20ASC.%20Army%20Studies%20Conference/JP-25%20ACOUSTIC%20DETECTION%20AND%20TRACKING%20OF%20SMALL%20LOW%20FLYING%20THREAT%20AIRCRAFT.pdf.

6. Kaushik and Nance, "A Review of the Role of Acoustic Sensors in the Modern Battlefield."

7. William Matthews, "Tracking Noises—with Light," *Defense News* (May 10, 2010), accessed 23 September 2012 at http://www.defensenews.com/story.php?i=4612633&c=FEA&s=TEC.

8. Correll, "Igloo White."

9. Steve Norton, I. J. Won, Alan Witten, Alex Oren, and Frank Funak (Geophex, Ltd.), "Time-Exposure Acoustics for Imaging Underground Structures," Final Report (September 30, 2003), accessed 23 September 2012 at http://handle.dtic.mil/100.2/ADA417769.

10. IUSS Caesar Alumni Association, "IUSSHistory 950–2010," accessed 23 September 2012 at http://www.iusscaa.org/history.htm.

11. Graphic from University of Rhode Island, "Discovery of Sound in the Sea," accessed 23 September 2012 at www.dosits.org/gallery/tech/bt/ha1.htm.

12. Gurlap Systems, "Broadband Seismometer," accessed 23 September 2012 at http://ida.ucsd.edu/pdf/cmg-3t.pdf.

13. National Research Council of the National Academies of Sciences, "The Comprehensive Nuclear Test Ban Treaty: Technical Issues for the United States" (Washington, DC: National Academies Press, 2012), 60, accessed 23 September 2012 at http://www.nap.edu/catalog.php?record_id=12849.

14. Ibid., 45.

15. James R. Shea, "Winnowing Wheat from Chaff," *Studies in Intelligence,* Vol. 13, No. 3 (Fall 1969), 20, accessed 23 September 2012 at https://www.cia.gov/library/center-for-the-study-of-intelligence/kent-csi/v0113n04/pdf/v13i4a03p.pdf.

16. National Research Council, "The Comprehensive Nuclear Test Ban Treaty," 61.

17. Kaushik and Nance, "A Review of the Role of Acoustic Sensors in the Modern Battlefield," 2.

18. Correll, "Igloo White."

19. From S. Tenney, Army Research Laboratory, quoted in Christopher Stubbs, "Tactical Infrasound," JASON Report JSR-03-520, The MITRE Corporation (May 9, 2005).

20. Ibid.

21. Gregory Crawford, "Netted Sensor Fence for Homeland Defense," accessed 23 September 2012 at www.mitre.org/news/events/tech04/briefings/1406.pdf.

22. Daniel Frei, "International Humanitarian Law and Arms Control," *International Review of the Red Cross,* (November–December 1988), 491–504, accessed 23 September 2012 at www.loc.gov/rr/frd/Military_Law/pdf/RC_Nov-Dec-1988 .pdf.

23. Andra M. Bobbitt and Sharon Nieukirk, "A Collection of Sounds from the Sea," NOAA Pacific Marine Environmental Laboratory, accessed 23 September 2012 at www.oceanexplorer.noaa.gov/explorations/sound01/background/seasounds/ seasounds.html.

24. Ibid.

25. Shea, "Winnowing Wheat from Chaff," 20.

26. National Research Council, "The Comprehensive Nuclear Test Ban Treaty," 111.

27. National Academy of Sciences, "Technical Issues Related to the Comprehensive Nuclear Test Ban Treaty" (Washington, DC: National Academy Press, 2002), 39.

28. Ibid., 42.

29. Ibid., 21.

30. Ibid., 44.

31. Lawrence Livermore National Laboratory, "Seismic Monitoring Techniques Put to a Test," *S&T Review* (April 1999), 18.

32. Kevin T. Malone, Loren Riblett, and Thomas Essenmacher, "Acoustic/Seismic Identifications, Imaging, and Communications in Steel Rattler," Sandia National Laboratories, published in *SPIE,* Vol. 3081, 158–165, accessed 19 July 2012 at http://lib.semi.ac.cn:8080/tsh/dzzy/wsqk/SPIE/v013081/3081–158.pdf.

33. Lieutenant-Commander David Finch, "Acoustic Surveillance and Maritime Domain Awareness," *Canadian Naval Review,* Vol. 3, No. 1 (Spring 2007), 15 accessed 15 September 2012 at http://naval.review.cfps.dal.ca/archive/3175534– 3196361/v013num1art4.pdf.

34. National Radiation Laboratory of New Zealand, "CTBT International Monitoring," accessed 23 September 2012 at www.nrl.moh.govt.nz/about/ctbtinternational monitoringsystem.pdf.

15. Materials Intelligence

This chapter discusses materials intelligence, which divides broadly into materials sensing and materials sampling.

Materials sensing makes use of devices that sense chemical or physical changes in the environment immediately surrounding the sensor. These sensors measure phenomena within an object or at short ranges and typically detect such things as temperature, contaminants, nuclear radiation, or electric or magnetic fields.

Materials sampling involves acquiring small quantities or traces of a material and using forensic processes to determine its nature. So materials sampling includes the collection and analysis of trace elements, particulates, effluents, and debris. Such materials are released into the atmosphere, water, or earth by a wide range of industrial processes, tests, and military activities. Air sampling equipment, carried aloft by reconnaissance aircraft to detect the debris from atmospheric nuclear tests, is an example of such a sampling activity.

Function

Materials sensing and sampling are important for many areas of intelligence interest. They support military planning and operations. They are used to identify nuclear testing, nuclear materials production and movement, and chemical warfare production. Economic intelligence uses materials sampling to assess factory production. Materials collection can also include sensing or sampling for environmental monitoring, which increasingly is an intelligence concern because some governments and industrial enterprises attempt to conceal their pollution activities. Materials sampling also has long been practiced in law enforcement, and one of its premier practitioners is fictional: Sherlock Holmes, who, as he modestly admitted, could "distinguish at a glance the ash of any known brand either of cigar or of tobacco."[1]

Following is a summary of the major intelligence functions of materials sensing and sampling.

NUCLEAR MATERIAL SENSING AND SAMPLING

Nuclear sensing and sampling for intelligence currently have two functions and a third possible function.

- The first is aimed at detecting nuclear weapons testing and assessing weapons performance; it relies mostly on aircraft or ground sites to collect air samples. Analysis of air samples confirmed that the Soviet Union had conducted its first atomic bomb test. Later analysis of fallout from the first Soviet hydrogen bomb test also revealed many details about that weapon's design.
- The second is aimed at detecting the production or movement of nuclear weapons material and relies primarily on collecting material samples in or near a suspect facility. This was a major issue in the events leading up to Operation Iraqi Freedom in 2003 and has been an ongoing issue between a U.S.-led coalition and Iran. In the aftermath of the 9/11 attacks, a concern has increased about the possibility of dirty bombs (explosives that disperse nuclear material) being used as a terrorist weapon. This concern has led to the proliferation of nuclear sensors at ports and borders.
- A third type of collection is possible but fortunately has yet to be employed: obtaining debris samples after a nuclear attack for the purpose of identifying the origin of the device used.

Any handling of nuclear material nearly always leaves a trace in the environment, even if the material has been removed and the facility cleaned up. Every nuclear explosion, even an underground explosion, leaves traces in the environment. This trace nuclear material can provide clues to its age, origin, intended use, and the way it was produced and handled. Such traces and clues can often be detected and analyzed with techniques provided by nuclear forensics, which functions much like medical forensics.

Loosely defined, nuclear forensics is the collection and analysis of a sample containing nuclear or radioactive material to determine the history or production process of the material. Nuclear forensics is most often used for combating nuclear smuggling, but it also helps with verification of arms control and disarmament frameworks, such as the Comprehensive Nuclear Test Ban Treaty and the Fissile Material Cut-off Treaty.[2]

CHEMICAL SENSING AND MATERIALS SAMPLING

Chemical signatures are widely used for environmental monitoring and in law enforcement. For example, the presence and source of water pollutants can be determined by remote sensing and water sampling to detect specific pollutant signatures. Similar techniques can be used for air pollution monitoring. Law enforcement uses such sensing to detect chemical signatures in the air that indicate the presence of illicit methamphetamine laboratories.

In intelligence, chemical signatures are used mostly to identify effluents from factories to determine what processes are being used in the factory. The most common requirement is to characterize facilities that are suspected of producing weapons of mass destruction. Such characterization relies heavily on the ability to identify the signatures of chemical effluents from these facilities. A gaseous diffusion plant that is intended to enrich uranium produces several effluent signatures; uranium hexafluoride and its decomposition products all have unique chemical signatures. A nuclear fuel reprocessing plant produces a wide range of effluents, each of which has a unique signature that can help identify the plant's purpose.[3] Nerve agents that are produced for chemical warfare purposes also produce effluents that have unique signatures and indicate the specific agent being produced.

Materials sampling also is used to conduct industrial espionage. Samples of metals and other compounds in or near a factory can reveal information about the processes being used to produce both military and civilian equipment.

Chemical sampling using special purpose sensors has come into prominence as a result of the growing worldwide threat of chemical terrorism. But chemical sampling has been used to provide intelligence for years. Many industrial processes generate and release telltale chemicals; their signatures can provide information about the activities taking place within a facility. The ability to detect the chemicals released into the environment from a facility can provide a powerful means for monitoring treaty compliance or detecting weapons production activities.

With the increasing importance of tracing explosives (especially those used in improvised explosive devices [IEDs]), materials sampling and analysis have become an even more valuable tool for intelligence organizations, the military, and law enforcement.

MAGNETIC MATERIAL SENSING

Magnetic field sensing can detect the presence or motion of vehicles, ships, or submarines at short ranges by the weak changes they create in the earth's magnetic field. Magnetic sensing only works against materials that react to magnets (known as ferromagnetic materials). These sensors can, at very close ranges, detect ferromagnetic objects such as weapons and some IEDs. They have been used for weapons screening at passenger checkpoints for years, though newer types of scanners are replacing them.

Process

PLANNING

Planning differs according to whether the collection is to be done by sampling or sensing. For sampling, human intelligence (HUMINT) assets must be identified and briefed to conduct either overt or clandestine sampling—during inspection tours or plant visits, for example. If sensing is to be used for collection, the sensors have to be deployed where there is a high probability of success. In the case of **magnetic anomaly detector (MAD)** or spectral sensing, for example, aircraft flights have to be planned for promising target areas.

COLLECTION

Materials sensing relies on some kind of sensor that can obtain a signature that is unique to the material. Sensors that can obtain such materials signatures typically detect either nuclear radiation or the presence of ferromagnetic material such as steel. All these sensors function only at relatively short ranges. Chemical signatures, though, can be collected remotely by spectral sensing as discussed in Chapter 10.

Sampling, as the name implies, uses no sensor; a physical sample of the material is collected and sent to a laboratory for processing. Both nuclear material and chemicals are collected by sampling. Some sampling is done overtly, but much of the sampling for intelligence purposes is done clandestinely, using HUMINT assets.

There are two ways of doing materials collection, as noted above. Collection of nuclear and chemical material signatures often is done by using sensors that can detect nuclear radiation or the spectral signature of the material. Sensors can be clandestinely emplaced near a factory or weapons facility, and the results can be communicated to a remote location for analysis. Alternatively, one can physically collect a sample of the material for subsequent exploitation and analysis. Collection of materials samples has been done by air, soil, and water sampling.

Nuclear Materials Sensing

Nuclear Materials Signatures. Nuclear signatures are the physical, chemical, and isotopic characteristics that distinguish one nuclear or radiological material from another. Radioactive materials emit one or more types of radiation, such as alpha particles (helium nuclei), beta particles (electrons or positrons), neutrons, and gamma rays. The specific combination of particles and rays emitted, along with the intensity of each type, constitutes a signature that allows for identification of the radioactive source material. The primary materials of intelligence concern are the three fissionable isotopes— uranium-233, uranium-235, and plutonium-239—though any radioactive material that could be used in a dirty bomb is of concern as well.

All nuclear reactions result in the emission of particles and waves—neutrons, electrons, ions, gamma rays, or X-rays. X-rays and gamma rays fall into the electromagnetic (EM) spectrum (being at shorter wavelengths than ultraviolet, or UV, radiation). But because they fit best in a discussion of the other types of nuclear radiation, they are included here.

The radiation is strongest from a surface or atmospheric nuclear detonation, but nuclear power reactors also emit. The strength and type of radiation allow one to characterize the emitter. A number of nuclear radiation detectors have been developed; one of the oldest is the Geiger counter, which operates by sensing the ionization effect caused by the presence of radiation. Modern solid-state radiation sensors are more sensitive and are capable of detecting concealed nuclear devices at close ranges. Some are quite small, the size of a shirt button.

In most cases, nuclear radiation detectors are effective only if they are relatively close to the source. For example, the signature from a plutonium weapon's spontaneous decay processes will be gamma rays and neutrons. But the threshold for detection of neutrons is about 15 meters from a nuclear weapon. Beyond that range, background noise (that is, the background of naturally occurring neutrons) overrides the weapon signature. Nuclear materials detectors therefore have relatively short detection ranges and are best suited for choke points and monitoring portals or where one has good a priori intelligence about the presence of the nuclear material.

Close-in Sensing. X-ray and gamma ray detectors are being developed to address a threat of increasing intelligence concern: Dirty bombs, using conventional explosives that spread radioactive materials such as cesium-137, can be developed by terrorist groups. Substantial supplies of radioactive material that could be made into dirty bombs exist worldwide.

Such weapons can be detected at choke points by a combination of gamma ray detectors and X-ray scanners. If the radiation source is unshielded, the gamma ray detector can sense it. If it is shielded (for example, by lead), then an X-ray scanner will observe a large opaque blob that can be further investigated. Any technique used to conceal radioactive material tends to make it more vulnerable to detection.[4]

Nuclear radiation sensors must deal with a trade-off that is common to many types of sensors: The device can be made to be extremely sensitive, but the number of false alarms then rises dramatically. Another challenge for such sensors is that they must distinguish between the signature produced by a nuclear device or nuclear material and the signature of legitimate goods, some of which naturally emit a low level of radiation. This has been a recurring problem in radiation monitors installed at ports and border checkpoints, where items that naturally emit radioactivity (such as cat litter, ceramic tile, and porcelain) have repeatedly triggered false alarms.[5]

Air Sampling. This method of detecting nuclear debris is often thought to date from the late 1940s, when the United States began to monitor atmospheric nuclear tests. Sampling actually began during World War II. Concerned about possible German development of an atomic bomb, the United States developed a capability to capture and analyze xenon-133, a radioactive gas that is emitted by operating nuclear reactors. The device was installed and tested on a B-26 light bomber. After the war, the sampling missions were assumed by USAF's Air Weather Service. The service first used specially equipped WB-29 aircraft and subsequently switched to RB-57s, which could fly at the higher altitudes that were more desirable for collecting nuclear debris samples.[6]

Air samples taken over the Pacific Ocean were used to detect the first Soviet nuclear test in late August 1949. Air sampling became even more important after the Limited Test Ban Treaty of 1963. The treaty banned its signatories from nuclear testing underwater, in the atmosphere, and in space. It did not provide for an independent international monitoring system; it instead depended on the major powers' satellite collection assets, the national technical means (NTM) discussed in Chapter 8. NTM assets were directed at keeping track of each government's nuclear programs and possible testing by new entrants into the nuclear weapons club.[7] These overhead assets may provide a warning, but they can miss carefully concealed test preparations (as they did in the Indian nuclear tests of 1998). Satellite sensors may even miss the test itself or give an ambiguous signature, as in the suspected South African or Israeli nuclear test discussed in Chapter 10. Therefore, air sampling, combined with underground acoustic monitoring, is important as a cross-check on the effectiveness of NTM.

Above-ground testing produces an abundant amount of radioactive isotopes (called radionuclides) that can be detected. But underground testing also releases radioactive substances into the atmosphere. It is very difficult to contain the gases released in a nuclear explosion. If a nuclear test occurs, radioactive particles and gases might be vented at the time of the test, or radioactive gases might subsequently seep out through the cracks in the rocks above the explosion. Past experience at the test sites shows that even the most skillfully conducted underground explosions may vent these gases unpredictably. All the Soviet underground tests at Novaya Zemlya and about half of the underground tests at the Semipalatinsk test site in Kazakhstan resulted in the release of radioactivity, according to Russian reporting;[8] more likely, all their tests did.

The noble gases—argon, xenon, and krypton—are the primary targets for collection and analysis to detect underground nuclear testing. These gases, like the noble gas helium, do not react chemically with other elements. Therefore, they will seep through rock cracks without being absorbed by the rock, and they will not be scrubbed out of the atmosphere by rain. Furthermore, they have different half-lives, which makes collection challenging but helps in exploitation and analysis. The challenge is to collect the samples before they decay—as all radioactive elements do. Argon-37 has a half-life of 35 days. Xenon-133 has a half-life of 5 days, and xenon-135 has a half-life of 9 hours. An intelligence collector has to be very quick to make a successful detection. But once the collection is made, the differing amounts of each isotope remaining help establish the length of time since the detonation.[9] For example, the ratio of the production of xenon-135 and xenon-133 in plutonium fission is known. Because xenon-135 decays much more rapidly than xenon-133, the ratio of their concentrations in the plume provides a rough measure of the number of xenon-135 half-lives and therefore the

time since the test.[10] The relative ratios also help determine the device's yield and whether the device used plutonium or uranium.

Radioactivity releases from tests can be detected in two ways: by specially equipped aircraft (as noted above) or by ground stations operated by the International Monitoring System (IMS).[11] The role of the IMS in seismic and acoustic sensing was discussed in Chapter 14. The IMS also has a radionuclide monitoring network that is primarily directed at monitoring atmospheric nuclear explosions.

On-Site Nuclear Sampling. While much information about nuclear material is available from sensing, some signature details can only be obtained from a physical sample. These detailed signatures allow researchers to identify the processes used to initially create a material and may allow identification of the source of the material—a critical issue in the field of intelligence.[12] The shape and size of uranium particles, for example, provide clues about the origin of the material. The amount of radiation emitted from a given sample can sometimes be used to tell when the material was produced.

With the current moratorium on nuclear testing, intelligence collection has shifted away from air sampling and moved to on-site sampling, aimed at verifying the safety of nuclear warheads, detecting signs of nuclear proliferation, and thwarting illicit trafficking of nuclear materials.[13] The collection of samples for nuclear forensics commonly uses a technique referred to as "wipe and swipe"—wiping suspicious areas with specially prepared cotton weave that is designed to collect dust particles. Inspectors from the International Atomic Energy Agency use specially prepared sample kits to collect a large number of such samples each year at nuclear power plants around the world. For countries that refuse to allow site visit inspections, clandestine sampling may be necessary.

Chemical Sensing and Materials Sampling. Chemical signatures can be obtained by either sensing or sampling. A few signatures can be acquired by remote spectral sensing of EM energy, as discussed in Chapter 10. Gases, for example, generally produce spectra by emitting radiant energy upon being heated by some external source of energy. This could be the sun or an external source such as that encountered in a chemical production process.

Most chemical signatures are obtained by materials sampling. But to deal with the threat of terrorist chemical attacks, we would prefer to have a sensor that can quickly and reliably detect chemical traces in the immediate area. A number of sensors already exist, and this is a rapidly changing field. Integrated optics sensors have demonstrated the ability to detect the presence of chemical agents in seconds. A typical sensor consists of a laser light source, a planar waveguide (essentially a small flat piece of glass through which the light travels), and a detector for monitoring light output. Chemicals react with the glass waveguide surface and thereby alter the speed of light through the waveguide. Signal processing software interprets the sensor's results and delivers information on the chemical's identity and quantity.[14]

The previous discussion focused on materials sensing at relatively close range. Another way to do materials collection is to obtain a sample of the material for either on-the-spot or subsequent processing and analysis. Sampling can be done openly or clandestinely. Some treaties, as the next example illustrates, provide for open sampling.

The Chemical Weapons Convention provides for on-site inspection to ensure that chemical warfare (CW) agents are not being produced in factories of signatory nations. Inspectors under the convention are allowed to take wipe-and-swipe samples from the surfaces of plant equipment, as well as to take liquid samples from the production process and the waste stream. All methods of CW production create wastes. Some of the CW material always is left over, and it will emerge in the waste stream. Flushing the reactors and pipes clean prior to an inspection doesn't work. The production of CW agents leaves behind traces of agents, precursor chemicals, and by-products in the rubber seals and gaskets. And a concrete floor absorbs chemicals like a sponge.[15]

Soil sampling can detect CW agents, even over a long term. Either the agent or its degradation products will persist. Soil samples taken from a Kurdish village in northern Iraq were analyzed and found to contain degradation products of sarin and mustard gas more than four years after the Iraqi government bombed the village in 1988.[16] Much of this soil and debris sampling is done by clandestine collection. For example:

- A controversial U.S. cruise missile attack on a Sudanese pharmaceutical factory in 1998 resulted from soil sampling and subsequent analysis. A soil sample was obtained by clandestine means near the Shifa pharmaceutical plant in Khartoum. Analysis of the sample indicated that it contained a chemical ingredient known as EMPTA. EMPTA, according to a U.S. intelligence official, has no commercial use except in the production of nerve gas.[17]
- The Soviet KGB was as adept as U.S. intelligence in clandestine materials sampling. During a Cold War visit to a U.S. aircraft factory, a Soviet guest applied adhesive to his shoes to obtain metal samples for subsequent analysis to determine the metal alloys used for new U.S. fighter planes.[18]

Materials
Intelligence

• Material samples provided the first firm evidence that the Soviets were using titanium for the hulls of their submarines. Titanium construction represented a major advance in submarine design because it could enable submarines to operate at greater depths. The first clues came from ground level and satellite photographs of hull sections at a Leningrad shipyard: The hull sections were too highly reflective to be steel, and they showed no signs of oxidation, as steel would. Prompted by the clues, an assistant U.S. Navy attaché was able in 1969 to obtain a sample of metal from the shipyard that proved to be a scrap of titanium, providing confirmation of the Soviet development.[19]

Sampling can also be used to track ships or submarines. As these vessels move through the water, they leave behind trace chemicals. Metals are continuously deposited into the water by the corrosion and erosion of the hull. Lubricants, waste flushed from sanitary tanks, and hydrogen gas discharged from a submarine's life support system are all deposited in a ship's wake. An example of the resulting track produced by leaking oil was shown earlier in Figure 12.12. Neutron radiation from a nuclear power generator can cause detectable changes in seawater. All these contaminants leave a "track" in the ocean that can be followed by the appropriate sensors located on a trailing ship or submarine. Such tracking is, of course, real-time and has more of a flavor of operational information than of intelligence. But tracking ships or submarines over time helps to establish operational patterns and to predict future ship or submarine movements—therefore, it has use in intelligence.

Magnetic Anomaly Detector (MAD). Magnetic field sensing, or magnetometry, is not the same as EM sensing. EM waves propagate and can be detected at great distances. Magnetic fields do not propagate; they typically can only be sensed at very short ranges. The field produced by a magnet, for example, can be noticed only at distances from a few inches up to a few feet unless special sensing equipment is used.

The device for sensing weak changes in the earth's magnetic field is called a **magnetometer**. Magnetometers work by detecting the changes in certain types of atoms when the atoms are subjected to an external magnetic field. A MAD is a specific type of magnetometer. In geology, a MAD is used to search for minerals by observing the disturbance of the earth's normal magnetic field. A MAD also can locate underground tunnels or structures because the empty space where rock would normally be creates a slight change in the earth's magnetic field. MAD operation is similar in principle to the metal detector used by treasure hunters or the devices used by utility companies to find underground pipes.

One of the most common military uses of MAD devices is in locating submerged submarines from aircraft. The aircraft must be very close to the submarine's position, almost overhead, to detect the anomaly. The detection range typically is no more than a few hundred meters. The submarine's size and its hull material composition determine the maximum detectable range. The direction traveled by both the aircraft and the submarine relative to the earth's magnetic field also affects detectability. The close proximity required for magnetic anomaly detection makes the MAD system very useful for pinpointing a submarine's position once the submarine has been geolocated to a specific area by other sources.

FIGURE 15.1 P-3 Orion Aircraft with MAD Boom

The detection range of the MAD sensor can also be affected by the operation of the aircraft that carries it. Electric motors and other electronics can produce so much aircraft RF interference that the submarine's magnetic signature is lost in the noise. MAD aircraft rely on special electronics to compensate for and eliminate this aircraft noise. Also, the MAD is placed as far as possible from the interfering sources. The result is that a MAD aircraft has a distinct tail extension, called the MAD boom. Figure 15.1 shows a P-3 Orion aircraft with its MAD boom.

MAD devices also can be used in a battlefield environment to detect concealed metallic objects—armored vehicles or artillery hidden under a forest canopy, for example.

PROCESSING AND EXPLOITATION

Materials and chemicals are identified through various techniques in a laboratory. Mass spectroscopy using the spectrometer (introduced in Chapter 7) is one of the most common methods. In mass spectroscopy, a sample is bombarded with an electron beam that has sufficient energy to break apart the sample into molecules. The positive molecules then are accelerated in a vacuum through a magnetic field, which separates them based on the ratio of their mass to their electric charge.

Materials
Intelligence

Nuclear Material Samples. In the case of nuclear material samples, screening for radioactive isotopes uses a technique called gamma spectrometry. Gamma spectrometry relies on the fact that most radioactive substances emit gamma rays, and the energy and count rate of gamma rays emitted provide information on the isotopes in the sample. For example, the radiation emitted by nuclear material can reveal its age (that is, the time since it was first processed). As radioactive elements decay, they produce radioactive isotopes that, in turn, produce other isotopes. A spectrometer can determine the ratios of all the isotopes in this mix and then use these ratios to establish how much time the original material has spent decaying.

Gamma spectrometry is capable of detecting as little as one microgram of uranium and often can estimate its level of enrichment.[20] A number of other methods also are used to obtain details about radioactive isotopes, including electron microscopy and X-ray diffraction. Following is an example of the processing of nuclear attack debris.

Nuclear Attack Debris. A nuclear attack delivered by missiles or aircraft would in most cases be traceable back to the country from which the attack originated. It would be more difficult to trace the origin of a terrorist nuclear attack, since such an attack is likely to result from a clandestinely emplaced device. There are two likely types of terrorist devices:

- A conventional nuclear bomb acquired from some country's nuclear stockpile or fabricated from stolen weapons-grade material
- A so-called dirty bomb comprising conventional explosives in a blast that spreads radioactive material over a wide area

In the first type of attack, forensics may be able to identify the nation that originated the fissile material or weapon and determine whether terrorists had fabricated the weapon on their own or obtained it from a nation's stockpile.[21] In a dirty bomb attack, forensics probably can identify the source of the radioactive material used. Nuclear forensics can do this because of the widespread practice of fingerprinting nuclear and radiological material to prevent the illegal smuggling and trafficking of materials that have potential for use in nuclear terrorism. In all cases, it is important to conduct prompt sampling of the debris from the attack and to process and exploit the samples quickly.

Processing and exploitation of the radioactive debris can provide a number of insights that would help to identify the perpetrators of an attack. In the case of a nuclear bomb detonation, the first question would be whether the weapon was based on highly enriched uranium or plutonium. That question can be answered fairly quickly. Within hours to weeks, the investigators would determine key details about the original nuclear material and then estimate the size, weight, and complexity of the bomb. For example:

- If the device used highly enriched uranium, then exploitation could determine the amount of uranium-235 that it contained.
- If the weapon used plutonium, then exploitation could determine how much time the fuel had spent in a nuclear reactor to create the bomb-grade plutonium isotopes, establish the length of time since an isotope was separated from spent nuclear fuel, and identify the unique signatures that indicate specific production and separation processes.
- Another important issue is the sophistication, or lack thereof, of the weapon. The exploitation team would make this judgment based on the efficiency of the plutonium or uranium fission and whether fusion reactions were employed to increase the yield.

By comparing isotopic data from the debris with similar data from plutonium or highly enriched uranium stockpiles or weapons, it is possible to conclude whether some of the fissile material comes from a specific arsenal. It also is possible, with sufficient time and access to actual weapons designs, to determine whether a particular type of weapon has been employed.[22]

MAD Processing. MAD processing must deal with extracting a very weak anomaly signal in the presence of noise and interference. False alarms inevitably increase as the sensitivity of the MAD device is increased.

DISSEMINATION

Dissemination of materials intelligence reporting is usually limited to a predefined customer set. Except for MAD collection, the product usually is not time-sensitive. Most materials intelligence requires extensive processing, so dissemination of reports does not happen quickly anyway.

As in other fields of technical intelligence, a detailed signature library is a critical part of the forensic process. For nuclear sampling, the goal is to compare a sample's signature against known signatures from uranium mines and fabrication plants. This depends on having a library of nuclear materials of known origin from around the world. U.S. scientists have assembled such a library using samples provided from domestic suppliers of nuclear materials (uranium hexafluoride and uranium oxide reactor fuel).[23]

A detailed chemical signature library is essential if the exploitation phase must identify the source of the chemical. The signature library needs to include location-specific signatures for chemicals, such as explosives, so that an analyst can identify the laboratory or plant that produced the chemical.

Biological agent strains also need to be recorded in a signature library for source identification. The signature of biological agents has to include their natural geographic distribution, so that intelligence can better track biological incidents and outbreaks. The 2001 anthrax attack described in Chapter 16 could be narrowed to a specific source because detailed analysis of that anthrax signature had been obtained.

In some cases, such as chemical agent forensics, the number of signatures of interest keeps changing, so a library requires constant updating. A library of existing molecular structure signatures is still being assembled, and new chemical compounds are constantly being created.

Structure

Like many other boutique collection efforts, materials sampling is a structurally diverse enterprise. Naval, law enforcement, and ground force units all do magnetic field sensing for their specialized purposes. Nuclear material sampling and chemical sampling are done by military, intelligence, and law enforcement units and by international treaty monitoring organizations. Monitoring the chemical weapons convention, for example, is a responsibility of an international body, the Organisation for the Prohibition of Chemical Weapons. Monitoring to detect illicit movement of chemical or nuclear material usually is handled at border checkpoints by customs officials.

Summary

Materials intelligence makes use of two collection techniques—materials sensing and materials sampling.

Materials sensing relies on devices to sense chemical or physical changes in the environment immediately surrounding the sensor. These sensors measure phenomena within an object or at short ranges and typically detect contaminants, nuclear radiation, or magnetic fields.

Materials sampling involves acquiring small quantities or traces of a material and using forensic processes to determine its nature. So materials sampling includes the collection and analysis of trace elements, particulates, effluents, and debris. Such materials are released into the atmosphere, water, or earth by a wide range of industrial processes, tests, and military activities.

Three general types of materials are of intelligence interest and are the focus of sensing and sampling efforts: nuclear material, certain chemicals, and magnetic material.

NUCLEAR MATERIAL SAMPLING AND SENSING

Any handling of nuclear material nearly always leaves a trace in the environment, even if the material has been removed and the facility cleaned up. Every nuclear explosion, even an underground explosion, leaves traces in the environment. This trace nuclear material can provide clues to its age, origin, and intended use and the way it was produced and handled. Such traces and clues can often be detected and analyzed with techniques provided by nuclear forensics, which functions much like medical forensics, and which has three main intelligence purposes:

- detecting nuclear weapons testing and assessing the weapons performance, which relies on aircraft or ground sites to collect air samples;
- detecting the production or movement of nuclear weapons material, which relies primarily on collecting material samples in or near a suspect facility; and
- obtaining debris samples after a nuclear attack for the purpose of identifying the origin of the device used.

All nuclear reactions result in the emission of particles and waves—gamma rays, x-rays, neutrons, electrons, or ions. The radiation is strongest from a surface or atmospheric nuclear detonation, but nuclear power reactors also emit. The strength and type of radiation allows one to characterize the emitter. Nuclear explosive devices can be identified by the presence of the fissionable isotopes uranium-235, plutonium-239, and uranium-233.

In most cases, nuclear radiation detectors are effective only if they are relatively close to the source. They encounter a problem that is common to many types of sensors: The sensor can be made extremely sensitive to allow detection at longer ranges, but the number of false alarms then rises dramatically.

CHEMICAL SAMPLING AND SENSING

Chemical sampling and sensing have become much more important due to the growing worldwide threat of chemical terrorism. Spectral sensing can detect many chemicals at a distance and is especially effective against gaseous effluents. Chemical production processes generate and release telltale chemical signatures that can provide information about the activities taking place within a facility. Sensors are widely used to detect and identify chemicals upon contact.

Materials sampling is used to identify the processes and products of a facility and in any location where there is reason to suspect chemical warfare agents have been produced or used.

MAGNETIC MATERIAL SENSING

A common example of short-range sensing is the MAD sensor used by many countries to locate submerged submarines from aircraft. The aircraft must be within a few hundred meters of the submarine's position to detect the change that the submarine causes in the earth's magnetic field. Magnetometers also are used to detect concealed weapons and IEDs.

NOTES

1. Sir Arthur Conan Doyle, "A Study in Scarlet," *The Complete Sherlock Holmes* (New York: Doubleday, 1985), 33.
2. Vitaly Fedchenko, "Weapons of Mass Analysis—Advances in Nuclear Forensics," *Jane's Intelligence Review,* (November 1, 2007).
3. Jack Allentuck and James R. Lemley, "Open Skies and Monitoring a Fissile Materials Cut-off Treaty," Brookhaven National Laboratory Report No. BNL-61355 (July 9, 1965).
4. Steven Johnson, "Stopping Loose Nukes," *Wired,* (2004), accessed 23 September 2012 at www.wired.com/wired/archive/10.11/nukes_pr.html.
5. Eric Lipton, "U.S. Security Devices at Ports to Be Replaced," *International Herald Tribune,* (Monday, May 9, 2005), accessed 23 September 2012 at http://www.nytimes.com/2005/05/08/world/americas/08iht-secure.html.
6. Luis W. Alvarez, *Alvarez: Adventures of a Physicist,* (New York: Basic Books, 1987), 120.
7. National Research Council of the National Academies of Sciences, "The Comprehensive Nuclear Test Ban Treaty: Technical Issues for the United States" (Washington, DC: National Academies Press, 2012), 2, accessed 23 September 2012 at http://www.nap.edu/catalog.php?record_id=12849.
8. National Academy of Sciences, "Technical Issues Related to the Comprehensive Nuclear Test Ban Treaty" (Washington, DC: National Academies Press, 2002), 45.
9. Ibid.
10. Richard L. Garwin and Frank N. von Hippel, "A Technical Analysis: Deconstructing North Korea's October 9 Nuclear Test," *Arms Control Today* (November 2006), accessed 23 September 2012 at www.armscontrol.org/act/2006_11/tech.

11. National Radiation Laboratory of New Zealand, "CTBT International Monitoring," accessed 23 September 2012 at www.nrl.moh.govt.nz/about/ctbtinternational monitoringsystem.pdf.

12. "Identifying the Source of Stolen Nuclear Materials," *Science and Technology Review,* Lawrence Livermore National Laboratory (January/February 2007), 13–18.

13. Jonathan Medalia, "Nuclear Terrorism: A Brief Review of Threats and Responses," CRS Report to Congress (February 10, 2005).

14. "Sensing Danger: Researchers Develop New Sensing Technologies to Improve Response to Chemical and Biological Attacks," *Research Horizons Magazine,* (November 23, 2004), accessed 23 September 2012 at http://gtresearchnews.gat ech.edu/newsrelease/danger.htm.

15. U.S. Congress, *Technologies Underlying Weapons of Mass Destruction,* OTA-BfP-ISC-115 (Washington, DC: U.S. Government Printing Office, December 1993), 48.

16. Ibid, 62.

17. "U.S.: Sudan Plant Sample Contains VX Nerve Gas Precursor," *CNN.com,* (August 24, 1998), accessed 23 September 2012 at www.cnn.com/WORLD/ africa/9808/24/bomb.damage/.

18. Gus W. Weiss, "The Farewell Dossier," CIA Center for the Studies of Intelligence, accessed 23 September 2012 at www.cia.gov/library/center-for-the-study-of-intelligence/csi-publications/csi-studies/studies/96unclass/farewell.htm.

19. Norman Polmar and Kenneth J. Moore, *Cold War Submarines* (Dulles, VA: Brassey's, 2004), 143.

20. Ibid.

21. Medalia, "Nuclear Terrorism."

22. William Donlop and Harold Smith, "Who Did It? Using International Forensics to Detect and Deter Nuclear Terrorism," *Arms Control Today* (October 2006), accessed 23 September 2012 at www.armscontrol.org/act/2006_10/CVRForensics.

23. Lawrence Livermore National Laboratory, "Identifying the Source of Stolen Nuclear Materials," *Science and Technology Review* (January/February 2007).

16. Biological, Medical, and Biometric Intelligence

The intelligence collection discussed in this chapter has two major purposes:

- to detect the presence of biological agents—microorganisms—in the environment, in humans, animals, or crops and to identify the microorganisms; and
- to identify humans or to assess their physical or emotional state.

This combination of specialized collection INTs may seem to be a "cats and dogs" mix, but it has a common theme: Biological and medical sampling and biometric sensing and sampling all involve intrusive collection, mostly targeted on humans.

Function

As was the case with chemical sensors in Chapter 15, biological sensors (often called biosensors) have become more important as a result of the growing threat of biological terrorism. Biological sampling and biosensors can provide warning of disease outbreaks. They can identify specific pathogens such as anthrax or smallpox. When malign biological agents are detected, the goal is to quickly and accurately trace their origin in order to determine if they are endemic to a particular region or who may have intentionally introduced them.

The National Center for Medical Intelligence (NCMI) has a long history of assessing the threats from outbreaks of diseases such as the H5N1 avian influenza. Intelligence collection and analysis in this field are necessary because some countries fail to report infectious diseases or even provide false information about them. China, in particular, has a history of hiding information about disease outbreaks. The Chinese government took great care to conceal information about the outbreak of Severe Acute Respiratory Syndrome in 2003.[1] Medical intelligence collection continues to be important because of the risk that government concealment of disease information could lead to a pandemic.

BIOLOGICAL SAMPLING AND SENSING

Biological intelligence is concerned with obtaining biological signatures for two purposes:

- to identify the microorganisms that cause disease and tracing the source of disease outbreaks, and
- to identify biological warfare (BW) agent manufacture or use.

Both intelligence agencies and public health services worldwide devote considerable effort to cataloging biological signatures because they permit the source of a disease outbreak to be tracked. The 2001 biological attack using anthrax in the U.S. postal system provides an example of the value of detail in signatures. Close on the heels of the September 11, 2001, terrorist attack, with Americans already fearful and off balance, letters were mailed to various news outlets and to two senators—all containing anthrax powder. The biological attack resulted in five deaths, including postal workers for whom the letters were not meant. Were it not for the thorough cataloging of signatures, attempts to identify the anthrax source might have been futile. Instead, the anthrax bacteria used in the attacks were identified as coming from a specific strain, the Ames strain, which only existed in specific laboratories, including the U.S. Army biodefense laboratory at Fort Detrick, Maryland. Using this knowledge, FBI investigators were able to zero in on a suspect at the laboratory, Dr. Bruce Ivins, who committed suicide just before being arrested.[2]

The other priority intelligence interest is identifying BW agent manufacture or use, and the ideal would be to immediately sense either. In the case of a BW agent release, medical responders have very little time to deal with the agent.

During the first Gulf War, the U.S. military, concerned about reports of BW agents in the Iraqi arsenal, deployed sampling teams to the Gulf region. The teams obtained air, soil, and water samples along with some blood and tissue samples. These field units obtained a number of false positives from the sampling exercise, including indications of anthrax and botulinum toxin. None of the positives could be duplicated in laboratory analysis.[3]

MEDICAL SAMPLING AND SENSING

Medical sampling has much the same objective as biological sampling, discussed above. It uses many of the same sampling techniques. But the focus is typically on assessing the condition of the individual being sampled, not on identifying a disease threat. Medical sampling is used for other purposes than detecting diseases—identifying chemical warfare agent production, for example. Chemical warfare agents can be detected in the urine or blood samples of plant workers who have been exposed to the agent.[4]

Both medical sampling and sensing are used to assess the mental and physical health of world leaders. These leaders value their public image, and the perception that a leader's health is failing can diminish his or her effectiveness. So leaders tend to protect their health information, and the job of intelligence is to pierce that veil of secrecy. A foreign government derives a political and diplomatic advantage by learning the true condition of an ailing leader. Knowing that a leader doesn't have much time left can be critical to another government for timing and influencing actions about possible successors, for example. And leaders having a terminal illness are prone to make impulsive decisions that can have lasting political consequences. Dr. Jerrold Post founded CIA's Center for the Analysis of Personality and Political Behavior. While at CIA, he prepared psychological profiles on a number of world leaders, including Israeli Prime Minister Menachem Begin. Dr. Post commented that two decisions Begin made on his deathbed—designation of Jerusalem as Israel's eternal capital and applying Israeli law to the Golan Heights—have complicated Middle East peace negotiations ever since.[5]

BIOMETRIC SAMPLING AND SENSING

Biometrics is the technology of measuring and statistically analyzing biological data about humans. It relies on automated methods for recognizing an individual based on his or her physical or behavioral characteristics.

All humans have a number of biological characteristics that uniquely identify them, and these are included in the term *biometric signatures.*

Fingerprints and deoxyribonucleic acid (DNA) are two well-known signatures. The retina and iris of the eye also are signatures unique to an individual. Other physical characteristics that are sensed for biometrics include facial characteristics, hand geometry, voice, and keystroke dynamics. The type of biometric sensor that works best will vary significantly from one application to another. Some types of biometric sampling closely resemble the medical sampling discussed earlier.

The biometrics concept—using a fingerprint, a hand shape, an eye structure, a voice pattern, or another physical characteristic as an identification token—has been around for many years. Its current popularity belies its age. Fingerprints were used as signatures in ancient civilizations. Digitized fingerprints and voiceprints have been used in human recognition for years, and their use is increasing.

Biometrics is important in intelligence for identifying people. It is particularly useful to support human intelligence (HUMINT) operations. The most useful signatures in intelligence are those that can be identified unobtrusively. Facial characteristics and scent and voice biometrics are examples of some currently used signatures that fit in this category.

Biometrics is used for many things besides intelligence. It is used to authenticate the identity of persons who request access to a facility or to information. It supports the identification of persons on watch lists at control points. It is widely used in law enforcement and immigration control. The military role of biometrics expanded greatly during the wars in Iraq and Afghanistan. Admiral Edmund Giambastiani, former vice chairman of the Joint Chiefs of Staff, has observed that identity management techniques and biometrics are the most significant tools the United States currently possesses in asymmetrical warfare. He noted that "employment of biometrics on the battlefield denies anonymity to the enemy and limits his freedom of movement. We realize that, in irregular warfare and counter-insurgency operations, we are fighting individuals, not traditional armies."[6]

Biometric recognition is becoming more popular worldwide, as successful biometric systems become cheaper and easier to use and as the need for enhanced security continues to grow. This helps intelligence and law enforcement organizations track terrorists and criminals as they move between countries.

While biometrics is proving valuable in these tactical and law enforcement applications, it has created problems for clandestine services. Clandestine HUMINT operatives depend on the ability to cross borders with assumed identities, and biometrics increasingly makes that a hazardous process. Former Israeli Mossad operative and Knesset member Rafi Eitan

has noted that "by 2015 most countries will have moved over to biometric identification methods, which are more thorough methods for checking a person's identity."[7]

BEHAVIORAL SENSING

The science of behavioral sensing and assessment is closely related to biometrics and is often combined with biometric sensing. This is a rapidly growing field that finds application in law enforcement and intelligence. Behavioral sensing is used not to identify a specific named individual but to identify a potential perpetrator. It is more than signatures; it is the study of patterns of behavior. The goal is to identify the perpetrator in a security setting before he or she has the chance to carry out the attack.

Patterns of suspicious behavior are well known in law enforcement. People can spend time apparently doing nothing while sitting on a park bench, and such behavior is considered normal. However, if people spend the same amount of time sitting in a parked car next to a secure facility, then their intentions are suspect.

Process

PLANNING

Biological sensing and sampling are ongoing processes, aimed at providing warning of disease outbreaks and epidemics in humans, animals, and food crops. Planning, therefore, has to ensure that the right geographical areas are being monitored for the right diseases. It must, for example, take into account any new diseases that may need to be included in the monitoring process.

Medical sensing and sampling for intelligence usually are focused on specific targets—world leaders who appear to be in questionable health or are known for aberrant behavior. So collection planning tends to be done against these targets when a need for such intelligence becomes apparent.

Biometrics collection has become a mass collection effort due to its extensive application in Iraq and Afghanistan. Most persons entering or leaving Afghanistan at the Kabul airport or at major border crossing points are fingerprinted and photographed, as are all detainees. Because of the size of the effort and because it is intrusive, extensive advance planning has to be done to develop, staff, and coordinate the collection effort and to deal with the diplomatic, social, and legal issues.

COLLECTION

Biological Sensing and Sampling. Biological sensing and sampling are conducted by medical and veterinary facilities worldwide for reasons of public health and to monitor disease outbreaks among crops and farm animals. Samples taken from humans, animals, and plants are used routinely to identify diseases. The United Nations' World Health Organization and the U.S. Centers for Disease Control and Prevention, for example, do extensive medical sampling. This collection is not done for intelligence purposes, but it provides the essential background for the more selective targeting done by intelligence agencies.

As an example of such targeting, intelligence collection is done to obtain indications of biological warfare agent production, and such collection may have to be done clandestinely. Sampling is most commonly done, because sensing of biological agents doesn't provide the desired level of detail about the production process.

Remote sensing of biological agents depends on the existence of a signature that can be remotely sensed, and for most agents no such signature exists. Biological agents are usually colorless and odorless. A number of biological detectors exist that can immediately indicate the presence of a biological agent by capturing samples, but the samples must be collected, taken to a lab, and then cultured to identify the pathogen. The whole process can take several hours.

Sensors that can quickly detect and possibly identify biological agents on contact are being tested. And though biological agents are more difficult to detect than chemical agents, the same sensor can sometimes be used to detect attacks for both. The integrated optics sensor for chemical agent detection described in Chapter 15 has been used to detect biological agents. The device measures the reaction of an agent with chemicals on the optical waveguide surface. A different design approach senses the rapid reaction of certain human cells to the presence of diseases such as anthrax, plague, and smallpox.[8] Frequent false alarms have been a problem for most biosensors, as noted earlier in the Gulf War sampling effort, but that is likely to change as the designs improve.

Medical Sampling. Medical sampling is closely related to biological sampling, but the focus is somewhat different. In intelligence, we typically want to know the medical condition of a specific person or to identify a specific person rather than to identify the threat posed by a disease. Usually, that person is a world leader or major shaper of international events. For assessing the health of world leaders, both sampling and sensing techniques are

employed. Sampling, where it can be done at all, usually has to be done using clandestine HUMINT. But sensing is done routinely based on videos and photos of leaders.

Medical sampling can be intrusive, as characterized by a detailed physical examination of disease victims. But collection can be done by any one of several clandestine sampling techniques. For example, it is possible to collect medical waste items, such as discarded bandages or syringes, or stool and urine samples from a building's plumbing system. Or it may be possible to acquire samples of blood or bodily fluids that have been sent to a laboratory for testing. Some world leaders travel abroad for medical testing, providing increased opportunities for such sampling.[9]

Medical sampling is routinely done worldwide by nongovernmental organizations (NGOs), such as Doctors Without Borders, as a part of their normal efforts to aid the sick. But relying on NGOs for intelligence collection has its risks, as the following example illustrates.

Case Study: The bin Laden Hunt. One of the more controversial instances of medical sampling for intelligence purposes was a part of the hunt for Osama bin Laden. A Pakistani doctor, Shakil Afridi, was hired to set up a vaccination program in the region around Abbottabad. The real purpose of the program was to collect blood samples from children in the compound suspected of concealing bin Laden. DNA testing would then determine if they were bin Laden's children. Whether the sampling program was a success has not been revealed. But Dr. Afridi was considered a traitor by the Pakistanis. He was arrested, tried, convicted on a charge of having links to a banned militant group, and imprisoned.[10]

The controversy in the United States concerned the apparent use of humanitarian aid as a cover for intelligence collection. A coalition of American humanitarian aid groups wrote a letter to CIA Director David Petraeus claiming that the operation "compromises the perception of U.S. NGOs as independent actors focused on a common good and casts suspicion on their humanitarian workers. The CIA's actions may also jeopardize the lives of humanitarian aid workers in Pakistan."[11]

Many NGOs are well positioned to conduct medical sampling; they do it routinely as part of their humanitarian efforts. But the Afridi case illustrates the risk of using NGOs or private citizens for clandestine collection. It also illustrates the point that medical sampling often is closely tied to other collection specialties—in this case, biometrics.

Biological and medical sampling are closely tied to each other. In some cases, it is necessary to do both. One of the more extensive sampling efforts, the "Yellow Rain" investigation in Southeast Asia, involved both biological and medical sampling.

Case Study: Yellow Rain. Starting in 1976 in Laos, 1978 in Cambodia (Kampuchea), and 1979 in Afghanistan, intelligence analysts began receiving reports of chemical or toxin weapons being used against the Hmong, the Khmer, and the Afghans, respectively. The alleged attacks were often described as a helicopter or plane flying over a village and releasing a colored cloud that would fall in a manner that looked, felt, and sounded like rain. The most commonly reported color was yellow. Thus, the reported attacks in the three nations became known as "Yellow Rain."

The similarities in the descriptions of attacks and subsequent symptoms among victims in the three countries raised suspicions that the same agent was being used. All three locations were linked in some manner to the Soviet Union. In Afghanistan, the Soviets were directly involved in a war; in Laos and Cambodia, they supported the Pathet Lao and Vietnamese forces.

Beginning in 1979, the United Nations, the United States, and other nations began investigating these allegations of chemical/toxin weapons use. U.S. government employees, with the assistance of volunteers and refugees from the affected countries, searched for evidence that might confirm or refute aspects of the refugee reports. They collected biomedical and environmental samples for laboratory analysis, acquired medical data on alleged victims, and administered questionnaires regarding alleged attacks. In 1981, the U.S. secretary of state announced that physical evidence had been found that showed mycotoxins (poisonous substances produced by fungi) supplied by the Soviet Union were being used as a weapon against civilians and insurgents in Southeast Asia and Afghanistan.

Not everyone concurred with the finding that Yellow Rain was a chemical/biological weapons (CBW) attack involving mycotoxins. During the investigation, the CIA obtained access to a defector: a Soviet-trained Vietnamese chemical officer who came from the top level of the Vietnamese Army's Chemical Branch. The defector demonstrated extensive knowledge of the Vietnamese organization, equipment, and activities for chemical, biological, and nuclear defense. He also reported that the Soviets absolutely refused to give the Vietnamese any chemical or biological weapons, and that the Vietnamese did not have the technical capacity to produce such weapons. A polygraph examination and repeated interrogation convinced the interrogation team that the defector was telling the truth.[12] Furthermore, some nations were unsuccessful in finding mycotoxins in their sample analysis. The United Nations found the evidence to be inconclusive, and an alternative

hypothesis emerged, suggesting that the "yellow rain" was actually just a naturally occurring phenomenon of a swarm of Asian honeybees defecating in flight.[13] The United States continued its investigation through the mid-1980s, collecting and analyzing pertinent information on the alleged attacks. The controversy about what actually happened has continued ever since.

Medical and Psychological Profiling. In contrast to sampling, medical sensing techniques can be very nonintrusive and broadly applied. Some of the simplest sensing for Severe Acute Respiratory Syndrome involved the biometric technique of remotely taking people's temperatures. During the 2003 outbreak, Japan installed infrared thermometers at Tokyo International Airport to monitor passengers and identify possible victims.[14]

In creating medical profiles of world leaders, videos are the preferred sensing tool. They are very useful for evaluation of outward signs of physical disability or disease. How the person walks, whether he or she favors certain limbs over others, skin color and texture, or symmetry of the face, all can indicate the presence of illnesses or recent strokes.

The methods for psychological profiling are well known. Over the years, psychologists have developed a number of techniques, drawing mostly on publicly collected information about leaders—their speeches, writings, biography, and observable behavior.[15] In assessing foreign leaders, collectors and analysts also draw on techniques from the professional discipline of cultural anthropology.

Biometrics Collection. At its most simple level, biometrics collection requires that a sensor take an observation. The type of sensor and its observation will vary by biometric type. For example, in facial recognition, the sensor is usually a camera and the observation is a picture of an individual's face.

Fingerprints have long been the leading biometric technique, since it is established that no two fingerprints are ever exactly alike. Fingerprint readers are now both inexpensive and widely available. In order for fingerprints to be transmitted, stored in a library, and searched, they have to be digitized according to some standard. The current standard fingerprint data format is one that has been adopted by both the FBI and Interpol.

A voice biometric or "voiceprint" is as unique to an individual as a finger or palm print. A voice impersonation that sounds like an exact match to the human ear will, in fact, have a significantly different voiceprint. A person's voice is unique because of the shape of the vocal cavities and the way the mouth moves when speaking. To be included in a voiceprint system, a person must either say the exact words or phrases that the system requires or give an extended speech sample so that the computer can identify the person no matter which words are spoken. The signature used in a voiceprint is called a **sound spectrogram** or sonogram. *Spectrogram* is the preferred term, because *sonogram* also is used to describe a diagnostic medical image created using ultrasound echoes. The spectrogram was introduced in Chapter 14 in connection with tracking ships and submarines. It is basically a graph that shows a sound's frequency on the vertical axis and time on the horizontal axis. Different speech sounds create different shapes within the graph.

A problem with using voiceprints is that, although the signature is unique, it can change when a person is tired or has a cold. And the media used to transmit or record the voice can affect the signature that is provided for exploitation.

Deoxyribonucleic acid (DNA) is the well-known double helix structure present in every human cell. A DNA sample can be analyzed to identify either a DNA fingerprint or a DNA profile. DNA is not currently useful for biometric surveillance because it is not an automated process. It takes several hours to create a DNA fingerprint. While there is only about one chance in 6 billion of two people having the same profile, DNA tests cannot distinguish between identical twins.

Retinal scanning analyzes the pattern of blood vessels at the back of the eye. Scanning involves using a low-intensity light source and an optical sensor. The resulting patterns can be read at a great level of accuracy. Scanning requires the user to remove his or her glasses, place an eye close to the device, and focus on a certain point. Retinal scanning is actually one of the older biometric ideas. An article appeared in 1935 in the *New York State Journal of Medicine* that suggested that the pattern of blood vessels on the retina could be used to identify an individual.[16]

Iris scans analyze the features that exist in the colored tissue surrounding the pupil. The iris is unique; no two irises are alike, even among identical twins, in the entire human population. In the iris alone, there are more than 400 distinguishing characteristics that can be quantified and used to identify an individual. Approximately 260 of those are currently captured and used in iris identification.

Retinal and iris scans can capture their respective signatures at a distance of up to 1 meter. This makes them useful at checkpoints but generally not usable in area surveillance.

Biometric facial recognition is probably the most rapidly growing area of biometrics. It has the substantial advantage of being done at a distance, unobtrusively. Facial recognition uses camera images, measuring distances and angles between points on the face—mouth extremities, nostrils, eye

Biological,
Medical, and
Biometric
Intelligence

corners—to create a faceprint that can be recognized in scanning a crowd of people. Biometric facial recognition currently is being used to control access to facilities, as well as to computers and gaming casinos, and at border crossing points around the world.[17]

Hand geometry uses the geometric shape of the hand for authenticating a user's identity. But unlike fingerprints, the human hand is not unique until observations get down to fine detail. One can use finger length, thickness, and curvature for the purposes of verification (confirming that a person is who he says he is), but this is not suitable for identification (as one cannot reliably search for a handprint in a database; there are too many likely matches).

Keystroke dynamics relies on measuring the unique ways a person enters information using a keyboard. As a biometric recognition technique, it has an antecedent that is more than a century old. As noted in Chapter 4, Morse code operators have long been able to recognize other operators by their characteristic pattern of keying the code, known as their "fist."

Scent identification is based on the ability to identify a unique signature based on scent in much the same way that dogs can distinguish the scents of specific humans and other dogs. This identification is accomplished by a technique called **chromatography**, which measures the relative proportions of chemicals in a gas. Researchers also are investigating the possible use of human scent to detect deception.[18]

The trend is to collect multiple biometric signatures using portable equipment and to electronically forward the results to a central processing unit that can access a library. An example is the Handheld Interagency Identity Detection Equipment (HIIDE), widely used in Afghanistan. Its use is illustrated in Figure 16.1. The device is used to take photos of a subject's face and iris and to collect 10 fingerprints with a sensor. It then can search the library within the device or wirelessly search databases for a match.[19] HIIDE is widely used by coalition forces in Afghanistan. The United Kingdom has deployed a similar device, called MForce—a portable biometrics system that combines identity and intelligence-gathering functions and can be set up quickly by military users in the field or at a forward operating base.

In combating insurgencies, it appears that biometrics collection has become a routine matter. By mid-2012, U.S. and Afghan government forces had compiled biometric records on more than 2.5 million of Afghanistan's 30 million people, primarily in the form of iris and fingerprint scans. The collection targets included laborers on military bases, border crossers, arrestees, and males of fighting age. A comparable number of records have been collected in Iraq.[20]

FIGURE 16.1 Biometric Collection[21]

Behavioral Sensing. Terrorists are often trained to conceal emotions, but some reactions of the human body are not subject to voluntary control. Skin temperature, blood-flow patterns, perspiration, and heart and breathing rates are difficult or impossible to control; the polygraph relies on these. New technologies are being developed to sense these signatures at a distance. The U.S. Department of Homeland Security (DHS) is reportedly developing an automated sensing system to detect hostile intent; the system would rely on an array of sensors to measure these signatures at a distance of approximately 2 meters.[22]

Another promising area of behavioral signatures is the field called microexpressions. These are fleeting facial expressions, typically lasting less than one-tenth of a second and involving a small part of the human face. Microexpressions are largely involuntary. There are about 40 known microexpressions, and some of these are believed to expose lying. Microexpressions are easily missed by human eyes, though the best professional poker players are expert at reading them. But such brief expressions may be subject to automated detection and classification. The apparent persistence of microexpressions across cultures makes them signatures of interest for both intelligence and law enforcement.[23]

PROCESSING, EXPLOITATION, AND ANALYSIS

Biological and Medical Samples. Biological and medical samples are both processed in much the same way—in medical laboratories, using tools and methodologies that are widely used within the medical profession. Processing of sensing data such as videos of world leaders is typically done by a medical expert or psychiatrist.

Biometric Processing. This depends on the creation of internationally standard ways to describe an observation mathematically—that is, a standard format for each type of biometric signature. The method will again vary by biometric type. The identification or verification part of the process requires

that a computer system feed the biometric signature into a comparison algorithm and compare it with one or more biometric signatures previously stored in its library. This step fails if the collected signature does not have the same format as the ones stored in the library.

Behavioral Sensing. Increasingly, behavioral signatures are being used for profiling and identifying possible terrorists. Today this type of exploitation is done by trained observers; law enforcement officers have done it that way for centuries. Current research is aimed at developing an exploitation system that can match faces, voices, bodies, and other biometric features against scientifically tested behavioral indicators to provide a numerical score of the likelihood that an individual may be about to commit a terrorist act.[24]

DISSEMINATION

Much biological, medical, and biometric data of intelligence interest are collected in foreign countries. This can make collection difficult, because it typically requires close cooperation with other states. The collection and storage of data on individuals is a sensitive issue for most countries because of civil rights and identity protection concerns. But the major challenges come when the information needs to be shared with allies. Biometric data, in particular, need to be shared for identity checks in other countries and at international borders. This can be a problem because of differing host nation cultures, laws, norms, and policies. Special handling instructions have to be developed for each subsequent international data-sharing agreement. One solution does not fit all partner nations in a coalition. Similar constraints and challenges apply when intelligence based on medical sampling must be shared with coalition partners.

Biological and medical reporting that is related to disease outbreaks is disseminated widely. Much such information is openly available through the World Health Organization (WHO). The NCMI publishes both classified and unclassified reports on disease outbreaks.

Biological agent strains also need to be recorded in a signature library for source identification. The signature of biological agents has to include their natural geographic distribution, so that intelligence can better track biological incidents and outbreaks. The 2001 anthrax attack described earlier could be narrowed to a specific source because detailed analysis of that anthrax signature had been obtained.

In contrast, medical reporting and psychological assessments of foreign leaders typically are classified and receive very limited distribution, depending on the sensitivity of the collection sources and the political sensitivity of the information. And reports on foreign leaders can be politically contentious. In 1993, CIA reportedly provided Congress with a psychological assessment of deposed Haitian president Jean-Bertrand Aristide. It concluded that Aristide had a history of mental illness and manic depression.[25] That conclusion resulted in considerable criticism of CIA from congressional members who supported Aristide's reinstatement as president.

Biometric reporting, by its nature, is first collected on individuals and stored in some form of library. Then identity queries have to be submitted to the library, where a search for a match is performed. Within the United States, the Department of Defense (DoD) manages much of the biometrics effort to build a library of signatures and to track individuals of intelligence interest. The challenge is to make the file formats for library entries standard so that sharing among international partners can work. It is also highly desirable that the files contain location information to support the tracking of individuals of intelligence interest.

Structure

Biological and medical sampling have fairly well-established structures; they've been done for years both within and outside of intelligence organizations. Medical sampling is performed by a number of governmental, commercial, and nongovernmental organizations. Internationally, the UN's WHO monitors disease outbreaks and has its own medical sampling effort. Very few countries maintain intelligence organizations that have a specific mission of medical sampling. In the United States, one such organization exists: the NCMI, located at Fort Detrick, Maryland. NCMI, formerly the Armed Forces Medical Intelligence Center (AFMIC), has a long history of providing medical intelligence. NCMI also handles biological warfare agent intelligence, supported by U.S. Army sampling teams in combat theaters.

Psychological assessments also have a well-established structure. CIA reportedly has a collection and analysis unit that provides such profiles. Some universities also have political departments that conduct psychological assessments.[26]

Biometrics is less established structurally, depending on the subdiscipline. Fingerprint collection and fingerprint libraries have been maintained for decades by the FBI, for example. But the newer fields of biometrics and behavioral sensing represent rapidly developing areas of intelligence, so the structure is in flux.

Within the United States, the Defense Department's Biometrics Identity Management Agency (BIMA) has the mission to coordinate biometrics efforts across the DoD and the U.S. intelligence community and to manage biometrics libraries. Law enforcement organizations have their own systems for capturing biometric data such as fingerprints and DNA and storing it in a central library.

The need to work closely with partner nations to collect and share biometric signatures requires that there be an international structure of some kind. But partner nations are sensitive about identity data on their nationals and concerned about who might have access to the data. India, for example, would be unlikely to share identity data with Pakistan and vice versa.

Summary

Biological and medical sampling and biometric sensing and sampling all require intrusive collection that is targeted on humans. Because the collection is done internationally and the results are shared with other countries, it raises civil rights and identity protection issues.

Biological collection has become much more prominent as a result of the growing worldwide threat of biological terrorism. Biological signatures are needed to identify the microorganisms that cause disease, for tracing the source of disease outbreaks, and to identify biological warfare agent manufacture or use. Most collection is done by sampling. Diagnostic sampling is performed in medical and veterinary facilities worldwide. Samples taken from humans, animals, and plants are used routinely to identify diseases. But biosensors are finding increasing use because they can identify specific pathogens such as anthrax and smallpox. When biological agents are detected, the goal is to quickly and accurately trace their origin in order to determine if they are endemic to a particular region and who may have intentionally introduced them.

Medical intelligence sampling is closely related to biological sampling, but the focus is on individuals rather than on detecting and identifying diseases. Medical sampling is used to identify exposure to chemical warfare agents. Both medical sampling and sensing are used to assess the mental and physical health of world leaders.

Biometrics is a separate discipline for obtaining and analyzing signatures about humans. It uses automated methods for recognizing an individual based on physical or behavioral characteristics. Specialized sensors can capture a number of physical characteristics to create biometric signatures, including fingerprints, facial characteristics, iris or retinal patterns, hand geometry, voice features, and keystroke dynamics.

Behavioral sensing and assessment is closely related to biometrics and is often combined with biometric sensing. It is more than signatures; it is the study of patterns of behavior. Behavioral sensing is used not to identify a specific named individual but to identify a potential perpetrator.

NOTES

1. Ellen Bork, "China's SARS Problem, and Ours," *The Daily Standard,* (April 4, 2003), accessed 24 September 2012 at www.weeklystandard.com/Content/Public/Articles/000/000/002/504jlpnl.asp.
2. "New Details on F.B.I.'s False Start in Anthrax Case," *New York Times,* (November 25, 2008), A23.
3. DoD, "Close-out Report, Biological Warfare Investigation" (February 13, 2001), accessed 7 April 2013 at http://www.gulflink.osd.mil/bw_ii/index.html.
4. U.S. Congress, *Technologies Underlying Weapons of Mass Destruction,* OTA-BfP-ISC-115 (Washington, DC: U.S. Government Printing Office, December 1993), 53.
5. Gary Thomas, "Spies Track Physical Illnesses of Foreign Leaders," *VOA News,* (September 19, 2011), accessed 3 September 2012 at www.voanews.com/content/article/171599.html.
6. DoD newsletter, "The Biometric Scan" (January 2008), accessed 9 September 2012 at http://www.biometrics.dod.mil/newsletter/issues/2008/Jan/v4issue1_a4.html.
7. Jonathan Lis, "Will Biometric Passports Limit the Reach of Israel's Intelligence?" *Haaretz* (February 19, 2010), accessed 28 July 2012 at http://www.haaretz.com/print-edition/news/will-biometric-passports-limit-the-reach-of-israel-s-intelligence-1.263599.
8. "Bio-sensor Quickly Detects Anthrax, Smallpox and Other Pathogens," *Science Daily,* (March 7, 2008), accessed 9 September 2012 at http://www.sciencedaily.com/releases/2008/03/080304120746.htm.
9. Gary Thomas, "Spies Track Physical Illnesses of Foreign Leaders" (September 20, 2011), *Voice of America,* accessed 21 September 2012 at http://www.voanews.com/english/news/usa/Spies-Track-Physical-Illnesses-of-Foreign-Leaders-130222673.html.
10. BBC News Asia, "Profile: Shakil Afridi" (September 11, 2012), accessed 17 September 2012 at http://www.bbc.co.uk/news/world-asia-18182990.
11. Saeed Shah, "Aid Groups Protest to CIA over bin Laden Scheme," *Miami Herald,* (March 3, 2012), accessed 17 September 2012 at http://www.miamiherald.com/2012/03/02/2672173/aid-groups-protest-to-cia-over.html.
12. Merle Pribbenow, "'Yellow Rain': Lessons from an Earlier WMD Controversy," *International Journal of Intelligence and Counterintelligence,* Vol. 19 (2006), 737–745.
13. U.S. Department of State, "Case Study: Yellow Rain," accessed 24 September 2012 at http://2001-2009.state.gov/t/vci/rls/prsrl/57321.htm.

14. NIC Assessment: *SARS: Down but Still a Threat,* ICA 2003-09 (August 2003), accessed 24 September 2012 at www.fas.org/irp/nic/sars.pdf.

15. Benedict Carey, "Teasing Out Policy Insight from a Character Profile," *New York Times,* (March 28, 2011), accessed 20 September 2012 at http://www.nytimes.com/2011/03/29/science/29psych.html.

16. Tiffany L. Vogel, "Security: Biometric Style," International Federation for Protection Officers (April 25, 2003), accessed 24 September 2012 at www.ifpo.org/articlebank/biometrics.html.

17. John D. Woodward Jr., "Super Bowl Surveillance: Facing Up to Biometrics," in *Intelligencer: Journal of U.S. Intelligence Studies* (Summer 2001), 37.

18. Shaun Waterman, "DHS Wants to Use Human Body Odor as Biometric Identifier, Clue to Deception," UPI.com (March 9, 2009), accessed 24 September 2012 at www.upi.com/Emerging_Threats/2009/03/09/DHS_wants_to_use_human_body_odor_as_biometric_identifier_clue_to_deception/UPI-20121236627329/.

19. Biometrics Task Force, "HIIDE Gets an Update," accessed 28 September 2012 at http://www.biometrics.dod.mil/Newsletter/issues/2008/Oct/v4issue4_pm.html.

20. Defense Systems, "Biometrics Now Way of Life in Afghanistan" (July 11, 2012), accessed 17 September 2012 at http://defensesystems.com/articles/2012/07/11/agg-biometrics-afghanistan.aspx.

21. Public domain image, accessed 28 September 2012 at http://warrior-police.blogspot.com/2010/05/hiide-seek-modern-army-style.html.

22. "If Looks Could Kill," *Economist.com,* (October 23, 2008), accessed 24 September 2012 at www.economist.com/science/displayStory.cfm?source=hptextfeature&story_id=12465303.

23. Ibid.

24. "Technology Would Help Detect Terrorists Before They Strike," *Science Daily,* (October 10, 2007), accessed 24 September 2012 at www.sciencedaily.com/releases/2007/10/071005185129.htm.

25. Benedict Carey, "Teasing Out Policy Insight from a Character Profile," *New York Times,* (March 28, 2011), accessed 20 September 2012 at http://www.nytimes.com/2011/03/29/science/29psych.html.

26. Ibid.

17. Materiel Acquisition and Exploitation

This chapter discusses a specialized field of technical collection that does not fit cleanly into any of the previous chapters but that contributes significantly in the areas of treaty monitoring, military operations and law enforcement. *Materiel* acquisition and testing is not to be confused with *materials* sampling that was discussed in Chapter 15—though each usually involves the help of a human intelligence (HUMINT) operation.

Materiel acquisition specifically refers to acquiring hardware (to include large items such as airplanes, missiles, or ships and small items such as integrated circuit chips or cell phones and computer chips).

Function

Materiel acquisition and exploitation have a long history in the military arena. The Hittites of Asia Minor in about 2000 BCE may have been the first targets of materiel acquisition efforts, as their iron weaponry was acquired and reverse engineered by the bronze-using Egyptians.[1] The Hittites were far from the last victims; military materiel acquisition is a routine occurrence and often is done by illicit means. As recently as 2012, a network of companies that illegally acquired U.S. microelectronics chips for Russia was broken up and the participants arrested. The network acquired advanced chips from U.S. suppliers using false end-user certificates and reportedly shipped them to the Russian armed forces and Russian's domestic intelligence agency, the Federal Security Service (FSB). The microelectronic devices were designed to be used in military and intelligence equipment—radar and surveillance systems, missile guidance systems, and detonation triggers.[2]

Most materiel acquisition usually has one of three intelligence purposes:

1. To reverse engineer a component or a piece of equipment (that is, disassemble it and analyze its structure, function, and processes) so that your own organization or country can reproduce it.
2. To complete a performance analysis, to determine the strengths and weaknesses of the equipment. Countries often acquire military hardware in order to develop countermeasures to it (for example, to determine the type of weapon needed to penetrate a tank's armor).
3. To identify the sources of the materiel and the volume of production. An example is illicit weapons traffic, usually weaponry that supports insurgencies. Every year, large quantities of light weapons are brought into conflict areas such as sub-Saharan Africa by gray arms traffickers. The markings on such equipment can often be used to identify the source and to support diplomatic or law enforcement operations to stop the weapons flow.

Process

The process for materiel acquisition is shown in Figure 17.1. It differs from that described in the preceding chapters on nonliteral collection. There is usually no processing and no signature library. You proceed directly from collection (acquisition) to exploitation. The dissemination phase may result in a database of exploitation reports, but that does not serve the same function as a signature library.

PLANNING

Often a military item may be known to exist, and intelligence questions about it need to be answered. The organization that needs the information will generate a requirement for collecting and exploiting the item. An example of such a requirement might be to identify or verify suspected external modifications to an enemy's main battle tank. The result would be a target folder that describes the item of interest, preferably with a photograph or

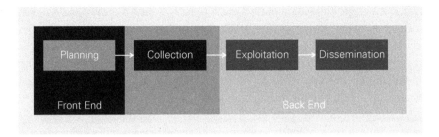

FIGURE 17.1 The Materiel Acquisition Structure and Process

sketch and possible acquisition sources or locations. The folder would also include exploitation and reporting instructions.[3]

In a few cases, however, acquisition is not planned for. Sometimes a collection opportunity suddenly arises and planning is conducted on a crash basis. The Foxbat exploitation, discussed later, illustrates how this can happen. Whether long-range or on a crash basis, precise planning and the involvement of all-source analysts usually is needed in the acquisition phase. The cases in this section illustrate that fact. Also, even when the acquisition was not planned for, exploitation is almost always carefully planned to take maximum advantage of the opportunity.

ACQUISITION (COLLECTION)

Materiel is collected overtly or using clandestine methods.

Overt Acquisition. Overt acquisition of military materiel usually means capturing the equipment as a result of combat. During the recent Mideast conflicts, U.S. intelligence organizations have had considerable success in capturing materiel for exploitation. In 1991, the Department of Defense set up the Joint Captured Materiel Exploitation Center (JCMEC). Foreign materiel exploitation specialists from all of the U.S. armed services along with U.K. specialists were assigned to the JCMEC during the two Gulf wars and the conflict in Afghanistan.

During Operation Iraqi Freedom, JCMEC teams collected, identified, exploited, and evacuated a large volume of captured enemy materiel throughout the Iraqi theater of operations. DIA personnel assigned to the JCMEC collected over $1 million worth of foreign short-range ballistic missiles, antitank guided missiles, and surface-to-air missiles. An Office of

Naval Intelligence team acquired more than 150 tons of armored vehicles, torpedoes, naval mines, and antiship cruise missiles for transport to the United States.[4] During Operation Enduring Freedom, the JCMEC again was active in acquiring foreign materiel. The JCMEC recovered foreign materiel in Afghanistan estimated to be worth $40 million and shipped the materiel back to the United States for detailed exploitation.[5]

These examples illustrate the norm—most military equipment is incidentally acquired in conflict. Initiating a military action specifically to acquire materiel is a rare occurrence. However, on occasion special operations have been mounted just for materiel acquisition, and the following case outlines one of the most successful that has been openly acknowledged. The full details of this World War II real-life spy thriller are given in Alfred Price's book, *Instruments of Darkness*.[6]

Overt Acquisition Example: The Bruneval Raid. In the fall of 1941, Britain's scientific intelligence officer, Dr. R. V. Jones, was zeroing in on a new German antiaircraft fire control radar that was believed to transmit on a frequency of 570 MHz. One of the more daring British reconnaissance pilots brought back a picture of a new radar located near Bruneval, France. The British realized that this radar was located less than 200 yards from the coast and quickly organized a commando raid to obtain detailed information about it.

The British assembled a company of paratroops to make an airborne assault. A naval assault was too risky because of the high cliffs around Bruneval, but a light naval force was assembled to handle the evacuation. Dr. Jones, meanwhile, had identified the German radar by name—*Würzburg*—but he still could not confirm that the radar was the source of the 570-MHz signals.

Jones specified in detail the parts he wanted his acquisition team—members of the Corps of Royal Engineers and a radar mechanic—to bring back. Of special interest were the feed antenna for the radar dish, which would establish the operating frequency of the radar, and the receiver and display equipment, which would reveal whether any antijamming circuits existed. He also asked for the transmitters because they would reveal the German technology for generating 570-MHz signals. Two radar operators were to be taken prisoner, if possible, so that they could be interrogated about radar operation. Finally, if equipment could not be removed, the labels and inspection stamps were to be taken because these would provide valuable background information.

On the night of February 27, 1942, the raid, codenamed Operation BITING, took place. Despite the errors and missed assignments that are inevitable in such an adventure, the raid was an unqualified success. The Bruneval force brought back exactly what Jones had asked for, except that only one radar operator was captured.[7]

The Bruneval Raid succeeded because the British knew exactly what they wanted to get. The acquisition team had an expert analyst in the loop at every step. Most successes in materiel acquisition since that time have involved carefully focused teams closely tied to analytical expertise. Most failures have resulted in cases where the collectors, compartmented from the analysts, had no real idea what they were trying to get or why.

Clandestine Acquisition. Though the Bruneval Raid was a victory, there is always an obvious drawback of a seizure that results from combat or special operations, like that of the *Würzburg.* The opponent knows about the operation's success and can take countermeasures to reduce the value of information gained. Given the choice, clandestine acquisition is the preferred collection technique. The gold standard is when the opponent is unaware of the effort altogether.

Clandestine materiel acquisition by governmental intelligence agencies is often by purchase, usually through middlemen to conceal the intended destination. In their heyday, the Soviets were very good at such clandestine materiel acquisition. They acquired a great deal of materiel for reverse engineering of both military and civilian products. On one occasion, they managed to acquire a new IBM computer before it was officially on the market. However, the result must have been less than satisfactory for the Soviets because none of the IBM sales or maintenance people they subsequently contacted knew how to make it work.

As previously noted, acquisition of military equipment often is a result of a successful HUMINT operation, as the acquisition is usually a clandestine effort. There are good reasons for making it clandestine. First, one wishes to protect sources and methods. Second, as we have already emphasized, the intelligence that is gained has less value if the opponent is aware of the acquisition. Both motivations are illustrated in the case of probably the most expensive clandestine materiel acquisition effort ever undertaken by the United States—the Glomar Explorer.

Clandestine Acquisition Example: The Glomar Explorer. In March 1968, a Soviet Golf-class submarine on patrol northwest of Hawaii was racked with explosions and sank in 17,000 feet of water, carrying all 90 men aboard down with it. Soviet salvage vessels were unable to locate the sunken craft, but the U.S. Navy subsequently pinpointed its location using more sophisticated search equipment. At this point, the CIA entered the picture, as a proposal had been made to recover the submarine. This was the beginning of the project that was reportedly codenamed Project Jennifer.

To accomplish the task, Howard Hughes's Summa Corporation built a 620-foot-long deep sea recovery vessel named the *Glomar Explorer*. The ship was equipped with huge derricks, along with a companion barge to conceal the submarine when it was recovered. The *Glomar Explorer* was built under the cover of a deep sea mining mission and was completed in 1973 at a cost of $200 million.

During July and August 1974, the *Glomar Explorer* began recovery operations. Cables were looped around the submarine, and winches began slowly pulling the submarine up toward the barge. About halfway up, the hull broke apart and two-thirds of the submarine fell back and was lost on the bottom. Though the sought-after prizes—the code books and nuclear warheads—were reportedly lost, the remaining one-third of the submarine was recovered and yielded valuable intelligence.[8]

The Glomar Explorer is an excellent example of two important points about clandestine operations. First, a great deal of effort was expended in keeping the success a secret, in the service of protecting sources and methods. Second, a consistent asset of U.S. intelligence collection is that U.S. collectors are innovative and unpredictable. In materiel acquisition, as in HUMINT generally, they try things that most services are too conservative or too risk-averse to try.

EXPLOITATION

The previous examples have focused on materiel acquisition. But once the materiel has been acquired, it must be exploited for its intelligence value. This usually is done by experts who are familiar with how the type of product is built. If collection has been done clandestinely (and sometimes when collection has been done by capturing the equipment), then the exploitation also should be concealed.

Exploitation often begins in the field, in the case of captured equipment. This initial and usually quick exploitation phase determines whether the opposing forces are really employing the equipment and whether further exploitation is necessary. If it is, the equipment may be sent to a field center for exploitation. The United States relies on Captured Materiel Exploitation Centers for such tactical intelligence exploitation. High-interest equipment may then be evacuated to the Scientific and Technical Intelligence centers maintained by individual U.S. services for detailed exploitation.[9]

Wherever the work is done, and with whatever tools or methods are available, there are standard goals for exploitation. Depending on whether the materiel can be brought to your territory, or you find a way to borrow it, or in the worst case, you are not able to physically touch it, there are a number of available exploitation methods. Three of them—product teardown, performance testing, and factory markings—are discussed here.

Product Teardown. Whether the end goal is performance analysis or reverse engineering, at some point in the exploitation process is a step called product teardown. Large commercial companies maintain product teardown rooms for this purpose. Government intelligence organizations may rely on industry or on their own equipment test facilities to do the same thing.

Product teardown is the practice of dismantling products into parts and analyzing those parts. It begins with a thorough analysis of the complete product. Next comes disassembly, with measurement, testing, and modeling of subassemblies at each step. Where possible, disassembly and testing are done nondestructively. At each step, the exploitation team takes photographs, measures, and makes drawings of each component or major subassembly. The final exploitation step may be performance analyses of individual parts. The process is much the same for both civilian products and military materiel, as the following example illustrates.

Product Teardown Example: The Foxbat Exploitation. Some materiel exploitation results from the acts of émigrés or defectors who transport the materiel with them. The most spectacular such incident occurs when a defector flies an aircraft out of country. Such a defection in 1976 provided U.S. intelligence with a close look at the Soviet Union's new jet fighter: the MiG-25 Foxbat.

In 1960, the U.S. Congress voted to fund the development of the North American XB-70 Valkyrie. The Soviet Union had no interceptor capable of attacking an aircraft designed to fly at Mach 3 at 70,000 to 80,000 feet. The MiG-25 Foxbat was originally designed in response to this future threat, with a planned capability of Mach 3.2 at 80,000 feet. The prototype first flew in April 1965. Production of the Foxbat fighter began in 1969, and the aircraft eventually entered Soviet service in 1973. Early U.S. intelligence assessments concluded that the Foxbat was a technically advanced and very fast fighter, capable of performing well against comparable U.S. combat aircraft.

On September 6, 1976, Soviet lieutenant Victor Belenko defected, flying his Foxbat to Hakodate Airport in Japan. The aircraft was Soviet property, and the Japanese would have to give it back. So the question became: How long would it take engineers and technicians to extract the most valuable intelligence by disassembling and studying the plane on the ground? U.S. experts believed that 30 days would suffice. The Japanese agreed to make the MiG-25 available for at least that long, provided that American specialists wore civilian clothes and acted as consultants working under Japanese supervision.[10]

U.S. experts knew they would have to return the plane eventually. They took it apart piece by piece. The Foxbat was disassembled and the engine, radar, computer, automatic pilot, fire control, electronic countermeasure, hydraulic, communications, and other systems were put on blocks and stands for mechanical, electronic, metallurgical, and photographic analysis.

The exploitation of the MiG-25 uncovered a series of surprises. In sum, the Foxbat was substantially less than the spectacular Soviet accomplishment described in intelligence estimates. It could function well as an interceptor against bombers, but it would perform poorly against U.S. fighters. It was a fuel hog, having fairly primitive avionics. The airplane had, in fact, been built for one specific mission—to intercept and shoot down the B-70 (which never went into production). Its resulting limitations included these:

- The massive turbojets could propel the aircraft to Mach 3, but it could barely maneuver at that speed.
- The pilot's visibility was severely limited; the pilots could basically see only what was directly in front of them.
- The avionics used vacuum tubes, at a time when U.S. combat aircraft relied on solid-state electronics.
- The construction techniques were crude by Western standards (for example, rivet heads sticking out and poor-quality welding).
- Advanced materials, such as titanium, were used sparingly and only where essential—nickel-steel alloy was used wherever possible.[11]

While the Americans and Japanese methodically took apart the MiG-25 and continued their exploitation and debriefing of Belenko, the Soviets were demanding the immediate return of the aircraft and pilot. The Japanese responded by noting that the aircraft had violated Japanese airspace; the issue, therefore, was complicated. There were precedents for returning the plane and precedents for keeping it. For the time being, the Japanese retained the aircraft as evidence while their investigation of the matter was ongoing.[12] Material evidence in a crime such as this plainly deserved the most careful going-over, perhaps even by experts from several countries. It was possible, after all, that the pilot was carrying contraband into the country. The aircraft would have to be searched in detail. When the Soviets demanded to be allowed to fly the plane out of Japan, the Japanese replied that this was impossible. A crime had been committed by the plane's intrusion into Japanese airspace. The Japanese government could not allow a repeat violation by permitting the plane to fly out. The Foxbat would have to be transported out by ship, in crates.

The Soviets escalated from protests and pleas to threats and actions. Soviet naval vessels began seizing Japanese fishing vessels and imprisoning their crews. These actions, along with other threats and the condescending Soviet attitude, had the opposite effect from what the Soviets intended. It infuriated the Japanese public and provoked the Japanese government into a defiant posture. In a formal note rejecting the Soviet protests and charges, the Japanese government expressed surprise that the Soviet Union had not apologized for violating Japanese airspace. As for all the Soviet demands that the MiG-25 be given back, a foreign ministry official said, "The Soviet Union should first explain what it thinks of the incident. It is no way for anyone to try to take back something he has thrown, even though inadvertently, into the yard of his neighbor."[13]

On November 12, 1976, more than two months after Belenko landed the Foxbat, the Soviets got it back—in pieces. Eight Japanese trucks delivered the crated parts to a Japanese port, where a Soviet freighter waited with a crew supplemented by technicians and KGB officers. The freighter remained in the port until the Russians inventoried all the parts.[14]

Performance Testing. Product teardown is one exploitation approach, widely used with consumer products and a necessary step in reverse engineering. But with larger items of materiel such as tanks, ships, missiles, and aircraft, it is highly desirable for exploitation to include performance testing on a test range. Major military powers maintain test ranges for their own combat equipment; such ranges are logical places to test an opponent's similar equipment. All the U.S. military services operate ranges where acquired equipment can be tested. The challenge is to protect the existence of the effort, since the equipment being tested often has been acquired clandestinely.

Continuing the Foxbat example, when the Pentagon learned that the Japanese had unexpectedly acquired a MIG-25, their objective was to do exactly that: bring the plane to the United States and run it through performance tests at a test range. Had the United States succeeded in borrowing the Foxbat for an extended period, it is likely it would have been exploited at Area 51, where previous aircraft acquired by the United States, such as the MiG-17 and MiG-21, reportedly have been exploited.[15] For political reasons, this was not possible.

Materiel
Acquisition and
Exploitation

Since actual performance testing of the MiG-25 was off the table, investigators turned to another INT: HUMINT, specifically defector debriefing. Much performance information came from debriefings of Lieutenant Belenko.

The combination of the debriefing information with the exploitation results provided a more complete picture of the aircraft's design and performance. For example, Belenko reported the following:

- The combat radius of the aircraft was at most 300 kilometers (186 miles)—by Western standards, an incredibly short range.
- In maneuvers, the aircraft could not take more than 2.2 Gs with full tanks—with more, the wings would rip off. Even with nearly empty tanks, 5 Gs was the turn limit. The Foxbat was clearly not designed to dogfight; it could not match the older U.S. F-4 Phantom in a turn.
- Top speed was theoretically Mach 2.8, well below the original speed goal of Mach 3.2. However, the pilots were forbidden to exceed Mach 2.5. At high speeds the engines tended to accelerate out of control; above Mach 2.8, the engines would overheat and burn up. Anytime the aircraft was flown near Mach 2.8, the engines were ruined and had to be replaced.[16]

Exploitation without Acquisition. Figure 17.1 shows a collection step, which usually involves physical acquisition. But materiel can be exploited without actually acquiring it. Sometimes, all you need is a good photograph or even a sketch. The shape of a tank, ship, or aircraft can tell a great deal about its performance. Photography has been used for decades to assess the performance of military equipment. Such photography is routinely acquired by military attachés worldwide and forwarded to their intelligence services for exploitation. Handheld photography could be considered imagery intelligence (IMINT), but it more logically fits as part of materiel exploitation.

As an example, handheld photography is often the initial source for estimating the performance of new military aircraft. The exploitation process typically starts with transmuting the photograph (preferably photographs from different angles) into a three-dimensional drawing. This is usually done by an imagery analyst. Then the drawing and the dimensions are used to produce an estimate of the aircraft weight. Engine exhaust ports are measured and the results used to calculate thrust. Clues such as rivet lines give the aircraft structural layout. Armament, electronic, and equipment specialists use the drawings along with features identified in the photographs to reconstruct the armament, electronic, and other component systems used in the plane. The aircraft shape is used to make drag calculations.[17] All these photography-based estimates, taken together, allow estimates to be made of performance and operational effectiveness.

It sometimes is not necessary to acquire materiel in order to obtain what are called factory markings that have intelligence value. Military equipment usually has identifying markings placed on it for inventory and quality control purposes. These markings allow exploitation teams to identify the source of the equipment, and the serial numbers often permit estimates to be made of production quantity. This type of materiel exploitation is well known to military intelligence organizations. During World War II, the United States and Britain used factory markings to estimate German V-2 rocket production. The Germans used them to estimate Soviet war materiel production, and the Soviets used them to estimate German tank production.[18]

The practice has continued in every war since then and during peacetime as well. The following example illustrates the acquisition and use of factory markings.

Exploitation Example: The Kidnapping of the Lunik. The following is an example of HUMINT-enabled collection that illustrates how factory markings are acquired. Like the MiG-25 example, it illustrates the point that it is not always necessary to acquire in order to exploit; borrowing may be sufficient.

> During the 1960s, the Soviet Union conducted a traveling exhibition of their industrial and economic achievements. At one stop on the tour, an unexpected shipment arrived from Moscow: the top stage of the new Lunik space vehicle. The Lunik vehicle was unpacked and placed on a pedestal.
>
> The appearance of the Lunik provoked a discussion among U.S. intelligence analysts. Would the Soviets risk exposing a production vehicle at a trade show or was the Lunik simply a specially made mockup? The first would have much potential intelligence value; the second would be worth very little. The decision was to gamble on the chance that the Lunik was not a mockup.
>
> After the exhibition closed at its first stop on the tour, a team of specialists clandestinely gained access to the Lunik for 24 hours. They found that it was, indeed, a production item from which the engine and most electrical and electronic components had been removed. They examined it thoroughly from the viewpoint of probable

Materiel Acquisition and Exploitation

performance, taking measurements, determining its structural characteristics and wiring format, and estimating engine size. The team then recommended a more detailed exploitation.

As the exhibition moved from one city to another, an intercepted shipping manifest showed an item listed as "models of astronomic apparatus," whose dimensions were approximately those of the Lunik crate. This information was sent to the CIA station nearest the destination with a request to try to arrange secure access if the Lunik should appear.

The Lunik crate arrived soon afterward and was delivered to the exhibition. The specialists that were brought in for the detailed exploitation came from a factory markings team, whose expertise was in exploiting factory-produced items and identifying their production source. On the basis of their experience at trade fairs and other exhibitions, the team preferred access to the item before the opening of an exhibition to examining it while in the exhibition hall or after it had left the grounds for another destination. The physical situation at the grounds, however, ruled out access to it prior to the show's opening. During the show, the Soviets provided their own 24-hour guard for the displays, so there was no possibility of making a surreptitious night visit.

This left only one chance: to get to the Lunik at some point after it left the exhibition grounds. After the exhibition, the displays would be carried by truck from the exhibition grounds to a railroad station and then loaded onto freight cars for their next destination.

It was arranged for the Lunik to be the last truckload of the day to leave the grounds. When it left, it was preceded by a CIA station car and followed by another; their assignment was to determine whether the Soviets were escorting it to the rail yard. When it was clear that there were no Soviets around, the truck was stopped at the last possible turnoff, a canvas was thrown over the crate, and a new driver took over. The local driver was escorted to a hotel room and kept there for the night.

Half the team then climbed into the front-nose end of the Lunik with a set of photographic equipment and a drop light. They removed one of the inspection windows in the nose section, took off their shoes so as to leave no telltale scars on the metal surface, and squeezed inside. They then photographed or hand-copied all markings and components. The other half of the team did the same in the aft engine compartment.

At 5:00 a.m., a driver came and moved the truck to a prearranged point. Here the canvas cover was removed and the original driver took over and drove to the rail yard. The Soviet who had been checking items as they arrived the previous day came to the yard at 7:00 a.m. and found the truck with the Lunik awaiting him. He showed no surprise, checked the crate in, and watched it being loaded onto a flatcar.[19]

The subsequent factory markings exploitation provided identification of the producer of the Lunik stage and the electronics producers. The equipment photographs allowed assessments to be made of the level of technology used in the stage.

Reverse Engineering the B-29. At first glance, reverse engineering would seem to be a productive way to make use of an acquired hardware, where it is more advanced than what your factories can build. After all, it is usually faster to produce a copy of a product than beginning from scratch. The following example illustrates the principle but also illustrates the major drawback of reverse engineering.

During 1944, three B-29s made emergency landings in Soviet territory after bombing raids on Japan and Japanese-occupied China. The Soviets were neutral with respect to Japan until almost the end of the war. So the bombers were interned and kept by the Soviets, despite American demands for their return. Stalin gave aircraft designer Andrei Tupolev the job of reverse engineering the aircraft. The interned B-29s were flown to Moscow and delivered to the Tupolev design bureau. One B-29 was fully dismantled, down to the rivets. Another was used for flight tests and training. A third aircraft was left intact as a standard. Tupolev produced 20 copies of the aircraft, which he named the TU-4, in just two years.[20] Figure 17.2 shows a comparison of the two aircraft.

The Tupolev story illustrates both the pluses and minuses of reverse engineering. The advantage is that you can produce a copy of the product much faster than if you had to start from scratch. The disadvantage is that you are perpetually in a catch-up position. In the case of the TU-4, by the time it was flying, it was obsolete; the United States by then was well along in building its first jet-powered strategic bomber, the B-47.

FIGURE 17.2 Reverse Engineering the B-29

DISSEMINATION

Military hardware exploitation results are disseminated at several levels. In the United States, JCMEC, which typically handles exploitation in the field, produces first-level exploitation reports. Where the need is to assess an opponent's combat hardware strengths and vulnerabilities, it is important to get the report out to the field quickly. The JCMEC reporting does that. These short reports, in the United States, take a form called an intelligence information report (IIR) format, and classification is kept at a low level so that the reports can get wide dissemination.[21]

In-depth military equipment exploitation is handled by U.S. Technical Intelligence Centers, and the results usually are disseminated in the form of a formal report that can be quite detailed. These typically go to the organizations that requested the exploitation. In cases where the exploitation is to support reverse engineering or countermeasures development, accuracy and detail become more important than speed. The need is to get all of the product details to the builder of the reverse engineered equipment or to the countermeasures developer.

Structure

This is the best example of a boutique INT. It is highly targeted, going after specific items for a specific purpose.

Clandestine acquisition is typically handled by a clandestine service, often by purchasing the materiel through middlemen. One of the best known examples is the KGB's Line X, which was very successful at acquiring Western technology until its operations were exposed by Colonel Vladimir Vetrov.

Military organizations are set up to acquire and exploit captured military equipment. In the United States, this responsibility is handled by DIA under the Department of Defense (DoD) Foreign Materiel Acquisitions and Exploitation Program. Service components typically handle the materiel that is of interest to that service. The U.S. Army, for example, assigned the National

Ground Intelligence Center (NGIC) as its executive agent for acquiring and exploiting foreign ground systems.[22]

But commercial firms now handle substantial quantities of military materiel acquisition and exploitation under government contracts. They manage the location, acquisition, equipment inspection, and all of the logistics associated with importing, repair, and maintenance of the equipment.[23]

Summary

Though the name sounds similar to materials intelligence discussed in Chapter 15, materiel acquisition is quite different. It involves acquiring a piece of equipment or a component—such as an integrated circuit chip, a vehicle, a computer, a missile, or a radar. The acquisition is usually for one of two purposes. The first purpose is to reverse engineer a component or a piece of equipment. The second purpose is for performance analysis, to determine the strengths and weaknesses of the equipment. This is the premier example of a boutique INT; whether for military or commercial purposes, materiel acquisition is targeted on specific items, and the exploitation is tailored to meet specific objectives.

Acquisition of military equipment often is a result of a successful HUMINT operation, as the acquisition is usually a clandestine effort. Clandestine acquisition is the preferred technique because the acquirer usually does not want the opponent to be aware of the effort. However, military equipment also is acquired as a result of combat operations or from defectors.

Once the materiel has been acquired, it must be exploited for its intelligence value. Exploitation often begins in the field, in the case of captured military equipment. Large items such as ground vehicles, radars, and aircraft subsequently receive detailed exploitation (performance testing) at test ranges. Small items usually are examined in laboratories.

In either case, after performance testing of the item, product teardown is the next exploitation step. The purpose here is to conduct a detailed examination of the design and the quality and function of components that it uses. If it hasn't already been done, the components of military hardware will be checked for factory markings that help identify equipment producers and production quantities.

Commercial firms typically acquire their competitors' products for exploitation. Usually they do this for performance testing to determine the product's strengths and weaknesses. Sometimes, they acquire in order to reverse engineer the product and to produce a duplicate.

Materiel
Acquisition and
Exploitation

NOTES

1. Ralph Linton, *The Tree of Culture* (New York: Alfred A. Knopf, 1955), 105.
2. "Feds: High-Tech Smuggling Ring Sent U.S. Electronics to Russian Spy, Military Agencies," *NBCNews.com* (October 4, 2012), accessed 4 October 2012 at http://usnews.nbcnews.com/_news/2012/10/04/14213457-feds-high-tech-smuggling-ring-sent-us-electronics-to-russian-spy-military-agencies?lite.
3. US Army FM 2-0, *Intelligence,* (March 2010), Chapter 13.
4. "Support to Operation Iraqi Freedom" (Washington, DC: Central Intelligence Agency, posted April 25, 2007), accessed 29 June 2012 at https://www.cia.gov/library/reports/archived-reports-1/Ann_Rpt_2003/iraq.html.
5. "Support to the War on Terrorism and Homeland Security" (Washington, DC: Central Intelligence Agency, posted April 30, 2007), accessed 29 June 2012 at https://www.cia.gov/library/reports/archived-reports-1/Ann_Rpt_2002/swtandhs.html.
6. Alfred Price, *Instruments of Darkness* (London, UK: William Kimber, 1967), 80–87.
7. Ibid.
8. *Newsday* (April 11, 1989), 2.
9. US Army FM 2-0, *Intelligence* (March 2010), Chapter 13.
10. "MiG-25 Foxbat," accessed 16 September 2012 at www.spyflight.co.uk/foxb.htm.
11. Global Aircraft, "MiG-25 Foxbat," accessed 16 September 2012 at http://www.globalaircraft.org/planes/mig-25_foxbat.pl.
12. John Barron, *MiG Pilot: The Final Escape of Lt. Belenko* (New York: McGraw-Hill, 1980).
13. Ibid.
14. Ibid.
15. T. D. Barnes, "Exploitation of Soviet MiGs at Area 51," accessed 28 July 2012 at http://area51specialprojects.com/migs_area51.html.
16. Barron, *MiG Pilot.*
17. Isadore Herman, "Estimating Aircraft Performance," *Studies in Intelligence* (Washington, DC: Center for the Study of Intelligence, posted May 8, 2007), accessed 29 June 2012 at https://www.cia.gov/library/center-for-the-study-of-intelligence/kent-csi/v016n01/html/v06i1a02p_0001.htm.
18. Arthur G. Volz, "A Soviet Estimate of German Tank Production," *The Journal of Slavic Military Studies,* Vol. 21, No. 3 (July 2008), 588–590.
19. Sydney Wesley Finer, "The Kidnapping of the Lunik," *Studies in Intelligence* (Washington, DC: Center for the Study of Intelligence), accessed 24 September 2012 at https://www.cia.gov/library/center-for-the-study-of-intelligence/kent-csi/v0111n01/html/v11i1a04p_0001.htm.
20. Kerber, Leonid. "TU-4 Bomber Epic." A compilation of articles published from 1988 to 1990 (in Russian). Accessed 29 June 2012 at http://militera.lib.ru/memo/russian/kerber/02.html. See also Wayland Mayo, "Russian B-29 Clone—The TU-4 Story," accessed 29 September, 2012 at http://www.rb-29.net/html/03RelatedStories/03.03shortstories/03.03.10contss.htm.
21. US Army FM 2-0, *Intelligence* (March 2010), Chapter 13.
22. US Army manual FM 34-37 (January 15, 1991), Chapter 8.
23. See, for example, the services offered commercially by SASI at http://www.sasi-corp.com/forsales.htm and by Culmen International at http://www.culmen.com/?page=pg&pid=18.

18. Managing Intelligence Collection

A large intelligence service, such as that of the United States, with its worldwide interests, many collection assets, and many targets, faces a daunting management challenge. This chapter discusses some of the issues in managing collection, with emphasis on management as it is practiced in the United States.

It is true that none of the steps in an intelligence system can occur without collection, at one time or another, preceding them. It is also true that the collection product cannot be delivered without a system of preceding steps:

- Intelligence priorities must be set. (Collectors are not involved in this step.)
- Requirements (or needs) have to be identified to accomplish those priorities.
- Collection priorities have to be created to satisfy those requirements.
- Collection strategies have to be decided upon in service to the priorities.
- After it is acquired, the collection product has to be processed, exploited, and disseminated.

What appears to be a straightforward, even simple list—is not.

Collectors like to think of the management of collection as having three phases (as noted in Chapter 1). In truth, the lines are blurred and some parts overlap, but for the purposes of this management chapter, we will honor the straight-line approach of most collectors. Generally, *front end* refers to the process of deciding what information to go after and what collection means to use: determining requirements (or needs) from national intelligence priorities, setting collection priorities based on those requirements, and forming a collection strategy. Ideally, an all-source analyst, the customer of collection, would (and should), as a coordinator, collaborate with collectors throughout these parts of the process. For this reason, the role of the analyst is included in this discussion. The front end section wraps up with a description of automated management tools that are intended to foster integration and interdependency among the players. The middle phase is described by collectors in simplest terms: collect or acquire the information.

Management thereafter (the *back end*) has to do with the processing, exploitation, and dissemination of the intelligence that has been collected. These core processes are complicated by management issues that hound any large intelligence community like that of the United States.

Managing across boundaries, managing customer expectations, and managing the process of bringing new capabilities online are other management issues in collection that are discussed herein. Collection evaluation wraps up the chapter.

Managing the Front End

INTELLIGENCE PRIORITIES

Intelligence priorities derive from national interests and priorities, which are usually expressed by the top levels of the executive branch, and increasingly the U.S. Congress. Intelligence priorities also must reflect existing and anticipated threats and opportunities as well as political, economic, and military constraints.

Intelligence priorities are particularly important to establish when collection assets can be allocated against a very large target set, and a subset must be selected for targeting. Almost all collection fits this definition. Almost any geographical location on earth can be targeted for visible or spectral imagery collection, but targeting all the earth would saturate overhead collection capabilities, and processing and exploitation of such worldwide collection simply could not be done. The same limitation applies to ELINT collection, with the added restriction that all available ELINT assets probably could not cover the entire radio frequency (RF) spectrum worldwide. In both cases, the collection problem has to be bounded, and intelligence priorities help to serve this purpose. The challenge, then, is to develop an effective system for establishing intelligence priorities.

Many attempts have been made to formalize intelligence priorities since the National Security Act of 1947. The following are some of them:

- During the early 1970s, the U.S. intelligence community developed a set of key intelligence questions (KIQs) that defined intelligence priorities.[1]
- During the mid-1970s, Director of Central Intelligence Directive 1/2 (DCID 1/2) created a matrix of intelligence targets and priorities that replaced the KIQs. Soon thereafter, it was replaced by the Foreign Intelligence Requirements, Categories, and Priorities (FIRCAP) system.[2]
- In 1992, the director of central intelligence (DCI) replaced FIRCAP with the national intelligence needs process, a hierarchical system for defining priorities. At the top level, these were very broadly defined, including issues such as political instability and weapons of mass destruction. At the bottom of the hierarchy, they were specific and measurable—issues such as the transparency and legitimacy of elections.[3]
- After the end of the Cold War, the United States reshaped its intelligence priorities to reflect the new realities. The initial result was Presidential Decision Directive 35 (PDD-35), which defined policy goals and intelligence needs. It separated intelligence requirements into two broad categories: so-called hard targets (such as Libya, Cuba, Iraq, Iran, and North Korea) and transnational issues (such as international crime, terrorism, and weapons proliferation). PDD-35 used a tier structure, with upper-tier countries having higher priority.[4] The PDD-35 priorities did not change for many years after 1995, despite changes in the international scene including the growth of the international terrorist threat.
- In 2003, the director of national intelligence (DNI) implemented the National Intelligence Priorities Framework (NIPF), discussed below, to replace PDD-35.

These priorities systems encounter pitfalls that are common to any intelligence organization:

- Collectors and analysts tend to focus their efforts on the top priorities in any prioritization system and leave little or no resources to address lower priorities.[5]
- Organizational survival dictates showing that the organization's collection or analysis efforts are addressing top priorities—after all, resources and budgets are at stake.

Past experience with a prioritization system illustrates how the problem develops. As noted earlier, in the 1970s the U.S intelligence community used DCID 1/2 to develop collection priorities. DCID 1/2 had a priorities scale of one to seven, with one being the highest priority. Senior policymakers and military commanders had to compete for satisfaction of their intelligence needs. All participants soon realized that if their priorities were ranked worse than two then collection wasn't likely to happen. An interagency committee met periodically to adjust the priorities. These meetings frequently devolved into heated arguments as advocates for a particular requirement argued for increasing its priority. Over time the great majority of requirements were ranked one or two, making the prioritization system almost useless. Eventually, the intelligence community leadership recognized that the system was broken and abandoned the DCID 1/2 approach.[6]

The NIPF is the current guidance from the DNI to the intelligence community on national intelligence priorities. It is reviewed by the National Security Council (NSC) and approved by the president. The NIPF guides prioritization for the operation, planning, and programming of U.S. intelligence collection and analysis. The NIPF is updated annually. It takes the form of a matrix of countries and nonstate actors of intelligence interest versus a set of intelligence topics. It is used to guide both collection and analysis of intelligence. Former National Intelligence Council Director Tom Fingar has described the NIPF as a matrix of

> 32 intelligence topics (subdivided into 3 prioritized bands) against roughly 220 countries and non-state actors. Each cell in the matrix receives a "score" ranging from zero to five, with zero meaning the cell is empty and that the topic will receive essentially no attention from the IC. One is the highest priority, and topics in that group will receive a great deal of attention. Category five topics are essentially "global coverage" accounts maintained to support diplomatic and other ongoing responsibilities, or "fire extinguisher" accounts maintained at a low level of effort because of their potential to flare up with significant implications for U.S. interests.[7]

Because the NIPF is reviewed at the NSC and not left to a subordinate interagency mechanism, it appears to be more successful than its predecessors. In the past, the urgency of many military requirements has tended to squeeze out the satisfaction of less time-sensitive, but nonetheless important, national requirements. But at the NSC the requirements of the Departments of State, Homeland Security, Justice, Treasury, Energy, CIA, and others get reviewed along with DoD requirements. The result is a longer term perspective on intelligence needs than that associated with immediate military operations support.[8]

REQUIREMENTS

The types of requirements that are commonly used need to be clarified. A collection management system has to be flexible to be able to adapt to rapidly changing situations. So, some provision has to be made for levying time-sensitive and ad hoc requirements based on new intelligence or for explaining the special circumstances surrounding a requirement. The imagery community refers to these requirements sets by the term *requirements decks,* but similar breakouts of requirements are used in most collection:

- *Standing* requirements are defined for continuing, long-term collection—often for repeated collection in the case of imagery or ELINT targets.
- *Time-sensitive* requirements need immediate collection action. Depending on the collection asset, this could mean a few minutes to a few days. A pending missile or nuclear weapon test would generate time-sensitive requirements.
- *Ad hoc* requirements are totally new, where no standing requirement exists. They usually are short term, on the order of a few days to a few weeks. Most materiel collection is ad hoc.
- *Amplification* of a requirement is often needed when conditions are imposed on how collection must be done (for example, at a certain time of day or a specific collector-to-target geometry). A good example is the detailed amplification associated with the Bruneval Raid described in Chapter 17.

Formal requirements structures are necessary in dealing with high volume overhead imagery intelligence (IMINT) and ELINT and with open source material, where a large number of potential targets exist, and where a large customer suite with competing priorities wants more collection than could be accomplished with the entire national budget.

This requirements structure has a problem, however, in dealing with priorities below the top level. It is important to understand that collection requirements form a hierarchy. Lower elements in the hierarchy are more specific and, in a well-drafted requirements hierarchy, are linked to the higher elements by some measures that indicate their relative value in the overall scheme of things. The number of specific, lower-level requirements will be in the dozens where the target is a specific company, in the hundreds for a small country or a consortium, and in the thousands for an illicit network target such as international narcotics. A typical requirement at the lower levels might read: "Geolocate all armored vehicles in the battlefield area" or "identify key members of the Sinaloa narcotics cartel."

In the United States, the NIPF establishes top-level priorities, but someone has to carry that priority structure down the requirements hierarchy.

That can be contentious, as the example of DCID 1/2 illustrates. Is a requirement to geolocate a coca field in Colombia more important than one to locate a poppy field in Afghanistan? How do those priorities compare with locating a mobile missile unit in Russia? This problem of establishing lower-level priorities has led senior U.S. intelligence officials to note, more than once, that everyone tasks the system, but no one prioritizes. And intelligence officers are reluctant to tell customers that "we do not need this badly enough to spend resources on it."[9]

Even when a sound, well-reasoned requirements hierarchy is put into place, a collection management issue can easily surface. When an issue has sufficiently high priority, it is relatively easy to ask for more collection resources than needed, and the collection system must respond—sometimes by taking resources away from lower-priority targets. Asking for a high-resolution optical imagery search over a large region to locate an airfield is a waste. An airfield can be located much more quickly and cheaply in lower-quality National Imagery Interpretability Rating Scale (NIIRS) 2 imagery and then imaged with high quality to obtain the needed level of detail. But a poorly designed requirements system can (and often does) result in such suboptimum resource allocation. So all participants in the requirements process—analysts, collectors, and customers—must exercise restraint and ask for what they need, not what would be nice to have.

COLLECTION PRIORITIES

Collection priorities are derived from intelligence priorities and requirements. But collection priorities are also informed by other considerations. Making the transition from NIPF (or any other system of defining intelligence priorities) to collection priorities is a challenge, for several reasons.

First, a collection gap must exist. This means that there must be a demonstrated inadequacy of alternative sources. Except in rare instances, the intelligence community should not use collection assets to obtain information that is already readily available. Specifically, if information is available from unclassified sources, intelligence collection assets should not be used to get it, except where cross-checking is essential—for example, in countering suspected deception. Increasingly, commercial sources such as commercial imaging satellites can do collection that once required national intelligence assets—and can do it more cheaply.

The key to making the transition from intelligence priorities to collection priorities is identifying and sorting collection gaps from all the other gaps. The material may already have been collected, but it has not been processed or exploited. Or it may have been processed and exploited, but it has not been analyzed. These latter cases are processing, exploitation, or analysis gaps—not collection gaps.

Second, there must be some probability of payoff. Collection assets should be allocated only where they are likely to produce a specific benefit or result for the policymaker or customer. Collection priorities have to reflect intelligence priorities and also involve information that the intelligence community can successfully obtain. Customers who possess high intelligence priorities naturally tend to demand the use of collection assets even when the probability of successful collection is nearly zero—a misuse, if not abuse, of limited resources. A collection manager has to be willing to stand up to customers—often to very powerful customers—and say, "That collection attempt would be a waste of our capabilities."

Collection priorities were a simpler problem during the Cold War. The Soviet Union always was the preeminent target, and first priority went to collecting against its nuclear and conventional military forces. Furthermore, the Soviet Union was a very predictable collection target. The locations of its military bases and test ranges were well known. The United States and the Soviet Union had a number of common interests and mutually understood patterns of behavior that limited the effects of the occasional misjudgments.

Collection priorities have become much more complex since then. The opponents in the war on terrorism are far less predictable. Their bases and attack capabilities are not well known and change rapidly. Furthermore, there are a sizable number of failed states where a situation that is inimical to U.S. interests could develop at any time with little warning. Consequently, collection priorities have become much more dynamic.

When collection priorities are not carefully thought through, the bulk of raw data collected is irrelevant. For example, much new overhead imagery contains information that is already known; natural terrain features and fixed structures change little, if at all, in the course of a year, though they may be imaged many times during that year.

However, all data that are collected must be processed to some extent, and the handling of this volume of irrelevant data chokes the processing and exploitation systems and often chokes the analyst as well.

COLLECTION STRATEGIES

For the sake of argument, let's say that national interests have been properly transformed into clear intelligence priorities, which have, in turn, been translated into a well-reasoned requirements hierarchy. The collection management system knows what it needs to do and turns to the *how* of getting it done.

A collection strategy can be described as a systematic plan to optimize the effective and efficient tasking of all capable, available, and appropriate collection assets and resources against requirements, where

- effectiveness is determined by analyzing the capability and availability of assets and resources to collect against specific targets, and
- efficiency is determined by comparing the appropriateness of all potential assets to collect against specific targets in a given environment.[10]

As an efficiency example, an intelligence imaging satellite might provide a greater NIIRS capability than is required to collect against a specific target. In this situation, a commercial imaging satellite might be quite capable of meeting the NIIRS requirement and would therefore serve as an appropriate substitute for the more capable imager, which could be more efficiently used elsewhere.

Another example is that a requirement could result in multiple tasking to collect specific data. For instance, a requirement related to human rights and war crimes might result in tasking for the collection of multiple communications, imaging of suspected burial sites, special reports from human sources with access, compilation of open source materials, and specialized technical collection.[11] Obtaining open source materials, in this example, is relatively easy and inexpensive. Imaging of suspected burial sites might come next in order of difficulty and cost, probably followed by communications intelligence (COMINT). The tasking of human sources, while not necessarily expensive, could be highly risky and therefore used as a last resort—that is, only if nothing else satisfies the requirement.

The point of these examples is that a collection strategy must consider all outstanding intelligence requirements, their relative priority, and the immediate situation in allocating scarce resources. And to repeat the point, an expensive or risky source should not be used when a cheaper or less risky one can do the job.

A few collection problems are easy. A missile silo needs to be checked to ensure that it is still operational. The collection involves getting an overhead optical image of the silo so that the image can be processed and exploited. This solution requires little thought and not much coordination.

However, as previously noted throughout this book, today's targets are more complex. If the target to be checked is a mobile missile instead of a fixed silo, then the missile must first be located. The immediate question becomes: What assets should be tasked to locate the missile? There are several choices—visible and synthetic aperture radar (SAR) imagery are two choices for obtaining imagery of the possible missile locations. Each has its advantages, depending on the possible missile locations, camouflage, and the size of the area to be imaged. ELINT or communications intercepts might be used to locate the missile. Human intelligence (HUMINT) collection might be possible, or some combination of these might be necessary. In some cases, on-site inspection may be an option for locating the missile because of an arms verification treaty. And of course, open source can sometimes provide clues to missile locations.

Given the range of possible collection scenarios for complex targets, it is necessary to develop a collection strategy before tasking collection assets. This means considering the utility of all possible collectors and coordinating their use across several different organizations.

Collection managers therefore try to develop strategies that integrate tasking and collection of multidisciplinary assets to obtain maximum value from the collection. The idea is to leverage the unique capabilities of each asset and to manage and allocate the collection resources to provide more value than independently developed strategies can achieve. Such collaborative strategies can use one of two approaches:[12]

• *Convergent collection:* Using different collection assets simultaneously against a target. Simultaneous COMINT and IMINT collection, for example, can provide a more complete picture of activity at a site than can either one taken individually.

• *Sequential collection:* Triggering collection by an asset based on information obtained from another technical, COMINT, or HUMINT asset; sequential collection also could mean staggering collection timing to obtain a benefit such as greater persistence of coverage.

These collaborative approaches result in more effective collection strategies, and they are often used. Some parts of the U.S. intelligence community have attempted to formalize this process with an initiative called, not surprisingly, collaborative collection strategies (CCS). CCS is basically a renaming of traditional multi-intelligence collection, intended to have collectors and analysts formally collaborate throughout the process to support cross-discipline collection and analysis operations—from identification of the problem through the development and execution of the specific strategy. CCS operations have for some time made use of COMINT–IMINT collaboration, and attempts are being made to include the other intelligence

Managing
Intelligence
Collection

community disciplines.[13] For example, HUMINT enables many other collection efforts, and vice versa:

- Construction of a new underground facility observed in imagery can be the basis of a request for HUMINT collection. The reverse is also true— HUMINT about the construction can be used to task imagery collection—but the timeliness problem sometimes intervenes. HUMINT can take time to get through the system, and imagery of the underground facility is far less valuable after the facility has been covered with earth or the excavation spoil removed.
- HUMINT reporting of suspicious aircraft landing and taking off at an airfield only during nighttime can be used to request the emplacement of acoustic sensors near the airfield to identify the aircraft.
- A HUMINT source might use a handheld camera to obtain a picture of a new radar antenna. Measurements of the antenna can allow analysts to estimate the operating frequency for ELINT targeting.

Such cross-cueing of collectors can be done in real time or near real time, and it has a special name in the intelligence business: it is called *tip-off*. In many cases, a collection target has a very fleeting lifetime. So planning for tip-off is an important part of collection strategy. The actual tip-off is done in the tasking phase, but it has to be planned for in the strategy phase. Coordinated tasking of collection from a variety of sensor platforms and regimes is crucial to solving tough intelligence problems. Sometimes, collection is only wanted if certain events occur. This is one purpose served by tip-off. For example, radar detection of an unidentified aircraft can be used to tip off ELINT collection against the aircraft's radar to help identify the aircraft.

Following are two other examples of collection strategies that are used to deal with difficult collection problems.

Swarm, Surge, or Blitz Collection Strategy. The problem of conducting reconnaissance is that, if the opponent can determine the reconnaissance pattern, the reconnaissance can then be defeated by careful timing of activities to avoid the times when collectors are present. This is a particular problem with overhead ELINT and IMINT collection. While there may not be enough assets to conduct surveillance, whatever is available can be allocated for a short time to provide intensive coverage of specific targets. The intelligence community has various names for this collection strategy, including *blitz, surge,* or *swarm* collection.

The customer of such collection—here, the analyst—has to recognize that the collected material is the result of a surge or blitz. Failure to understand this can lead to erroneous analysis, as it did in one conclusion of the national intelligence estimate on Iraqi weapons of mass destruction. Analysts concluded that there had been an increase in activity at suspect Iraqi chemical facilities; the Weapons of Mass Destruction Commission report concluded that the apparent increase in activity may have been simply a result of increased imagery of the facilities.[14]

Probing Strategy. Against targets that practice denial and deception, provocative probing can sometimes be of benefit. In the U.S. Air Force airborne reconnaissance programs dating back to the 1950s, probing was used effectively to overcome the practice of emissions control by the Soviet Union. In emissions control, all nonessential signals were kept off the air until the signals intelligence (SIGINT) collector had left the area. The U.S. response was to send an aircraft on a penetration course toward the Soviet border, for example, and turn away at the last minute, after the Soviets had turned on their entire air defense network to deal with the threat. Probing an opponent's system and watching the response is a useful tactic for learning more about the system. The reaction to probing may have its own set of undesirable consequences, however: The Soviets would occasionally chase and shoot down the reconnaissance aircraft to discourage the probing practice.

THE ALL-SOURCE ANALYST ROLE

The idea of a front end was introduced in Chapter 1. It is a term of art in intelligence collection, referring to the process that involves everything that we have discussed so far. An integral player in managing the front end of collection is the all-source analyst.

Even a large and bureaucratic collection network such as that of the United States can be responsive. But the intelligence analyst has to play a more significant role in making it so. The Weapons of Mass Destruction Commission noted that analysts—the customers of collection—should have a role in formulating collection strategy:

> Analysts must be willing to admit what they don't know in order to focus future collection efforts.[15]

That is presumably a goal of the collaborative collection strategies project described in the previous section. Analysts can bring a unique expertise and understanding of the target to the process. Helping to focus collection has a high payoff for the analyst, and analysts bring a unique asset to the table. As a part of their normal jobs, they have to create both a problem breakdown model and a target model. By sharing these models with collectors so that the collectors can identify gaps in knowledge, the analyst better equips them to effectively fill the gaps. Tracking the status of collection requests, finding out who else is asking for the same information (and thereby is part of a community of interest), and obtaining access to others' research results all are facilitated by a common system such as proposed by the collaborative collection strategies.

In the last two decades, some intelligence organizations have defined a specialized career field called *targeting analyst* to meet this need. In this terminology, the *target* often is a person who possesses information of intelligence value, but it can also mean networks, organizations, communications systems, or facilities. The job of the targeting analyst is to translate intelligence needs into potential targets, identify gaps in knowledge, identify collection assets that can be used against the target, and develop a collection plan. In essence, one analyst handles all these steps. The targeting analyst clearly does not plan for mass collection, such as imagery or ELINT collection, which is best done by automated systems. The analyst concentrates on what was earlier described as targeted collection, and is most likely to be focused on a single target of very high intelligence value.

A formal and elaborate requirements system tends not to be very responsive. Because of the failure to prioritize in detail, and because there are more requirements than collection assets can handle, many requirements simply are not satisfied. When analysts and collectors work together to provide background, justification, detailed guidance, and follow-up evaluations, the system can be very responsive. And any collection system rewards analysts who take the time to cultivate collectors and to provide feedback on the value of collection products.

TASKING

The next step in the front-end process is tasking of collection assets. Tasking involves providing specific guidance to a specific collector. A collection requirement might request "an image of Latakia harbor at sufficient quality to identify cargo vessels in the harbor." The tasking to support this requirement might specify "U-2 mission 1037: collect NIIRS 6.5 visible imagery, 2 × 2 NM frame centered on 35° 32' N, 35° 46' E at approximately 0200Z hours on 27 July 2013."

Missile and aircraft foreign instrumentation signals intelligence (FISINT) tasking is more event-oriented; collection can occur only during or immediately before flight times. ELINT tasking is somewhere in between—automated but with tasking controlled by events. One seldom knows when a signal of high importance will suddenly appear.

An example of how software handles automated imagery tasking is the algorithm developed to handle tasking of the Hyperion hyperspectral imager that is on NASA's EO-1 satellite. The software has available cloud data generated by the Air Force Weather Agency and uses it to task Hyperion so that the sensor won't attempt to image clouded areas. It is designed to manage the convergent and sequential collection strategies discussed earlier. That is, it can support ad hoc tasking. It can identify available collection resources, recommend how they should be allocated against targets, and time individual collectors to get the best geolocation accuracy and image resolution.[16]

Tasking must not only be specific, as the U-2 example above illustrates. It must often include background information to help the collector. Many requirements need amplification or explanation. A formal requirements system too often does not allow the needed level of amplification. It is difficult to provide for all the nuances and conditions that accompany a requirement. Both materiel and materials collection, for example, require very specific guidance; most successful collections occur when the collectors fully understand the what, when, where, and why. Consider R.V. Jones's tasking on collection against the Würzburg radar, discussed in the case study of Chapter 17. The guidance was highly specific on what parts to bring back. Sometimes, the collectors even need advice about how to collect. For example, the collection of a biological sample or factory effluent may require collection under very specific conditions, and the sample may need to be handled, stored, or transported only in a certain fashion. As another example from Chapter 13, FISINT collected after the second-stage burnout of a ballistic missile has far less intelligence value than FISINT collected up to that point.

COLLECTION MANAGEMENT TOOLS

The preceding sections illustrate the complexity of front-end management. In an attempt to manage this complex front-end process for large collection systems with many customers, the U.S. intelligence community has developed many automated collection management tools. Sometimes these tools also are used to manage the back-end processes discussed in the next section. Over the years, a number of efforts have been made to transition from the plethora of individual tools to a set of intelligence community–wide collection management tools that would do integrated collection management.

Managing
Intelligence
Collection

In 1994, the DoD began development of the joint collection management tools (JCMT), intended to be a DoD system for all-source collection management, combining IMINT, SIGINT, measurements and signatures (MASINT), and HUMINT tasking. This software package supported the gathering, organizing, and tracking of intelligence collection requirements for all these disciplines. The JCMT replaced a number of existing collection management systems, including the

- Army's Collection Management Support Tools,
- Defense Intelligence Agency's Collection Requirements Management Application,
- Operational Support Office's National Exercise Support Terminal,
- United States Southern Command's Intelligence Support Processing Tool, and
- USAF National Air Intelligence Center's Collection Requirements Management System.[17]

The complex human-machine interface, message parsing problems, and heavy database maintenance requirements resulted in JCMT being terminated in 2000. It was incorporated into the Intelligence Community Multi-intelligence Acquisition Program (IC-MAP), subsequently renamed the Intelligence Community Analysis and Requirements System (ICARS).[18]

The ICARS program reportedly was terminated in 2009. But it illustrates how an integrated system might function. The concept was to build a Web-based collection requirements management environment that provides a single point of entry for analysts to shape collection. It was intended to connect all intelligence community collection requirements management systems and make it easier for analysts to submit their collection needs or describe intelligence gaps. Also, analysts would have been able to search and view existing requirements that complement their own. ICARS was intended to foster collaboration across organizational boundaries, as analysts subscribe to each other's requests and work together with collectors to formulate optimal collection strategies.[19]

Another example of a cross-agency requirements system is a joint National Geospatial-Intelligence Agency (NGA) and National Security Agency (NSA) effort called *Integrated Collection Management* (ICM). ICM is intended to synchronize these agencies' collection and exploitation efforts through all phases of the process—tasking, collection, production, exploitation, and dissemination—with a vision to do so across all intelligence disciplines.[20]

At the time of this writing, a number of discipline-specific requirements management systems continue to exist at the national level, and a number of parallel systems exist within DoD:

- The Requirements Management System (RMS) is used to manage and task imagery collection, exploitation, and production. It is managed by NGA.[21]
- The MASINT requirements system (MRS) performs a similar function for MASINT collection.[22]
- The National SIGINT Requirements Process (NSRP) is a system for requesting SIGINT (including ELINT and FISINT) collection and processing. It evaluates and prioritizes requirements.[23]
- The Open Source Requirements Management System (OSRMS) is handled by the director of national intelligence's Open Source Center (which is organizationally within CIA). This system allows users to research existing open source requirements, submit new ones, and track their status.[24]

Exactly what sort of management tool will emerge from these programs, and what it will look like, remains an open issue. However, the uniform goal of these efforts paints a picture of what the ideal collection management system would look like. In this picture, analysts and collectors would be able to work in concert to manage opportunities and diminish duplication. Collectors would know what other collectors are doing so that they could anticipate synergistic opportunities. And the system would function effectively across many different classification levels.

Managing the Back End

A critical phase of collection is the processing and exploitation of the raw intelligence that has been collected. This phase has to be planned for, and resources allocated for it, before a collection system becomes operational. And yet this part of the overall collection effort often is the most difficult to know how to plan for. It is relatively easy to assess the potential value of collection systems; what they can do usually is well understood in advance. But the value added by processing and exploitation is not as well understood. The processing of literal intelligence information (primarily from open source, HUMINT, and COMINT) is fairly straightforward. It usually involves translation of text. In contrast, nonliteral information can require the continuing efforts of technical experts and the development and maintenance of large software packages. Processing and exploitation of hyperspectral and SAR imagery can be very expensive. And the changing target set forces additional modifications. For example, when a country deploys new radars, the ELINT processing and exploitation system may have to be updated to accommodate these new targets—often at a substantial cost because it has to be done quickly.

Furthermore, with new types of collection, planners may not know in advance how to best design processing and exploitation. Also, new ways to use collection are sometimes discovered after the collection system has been in operation for a while. These factors all tend to make the back-end development lag behind the collection system itself.

The exploitation of nonliteral collection often requires correlating a signature with a signature database for identification purposes. As discussed in Part II, this requires a signature library: a large database of processed, exploited, and accessible material that can be used to monitor activity and detect significant changes in signatures or patterns. So, complete and up-to-date signature libraries are critical components of the back end. The importance of signature libraries has been stressed throughout Part II. A large number of such libraries is needed, including a basic IMINT library, ELINT and FISINT libraries, and hyperspectral and acoustic signature libraries.

Managing the signature libraries is a continuing challenge. The libraries must be constantly updated and made available to all potential users. The challenge is much like that of managing the FBI's fingerprint library, which also must be constantly updated and available to a large number of law enforcement agencies. Collaborative sharing and exploitation of the signatures has resulted in better intelligence wherever it has been tried. The law enforcement community recognizes the value of sharing fingerprint libraries. In contrast, intelligence collection organizations have in the past tended to protect and compartment their libraries. This natural tendency to protect against the loss of sources limits the potential value of the libraries and the potential for better use of the intelligence they provide.[25]

Managing Across Boundaries

Commercial companies sometimes speak of their organizational culture as having "silos." The reference is to those huge metal cylinders found in rural farm areas where large quantities of grain are stored, keeping the grain separate from any outside elements. Grain is funneled out in small batches from a small opening, only when needed. Businesses normally use the metaphor in a pejorative sense to mean that their departments are isolated from each other, thereby inhibiting creativity, collaboration, and the potential benefits from partnerships. In the intelligence community, we use the term stovepipes to describe a similar phenomenon that has grown up over many decades.

There is no argument that a need exists for real-time cross-community collaboration. And stovepipes do make it hard to allocate requirements to assets and to collaborate in ways that would produce synergy. But stovepipes were a natural result of a growing intelligence community. Professor Peter Oleson describes it this way:

> As the U.S. intelligence community evolved after World War II, specific organizations grew up surrounding collection disciplines and technical specialties within them. For example, the NSA focused on SIGINT—especially the collection, processing, decryption, and analysis of adversaries' communications. CIA's Directorate of Operations developed the expertise surrounding the spotting, recruitment, vetting, tasking, and running of clandestine human sources, including the ability to communicate covertly (HUMINT). CIA's National Photographic Interpretation Center (NPIC) became the technical experts at the interpretation of satellite and other imagery (IMINT). These specialty organizations became known as *stovepipes*. They managed the process of their specialties from cradle to grave.
>
> As intelligence grew in importance, size, and complexity, multiple agencies became involved in each technical specialty. Duplication of effort and wasted resources were inevitable results. While the secretary of defense was the government's executive agent for SIGINT, and NSA was vested in carrying out that responsibility, CIA and the services were also involved in SIGINT activities. DIA and the services also conducted HUMINT activities. Similarly, DIA and the services were heavily involved in IMINT for satisfying their own requirements. Arguments between organizations, especially over investment and budget allocations, were legend. Congress often challenged the executive branch to better manage its duplicative efforts.[26]

The intelligence community (IC) stovepipes are sometimes mistakenly thought of as collection stovepipes, that is, as being divided by collection INT.[27] The stovepipes exist, but they should not be thought of as being just HUMINT or COMINT stovepipes, for example. There are, in fact, four types of stovepipes: organizational, compartmented, technical, and international. All four of these have valid reasons to exist. The challenge is to make the collection system function more effectively with stovepipes, because they are not likely to disappear.

ORGANIZATIONAL STOVEPIPES

Organizational separation creates the dominant stovepipes within the U.S. intelligence community. A large number of IC organizations do collection. Major collection assets are owned by the CIA, DIA, NGA, NRO, NSA, and

military services. Nonliteral collection in particular does not have a single champion agency in the sense that traditional HUMINT and COMINT do (though parts of technical collection, such as IMINT and ELINT, have their champions). There is no national processing and exploitation center to provide visibility for nonliteral collection, no senior authority, and no clear ownership.

Powerful incentives to retain stovepipes are pervasive in any business, corporation, or industry, or in academia, for that matter. They are easy to understand in the realm of intelligence organizations:

- Military combat units all strongly prefer to have their own intelligence collection and analysis units. A long-standing principle of military commanders is summed up by this statement: "If I don't control it, I can't rely on it." The assumption is that only one of their own can properly understand their unique needs.
- All organizations want their intelligence successes to be recognized and find it difficult to see another organization take even partial credit. Managers naturally tend to highlight their successes and downplay the contributions of other organizations. This general disinclination to share the fruits of successes hurts the potential for collaboration.
- A closely related incentive is provided by the competition for funding. Funding decisions depend on achieving recognition by the organization providing funds—in this case, the U.S. Congress. Groups that Congress regards as providing highly valuable intelligence tend to get funded; less visible contributors see their funding cut.

As a result, collection is a continuing focus for bureaucratic infighting or competition over ownership of the assets.[28] The ideal would be to manage by issue across all collection with a collaborative focus on targets, addressing the priorities discussed in previous sections, so that the available assets can complement each other. Such a level of collaboration requires a common objective, compatible policies among agencies, and interoperable systems. Information sharing among collectors has improved in recent years, but it has room to improve yet.

Nevertheless, there have been attempts to manage collection across organizational stovepipes. The initial attempt to do all-source collection management resulted from Presidential Executive Order 12036 in 1977. It established the National Intelligence Tasking Center (NITC) under the direction, control, and management of the director of central intelligence for coordinating and tasking national foreign intelligence collection activities by all elements of the intelligence community, including the DoD and FBI.

The effort was generally opposed by other agencies and ultimately just disappeared.[29]

The DNI has established the National Intelligence Coordination Center (NIC-C) to oversee the use of all IC collection assets and to facilitate collaboration among collection organizations. The NIC-C has an ambitious agenda that includes front-end management, coordination, and collection evaluation. It appears to have the goal of achieving the ideal collection management system described at the beginning of this chapter. Whether it can succeed where the NITC did not, given the tenacity of the organizational stovepipes, is an open question. Strong incentives exist to maintain these stovepipes. Until the incentives are dealt with, an organization like NIC-C faces continuing challenges to its authority. Meanwhile, much of the success in collaboration appears to come from individuals in the intelligence community who work across the organizational boundaries, respecting the sensitivities of their partners and understanding their cultural mores.

COMPARTMENTED STOVEPIPES

The U.S. intelligence and defense communities have a large number of **special access programs (SAPs)**, often called *black programs*. These programs also are referred to as compartmented programs because they are protected by special security compartments to which access is highly restricted. Compartmentation has an obvious benefit: The program's success is usually dependent on an opponent being unaware of its existence or what it does. The steady loss of collection assets supports those who argue for more compartments, and, in fact, the compartments continue to proliferate. But compartmentation stovepipes have their price:

- Compartmentation often keeps intelligence from getting to those who need it—other collectors, analysts, and customers. The guardians of compartmented intelligence programs face a constant trade-off between protecting their source and making the product available. They have to balance security versus effectiveness.[30]

- Compartmentation means that different security levels must somehow coexist in the overall system. The difficulty of achieving multilevel security in information networks makes collaboration difficult.[31]

- Compartmentation tends to protect the stovepipes from pressures to change, and competition for funding provides an incentive to maintain the stovepipe and make it stronger. IC managers naturally focus on protecting their special compartments.

Compartmentation has an added dimension when intelligence must support law enforcement agencies and homeland security. Few people in these organizations have any security clearances at all. So the intelligence product requires sanitization, which creates policy, security, and oversight issues that are not easily addressed.

TECHNICAL STOVEPIPES

Technical stovepipes exist because of the need to pull together pools of expertise on tough collection issues. But the specialists in one field of collection usually do not have in-depth knowledge of the other fields and so often do not recognize the opportunities for cooperation. As an example, optical and SAR imagery collection are usually under a single overall organizational stovepipe—NGA in the United States. But the required technical expertise is quite different for collection and processing of these two types of imagery. Optical engineers work in the former, and radar engineers are needed in the latter. Across all of technical collection, the different INTs require a wide variety of skill sets, and practitioners typically have little in common in the different subdisciplines. Also, collection is characterized by a wide range of cultures speaking in different tongues; communication across disciplines is difficult—mirroring a problem that exists in the world of basic and applied research. Furthermore, because many of the technical collection assets are poorly understood, and because there are so many of them, users do not take advantage of their potential. It is difficult to task and to exploit the results of tasking.

The signature libraries that characterize nonliteral collection may be the most stovepiped part of a stovepiped community. Each library is designed for effective use by the subdiscipline that it supports. The result is that any effort to reach across libraries in collaborative analysis efforts is very frustrating. Analytical software that can access one library generally cannot make use of any other library.

In spite of the problems created by technical stovepipes, they fill an important need. A critical mass of expertise is necessary for progress in any collection discipline, and technical stovepipes serve this purpose.

INTERNATIONAL STOVEPIPES

An important part of collection management is managing collection and product sharing across national boundaries.

U.S. intelligence does a superb job in leveraging the assets, capabilities, and territory of its international partners. Partnerships may be the single biggest U.S. collection advantage over its adversaries. Of course, the resultant sharing of intelligence benefits the partners as well. The Soviet Union also had liaison relationships with its satellite intelligence agencies in Eastern Europe, but this was not a true partnership. The KGB tended to dominate the relationship and reap most of the benefits.[32]

Increasingly, the United States shares collection with its international partners and in turn depends on these partners for collection. For ELINT and COMINT, this is not new. The United States has collaborated with the British, Australians, Canadians, and New Zealanders in this area for years. Some collection sensors must be deployed on the territory of allies. Such sensors usually are deployed via cooperative operations with foreign military or intelligence services. The AN/FPS-95, described in Chapter 11, was deployed in the United Kingdom. The IUSS, discussed in Chapter 14, was deployed with the assistance of Canada, the United Kingdom, and Iceland.[33] The X band radar, described in Chapter 11, has been deployed to Japan.[34] And the Japanese cooperation in exploitation of the MiG-25 illustrates the beneficial results to the United States of these relationships. Such sharing of collection assets necessitates a great deal of planning and collaboration.

Furthermore, the increasing frequency of multinational operations has forced sharing with a wider range of coalition partners. Treaty monitoring agreements often require international collaboration; an example is the IMS network for monitoring nuclear testing that was discussed in Chapter 14. The United States increasingly relies on a multinational network of collectors or processing and exploitation staff for load-sharing and especially for language translation. The growing U.S. network of foreign partners has a number of benefits but also raises some concerns:

- Foreign partners can be encouraged to carry out certain missions, but they cannot be directed to do so.
- Over time, these partners learn a great deal about U.S. collection assets and capabilities; some partners potentially are a source of leaks that reduce the effectiveness of these collection assets.
- Sharing of intelligence with coalition foreign partners is increasingly important but appears to lack a coherent policy. Many U.S. intelligence organizations have direct liaison relationships with many countries. The closest analogue would be if each department of the U.S. government dealt directly with its foreign counterparts, independent of the State Department.

Managing
Intelligence
Collection

FUNCTIONAL MANAGEMENT OF STOVEPIPES

So today, collection is spread across organizational and national boundaries and security compartments. We would like to achieve synergy in collection, which means real-time cross-INT collaboration among all collection groups. But the boundaries, or stovepipes, make it harder to allocate requirements to assets and to collaborate in collection to achieve synergy.

As the preceding sections discuss, stovepipes serve an essential purpose. They create a management structure for collection. They prepare and defend collection budgets. Almost no one suggests eliminating them. Instead, the focus has been on eliminating the barriers they pose to cross-INT innovation and the adoption of new approaches, as discussed in the preceding section on organizational stovepipes.

What evolved out of this need for change was a new management model (a hybrid approach) referred to as functional management. It began in the DoD when DIA was assigned the budget planning authority for general military intelligence in the mid-1970s. The director of DIA was named as the functional manager of the General Defense Intelligence Program (GDIP), which incorporated the non-SIGINT programs of DIA and the four services. The director of NSA became the functional manager for SIGINT, with oversight and influence over the allocation of funds and program priorities for SIGINT efforts in the services, the National Reconnaissance Office, and CIA.[35]

Within the intelligence community, there are now numerous functional managers for different collection and analysis disciplines. An example during the last decade was the concept of functionally managing geospatial intelligence (GEOINT). The director of NGA is the GEOINT functional manager. But GEOINT involves both collection and all-source analysis, so GEOINT activities are conducted outside of NGA by all of the military services, DIA, CIA, the National Reconnaissance Office (NRO), FBI, and a host of other government agencies—not all of whom are intelligence organizations (for example, the U.S. Geological Survey).[36]

Managing Customer Expectations

Customers occasionally develop an unrealistic perception of what intelligence collection can do. So an important part of a collection manager's job is ensuring that customers understand both the constraints that limit collection and the opportunities that it can provide.

After a collection capability has been operating for many years, the customer set understands what it can do. The customers have integrated that capability into their own planning. They depend on the continuing existence of the capability—which is both an asset and a liability, because it leads to the *legacy system* problem. It is very difficult to drop a capability even though it may have declined in overall value, because the customers depend on it. But in times of constrained budgets, the funds spent on maintaining legacy systems are not available to develop new and more effective collection systems.

New collection assets, though, have a quite different problem. Users do not understand how new systems work or what value the collection has, so they are slow to ask for or use collection from those systems. They have to learn the capabilities and limitations of new collection, and that takes time. So the U.S. intelligence community faces the continuing challenge of educating customers about the capabilities of new collection assets. That, of course, is a primary purpose of this book.

KNOWLEDGE OF COLLECTION VALUE

Customers include both the all-source analysts who must use the collection product and their customers in the military, law enforcement, and national policy communities who must accept the results—and are unlikely to rely on systems that they do not understand. That is not a great problem for literal intelligence, which is generally well understood. But much of the non-literal collection product, except for visible imagery, is poorly understood. Among analysts, the understanding of nonliteral collection varies according to the analytic specialty:

- Scientific, technical, and weapons systems analysts are the most comfortable with technical collection disciplines. They depend on the collection product for assessing foreign weapons systems and weapons proliferation issues.
- Military analysts are next in line in understanding. They have relied for years on materiel exploitation, for example. And technical collection is of particular value for countering denial and deception (D&D) because a typical target has multiple signatures, and it is difficult to hide or simulate them all. The fact that some techniques are poorly understood by foreign intelligence services helps here.
- Political and economic analysts, in contrast, tend to rely less on technical collection and have less understanding of its potential value for helping to answer their questions.

Even among its users, though, nonliteral collection often is poorly understood, in part because it is highly technical, in part because it covers a broad range of intelligence disciplines having a highly diverse customer set. A large expertise gap exists between the practitioners (collectors and processors) and users of the product. The practitioners rely heavily on technical jargon that all-source analysts find difficult to understand. End users can sometimes view, and discuss with all-source analysts, the product of COMINT, HUMINT, or open source reporting. But except for visible imagery, the end users of intelligence seldom see the product of technical collection and would struggle with it if they did. Even visible imagery, which most users can understand, needs some analysis of the signatures involved.

Because technical collection is poorly understood, end users often do not recognize its value, lack confidence in the product, and are slow to accept it. It often does not get the respect that it deserves, and it does not have a strong customer base. Some end users refer to the more arcane technical intelligence products as "witchcraft" or "voodoo-INT." As the intelligence community becomes familiar with the products over time, some established technical collection capabilities gain acceptance. However, the rapidly advancing technologies in many collection areas mean that the understanding problem will continue to exist for new capabilities coming into the inventory.

So collection managers must reach out to and continually educate these customers. The analyst–collector relationship needs to be strengthened. The knowledge problem is especially severe in the high-tech disciplines covered in this book, but it varies significantly in specific disciplines. For example, visible imagery is well understood by customers, but disciplines such as radar intelligence and acoustic and material signature collection and analysis are poorly understood.[37]

DEALING WITH TIMELINESS PRESSURES

The customers of intelligence continue to demand more timely access to intelligence, for several reasons:

- Policymakers always want intelligence *now*, and they often are reacting to current events—meaning that their needs are unpredictable. Today, it is Sri Lanka; tomorrow, it is Vanuatu; next week, it is Pakistan.
- Combat operations units increasingly are customers and reliant on national collection assets for targeting. Like policymakers, these customers have a timeliness requirement, but they have more predictable needs. Intelligence as a result is becoming more closely tied to operations, even pulling the trigger in some military operations (for example, CIA using

Hellfire missile–equipped Predator unmanned aerial vehicles [UAVs] to target terrorists).

- The law enforcement community is increasingly reliant on intelligence, and law enforcement operates at a fast pace. One hour of delay often is too much.

Intelligence analysts get the most pressure from these timeliness demands because they are close to the customer, but the collectors also feel it. Many of the literal intelligence sources have difficulty meeting these demands for timeliness because language translation often is required.

Technical collection, though, is able to deliver real-time or near real-time products directly to operational units and policymakers. ELINT and imagery sources routinely do so today. Some of the newer technical collection capabilities require extensive processing to obtain the signature because they rely on experimental and immature technology. The associated processes are technology-intensive, dependent on specialized expertise, and therefore slow. The trend as these technologies mature, though, is to automate the processing and disseminate the product in near real time.

Bringing New Collection Capabilities Online

The exciting aspect of collection is that it is so reliant on new technologies and new techniques. The advance of technology affects all collection positively in two ways:

- The proliferation of new technologies worldwide means that there are more opportunities for collection; the collection targets exhibit new vulnerabilities over time. There are more signatures, as electronic systems like radars, communications means, and personal digital assistants (PDAs) proliferate. To illustrate, if the collection target was an Old Order Amish community (admittedly, a highly unlikely intelligence target), you would almost be reduced to HUMINT, biometrics, and open source for collection; the Amish tend not to use a wide range of modern technologies. But the typical person, object, organization, or installation today offers a rich set of potential access points for collection and exploitation.
- New technologies and techniques can be applied to obtain better collection from existing sources or to develop new sources. The Internet, radio-frequency identification (RFID) tags, hyperspectral and ultraspectral imaging, radar and optical polarimetry, and a number of materials-sensing techniques all did not exist during most of the Cold War.

To take advantage of these opportunities, an intelligence organization must do at least three things: maintain a technological edge; shorten the research, development, test, and evaluation (RDT&E) cycle in order to get collection, processing, and exploitation systems into the field more quickly; and effectively manage the difficult transition from research and development (R&D) into operational systems.

MAINTAINING A TECHNOLOGICAL EDGE

Collection assets have a finite useful lifetime, and sometimes a very short one. Revelations tend to reduce the value of collection assets, especially in the United States. No other country seems to compromise its intelligence assets as quickly as the United States does, and the impact on technical collection is especially heavy. The consequence is that new technologies need to be developed and applied constantly, which requires a robust R&D effort. There are some challenges, though, in maintaining this technological edge.

First, the pressure from customers (cited previously) encourages collectors to rely on known sources, technology, and targets instead of developing new ones. The legacy system issue encourages collectors to rely on traditional sources and traditional ways of doing business. Searching for new radar signals, for example, often is not encouraged in ELINT; all assets are consumed by the existing signals, and the demands for coverage of known targets make it difficult to search for new ones. Analysts support this inclination by demanding more of the same. Once there is an established set of customers for any set of targets, it is difficult to stop providing that intelligence. The customers often depend on continuing to receive the information. For example, if the military's precision targeting systems depend on the existence of multispectral imagery of the target with a certain level of accuracy, then halting the collection of such imagery kills the effectiveness of an important military capability.

Second, when new collection systems are developed, the workforce has to be trained to use them. So the intelligence community faces a continuing need to train its workforce to employ new technologies and to use the capabilities of new collection assets.

Finally, the U.S. intelligence community must deal with consequences of a long-standing not-invented-here (NIH) attitude. Many of the IC components have been reluctant to adopt either commercial technologies or those developed by other U.S. government agencies. For many decades, this worked; the IC was ahead of the commercial world in developing and applying new technologies. But today, commercial entities lead in several collection areas. Las Vegas gambling casinos were leaders in the application of facial recognition. Microsoft and other companies took the lead in developing and applying information technology. Google Earth has raced ahead in the geospatial arena. Accustomed to being leaders, some IC segments have not adjusted easily to being followers.

Change is hard on all participants, and managing change is especially difficult. There are entire books written on how to deal with it. But, in the end, it becomes a simple proposition for every IC manager. Remaining the premier intelligence force in the world hinges on maintaining a technological edge.

ACCELERATING THE RDT&E CYCLE

Closely related to maintaining a technological edge is accelerating the RDT&E cycle. But the RDT&E cycle through which new systems must go can take a very long time. Satellites, ships, and aircraft have a development cycle measured in years. Ground sites such as the Maui space surveillance facility discussed in Chapter 8 have a development cycle measured in decades. The time frame, especially for large systems, seems to be becoming longer. One legitimate reason for this is the increasing complexity of the systems. But part of the delay has to do with the process and length of program reviews and approvals.

It is possible to shorten the development time frame by using an accelerated process. The U.S. Air Force coined the term *quick reaction capability* (QRC) for this fast-track process back in the late 1950s, and the process is still used today, sometimes under other names. The QRC concept is to dispense with many of the formal acquisition and systems engineering processes in order to get a piece of equipment into the field quickly. For small items such as sensors, the QRC process has been demonstrated to work and even to be less costly than the normal development cycle. QRC is more difficult but still possible for a large and complex system, where a great deal of systems engineering needs to be done.

Accelerating the RDT&E cycle seems to be an attractive option, but it has its risks. Some of the most advanced technical sensors are little more than experimental prototypes. They are technologically immature and are not readily deployed or used in the field. This deploy-before-ready approach helps the United States maintain an R&D edge, but supporting the deployment can be very expensive.

Managing
Intelligence
Collection

MANAGING THE TRANSITION
TO AN OPERATIONAL COLLECTION SYSTEM

Some types of collection systems have been around for years. Electronic COMINT dates back to the beginning of telegraphy. ELINT and optical imagery have been developed and steadily improved since the 1940s. For systems with such a history, no great difficulty exists in moving the improvements into operational status. The entire intelligence organization is already familiar with the collection system and what it can do. Improvements are readily accepted, even demanded. Intelligence analysts, for example, want more of the same optical imagery but with better NIIRS quality, and they want it to cover a larger area more often. The resulting transition of such user-demanded improvements to operations is relatively smooth.

New types of collection systems face a different, far more difficult, process. For these new and highly technical assets, there are many barriers in getting to operational status. It is typically difficult to move sophisticated technical sensors from R&D to an operational system for several reasons:

- Customers typically do not understand what the new system can offer or how to use the product, so there is no customer demand. The U.S. intelligence community was very slow to recognize the potential of SAR, and the program to develop a SAR almost died several times for lack of funding.

- As noted earlier, there is a continuing demand for existing collection, and customers are unwilling to abandon existing programs. These legacy programs have to be funded, taking away funding for new initiatives. No matter how big the collection system budget, it eventually will be consumed by legacy programs, so no new starts occur unless they are forced.

- Processing and exploitation typically must be developed from scratch. Many of the new collection techniques require intensive processing and exploitation, along with specialized technical expertise, which is in short supply.

- Finally, new systems face an obstacle that system improvements do not have to deal with, an obstacle so prevalent that it has the ominous name of the *valley of death*.

The term *valley of death* comes to us from the commercial world. There, the road from a discovery generated from basic research to a commercial product or process is long and, according to some, rife with significant roadblocks. Innovators describe the valley as a funding gap that exists at an intermediate stage of the development process, between basic research and commercialization of a new product. In this intermediate stage of the innovation process, there is a dearth of funding for technology projects that no longer count as basic research but are not yet far enough along for the benefits to be readily recognized. As one source describes it, this valley is "where good lab discoveries go to die because they lack the funding necessary to become a commercial product."[38]

The same valley of death occurs in the intelligence community's RDT&E process. It is an inevitable consequence of the ease of funding R&D and the difficulty of getting funding to transfer a project into the much more expensive acquisition phase. But the valley of death is not necessarily a bad thing. Not infrequently, collection projects move into the acquisition phase, only to die there amid cost overruns. In such cases, an earlier death would have been a good thing for them.

Evaluating Collection

Because a large part of any intelligence service's budget is spent on collection, those services want to know that they are getting their money's worth. So, collection performance must be evaluated both prospectively and retrospectively.

Prospective evaluation for technical collection typically employs simulation modeling; it is often used before a collection system is developed, especially for evaluating the potential of overhead collection systems. These systems are very expensive, so the simulations are well worth the costs of development and operation.

Once a collection system is in use, three methods have been used to evaluate the collection product retrospectively:

- Survey the analysts, asking them to evaluate collection reports that were used in finished intelligence (which consumes valuable analyst time).
- Audit access to the raw intelligence databases. Multiple accesses by the same person in some defined time frame indicate that a report has more value. (A problem with this method is that the most valuable reports often are accessed once and then printed, so you also need to know when a report is printed.)
- Use citation analysis, that is, count the number of times a report is cited in finished intelligence. But the most useful reports are not necessarily cited, and highly compartmented reports are typically used as background since they cannot be used in lower-classification reporting.

All these evaluation techniques depend on having some form of metrics—things that can be assigned numbers, where the numbers indicate relative value. Metrics are used wherever possible in evaluating collection because Americans seem to have a passion for quantifying almost anything. So evaluators have to know what to measure and how to measure it. The customary metric is some type of measure of user satisfaction.

Measures of user satisfaction can be taken after collection to evaluate how well the intelligence process performed against a need or closed a gap. Expressed another way, the measurement is a quantification of how well a particular requirement or condition has been satisfied. Meaningful measures of user satisfaction could be answers to such questions as these:

- What percentage of all Iranian mobile missiles were located?
- Where are the petroleum industry's planned oil exploration regions?
- What is the expected size of the 2014 opium crops in Pakistan, Laos, Mexico, Thailand, Afghanistan, and Burma? Where are the opium processing centers in these countries, and how much can they process?
- Where are the concealed weapons of mass destruction production centers in Iran?

All these questions call for analytic conclusions, but all lead to more specific definitions of measures of user satisfaction.

A poor example of a measure of user satisfaction would be: "How much of the target area was searched in imagery at a given resolution?" One hundred percent of the target area could be searched without turning up a single item of useful intelligence. Collectors are fond of using such quantitative measures because they provide a firm and technically computable measure. As a result, many collection organizations have become fixated on numbers—on both quality and quantity of collection—and insufficiently concerned with content. For example:

- Collectors often have their performance rated by the number of reports submitted, encouraging the submission of many short reports instead of a few comprehensive ones.
- A COMINT collector probably gets credit for continuous copy of a complete conversation, even if the entire transmission was unbreakably encrypted and provides no intelligence.
- If the IMINT collectors take 100 pictures of a critical installation, they might get credit for each image in their collection performance ratings, even if the last 99 pictures contain nothing new.

The first example above illustrates a flaw that is common to metrics-based systems: They can be gamed, that is, collection and reporting can be shaped to make the metric look good, not to provide better intelligence. The problem is especially severe where the metric is used for determining budgets. *Any metric can and will be gamed if it is used for resource allocation.*

In summary, formal collection metrics tend to focus more on what can be easily counted than on what is important. Content, not quantity, is the critical measure, and formal requirements structures do not handle content evaluation well. Analysts and customers have to evaluate content and place a value on collection. Done properly, such evaluation can effectively control gaming.

Conclusion

The collection management challenges discussed in this chapter stem in part from the success that the United States has had in developing collection assets and the wide range of U.S. interests. Intelligence literature often makes a point of criticizing U.S. intelligence collection capabilities as being cumbersome and inefficient. It is true that some small government intelligence services, such as Israel's Mossad, and a number of multinational corporations can be successful within the areas where they have concentrated their intelligence expertise. They also have all the advantages that accrue to a small, tightly knit organization. Still, U.S. government collection capabilities remain the best in the world. The U.S. intelligence community has the most resources and does the best systems planning. It innovates constantly and attempts things few other services would try. In breadth and depth of coverage, the United States is the benchmark worldwide.

Summary

The ideal collection management system would maintain a current understanding of customers' needs for information and the gaps in knowledge. It would develop coordinated requirements and allocate collection assets to maximize the value of intelligence collected. All collectors would be aware of what the other collectors are doing so that collection assets are used synergistically. The system would function effectively across many different classification levels. The processing, exploitation, and analysis of the product would be done quickly and accurately so that the results get to customers in time to be of use.

All national intelligence services find that the ideal is difficult to achieve. Getting closer to it requires dealing with the challenges of

- matching priorities to requirements and transitioning them into collection strategies;
- objectively evaluating collection performance;
- managing the entire process across organizational, compartmented, technical, and national boundaries;
- managing customer expectations, especially in dealing with timeliness pressures; and
- bringing new technologies and capabilities online.

Collection management begins at the front end—that part of the process that involves collection planning. National priorities have to be translated into intelligence priorities and then into specific requirements. From these, collection strategies have to be developed and specific collectors tasked to obtain the needed information.

The first step is to establish national intelligence priorities. Many attempts have been made to establish such priorities over the last several decades. The current system in use is called the National Intelligence Priorities Framework. Like its predecessors, the NIPF has to deal with a natural tendency of collectors to focus on top priorities at the expense of lesser ones.

The requirements that derive from national intelligence priorities form a hierarchy. Formal requirements structures are necessary in dealing with high-volume satellite IMINT and ELINT and with open source material. Requirements can take several forms. Standing requirements are long-term and usually involve continuing or repeated collection; time-sensitive requirements need immediate collection action and are usually focused on a single event; ad hoc requirements are totally new (and may also be time-sensitive).

The key to making the transition from intelligence priorities or needs to collection priorities is identifying and sorting collection gaps from all the other gaps. After this is done, there must be some assessment of the probability of successful collection before proceeding to collection strategy.

A collection strategy can be described as a systematic plan to optimize the effective and efficient tasking of all capable, available, and appropriate collection assets and resources against requirements. Given the range of possible collection scenarios for complex targets, it is necessary to develop a collection strategy before tasking collection assets. Collection strategies therefore try to integrate tasking and collection of multidisciplinary assets to obtain maximum value from the collection. Coordinated strategies that have been successful in the past include swarm, surge, blitz, and provocative probing.

The last step in the front-end process is tasking of collection assets. Tasking involves providing specific guidance to a specific collector. Tasking must be specific and it must often include background information to help the collector. Many requirements need amplification or explanation.

In an attempt to manage this complex front-end process for large collection systems with many customers, the U.S. intelligence community has developed many collection management tools. Sometimes these tools also are used to manage the back-end processes also. Over the years, a number of efforts have been made to transition from the plethora of individual tools to a set of IC-wide collection management tools that would do integrated collection management.

The other major phase of collection is the back end, which involves processing and exploitation of the raw intelligence that has been collected. This phase has to be planned for and resources allocated for it before a collection system becomes operational. This part of the overall collection effort often is not planned for in advance, at least not to the degree of collection itself. With new types of collection, planners may not know in advance how to best design processing and exploitation. Also, new ways to use technical collection are sometimes discovered after the collection system has been in operation for some time.

Collection is spread across organizational and national boundaries and security compartments. These boundaries can hinder the effective allocation of requirements to assets and the needed collaboration. The problem is so well known that these barriers to collaboration have a special name in the intelligence community: *stovepipes*. There are, in fact, four types of stovepipes: organizational, compartmented, technical, and international. All four of these have valid reasons to exist. The challenge is to make the collection system function effectively, given that the stovepipes are not likely to disappear. In the United States, the response has been to create a new management model (a hybrid approach) referred to as functional management. Within the U.S. intelligence community, there are now numerous functional managers for different collection and analysis disciplines.

After a collection capability has been operating for many years, it develops a customer set that understands what it can do. New collection assets, though, have a quite different problem. Users do not understand how new systems work or what value the collection has. They need to learn the capabilities and limitations of new collection types. The customers of

Managing
Intelligence
Collection

intelligence continue to demand more timely access to intelligence, both for policy decisions and to support modern fast-reaction battlefield needs.

All collection relies heavily on new technologies. The advance of technology affects collection positively in providing new targets for collection in other countries and in providing new collection means. Collection assets have a finite useful lifetime, so it is necessary to maintain a technological edge. This means keeping the RDT&E cycle short to get new equipment in the field rapidly and to find a mechanism for transitioning promising research into operational collection systems.

Collection systems performance must be evaluated both prospectively and retrospectively. Simulation modeling is used to predict the performance of very expensive systems. Content-based measures of user satisfaction can be used for retrospective evaluation, but they should be done by involving all-source analysts and customers, not by collectors alone.

NOTES

1. Center for the Study of Intelligence, Intelligence Monograph, "Critique of the Codeword Compartment in the CIA" (March 1977), accessed 24 September 2012 at www.fas.org/sgp/othergov/codeword.html.
2. Douglas Gartoff, *Directors of Central Intelligence as Leaders of the U.S. Intelligence Community*, Center for the Study of Intelligence (March 16, 2007), Chapter 12, accessed 24 September 2012 at www.cia.gov/library/center-for-the-study-of-intelligence/csi-publications/books-and-monographs/directors-of-central-intelligence-as-leaders-of-the-u-s-intelligence-community/chapter_12.htm.
3. Ibid.
4. Thomas C. Bruneau and Steven C. Boraz, *Reforming Intelligence: Obstacles to Democratic Control and Effectiveness* (Austin: University of Texas Press, 2007), 41–45.
5. U.S. House of Representatives, Permanent Select Committee on Intelligence Staff Study, "IC21: The Intelligence Community in the 21st Century" (June 5, 1996), Section III: Intelligence Requirements Process.
6. Private communication from Professor Peter Oleson, University of Maryland University College (2013).
7. Thomas Fingar, "Analysis in the U.S. Intelligence Community: Missions, Masters, and Methods" in *Intelligence Analysis: Behavioral and Social Scientific Foundations*, Baruch Fischoff and Cherie Chauvin, eds. (Washington, DC: National Academies Press, 2011), 18, accessed 24 September 2012 at http://www.nap.edu/catalog/13062.html.
8. Private communication from Professor Peter Oleson, University of Maryland University College (2013).
9. Roy Godson, *Intelligence Requirements for the 1990s* (Lanham, MD: Lexington Books, 1989), 68.

10. DoD Joint Publication 2-01, "Joint and National Intelligence Support to Military Operations" (January 5, 2012), Chapter 3, accessed 24 September 2012 at http://www.dtic.mil/doctrine/new_pubs/jp2_01.pdf.

11. Private communication from Professor Peter Oleson, University of Maryland University College (2013).

12. IC21, Section IV: Collection Synergy.

13. Scott C. Poole, "Integrated Collection Management Accelerates Interagency Cooperation," *NGA Pathfinder*, Vol. 6, No. 3 (May/June 2008), 8, accessed 24 September 2012 at http://www.dtic.mil/cgi-bin/GetTRDoc?AD=ada493139.

14. "Report of the Commission on the Intelligence Capabilities of the United States Regarding Weapons of Mass Destruction," 125, accessed at http://www.gpo.gov/fdsys/pkg/GPO-WMD/content-detail.html.

15. Ibid., 12.

16. Mark Abramson, David Carter, Brian Collins, Stephan Kolitz, John Miller, Peter Scheidler, and Charles Strauss, "Operational Use of EPOS to Increase the Science Value of EO-1 Observation Data," accessed 24 September 2012 at http://esto.nasa.gov/conferences/ESTC2006/papers/a3p1.pdf.

17. GlobalSecurity.org, "Joint Collection Management Tools," accessed 4 April 2013 at www.globalsecurity.org/intell/systems/jcmt.htm.

18. Ibid.

19. Office of the Director of National Intelligence, "FY2008–2009 Congressional Budget Justification," Vol. 12 (February 2007), 27–28, accessed 24 September 2012 at http://www.fas.org/irp/dni/cbjb-2008.pdf.

20. Poole, "Integrated Collection Management Accelerates Interagency Cooperation," 8.

21. NGA Publication 1.0, "National System for Geospatial Intelligence: Geospatial Intelligence (GEOINT) Basic Doctrine" (September 2006), 21, accessed 24 September 2012 at http://www.fas.org/irp/agency/nga/doctrine.pdf.

22. DoD Joint Publication 2-01, "Joint and National Intelligence Support to Military Operations."

23. *U.S. Commission on National Security/21st Century*, Vol. 6, "Intelligence Community" (April 15, 2001), chapter on National Security Agency/Central Security Service, 12, accessed 24 September 2012 at http://govinfo.library.unt.edu/nssg/addedum/Vol_VI_Intel.pdf.

24. Richard A. Best, Jr., "Open Source Intelligence (OSINT): Issues for Congress," Congressional Research Service (January 28, 2008), accessed 24 September 2012 at http://www.dtic.mil/cgi-bin/GetTRDoc?AD=ADA488690.

25. Mark M. Lowenthal, *Intelligence: From Secrets to Policy*, 4th ed. (Washington, DC: CQ Press, 2009), 76.

26. Private communication from Professor Peter Oleson, University of Maryland University College (2013).

27. Gregory F. Treverton, "Toward a Theory of Intelligence" (RAND, 2006), 24, accessed 24 September 2012 at http://www.rand.org/pubs/conf_proceedings/2006/RAND_CF219.pdf.

28. Pamela Hess, "Intelligence Agencies in Turf War," Associated Press Report (May 28, 2008), accessed 24 September 2012 at http://www.foxnews.com/wires/2008May28/0,4670,IntelligenceTurfWar,00.html.

29. Gartoff, *Directors of Central Intelligence as Leaders of the U.S. Intelligence Community*, Chapter 8, accessed 3 April 2013 at https://www.cia.gov/library/center-for-the-study-of-intelligence/csi-publications/books-and-monographs/directors-of-central-intelligence-as-leaders-of-the-u-s-intelligence-community/chapter_8.htm.

30. "Report of the Commission on the Intelligence Capabilities of the United States Regarding Weapons of Mass Destruction" (March 31, 2005), 444.

31. Ibid., 439.

32. GlobalSecurity.org, "Intelligence and Counterintelligence," accessed 24 September 2012 at www.globalsecurity.org/intell/world/russia/kgb-su0522.htm.

33. IUSS Caesar Alumni Association, "IUSSHistory 950-2010," accessed 23 September 2012 at http://www.iusscaa.org/history.htm.

34. "Forward-Based X-Band Radar–Transportable," *Missilethreat.com*, accessed 24 September 2012 at www.missilethreat.com/missiledefensesystems/id.19/system_detail.asp.

35. Private communication from Professor Peter Oleson, University of Maryland University College (2013).

36. Ibid.

37. Mark M. Lowenthal, *Intelligence: From Secrets to Policy*, 4th ed. (Washington, DC: CQ Press, 2009), 107.

38. J. Heller and C. Peterson, "Valley of Death," in *Nanotechnology Investing*, Foresight Nanotech Institute, accessed 24 September 2012 at www.foresight.org/policy/brief8.html.

Glossary

Absorption	Reduction in the strength of a wave propagating through a medium.
Accuracy	Describes how close a measurement is to the true value of the quantity being measured.
Acoustic intelligence	Intelligence derived from the collection and processing of acoustic phenomena. Also called ACINT for sound in water, and ACOUSTINT for sound in air.
Activity-based intelligence	A type of all-source analysis that is focused on activity and transactions associated with an entity, population, or area of interest.
Adaptive optics	An optical technique that cancels the atmospheric turbulence-induced distortions of an object's image. Adaptive optics uses movable mirror segments or deformable continuous mirrors to compensate for image degradation.
Aerostat	A lighter-than-air vehicle that can remain stationary in the air.
All-source analysis	A process or analytic product making use of all available and relevant sources of information; also called finished intelligence.

Angular resolution	The minimum angular separation between distinguishable objects observed by a sensor.
Antenna	Device to radiate or receive radio frequency energy.
Apogee	The point at which an object in orbit around the earth—a satellite or other body—is at the greatest distance from the earth.
Artifact	In synthetic aperture radar usage, a distortion resulting from the target violating one of the assumptions used in radar processing. *See* multibounce and layover for examples.
Ascending pass	A satellite's travel northward on one side of the earth.
Aspect angle	Description of the geometric orientation in the horizontal plane of an object in the scene.
Atmospheric windows	Wavelengths in the millimeter wave or optical part of the spectrum where the atmosphere is transparent or nearly so.
Attenuation	Decrease in the strength of an EM signal.
Azimuth	The relative position of an object horizontally within the field of view, usually measured from true North.
Azimuth resolution	The minimum azimuthal separation between distinguishable objects observed by a sensor.
Backdoor	A software implant allowing access to a computer network or individual computer, bypassing security procedures. Often called an exploit.
Backscatter	The signal reflected by elements of an illuminated scene back in the direction of the sensor.
Ballistic coefficient	A performance measure for ballistic missile reentry vehicles based on the vehicle's weight, drag, and cross-section; vehicles with a high ballistic coefficient penetrate the atmosphere more quickly than those with a low ballistic coefficient. Also called beta.
Bandwidth	A measure of the span of frequencies that are available in a signal or can be collected by a sensor.
Baseline	*See* basic encyclopedia.
Basic encyclopedia	A compendium of installations worldwide that might be of interest to intelligence agencies and to the operational and planning staffs of military commands. Also called a baseline.
Beamwidth	A measure of the width of the radiation pattern of an antenna.
Beta	Term used to refer to the ballistic coefficient of a reentry vehicle.

Bhangmeter	An optical sensor deployed on satellites to detect the dual flash that characterizes atmospheric nuclear explosions.
Biometric signature	A biological identifying characteristic, customarily used in reference to humans.
Biometrics	The science and technology of measuring and analyzing biological data.
Bistatic radar	A radar with transmitter and receiver widely separated in order to obtain a different signature from that of a monostatic radar or to defeat jamming.
Black program	A name applied to highly compartmented or special access programs.
Blackbody	An object that absorbs all incident electromagnetic energy and consequently radiates perfectly; such an object would be completely black, reflecting no energy.
Blitz	A technique for allocating collection assets to provide relatively brief but intensive coverage of specific targets.
Botnet	A set of computers controlled by a "command-and-control" (C&C) computer to execute commands as directed. Computers in a botnet are called nodes or zombies.
C band	Microwave radar band between 5250 and 5925 MHz.
Calibration	The process of quantitatively defining the system responses to known, controlled signal inputs.
Case officer	A professionally trained employee of an intelligence service with responsibility for managing human agents and agent networks.
Change detection	Any technique for observing changes in an image over time.
Charge-coupled devices (CCDs)	The name applied to an array of solid-state devices that detect incoming photons in an image sensor.
Chirped pulse	Frequency modulation applied to a radar pulse for the purpose of obtaining high-range resolution with a long pulse. Often called linear frequency modulation (LFM).
Chromatography	A laboratory technique for separating the chemical components of a mixture.
Cipher	An algorithm for performing encryption of a message.
Clandestine	An operation characterized by the opponent being unaware that the operation happened at all.
Clandestine service	The arm of an intelligence organization responsible for the conduct of clandestine operations.
Coherent	A property of a signal such that the signal phase is measurable (for example, over many pulses of a radar).

Coherent change detection (CCD)	Using a synthetic aperture radar to, in effect, overlay two radar images, in order to produce a picture of what changed in the time between the two images. It does this by measuring and storing both the intensity and phase (phase history data) of each image pixel.
Collateral	Material or information that is extrinsic to a collection organization, usually reporting or intelligence that is produced by another collection INT.
Communications intelligence (COMINT)	Intelligence information derived from the intercept of communications by other than the intended recipients.
Competitive intelligence	Intelligence collected about business competitors, including their plans, strategy, and products.
Contrast	Difference between the tone of two neighboring regions in an image.
Contrast enhancement	A processing technique that involves increasing the tonal distinction between various features in a scene.
Covert	An operation wherein the results are apparent, but the source of the operation either is not apparent or has plausible deniability.
Cross-track scanner	Also known as an optical-mechanical or "whiskbroom" scanner; it uses a scanning mirror that projects the image of a surface resolution element onto a single detector.
Cryptanalysis	The process of "breaking encryption" or decrypting encrypted messages by other than the intended recipients.
Dangle	An attractive potential recruit intentionally placed in front of a hostile intelligence service.
Data cube	A three-dimensional representation of a hyperspectral image.
Descending pass	The part of a satellite orbit traveling southward.
Detection threshold	The minimum level of signal intensity that a sensor can detect.
Diffuse	Reflection typically made up of many individual reflections of energy having random phase with respect to each other, such as from a natural forest canopy or agricultural field. The term is also used to describe a surface that reflects electromagnetic illumination in this fashion. The opposite term is *specular*.
Digital image	An image that has been placed in a digital file with brightness values of picture elements (pixels) representing brightness of specific positions within the original scene.
Direction finding (DF)	Measurement of the direction of arrival of a signal.
Dissemination	The communication of processed and exploited raw intelligence to customers in paper or electronic form.

Doppler	A shift in frequency caused by relative motion along the line of sight between the sensor and the target.
Doppler effect (Doppler shift)	A change in the observed frequency of an acoustic or electromagnetic signal emitted by or reflected from an object, when the object and the observer are in motion relative to each other.
Drive-by download site	A website containing malicious software that takes advantage of vulnerabilities in web browsers and browser add-ons.
Dwell time	Length of time that a sensor can maintain access to a target.
Dynamic range	The ratio of the maximum to the minimum observable signal. The maximum signal is the signal at which the system saturates, while the minimum signal is usually defined as the noise floor.
Edge enhancement	An imagery enhancement technique commonly used in processing images for intelligence, characterized by highlighting the edges of target objects.
Electromagnetic (EM) wave	A wave described by variations in electric and magnetic fields. Light waves, radio waves, and microwaves are examples. All such waves propagate at the speed of light in free space.
Electronic intelligence (ELINT)	Information derived from the intercept of intentional electromagnetic radiations, primarily radar, that do not fall into the categories of COMINT or FISINT.
Electro-optical (EO) imagers	An imaging sensor that converts incoming light energy to an electrical signal for transmission and storage.
Elicitation	The practice of obtaining information about a topic from conversations, preferably without the source knowing what is happening.
Ellipsometry	Another name for optical polarimetry.
Emissive band	The optical spectrum band extending from mid-wavelength infrared through long-wavelength IR and into the far IR region.
Emissivity	A property of an object that describes how its thermal emissions deviate from the ideal of a blackbody.
Error ellipse	In geolocation, an ellipse on the earth's surface within which a target of interest has a 50% probability of being located.
Exploit	Malware that takes advantage of software vulnerabilities to infect, disrupt, or take control of a computer without the user's consent and preferably without the user's knowledge; often called a backdoor.
Exploitation	The transformation of processed collection results into a product that can be used by customers or all-source analysts.
f number	In optics, the ratio of focal length to aperture diameter.

Factory markings	Identifying markings placed on military equipment for inventory and quality control purposes. Such markings have intelligence value because they can identify the source of the equipment and the quantity produced.
False alarm	A noise or interfering signal that is mistaken for the desired signal.
False color	An image that depicts a subject in colors that differ from those a faithful full-color photograph would show, usually by shifting the colors in each pixel to longer wavelengths.
False negative	A desired signal that is discarded as interference or noise.
False positive	Another term for false alarm.
Far infrared	The infrared band lying between 15 μm wavelength and the millimeter wave band.
Field of regard	The total area that a collection platform is capable of seeing.
Field of view	A defined volume of space that a sensor can see at any instant.
Fluidics	The technology of using pressures and flows of fluids for sensing and control. In intelligence, the collection of sound traveling in conduits for acoustic monitoring.
Focal length	In optical systems, the distance between the entrance aperture and the focal plane.
Focal plane	The surface at which an optical image is in focus.
Focal plane array	A planar array of optical sensors placed at the point where the optics focus incoming light energy.
Foreign instrumentation signals intelligence (FISINT)	Information derived from the intercept of foreign instrumentation signals by other than the intended recipients. Foreign instrumentation signals include but are not limited to signals from telemetry, tracking/fusing/arming/firing command systems, and video data links.
Forward-looking infrared (FLIR)	An infrared imaging system designed to operate at night, so called because it is usually mounted on an aircraft or vehicle and looking in the direction of travel.
Framing camera	A camera using conventional optics with a planar array of detectors located in the camera focal plane.
Frequency	Rate of oscillation of a wave, measured in hertz (oscillations per second).
Frequency difference of arrival (FDOA)	A technique for geolocating an emitter by measuring and comparing the Doppler shifts at different receivers where relative motion exists between the emitter and the receivers.
Frequency division multiplexing	Multiplexing done by allocating a different part of the radio frequency spectrum to each stream of communication.

Frequency hopping	A radar technique where the signal periodically moves to a different frequency (often with each pulse transmitted).
Frequency-independent antenna	An antenna that maintains almost constant beamwidth over a very wide frequency band (the upper-frequency limit being several times the lower-frequency limit).
Frequency resolution	A measure of the ability to distinguish two signals that are closely spaced in frequency.
Front end	The process that involves collection planning, specifically the development of requirements, collection priorities, collection strategies, and tasking of collectors.
Fully polarimetric	Transmitting and receiving both polarizations simultaneously; used to describe a type of SAR.
Gain	Change in signal level due to processing functions that increase the magnitude of the signal.
Geolocation	The process of pinpointing the location of an object on the earth or in space.
Geolocation accuracy	The accuracy of measuring the location of an object on the earth or in space.
Geophone	A type of microphone used to measure seismic disturbances.
Geospatial intelligence (GEOINT)	The all-source analysis of imagery and geospatial information to describe, assess, and visually depict physical features and geographically referenced activities on the earth.
Geostationary orbit (GEO)	An orbit above earth's equator at an altitude of 35,800 km, where the orbital period is 24 hours, equal to that of the earth's rotation.
Glint	A brief strong radar return, caused when the radar cross-section of a target suddenly becomes very large.
Global coverage	In intelligence, maintaining awareness of opportunities and threats to national interests worldwide.
Grazing angle	The minimum angle of elevation, measured from a ground target to a satellite, at which the satellite can observe the target.
Ground moving target indicator (GMTI)	*See* moving target indicator.
Ground sample distance (GSD)	The distance between the center of adjacent pixels in a sensor image.
Highly elliptical orbit (HEO)	An extremely elongated orbit characterized by a relatively low-altitude perigee and an extremely high-altitude apogee. These orbits can have the advantage of long dwell times during the approach to and descent from apogee.

Human intelligence (HUMINT)	Intelligence information derived from the use of human beings as both sources and collectors, and where the human being is the primary collection instrument.
Hydrophone	A microphone designed to be used underwater for recording or listening to underwater sound.
Hyperspectral images (HSI)	Optical imagery that uses hundreds of spectral bands.
Image	Mapping of the radar or optical reflectivity of a scene.
Image enhancement	Processing technique used to improve the appearance of the imagery to assist in visual interpretation and analysis.
Imagery intelligence (IMINT)	Intelligence information derived from the collection by visual photography, infrared sensors, lasers, electro-optics, and radar sensors, such as synthetic aperture radar, wherein images of objects are reproduced optically or electronically on film, on electronic display devices, or in other media.
Imaging radiometer	A sensor that measures the intensity of EM radiation while obtaining an image of the target. It creates, in effect, a "radiometric map."
Imaging spectrometer	A sensor that obtains an image of a target while measuring the spectral characteristics of each object in the image.
Incidence angle	Angle between the line of sight from the sensor to the target and a vertical direction measured from the target surface.
Inclination	In space systems terminology, the angle of a satellite's orbit measured counterclockwise from the equatorial plane.
Incoherent (or noncoherent)	Property of a signal in which the phases of the constituents are not statistically correlated or systematically related in any fashion.
Incoherent change detection	In radar imagery, observing changes to a scene between imaging events that are caused by changes in the intensity of energy returned from target pixels. Contrast with coherent change detection.
Infrared intelligence (IRINT)	Intelligence information associated with emitted or reflected energy derived from monitoring the electromagnetic infrared spectrum.
Instantaneous field of view (IFOV)	The angular aperture within which one pixel of a sensor is sensitive to electromagnetic radiation, measured in degrees.
Integrated undersea surveillance system (IUSS)	A network of acoustic arrays, some towed behind ships and submarines and some fixed to the seafloor, designed to locate and track submarines at long distances. *See* sound surveillance system (SOSUS).
Intensity accuracy	The degree to which a sensor can resolve differences in intensity.
Intensity coverage	The range of intensity that a sensor can receive and process linearly. *See* dynamic range, which has the same meaning.

Intensity resolution	The measure of the difference in signal intensity that can be detected and recorded by a sensor. Also called radiometric resolution.
Interferometer	A sensor that receives EM energy over two or more different paths and deduces information from the coherent interference between the received signals.
Interpretability	The ability to identify and distinguish objects, features, patterns, and textures within an image and to determine their significance.
Inverse synthetic aperture radar (ISAR)	A technique to generate a two-dimensional image of a moving object from a fixed radar location by coherently processing echoes from the object as it moves.
Keystroke logger	Malware that captures and records keystrokes.
L band	Microwave radar band between 1215 and 1400 MHz.
Layover	In synthetic aperture radar, an extreme form of elevation displacement or foreshortening in which the top of a reflecting object (such as a mountain) appears closer to the radar (in slant range) than do the lower parts of the object. The image of such a feature appears to have fallen over toward the radar.
Legacy system	An existing collection effort with an established customer set, where customer demand makes it difficult to terminate the effort.
Library	A repository of raw intelligence, usually of signatures resulting from nonliteral collection.
Linear frequency modulation (LFM)	Modulation on a signal causing it to increase or decrease linearly in frequency over time. Also known as chirp.
Literal information	Information in a form that humans use for communication.
Low earth orbit (LEO)	Satellite orbits between 200 and 1500 km above the earth's surface.
Low probability of intercept (LPI)	The use of transmitted power management or signal modulation to make it difficult for SIGINT systems to collect RF signals.
Magnetic anomaly detector (MAD)	A magnetometer that is used by military forces to detect submarines or in geology to search for minerals by observing the disturbance of the earth's normal magnetic field.
Magnetometer	A device that senses weak changes in the earth's magnetic field.
Magnetometry	The science of sensing magnetic fields.
Materials	As used in intelligence, physical or biological samples acquired for exploitation.
Materiel	In collection, physical objects and equipment acquired for intelligence purposes, usually clandestinely.

Measurements and signatures intelligence (MASINT)	Intelligence information obtained by quantitative and qualitative analysis of data derived from specific technical sensors for the purpose of identifying any distinctive features associated with the source, emitter, or sender, and to facilitate subsequent identification and/or measurement of the same.
Medium earth orbit (MEO)	Satellite orbits typically between 10,000 and 20,000 km altitude.
Microexpressions	Fleeting facial expressions, typically lasting less than one-tenth of a second and involving a small part of the human face.
Microwave	An electromagnetic frequency between 1 and 300 GHz.
Mole	An intelligence service employee who is an agent for a foreign intelligence service.
Moving target indicator (MTI)	A feature that allows a radar to detect target motion. It also is called a ground moving target indicator (GMTI).
Multibounce	A scattering mechanism in which the electromagnetic wave reflects off more than one point before returning to the sensor. The simplest example is double-bounce scattering.
Multifunction radars	In radar use, a radar that can perform more than one of the four functions of search, track, imaging, and target measurement.
Multilateration	Also known as hyperbolic positioning, it is the process of locating an object by computing the time difference of arrival (TDOA) of a signal at different receivers.
Multipath	Another term for multibounce, usually referring to a radar or communications signal that bounces off multiple surfaces before being received.
Multiplexing	The combining of independent streams of communication into a single transmission; used to transmit telemetry.
Multispectral images (MSI)	Imagery collected by a single sensor in multiple regions (bands) of the electromagnetic spectrum. Typically used to refer to the collection of fewer than 100 bands, to distinguish it from hyperspectral imagery.
Multispectral scanner	An imaging sensor that scans several spectral bands simultaneously to form multiple images of a scene.
Nadir	A point on the earth's surface directly below the satellite.
National Imagery Interpretability Rating Scale (NIIRS)	A 10-level rating scale that defines the ability to identify certain features or targets within an image. The NIIRS defines and measures the quality of images and performance of imaging systems.
National technical means (NTM)	A euphemism for satellite collection assets, derived from a term used in the Limited Test Ban Treaty of 1963.

Near-polar orbit	A satellite orbit that passes near the north and south poles.
Near real time	Refers to the brief delay caused by automated processing and display between the occurrence of an event and reception of the data at some other location. The term typically describes a delay of a few seconds to a few minutes.
Noise	Any unwanted or contaminating signal competing with the desired signal. Noise may be generated within the sensor or may enter the sensor from the outside.
Nonliteral information	Information in a form that is not customarily used for human communication.
Nuclear forensics	The collection and analysis of a sample containing nuclear or radioactive material to determine the history or production process of the material.
Nuclear intelligence (NUCINT)	Intelligence information derived from the collection and analysis of radiation and other effects resulting from radioactive sources.
Open source	Material that is publicly available in print or electronic form.
Operational ELINT (OPELINT)	ELINT that is primarily intended to directly support ongoing military or law enforcement operations.
Optical intelligence (OPTINT)	Intelligence information derived from radiometric and spectroscopic exploitation of optical energy (ultraviolet, visible, and near infrared) resulting in a spatial, temporal, or spectral signature of targets.
Optical spectrum	That part of the electromagnetic spectrum where optics, rather than antennas, are used to receive energy (wavelengths shorter than about 300 microns)
Orbit cycle	The period of time until a satellite retraces its path, passing over the same point on the earth's surface directly below the satellite (the nadir point) for a second time.
Overhead collection	Term commonly used in intelligence literature to refer to collection from satellites.
Overhead nonimaging infrared (ONIR)	*See* overhead persistent infrared (OPIR).
Overhead persistent infrared (OPIR)	A term applied to spaceborne sensors that detect and track intense emissions of IR energy over a large area of the earth. Replaces the term *overhead nonimaging infrared (ONIR)*.
P wave	In seismic sensing, a pressure (compressional) wave created by an underground explosion.
Panchromatic imagery	Black-and-white imagery that spans an area of the electromagnetic spectrum, typically the visible region.

Pattern	The product of analysis (frequently of signatures).
Perigee	The point at which an object in orbit around the earth—a satellite or other body—makes its closest approach to the earth.
Period	Time duration of one cycle of a wave or one cycle of any regularly recurring pattern. Period is inversely equal to frequency.
Phase coding	A type of modulation on a radar pulse caused by periodically changing the phase of the transmitted signal to improve range resolution.
Phase history data (PHD)	The raw data collected by a SAR system prior to range and azimuth compression. Slight differences in frequency, or phase differences, are noted, and the signal intensity and phase differences are recorded to create PHD.
Phased array	A group of antenna elements in which the relative phases of the respective signals feeding the elements are varied in such a way that the main beam of the array is steered in a desired direction.
Photometry	Measurement of the intensity of light emitted from or reflected by an object.
Pitch	Vertical rotation of a sensor platform in a "nose up and down" fashion.
Pixel	Picture element, the smallest element of a digital image.
Polar orbit	A 90-degree inclination orbit, which crosses the equator moving directly north or south and crosses directly over the poles.
Polarimetric SAR	A synthetic aperture radar that is capable of transmitting and/or receiving multiple polarizations.
Polarimetry	The measurement and interpretation of the polarization of transverse waves, most notably electromagnetic waves such as radio waves and light.
Polarization	Orientation of the electric vector in an electromagnetic wave. In the RF bands, polarization is established by the antenna, which may be adjusted to be different on transmit and on receive.
Precision	A measure of the detail in which a quantity is expressed.
Preprocessing	In IMINT, making radiometric or geometric corrections before the main data analysis and extraction of information are done.
Product teardown	The practice of dismantling commercial products or materiel of intelligence interest for detailed exploitation.
Propagation	The movement of energy in the form of waves through space or other media.
Pulse	A group of waves with a distribution confined to a short interval of time. Such a distribution is described by its time duration and its amplitude or magnitude.
Pulse compression	A technique used in radar and sonar to improve the range resolution and signal-to-noise ratio of the sensor, by modulating the transmitted pulse.

Pulse repetition frequency (PRF)	Rate of recurrence of the pulses transmitted by a radar.
Pulse repetition interval (PRI)	The time interval between successive pulses transmitted by a radar.
Pulse train deinterleaving	In ELINT, a processing technique for separating incoming radar pulses and assigning them to specific radar targets.
Pushbroom imager	An imager that makes use of the motion of a detector array along the ground; the imaging effect resembles the bristles of a broom being pushed along a floor.
Quick reaction capability (QRC)	A USAF program designed to suspend normal contract procedures in order to get a weapons system or subsystem into the field rapidly.
Radar	Electromagnetic sensor characterized by transmitting a signal and receiving the reflection from a target; the acronym is derived from radio detection and ranging.
Radar cross-section (RCS)	Measure of radar reflectivity, expressed in terms of the physical size of a hypothetical perfect sphere that would give rise to the same level of reflection as that observed from the sample target.
Radar intelligence (RADINT)	Intelligence information derived from data collected by radar.
Radar resolution cell	A volume defined by range and angular resolution for a radar.
Radiation	Act of giving off electromagnetic energy.
Radio frequency flooding	The use of RF signals (generally microwave) to illuminate a target and collect audio modulations on the signal reflected from the target.
Radiometer	A passive sensor that receives an records the electromagnetic energy that is naturally emitted from objects.
Radiometric imager	An EM sensor that both creates an image and measures the intensity of received energy in each pixel of the image.
Radiometric resolution	The ability of a sensor to distinguish different levels of signal intensity.
Range	Line-of-sight distance, usually between a sensor and its target.
Range resolution	In radar, this is the resolution characteristic of the range dimension. Range resolution is fundamentally determined by the radar bandwidth.
Real time	The absence of delay, except for the time required for the transmission by electromagnetic energy, between the occurrence of the event or the transmission of data, and the knowledge of an event, or reception of the data at some other location. Contrasts with near real time, which has an additional delay.

Reconnaissance	Periodic observation of a target area; contrast with surveillance.
Reference emitter	An EM signal from a known location, used as a reference to reduce the geolocation error of the desired target signal.
Reflected infrared	The main infrared component of the solar radiation reflected from the earth's surface.
Reflective band	The UV, visible, near IR (NIR), and short wavelength IR (SWIR) bands.
Reflectivity	Property of illuminated objects to reradiate a portion of the incident energy.
Regional coverage	In intelligence, maintaining awareness of opportunities and threats to national interests in a specific geographical region.
Regional wave	A seismic wave that is sensed relatively close to its source. Compare with teleseismic waves, which are sensed at long distances.
Remote sensing	Sensing, primarily from the electromagnetic spectrum, that is done at long distances (on the order of tens to thousands of kilometers).
Resolution	The ability of a system to differentiate two signatures—a unit of granularity.
Resolution cell	A three-dimensional volume surrounding each point in a scene. Two separate targets located in the same resolution cell cannot be distinguished.
Retrograde orbit	A satellite orbit having more than 90 degrees inclination. The satellite moves in the opposite direction from the earth's rotation.
Revisit time	The time that elapses before a collection asset can collect against a target for a second time. This is also called revisit period.
Roll	Rotation of a sensor platform around the flight vector, hence in a "wing up or down" direction.
Rootkit	Software code designed to take control of a computer while avoiding detection.
Roughness	In imagery, the variation of surface height within an imaged resolution cell. A surface appears "rough" to illumination when the height variations become larger than a fraction of the EM wavelength.
S band	The two microwave radar bands between 2300 and 2500 MHz and between 2700 and 3700 MHz.
S wave	In seismic sensing, a shear (transverse) wave created by earthquakes.
Safe house	In intelligence, a residence, hotel room, or similar facility used to conduct clandestine meetings.
SAR interferometry	Using two antennas on a SAR platform or two SARs flying in formation to receive independent images of a target. The two images can be processed to detect moving targets or for terrain mapping.

Scanner	A sensor with a narrow field of view that sweeps over the terrain to build up and produce a two-dimensional image of the surface.
Scene	The ground area observed by a sensor.
Seismic sensing	Detecting sound that travels through the earth. *See* seismic waves.
Seismic waves	Waves that travel through the earth (for example, as a result of an earthquake or explosion).
Seismometer	A type of microphone used to sense teleseismic waves.
Shadowing	In SAR, a region hidden behind an elevated feature in the scene that shows up as black on the SAR image. This region is not illuminated by the radar energy and thus is also not visible in the resulting radar image.
Signal-to-noise ratio (SNR)	Quantitative basis for comparing the relative level of a desired signal to an unwanted element such as noise. SNR can also be defined as the ratio of the power in a desired signal to the undesirable noise present in the absence of a signal.
Signals intelligence (SIGINT)	A category of intelligence comprising communications intelligence (COMINT), electronic intelligence (ELINT), and foreign instrumentation signals intelligence (FISINT).
Signature	A set of distinctive characteristics of persons, objects, or activities that result from processing of collected intelligence.
Signature library	A database of signatures associated with a specific person, activity, or class of objects so that when a signature is identified, it can be associated with a specific person, phenomenon, object, or class of objects in the database.
Single-source analysis	An analytic product produced by a collection organization that relies primarily on its collection; COMINT, open source, and imagery analysis are examples.
Smearing	In SAR, image distortion caused by a target accelerating toward or away from the radar.
Sniffers	Software programs or human administrators that search for unauthorized access to computers and networks.
Sound spectrogram	A graph of the intensity versus frequency of sound, used in voice recognition.
Sound surveillance system (SOSUS)	A network of hydrophone arrays mounted on the seafloor throughout the Atlantic and Pacific oceans. Now part of the integrated undersea surveillance system (IUSS).
Space object identification (SOI)	A combination of techniques used to obtain additional information about satellites, reentry vehicles, and space debris.
Spatial accuracy	The accuracy of a sensor's location of a target on the earth or in space.

Spatial coverage	A measure of the area on the earth's surface or the volume of space that a sensor can view in a given time.
Spatial filtering	A processing technique used to enhance (or suppress) specific spatial patterns in an image.
Spatial resolution	Ability of a sensor to resolve or separate two objects spatially, usually stated as a measure of distance on the ground.
Special access program (SAP)	A term used by the DoD and the intelligence community to refer to highly classified programs, usually protected by special classification compartments; also known as a black program.
Specific emitter identification	Also known as fingerprinting, a processing technique for identifying RF emitters based on unique features of their signals.
Spectral accuracy	A measure of the accuracy with which a sensor can determine the frequency or wavelength of a signal.
Spectral coverage	A measure of the amount of the electromagnetic spectrum that a sensor can observe.
Spectral emissivity curve	A spectral signature created by thermal emissions from a target.
Spectral imager	A set of imaging radiometers, each operating at a different wavelength and thereby creating many simultaneous images of a scene.
Spectral resolution	The ability of a sensor to distinguish among energies of varying wavelengths emitted by or reflected from a target.
Spectral response	A measure of the sensitivity of a sensor to different wavelengths of EM radiation.
Spectral response curve	A spectral signature created by EM energy reflected from a target.
Spectral signature	A signature created by emission or reflection of electromagnetic energy at specific wavelengths from a target.
Spectrometer	An instrument used to measure the intensity and wavelength of light.
Spectroscope	An optical device that splits incoming light according to its wavelength.
Spectrum analyzer	A device used to examine the spectral composition of an electrical wave form; it is the radio frequency equivalent of the spectrometer.
Specular reflection	Coherent reflection from a smooth surface in a plane normal to the surface at an angle opposite to the incidence angle. A mirror is a specular reflector.
Spotlight mode	A mode of SAR operation where the radar antenna is rotated to stay aimed at a target area during flight to increase the integration time and therefore the azimuth resolution.

Spread spectrum	A signal transmission that deliberately uses more frequency bandwidth than needed, for the purpose of avoiding detection, defeating interference, or obtaining more favorable signal reception.
Squint	In SAR, the angle measured from perpendicular (broadside) to the direction of flight (the broadside direction being called zero squint). Forward of broadside (in the direction of flight) is called positive squint; aft of broadside is called negative squint.
Steganography	The art and science of hiding information by embedding messages within other, seemingly innocent messages.
Stereograph	A combination of two photographs of the same scene taken from slightly different angles to provide a 3-D view of the scene.
Stereoscope	A device that simultaneously presents the left photograph to the viewer's left eye and the right photograph to the viewer's right eye for the purpose of viewing a 3-D image.
Stovepipe	A term for maintaining a separate collection or analysis process based on organizational, compartmentation, or technical factors.
Strip map imager	A SAR imaging technique where the antenna points in a fixed direction (normally perpendicular to the direction of aircraft or satellite movement).
Sun-synchronous orbit	A satellite orbit designed so that the satellite passes over a given point on the earth at approximately the same time every day.
Surface-wave radar	A type of over-the-horizon radar that depends on the propagation of EM waves that "bend" along the sea surface instead of traveling line-of-sight.
Surveillance	The continuous observation of a target or target area by visual, aural, electronic, photographic, or other means. Contrast with reconnaissance.
Synoptic coverage	Obtaining sensor coverage of a large region nearly simultaneously.
Synthetic aperture radar (SAR)	A radar that achieves high azimuth resolution by obtaining a set of coherently recorded signals such that the radar is able to function as if it had a very large antenna aperture.
Target	An entity (country, area, object, installation, agency, or person) against which intelligence collection is directed.
Target displacement	In synthetic aperture radar imagery, a target appearing in an incorrect position as a result of the target's movement during the imaging process.
Targeting	The process of selecting collection targets and matching the appropriate collection response to them, taking account of requirements and capabilities.
Technical ELINT	RF collection and analysis that is used to assess the capabilities and performance of an electronic system (usually a radar).

Telemetry	Instrumentation readings transmitted from a satellite or from a missile or aircraft undergoing testing.
Telemetry externals	Changes in a telemetry signal caused by the flight profile of the vehicle.
Telemetry internals	The values of the measurements made by flight instrumentation.
Teleseismic sensing	The collection of infrasound that travels deep in the earth. *See* teleseismic wave.
Teleseismic wave	A seismic wave that is recorded far from its source.
Temporal accuracy	The measurement accuracy of a signal's arrival time at a sensor.
Temporal coverage	The duration of a sensor's coverage.
Temporal resolution	The span of time between successive collections against a target. Can refer either to the time that elapses before a collection asset can sense a target for a second time or to the ability to separate two closely spaced events in a signature.
Terminator condition	A satellite observation situation where the ground site is in darkness while the sun illuminates the target.
Thermal imaging	Imagery in the infrared spectrum based on emitted radiation (that is, it does not depend on the presence of an illuminator).
Thermal infrared	The MWIR and LWIR bands of the IR spectrum.
Time difference of arrival (TDOA)	A measurement of the relative arrival times of a signal at dispersed geographic points, used to geolocate the signal.
Time division multiplexing	Transmitting multiple communications streams where each stream periodically gets to use the entire frequency bandwidth of the transmitter for a short time interval.
Tip-off	Using intelligence from one collection source to cue collection by another source.
Tradecraft	The skills acquired through experience in an intelligence discipline, such as in analysis or clandestine operations.
Traffic analysis	A COMINT technique used to build a model of a communications network by communications pattern analysis
Trojan horse	A seemingly innocent program that conceals its primary purpose of infecting a computer with malware.
Two-color multiview	The technique shows objects that appeared in the first image but have left the scene in the second image, in one color. Objects that have appeared in the scene since the first image are shown in a second color.
Ultraspectral Images (USI)	Measurement of thousands of spectral bands.

Unmanned aerial vehicle (UAV)	A powered aeronautical vehicle that does not carry a human operator and can fly autonomously or be piloted remotely. Ballistic or cruise missiles and artillery projectiles are not considered UAVs.
Valley of death	Term used to describe the gap between R&D and the creation of a product, so named because most research projects die at this stage.
Van Allen radiation belt	A torus of energetic charged particles around earth, held in place by the earth's magnetic field. The inner belt extends from about 700 to 10,000 km above earth; the weaker outer belt extends from about 3 to 10 earth radii.
Vibrometry	A radar technique for remotely sensing vibrations from a target.
Visual magnitude (m_v)	Measure of the relative brightness of an object; a first magnitude star, the brightest in the sky, is 100 times as bright as a sixth magnitude star.
Walk-in	A person who simply shows up (often at a country's overseas embassy) and volunteers to spy.
Wave	Propagating periodic displacement of an energy field. At any instant of time, a wave is described by its "height" (amplitude) and its "length" (wavelength).
Wavelength	Minimum distance between two events of a recurring feature in a periodic sequence, such as the crests in a wave.
Whiskbroom scanner	An imaging sensor that uses a scanning mirror to create an image using a single detector. Also called a cross-track or optical-mechanical scanner.
Worm	Malware that is designed to be completely concealed, instead of masquerading as an innocent program as a Trojan horse does.
Wullenweber	Large circular antenna array used by the military to triangulate HF (3–30 MHz) radio signals; also known as a circularly disposed antenna array (CDAA).
X band	Microwave radar band between 8500 and 10680 MHz.
Yaw	Rotation of a sensor platform in the horizontal plane, hence in a "nose right or left" direction.

Index

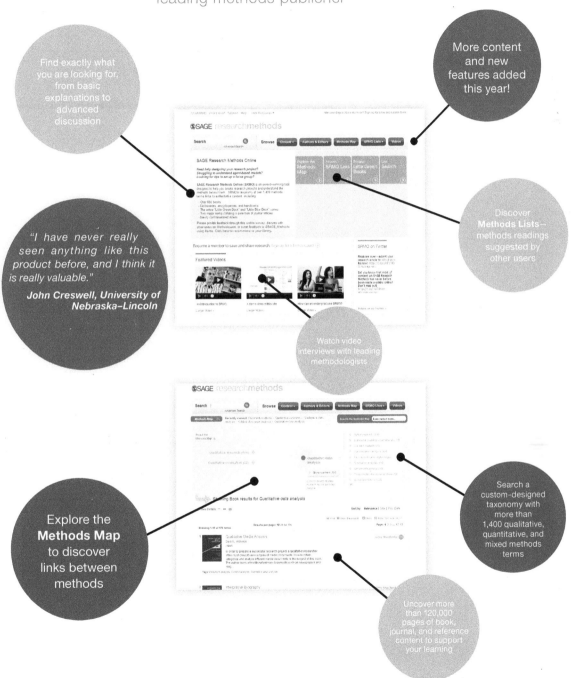

⑤SAGE researchmethods

The essential online tool for researchers from the world's leading methods publisher

Find exactly what you are looking for, from basic explanations to advanced discussion

More content and new features added this year!

"I have never really seen anything like this product before, and I think it is really valuable."

John Creswell, University of Nebraska–Lincoln

Discover **Methods Lists**— methods readings suggested by other users

Watch video interviews with leading methodologists

Explore the **Methods Map** to discover links between methods

Search a custom-designed taxonomy with more than 1,400 qualitative, quantitative, and mixed methods terms

Uncover more than 120,000 pages of book, journal, and reference content to support your learning

Find out more at
www.sageresearchmethods.com

CPSIA information can be obtained
at www.ICGtesting.com
Printed in the USA
BVHW020445140723
667182BV00001B/6

9 781452 271859